# Guide to
# U.S. Map Resources

# Guide to
# U.S. Map Resources

compiled by

## DAVID A. COBB

Map and Geography Round Table

American Library Association

## American Library Association

CHICAGO AND LONDON

Cover designed by Charles Bozett

Composed by Kitezh Typesetting
  in Century Schoolbook
  Display type, Trump Medieval,
  composed by Pearson Typographers

Printed on 50-pound Glatfelter,
  a pH-neutral stock, and bound
  in B-Grade Holliston linen cloth by
  Edwards Brothers, Inc.

**Library of Congress Cataloging-in-Publication Data**

Cobb, David A.
  Guide to U.S. map resources.

  Includes index.
  1. Map collections—United States—Directories.
  I. Title.
  GA193.U5C62  1985     026'.912'0973     85-22958
  ISBN 0-8389-0439-4

Second printing, November 1986

# Contents

# *Foreword*

It is indeed a pleasure to write the foreword for this first MAGERT publication, appropriately enough a guide to U. S. map resources. Among the many reasons that it is a pleasure for me to perform this task is that it is, relatively speaking, so undemanding compared with the considerable efforts of the persons who have worked on this volume, all above and beyond the call of tenure. During the years that the Guide was being put together, I was endeavoring to advance by degrees, and thus miraculously escaped doing anything other than contributing a suitably brief foreword after everyone else had done all the work. Of course, any muttered comments to the effect that, upon hearing of the Guide project, I, in an excess of cowardice, immediately and gratefully enrolled in the nearest graduate school, are base calumnies.

Let us move from applauding the compilers to examining the volume. Holding this work, you hold the world of United States map libraries. Contained between its covers are millions of maps and remote sensing images, all of the map libraries' globes, relief models, cartographic books and serials, and special collections. The main purpose of this Guide is to link all of the above together, so that instead of depending on some vague remembrance from an all-too-brief conference meeting, we may with confidence refer our map library user to the appropriate collection.

There is one more point that must be made. Persons not fortunate enough to work in libraries see such reference works as this as being incredibly dull, only recognizing the value of such works when they desperately need the information in the book. But we librarians see not just the book; rather, we see its contents. When I look at these entries, I see not just the numbers of maps and so forth, but rather the beauty of the cartographic materials themselves, from the complexity and subtlety of, say, the Swiss topographic sheets to the occasionally garish but always arresting hues of U. S. Geological Survey geologic sheets. I see yet more. In the printed names of the map curators, I see the persons they are – the hard work, good times, and arguments we've had over the years; and I wonder once again if it is that cartographic materials draw together the best persons, or if the media somehow enoble us, in a sort of reverse Jekyll-Hyde syndrome.

All of the abilities of the nation's map librarians, all of the substantial resources of its map collections, are summarized in this volume. It is through such works as this that we librarians realize that there is no need for a farewell to Alexandria. Because we, all of us together, *are* Alexandria, or are at least on our way there. And since we are fortunate enough to be map librarians, we have an intellectual flying carpet – the map – to get us there. Godspeed.

Mary Larsgaard
Colorado School of Mines

# *Introduction*

Maps represent one of the oldest forms of communication known. The technique of map making has progressed from the earliest "stick charts," used for ocean navigation to the space imagery and computer digital products of the present day. An increasing number of maps are being compiled, edited, and produced by automated techniques with little human intervention. Maps truly represent a cultural mirror of the society which produces them. Maps may be used to trace not only the growth of geographical knowledge in a particular nation but also geographical exploration, development of printing techniques, use of coloring, urban growth, transportation patterns, etc.

The storage of maps in U. S. libraries is a relatively recent phenomena. Although a few major collections were established in the nineteenth century (i.e., American Geographical Society, Harvard University, and the Library of Congress), the majority of the collections in this guide were developed after World War II. The growth may be attributed mainly to the surplus maps distributed by the U. S. Army Map Service (now the Defense Mapping Agency) immediately after World War II and, most recently, to the expansion of depository programs by the U. S. Geological Survey, the Government Printing Office, and others. A review of the *American Library Directory* reveals that hundreds of libraries include maps in their holdings. Maps are no longer viewed as appendages to books, and, since maps are prominent conveyors of information in increasing numbers, libraries should include cartographic materials in their collection development policies.

Unfortunately, the field of map librarianship has lacked the most basic of reference sources—a comprehensive guide to these collections nationwide coupled with substantial lists of cartographic information and resources. Past attempts to list map collections have been incomplete, regional in scope, and the information has become quickly dated due to the lack of regular revisions. *Guide to U. S. Map Resources* is the initial attempt of the American Library Association Map and Geography Round Table to produce a thorough survey of the nation's map collections with revisions planned for every five years (i.e., 1990, 1995, etc.)

## Criteria

Questionnaires were mailed to over 3,000 libraries, the largest survey to determine the extent of map holdings in the United States. The library holdings listed in the guide can be divided into six general categories: academic, public, geoscience, state-federal, historical societies, and private libraries. With few exceptions, company libraries (i.e., oil companies) were excluded from this initial edition.

Academic libraries were identified in the U. S. Department of Education *Education Directory, Colleges and Universities 1981–82;* only four-year institutions with enrollments exceeding 1,500 were included. Generally, professional schools (i.e., medical, theology, etc.)

were excluded when readily identified. Public libraries were identified in the 1982 *American Library Directory* for which survey questionnaires were sent to all libraries with 100,000 or more volumes. Geoscience departments were identified in the American Geological Institute 1981–82 *Directory of Geoscience Departments, U. S. and Canada* and the Association of American Geographers 1982–83 *Guide to Graduate Departments of Geography in the United States and Canada.* All institutions offering graduate programs were surveyed.

The address files for the remaining three categories were provided by specialist editors familiar with each respective area. All state libraries and state geological survey offices were sent questionnaires. In addition, Arlyn Sherwood (Illinois State Library) recommended other state agencies and federal libraries to be surveyed. Similarly, all state historical societies were surveyed and additional collections were recommended by Jon Walstrom (Minnesota Historical Society). Lacking any specialized list of private libraries, Robert Karrow (The Newberry Library, Chicago) provided the project with a list of these potentially important collections.

## Organization and Compilation

The momentum for this publication began at the 1983 ALA Midwinter meetings in San Antonio. A core group soon developed a preliminary questionnaire and organizational framework. It was agreed from the beginning that a series of regional editors would follow up the questionnaires when necessary and contribute additional locations for each region not included in the general criteria outlined earlier. Second mailings were considered ineffective and telephone follow-ups could only be justified if performed on a regional basis.

Thus, the regional editors were the "first line" of return for the questionnaires after they were mailed from the general editor's address at the University of Illinois. Each region's questionnaires were initially returned to the regional editor, who checked them for completeness, contacted libraries for additional information, and initiated telephone follow-ups. (Information in entries marked with an asterisk [*] was provided by regional editors.) Then the questionnaires were sent to the University of Illinois for encoding and data input.

After reviewing the first few hundred questionnaires the general editor adopted two general guidelines:
1. With few exceptions, entries would not be included for libraries with less than 500 maps.
2. Subject specialities had to be eliminated since there was considerable confusion and exaggeration of specialities by many libraries.

## Analysis

The combined efforts of all of these persons has resulted in the most comprehensive guide to map collections in the United States. A total of 919 collections are included in this first edition of the *Guide to U. S. Map Resources.* The contents have been arranged alphabetically by state and then city.

An analysis of the data reveals that nineteen collections have more than 250,000 printed maps as of January 1, 1984 (see Table 1).

The collections above represent a total of 12,385,498 maps; the top three federal libraries in Washington alone account for 56 percent of this total. These nineteen collections average 651,868 maps, but a more realistic average of 337,865 is reached when the three large federal libraries are excluded. Further breakdowns show 78 percent of the collections contain less than 50,000 maps, 88 percent less than 100,000 and 97 percent have less than 200,000 maps.

The top ten libraries in each of the six categories are shown in Tables 2–7.

TABLE 1: *Libraries with 250,000 Printed Maps*

| Library/Location | Size |
|---|---|
| 1. Library of Congress/Washington, D.C. | 3,800,000 |
| 2. National Archives/Washington, D.C. | 2,000,000 |
| 3. Defense Mapping Agency/Washington, D.C. | 1,179,656 |
| 4. UCLA Map Library/Los Angeles | 506,547 |
| 5. Harvard Univ./Cambridge | 500,000 |
| 6. Louisiana State Univ./Baton Rouge | 500,000 |
| 7. Univ. of Wisconsin—AGS/Milwaukee | 400,000 |
| 8. New York Public Library/New York | 355,402 |
| 9. Univ. of Florida/Gainesville | 334,685 |
| 10. Univ. of Illinois/Urbana | 325,208 |
| 11. Univ. of California/Santa Barbara | 300,000 |
| 12. Univ. of Georgia/Athens | 290,000 |
| 13. U. S. Geological Survey/Reston, Va. | 290,000 |
| 14. Illinois State Univ./Normal | 275,000 |
| 15. Univ. of Chicago/Chicago | 275,000 |
| 16. Penn State/State College | 274,000 |
| 17. Indiana Univ.—Geology Library/Bloomington | 270,000 |
| 18. Univ. of Michigan/Ann Arbor | 260,000 |
| 19. Univ. of Tennessee—Geography Dept./Knoxville | 250,000 |

TABLE 2: *Largest State-Federal Libraries*

| | |
|---|---|
| Library of Congress/Washington, D.C. | 3,800,000 |
| National Archives/Washington, D.C. | 2,000,000 |
| Defense Mapping Agency/Washington, D.C. | 1,179,656 |
| U. S. Geological Survey/Reston, Va. | 290,000 |
| New York State Library/Albany | 160,000 |
| Illinois State Library/Springfield | 95,000 |
| Indiana State Library/Indianapolis | 91,208 |
| Virginia State Library/Richmond | 85,528 |
| Kentucky Dept. of Transportation/Lexington | 80,000 |
| Total | 7,781,391 |
| Average | 864,599 |

(Only nine libraries are listed in Table 2 since too many collections reported holdings of 75,000 maps.)

TABLE 3: *Largest Academic Libraries*

| | |
|---|---|
| UCLA Map Library/Los Angeles | 506,547 |
| Harvard Univ./Cambridge | 500,000 |
| Louisiana State Univ./Baton Rouge | 500,000 |
| Univ. of Wisconsin—AGS/Milwaukee | 400,000 |
| Univ. of Florida/Gainesville | 334,685 |
| Univ. of Illinois/Urbana | 325,208 |
| Univ. of California/Santa Barbara | 300,000 |
| Univ. of Georgia/Athens | 290,000 |
| Illinois State Univ./Normal | 275,000 |
| Univ. of Chicago/Chicago | 275,000 |
| Total | 3,706,440 |
| Average | 370,644 |

TABLE 4: *Largest Geoscience Libraries*

| | |
|---|---:|
| Univ. of Tennessee/Knoxville | 250,000 |
| Univ. of Wisconsin/Madison | 207,500 |
| Carleton College/Northfield, Minn. | 200,000 |
| Middlebury College/Middlebury, Vt. | 200,000 |
| San Jose State Univ./San Jose | 200,000 |
| Western Washington Univ./Bellingham | 172,000 |
| Indiana State Univ./Terre Haute | 160,000 |
| Western Illinois Univ./Macomb | 150,000 |
| Clark Univ./Worcester, Mass. | 139,000 |
| Univ. of Wisconsin/Eau Claire | 120,000 |
| Univ. of California/Berkeley | 120,000 |
| Total | 1,918,500 |
| Average | 191,850 |

TABLE 5: *Largest Public Libraries*

| | |
|---|---:|
| New York Public Library | 355,402 |
| Detroit Public Library | 161,318 |
| Public Library of Cincinnati | 137,951 |
| Free Library of Philadelphia | 130,000 |
| Milwaukee Public Library | 120,000 |
| Cleveland Public Library | 111,275 |
| St. Louis Public Library | 106,678 |
| Enoch Pratt Public Library/Baltimore | 101,362 |
| Buffalo and Erie County Public Library | 100,000 |
| Oakland (Calif.) Public Library | 100,000 |
| Total | 1,423,986 |
| Average | 142,398 |

TABLE 6: *Largest Private Libraries*

| | |
|---|---:|
| National Geographic Society/Washington, D.C. | 105,000 |
| Rand McNally & Co./Skokie, Ill. | 90,000 |
| United Nations/New York | 80,000 |
| Linda Hall Library/Kansas City | 62,000 |
| Museum of New Mexico/Albuquerque | 40,000 |
| California Academy of Science/San Francisco | 25,000 |
| Bishop Museum/Honolulu | 20,000 |
| World Bank/Washington, D.C. | 15,000 |
| Hammond Inc./Maplewood, N.J. | 13,000 |
| Amoco Library/Houston | 11,000 |
| Total | 461,000 |
| Average | 46,100 |

TABLE 7: *Largest Historical Society Libraries*

| | |
|---|---:|
| Minnesota Historical Society/St. Paul | 30,000 |
| New York Historical Society/New York | 30,000 |
| State Historical Society of Wisconsin/Madison | 23,000 |
| Utah State Historical Society/Salt Lake City | 18,000 |
| Oregon Historical Society/Portland | 15,000 |
| Ohio Historical Society/Columbus | 14,000 |
| Kansas State Historical Society/Topeka | 12,996 |
| South Dakota State Historical Society/Pierre | 8,000 |
| Idaho State Historical Society/Boise | 8,000 |
| Montana Historical Society/Helena | 6,000 |
| Total | 164,996 |
| Average | 16,499 |

As important as the holdings are, the lack of statistics in some categories is equally illuminating. For example, over 75 percent of the collections have no manuscripts; 28 percent have no atlases; 50 percent have no globes; 50 percent have no books; 48 percent have no gazetteers; and 60 percent have no aerial photographs. Although only 40 percent of the libraries have aerial photographs, they are an important type of cartographic material and are actively collected by many libraries, as shown in Table 8.

TABLE 8: *Largest Aerial Photograph Collections*

| | |
|---|---:|
| EROS Data Center/Sioux Falls, S.D. | 520,000 |
| Whittier College/Whittier, Calif. | 411,000 |
| Washington Dept. of Natural Resources/Olympia | 350,000 |
| Univ. of Oregon/Eugene | 333,388 |
| Univ. of California/Santa Barbara | 300,000 |
| Lunar & Planetary Institute/Houston | 275,000 |
| Kentucky Dept. of Transportation/Lexington | 200,000 |
| Univ. of Georgia/Athens | 190,000 |
| Univ. of Florida/Gainesville | 169,131 |
| Univ. of Minnesota/Minneapolis | 154,519 |
| Total | 5,806,076 |
| Average | 580,607 |

The remaining analyses are presented in Tables 9–14. Table 9 gives averages for each of the six collection categories and a composite average for further comparison (decimal figures have been rounded). Few persons work in or for the map collection full time, but unfortunately a high percentage (37.5) spend less than 10 percent of their time on maps.

TABLE 9: *Staffing*

| Employees | Average | Academic | Public | State-Fed. | Geosci. | Hist. Soc. | Priv. |
|---|---|---|---|---|---|---|---|
| Full Time Prof. | 43% | 45% | 43% | 15% | 48% | 44% | 55% |
| Part-time Prof. | 36% | 39% | 35% | 32% | 30% | 23% | 34% |
| Full Time Non-Prof. | 23% | 30% | 16% | 6% | 31% | 17% | 8% |
| Part Time Non-Prof. | 54% | 69% | 33% | 74% | 34% | 37% | 21% |

TABLE 10: *Cataloging & Classification*

|  | Average | Academic | Public | State-Fed. | Geosci. | Hist. Soc. | Priv. |
|---|---|---|---|---|---|---|---|
| Cataloged | | | | | | | |
| Yes | 55% | 59% | 41% | 46% | 60% | 74% | 75% |
| Classification | | | | | | | |
| LC | 22% | 37% | 6% | 8% | 9% | 16% | 17% |
| Dewey | 7% | 2% | 20% | 2% | 6% | 5% | 9% |
| Other | 29% | 19% | 23% | 37% | 45% | 51% | 51% |
| Utility | | | | | | | |
| OCLC | 16% | 24% | 12% | 5% | 13% | 4% | 13% |
| RLIN | 2% | 3% | 1% | 0% | 0% | 2% | 0% |

Table 10 leaves little doubt that the LC classification predominates, although public libraries seem to favor the traditional Dewey system despite its severe limitations for cartographic materials. It is disconcerting to learn that 45 percent of the collections are uncataloged and that nearly 75 percent of the libraries are not using either of the automated utilities. In addition, the majority of the collections (48 percent) maintain card format catalogs, if any; only 5 percent employ an online catalog.

TABLE 11: *Preservation Techniques*

| Type | Average | Academic | Public | State-Fed. | Geosci. | Hist. Soc. | Priv. |
|---|---|---|---|---|---|---|---|
| Encapsulation | 27% | 29% | 19% | 8% | 32% | 44% | 60% |
| Lamination | 16% | 14% | 20% | 14% | 21% | 9% | 11% |
| Chartex | 12% | 10% | 10% | 22% | 10% | 23% | 15% |
| Edging | 5% | 6% | 2% | 8% | 5% | 4% | 4% |
| Deacidification | 13% | 8% | 8% | 2% | 21% | 32% | 47% |

TABLE 12: *Federal Depository Collections*

| Agency | Average | Academic | Public | State-Fed. | Geosci. | Hist. Soc. | Priv. |
|---|---|---|---|---|---|---|---|
| USGS topo | 54% | 71% | 44% | 57% | 42% | 12% | 21% |
| USGS geol | 33% | 49% | 13% | 46% | 23% | 5% | 4% |
| DMA topo | 25% | 40% | 13% | 29% | 6% | 2% | 0% |
| DMA aero | 17% | 28% | 9% | 18% | 5% | 0% | 0% |
| DMA hydro | 15% | 25% | 8% | 16% | 4% | 0% | 0% |
| GPO | 30% | 50% | 26% | 5% | 13% | 0% | 0% |
| NOS | 9% | 17% | 3% | 3% | 2% | 0% | 0% |
| Canada topo | 4% | 6% | 0% | 3% | 2% | 2% | 0% |
| Canada geol | 4% | 5% | 1% | 3% | 6% | 0% | 2% |

TABLE 13: *Circulation, Use & Interlibrary Loan*

| | Average | Academic | Public | State-Fed. | Geosci. | Hist. Soc. | Priv. |
|---|---|---|---|---|---|---|---|
| Circulate | 45% | 56% | 40% | 70% | 23% | 9% | 2% |
| Annual Circulation | 250 | 300 | 150 | 101 | 362 | 590 | 500 |
| Monthly use | 31 | 49 | 49 | 20 | 29 | 10 | 20 |
| Interlibrary loan | 32% | 47% | 29% | 18% | 21% | 9% | 6% |

Although the statistics shown in Tables 11–13 are interesting for comparative purposes, they are skewed by the lack of samples, especially in the historical society and private library categories. Specifically, statistical analysis is difficult when 45 percent of the total libraries circulate maps but 66 percent do not provide figures. It is simply one of many statistics that map collections should pay more attention to in the future. If we are to use these statistics for comparative purposes, map librarians must pay closer attention to statistics for the use of others and for their own collections.

TABLE 14: *Equipment and Space*

| Type | Average | Academic | Public | State-Fed. | Geosci. | Hist. Soc. | Priv. |
|---|---|---|---|---|---|---|---|
| 5-drawer map cabinets | 12 | 19 | 3 | 24 | 12 | 8 | 8 |
| Vertical map cabinets | 2 | 3 | 2 | 2 | 2 | 1 | 2 |
| Copying machine | 87% | 93% | 90% | 64% | 81% | 91% | 89% |
| Square Footage | 325 | 600 | 50 | 700 | 249 | 200 | 150 |

## Summary

Despite the computer's methodical analysis of mounds of data, it became all too obvious that many librarians not only are unaware of the number of maps in their collections but are also confused regarding other important items such as subject specialities, equipment, cataloging, and even how much square footage their collections occupy. This is true of the smaller collections, but those responsible for larger collections are equally unfamiliar with the most basic characteristics of their collections and approximate figures with "many zeros" at the end. Careful comparisons between these 1984 statistics and those of earlier sources reveal some astonishing growth rates which could be described as suspicious at best. Although such figures are questionable, the editors believed that we should print the statistics provided to us.

It is hoped that users of this guide will provide the editors with suggestions to improve our statistical gathering for future editions, review their own statistics, and report any inaccuracies to the Map and Geography Round Table.

## Acknowledgments

One does not attempt, much less complete, a project of this magnitude without the expertise and experience of many colleagues. Thankfully, it was determined from the outset that regional editors would be selected to assist the general editor with specific regions in the United States. I cannot overemphasize their value to the compilation and completion of this publication. They willingly gave of their personal time, provided additional essential information and are the reason this is the comprehensive guide that it is. The following persons worked as regional editors on this project: Suzanne Clark (University of Vermont); Alice Hudson and Brent Allison (New York Public Library); Susan Tulis (University of Virginia); Mary Nell Maule (Georgia Tech); Dan Seldin (Indiana University); Pat Moore (University of Illinois); Pat Wilkinson (University of Northern Iowa); Richard Green (University of Iowa); Leslie Steele and Judy Reike (Texas A & M); Carol Collier (University of Wyoming); Steve Hiller (University of Washington); Linda Newman (University of Nevada); Philip Hoehn (UC, Berkeley); and Stan Stevens (UC, Santa Cruz). As mentioned earlier, the specialist editors were Arlyn Sherwood, Robert Karrow, and Jon Walstrom.

I would like also to thank the University of Illinois Library for computer support and the University of Illinois Research Board for the financial resources to support a graduate assistant. The initial mailing address file was compiled by Brent Allison while serving as my graduate assistant, and he struggled through various "printer problems" to have the questionnaire mailed in January 1984. A special thanks is also due Carol Berteotti, who input the greater part of this data from the questionnaires into a personal computer.

Projects such as this tend to prolong themselves far beyond original expectations, and the support of colleagues is especially valuable to keep one going. Two persons deserve special attention in this regard: both Donna Koepp and Charley Seavey have made the difficult times easier and always kept me thinking positively. Finally, a note of sympathy is given to Karen Sommerlad, who shared this project as much as anyone and provided the special support needed to continue.

David A. Cobb
University of Illinois
at Urbana-Champaign

**Regional and Specialist Editors**

Brent Allison, New York Public Library
Suzanne Clark, University of Vermont
Carol Collier, University of Wyoming
Richard Green, University of Iowa
Steve Hiller, University of Washington
Philip Hoehn, University of California, Berkeley
Alice Hudson, New York Public Library
Robert Karrow, Newberry Library
Mary Nell Maule, Georgia Tech University
Patricia Moore, University of Illinois
Linda Newman, University of Nevada
Judy Rieke, Texas A&M University
Dan Seldin, Indiana University
Arlyn Sherwood, Illinois State Library
Leslie Steele, Texas A&M University
Stan Stevens, University of California, Santa Cruz
Susan Tulis, University of Virginia
Jon Walstrom, Minnesota Historical Society
Pat Wilkinson, University of Northern Iowa

# Collection Directory

**Alabama**

**1**

Auburn University
Ralph B. Draughon Library
Special Collections Department
Auburn, AL 36849
Tel. (205) 826-4500
Responsible Person: Geiger, Gene,
  Special Collections Lib.
Special Strengths: Alabama
Holdings:
  96500 Printed Maps
  40000 Aerial Photographs
    100 Satellite Imagery
     20 Atlases
      1 Globe
     10 Wall Maps
     10 Raised Relief Maps
    260 Books
     40 Gazetteers
      5 Serial Titles
Chronological Coverage: 1% pre 1900;
  99% post 1900
Map collection is catalogued 2%
Classification: LC     Utility: OCLC
Formats: Cards
Preservation methods:
  Encapsulation, Lamination
Available to: Public, Students, Faculty
Circulates to: Students, Faculty
Average monthly use: 300
Average annual circulation:
  Maps: 350; Books: 50; Aerial
  Photographs: 25
Interlibrary loan available
  Only books circulate
Copying Facilities: Copying machine
Equipment:
  75 5-drawer cabinets
  12 vertical map cabinets

    1 stereoscope
Square Footage: 750
Map Depositories: USGS (topo);
  USGS (geol); DMA (topo); DMA
  (aero); DMA (hydro); GPO

**2**

Birmingham Public Library
Rucker-Agee Cartographic Collection
2020 Park Pl.
Birmingham, AL 35203
Tel. (205) 254-2534
Hours: 2–6 Su; Win 9–8, M–Th; 9–6, F,
  Sa; Sum 9–8, M, T; 9–6, W–Sa
Responsible Person: Scott, Virginia K.
Special Strengths: Southeast (Historical
  cartography discovery & exploration,
  Civil War)
Employees: Full Time     Part Time
  Prof.            0              1
Holdings:
  2995 Printed maps
   130 Aerial Photographs
   655 Atlases
     7 Globes
    17 Wall Maps
     6 Raised Relief Maps
  2123 Books
     8 Serial Titles
Chronological Coverage: 90% pre 1900;
  10% post 1900
Classification: Dewey
Formats: Cards, COM
Preservation methods:
  Encapsulation, Lamination, Chartex
  or Fabric Mounting
Available to: Public
Average monthly use: 25
Copying Facilities: Copying machine,

Photographic reproduction
Equipment:
  10 5-drawer cabinets

**3**

Samford University
Harwell G. Davis Library
800 Lakeshore Dr.
Birmingham, AL 35229
Tel. (205) 870-2748
Hours: 8–4:30, M–F
Responsible Person: Wells, Elizabeth C.
Special Strengths: Alabama, Southeast,
  Ireland
Special Collections: Casey Collection
  of Irish History & Genealogy
Employees: Full Time     Part Time
  Non-Prof.        1              3
Holdings:
  3750 Printed Maps
Chronological Coverage: 30% pre 1900;
  70% post 1900
Map collection is cataloged 75%
Available to: Public, Students, Faculty
Average monthly use: 20
Copying Facilities: Copying machine,
  Microform, Photographic reproduction
Equipment:
  5 5-drawer cabinets
Square Footage: 24

**4**

Huntsville-Madison County Public Library
Huntsville Heritage Room
P.O. Box 443
Huntsville, AL 35804
Tel. (205) 536-0021
Hours: 9–9, M–Th; 9–5, F, Sat; 1–5, Su

Responsible Person: Fuller,
    Annewhite, T., Dept. Head
Special Strengths: United States (Civil
    War), Alabama (1816–present)
Employees: Full Time    Part Time
    Non-Prof.    2        4
Holdings:
    319 Printed Maps
    100 Aerial Photographs
    20 Atlases
    50 Wall Maps
    4 Gazetteers
Chronological Coverage: 70% pre 1900;
    30% post 1900
Map collection is cataloged 90%
Formats: Printed guide
Preservation methods:
    Encapsulation, Lamination,
    Deacidification
Available to: Public
Copying Facilities: Copying machine
Equipment:
    1 5-drawer cabinet
    Acid free storage boxes
Square Footage: 10

5
Jacksonville State University Library
Jacksonville, AL 36265
Tel. (205) 435-9820
Hours: 7:30–10:30, M–F; 9–2, Sa;
    3–9 Su
Responsible Person: Cain, Linda L.
Special Strengths: Alabama
Employees: Full Time    Part Time
    Non-Prof.    0        5
Holdings:
    1156 Printed Books
    4 Aerial Photographs
    97 Atlases
    1 Globe
    3 Wall Maps
    12 Microforms
    133 Books
    12 Gazetteers
Chronological Coverage: 1% pre 1900;
    99% post 1900
Available to: Public, Students, Faculty
Copying Facilities: Copying machine
Equipment:
    4 5-drawer cabinets

6
Jacksonville State University
Map Library, Dept. of Geog. & Geol.
Jacksonville, AL 36265
Tel. (205) 435-9820
Hours: 8–3, M–F
Responsible Person: Baucom, Dr.
    Thomas F.
Special Strengths: Alabama
Employees: Full Time    Part Time
    Prof.    0        1
    Non-Prof.    0        1
Holdings:

2000 Printed Maps
    100 Aerial Photographs
    20 Satellite Imagery
    100 Raised Relief Maps
    5 Microforms
Chronological Coverage: 100% post 1900
Available to: Public, Students, Faculty
Circulates to: Faculty
Average monthly use: 2
Equipment:
    10 5-drawer cabinets
    2 vertical map cabinets
    Map-O-Graph, Stereo-Zoom Transfer
    Scope, mirror stereoscopes
Square Footage: 24
Map Depositories: USGS (topo); USGS
    (geol); DMA (topo); DMA (aero);
    DMA (hydro)

7
Mobile Public Library
701 Government St.
Mobile, AL 36602
Tel. (205) 438-7081
Hours: 9–9, M–Th; 9–6, F, Sa
Responsible Person: Curry, Janette
Special Strengths: Alabama, Gulf Coast
Holdings:
    2366 Printed Maps
    114 Atlases
    1 Globe
    1 Wall Map
    5 Books
    Gazetteers
Chronological Coverage: 2% pre 1900;
    98% post 1900
Available to: Public
Circulates to: Public
Copying Facilities: Copying machine
Equipment:
    1 5-drawer cabinet
Square Footage: 16

8
Mobile Public Library
Special Collections Division
704 Government St.
Mobile, AL 36604
Tel. (205) 438-7093
Hours: 9–6, M–T
Responsible Person: Higginbotham, Jay
Special Strengths: Gulf Coast
    (1520–present)
Employees: Full Time    Part Time
    Prof.    0        1
Holdings:
    500 Printed Maps
    100 Manuscript Maps
    50 Aerial Photographs
    4 Atlases
    2 Wall Maps
    1 Microform
    2 Books
    2 Gazetteers
Chronological Coverage: 80% pre 1900;

20% post 1900
Preservation methods:
    Encapsulation, Lamination
Available to: Public
Copying Facilities: Copying machine
Equipment:
    4 5-drawer cabinets
    1 vertical map cabinet
Square Footage: 81

9
Alabama Department of Archives & History
624 Washington Ave.
Montgomery, AL 36130-3601
Tel. (205) 261-4361
Hours: 8–5, M–F; 9–5, Sa
Responsible Person: Cox, Richard J.
Special Strengths: Alabama,
    Southeastern Ststes (19th–20th
    century)
Holdings:
    66 Atlases
    33 Books
Chronological Coverage: 50% pre 1900;
    50% post 1900
Preservation methods:
    Encapsulation, Lamination, Chartex
    or Fabric Mounting
Available to: Public, Students, Faculty
Average monthly use: 20
Average annual circulation: Maps: 240
Copying Facilities: Copying machine,
    Microform, Photographic reproduction
Equipment:
    5 5-drawer cabinets
    Multi drawer mahogany map cases
Square Footage: 230

10
Auburn University at Montgomery Library
Montgomery, AL 36193
Tel. (205) 271-9653
Hours: 7:45–9:45, M–Th; 8–4:45, F;
    1–4:45, Sa; 1–6:45, Su
Responsible Person: Dekle, Barbara W.,
    Head, Public Services
Holdings:
    1004 Printed Maps
    48 Atlases
    2 Globes
    3 Wall Maps
    32 Books
Chronological Coverage: 3% pre 1900;
    97% post 1900
Map collection is cataloged 100%
Classification: Local    Utility: OCLC
Formats: Cards
Available to: Public, Students, Faculty
Average monthly use: 4
Copying Facilities: Copying machine,
    Microform
Equipment:
    10 5-drawer cabinets
    3 vertical map cabinets
    Hanging files

Square Footage: 300
Map Depositories: DMA (topo); DMA
   (aero); DMA (hydro); GPO


### 11
Montgomery City-County Public Library
445 S. Lawrence St.
Montgomery, AL 36104
Tel. (205) 832-2884
Hours: 9–9, M–Th; 9–6, F; 9–5, Sa;
   1–6, Su
Responsible Person: Rutledge, Julia Nell
Special Strengths: Alabama
Employees: Full Time     Part Time
   Non-Prof.     1              2
Holdings:
   550 Printed Maps
   75 Atlases
   3 Globes
   4 Wall Maps
   25 Books
   10 Gazetteers
Chronological Coverage: 1% pre 1900;
   99% post 1900
Available to: Public, Students, Faculty
Circulates to: Public, Students, Faculty
Average monthly use: 40
Average annual circulation: Maps: 50
Copying Facilities: Copying machine
Equipment:
   1 5-drawer cabinet
   1 vertical map cabinet


### 12
Troy State University, Reference Dept.
Troy, AL 36082
Tel. (205) 566-3000
Hours: 7:45–10, M–Th; 7:45–5, F;
   10–2, Sa; 2–10, Su
Responsible Person: Bassett, Nell
Employees: Full Time     Part Time
   Non-Prof.     1              5
Holdings:
   1539 Printed Maps
   138 Atlases
   62 Books
   2 Gazetteers
Chronological Coverage: 10% pre 1900;
   90% post 1900
Map colleciton is cataloged 10%
Classification: LC     Utility: OCLC
Formats: Cards
Available to: Public, Students, Faculty
Average monthly use: 40
Copying Facilities: Copying machine
Equipment:
   2 5-drawer cabinets
Square Footage: 42


### 13
Geological Survey of Alabama, Library
P.O. Box O, University Station
Tuscaloosa, AL 35486
Tel. (205) 349-2852

Hours: 8–5, M–F
Responsible Person: Sartwell,
   Alexander F.
Special Collections: State Geologic maps,
   Out of print topo maps of Alabama,
   USDA Soils Maps of Alabama, USGS
   Folios, Alabama County Highway Maps.
   Alabama River Navigation Charts
Holdings:
   25000 Printed Maps
   50 Atlases
   1 Globe
   25 Wall Maps
   20 Raised Relief Maps
Chronological Coverage: 25% pre 1900;
   75% post 1900
Available to: Public, Students, Faculty
Copying Facilities: Copying machine
Equipment:
   64 various drawers
Map Depositories: USGS (geol)


### 14
University of Alabama
Map Library, Department of Geography
Box 1982, University of Alabama
University, AL 35486
Tel. (205) 348-5047
Hours: Noon–4:30, M–F
Responsible Person: Tamarin, Pat
Special Strengths: United States,
   Alabama (Aerial photography)
Employees: Full Time     Part Time
   Prof.         0              2
   Non-Prof.     0              2
Holdings:
   80000 Printed Maps
   2400 Aerial Photographs
   20 Atlases
   3 Globes
   60 Wall Maps
   20 Raised Relief Maps
Chronological Coverage: 100% post 1900
Available to: Public, Students, Faculty
Circulates to: Public, Students, Faculty
Average monthly use: 30
Average annual circulation: Maps: 300
Copying Facilities: Copying machine,
   Photographic reproduction
Equipment:
   16 5-drawer cabinets
   2 vertical map cabinets
   B&L Zoom Transferscope,
   Kail Enlarger/Reducer
Square Footage: 2000
Map Depositories: USGS (topo);
   DMA (topo)


### 15
University of Alabama
Wm. Stanley Hoole Special Collection
   Library
Amelia Gayle Gorgas Library
University, AL 35486
Tel. (205) 348-5512

Hours: 8–5, M–F; 6–10, Th
Responsible Person, Lamont, Joyce
Special Strengths: Southeast
   (16th–17th century)
Special Collections: Sanborn Fire
   Insurance Maps for Alabama Towns
Holdings:
   7500 Printed Maps
   10000 Manuscript Maps
   200 Atlases
   50 Wall Maps
   200 Books
   10 Serial Titles
Chronological Coverage: 50% pre 1900;
   50% post 1900
Map collection is cataloged 25%
Classification: LC
Utility: OCLC
Formats: Cards
Preservation methods:
   Encapsulation, Deacidification,
   Acid free folders
Available to: Public, Students, Faculty
Copying Facilities: Copying machine,
   Microform, Photographic reproduction
Equipment:
   18 5-drawer cabinets
   15 vertical map cabinets
   10 Highsmith cabinets
   2 12-drawer wood cabinets
Square Footage: 800


## Alaska
### 16
Anchorage Historical & Fine Arts
   Museum Archives
121 W. Seventh Ave.
Anchorage, AK 99501
Tel. (907) 264-4326
Hours: 9–5, M–F
Responsible Person: Brenner, M. Diane,
   Museum Archivist
Special Strengths: Alaska
Holdings:
   250 Printed Maps
   2 Manuscript Map
   40 Aerial Photographs
   3 Atlases
   2 Wall Maps
   1 Raised Relief Maps
   1 Gazetteer
Chronological Coverage: 10% pre 1900;
   90% post 1900
Map collection is cataloged 90%
Classification: LC
Formats: Cards
Available to: Public
Copying Facilities: Photographic
   reproduction
Equipment:
   4 5-drawer cabinets
   2 vertical map cabinets
Square Footage: 50

17
University of Alaska
Elmer E. Rasmuson Library
Documents & Maps Collection
Fairbanks, AK 99701
Tel. (907) 479-7624
Hours: 7:30–11, M–Th; 7:30–9, F;
  10–6, Sa; 12–10, Su
Responsible Person: Gunter, Pauline
Holdings:
  7762 Printed Maps
  500 Aerial Photographs
  495 Atlases
  3 Globes
  1 Raised Relief Map
  350 Books
  5 Serial Titles
Chronological Coverage: 25% pre 1900;
  75% post 1900
Classification: LC
Formats: Cards
Preservation methods:
  Chartex or Fabric Mounting
Available to: Public, Students, Faculty
Average monthly use: 100
Copying Facilities: Copying machine,
  Microform
Equipment:
  10 5 drawer cabinets
  Light table
Map Depositories: USGS (topo);
  USGS (geol); GPO; NOS; NOAA

18
Alaska Historical Library
Pouch G
Juneau, AK 99811
Hours: 8–5, M–F
Responsible Person: DeMuth, Phyllis,
  Librarian
Special Strengths: Alaska/Arctic
  Regions
Special Collection: Alaska USGS topo-
  graphic map microfilm rolls, Alaska
  Packers Association Collection of
  Alaska Plat Maps, Alaska fish trap &
  cannery locations
Holdings:
  4200 Printed Maps
  608 Manuscript Maps
  63 Atlases
  2 Raised Relief Maps
  256 Microforms
  500 Books
Chronological Coverage: 20% pre 1900;
  80% post 1900
Map collection is cataloged 50%
Formats: Cards, Computer Printout:
  Published Catalog
Preservation methods:
  Encapsulation, Lamination
Available to: Public
Copying Facilities: Copying machine,
  Microform, Photographic reproduction
Equipment:
  11 5-drawer cabinets
  1 vertical map cabinets
Map Depositories: USGS (topo);

USGS (geol); NOAA; Canada (geol)

19
Matanuska-Susitna Community College
  Library
Pouch 5001
Palmer, AK 99645
Tel. (907) 745-4255
Responsible Person: Madsen, Leza,
  Librarian
Special Strengths: Oregon, Washington,
  Hawaii, Alaska
Holdings:
  450 Printed Maps
  12 Aerial Photographs
  40 Atlases
  1 Globe
  15 Books
  3 Gazetteers
Chronological Coverage:
  100% post 1900
Available to: Public, Students, Faculty
Circulates to: Faculty
Average monthly use: 1
Average annual circulation: Maps: 6;
  Books: 12
Copying Facilities: Copying machine
Equipment:
  1 5-drawer cabinet
Square Footage: 6
Map Depositories: USGS (topo)

**Arizona**

20
Museum of Northern Arizona Library
Route 4, Box 720
Flagstaff, AZ 86001
Tel. (602) 774-5211
Hours: 9–5, M–F
Responsible Person: House, Dorothy,
  Librarian
Special Strengths: Arizona
Employees: Full Time    Part Time
Non-Prof.    2    4
Holdings:
  6000 Printed Maps
Formats: Cards
Available to: Public, Students, Faculty
Copying Facilities: Copying machine
Equipment:
  4 20-drawer map cases

21
Northern Arizona University Libraries
Map Collection
CU Box 6022
Flagstaff, AZ 86011
Tel. (602) 523-2171
Hours: 7:30–11, M–Th; 7:30–6, F;
  8–6, Sa; 1–11, Su
Responsible Person: Hassell, Hank
Special Strengths: Arizona (Geology)
Employees: Full Time    Part Time
Non-Prof.    0    3

Holdings:
  10000 Printed Maps
  400 Aerial Photographs
  60 Satellite Imagery
  6 Wall Maps
  12 Raised Relief Maps
  50 Books
Chronological Coverage: 5% pre 1900;
  95% post 1900
Map collection is cataloged 20%
Classification: LC
Formats: Cards
Preservation methods:
  Lamination, Chartex or Fabric
  Mounting
Available to: Public, Students, Faculty
Circulates to: Public, Students
Average monthly use: 1000
Average annual circulation: Maps: 50
Interlibrary loan available
  Library use only
Copying Facilities: Copying machine,
  Microform
Equipment:
  15 5-drawer cabinets
  2 file cabinets
Square Footage: 450
Map Depositories: USGS (topo);
  USGS (geol); GPO; NOAA

22
Northern Arizona University
Special Collections Library
C.U. Box 6022
Flagstaff, AZ 86011
Tel. (602) 523-5551
Hours: 8–5, M–F
Responsible Person: Whiteley, Peter M.
Special Strengths: Arizona (pre 1900);
  Colorado Plateau (pre 1900)
Special Collections: Manuscript Atlases
  (concern Arizona & Colorado Plateau
  explorations), (Wheeler) Atlases
  (printed)
Employees: Full Time    Part Time
Non-Prof.    2    2
Holdings:
  750 Printed Maps
  250 Manuscript Maps
  50 Aerial Photographs
  40 Atlases
  12 Wall Maps
  20 Raised Relief Maps
  26 Books
  3 Serial Titles
Chronological Coverage: 75% pre 1900;
  25% post 1900
Map collection is cataloged 100%
Classification: LC    Utility: OCLC
Formats: Cards
Preservation methods:
  Encapsulation, Lamination,
  Deacidification
Available to: Public, Students, Faculty
Average monthly use: 75
Copying Facilities: Copying machine

Equipment:
  30 5-drawer cabinets
  8 linear feet of vertical
  shelving, 3 12-drawer map cabinets
Square Footage: 50


## 23
Grand Canyon Study Collection
Map Library
P. O. Box 129
Grand Canyon NP, AZ 86023
Hours: 8–5, M–F
Responsible Person: Chamberlin,
  Edward M., Museum Tech.
Special Strengths: Grand Canyon NP,
  Arizona, Colorado River
Special Collections: The collection is
  for the storage of all (Grand Canyon)
  materials & only Grand Canyon NP
  materials.
Employees: Full Time    Part Time
Non-Prof.    0          2
Holdings:
  150 Printed Maps
  50 Manuscript Maps
  2000 Aerial Photographs
  2 Satellite Imagery
  1 Raised Relief Map
Chronological Coverage: 1% pre 1900;
  99% post 1900
Map collection is cataloged 2%
Classification: NPS System
Formats: Cards
Preservation methods:
  Encapsulation, Deacidification
Average monthly use: 1
Copying Facilities: Copying machine,
  Microform
Equipment:
  8 5-drawer cabinets
  acid free folders
Square Footage: 52
Map Depositories:
  Grand Canyon maps incl.
  developmental plans


## 24
Mesa Public Library
64 E. 1st St.
Mesa, AZ 85201
Tel. (602) 834-2715
Hours: 9:30–9, M–Th; 9:30–5:30, F, Sa
Responsible Person: Snelson, Lanty C.
Special Strengths: Arizona, Mesa
Employees: Full Time    Part Time
Non-Prof.    0          1
Holdings:
  1500 Printed Maps
  40 Atlases
  1 Globe
  7 Wall Maps
  15 Raised Relief Maps
  5 Books
  2 Gazetteers
Chronological Coverage: 2% pre 1900;

98% post 1900
Available to: Public
Average monthly use: 50
Copying Facilities: Copying machine,
  Microform
Equipment:
  12 5-drawer cabinets
  2 atlas cases
Square Footage: 140


## 25
Arizona Dept. of Library Archives &
  Public Records, Map Services
1700 W. Washington, State Capital
Phoenix, AZ 85007
Tel. (602) 255-4046
Hours: 8–5, M–F
Responsible Person: Rowan, Atifa,
  Head, Maps & Documents
Special Strengths: Arizona, Southwest
Special Collections: Landsat Imagery
  of United States
Holdings:
  10000 Printed Maps
  50 Manuscript Maps
  300 Satellite Imagery
  25 Atlases
  3 Globes
  10 Wall Maps
  60 Raised Relief Maps
  1300 Microforms
  10 Books
  150 Gazetteers
Chronological Coverage: 50% pre 1900;
  50% post 1900
Map collection is cataloged 50%
Classification: LC    Utility: OCLC
Formats: Cards
Preservation methods:
  Encapsulation
Available to: Public
Average monthly use: 90
Copying Facilities: Copying machine,
  Microform
Equipment:
  2 vertical map cabinets
  9 various map cabinets
Map Depositories: USGS (topo);
  USGS (geol); DMA (topo); GPO


## 26
Arizona State Dept. of Mines & Mineral
  Resources, Map Collection
Mineral Resources Building: Fairgrounds
Phoenix, AZ 85007
Tel. (602) 255-3791
Hours: 8–5, M–F
Responsible Person: Jett, John, Director
Special Strengths: Arizona (Mining)
Special Collections: Unique Maps of
  Mines contained in Mine Files
Holdings:
  2500 Printed Maps
  2000 Manuscript Maps
  11 Atlases

50 Wall Maps
2000 Microforms
2 Books
4 Gazetteers
Chronological Coverage: 10% pre 1900;
  90% post 1900
Map collection is cataloged 90%
Formats: Cards, Computer Printout
Preservation methods:
  Lamination
Available to: Public, Students, Faculty
Copying Facilities: Copying machine
Equipment:
  6 5-drawer cabinets
  Light table


## 27
Yavapai College Library
1100 E. Sheldon
Prescott, AZ 86301
Tel. (602) 445-7300
Hours: 7–10, M–Th; 7–6, F; 1–9, Su
Responsible Person: Brenna, Charlotte,
  Library Director
Special Strengths: Arizona
Holdings:
  800 Printed Maps
  15 Atlases
  1 Globe
  2 Wall Maps
  1 Book
Chronological Coverage:
  100% post 1900
Map collection is cataloged 75%
Classification: LC
Formats: Cards, COM
Available to: Public, Students, Faculty
Circulates to: Public, Students, Faculty
Average monthly use: 30
Average annual circulation: Maps: 50
Copying Facilities: Copying machine
Equipment:
  1 vertical map cabinet
Square Footage: 30
Map Depositories: USGS (topo); GPO


## 28
Arizona State University
Noble Science & Engineering Library
Map Collection
Tempe, AZ 85287
Tel. (602) 965-3582
Hours: 8–8, M–Th; 8–5, F; 1–5, Su
Responsible Person: Miller, Rosanna,
  Head, Map Collection
Special Strengths: Arizona, Southwest,
  Mexico
Employees: Full Time    Part Time
Prof.        1          0
Non-Prof.    3          1
Holdings:
  110000 Printed Maps
  1650 Aerial Photographs
  50 Satellite Imagery
  1055 Atlases

1 Globe
10 Wall Maps
55 Raised Relief Maps
240 Books
273 Gazetteers
12 Serial Titles
Chronological Coverage: 8% pre 1900;
92% post 1900
Preservation methods:
Encapsulation, Deacidifcation
Available to: Public, Students, Faculty
Circulates to: Public, Students, Faculty
Average monthly use: 250
Average annual circulation: Maps: 3350
Interlibrary loan available
Copying Facilities: Copying machine
Equipment:
220 5-drawer cabinets
Square Footage: 4966
Map Depositories: USGS (topo);
USGS (geol); DMA (topo); DMA
(aero); DMA (hydro); GPO; NOS;
NOAA

### 29
Tempe Public Library
3500 S. Rural Rd.
Tempe, AZ 85282
Tel. (602) 968-8231
Hours: 10–9, M–Th; 10–5:30, F, Sa;
1:30–5:30, Su
Special Strengths: Arizona
Holdings:
695 Printed Maps
75 Atlases
1 Globe
6 Books
3 Gazetteers
Chronological Coverage: 2% pre 1900;
98% post 1900
Map collection is cataloged 13%
Classification: Dewey    Utility: OCLC
Formats: Cards
Available to: Public
Copying Facilities: Copying machine,
Microform
Equipment:
3 vertical map cabinets
Square Footage: 30

### 30
Arizona Bureau of Geology & Mineral
Technology
845 N. Park
Tucson, AZ 85710
Tel. (602) 621-7906
Hours: 8:30–5, M–F
Special Strengths: Arizona
Employees: Full time    Part Time
Non-Prof.    1          2
Holdings:
9700 Printed Maps
200 Aerial Photographs
24 Wall Maps
1 Raised Relief Map

1 Microform
Chronological Coverage:
100% post 1900
Map collection is cataloged 50%
Formats: Cards
Available to: Public, Students, Faculty
Copying Facilities: Copying machine
Equipment:
11 5-drawer cabinets
4 vertical map cabinets
Square Footage: 150
Map Depositories: USGS (topo);
USGS (geol)

### 31
Arizona Heritage Center
Research Library (Maps)
949 E. Second St.
Tucson, AZ 85719
Tel. (602) 628-5774
Hours: 10–4, M–F; 10–1, Sa
Responsible Person: Bock, Jean
Special Strengths: Southwest & Sonora
(18th–19th century), Arizona
(18th–19th century)
Employees: Full Time    Part Time
Prof.         0            1
Non-Prof.     0            1
Holdings:
3500 Printed Maps
15 Manuscript Maps
200 Aerial Photographs
2 Satellite Imagery
25 Atlases
8 Wall Maps
2 Raised Relief Maps
1900 Microforms
15 Books
2 Gazetteers
2 Serial Titles
Chronological Coverage: 70% pre 1900;
30% post 1900
Map collection is cataloged 75%
Formats: Cards
Preservation methods:
Encapsulation
Available to: Public, Students, Faculty
Copying Facilities: Copying machine,
Microform, Photographic reproduction
Equipment:
13 5-drawer cabinets
1 3-drawer, 1 7-drawer
1 12-drawer, 2 10-drawer
Square Footage: 272

### 32
National Park Service
Western Archeological & Conservation
Center
P. O. Box 41058
Tucson, AZ 85717
Tel. (602) 629-6995
Hours: 8–4:30, M–F
Responsible Person: Horn, W. Richard,
Librarian

Special Strengths: Southwest United
States
Holdings:
1800 Printed Maps
100 Aerial Photographs
5 Atlases
5 Books
1 Gazetteer
Chronological Coverage:
100% post 1900
Available to: Public, Students
Average monthly use: 10
Average annual circulation: Maps: 150;
Books: 600
Interlibrary loan available
Copying Facilities: Photographic
reproduction
Equipment:
13 5-drawer cabinets
6 vertical map cabinets
Square Footage: 64

### 33
Tucson Public Library
200 S. Sixth Ave., P. O. Box 27470
Tucson, AZ 85726
Tel. (602) 791-4393
Hours: 9–9, M–Th; 9–5, F, Sa; 1:30–5, Su
Responsible Person: Barber, Carroll G.,
Map Librarian
Special Strengths: Arizona
Employees: Full Time    Part Time
Prof.         0            1
Non-Prof.     0            1
Holdings:
1200 Printed Maps
50 Atlases
1 Globe
2 Wall Maps
22 Raised Relief Maps
40 Books
4 Gazetteers
Chronological Coverage: 1% pre 1900;
99% post 1900
Preservation methods:
Lamination
Available to: Public
Average monthly use: 300
Copying Facilities: Copying machine
Equipment:
3 5-drawer cabinets
Atlas case
Square Footage: 100
Map Depositories: USGS (topo)

### 34
University of Arizona,
Space Imagery Center
Lunar & Planetary Laboratory
Tucson, AZ 85721
Tel. (602) 621-4861
Hours: 8–5, M–F
Responsible Person: Georgenson, Gail S.
Special Strengths: Planets (geologic,
shaded relief, controlled photomosaics,

etc.)
Special Collections: Satellite imagery
    from planetary probes
Employees: Full Time      Part Time
Prof.            0              2
Holdings:
        500 Printed Maps
        1000 Aerial Photographs
        500000 Satellite Imagery
        25 Atlases
        8 Globes
        20 Computer Tapes
        150 Books
Chronological Coverage:
    100% post 1900
Map collection is cataloged 100%
Classification: USGS
Formats: Cards
Available to: Public, Students, Faculty
Average monthly use: 10
Copying Facilities: Copying machine,
    Photographic reproduction
Equipment:
    20 5-drawer cabinets
Square Footage: 1100
Map Depositories: USGS (topo);
    USGS (geol); DMA (topo)


35
University of Arizona
University Library, Map Collection
Tucson, AZ 85721
Tel. (602) 626-2596
Hours: 8–5, M–F; 9–1, Sa
Responsible Person: Minton, James O.,
    Map Librarian
Special Strengths: Arizona, Southwestern
    United States, Mexico
Special Collections: LANDSAT: approx.
    2126 reels of 70 mm. negative film,
    providing complete coverage of land
    surfaces of the earth, images taken
    primarily between 1975 & 1977
Employees: Full Time      Part Time
Prof.            3              0
Non-Prof.        1              5
Holdings:
        165000 Printed Maps
        16331 Aerial Photographs
        2126 Satellite Imagery
        2000 Atlases
        13 Globes
        162 Wall Maps
        60 Raised Relief Maps
        23 Microforms
        880 Books
        420 Gazetteers
        55 Serial Titles
Chronological Coverage: 1% pre 1900;
    99% post 1900
Map collection is cataloged 100%
Classification: LC      Utility: OCLC
Formats: Cards
Preservation methods:
    Encapsulation, Lamination,
    Chartex or Fabric Mounting, Edging

Available to: Public, Students, Faculty
Circulates to: Public, Students, Faculty
Average monthly use: 600
Average annual circulation:
    Maps: 11600
Interlibrary loan available
Copying Facilities: Copying machine
Equipment:
    27 5-drawer cabinets
    60 vertical map cabinets
    11 5-drawer vertical files
    6 4-drawer vertical files
    drafting table, light table, single path
    light table
Square Footage: 5807
Map Depositories: USGS (topo);
    USGS (geol); DMA (topo); DMA
    (aero); DMA (hydro); GPO


## Arkansas
36
University of Central Arkansas
Department of Geography, Map Library
Old Main
Conway, AR 72032
Tel. (501) 450-3164
Responsible Person: Butt, Paul L.
Special Strengths: Arkansas
Employees: Full Time      Part Time
Non-Prof.        0              2
Holdings:
        50000 Printed Maps
        10 Atlases
        50 Wall Maps
        20 Raised Relief Maps
Chronological Coverage:
    100% post 1900
Map collection is cataloged 95%
Available to: Public, Students, Faculty
Circulates to: Public, Students, Faculty
Average monthly use: 70
Average annual circulation: Maps: 200
Equipment:
    11 5-drawer cabinets
    6 24-drawer cabinets
Square Footage: 400
Map Depositories: USGS (topo)


37
University of Arkansas
University Libraries
Reference & Government Documents,
Map Library
Fayetteville, AR 72701
Tel. (501) 575-4101
Hours: 7–11, M–Th; 7–6, F; 9–6, Sa;
    10–11, Su
Responsible Person: Bailey, Alberta,
    Reference Librarian
Special Strengths: Arkansas &
    surrounding states, United States
Employees: Full Time      Part Time
Prof.            0              3
Non-Prof.        0              2
Holdings:

        104000 Printed Maps
        130 Atlases
        1 Globe
        1 Wall Map
        6 Raised Relief Maps
        510 Microforms
        60 Books
        10 Gazetteers
        1 Serial Title
Chronological Coverage: 10% pre 1900;
    90% post 1900
Map collection is cataloged 90%
Classification: LC      Utility: OCLC
Formats: Cards
Available to: Public, Students, Faculty
Circulates to: Students, Faculty
Average monthly use: 100
Average annual circulation: Maps: 100
Copying Facilities: Copying machine
Equipment:
    95 5-drawer cabinets
Square Footage: 2000
Map Depositories: USGS (topo);
    USGS (geol); DMA (topo); DMA
    (aero); DMA (hydro); GPO; NOAA;
    US Bureau of Census; US Soil Cons.
    Serv.; US National Forest System


38
Arkansas Geological Commission
3815 W. Roosevelt Rd.
Little Rock, AR 72204
Tel. (501) 371-1488
Hours: 8–4:30, M–F
Responsible Person: Sproul, Oleta
Special Strengths: Arkansas (Geology,
    Topography & Hydrology)
Holdings:
        12000 Printed Maps
        100 Satellite Imagery
        20 Atlases
Chronological Coverage: 15% pre 1900;
    85% post 1900
Available to: Public
Average monthly use: 25
Interlibrary loan available
    Rare do not circulate
Copying Facilities: Copying machine
Equipment:
    36 5-drawer cabinets
    1 vertical map cabinet
    Book shelving
    48 tube cabinets
Square Footage: 674
Map Depositories: USGS (topo);
    USGS (geol)


39
Central Arkansas Library System
Reference Services
700 Louisiana
Little Rock, AR 72201
Tel. (501) 370-5952
Hours: 8:30–9, M, T, Th; 8:30–6, W, F, Sa
Responsible Person: Ziegenbein, Sarah B.

Special Strengths: Arkansas
Holdings:
  1600 Printed Maps
    1 Aerial Photograph
    19 Atlases
    1 Globe
    3 Wall Maps
    2 Raised Relief Maps
    1 Gazetteers
Chronological Coverage: 1% pre 1900;
  99% post 1900
Map collection is cataloged 100%
Formats: Cards
Available to: Public
Average monthly use: 5
Copying Facilities: Copying machine
Equipment
  3 10-drawer cabinets
Square Footage: 36

### 40
Arkansas State University
Dean B. Ellis Library
P. O. Box 2040
State University, AR 72467
Tel. (501) 972-3077
Hours: 7:30–4:30, M–F
Special Strengths: Arkansas
Employees: Full Time    Part Time
  Prof.        0            1
  Non-Prof.    0            1
Holdings:
  800 Printed Maps
    2 Atlases
Chronological Coverage: 2% pre 1900;
  98% post 1900
Preservation methods:
  Encapsulation
Average monthly use: 10
Copying Facilities: Copying machine,
  Microform
Equipment:
  6 5-drawer cabinets
Square Footage: 240
Map Depositories: USGS (topo);
  GPO

### California
### 41
Alameda Free Library*
1433 Oak St.
Alameda, CA 94501
Tel. (415) 522-3578
Hours: 10–9, M, W, Th; 10–5:30, T, Sa;
  1–5:30, F
Holdings:
  5318 Printed Maps
Available to: Public
Copying Facilities: Copying machine
Map Depositories: USGS (topo)

### 42
Humboldt State University
University Library, Map Collection
Arcata, CA 95521
Hours: 8–9, M–Th; 8–5, F; 1–5, Sa, Su
Responsible Person: Sathrum, Robert L.,
  Map Librarian
Special Strengths: Northwestern
  California, Northeastern California
Holdings:
  13700 Printed Maps
    4500 Aerial Photographs
    300 Atlases
    3 Globes
    15 Raised Relief Maps
    50 Microforms
Chronological Coverage: 2% pre 1900;
  98% post 1900
Map collection is cataloged 100%
Classification: LC
Formats: Computer Printout
Preservation methods:
  Chartex or Fabric Mounting
Available to: Public, Students, Faculty
Circulates to: Students, Faculty
Average annual circulation:
  Maps: 13125
Interlibrary loan available
Copying Facilities: Copying machine,
  Microform
Equipment:
  24 5-drawer cabinets
  2 vertical map cabinets
  mirror stereoscope
Square Footage: 1000
Map Depositories: USGS (topo);
  USGS (geol); DMA (topo); DMA
  (aero); DMA (hydro); GPO; NOS

### 43
Kern County Library
Geology-Mining-Petroleum Library
1315 Truxtun Ave.
Bakersfield, CA 93301
Tel. (805) 861-2136
Hours: 10–9, M–Th; 10–6, F, Sa
Responsible Person: Haas, Mary,
  G-M-P Librarian
Special Strengths: California, Western
  States
Employees: Full Time    Part Time
  Prof.        0            1
Holdings:
  8121 Printed Maps
  18377 Books
    26 Serial titles
Chronological Coverage:
  100% post 1900
Available to: Public
Average monthly use: 60
Average annual circulation: Books: 350
Copying Facilities: Copying machine,
  Microform
Equipment:
  8 5-drawer cabinets
  5 vertical map cabinets

Map Depositories: CA's Divisions of
  Mines & Geology, Oil & Gas, U.S.
  Bureau of Mines

### 44
Berkeley Public Library, Main Branch
2090 Kittredge
Berkeley, CA 94704
Tel. (415) 644-6648
Hours: 10–8, M–Th; 10–6, Sa; 1–5, Su
Responsible Person: Saunderson, Robert
Special Strengths: California, United
  States (state & city road maps)
Employees: Full Time    Part Time
  Prof.        0            1
  Non-Prof.    0            1
Holdings:
  7000 Printed Maps
    280 Atlases
    2 Globes
    8 Wall Maps
    3 Raised Relief Maps
    20 Books
    2 Gazetteers
Chronological Coverage: 1% pre 1900;
  99% post 1900
Available to: Public
Circulates to: Public
Copying Facilities: Copying machine,
  Microform
Equipment
  3 5-drawer cabinets
  3 vertical map cabinets
Square Footage: 40

### 45
U. S. Forest Service Library
P. O. Box 245
Berkeley, CA 94701
Tel. (415) 486-3382
Hours: 7:45–4:15, M–F
Responsible Person: Galvin, Dennis
Special Strengths: California (Soil-
  Vegetation maps, Timber Stands)
Employees: Full Time    Part Time
  Prof.        0            1
  Non-Prof.    0            1
Holdings:
  1200 Printed Maps
    100 Manuscript Maps
    300 Microforms
Chronological Coverage:
  100% post 1900
Preservation methods:
  Chartex or Fabric Mounting
Available to: Faculty
Average monthly use:12
Copying Facilities: Copying machine
Equipment:
  6 5-drawer cabinets
  Microfiche readers
Square Footage: 100
Map Depositories: CA Dept. of Forestry,
  U. S. Forest Service

46
University of California, Berkeley
Department of Geography Library
501 Earth Science Building
Berkeley, CA 94720
Tel. (415) 642-3903
Hours: 1–5, M–F
Responsible Person: Holmes, Daniel O.
Special Strengths: California
Employees: Full Time    Part Time
  Prof.        0            1
  Non-Prof.    0            1
Holdings:
  120000 Printed Maps
    100 Manuscript Maps
  90000 Aerial Photographs
    35 Atlases
    5 Globes
  1000 Wall Maps
    200 Raised Relief Maps
    5 Microforms
    100 Books
    20 Gazetteers
    30 Serial Titles
Chronological Coverage: 10% pre 1900;
  90% post 1900
Map collection is cataloged 20%
Formats: Cards, Computer Printout
Preservation methods: Encapsulation,
  Chartex or Fabric Mounting
Available to: Public, Students, Faculty
Circulates to: Students, Faculty
Average monthly use: 40
Average annual circulation:
  Maps: 3000; Aerial Photographs: 100
Copying Facilities: Copying machine,
  Photographic reproduction
Equipment:
  60 5-drawer cabinets
  12 shelved cabinets
  Stereoscopes, Kail projector, digitizer
Square Footage: 1400


47
University of California, Berkeley
Earth Sciences Library
230 Earth Sciences Building,
Dept. of Geology & Geophysics
Berkeley, CA 94720
Tel. (415) 642-2997
Hours: 9–7, M–Th; 9–5, F; 10–5, Sa, Su
Responsible Person: Rinaldi, Julie F.
  Acting Head
Special Strengths: Western United
  States, especially California (20th
  century)
Employees: Full Time    Part Time
  Non-Prof.    1            6
Holdings:
  46579 Printed Maps
    2 Globes
Chronological Coverage: 5% pre 1900;
  95% post 1900
Map collection is cataloged 100%
Classification: LC    Utility: OCLC
Formats: Cards, COM, Online

Preservation methods:
  Encapsulation
Available to: Public, Students, Faculty
Circulates to: Public, Students, Faculty
Average annual circulation:
  Books: 32000
Interlibrary loan available
  A small percentage of collection is
  designated as non-circulating
Copying Facilities: Copying machine
Equipment:
  42 5-drawer cabinets
  11 5-drawer cabinets
  5 closets for rolled maps
Square Footage: 716
Map Depositories: USGS (topo);
  USGS (geol); Canada (geol); Australia,
  Japan, New Zealand, South Africa


48
University of California, Berkeley
East Asiatic Library
Berkeley, CA 94720
Tel. (415) 642-2556
Hours: 9–7, M–Th; 9–5, F, Sa
Responsible Person: Shively, Donald
Special Strengths: Japan & East Asia
  (1650–1912)
Holdings:
  2000 Printed Maps
    100 Aerial Photographs
Chronological Coverage: 90% pre 1900;
  10% post 1900
Map collection is cataloged 80%
Formats: Cards
Preservation methods: Encapsulation
Available to: Public, Students, Faculty
Copying Facilities: Microform,
  Photographic reproduction


49
University of California, Berkeley
Forestry Library
Berkeley, CA 94720
Tel. (415) 642-2936
Hours: 9–9, M–Th; 9–5, F; 1–5, Sa, Su
Responsible Person: Evans, Peter
Special Strengths: California, Vegetation
Special Collections: California Soil-
  Vegetation Maps
Holdings:
  1800 Printed Maps
    24 Atlases
Chronological Coverage:
  100% post 1900
Map collection is cataloged 90%
Available to: Public, Students, Faculty


50
University of Californa, Berkeley
General Library, Map Room
Berkeley, CA 94720
Tel. (415) 642-4940
Hours: 10–5, M–F; 1–5, Sa

Responsible Person: Hoehn, Philip,
  Map Librarian
Special Strengths: California, Mexico,
  Central America, Western United
  States, Canada
Employees: Full Time    Part Time
  Prof.        0            1
  Non-Prof.    0            6
Holdings:
  237692 Printed Maps
  21882 Aerial Photographs
    2300 Atlases
    2 Globes
  1000 Wall Maps
    500 Raised Relief Maps
  6425 Microforms
    345 Books
    340 Gazetteers
Chronological Coverage: 10% pre 1900;
  90% post 1900
Map collection is cataloged 100%
Classification: LC    Utility: OCLC
Formats: Cards, COM, Online
Preservation methods: Encapsulation
Available to: Public, Students, Faculty
Circulates to: Public, Students, Faculty
Average monthly use: 540
Average annual circulation:
  Maps: 16114; Books: 2170;
  Microfiche: 103
Interlibrary loan available
  Rare & reference maps do not circulate
Copying Facilities: Copying machine,
  Microform, Photographic reproduction,
  slides
Equipment:
  286 5-drawer cabinets
  3 vertical map cabinets
  1 9-drawer, 30 4-drawer
  6 4-drawer vertical files
  stereoscopes, planimeter, map wheel
  (distance measuring), 'Topo Aid'
Square Footage: 5600
Map Depositories: USGS (topo); DMA
  (topo); DMA (aero); GPO; NOS,
  NOAA; CA (Lib. Depos. Act)


51
University of California, Berkeley
Museum of Paleontology, Map File
Berkeley, CA 94720
Tel. (415) 642-3733
Hours: 8–5, M–F
Responsible Person: Hutchinson, J. H.
Special Strengths: California, Nevada,
  Oregon, Montana, Wyoming, Western
  United States, France, Argentina,
  Mexico
Holdings:
  3000 Printed Maps
    100 Aerial Photographs
    2 Atlases
    2 Wall Maps
    4 Raised Relief Maps
Chronological Coverage: 2% pre 1900;
  98% post 1900

Map collection is cataloged 70%
Classification: Scale/Name
Formats: Cards, Computer Printout
Available to: Students, Faculty
Average monthly use: 15
Copying Facilities: Copying machine
Equipment:
  6 5-drawer cabinets
Square Footage: 40

#### 52

University of California, Berkeley
The Bancroft Library
Berkeley, CA 94720
Tel. (415) 642-6481
Hours: 9–5, M–F; 1–5, Sa
Responsible Person: Hoehn, Philip,
  Map Librarian
Special Strengths: California, The West,
  Mexico (pre-1900) land grants, mines
  & mining, land ownership)
Employees: Full Time    Part Time
  Prof.        0            1
Holdings:
  20499 Printed Maps
    59 Aerial Photographs
   500 Atlases
     6 Globes
  1300 Microforms
   500 Books
    50 Gazetteers
     2 Serial Titles
Chronological Coverage: 75% pre 1900;
  25% post 1900
Map collection is cataloged 100%
Classification: LC    Utility: OCLC
Formats: Cards, COM, Online
Preservation methods: Encapsulation
Available to: Public, Students, Faculty
Average monthly use: 50
Average annual circulation:
  Maps: 3700
Interlibrary loan available
  Only photo- or microcopies loaned
Copying Facilities: Copying machine,
  Microform, Photographic reproduction,
  slides
Equipment:
  52 5-drawer cabinets
  4 10-drawer cabinets
Square Footage: 850

#### 53

University of California, Berkeley
Water Resources Center Archives
410 O'Brien Hall
Berkeley, CA 94720
Tel. (415) 642-2666
Hours: 8–5, M–F
Responsible Person: Giefer, Gerald J.
Special Strengths: California (1890–
  1940); Water Resources, Irrigation,
  Reclamation)
Employees: Full Time    Part Time
  Non-Prof.    2            1

Holdings:
  2000 Printed Maps
  3142 Manuscript Maps
   350 Aerial Photographs
    10 Atlases
     1 Globe
     8 Wall Maps
     2 Raised Relief Maps
     1 Gazetteer
Chronological Coverage: 5% pre 1900;
  95% post 1900
Map collection is cataloged 100%
Formats: Cards, Online
Available to: Public, Students, Faculty
Average annual circulation:
  Books: 15000
Interlibrary loan available
Copying Facilities: Copying machine,
  Photographic reproduction
Equipment:
  13 5-drawer cabinets
  1 vertical map cabinet
Square Footage: 100

#### 54

Burlingame Public Library*
480 Primrose Rd.
Burlingame, CA 94010
Tel. (415) 344-7107
Hours: 9–9, M–F; 9–6, Sa; 1–5, Su
Holdings:
  1379 Printed Maps
Available to: Public
Copying Facilities: Copying machine

#### 55

California State University, Chico
Geographical Services
Department of Geography
Chico, CA 95929
Tel. (916) 895-5969
Hours: 8–Noon, 1–5, M–F
Responsible Person: Nelson, Charles,
  Cartographic Technician
Special Strengths: Northern California
Employees: Full Time    Part Time
  Non-Prof.    0            3
Holdings:
  14984 Printed Maps
   245 Manuscript Maps
  3900 Aerial Photographs
    55 Satellite Imagery
    15 Atlases
     5 Globes
   250 Wall Maps
    70 Raised Relief Maps
Chronological Coverage: 1% pre 1900;
  99% post 1900
Preservation methods: Chartex or
  Fabric Mounting
Available to: Public, Students, Faculty
Circulates to: Public, Students, Faculty
Average monthly use: 860
Average annual circulation:
  Maps: 9750; Aerial Photographs: 2450

Copying Facilities: Copying machine,
  Photographic reproduction, Diazo
Equipment:
  44 5-drawer cabinets
  4 cabinets (aerials)
  Variscan enlargement machine,
  map-o-graph, mirror stereoscopes
Square Footage: 780

#### 56

California State University, Chico
Meriam Library—Maps
Chico, CA 95929
Tel. (916) 895-6803
Hours: 8–8, M–Th; 8–5, F; 1–5, Su
Responsible Person: Crotts, Joe
Special Strengths: California
Employees: Full Time    Part Time
  Prof.        1            1
Holdings:
  100000 Printed Maps
    10 Aerial Photographs
   500 Atlases
     2 Globes
    10 Wall Maps
    60 Raised Relief Maps
    20 Books
   175 Gazetteers
     4 Serial Titles
Chronological Coverage: 1% pre 1900;
  99% post 1900
Map collection is cataloged 100%
Classification: LC    Utility: OCLC
Formats: Cards
Preservation methods: Encapsulation,
  Lamination, Chartex or Fabric
  Mounting
Available to: Public, Students, Faculty
Circulates to: Students, Faculty
Average monthly use: 300
Average annual circulation: Maps: 300
Interlibrary loan available
  Northern California
Copying Facilities: Copying machine
Equipment:
  107 5-drawer cabinets
  1 vertical map cabinet
  16 5-drawer file cabinets
  2 light tables, 1 polar planimeter
Square Footage: 4400
Map Depositories: USGS (topo);
  USGS (geol); DMA (topo); DMA
  (aero); DMA (hydro); GPO, CA Div.
  of Mines & Geology; CA State Printing
  Office

#### 57

University of California, Davis
Physical Sciences Library
Geological Map Collection
Davis, CA 95616
Tel. (916) 752-0519
Hours: 9–5, M–F
Responsible Person: Jester, Edward C.
Special Strengths: California, World

(Geology)
Holdings:
    7600 Printed Maps
      20 Serial Titles
Chronological Coverage:
    100% post 1900
Map collection is cataloged 37%
Classification: LC        Utility: OCLC
Formats: Cards
Available to: Public, Students, Faculty
Circulates to: Public, Students, Faculty
Average monthly use: 50
Average annual circulation: Maps: 650
Interlibrary loan available
Copying Facilities: Copying machine
Equipment:
    10 5-drawer cabinets
     8 vertical map cabinets
Square Footage: 187
Map Depositories:  USGS (geol)

### 58

University of California, Davis
Shields Library, Map Section
Davis, CA 95616
Tel. (916) 752-1624
Hours: 8–5, M–F; 7–10, M, W;
    1–5, Sa, Su
Responsible Person: Lundquist, David,
    Map Librarian
Special Strengths: World (Wine)
Employees: Full Time      Part Time
    Prof.           0              1
    Non-Prof.    0              4
Holdings:
    77434 Printed Maps
        1 Manuscript Map
    20000 Aerial Photographs
      100 Satellite Imagery
       61 Atlases
        4 Globes
      250 Wall Maps
       47 Raised Relief Maps
    18328 Microforms
      320 Books
      158 Gazetteers
      457 Serial Titles
Chronological Coverage: 10% pre 1900;
    90% post 1900
Map collection is cataloged 40%
Classification: LC        Utility: OCLC
Formats: Cards
Preservation methods: Encapsulation,
    Chartex or Fabric Mounting
Available to: Public, Students, Faculty
Circulates to: Public, Students, Faculty
Average monthly use: 350
Average annual circulation:
    Maps: 3000; Aerial Photographs: 50
Interlibrary loan available
    Rare or fragile materials
Copying Facilities: Copying machine
Equipment:
    60 5-drawer cabinets
     8 vertical file cabinets
     1 microfiche

Square Footage: 800
Map Depositories: USGS (topo);
    USGS (geol); DMA (topo); DMA
    (aero); DMA (hydro); GPO; NOS

### 59

Solano County Library*
1150 Kentucky St.
Fairfield, CA 94533
Tel. (415) 429-6601
Hours: 10–9, M–Th; 10–6, F; 10–5, Sa;
    1–5, Su
Holdings:
    2638 Printed Maps
Available to: Public
Copying Facilities: Copying machine,
    Microform

### 60

California State University, Fresno
Henry Madden Library, Map Library
Fresno, CA 93740
Tel. (209) 294-2174
Responsible Person: Fox, Herbert S.,
    Map Librarian
Special Strengths: Central California
Employees: Full Time      Part Time
    Prof.           0              1
    Non-Prof.    0              1
Holdings:
    103850 Printed Maps
      1200 Aerial Photographs
        20 Satellite Imagery
       550 Atlases
         5 Globes
         5 Wall Maps
        30 Raised Relief Maps
         5 Microforms
       220 Gazetteers
Chronological Coverage: 1% pre 1900;
    99% post 1900
Preservation methods: Lamination,
    Chartex of Fabric Mounting; Acid
    free folders
Available to: Public, Students, Faculty
Circulates to: Public, Students, Faculty
Average monthly use: 210
Interlibrary loan available
    No atlases, gazetteers, raised relief
    maps, DMA maps or O.P. maps
Copying Facilities: Copying machine,
    Microform
Equipment:
    63 50-drawer cabinets
     8 vertical file cabinets
Square Footage: 3500
Map Depositories: USGS (topo);
    USGS (geol); DMA (topo); DMA
    (aero); DMA (hydro); GPO; CA Division
    of Mines & Geology

### 61

California State University Library,
Fullerton

Collection for the History of Cartography,
P.O. Box 4150
Fullerton, CA 92634
Tel. (714) 773-2714
Hours: By appointment
Responsible Person: Boswell, Roy V.,
    Curator & Founder
Holdings:
    1427 Printed Maps
Chronological Coverage: 100% pre 1900
Map collection is cataloged 100%
Classification: LC
Formats: Cards
Preservation methods: Encapsulation,
    Deacidification, Acid free folders

### 62

Glendale Central Library,
Reference Section
222 E. Harvard
Glendale, CA 91205
Tel. (818) 956-2027
Hours: 10–9, M–Th; 10–6, F, Sa
Responsible Person: Peterson,
    Margaret V.
Special Strengths: Glendale, California
Special Collections: Soil Surveys of
    various United States counties
    (1910–present)
Employees: Full Time      Part Time
    Prof.           0              1
    Non-Prof.    0              1
Holdings:
    4620 Printed Maps
       2 Aerial Photographs
       3 Satellite Imagery
     160 Atlases
       1 Globe
       3 Raised Relief Maps
       8 Books
      19 Gazetteers
Chronological Coverage: 1% pre 1900;
    99% post 1900
Preservation methods: Lamination,
    Chartex or Fabric Mounting
Available to: Public, Students, Faculty
Circulates to: Public, Students, Faculty
Average monthly use: 60
Interlibrary loan available
    Topographic maps do not circulate
Copying Facilities: Copying machine
Equipment:
    20 5-drawer cabinets
     6 vertical map cabinets
     2 atlas cases
Square Footage: 200

### 63

California State University, Hayward
Reference Department, Library
Hayward, CA 94542
Tel. (415) 881-3765
Hours: 8–9, M–Th; 8–5, F; 10–5, Sa;
    1–6, Su
Responsible Person: Kwan, Barbara

Employees: Full Time    Part Time
  Prof.       0          1
Holdings:
  8200 Printed Maps
    2 Aerial Photographs
  585 Atlases
    2 Globes
    4 Raised Relief Maps
    2 Gazetteers
Chronological Coverage: 1% pre 1900;
  99% post 1900
Map collection is cataloged 100%
Formats: Cards
Available to: Public, Students, Faculty
Circulates to: Public, Students, Faculty
Copying Facilities: Copying machine
Equipment:
  20 5-drawer cabinets
  light table
Map Depositories: USGS (topo)

### 64

University of California, Irvine
Main Library
Irvine, CA 92713
Responsible Person: Gelfand, Julia,
  Reference Dept.
Special Strengths: California, Arizona
Holdings:
  600 Printed Maps
  400 Atlases
    3 Globes
  100 Microforms
  2400 Books
  145 Gazetteers
    28 Serial Titles
Chronological Coverage: 20% pre 1900;
  80% post 1900
Available to: Public, Students, Faculty
Average monthly use: 40
Copying Facilities: Copying machine,
  Microform, Photographic reproduction
Equipment:
  2 5-drawer cabinets
  2 4-drawer file cabinets
Square Footage: 120
Map Depositories: USGS (topo);
  USGS (geol); GPO

### 65

California State University, Los Angeles
The Geography Map Library
Geography & Urban Studies Dept.
5151 State University Dr.
Los Angeles, CA 90032
Hours: 8:30–6, M–Th; 8:30–12:30, F
Responsible Person: Mazzucchell,
  Dr. Vincent G.
Special Strengths: Western United
  States, California, Los Angeles
Employees: Full Time    Part Time
  Non-Prof.   1         3
Holdings:
  64000 Printed Maps
  18000 Aerial Photographs

    400 Satellite Imagery
    270 Atlases
      7 Globes
    640 Wall Maps
    217 Raised Relief Maps
     30 Microforms
  1940 Books
     11 Gazetteers
     10 Serial Titles
Chronological Coverage: 5% pre 1900;
  95% post 1900
Map collection is cataloged 100%
Classification: LC    Utility: OCLC
Formats: Cards
Preservation methods: Chartex or
  Fabric Mounting
Available to: Public, Students, Faculty
Circulates to: Students, Faculty
Average monthly use: 75
Average annual circulation: Maps: 326
Copying Facilties: Copying machine
Equipment:
  61 5-drawer cabinets
  5 5-drawer vertical files
  4 2-drawer storage cabinets
  Microfiche & Microfilm Readers
Square Footage: 2327
Map Depositories: USGS (topo);
  DMA (aero)

### 66

Los Angeles Public Library
Mary Helen Peterson Map Room,
History Dept.
630 W. 5th St.
Los Angeles, CA 90071
Tel. (213) 626-7461
Hours: 10–5:30, M, W, F, Sa; 12–8, T, Th
Responsible Person: Pratt, Mary S.
Special Strengths: Los Angeles (19th &
  20th century)
Employees: Full Time    Part Time
  Prof.       0          1
  Non-Prof.   0         1
Holdings:
  75000 Printed Maps
    20 Aerial Photographs
  1500 Atlases
     1 Globe
    500 Wall Maps
      6 Raised Relief Maps
    200 Microforms
    500 Books
  1000 Gazetteers
     10 Serial Titles
Chronological Coverage: 10% pre 1900;
  90% post 1900
Map collection is cataloged 5%
Classification: Dewey
Formats: Cards
Preservation methods: Chartex or
  Fabric Mounting
Available to: Public
Circulates to: Public
Average monthly use: 1000
Average annual circulation: Maps: 250

Copying Facilities: Copying machine
Equipment:
  89 5-drawer cabinets
  14 roller cases
  6 vertical file cabinets
Square Footage: 1092
Map Depositories: USGS (topo); DMA
  (topo); DMA (aero); DMA (hydro);
  GPO; NOS; NOAA

### 67

University of California, Los Angeles
Dept. of Geography
Bunche Hall 1255
Los Angeles, CA 90024
Tel. (213) 206-8188
Hours: By appointment
Responsible Person: Diaz, Noel L.,
  Staff Cartographer
Special Collections: Fairchild Aerial
  Surveys, Inc. Collection of Aerial
  Photos
Holdings:
  126973 Aerial Photographs
Chronological Coverage:
  100% post 1900
Map collection is cataloged 100%
Formats: Printed catalog

### 68

University of Californa, Los Angeles
Map Library
Los Angeles, CA 90024
Tel. (213) 825-3526
Hours: 10–3, M–F
Responsible Person: Hagen, Carlos B.,
  Director
Special Strengths: Latin America,
  Pacific Ocean, Near East, California
Employees: Full Time    Part Time
  Prof.       1          0
  Non-Prof.   3         1
Holdings:
  506547 Printed Maps
    550 Manuscript Maps
  10424 Aerial Photographs
  2550 Atlases
     4 Globes
    61 Raised Relief Maps
    38 Microforms
  6601 Books
    311 Serial Titles
Chronological Coverage: 20% pre 1900;
  80% post 1900
Preservation methods: Encapsulation
Available to: Public, Students, Faculty
Circulates to: Faculty
Average monthly use: 400
Average annual circulation:
  Maps: 4000
Interlibrary loan available
  Restricted materials need permission
Copying Facilities: Copying machine
Equipment:
  418 5-drawer cabinets

87 bookshelves, 27 filing
cabinets, special atlas case,
Map-O-Graph, drafting tables,
light tables
Square Footage: 3943
Map Depositories: USGS (topo);
USGS (geol); DMA (topo); DMA
(aero); DMA (hydro); GPO; NOS;
NOAA; Canada (topo); Australia

### 69

University of California, Los Angeles
Wm. A. Clark Memorial Library
2520 Cimarron St.
Los Angeles, CA 90024
Tel. (213) 731-8529
Hours: 9–4:45, M–F
Responsible Person: Bidwell, John,
Reference Librarian
Special Strengths: Great Britain, World,
California, New Mexico
Holdings:
75 Printed Maps
2 Manuscript Maps
10 Atlases
3 Globes
150 Books
20 Gazetteers
Classification: LC
Formats: Cards
Available to: Public
Average monthly use: 4
Copying Facilities: Copying machine,
Photographic reproduction
Equipment:
8 map drawers

### 70

University of California, Los Angeles
Wm. C. Putnam Map Room
Geology-Geophysics Library
4697 Geology Building
Los Angeles, CA 90024
Tel. (213) 825-1055
Hours: By request, 8–5, M–F
Responsible Person: How, Sarah E.,
Head, Geology-Geophysics
Special Strengths:
California (Geology), Nevada (Geology)
Employees: Full Time     Part Time
Non-Prof.     0             1
Holdings:
100000 Printed Maps
155 Wall Maps
31 Raised Relief Maps
Chronological Coverage:
100% post 1900
Available to: Public, Students, Faculty
Circulates to: Public, Students, Faculty
Average annual circulation:
Maps: 1100
Equipment:
44 5-drawer cabinets
14 vertical map cabinets
20 4-drawer file cabinets

6 12-drawer cabinets
Square Footage: 977
Map Depositories: USGS (topo);
USGS (geol)

### 71

University of Southern California
Doheny Library, Reference Dept.
Los Angeles, CA 90089
Tel. (213) 743-2540
Hours: 8–12, M–Th; 8–5, F; 9–5, Sa;
1–12, Su
Responsible Person: Thompson, Don,
Head
Special Strengths: California
Holdings:
7500 Printed Maps
Chronological Coverage: 2% pre 1900;
98% post 1900
Classification: LC
Formats: Cards
Available to: Public, Students, Faculty
Average monthly use: 10
Interlibrary loan available
Copying Facilities: Copying machine
Equipment:
45 5-drawer cabinets
Map Depositories: USGS (topo);
DMA (topo)

### 72

U.S. Geological Survey Library,
Menlo Park
345 Middlefield Road, MS 55
Menlo Park, CA 94025
Tel. (415) 323-8111
Hours: 7:45–4:15, M–F
Responsible Person: Sanders, William,
Map Curator
Special Strengths: Western United
States (Geology)
Employees: Full Time     Part Time
Non-Prof.     6             4
Holdings:
66500 Printed Maps
135000 Aerial Photographs
500 Atlases
3 Globes
25 Raised Relief Maps
50 Microforms
500 Books
300 Gazetteers
300 Serial titles
Chronological Coverage: 10% pre 1900;
90% post 1900
Map collection is cataloged 100%
Classification: Local     Utility: OCLC
Local
Formats: Cards
Available to: Public
Average monthly use: 500
Average annual circulation:
Maps: 1500; Books: 25000; Aerial
Photographs: 1500
Interlibrary loan available

Copying Facilities: Copying machine
Equipment:
92 5-drawer cabinets
28 vertical map cabinets
80 shelves
Square Footage: 1350
Map Depositories: USGS (topo);
USGS (geol); GPO; Canada (geol)

### 73

Mill Valley Public Library*
375 Throckmorton Ave.
Mill Valley, CA 94941
Tel. (415) 388-2190
Hours: 12–9, M; 10–9, T, Th; 10–6, W;
12–6, F; 10–6, Sa
Holdings:
1053 Printed Maps
Available to: Public
Copying Facilities: Copying machine

### 74

Stanislaus County Free Library*
1500 I St.
Modesto, CA 95354
Tel. (209) 571-6823
Hours: 9–9, M–Th; 9–5, Sa
Holdings:
2184 Printed Maps
Available to: Public
Copying Facilties: Copying machine

### 75

Napa City-County Library
1150 Division St.
Napa, CA 94559
Tel. (707) 253-4241
Hours: 10–5:30, M, T, F; 10–9, W, Th
Responsible Person: Wilson, Nadina
Special Strengths: California, West
Coast, San Francisco Bay Area
Special Collections: Napa County
Historical Maps
Holdings:
600 Printed Maps
100 Atlases
5 Books
5 Gazetteers
Chronological Coverage: 10% pre 1900;
90% post 1900
Map collection is cataloged 5%
Classification: Local
Formats: Cards, Online
Available to: Public
Average monthly use: 100
Copying Facilities: Copying machine
Equipment:
1 5-drawer cabinet
1 vertical map cabinet
Square Footage: 32

76
California Railway Museum Library
1802 East 23rd St.
Oakland, CA 94606
Tel. (415) 534-0071
Hours: By appointment
Responsible Person: Sappers, Vernon J.,
    Curator
Special Strengths: California (1860–
    present, Railroads), Alameda County
    & Oakland (1860–1900)
Employees: Full Time    Part Time
Prof.            0            1
Non-Prof.        0            1
Holdings:
    5000 Printed Maps
    100 Wall Maps
Chronological Coverage: 15% pre 1900;
    85% post 1900
Available to: Public
Copying Facilities: Copying machine
Equipment: 10 5-drawer cabinets


77
Merritt College Library
12500 Campus Dr.
Oakland, CA 94605
Tel. (415) 531-4911
Hours: 9–3, M–F
Responsible Person: Fleischman, Al
Employees: Full Time    Part Time
Non-Prof.        0            1
Holdings:
    1500 Printed Maps
    50 Atlases
Chronological Coverage: 100% post 1900
Map collection is cataloged 40%
Formats: Cards
Available to: Students, Faculty
Average annual circulation: Maps: 50
Interlibrary loan available
Copying Facilities: Copying machine
Equipment:
    1 5-drawer cabinet
    4 vertical map cabinets
    1 7-drawer unit
Map Depositories: USGS (topo)


78
Oakland Public Library
125 14th St.
Oakland, CA 94612
Tel. (415) 273-3136
Hours: 12–8:20, M; 10–8:30, T, W, Th;
    10–5:30, F, Sa
Responsible Person: Hausler, Donald
Special Strengths: Oakland (1850–1980),
    Alameda County (1850–1980),
    California (1850–1980)
Holdings:
    100000 Printed Maps
    100 Manuscript Maps
    100 Aerial Photographs
    50 Atlases
    2 Globes

    50 Wall Maps
    2 Raised Relief Maps
    50 Books
    100 Gazetteers
    1 Serial Title
Chronological Coverage: 5% pre 1900;
    95% post 1900
Map collection is cataloged 20%
Classification: Dewey
Formats: Cards
Preservation methods: Lamination
Available to: Public
Circulates to: Public
Average monthly use: 300
Average annual circulation:
    Maps: 1500; Books: 600
Interlibrary loan available
Copying Facilities: Copying machine
Equipment:
    5 vertical map cabinets
Square Footage: 600
Map Depositories: USGS (topo);
    DMA (topo); DMA (aero)


79
Butte County Library*
1820 Mitchell
Oroville, CA 95965
Tel. (916) 534-4641
Hours: 1–9, M, W; 10–5, T, Th–Sa
Holdings:
    1905 Printed Maps
Available to: Public
Copying Facilities: Copying machine


80
Palm Springs Public Library
300 S. Sunrise Way
Palm Springs, CA 92262
Tel. (619) 323-8294
Hours: 9–8, M–Th; 9–5:30, F, Sa
Responsible Person: Roades, Margaret,
    Reference Coordinator
Special Strengths: Palm Springs Region
Holdings:
    600 Printed Maps
    35 Atlases
    1 Globe
    2 Wall Maps
    3 Gazetteers
Chronological Coverage:
    100% post 1900
Available to: Public, Students, Faculty
Copying Facilities: Copying machine,
    Microform
Equipment:
    1 12-drawer map cabinet
Square Footage: 10
Map Depositories: GPO


81
Palo Alto City Library
1213 Newell Rd.
Palo Alto, CA 94303

Tel. (415) 329-2664
Hours: 10–9, M–F; 10–6, Sa; 1–5, Su
Responsible Person: Henderson, Susan
Holdings:
    3600 Printed Maps
    73 Atlases
    1 Globe
    3 Gazetteers
Chronological Coverage:
    100% post 1900
Available to: Public
Circulates to: Public
Copying Facilities: Copying machine
Map Depositories: USGS (topo)


82
California Institute of Technology
Geology Library (Geology Map Room)
Division of Geological & Planetary
    Sciences
Pasadena, CA 91125
Tel. (213) 356-6699
Responsible Person: Plane, Daphne,
    Geology Librarian
Employees: Full Time    Part Time
Non-Prof.        0            1
Holdings:
    73000 Printed Maps
    1 Globe
Chronological Coverage:
    100% post 1900
Available to: Public, Students, Faculty
Circulates to: Students, Faculty
Copying Facilities: Copying machine
Equipment:
    24 5-drawer cabinets
    49 vertical map cabinets
    6 2-drawer steel cases
    10 4-drawer steel cases
Square Footage: 594
Map Depositories: USGS (topo);
    USGS (geol); Australia


83
Regional Planetary Image Facility
Jet Propulsion Laboratory
4800 Oak Grove Dr., Mail Stop 264-115
Pasadena, CA 91104
Hours: 9–5, M–F
Responsible Person: Pieri, Leslie, J.
Special Strengths: Solar System except
    Earth, stars, & sun (planetary, geology)
Employees: Full Time    Part Time
Prof.            2            2
Holdings:
    500 Printed Maps
    225000 Satellite Imagery
    10 Globes
    200 Raised Relief Maps
    200 Books
Chronological Coverage:
    100% post 1900
Map collection is cataloged 90%
Classification: Internal, DBASE II
Formats: Online, Computer Printout

Available to: Public, Students, Faculty
Average monthly use: 120
Copying Facilities: Copying machine
Equipment:
  5 5-drawer cabinets
  2 vertical map cabinets
Square Footage: 2500
Map Depositories: USGS (topo):
  USGS (geol); DMA (topo); DMA
  (aero); DMA (hydro)

### 84

Contra Costa County Library
1750 Oak Park Blvd.
Pleasant Hill, CA 94523
Tel. (415) 944-3434
Hours: 10–9, M–Th; 10–6, F, Sa
Responsible Person: Gates, T. F.,
  History Librarian
Special Strengths: Contra County, CA
  (1850–present)
Special Collections: Contra Costa
  County California Historical Map
  Collection
Holdings:
  4335 Printed Maps
  50 Atlases
  2 Gazetteers
Chronological Coverage: 50% pre 1900;
  50% post 1900
Map collection is cataloged 100%
Formats: Cards
Preservation methods: Lamination
Available to: Public
Copying Facilities: Copying machine
Equipment:
  1 5-drawer cabinet
Square Footage: 20
Map Depositories: USGS (topo)

### 85

Diablo Valley College
321 Golf Club Road
Pleasant Hill, CA 94523
Tel. (415) 685-1230
Hours: 7:45–10, M–Th; 7:45–5, F
Responsible Person: Dolven, Mary
Holdings:
  2439 Printed Maps
Available to: Public
Copying Facilities: Copying machine
Map Depositories: USGS (topo)

### 86

Pomona Public Library
625 S. Garey Ave.
Pomona, CA 91766
Hours: 10–9, M, T; 10–6, W, Th; 10–5,
  F; 12–5, Sa
Responsible Person: Christmas, Gary
Special Strengths: California
Employees: Full Time    Part Time
  Prof.       0           2
Holdings:

6436 Printed Maps
Available to: Public
Copying Facilities: Copying machine,
  Microform, Photographic reproduction
Equipment:
  6 5-drawer cabinets
  8 vertical map cabinets
Map Depositories: USGS (topo)

### 87

University of Redlands
Armacost Library, Irvine Map Room
Redlands, CA 92374
Tel. (714) 793-2121
Hours: 8–10, M–Th; 8–5, F; 10–5, Sa;
  1–10, Su
Responsible Person: Reasoner, Lynne
Special Strengths: California, Arizona,
  Nevada, Oregon
Employees: Full Time    Part Time
  Prof.         0           1
  Non-Prof.     0           1
Holdings:
  14750 Printed Maps
  35 Aerial Photographs
  11 Globes
  258 Wall Maps
  60 Raised Relief Maps
Chronological Coverage:
  100% post 1900
Map collection is cataloged 10%
Classification: LC    Utility: OCLC
Formats: Cards
Available to: Public, Students, Faculty
Copying Facilities: Copying machine,
  Microform
Equipment:
  54 5-drawer cabinets
Square Footage: 800
Map Depositories: USGS (topo); GPO

### 88

Richmond Public Library
Richmond, CA 94804
Hours: 9–9, M–W; 9–6, Th–Sa; 2–5, Su
Special Strengths: California
Holdings:
  2200 Printed Maps
  75 Atlases
  3 Gazetteers
Chronological Coverage: 10% pre 1900;
  90% post 1900
Classification: Dewey
Formats: Cards
Available to: Public, Students, Faculty
Circulates to: Public, Students, Faculty
Interlibrary loan available
  Reference items do not circulate
Copying Facilities: Copying machine
Equipment:
  2 vertical map cabinets
Map Depositories: USGS (topo)

### 89

University of California, Riverside
Government Publications Department
P. O. Box 5900
Riverside, CA 92517
Tel. (714) 787-3226
Hours: 8–9, M–Th; 8–5, F; 1–5, Sa, Su
Responsible Person: Beaumont, Richard
Special Strengths: California, Riverside
  County
Holdings:
  60000 Printed Maps
  100 Aerial Photographs
  500 Atlases
  2 Globes
  2 Wall Maps
  150 Gazetteers
Chronological Coverage: 5% pre 1900;
  95% post 1900
Classification: LC
Formats: Cards, Computer Printout
Preservation methods: Lamination
Available to: Public, Students, Faculty
Circulates to: Public, Students, Faculty
Average monthly use: 40
Average annual circulation: Maps: 600
Copying Facilities: Copying machine
Equipment:
  45 5-drawer cabinets
  1 vertical map cabinet
Square Footage: 1000
Map Depositories: USGS (topo); DMA
  (topo); GPO

### 90

University of California, Riverside
Physical Sciences Library
P. O. Box 5900
Riverside, CA 92517
Tel. (714) 787-3511
Hours: 9–10, M–Th; 8–6, F; 10–6, Sa;
  1–10, Su
Responsible Person: Vierich, Richard
Special Strengths: United States
  (Geology)
Holdings:
  9000 Printed Maps
  12 Aerial Photographs
  100 Atlases
  12 Books
  3 Gazetteers
Chronological Coverage: 100% post 1900
Available to: Public, Students, Faculty
Circulates to: Public, Students, Faculty
Interlibrary loan available
Copying Facilities: Copying machine
Map Depositories: USGS (geol); CA
  Division of Mines & Geology

### 91

California Dept. of Transportation
Office Engineer's Drafting Cartographic
  Services
1120 N St.
Sacramento, CA 95814

Tel. (916) 445-3110
Hours: 7–4, M–F
Responsible Person: Wulff, Paul
Special Strengths: California
Holdings:
    1600 Printed Maps
Available to: Public

92
California State Archives
1020 O St.
Sacramento, CA 95814
Tel. (916) 445-4293
Hours: 8–5, M–F
Responsible Person: Burns, John F.,
    Chief
Special Strengths: California (1850–
    1930, Railroads); California (1820–
    1845, Spanish Land Grants)
Special Collections: Public Utilities
    Commission, Spanish Land Grants
Holdings:
    12000 Manuscript Maps
Chronological Coverage: 10% pre 1900;
    90% post 1900
Map collection is cataloged 90%
Formats: Cards, Map Index Worksheets
Preservation methods: Encapsulation,
    Lamination, Deacidification
Available to: Public, Students, Faculty
Average monthly use: 10
Copying Facilities: Copying machine,
    Photostatic Copies
Equipment:
    15 5-drawer cabinets
    6 64-hole rolled map cabinets
Square Footage: 500

93
California State Land Map Library
    at Sacramento
1807 13th St.
Sacramento, CA 95814
Tel. (916) 332-3317
Hours: 9–3, M–F
Responsible Person: Minnick, Roy
Special Strengths: California (1850–
    present, property boundaries)
Special Collections: Negative and
    positives of Hydro & Topo Charts
    from 1845 to 1935, published by USC
    and GS
Employees: Full Time    Part Time
Non-Prof.    2            2
Holdings:
    16000 Printed Maps
    1000 Manuscript Maps
    4000 Aerial Photographs
    10 Wall Maps
    100 Books
Chronological Coverage: 60% pre 1900;
    40% post 1900
Map collection is cataloged 100%
Formats: Cards, Computer Printout,
    Bibliography

Available to: Public, Students, Faculty
Average monthly use: 80
Copying Facilities: Copying machine,
    Photographic reproduction, Local
    contractor
Equipment:
    30 5-drawer cabinets
    6 roll files
Square Footage: 2500

94
California State Library, Sacramento
California Section
914 Capitol Mall
Sacramento, CA 95814
Tel. (916) 324-4871
Hours: 8–5, M–F
Responsible Person: Fante, Thomas M.,
    Senior Librarian
Special Strengths: California (pre 1900)
Employees: Full Time    Part Time
    Prof.        0            4
    Non-Prof.    0            4
Holdings:
    5000 Printed Maps
    300 Manuscript Maps
    300 Microforms
Chronological Coverage: 90% pre 1900;
    10% post 1900
Map collection is cataloged 95%
Classification: Dewey
Formats: Cards
Preservation methods: Encapsulation,
    Lamination, Chartex or Fabric
    Mounting
Available to: Public
Average monthly use: 50
Copying Facilities: Copying machine,
    Photographic reproduction
Equipment:
    45 5-drawer cabinets
Square Footage: 800

95
California State Library, Sacramento
Government Publications Section
P. O. Box 2037
Sacramento, CA 95809
Tel. (916) 322-4572
Hours: 8–5, M–F
Responsible Person: Cully, John
Special Strengths: California
Employees: Full Time    Part Time
    Prof.        0            6
    Non-Prof.    0            10
Holdings:
    62657 Printed Maps
    150 Atlases
    1 Globe
    100 Raised Relief Maps
Chronological Coverage: 30% pre 1900;
    70% post 1900
Classification: LC
Formats: Cards
Preservation methods: Encapsulation

Available to: Public
Average monthly use: 65
Copying Facilities: Copying machine,
    Photographic reproduction
Equipment:
    35 5-drawer cabinets
Square Footage: 1800
Map Depositories: USGS (topo);
    USGS (geol); GPO

96
California State Railroad Museum
    Library
111 I St.
Sacramento, CA 95814
Tel. (916) 323-8073
Hours: 1–5, T–Th
Responsible Person: Gray, Walter P. III,
    Archivist
Special Strengths: California (1830–
    present, Railroads)
Special Collections: California Railroad
    Valuation Maps
Employees: Full Time    Part Time
    Non-Prof.    0            1
Holdings:
    8000 Printed Maps
    100 Manuscript Maps
    30 Atlases
    50 Wall Maps
Chronological Coverage: 10% pre 1900;
    90% post 1900
Available to: Public
Average monthly use: 5
Copying Facilities: Copying machine,
    Photographic reproduction
Equipment:
    21 5-drawer cabinets
Square Footage: 100

97
California University, Sacramento
Social Science & Business, Map Room
Administration Reference Dept.
The Library
2000 Jed Smith Dr.
Sacramento, CA 95819
Tel. (916) 454-6632
Hours: 8–9, M–Th; 8–4:30, F;
    1–4:30, Sa, Su
Responsible Person: Kristie, Bill
Special Strengths: California, Sacramento
Holdings:
    15787 Printed Maps
Chronological Coverage: 10% pre 1900;
    90% post 1900
Preservation methods: Chartex or
    Fabric Mounting
Available to: Public, Students, Faculty
Copying Facilities: Copying machine
Equipment:
    15 5-drawer cabinets
    2 file cabinets
Square Footage: 1400
Map Depositories: USGS (topo)

**98**
Sacramento History Center/Sacramento
    Museum & History Division
1930 J St.
Sacramento, CA 95814
Tel. (916) 447-2958
Hours: 8–12, M–F
Responsible Person: Searcy, Susan,
    Archivist
Special Strengths: Sacramento (1880–
    1950, gold dredging, reclamation),
    Old & New Worlds (1500–1700, 'CA
    as an Island' general exploration),
    United States (1700–1860, general,
    travel routes to CA, gold rush fields)
Special Collections: Sacramento County
    Recorder Collection (Land grants,
    subdivision, surveys); Eleanor
    McClatchy Collection (Old & New
    Worlds), Natomas Company Collection
    (Sacramento)
Employees: Full Time    Part Time
Non-Prof.    0         5
Holdings:
    4000 Printed Maps
    500 Manuscript Maps
    20 Aerial Photographs
    2 Atlases
    300 Microforms
    200 Books
Chronological Coverage: 50% pre 1900;
    50% post 1900
Map collection is cataloged 70%
Formats: Cards
Preservation methods: Encapsulation,
    Deacidification
Available to: Public
Average monthly use: 30
Average annual circulation:
    Maps: 500; Books: 500
Copying Facilities: Copying machine,
    Photographic reproduction
Equipment:
    20 5-drawer cabinets
Square Footage: 77

**99**
Sacramento Public Library*
828 I St.
Sacramento, CA 95814
Tel. (916) 449-5203
Hours: 9–6, M, F; 9–9, T, Th;
    10–6, W; 9–5:30, Sa
Holdings:
    2145 Printed Maps
Available to: Public

**100**
San Diego Public Library
820 E St.
San Diego, CA 92101
Tel. (619) 236-5800
Hours: 10–9, M–Th; 9:30–5:30, F–Sa
Responsible Person: Anderson, Joanne,
    Science Section

Special Strengths: California, San Diego,
    Baja California, Mexico, Western
    United States
Special Collections: Sanborn Fire
    Insurance Maps for the City of San
    Diego (1887, 1920–40)
Holdings:
    29769 Printed Maps
    6 Aerial Photographs
    371 Atlases
    1 Globe
    19 Wall Maps
    13 Raised Relief Maps
    245 Books
    304 Gazetteers
    1 Serial Title
Chronological Coverage: 10% pre 1900;
    90% post 1900
Classification: Dewey
Formats: Cards, COM
Preservation methods: Encapsulation,
    Lamination
Available to: Public
Circulates to: Public
Copying Facilities: Copying machine
Equipment:
    30 5-drawer cabinets
    Filing Cabinets
Map Depositories: USGS (topo); GPO

**101**
San Diego State University
University Library, Map Collection
San Diego, CA 92182
Tel. (619) 265-5832
Hours: 8–4:30, M–F
Responsible Person: Strickland, Muriel
Special Strengths: California, San Diego
    County
Holdings:
    135000 Printed Maps
    200 Aerial Photographs
    600 Atlases
    3 Globes
    50 Wall Maps
    2 Raised Relief Maps
    100 Books
    100 Gazetteers
Chronological Coverage: 1% pre 1900;
    99% post 1900
Available to: Students, Faculty
Average monthly use: 250
Average annual circulation:
    Maps: 11000
Interlibrary loan available
    Except fragile items
Copying Facilities: Copying machine
Equipment:
    88 5-drawer cabinets
    Light table
Square Footage: 1300
Map Depositories: USGS (topo);
    USGS (geol); DMA (topo); DMA
    (aero); DMA (hydro); GPO

**102**
University of California, San Diego
Map Section C-075P
University Library
San Diego, CA 92093
Tel. (619) 452-3338
Hours: 8–10, M–F
Responsible Person: Cruse, Larry
Employees: Full Time    Part Time
Prof.        0          1
Non-Prof.    0          5
Holdings:
    155000 Printed Maps
    1712 Aerial Photographs
    20 Atlases
    3 Globes
    20 Wall Maps
    300 Raised Relief Maps
    4000 Microforms
    300 Books
    308 Gazetteers
Chronological Coverage: 10% pre 1900;
    90% post 1900
Map collection is cataloged 100%
Classification: LC
Formats: Cards
Preservation methods: Encapsulation
Available to: Public, Students, Faculty
Circulates to: Students, Faculty
Average monthly use: 300
Average annual circulation: Maps: 300
Interlibrary loan available
Copying Facilities: Copying machine,
    Microform, Micro
Equipment:
    97 5-drawer cabinets
    1 microfiche reader
    1 microfilm reader
    Pocket stereoscope
Square Footage: 3000
Map Depositories: USGS (topo);
    USGS (geol); DMA (topo); DMA
    (aero); GPO; NOS; NOAA; Auto Club,
    S. Calif.; Cal. State Auto Club

**103**
California Academy of Sciences
J. W. Mailliard Jr. Library
Golden Gate Park
San Francisco, CA 94118
Tel. (415) 221-5100
Hours: 9–12, 1–5, M–F
Responsible Person: Jackson, James E.,
    Assistant Librarian
Special Collections: Baja California
Employees: Full Time    Part Time
Non-Prof.    0          1
Holdings:
    25000 Printed Maps
    25 Atlases
    50 Raised Relief Maps
    100 Books
    175 Gazetteers
Chronological Coverage: 5% pre 1900;
    95% post 1900
Available to: Public, Students, Faculty

Copying Facilities: Copying machine
Equipment:
28 5-drawer cabinets
Square Footage: 400
Map Depositories: USGS (topo);
USGS (geol); New Zealand, Australia
Geological Survey Maps

104
California Division of Mines & Geology,
Library
Ferry Building, Room 2022
San Francisco, CA 94111
Tel. (414) 557-0308
Hours: 8–4:30, M–F
Responsible Person: Brunton, Angela
Special Strengths: California (Geology)
Holdings:
10000 Printed Maps
100 Atlases
1 Wall Maps
100 Microforms
200 Books
3 Serial Titles
Chronological Coverage: 5% pre 1900;
95% post 1900
Map collection is cataloged 50%
Classification: LC
Formats: Cards
Available to: Public
Interlibrary loan available
USGS Topographical maps do not
circulate
Copying Facilities: Copying machine
Equipment:
21 5-drawer cabinets
Square Footage: 50
Map Depositories: USGS (geol);
Canada (geol)

105
California Historical Society Library*
2099 Pacific Ave.
San Francisco, CA 94109
Tel. (415) 567-1848
Hours: 10–4, W–Sa
Responsible Person: Johnston, Bruce L.
Special Strengths: California
Holdings:
3280 Printed Maps
Preservation methods: Chartex or
Fabric Mounting
Available to: Public, Students, Faculty
Copying Facilities: Copying machine

106
California State Library, Sutro Library
Winston Drive
San Francisco, CA 94321
Tel. (415) 931-4477
Hours: 10–5, M–F
Responsible Person: Kurutz, Gary
Special Strengths: New World (17th–
19th century)

Holdings:
300 Printed Maps
100 Manuscript Maps
100 Atlases
1 Globe
10 Wall Maps
3 Raised Relief Maps
75 Books
Chronological Coverage:
100% pre 1900
Preservation methods: Encapsulation,
Lamination, Chartex or Fabric
Mounting
Available to: Public, Students, Faculty
Average monthly use: 1
Copying Facilities: Copying machine,
Photographic reproduction
Equipment:
1 5-drawer cabinet

107
National Maritime Museum
J. Porter Shaw Library
Building E, 3rd Floor, Fort Mason
San Francisco, CA 94123
Hours: 1–5, T–F
Responsible Person: Hull, David,
Principle Librarian
Special Strengths: Pacific Basin
(Nautical Charts)
Holdings:
750 Printed Maps
5 Atlases
50 Books
5 Gazetteers
Chronological Coverage: 40% pre 1900;
60% post 1900
Map collection is cataloged 80%
Formats: Cards
Available to: Public, Students, Faculty
Copying Facilities: Copying machine,
Photographic reproduction
Equipment:
10 5-drawer cabinets
Square Footage: 200

108
San Francisco Public Library
Civic Center
San Francisco, CA 94102
Tel. (415) 558-4927
Hours: 10–6, M, F, Sa; 10–9, T–Th;
1–5, Su
Responsible Person: Casserly, Joan
Special Strengths: California, San
Francisco
Special Collections: San Francisco
Archives
Employees: Full Time     Part Time
Prof.            0            11
Non-Prof.        0            24
Holdings:
61300 Printed Maps
400 Atlases
5 Globes

528 Wall Maps
4 Raised Relief Maps
50 Books
50 Gazetteers
Chronological Coverage: 25% pre 1900;
75% post 1900
Map collection is cataloged 30%
Classification: Dewey     Utility: RLIN
Formats: Cards
Preservation methods: Encapsulation,
Chartex or Fabric Mounting
Available to: Public, Students, Faculty
Average monthly use: 750
Interlibrary loan available
Atlases only
Copying Facilities: Copying machine
Equipment:
10 5-drawer cabinets
Vertical files, Shelves
Square Footage: 300
Map Depositories: USGS (topo);
USGS (geol)

109
San Francisco State University Library
Maps & Atlases
Government Publications Dept.
1630 Holloway Ave.
San Francisco, CA 94132
Tel. (415) 469-1557
Hours: 8–10, M–Th; 8–5, F; 1–5, Sa, Su
Responsible Person: Jacobsen, LaVonne
Employees: Full Time     Part Time
Prof.            0            1
Non-Prof.        0            1
Holdings:
10000 Printed Maps
500 Atlases
15 Globes
10 Wall Maps
25 Raised Relief Maps
10 Books
60 Gazetteers
Chronological Coverage:
100% post 1900
Map collection is cataloged 25%
Classification: LC
Formats: Cards, Computer Printout
Available to: Public
Circulates to: Students, Faculty
Average annual circulation:
Maps: 3400
Copying Facilities: Copying machine,
Microform, Photographic reproduction,
Art-o-graph
Equipment:
35 5-drawer cabinets
4 file cabinets
Square Footage: 900
Map Depositories: DMA (topo); DMA
(aero); DMA (hydro); GPO

110
San Francisco State University
Map Library-Geography Department

1600 Holloway Ave.–HLL 289
San Francisco, CA 94132
Tel. (415) 469-1145
Hours: 8:30–4:30 M–F
Responsible Person: Montgomery,
  Richard
Special Strengths: Western States,
  Moon
Employees: Full Time    Part Time
  Prof.        0            2
Holdings:
  50000 Printed Maps
  2500 Aerial Photographs
  100 Atlases
  8 Globes
  800 Wall Maps
  200 Raised Relief Maps
Chronological Coverage:
  100% post 1900
Preservation methods: Lamination,
  Chatex or Fabric Mounting, Acid
  free folders
Available to: Public, Students, Faculty
Circulates to: Public, Students, Faculty
Copying Facilities: Copying machine,
  Microform
Equipment:
  71 5-drawer cabinets
  1 vertical map cabinet
  6 vertical files
  4 stereo viewers with parallax bars
Square Footage: 1132
Map Depositories: USGS (topo)

111
USDA Forest Service
630 Sansome St.
San Francisco, CA 94111
Tel. (415) 556-1022
Hours: 7:30–4, M–F
Responsible Person: Ambacher, Alan
Special Strengths: California
  (Air Photographs, 1970–present)
Holdings:
  30 Printed Maps
  40000 Aerial Photographs
Chronological Coverage:
  100% post 1900
Preservation methods: Encapsulation,
  Deacidification, Acid free folders
Average monthly use: 50
Copying Facilities: Copying machine
Equipment:
  Stereoscopes, Microfiche reader
Square Footage: 100

112
San Jose State University Library*
250 S. 4th St.
San Jose, CA 95192
Tel. (408) 277-3385
Hours: 8–10, M–Th; 8–5, F; 10–5, Sa;
  12–5, Su
Responsible Person: Enrici, Pam
Holdings:

4937 Printed Maps
Preservation methods: Lamination,
  Chartex or Fabric Mounting
Available to: Public, Students, Faculty

113
San Jose State University
Department of Geology, Map Room
San Jose, CA 95192
Tel. (408) 277-2387
Hours: 7–5, M–F
Responsible Person: Curtis, George
Holdings:
  200000 Printed Maps
  1000 Manuscript Maps
  1000 Aerial Photographs
  100 Satellite Imagery
  10 Atlases
  10 Globes
  30 Wall Maps
  500 Raised Relief Maps
  10 Books
  50 Serial Titles
Chronological Coverage: 10% pre 1900;
  90% post 1900
Available to: Public, Students, Faculty
Circulates to: Public, Students, Faculty
Average monthly use: 200
Average annual circulation: Maps: 5000;
  Books: 1500; Aerial Photographs: 100
Copying Facilities: Copying machine
Equipment:
  75 5-drawer cabinets
  6 vertical map cabinets
  Radial line plotter
Square Footage: 700

114
Santa Clara County Free Library*
1095 N. 7th St.
San Jose, CA 95112
Tel. (408) 293-2326
Hours: 12–9, M, T; 10–9, W; 10–6, Th–Sa
Holdings:
  1172 Printed Maps
Available to: Public, Students, Faculty
Copying Facilities: Copying machine

115
San Leandro Community Library*
300 Estudillo Ave.
San Leandro, CA 94577
Tel. (415) 483-1511
Hours: 10–9, M–Th; 10–5:30, F; 10–5, Sa
Holdings: 2617 Printed Maps
Preservation methods: Chartex or
  Fabric Mounting
Available to: Public, Students, Faculty
Copying Facilities: Copying machine

116
California Polytechnic State University
  Library

Documents & Maps Department
San Luis Obispo, CA 93407
Tel. (805) 546-1354
Hours: 7:30–11, M–F
Responsible Person: Kim, Chi Su
Employees: Full Time    Part Time
  Prof.        0            1
Holdings:
  18128 Printed Maps
  61 Aerial Photographs
  7 Satellite Imagery
  430 Atlases
  2 Globes
  57 Wall Maps
  47 Raised Relief Maps
  86 Microforms
Chronological Coverage:
  100% post 1900
Map collection is cataloged 100%
Classification: LC    Utility: OCLC
Formats: Cards
Preservation methods: Chartex or
  Fabric Mounting
Available to: Public
Average monthly use: 60
Average annual circulation: Maps: 300;
  Aerial Photographs: 30
Copying Facilities: Copying machine,
  Microform
Equipment:
  18 5-drawer cabinets
  8 vertical map cabinets
Square Footage: 225
Map Depositories: USGS (topo); GPO

117
Huntington Library
San Marino, CA 91108
Tel. (213) 792-6141
Hours: 8:30–4:30, M–Sa
Responsible Person: Lange, Thomas V.,
  Assistant Curator
Special Strengths: California, Western
  Americana
Holdings:
  5000 Printed Maps
  2500 Aerial Photographs
  500 Atlases
  10 Globes
Chronological Coverage: 90% pre 1900;
  10% post 1900
Map collection is cataloged 90%
Formats: Cards
Average monthly use: 5
Copying Facilities: Copying machine,
  Microform, Photographic reproduction,
  Slides
Equipment: Acid Free Folders
Square Footage: 130

118
San Mateo County Historical Association
  & Museum
1700 W. Hillsdale Blvd.
San Mateo, CA 94402

Tel. (415) 574-6441
Hours: 10–4:30, W, Th, F
Responsible Person: Holmes, Marion C.,
   Archivist
Special Strengths: San Mateo County
   (California)
Holdings:
   1248 Printed Maps
Preservation methods: Encapsulation
Available to: Public, Students, Faculty
Copying Facilities: Copying machine,
   Photographic reproduction
Equipment:
   5 5-drawer cabinets
Square Footage: 20

## 119
San Mateo Public Library*
55 W. Third Ave.
San Mateo, CA 94402
Tel. (415) 574-6952
Hours: 10–9, M–W; 10–6, Th; 10–5, F;
   9–5, Sa
Holdings:
   4413 Printed Maps
Available to: Public
Copying Facilities:
   Copying machine

## 120
University of California, Santa Barbara
Map & Imagery Laboratory
Santa Barbara, CA 93106
Tel. (805) 961-2779
Hours: 8–5, 7–10, M–Th;, 8–5, F
Responsible Person: Carver, Larry,
   Department Head
Special Strengths: World (Ocean &
   Land areas), Physical, Biological
   sciences, Topography, Land use,
   Environmental conditions, Urban
   planning, Resource development
Special Collections: Landsat 2 imagery
   in 70mm master negative covering
   much of the world from November,
   1975 to November, 1978
Employees: Full Time    Part Time
   Prof.        1            0
   Non-Prof.    3            4
Holdings:
   300000 Printed Maps
   300000 Aerial Photographs
   120000 Satellite Imagery
   1800 Atlases
   9 Globes
   10 Wall Maps
   300 Raised Relief Maps
   21000 Microforms
   275 Computer Tapes
   570 Books
   130 Gazetteers
   25 Serial Titles
Chronological Coverage: 1% pre 1900;

99% post 1900
Map collection is cataloged 20%
Classification: LC
Formats: Cards
Available to: Public, Students, Faculty
Circulates to: Public, Students, Faculty
Average monthly use: 3000
Average annual circulation: 35000
Interlibrary loan available
   Very limited–Education only–No O.P.,
   No imagery
Copying Facilities: Copying machine,
   Microform, 3 camera systems
Equipment:
   351 5 drawer cabinets
   20 vertical map cabinets
   79 single side stack units
   Zoom Transfer scope, stereoscopes,
   multispectral additive color viewer
Square Footage: 12000
Map Depositories: USGS (topo);
   USGS (geol); DMA (topo); DMA
   (aero); DMA (hydro); GPO; NOS;
   NOAA; Over 50 worldwide agencies

## 121
Santa Clara Public Library*
2635 Homestead Rd.
Santa Clara, CA 95051
Tel. (408) 984–3236
Hours: 9–9, M–F; 9–6, Sa; 1–5, Su
Holdings:
   2157 Printed Maps
Available to: Public, Students, Faculty
Copying Facilities: Copying machine
Map Depositories: USGS (topo)

## 122
University of Santa Clara
Michael Orradra Library
Santa Clara, CA 95053
Tel. (408) 984-4415
Hours: 8–Midnight, M–F; 9–10, Sa;
   10:30–Midnight, Su
Responsible Person: Bazan, Lorraine
Employees: Full Time    Part Time
   Prof.        0            1
Holdings:
   4372 Printed Maps
Classification: LC
Formats: Cards
Available to: Public
Circulates to: Students, Faculty
Copying Facilities: Copying machine
Equipment:
   6 5-drawer cabinets
Square Footage: 400
Map Depositories: USGS (topo); U. S.
   Forest Service

## 123
Santa Cruz Public Library
Reference Department
224 Church St.

Santa Cruz, CA 95060
Tel. (408) 429-3526
Hours: 9–9, M–Th; 9–5, F, Sa
Responsible Person: Jones, Debra
Special Strengths: Santa Cruz County
Employees: Full Time    Part Time
   Prof.        0            1
   Non-Prof.    0            1
Holdings:
   2000 Printed Maps
   3 Globes
   3 Wall Maps
Chronological Coverage:
   100% post 1900
Available to: Public
Circulates to: Public
Interlibrary loan available
Copying Facilities: Copying machine
Equipment:
   1 5-drawer cabinet
   3 vertical map cabinets
Square Footage: 100

## 124
University of California, Santa Cruz
Map collection, University Library
Santa Cruz, CA 95064
Tel. (408) 429-2364
Hours: 9–12, 1–5, M–F
Responsible Person: Stevens, Stanley D.
Special Strengths: Monterey Bay Area
   (1789–Present), Monterey Bay Area
   (Aerial Photographs, 1925–Present)
Special Collections: Santa Cruz County
   Land Ownership Maps, Comprehensive
   Collection of Aerial Photos–5 County
   Region
Employees: Full Time    Part Time
   Prof.        1            0
   Non-Prof.    0            1
Holdings:
   107763 Printed Maps
   500 Manuscript Maps
   20164 Aerial Photographs
   4 Satellite Imagery
   500 Atlases
   6 Globes
   300 Wall Maps
   100 Raised Relief Maps
   9366 Microforms
   500 Books
   100 Gazetteers
Chronological Coverage: 10% pre 1900;
   90% post 1900
Map collection is cataloged 50%
Classification: LC
Formats: Cards
Available to: Public
Circulates to: Public, Students, Faculty
Average monthly use: 75
Average annual circulation:
   Maps: 400
Interlibrary loan available
   No manuscript & other rare items
Copying Facilities: Copying machine
Equipment:

64 5-drawer cabinets
2 Std. 3-drawer map cabinets
1 5-drawer oversized cabinet
Stereoscopes; light table; misc. tools
(drafting & reading)
Square Footage: 1761
Map Depositories: USGS (topo);
   USGS (geol); DMA (topo); DMA
   (aero); GPO; Canada (topo); CA Div.
   Mines & Geol.

### 125
Santa Monica Public Library
1343 6th St.
Santa Monica, CA 90401
Hours: 10–9, M–Th; 10–5:30, F, Sa
Responsible Person: Freeman, Gera
Special Strengths: California
Employees: Full Time    Part Time
   Prof.          0          1
Holdings:
   1868 Printed Maps
     59 Atlases
      2 Globes
      2 Raised Relief Maps
Chronological Coverage:
   100% post 1900
Available to: Public
Copying Facilities: Photographic
   reproduction
Equipment:
   8 5-drawer cabinets

### 126
Sonoma County Library
3rd & E St.
Santa Rosa, CA 95404
Tel. (707) 545-0831
Hours: 9:30–9, M–Th; 9:30–6, F, Sa;
   2–6, Su
Responsible Person: Herman, Audrey
Special Strengths: Sonoma County
   (1900–present)
Special Collections: Sonoma County
   Recorder Archival Maps, Sonoma
   County Surveyor Archival Maps
Holdings:
   200 Printed Maps
Chronological Coverage: 10% pre 1900;
   90% post 1900
Map collection is cataloged 5%
Formats: Cards
Available to: Public
Copying Facilities: Copying machine
Equipment:
   8 5-drawer cabinets
   8 vertical map cabinets
Square Footage: 400
Map Depositories: USGS (topo); GPO

### 127
Hoover Institution on War, Revolution
   & Peace
Stanford University

Stanford, CA 94305
Tel. (415) 497-2058
Hours: 8–5, M–F
Responsible Person: Heron, David W.,
   Head of Readers' Service
Special Strengths: Europe, Soviet Union
Holdings:
   3000 Printed Maps
      4 Manuscript Maps
Chronological Coverage: 3% pre 1900;
   97% post 1900
Available to: Students, Faculty
Copying Facilities: Copying machine,
   Microform
Equipment:
   8 5-drawer cabinets
Square Footage: 70

### 128
Stanford University
Branner Earth Sciences Library
Map Collection
Stanford, CA 94305
Tel. (415) 497-2746
Hours: 8–10, M–Th; 9–6, F; 10–5, Sa;
   1–10, Su
Responsible Person: Noga, Michael
Special Strengths: Australia, California,
   France, Japan, Canada, New Zealand,
   Geology
Special Collections: Alaska National
   Petroleum Reserve Seismograms,
   Central Geological Survey, Broken
   Hill, (New South Walls): mining plans
   & sections (1939)
Employees: Full Time    Part Time
   Prof.          2          0
   Non-Prof.      0          2
Holdings:
   83878 Printed Maps
      15 Manuscript Maps
     145 Atlases
       4 Raised Relief Maps
       3 Microforms
     245 Books
      28 Gazetteers
     231 Serial Titles
Chronological Coverage: 1% pre 1900;
   99% post 1900
Map collection is cataloged 1%
Classification: LC      Utility: RLIN
Formats: Cards, Online, Computer
   Printout
Preservation methods: Lamination
Available to: Public
Circulates to: Students, Faculty
Average monthly use: 200
Average annual circulation:
   Maps: 1268
Interlibrary loan available
Copying Facilities: Copying machine
Equipment:
   101 5-drawer cabinets
    20 vertical map cabinets
   light table
Square Footage: 2450

Map Depositories: USGS (topo);
   USGS (geol); Canada (geol); Geol.
   surveys from Japan, Ontario, New
   Zealand & CA

### 129
Stanford University
C. H. Green Library, Reference Dept.
Central Map Collection
Stanford, CA 94305
Tel. (415) 497-1811
Hours: 9–11:30 a.m., M–Th
Responsible Person: Tongye, Karyl A.,
   Library Specialist
Employees: Full Time    Part Time
   Non-Prof.      0          2
Holdings:
   77000 Printed Maps
      25 Atlases
       4 Globes
     130 Wall Maps
      75 Raised Relief Maps
     100 Books
     190 Gazetteers
      10 Serial Titles
Chronological Coverage: 25% pre 1900;
   75% post 1900
Map collection is cataloged 75%
Classification: LC
Formats: Cards
Available to: Public
Circulates to: Students, Faculty
Average monthly use: 52
Average annual circulation:
   Maps: 400
Interlibrary loan available
   U. C. & RLG libraries only
Copying Facilities: Copying machine
Equipment:
   110 5-drawer cabinets
     4 vertical map cabinets
Map Depositories: DMA (topo); DMA
   (aero); DMA (hydro); GPO

### 130
Stockton-San Joaquin County Public
   Library*
605 N. El Dorado St.
Stockton, CA 95202
Tel. (209) 944-8364
Holdings: 8501 Printed Maps
Available to: Public, Students, Faculty
Copying Facilities: Copying machine
Map Depositories: USGS (topo)

### 131
University of the Pacific
University Library, Reference Dept.
Stockton, CA 95211
Tel. (209) 946-2431
Hours: 8–11, M–Th; 8–10, F, 9–10, Sa;
   10–11, Su
Responsible Person: Bender-Lamb,
   Sylvia

Special Strengths: California
Holdings:
   500 Printed Maps
   125 Atlases
   1 Globe
   3 Books
   5 Gazetteers
Chronological Coverage:
   100% post 1900
Map collection is cataloged 100%
Classification: LC     Utility: RLIN
Formats: Cards
Available to: Public
Circulates to: Students, Faculty
Interlibrary loan available
Copying Facilities: Copying machine,
   Microform
Equipment:
   1 5-drawer cabinet
Square Footage: 50


132
Sunnyvale Public Library*
665 W. Olive Ave., P. O. Box 607
Sunnyvale, CA 94086
Tel. (408) 738-5585
Hours: 10–9, M–Th; 10–6, F, Sa;
   1–5, Su
Holdings:
   8000 Printed Maps
Available to: Public, Students, Faculty
Copying Facilities: Copying machine
Map Depositories: USGS (topo)


133
California State College, Turlock
Stanislaus Library
800 Monk Vista Ave.
Turlock, CA 95380
Tel. (209) 667-3233
Hours: 7:30–11, M–Th; 7:30–5, F;
   9–5 Sa; 10–9, Su
Responsible Person: Tamimi, Judith A.
Special Strengths: California
Employees: Full Time     Part Time
   Prof.         0              1
Holdings:
   1320 Printed Maps
   315 Atlases
   1 Globe
   3 Raised Relief Maps
   50 Books
   10 Gazetteers
Chronological Coverage: 10% pre 1900;
   90% post 1900
Available to: Public, Students, Faculty
Circulates to: Public, Students, Faculty
Interlibrary loan available
Copying Facilities: Copying machine
Equipment:
   8 5-drawer cabinets
Square Footage: 65


134
Solono County Library System
John F. Kennedy Library
505 Santa Clara St.
Vallejo, CA 94590
Tel. (707) 553-5568
Hours: 12–9, M, Th; 10–6, T, W, F;
   10–5, Sa
Responsible Person: Shaftel, Roberta,
   Reference Librarian
Special Strengths: California
Employees: Full Time     Part Time
   Non-Prof.      0             1
Holdings:
   1300 Printed Maps
   2 Satellite Imagery
   70 Atlases
   1 Globe
   4 Wall Maps
   6 Raised Relief Maps
   15 Books
   20 Gazetteers
Chronological Coverage: 20% pre 1900;
   80% post 1900
Preservation methods: Lamination
Available to: Public
Circulates to: Public
Average monthly use: 60
Average annual circulation: Maps: 30
Interlibrary loan available
Copying Facilities: Copying machine
Equipment:
   6 5-drawer cabinets
   11 vertical files
Square Footage: 15
Map Depositories: USGS (topo); DMA
   (topo); GPO


135
Whittier College
Dept. of Geological Sciences
Whittier, CA 90608
Tel. (213) 693-0771
Hours: By appointment
Responsible Person: Rhodes, Prof. Dallas
Special Collections: Fairchild Aerial
   Surveys, Inc. Photo Collection
   (1925–1945)
Employees: Full Time     Part Time
   Prof.         0              1
   Non-Prof.     0              1
Holdings:
   411000 Aerial Photographs
Chronological Coverage:
   100% post 1900
Available to: Public
Circulates to: Students, Faculty


## Colorado
136
Adams State College Library
Alamosa, CO 81101
Tel. (303) 589-7781
Hours: 8–10, M–Th; 8–5, F; 1–5, Sa;
   2–10, Su


Responsible Person: Halpin,
   Jerome H., Jr.
Special Strengths: Colorado
Holdings:
   1370 Printed Maps
Chronological Coverage: 1% pre 1900;
   99% post 1900
Map collection is cataloged 100%
Formats: Cards
Available to: Public
Circulates to: Public, Students, Faculty
Copying Facilities: Copying machine
Equipment:
   2 12-drawer map cabinets
Square Footage: 25


137
Carnegie Branch Library for Local
   History
P. O. Drawer H
Boulder, CO 80306
Tel. (303) 441-3110
Hours: 11–5, M, T, Th–Sa; 1–9, W
Responsible Person: Anderton, Lois,
   Librarian/Archivist
Special Strengths: Colorado (1870–
   present)
Employees: Full Time     Part Time
   Prof.          0             2
   Non-Prof.      0             2
Holdings:
   225 Printed Maps
   10 Manuscript Maps
   150 Aerial Photographs
   3 Atlases
   7 Wall Maps
   1 Raised Relief Map
   2 Microforms
   5 Books
Chronological Coverage: 25% pre 1900;
   75% post 1900
Available to: Public, Students, Faculty
Average monthly use: 10
Copying Facilities: Copying machine
Equipment:
   3 rolled map cabinets
Square Footage: 9


138
University of Colorado
University Libraries, Map Library
Campus Box 184
Boulder, CO 80309
Tel. (303) 492-7578
Hours: 9–5, 7–9, M–Th; 9–5, F
Responsible Person: Fagerstrom,
   David M.
Special Strengths: Colorado (1870–
   present), United States
Employees: Full Time     Part Time
   Non-Prof.      0             1
Holdings:
   122000 Printed Maps
   250 Aerial Photographs
   10 Atlases

Chronological Coverage: 10% pre 1900;
90% post 1900
Available to: Public, Students, Faculty
Average monthly use: 250
Interlibrary loan available
Copying Facilities: Copying machine,
Photographic reproduction
Equipment:
113 5-drawer cabinets
14 4-drawer, 2 2-drawer,
1 40-drawer wooden cabinet,
1 light table
Square Footage: 2280
Map Depositories: USGS (topo);
USGS (geol); DMA (topo); DMA
(aero); DMA (hydro); NOAA

141
Pikes Peak Library District
Local History & Colorado Map Collection
20 N. Cascade
Colorado Springs, CO 80901
Tel. (303) 473-2080
Hours: 10–9, M–Th; 10–6, F, Sa
Responsible Person: Mobley, Ree.
Local History Librarian
Special Strengths: Colorado
Employees: Full Time    Part Time
Non-Prof.       0              4
Holdings:
1500 Printed maps
5 Manuscript Maps
20 Aerial Photographs
30 Atlases
5 Wall Maps
20 Books
5 Gazetteers
Chronological Coverage: 5% pre 1900;
95% post 1900
Map collection is cataloged 90%
Formats: Cards, Online
Available to: Public
Average monthly use: 20
Copying Facilities: Copying machine
Equipment:
2 20-drawer cabinets
Square Footage: 50

139
Air Force Academy Library
United States Air Force Academy
Colorado Springs, CO 80840
Tel. (303) 472-4406
Responsible Person: Mehlhaff, Carol J.
Holdings:
2000 Printed Maps
270 Atlases
1 Globe
70 Books
200 Gazetteers
56 Serial Titles
Chronological Coverage: 1% pre 1900;
99% post 1900
Preservation methods: Lamination
Available to: Public, Students, Faculty
Circulates to: Students, Faculty
Copying Facilities: Copying machine
Equipment:
6 5-drawer cabinets
6 open shelf cabinets
Square Footage: 450

140
Colorado College, Tutt Library
Colorado Springs, CO 80907
Tel. (303) 473-2233
Hours: 8–5, Everyday
Responsible Person: Satterwhite, Robin
Special Strengths: United States
(Geology), Western United States
Employees: Full Time    Part Time
Prof.          0              2
Non-Prof.      0              2
Holdings:
17419 Printed Maps
100 Atlases
1 Globe
10 Raised Relief Maps
30 Gazetteers
Chronological Coverage: 15% pre 1900;
85% post 1900
Available to: Public, Students, Faculty
Average monthly use: 15
Interlibrary loan available
Folded maps only
Copying Facilities: Copying machine,

Microform
Equipment:
44 5-drawer cabinets
Map Depositories: USGS (topo);
USGS (geol); GPO

142
United States Air Force Academy
Map Depository
USAFA/DFSDG (Dean of Faculty
Support, Department of Geography)
Colorado Springs, CO 80840
Tel. (303) 472-2381
Hours: 7–4, M–F
Responsible Person: Slaydon, Captain
Stanley T.
Special Strengths: Comprehensive,
Wall Maps
Holdings:
14270 Printed Maps
103 Manuscript Maps
500 Aerial Photographs
200 Satellite Imagery
10 Atlases
13 Globes
450 Wall Maps
500 Raised Relief Maps
50 Microforms
15 Books
146 Gazetteers
Chronological Coverage: 10% pre 1900;
90% post 1900
Map collection is cataloged 100%
Classification: Numerical Indexing

Formats: Cards, Computer Printout
Preservation methods: Encapsulation,
Lamination, Deacidification
Available to: Public, Students, Faculty
Circulates to: Students, Faculty
Average monthly use: 125
Equipment:
64 5-drawer cabinets
5 vertical map cabinets
1 wooden cabinet
8 light tables
Square Footage: 2010
Map Depositories: USGS (topo);
USGS (geol); DMA (topo); DMA
(aero); DMA (hydro); GPO; NOAA;
Central Intelligence Agency, NASA,
Gt. Br. Ordnance Survey

143
University of Colorado
Colorado Springs Library
Austin Bluffs Parkway
P. O. Box 7150
Colorado Springs, CO 80933-7150
Tel. (303) 593-3290
Hours: 8–9, M–Th; 8–4, F; 9–5, Sa;
1–5, Su
Responsible Person: Haug, Mary Ellen
Young
Special Strengths: Colorado
Employees: Full Time    Part Time
Prof.          0              1
Non-Prof.      0              2
Holdings:
3816 Printed Maps
10 Satellite Imagery
140 Atlases
1 Globe
3 Wall Maps
50 Microforms
80 Books
5 Gazetteers
4 Serial Titles
Chronological Coverage: 5% pre 1900;
95% post 1900
Map collection is cataloged 95%
Classification: LC    Utility: OCLC
Formats: Cards
Available to: Public, Students, Faculty
Circulates to: Public, Students, Faculty
Average monthly use: 20
Average annual circulation:
Maps: 60
Interlibrary loan available
Copying Facilities: Copying machine,
Microform
Equipment:
2 5-drawer cabinets
Square Footage: 2268
Map Depositories: USGS (topo);
USGS (geol)

144
Colorado Department of Local Affairs
Division of Local Government

1313 Sherman St., Room 520
Denver, CO 80203
Tel. (303) 866-3005
Hours: 8–5, M–F
Responsible Person: Martinez, Robert
Special Strengths: Colorado
Holdings:
  5000 Printed Maps
  1824 Aerial Photographs
Chronological Coverage:
  100% post 1900
Preservation methods: Encapsulation,
  Lamination, Chartex or Fabric
  Mounting
Available to: Public
Average monthly use: 30
Copying Facilities: Copying machine
Equipment:
  12 5-drawer cabinets
  1 tube rack
Copying Facilities: Copying machine,
Square Footage: 100
Map Depositories: USGS (topo)

### 145
Colorado Dept. of Highways
Division of Transportation Planning
4201 E. Arkansas Ave.
Denver, CO 80222
Tel. (303) 757-9523
Hours: 8–4, M–F
Responsible Person: Mier, Fred P.
Special Strengths: Colorado
Holdings:
  1000 Manuscript Maps
  3 Atlases
  1500 Microforms
Chronological Coverage:
  100% post 1900
Preservation methods: Encapsulation
Available to: Public
Average monthly use: 50
Copying Facilities: Copying machine,
  Microform, Photographic reproduction
Equipment:
  16 5-drawer cabinets
  1 vertical map cabinet
  2 7 shelf cabinets
  microfilm reader/printer
Square Footage: 500

### 146
Colorado Geological Survey
1313 Sherman St., Room 715
Denver, CO 80203
Tel. (303) 866-2611
Hours: 8–5, M–F
Responsible Person: Slade, Louise
Special Strengths: Colorado (Geology)
Employees: Full Time    Part Time
  Non-Prof.    0              3
Holdings:
  1000 Printed Maps
  500 Manuscript Maps
  3500 Aerial Photographs

250 Satellite Imagery
100 Raised Relief Maps
500 Microforms
Chronological Coverage: 5% pre 1900;
  95% post 1900
Map collection is cataloged 25%
Available to: Public
Average monthly use: 15
Copying Facilities: Copying machine
Equipment:
  20 5-drawer cabinets
  Stereoscopes
Square Footage: 250
Map Depositories: USGS (topo);
  USGS (geol); CO Geological Survey

### 147
Colorado Historical Society
Office of Archaeology & Historic
  Preservation
1300 Broadway
Denver, CO 80203
Tel. (303) 866-4675
Hours: 8–5, M–F
Responsible Person: Gauss, Nancy
Special Strengths: Colorado
Holdings:
  2300 Printed Maps
Chronological Coverage:
  100% post 1900
Preservation methods: Chartex or
  Fabric Mounting
Available to: Public, Students, Faculty
Average monthly use: 75
Copying Facilities: Copying machine
Equipment:
  6 5-drawer cabinets
  2 vertical map cabinets
Square Footage: 81
Map Depositories: USGS (topo)

### 148
Colorado Historical Society
Stephen Hart Library, Books & Ephemera
1300 Broadway
Denver, CO 80203
Tel. (303) 866-2306
Hours: 10–4:30, T–Sa
Responsible Person: Sharp, Alice L.,
  Librarian
Special Strengths: Colorado (1859–
  present)
Holdings:
  2600 Printed Maps
  400 Manuscript Maps
  2 Aerial Photographs
  1 Satellite Imagery
  80 Atlases
  75 Wall Maps
  14 Raised Relief Maps
  8 Books
  3 Gazetteers
  5 Serial Titles
Chronological Coverage: 10% pre 1900;
  90% post 1900

Map collection is cataloged 33%
Classification: LC    Utility: OCLC
Formats: Cards
Preservation methods: Encapsulation,
  Deacidification
Available to: Public
Average monthly use: 10
Copying Facilities: Copying machine,
  Photographic reproduction,
  Autopositive
Equipment:
  13 5-drawer cabinets
Square Footage: 363

### 149
Denver Public Library
Map Collection, Government Publ. Dept.
1357 Broadway
Denver, CO 80203
Tel. (303) 571-2000
Hours: 10–9, M–W; 10–5:30, F, Sa
Responsible Person: Ashton, Dr. Rick,
  Director
Special Strengths: Denver
Employees: Full Time    Part Time
  Prof.        0              1
  Non-Prof.    0              1
Holdings:
  88000 Printed Maps
  150 Manuscript Maps
  3500 Aerial Photographs
  105 Satellite Imagery
  1200 Atlases
  2 Globes
  7 Wall Maps
  7 Raised Relief Maps
  1000 Microforms
  25 Books
  300 Gazetteers
  10 Serial Titles
Chronological Coverage:
  100% post 1900
Map collection is cataloged 10%
Classification: LC    Utility: OCLC
Formats: Cards, COM
Available to: Public
Circulates to: Public
Average monthly use: 500
Interlibrary loan available
  Except fragile items
Copying Facilities: Copying machine,
  Microform, Photographic reproduction
Equipment:
  51 5-drawer cabinets
  3 rolled map cabinets
Square Footage: 1982
Map Depositories: USGS (topo);
  USGS (geol); DMA (topo); DMA
  (aero); DMA (hydro); GPO

### 150
Denver Public Library
Western History Department
1357 Broadway
Denver, CO 80203

Tel. (303) 571-2000
Hours: 10–9, M–W; 10–5:30, F, Sa
Responsible Person: Gehres, Eleanor M.,
  Manager
Special Strengths: Colorado (pre-1900),
  Rocky Mountain States (1890–present)
Special Collections: Rocky Mountain
  Fuel Company Map Collection
Employees: Full Time    Part Time
  Prof.        0            1
Holdings:
  3000 Printed Maps
   800 Manuscript Maps
   150 Atlases
    50 Wall Maps
    25 Books
    10 Gazetteers
Chronological Coverage: 70% pre 1900;
  30% post 1900
Map collection is cataloged 90%
Classification: LC    Utility: OCLC
Formats: Cards, COM
Preservation methods: Encapsulation
Available to: Public
Average monthly use: 25
Copying Facilities: Copying machine,
  Photographic reproduction
Equipment:
  8 5-drawer cabinets
  8 vertical map cabinets
Square Footage: 100


151
U. S. Geological Survey Library, Denver
Mail Stop 914, Box 25046
Denver Federal Center
Denver, CO 80225
Tel. (303) 236-0300
Hours: 7:30–4, M–F
Responsible Person: Bier, Robert A., Jr.
Special Strengths: United States
  (Geosciences)
Employees: Full Time    Part Time
  Non-Prof.    0           2
Holdings:
  74000 Printed Maps
    200 Atlases
     10 Globes
    150 Raised Relief Maps
    200 Books
    500 Gazetteers
      5 Serial Titles
Chronological Coverage: 5% pre 1900;
  95% post 1900
Map collection is cataloged 65%
Classification: Other    Utility: OCLC
Formats: Cards
Preservation methods: Edging
Available to: Public, Studnets, Faculty
Average monthly use: 800
Average annual circulation: Maps: 360
Interlibrary loan available
Copying Facilities: Copying machine
Equipment:
  178 5-drawer cabinets
  Regular shelves

Square Footage: 2500
Map Depositories: USGS (topo);
  USGS (geol); Canada (geol)


152
United States Geological Survey
Field Records Collection
Mail Stop 914, Box 25046
Denver Federal Center
Denver, CO 80225
Tel. (303) 236-0305
Hours: 7:30–4, M–F
Responsible Person: Rowen, Deborah,
  Section Head
Special Strengths: United States (1871–
  present, Maps & Field Notebooks)
Special Collection: Original Geologic
  Maps & Field Notebooks
Holdings:
  12000 Printed Maps
  60000 Aerial Photographs
Chronological Coverage: 5% pre 1900;
  95% post 1900
Map collection is cataloged 90%
Formats: Cards
Preservation methods: Encapsulation,
  Deacidifiction
Available to: Public
Copying Facilities: Copying machine
Equipment:
  95 5-drawer cabinets
  70 cases for rolled maps
Square Footage: 1400


153
University of Denver
Department of Geography
Denver, CO 80208-0183
Phone: (303) 753-2513
Hours: 8–12, 1–4, M–F
Responsible Person: Herold, Laurance C.
Employees: Full Time    Part Time
  Non-Prof.    0           2
Holdings:
  52700 Printed Maps
     25 Atlases
    150 Wall Maps
     50 Raised Relief Maps
    143 Gazetteers
Chronological Coverage:
  100% post 1900
Available to: Students, Faculty
Average monthly use: 5
Equipment:
  35 5-drawer cabinets
Square Footage: 700
Map Depositories: DMA (topo)


154
Fort Lewis College Library
Durango, CO 81301
Tel. (303) 247-7914
Hours: 8–11 Daily
Responsible Person: Engle, Monica

Special Strengths: Colorado, Arizona,
  Utah, New Mexico
Employees: Full Time    Part Time
  Non-Prof.    0           1
Holdings:
  5554 Printed Maps
    50 Atlases
     1 Globe
     6 Wall Maps
    20 Books
    15 Gazetteers
    26 Serial Titles
Chronological Coverage: 2% pre 1900;
  98% post 1900
Classification: Other    Utility: OCLC
Formats: Cards
Preservation methods: Encapsulation,
  Edging
Available to: Public, Students, Faculty
Average monthly use: 100
Copying Facilities: Copying machine,
  Photographic reproduction
Equipment:
  3 5-drawer cabinets
  7 file cabinets
  1 rolled map case
Square Footage: 400
Map Depositories: USGS (topo);
  USGS (geol); GPO


155
Colorado State University Libraries
Documents Division, Map Collection
Fort Collins, CO 80523
Tel. (303) 491-5911
Hours: 7:30–Midnight, M–Th;
  7:30–10, F; 9–6, Sa; Noon–Midnight, Su
Responsible Person: Schmidt, Fred,
  Documents Librarian
Special Strengths: Colorado
Special Collection: Landsat II
  Satellite Images on film
Employees: Full Time    Part Time
  Non-Prof.    0           1
Holdings:
   40000 Printed Maps
  185000 Satellite Imagery
      50 Atlases
       1 Globe
      20 Raised Relief Maps
    2000 Microforms
      10 Books
     250 Gazetteers
Chronological Coverage:
  100% post 1900
Map collection is cataloged 15%
Classification: LC    Utility: RLIN
Formats: Cards
Available to: Public, Students, Faculty
Circulates to: Public, Students, Faculty
Average monthly use: 200
Average annual circulation: Maps: 750
Copying Facilities: Copying machine,
  Photographic reproduction
Equipment:
  5 5-drawer cabinets

open cabinets
shelves w/ special folders
Square Footage: 250
Map Depositories: USGS (topo);
 USGS (geol); DMA (topo); GPO

## 156
Colorado School of Mines
Arthur Lakes Library, Map Room
Golden, CO 80402
Phone: (303) 273-3697
Hours: 8–5, M–F
Responsible Person: Larsgaard, Mary
Special Strengths: Colorado (1890–
 1930, Mines), Western United States
 (Oil Wells), Western United States
 (1950–present, Geology)

Employees: Full Time    Part Time
 Prof.       1            0
 Non-Prof.   0            2

Holdings:
 115000 Printed Maps
  3000 Aerial Photographs
    30 Satellite Imagery
   350 Atlases
     2 Globes
    19 Raised Relief Maps
   136 Microforms
  1000 Books
   250 Gazetteers
    10 Serial Titles
Chronological Coverage: 2% pre 1900;
 98% post 1900
Map collection is cataloged 92%
Classification: LC    Utility: OCLC
Formats: Cards, Online
Preservation methods: Encapsulation
Available to: Public, Students, Faculty
Circulates to: Public, Students, Faculty
Average monthly use: 150
Average annual circulation:
 Maps: 2000; Aerial Photographs: 10;
 500 Well Completion Cards
Interlibrary loan available
 Except rare or fragile material
Copying Facilities: Copying machine
Equipment:
 108 5-drawer cabinets
 Vertical Files, Vertical cases
 14 4-drawer files
Square Footage: 1880
Map Depositories: USGS (topo);
 USGS (geol); DMA (topo); DMA
 (aero); DMA (hydro); GPO; NOS;
 United States Bureau of Land
 Management

## 157
University of Northern Colorado
James A. Michener Library
Reference Department, Map Collection
Greeley, CO 80639
Tel. (303) 351-2562
Hours: 8–5, 6:30–10, M–Th; 8–5, F;
 1–5, Sa; 12–5, 6:30–9, Su

Responsible Person: Greer, Arlene
Special Strengths: Colorado
Holdings:
 50000 Printed Maps
   200 Aerial Photographs
    10 Satellite Imagery
   500 Atlases
     6 Globes
    12 Wall Maps
   400 Microforms
    40 Books
    18 Gazetteers
     3 Serial Titles
Chronological Coverage: 1% pre 1900;
 99% post 1900
Available to: Public, Students, Faculty
Circulates to: Public, Students, Faculty
Average monthly use: 40
Average annual circulation: Maps: 300
Interlibrary loan available
Copying Facilities: Copying machine,
 Microform
Equipment:
 36 5-drawer cabinets
  4 vertical map cabinets
Square Footage: 3750
Map Depositories: USGS (topo);
 USGS (geol); DMA (aero); NOS

## 158
Western State College
Geology Department
Gunnison, CO 81230
Tel. (203) 943-2138
Hours: 8–5, M–F
Responsible Person: Bartleson, Bruce
Special Strengths: Colorado, Wyoming,
 New Mexico, Arizona, Utah

Employees: Full Time    Part Time
 Non-Prof.   0            1

Holdings:
 30000 Printed Maps
Chronological Coverage: 5% pre 1900;
 95% post 1900
Map collection is cataloged 100%
Available to: Public, Students, Faculty
Circulates to: Public, Students, Faculty
Average monthly use: 10
Average annual circulation: Maps: 30
Copying Facilities: Copying machine
Equipment:
 4 5-drawer cabinets
 4 vertical map cabinets
 Wooden vertical cabinets
Square Footage: 100
Map Depositories: USGS (topo);
 USGS (geol)

## 159
Lakewood Library
10200 W. 20th Ave.
Lakewood, CO 80215
Tel. (303) 232-7833
Hours: 10–8, M, T, Th; 12–8, W;
 10–5, F, Sa

Responsible Person: Lamprey, Patricia
Special Strengths: Colorado
Holdings:
 2000 Printed Maps
   40 Atlases
    1 Globe
    1 Wall Map
   20 Raised Relief Maps
   30 Microforms
    5 Books
    4 Gazetteers
Chronological Coverage:
 100% post 1900
Map collection is catloged 50%
Classification: LC
Formats: Computer Printout
Available to: Public
Circulates to: Public
Average monthly use: 20
Average annual circulation: Maps: 500
Interlibrary loan available
Copying Facilities: Copying machine
Equipment:
 3 4-drawer file cabinets
Square Footage: 8
Map Depositories: USGS (topo);
 USGS (geol); DMA (topo)

## 160
University of Southern Colorado
 LRC/Library
2200 Bonforte Blvd.
Pueblo, CO 81001
Tel. (303) 549-2451
Hours: 7–9, M–Th; 7–5, F; 1–9, Su
Responsible Person: Sullivan, Dan
Special Strengths: Colorado, United
 States

Employees: Full Time    Part Time
 Prof.       0            1
 Non-Prof.   0            2

Holdings:
 7000 Printed Maps
  175 Atlases
    3 Wall Maps
  693 Books
   14 Gazetteers
   44 Serial Titles
Chronological Coverage:
 100% post 1900
Available to: Public, Students, Faculty
Copying Facilities: Copying machine,
 Photographic reproduction
Equipment:
 8 5-drawer cabinets
 4 vertical map cabinets
Square Footage: 40
Map Depositories: USGS (topo);
 USGS (geol); DMA (topo)

## Connecticut
## 161
Bridgeport Public Library
925 Broad St.
Bridgeport, CT 06604

Tel. (203) 576-7403
Hours: 9–9, M, W; 9–5, T, Th–Sa
Responsible Person: Fredericks, Valeri
Special Strengths: Bridgeport, CT
Holdings:
    3860 Printed Maps
        10 Manuscripts Maps
        40 Aerial Photographs
        380 Atlases
        4 Globes
        3 Wall Maps
        6 Gazetteers
Chronological Coverage: 5% pre 1900;
    95% post 1900
Preservation methods: Chartex or
    Fabric Mounting
Available to: Public, Students, Faculty
Circulates to: Public, Students, Faculty
Average monthly use: 300
Copying Facilities: Copying machine
Equipment:
    23 5-drawer cabinets
Square Footage: 192
Map Depositories: USGS (topo)

162
Connecticut Historical Society
1 Elizabeth St.
Hartford, CT 06105
Tel. (203) 236-5621
Hours: 9–5, M–Sa
Responsible Person: McCain, Diana,
    Book Catalog Librarian
Special Strengths: Connecticut (1635–
    present)
Holdings:
    500 Printed Maps
        50 Manuscript Maps
        50 Aerial Photographs
        70 Atlases
        200 Books
        40 Gazetteers
        5 Serial Titles
Chronological Coverage: 90% pre 1900;
    10% post 1900
Map collection is cataloged 50%
Formats: Cards
Preservation methods: Encapsulation,
    Chartex of Fabric Mounting,
    Deacidification
Available to: Public, Students, Faculty
Average monthly use: 10
Copying Facilities: Copying machine,
    Microform, Photographic reproduction
Equipment:
    3 5-drawer cabinets

163
Connecticut State Library, Archives
History & Genealogy Unit
231 Capitol Ave.
Hartford, CT 06106
Tel. (203) 566-3690
Hours: 8:30–5, M–F; 9–1, Sa
Responsible Person: Wohlsen,

Theodore O., Jr., Unit Head
Special Strengths: Connecticut
    (History)
Special Collections: William Brownell
    Goodwin Collection, 1934–1949
    (Record Group 69:15)
Employees: Full Time    Part Time
    Prof.           0           4
    Non-Prof.       0           2
Holdings:
    24000 Printed Maps
    33000 Aerial Photographs
        10 Serial Titles
Chronological Coverage: 60% pre 1900;
    40% post 1900
Map collection is cataloged 50%
Classification: Dewey
Formats: Cards
Preservation methods: Encapsulation,
    Deacidification
Available to: Public, Students, Faculty
Average monthly use: 12
Copying Facilities: Copying machine
Equipment:
    24 5-drawer cabinets
Square Footage: 250
Map Depositories: USGS (topo)

164
Hartford Public Library
Reference Department
500 Main St.
Hartford, CT 06103
Tel. (203) 525-9121
Hours: 9–9, M–Th; 9–5, F, Sa
Responsible Person: Nolan, Martha O.
Special Strengths: New England, New
    York, World
Employees: Full Time    Part Time
    Prof.           0           2
    Non-Prof.       0           1
Holdings:
    10000 Printed Maps
        200 Atlases
Chronological Coverage: 10% pre 1900;
    90% post 1900
Available to: Public
Copying Facilities: Copying machine
Equipment:
    35 5-drawer cabinets
    2 vertical map cabinets
    6 10-drawer cases
Square Footage: 858
Map Depositories: USGS (topo);
    DMA (topo); GPO

165
Trinity College, Watkinson Library
300 Summit St.
Hartford, CT 06106
Tel. (203) 527-3151
Hours: 8:30–4:30, M–F
Responsible Person: Kaimowitz, Dr.
    Jeffrey H., Curator
Special Strengths: United States

(18th–19th century, Civil War)
Employees: Full Time    Part Time
    Prof.           2           1
    Non-Prof.       0           8
Holdings:
    700 Printed Maps
        10 Manuscript Maps
        185 Atlases
        100 Books
Chronological Coverage: 90% pre 1900;
    10% post 1900
Map collection is cataloged 100%
Classification: Other
    Watkinson Library
Formats: Cards
Preservation methods: Encapsulation,
    Deacidification
Available to: Public, Students, Faculty
Copying Facilities: Copying machine,
    Microform, Photographic reproduction
Equipment:
    6 5-drawer cabinets
    10 MS boxes for small maps
Square Footage: 77

166
Wesleyan University
Science Library
Middletown, CT 06457
Tel. (203) 347-9411
Hours: 7–2 a.m., M–Th; 7–Midnight, F;
    9–Midnight, Sa; 10–2 a.m., Su
Responsible Person: Calhoon, William
Employees: Full Time    Part Time
    Non-Prof.       0           2
Holdings:
    125000 Printed Maps
        125 Atlases
        1 Globe
        2 Wall Maps
        10 Books
        3 Gazetteers
Chronological Coverage: 5% pre 1900;
    95% post 1900
Available to: Public, Students, Faculty
Average monthly use: 10
Copying Facilities: Copying machine
Equipment:
    32 5-drawer cabinets
    4 vertical map cabinets
    1 3-drawer map cabinet
Square Footage: 800
Map Depositories: USGS (topo);
    USGS (geol); DMA (topo); DMA
    (aero)

167
G. W. Blunt White Library
Mystic Seaport Museum, Inc.
Greenmanville Ave.
Mystic, CT 06355
Tel. (203) 572-0711
Hours: 9–5, M–Th
Responsible Person: Allen, Virginia
Special Strengths: North America

(Navigation)
Special Collections: Over 5000 Nautical
charts
Employees: Full Time    Part Time
Non-Prof.    0             2
Holdings:
5814 Printed Maps
40 Atlases
2 Globes
1 Raised Relief Map
14 Books
1 Gazetteer
Chronological Coverage: 45% pre 1900;
55% post 1900
Map collection is cataloged 100%
Classification: Boggs & Lewis
Formats: Cards
Available to: Public, Students, Faculty
Copying Facilities: Copying machine,
Photographic reproduction
Equipment:
1 5-drawer cabinet

168
Central Connecticut State College
Department of Geography, Map Library
New Britain, CT 06268
Tel. (203) 827-7457
Hours: 2–4, M–F
Responsible Person: Snaden, Dr. James N.
Special Strengths: United States,
Europe, India, Japan
Holdings:
22000 Printed Maps
15 Atlases
3 Globes
110 Wall Maps
40 Raised Relief Maps
100 Gazetteers
Chronological Coverage:
100% post 1900
Classification: Other
DMA
Preservation methods: Lamination,
Chartex or Fabric Mounting
Available to: Public, Students, Faculty
Average monthly use: 2
Copying Facilities: Copying machine,
Photographic reproduction
Equipment:
25 5-drawer cabinets
Light table, stereoscope, Salzman
enlarger & reducer
Square Footage: 200
Map Depositories: USGS (topo);
USGS (geol); DMA (topo); DMA
(aero); DMA (hydro)

169
New Haven Free Public Library
133 Elm Street
New Haven, CT 06510
Tel. (203) 787-8130
Responsible Person: Morris, Betsy
Special Strengths: New England

Employees: Full Time    Part Time
Prof.        0             1
Holdings:
2200 Printed Maps
150 Atlases
5 Globes
15 Gazetteers
Chronological Coverage: 5% pre 1900;
95% post 1900
Available to: Public
Circulates to: Public
Average monthly use: 25
Average annual circulation: Maps: 10
Interlibrary loan available
Duplicates only
Copying Facilities: Copying machine
Equipment:
3 5-drawer cabinets
Map Depositories: USGS (topo)

170
Southern Connecticut State University
Buley Library, Reference Department
New Haven, CT 06515
Tel. (203) 397-4511
Hours: 8–4, M–F
Responsible Person: Clarie, Thomas C.
Special Strengths: New England, New
York
Employees: Full Time    Part Time
Non-Prof.    0             1
Holdings:
3350 Printed Maps
240 Aerial Photographs
225 Atlases
4 Globes
5 Wall Maps
5 Raised Relief Maps
25 Books
5 Gazetteers
4 Serial Titles
Chronological Coverage: 1% pre 1900;
99% post 1900
Available to: Public, Students, Faculty
Circulates to: Students, Faculty
Average monthly use: 60
Average annual circulation: Maps: 30
Copying Facilities: Copying machine
Equipment:
12 5-drawer cabinets
Map Depositories: USGS (topo);
USGS (geol); DMA (topo); DMA
(aero)

171
Yale University Library, Map Collection
Box 1603A Yale Station
New Haven, CT 06520
Tel. (203) 436-8638
Hours: 10–12, 1–5, M–F
Responsible Person: McCorkle,
Barbara B., Map Curator
Special Strengths: New England
(18th–19th century), Colonial
America (18th–19th century)

Special Collections: Karpinski
photographs/photostats, Stevenson
collection of glass negatives
Employees: Full Time    Part Time
Prof.        0             1
Non-Prof.    0             3
Holdings:
200000 Printed Maps
500 Manuscript Maps
3 Aerial Photographs
2500 Atlases
12 Globes
500 Wall Maps
24 Raised Relief Maps
500 Books
14 Serial Titles
Chronological Coverage: 15% pre 1900;
85% post 1900
Map collection is cataloged 95%
Classification: Yale
Utility: RLIN
Formats: Cards
Preservation methods: Encapsulation
Deacidification
Available to: Public, Students, Faculty
Average monthly use: 75
Copying Facilities: Copying machine,
Microform, Photographic reproduction
Equipment:
54 5-drawer cabinets
3 vertical map cabinets
Oak storage cases
Square Footage: 3100
Map Depositories: USGS (topo);
DMA (topo); DMA (hydro); NOS;
NOAA

172
Yale University, Geology Library
210 Whitney Avenue, P. O. Box 6666
New Haven, CT 06511
Tel. (203) 436-2480
Hours: 8:30–5, M–F
Responsible Person: Scammell,
Harry D., Librarian
Special Strengths: Comprehensive
(Geology, Topography)
Holdings:
170000 Printed Maps
Chronological Coverage: 1% pre 1900;
99% post 1900
Map collection is cataloged 100%
Classification: Yale Geology
Formats: Cards
Preservation methods: Encapsulation
Available to: Public
Average monthly use: 200
Copying Facilities: Copying machine,
Microform, Photographic reproduction
Equipment:
163 5-drawer cabinets
32 4-drawer cabinets
Square Footage: 900
Map Depositories: USGS (geol)

173
Ferguson Library
96 Broad St.
Stamford, CT 06901
Tel. (203) 964-1000
Hours: 9–9, M–F; 9–5:30, Sa; 1–5, Su
  (Oct.–May)
Responsible Person: Dershowitz, Hope
Special Strengths: Stamford,
  Connecticut & adjacent states
Holdings:
  400 Printed Maps
  150 Atlases
    1 Globe
    1 Wall Map
Chronological Coverage: 2% pre 1900;
  98% post 1900
Available to: Public
Average monthly use: 60
Copying Facilities: Copying machine
Equipment:
  1 5-drawer cabinet
  1 vertical map cabinet
  Vertical files
Square Footage: 20
Map Depositories: USGS (topo)

174
University of Connecticut
University Library, Map Library U-5M
19 Fairfield Rd.
Stoors, CT 06268
Tel. (203) 486-4589
Hours: 9–5, M–F; 1–5, M–F during
  breaks
Responsible Person: McGlamery,
  Thornton P.
Special Strengths: Connecticut,
  New England
Special Collections: Sanborn Microfirm
  of Connecticut, Petersen Collection
  (Negative photostats of New England
  towns 185 –)
Holdings:
  100000 Printed Maps
    10 Satellite Imagery
    8 Globes
    40 Raised Relief Maps
    100 Microforms
    1000 Books
    350 Gazetteers
    2 Serial Titles
Chronological Coverage: 5% pre 1900;
  95% post 1900
Map collection is cataloged 75%
Classification: LC    Utility: OCLC
Formats: Cards
Preservation methods: Encapsulation,
  Deacidification
Available to: Public, Students, Faculty
Circulates to: Faculty
Average monthly use: 350
Average annual circulation: Maps: 200;
  Books: 300; Aerial Photographs: 100
Interlibrary loan available
  Current Material Only

Copying Facilities: Copying machine
Equipment:
  47 5-drawer cabinets
  16 vertical map cabinets
  12 files
  2 light tables, 3 lighted magnifying
    glasses, 1 stereoscopic viewer
Map Depositories: USGS (topo);
  USGS (geol); DMA (topo); GPO;
  Metro District; Hartford, CT area

**Delaware**
175
Delaware State Archives
Hall of Records
Dover, DE 19901
Tel. (302) 736-5318
Hours: 8:30–12, 1–4:15, T–F; 8–12:30,
  1–3:45, Sa
Responsible Person: Mattern, Joanne A.,
  Supervisor
Special Strengths: Delaware (18th
  century)
Employees: Full Time    Part Time
  Prof.        0            2
  Non-Prof.    0            2
Holdings:
  3500 Printed Maps
  100 Manuscript Maps
  5000 Aerial Photographs
  25 Atlases
  40 Wall Maps
  100 Microforms
  25 Books
  5 Gazetteers
Chronological Coverage: 50% pre 1900;
  50% post 1900
Map collection is cataloged 90%
Classification: Local
Formats: Cards
Preservation methods: Lamination,
  Chartex or Fabric Mounting,
  Deacidification
Available to: Public, Students, Faculty
Average monthly use: 40
Copying Facilities: Copying machine,
  Microform, Photographic reproduction
Equipment:
  3 5-drawer cabinets
  1 vertical map cabinet
  50 oversize boxes
Square Footage: 68

176
Eleutherian Mills-Hagley Foundation
Hagley Museum & Library
P. O. Box 3630, Greenville
Wilmington, DE 19807
Tel. (302) 658-2400
Hours: 8:30–4:30, M–F; 9–4:30 second
  Saturday each month
Responsible Person: Williams,
  Richmond D., Deputy Director
Special Collections: Dallin Aerial
  Survey Company Collection (in

Pictorial Collections Dept.)
Holdings:
  925 Printed Mpas
  1500 Manuscript Maps
  15000 Aerial Photographs
  225 Atlases
  250 Books
  30 Gazetteers
Chronological Coverage: 55% pre 1900;
  45% post 1900
Classification: LC    Utility: OCLC
Formats: Cards
Preservation methods: Encapsulation,
  Chartex or Fabric Mounting,
  Deacidification
Available to: Public
Average monthly use: 50
Average annual circulation:
  Books: 10000
Interlibrary loan available
  Books only
Copying Facilities: Copying machine,
  Microform, Photographic reproduction
Equipment:
  18 5-drawer cabinets
  1 vertical map cabinet

**District of Columbia**
177
Association of American Railroads
Economics & Finance Dept. Library
1920 L St. N.W., Room 523
Washington, DC 20036
Tel. (202) 835-9387
Hours: 9–4, M–F
Responsible Person: Rowland,
  Helen M., Supervisor
Holdings:
  1116 Printed Maps
  9 Atlases
  2 Wall Maps
Chronological Coverage: 5% pre 1900;
  95% post 1900
Classification: LC
Formats: Cards
Copying Facilities: Copying machine
Equipment:
  8 vertical map cabinets

178
Columbia Historical Society Library
1307 New Hampshire Ave., N.W.
Washington, D.C. 20036
Tel. (202) 785-2068
Hours: 10–4, W, F; Noon–4, Sa
Responsible Person: Miller,
  Elizabeth, J., Curator
Special Strengths: Washington, D.C.
  (1880–1930), Metropolitan
  Washington (Aerial photos, 1955–58)
Holdings:
  300 Printed Maps
  2000 Aerial Photographs
  50 Atlases
  30 Books

Chronological Coverage: 50% pre 1900;
50% post 1900
Available to: Public, Students, Faculty
Equipment:
1 18-drawer open storage
Square Footage: 50

### 179
Defense Mapping Agency Hydrographic/-
Topographic Center
Scientific Data Dept., Support Division
6500 Brookes Lane
Washington, D.C. 20315
Tel. (202) 227-2109
Hours: 8:30–3, M–F
Responsible Person: Lozupone,
Frank P., Chief
Special Strengths: World
(Comprehensive)
Holdings:
1179656 Printed Maps
250 Atlases
27690 Books
850 Serial Titles
Chronological Coverage:
100% post 1900
Map collection is cataloged 100%
Formats: Cards, Computer Printout
Preservation methods: Lamination
Average monthly use: 1100
Average annual circulation:
Maps: 66000; Books: 16000
Interlibrary loan available
Special arrangement
Copying Facilities: Copying machine,
Microform, Photographic reproduction
Equipment:
1008 5-drawer cabinets
5000 linear feet movable library
shelves
Square Footage: 12000

### 180
District of Columbia DOT Library
Room 519 Presidential Building
415 12th St. N.W.
Washington, D.C. 20004
Tel. (202) 727-2157
Hours: 9–4:30, M–F
Responsible Person: Sorrel, Lorraine
Special Strengths: Washington
Metropolitan Area

| Employees: | Full Time | Part Time |
|---|---|---|
| Prof. | 0 | 2 |

Holdings:
150 Printed Maps
2000 Aerial Photographs
100 Wall Maps
1000 Computer Tapes
10 Books
Chronological Coverage:
100% post 1900
Available to: Public, Students, Faculty
Circulates to: Puboic
Average monthly use: 20

Copying Facilities: Copying machine,
Photographic reproduction
Equipment:
20 5-drawer cabinets
Square Footage: 300

### 181
Folger Shakespeare Library
201 E. Capitol St., S.E.
Washington, D.C. 20003
Tel. (202) 544-4600
Hours: 8:45–4:45, M–F; 8:45–4:30, Sa
Responsible Person: Knachel,
Dr. Philip A., Acting Director
Special Strengths: Great Britain
(16th–17th centuries)
Holdings:
267 Printed Maps
1 Manuscript Map
30 Atlases
2 Globes
280 Books
10 Gazetteers
3 Serial Titles
Chronological Coverage: 80% pre 1900;
20% post 1900
Map collection is cataloged 85%
Formats: Cards
Preservation methods: Chartex or
Fabric Mounting
Copying Facilities: Copying machine,
Photographic reproduction
Equipment:
3 5-drawer cabinets

### 182
George Washington University
Gelman Library, Reference Department
2130 H St. NW
Washington, D.C. 20052
Tel. (202) 676-6455
Hours: 8:30–10, M–Th; 8:30–6, F;
10–6, Sa; Noon–10, Su
Responsible Person: Maxwell, Barbara,
Government Documents
Special Strengths: Washington, D.C.
Holdings:
15600 Printed Maps
1 Globe
Chronological Coverage:
100% post 1900
Available to: Public, Students, Faculty
Average monthly use: 2
Average annual circulation: Maps: 6
Copying Facilities: Copying machine
Equipment:
16 5-drawer cabinets
Square Footage: 80
Map Depositories: USGS (topo);
DMA (topo); DMA (aero)

### 183
Library of Congress
Geography & Map Division

Washington, D.C. 20540
Tel. (202) 287-8530
Hours: 8:30–5, M–F; 8:30–12:30, Sa
Responsible Person: Wolter, Dr. John A.,
Chief
Special Strengths: World,
Comprehensive

| Employees: | Full Time | Part Time |
|---|---|---|
| Prof. | 23 | 2 |
| Non-Prof. | 12 | 1 |

Holdings:
3800000 Printed Maps
4000 Manuscript Maps
650 Satellite Imagery
47000 Atlases
300 Globes
40 Wall Maps
2258 Raised Relief Maps
58000 Microforms
8000 Books
295 Serial Titles
Chronological Coverage: 25% pre 1900;
75% post 1900
Map collection is cataloged 10%
Classification: LC
Formats: Cards, Online, Computer
Printout
Preservation methods: Encapsulation,
Deacidification
Available to: Public
Average monthly use: 2626
Average annual circulation:
Maps: 11112
Interlibrary loan available
Except items that are rare, in poor
condition, or in heavy demand
Copying Facilities: Copying machine,
Microform, Photographic reproduction,
Transparencies
Equipment:
5500 5-drawer cabinets
1 vertical map cabinet
Square Footage: 93000
Map Depositories: USGS (topo);
USGS (geol); DMA (topo); DMA
(aero); DMA (hydro); GPO; NOS;
NOAA; Canada (topo); Canada (geol);
Official depository for all Federal
map producing agencies

### 184
National Capitol Planning Commission
1325 G. St. N.W.
Washington, D.C. 20507
Tel. (202) 724-0211
Hours: 8–4, M–F
Responsible Person: Zenthe, Andrea J.
Special Strengths: National Capital
Region
Special Collections: Special purpose
maps concerning Federal Facilities
in the National Capital Region

| Employees: | Full Time | Part Time |
|---|---|---|
| Prof. | 0 | 1 |
| Non-Prof. | 0 | 1 |

Holdings:

15000 Printed Maps
   300 Aerial Photographs
    15 Atlases
  80000 Microforms
Chronological Coverage: 2% pre 1900;
  98% post 1900
Map collection is cataloged 85%
Formats: Cards
Available to: Public, Students, Faculty
Circulates to: Public, Students, Faculty
Average monthly use: 50
Average annual circulation:
  Maps: 1500; Aerial Photographs: 1500
Interlibrary loan available
Copying Facilities: Copying machine,
  Microform, Photographic reproduction
Equipment:
  10 5-drawer cabinets
  6 vertical map cabinets
  Tubular Files
Square Footage: 300


### 185

National Geographic Society
Map Library
1146 16th St., N.W.
Washington, D.C. 20036
Tel. (202) 857-7000
Hours: 8:30–5, M–F
Responsible Person: Barkdull,
  Margery K., Map Librarian
Special Strengths: United States
  (1970–present)
Holdings:
  105000 Printed Maps
    250 Aerial Photographs
     50 Satellite Imagery
    600 Atlases
    204 Raised Relief Maps
    760 Books
     40 Gazetteers
      7 Serial Titles
Chronological Coverage: 1% pre 1900;
  99% post 1900
Map collection is cataloged 95%
Formats: Cards
Preservation methods: Encapsulation
Available to: Public
Average monthly use: 150
Average annual circulation:
  Maps: 4000; Books: 375
Interlibrary loan available
  Subject to staff requirements
Copying Facilities: Copying machine
Equipment:
  80 5-drawer cabinets
  34 vertical map cabinets
  3 extra wide vertical files
  1 Suspendex vertical file
  Microfiche reader
Square Footage: 2500
Map Depositories: USGS (topo);
  DMA (too); Canada (topo); Australia
  Division of National Mapping; New
  Zealand Dept. of Lands & Surv.

### 186

Public Library of District of Columbia
History Division
901 G St. N.W.
Washington, D.C. 20001
Tel. (202) 727-1161
Hours: 9–9, M–Th; 9–5:30, F, Sa;
  1–5, Su
Responsible Person: Bartlett, Eleanor A.
Holdings:
  5713 Printed Maps
   250 Atlases
    1 Globe
    1 Serial Title
Chronological Coverage:
  100% post 1900
Available to: Public
Circulates to: Public
Average monthly use: 20
Average annual circulation: Maps: 100
Copying Facilities: Copying machine
Equipment:
  16 5-drawer cabinets
  1 vertical map cabinet
Square Footage: 104
Map Depositories: USGS (topo)


### 187

Society of the Cincinnati Library
2118 Massachusetts Ave., N.W.
Washington, D.C. 20008
Tel. (202) 785-0540
Hours: 10–4, M–F
Responsible Person: Kilbourne, John D.,
  Director
Special Strengths: East Coast (1760–
  1783)
Employees: Full Time    Part Time
  Prof.     1          1
  Non-Prof.  0         1
Holdings:
  350 Printed Maps
    5 Manuscript Maps
  150 Atlases
    2 Globes
   25 Books
   12 Gazetteers
Chronological Coverage: 90% pre 1900;
  10% post 1900
Map collection is cataloged 100%
Classification: Chronological
Formats: Cards
Preservation methods: Chartex or
  Fabric Mounting
Available to: Public
Average monthly use: 2
Copying Facilities: Copying machine,
  Photographic reproduction
Equipment:
  2 5-drawer cabinets


### 188

U. S. National Archives & Records Service
Special Archives Division

Cartographic & Architectural Branch
Washington, D.C. 20408
Tel. (703) 756-6700
Hours: 8–4:30, M–F
Responsible Person: Cunliffe,
  William H., Chief
Special Strengths: United States,
  Comprehensive
Employees: Full Time    Part Time
  Non-Prof.   5         3
Holdings:
  2000000 Printed Maps
   100000 Aerial Photographs
Chronological Coverage: 65% pre 1900;
  35% post 1900
Formats: Cards, Listings
Preservation methods: Encapsulation,
  Lamination, Deacidification
Available to: Public
Copying Facilities: Copying machine,
  Photographic reproduction
Equipment:
  1300 5-drawer cabinets
  2500 10-drawer cabinets
  900 4-drawer cabinets


### 189

U.S.M.C. Historical Center
Personal Papers Collection
Building 58, Navy Yard
Washington, D.C. 20374
Tel. (202) 433-3447
Hours: 8:30–4, M–F
Responsible Person: Miller, J. Michael
Special Strengths: Pacific Islands
  (1940–45); Korea (1950–53); Vietnam
  (1963–73)
Special Collections: This collection is
  mostly specialized in maps of Marine
  Corps military operations.
Holdings:
  3000 Printed Maps
   200 Manuscript Maps
    40 Aerial Photographs
    40 Raised Relief Maps
Chronological Coverage: 2% pre 1900;
  98% post 1900
Preservation methods: Encapsulation,
  Deacidification
Average monthly use: 4
Copying Facilities: Copying machine
Equipment:
  4 5-drawer cabinets
Square Footage: 200


### 190

World Bank
Cartography Library
1818 H Street N.W.
Washington, D.C. 20433
Tel. (202) 676-0229
Hours: 8–4:30, M–F
Responsible Person: Windheuser,
  Christine S.

Special Strengths: Third World
  Countries
Special Collections: Satellite Imagery
  & tape library
Holdings:
  15000 Printed Maps
  2500 Satellite Imagery
  150 Atlases
  1 Globe
  400 Computer Tapes
  500 Books
  200 Gazetteers
  10 Serial Titles
Chronological Coverage:
  100% post 1900
Map collection is cataloged 100%
Classification: Titling, Minisis
Formats: Cards
Average monthly use: 150
Copying Facilities: Copying machine,
  Photographic reproduction, Color
  Xerox
Equipment:
  30 5-drawer cabinets
  Zoom transfer scope
Square Footage: 900

**Florida**

191
Florida Atlantic University Library
Reference Department
P. O. Box 3092
Boca Raton, FL 33431
Tel. (305) 393-3785
Hours: 8–Midnight, M–Th; 8–6, F;
  9–6, Sa; Noon–Midnight, Su
Responsible Person: Wiler, Linda,
  Head of Reference
Special Strengths: Florida, Southeast
  Region
Employees: Full Time     Part Time
  Non-Prof.      0              1
Holdings:
  16771 Printed Maps
  3 Globes
  2 Wall Maps
Chronological Coverage:
  100% post 1900
Available to: Public, Students, Faculty
Average monthly use: 10
Copying Facilities: Copying machine,
  Microform
Equipment:
  32 5-drawer cabinets
  1 vertical map cabinet
  Light table
Square Footage: 700
Map Depositories: USGS (topo);
  USGS (geol); DMA (topo); DMA
  (aero); DMA (hydro); GPO; NOS;
  NOAA

192
University of Miami, Map Collection
Government Publications Department

Otto G. Richter Library
Coral Gables, FL 33124
Tel. (305) 284-3155
Hours: 8–9, M–F
Responsible Person: Wise, Mary
Employees: Full Time     Part Time
  Prof.          0              1
  Non-Prof.      0              1
Holdings:
  700 Printed Maps
Chronological Coverage:
  100% post 1900
Available to: Public, Students, Faculty
Interlibrary loan available
Copying Facilities: Copying machine
Equipment:
  2 5-drawer cabinets
  1 vertical map cabinet
Square Footage: 300
Map Depositories: USGS (topo);
  GPO

193
University of Miami
Otto G. Richter Library
Archives & Special Collections Dept.
Coral Gables, FL 33124
Tel. (305) 284-3247
Hours: 9–4, M–F
Responsible Person: Purdy, Helen,
  Head
Special Strengths: Florida, Caribbean,
  South America
Holdings:
  355 Printed Maps
  26 Manuscript Maps
  6 Atlases
  1 Wall Map
Chronological Coverage: 38% pre 1900;
  62% post 1900
Preservation methods: Encapsulation
Available to: Students, Faculty
Copying Facilities: Copying machine
Equipment:
  12 5-drawer cabinets
Square Footage: 275

194
Stetson University
DuPont-Ball Library
421 North Blvd., University Box 8418
DeLand, FL 32730
Tel. (904) 734-4121
Hours: 8–11, M–Th; 8–5, F; 9–5, Sa;
  1–11, Su
Responsible Person: Kline, Sims,
  Acting Director
Special Strengths: Florida
Employees: Full Time     Part Time
  Prof.          0              1
Holdings:
  2500 Printed Maps
  150 Atlases
  1 Globe
  5 Wall Maps

45 Books
5 Gazetteers
12 Serial Titles
Chronological Coverage:
  100% post 1900
Available to: Public, Students, Faculty
Circulates to: Public, Students, Faculty
Average monthly use: 25
Copying Facilities: Copying machine,
  Microform
Equipment:
  12 5-drawer cabinets
Square Footage: 200
Map Depositories: USGS (topo);
  GPO

195
University of Florida Libraries
Map Library
University of Florida
Gainesville, FL 32611
Tel. (904) 392-0803
Hours: 8:30–5, M–F
Responsible Person: Armstrong,
  Dr. Helen Jane
Special Strengths: Latin America,
  Florida (Aerial photography)
Special Collections: Florida Sanborn
  Fire Insurance Maps, NASA Aerial
  Film Library (9″ rolls & 70 mm film,
  low level, Color-CIR-B&W–mainly
  FL), Remote Sensing Imagery
  Collection, Erwin Raisz Personal
  Maps & Books
Employees: Full Time     Part Time
  Prof.          1              1
  Non-Prof.      0              5
Holdings:
  334685 Printed Maps
  100 Manuscript Maps
  169131 Aerial Photographs
  1223 Satellite Imagery
  745 Atlases
  17 Globes
  48 Wall Maps
  94 Raised Relief Maps
  68 Microforms
  709 Books
  275 Gazetteers
  8 Serial Titles
Chronological Coverage: 1% pre 1900;
  99% post 1900
Map collection is cataloged 32%
Classification: LC     Utility: OCLC
Formats: Cards, Online
Preservation methods: Encapsulation,
  Chartex or Fabric Mounting
Available to: Public, Students, Faculty
Circulates to: Students, Faculty
Average monthly use: 1060
Average annual circulation:
  Maps: 12370
Interlibrary loan available
  Within Florida only
Copying Facilities: Copying machine
Equipment:

168 5-drawer cabinets
39 vertical files
4 10-drawer units
Multi-Format Photo Interpretation
Station
Square Footage: 4965
Map Depositories: USGS (topo);
USGS (geol); DMA (topo); DMA
(aero); DMA (hydro); GPO; NOS;
Spain (Geol.), FL State Agencies

**196**
University of Florida
P. K. Yonge Library of Florida History
Map Collection
404 Library West
Gainesville, FL 32611
Tel. (904) 392-0319
Hours: 8–4:45, M–F
Responsible Person: Alexander,
Elizabeth, Librarian
Special Strengths: Florida (1500–1945),
Southeast United States (1500–1945)
Employees: Full Time    Part Time
Prof.           0              2
Non-Prof.    0              2
Holdings:
1700 Printed Maps
300 Manuscript Maps
Chronological Coverage: 80% pre 1900;
20% post 1900
Map collection is cataloged 100%
Formats: Cards
Preservation methods: Encapsulation
Available to: Public, Faculty
Average monthly use: 10
Equipment:
15 5-drawer cabinets
Square Footage: 400

**197**
Jacksonville Public Library System
Haydon Burns Library
122 N. Ocean St.
Jacksonville, FL 32202
Tel. (904) 633-3926
Hours: 9–9, M–F; 9–6, Sa
Responsible Person: Evans, Valerie
Special Strengths: United States,
Florida, Atlantic Coast
Holdings:
1605 Printed Maps
1 Globe
Chronological Coverage: 10% pre 1900;
90% post 1900
Available to: Public
Circulates to: Public
Average annual circulation: Maps: 68
Interlibrary loan available
Copying Facilities: Copying machine,
Microform
Equipment:
18 5-drawer cabinets
Square Footage: 60
Map Depositories: USGS (topo);

USGS (geol); GPO; NOAA

**198**
University of North Florida Library
P. O. Box 17605
Jacksonville, FL 32216
Tel. (904) 646-2616
Hours: 9–9, M–Th; 9–5, F; 11–4, Sa;
1–10, Su
Responsible Person: Davis, Mary L.,
Reference Librarian
Special Strengths: United States,
Florida
Holdings:
4600 Printed Maps
60 Atlases
1 Globe
15 Wall Maps
Chronological Coverage:
100% post 1900
Map collection is cataloged 90%
Classification: LC    Utility: OCLC
Formats: Cards, Online
Available to: Public, Students, Faculty
Average monthly use: 30
Copying Facilities: Copying machine,
Photographic reproduction
Equipment:
13 5-drawer cabinets
Map Depositories: USGS (topo);
USGS (geol)

**199**
Florida Institute of Technology Library
150 W. University Blvd.
Melbourne, FL 32901
Tel. (305) 723-3701
Hours: 9–10, M–Th; 9–5, F; 2–10, Su
Responsible Person: Melnicove,
Annette R., Acting Map Librarian
Special Strengths: Florida
Employees: Full Time    Part Time
Prof.           1              1
Non-Prof.    1              1
Holdings:
527 Printed Maps
25 Atlases
2 Globes
48 Books
10 Gazetteers
Chronological Coverage:
100% post 1900
Map collection is cataloged 100%
Classification: LC    Utility: OCLC
Formats: Cards
Preservation methods: Lamination
Available to: Public, Students, Faculty
Circulates to: Public, Students, Faculty
Average monthly use: 30
Average annual circulation: Maps: 60
Interlibrary loan available
Copying Facilities: Copying machine,
Microform
Equipment:
6 5-drawer cabinets

Light table
Map Depositories: USGS (topo);
USGS (geol); DMA (aero); DMA
(hydro); GPO

**200**
Florida International University Library
Documents Section
Tamiami Campus
Miami, FL 33199
Tel. (305) 554-2461
Hours: 8–5, M–F
Responsible Person: Rodriguez,
J. Hortensia, Documents Librarian
Special Strengths: Southeastern
United States
Holdings:
7344 Printed Maps
300 Atlases
2 Globes
35 Wall Maps
20 Raised Relief Maps
3 Books
5 Gazetteers
Chronological Coverage:
100% post 1900
Available to: Public, Students, Faculty
Interlibrary loan available
Copying Facilities: Copying machine
Equipment:
20 5-drawer cabinets
2 vertical map cabinets
Square Footage: 125
Map Depositories: USGS (topo); GPO

**201**
Historical Association of Southern Florida
101 W. Flagler St.
Miami, FL 33130
Tel. (305) 372-7747
Hours: By appointment, M–F
Responsible Person: Smith, Rebecca A.,
Curator of Research
Special Strengths: Florida & Caribbean
(1500–present)
Employees: Full Time    Part Time
Non-Prof.    0              2
Holdings:
1400 Printed Maps
100 Manuscript Maps
1000 Aerial Photographs
25 Satellite Imagery
5 Atlases
10 Wall Maps
15 Books
10 Gazetteers
Chronological Coverage: 40% pre 1900;
60% post 1900
Preservation methods: Encapsulation
Available to: Public, Students, Faculty
Copying Facilities: Copying machine,
Photographic reproduction
Equipment:
9 5-drawer cabinets

202
Miami-Dade Public Library
Main Library
One Biscayne Blvd.
Miami, FL 33132
Tel. (305) 579-5001
Hours: 9–6, M–Sa
Responsible Person: Freier, Arlene
Special Strengths: Florida
Employees: Full Time    Part Time
 Prof.           0              1
 Non-Prof.      0              1
Holdings:
 500 Printed Maps
 75 Atlases
 4 Globes
 4 Wall Maps
 15 Books
 10 Gazetteers
 1 Serial Title
Chronological Coverage: 2% pre 1900;
 98% post 1900
Preservation methods: Lamination
Available to: Public
Circulates to: Public
Average monthly use: 35
Average annual circulation: Maps: 50
Copying Facilities: Copying machine
Equipment:
 2 5-drawer cabinets
 6 vertical map cabinets
Square Footage: 20


203
University of Miami, Library
Rosenstiel School of Marine &
 Atmospheric Science
4600 Rickenbacker Causeway
Miami, FL 33149
Tel. (305) 361-4007
Hours: 8:30–5, M–F
Responsible Person: Hale, Kay K.,
 Librarian
Special Strengths: Caribbean, Atlantic
 & Gulf Coasts (Nautical Charts),
 World
Employees: Full Time    Part Time
 Prof.           0              1
 Non-Prof.      0              2
Holdings:
 2500 Printed maps
 200 Atlases
 2 Globes
 5 Books
 2 Gazetteers
Chronological Coverage: 2% pre 1900;
 98% post 1900
Map collection is cataloged 100%
Classification: LC     Utility: OCLC
Formats: Cards, Index Lists
Available to: Public, Students, Faculty
Circulates to: Students, Faculty
Average monthly use: 40
Average annual circulation: Maps: 200
Interlibrary loan available
 Charts are not loaned—only cataloged

materials
Copying Facilities: Copying machine
Equipment:
 15 5-drawer cabinets
 3 atlas cabinets
Square Footage: 80


204
Barry University
Msgr. William Barry Library
11300 Northeast 2nd Ave.
Miami Shores, FL 33161
Tel. (305) 758-3392
Hours: 9–10, M–Th; 9–5, F; 1–9, Su
Responsible Person: Dodge, Timothy
Special Strengths: United States
 (Aeronautical & Nautical), World
 (Aeronautical)
Employees: Full Time    Part Time
 Non-Prof.      1              2
Holdings:
 750 Printed Maps
 17 Atlases
 1 Globe
 45 Wall Maps
Chronological Coverage:
 100% post 1900
Formats: Cards
Available to: Public, Students, Faculty
Copying Facilities: Copying machine
Equipment:
 8 5-drawer cabinets
 4 vertical map cabinets
Map Depositories: U. S. Coast &
 Geodetic Survey


205
Orlando Public Library
10 N. Rosalind
Orlando, FL 52801
Tel. (305) 425-4694
Special Strengths: Florida
Holdings:
 2000 Printed Maps
 100 Atlases
 1 Globe
 12 Wall Maps
 1 Gazetteer
Chronological Coverage: 1% pre 1900;
 99% post 1900
Available to: Public
Circulates to: Public
Equipment:
 1 5-drawer cabinet
 1 vertical map cabinet


206
University of Central Florida
Library–Documents
P. O. Box 25000-0666
Orlando, FL 32816
Tel. (305) 275-2593
Hours: 8–11, M–Th
Responsible Person: Lloyd, Elizabeth W.

Employees: Full Time    Part Time
 Prof.           0              2
 Non-Prof.      1              2
Holdings:
 1589 Printed Maps
 151 Atlases
 4 Globes
 16 Wall Maps
 5 Raised Relief Maps
 70 Books
 5 Gazetteers
Chronological Coverage:
 100% post 1900
Classification: Other    Utility: OCLC
Formats: COM, Online
Available to: Public, Students, Faculty
Circulates to: Students, Faculty
Copying Facilities: Copying machine
Equipment:
 2 5-drawer cabinets


207
University of West Florida
John C. Pace Library
Pensacola, FL 32504
Tel. (904) 474-2414
Hours: 8–8:30, M–Th; 8–5, F, Sa;
 1–6, Su
Responsible Person: Pedue, Robert W.
Special Strengths: West Florida, Coastal
 West Florida (Aerial phtographs),
 Southeast
Employees: Full Time    Part Time
 Prof.           0              2
 Non-Prof.      0              1
Holdings:
 10000 Printed Maps
 3000 Aerial Photographs
 200 Atlases
 2 Globes
 20 Wall Maps
 30 Books
 5 Gazetteers
 5 Serial Titles
Chronological Coverage: 15% pre 1900;
 85% post 1900
Available to: Public, Students, Faculty
Average monthly use: 75
Copying Facilities: Copying machine,
 Photographic reproduction
Equipment:
 25 5-drawer cabinets
 2 vertical map cabinets
 1 stereoscope
Square Footage: 300
Map Depositories: USGS (geol);
 NOAA


208
St. Petersburg Public Library
Reference Department
3745 9th Ave., No.
St. Petersburg, FL 33713
Tel. (813) 893-7724
Hours: 9–9, M–Th; 9–5:30, F, Sa

Responsible Person: Everett,
Caroline W., Librarian
Holdings:
720 Printed Maps
75 Atlases
1 Globe
4 Books
2 Gazetteers
Chronological Coverage:
100% post 1900
Map collection is cataloged 50%
Classification: SuDocs
Available to: Public
Circulates to: Public, Students, Faculty
Interlibrary loan available
Copying Facilities: Copying machine,
Microfiche copier
Equipment:
3 5-drawer cabinets
Vertical file cabinets

209
Florida Bureau of Geology
903 W. Tennessee St.
Tallahassee, FL 32304
Tel. (904) 488-9380
Hours: 8:30–5:30, M–F
Responsible Person: Lewis, Alison M.,
Librarian
Special Strengths: Florida (Geology)
Employees: Full Time    Part Time
Non-Prof.    0    1
Holdings:
13100 Printed Maps
1500 Aerial Photographs
5 Atlases
110 Microforms
500 Books
Chronological Coverage: 2% pre 1900;
98% post 1900
Available to: Public, Students, Faculty
Average monthly use: 40
Interlibrary loan available
Only duplicates
Copying Facilities: Copying machine
Equipment:
12 5-drawer cabinets
PAM boxes
Map Depositories: USGS (topo);
USGS (geol); Fl. Bureau of Geology

210
Florida State University
R. M. Strozier Library, Maps. Dept.
Documents-Maps-Micromaterials Dept.
Tallahassee, FL 32306
Tel. (904) 644-6061
Responsible Person: Donnell, Marianne,
Maps Librarian
Special Strengths: Florida,
Southeastern United States
Holdings:
136103 Printed Maps
2083 Atlases
15 Globes

12 Wall Maps
12 Raised Relief Maps
3 Microforms
660 Gazetteers
14 Serial Titles
Chronological Coverage: 25% pre 1900;
75% post 1900
Map collection is cataloged 100%
Classification: LC
Formats: Cards
Preservation methods: Encapsulation
Available to: Public, Students, Faculty
Circulates to: Public, Students, Faculty
Average monthly use: 500
Average annual circulation:
Maps: 13000
Interlibrary loan available
Except pre-1920 maps and reference
materials
Copying Facilities: Copying machine
Equipment:
31 5-drawer cabinets
Light table
Square Footage: 1668
Map Depositories: USGS (topo);
USGS (geol); DMA (topo); DMA
(aero); DMA (hydro); GPO; NOS;
NOAA; FL Bureau of Geol. Map series

211
Leon County Public Library
1940 Monroe St.
Tallahassee, FL 32303
Tel. (904) 487-2665
Hours: 9–9, M, Tu, F; 12–9, W, Th;
9–6, Sa
Responsible Person: DeHoff, Julia
Special Strengths: Florida
Employees: Full Time    Part Time
Non-Prof.    0    1
Holdings:
1160 Printed Maps
60 Atlases
4 Globes
2 Wall Maps
5 Gazetteers
Chronological Coverage: 1% pre 1900;
99% post 1900
Map collection is cataloged 84%
Classification: LC
Formats: Cards
Preservation methods: Chartex or
Fabric Mounting
Available to: Public
Circulates to: Public
Average annual circulation: Maps: 20
Interlibrary loan available
Copying Facilities: Copying machine
Equipment:
3 5-drawer cabinets
Square Footage: 40

212
State Library of Florida
Florida Collection

R. A. Gray Building
Tallahassee, FL 32301-8021
Tel. (904) 487-2651
Hours: 8–5, M–F
Responsible Person: McRory, Mary,
Librarian
Special Strengths: Florida (18th–early
20th century)
Employees: Full Time    Part Time
Non-Prof.    0    1
Holdings:
750 Printed Maps
1 Manuscript Map
16 Aerial Photographs
2 Atlases
3 Books
6 Gazetteers
Chronological Coverage: 50% pre 1900;
50% post 1900
Map collection is cataloged 98%
Formats: Cards
Preservation methods: Encapsulation,
Lamination, Deacidification
Available to: Public, Students, Faculty
Average monthly use: 20
Copying Facilities: Copying machine
Equipment:
4 5-drawer cabinets
Square Footage: 36

213
University of South Florida Library
Special Collections & Florida Historical
Society Library
Tampa, FL 33620
Tel. (813) 974-2731
Hours: 8–9, M–Th; 8–5, F
Responsible Person: Dobkin, J. B.,
Special Collections Librarian
Special Strengths: Florida (1521–1901)
Employees: Full Time    Part Time
Non-Prof.    3    3
Holdings:
3000 Printed Maps
100 Manuscript Maps
150 Aerial Photographs
100 Atlases
1 Globe
7 Wall Maps
1 Microform
250 Books
17 Gazetteers
Chronological Coverage: 40% pre 1900;
60% post 1900
Map collection is cataloged 80%
Formats: Cards, In-house typed lists
Preservation methods: Encapsulation
Available to: Public, Students, Faculty
Average monthly use: 400
Average annual circulation:
Maps: 1200; Books: 11000
Copying Facilities: Copying machine,
Photographic reproduction
Equipment:
9 5-drawer cabinets
1 vertical map cabinet

Atlas case, 7 sliding drawers,
37 flat shelves
Magnifying glasses

### 214
University of South Florida, Map Library
Tampa, FL 33620
Tel. (813) 974-2726
Hours: 8–10, M–F
Responsible Person: Schwartz, Julia
Special Strengths: Florida
Employees: Full Time    Part Time
Non-Prof.    0        1
Holdings:
67400 Printed Maps
70 Atlases
1 Globe
4 Wall Maps
110 Books
6 Gazetteers
Chronological Coverage:
100% post 1900
Available to: Public, Students, Faculty
Circulates to: Public, Students, Faculty
Average monthly use: 15
Average annual circulation: Maps: 210
Interlibrary loan available
Copying Facilities: Copying machine
Equipment:
48 5-drawer cabinets
Square Footage: 1200
Map Depositories: USGS (topo);
DMA (topo); DMA (aero); GPO

## Georgia
### 215
Georgia Southwestern College
Dept. of Geology, Map Library
Americus, GA 31709
Tel. (912) 928-1252
Hours: 8–5, M–F
Responsible Person: Manker, Dr. Phil
Special Strengths: Georgia, Eastern
United States
Holdings:
4300 Printed Maps
10 Atlases
3 Globes
20 Wall Maps
150 Raised Relief Maps
Chronological Coverage:
100% post 1900
Available to: Students, Faculty
Circulates to: Students, Faculty
Average monthly use: 10
Copying Facilities: Copying machine
Equipment:
1 5-drawer cabinet
35 wooden cases
Planimeter, stereo viewer
Square Footage: 700

### 216
University of Georgia Libraries

Science Library, Map Collection
Athens, GA 30602
Tel. (404) 542-4535
Hours: 8–10, M–Th; 8–6, F; 1–6, Sa;
2–10, Su
Responsible Person: Sutherland, John
Special Strengths: Georgia (1880–
present), Georgia (Aerial photography),
Southeast U. S., United States, Central
& South America
Special Collections: Sanborn Fire
Insurance Maps of Georgia (7100
Sheets)
Employees: Full Time    Part Time
Prof.        2        0
Non-Prof.    1        3
Holdings:
290000 Printed Maps
100 Manuscript Maps
190000 Aerial Photographs
250 Satellite Imagery
900 Atlases
5 Globes
50 Raised Relief Maps
10000 Microforms
400 Books
200 Gazetteers
5 Serial Titles
Chronological Coverage: 1% pre 1900;
99% post 1900
Map collection is cataloged 85%
Classification: LC    Utility: OCLC
Formats: Cards
Preservation methods: Encapsulation,
Chartex or Fabric Mounting
Available to: Public, Students, Faculty
Circulates to: Public, Students, Faculty
Average monthly use: 750
Average annual circulation:
Maps: 6000; Aerial Photographs: 1500
Interlibrary loan available
Except Sanborn Fire Insurance maps,
air photo mosaics, & selected items
Copying Facilities: Copying machine
Equipment:
241 5-drawer cabinets
26 vertical file cabinets
stereoscopes, distance measure,
3 light tables, map reading devices
Square Footage: 7000
Map Depositories: USGS (topo);
USGS (geol); DMA (topo); DMA
(aero); DMA (hydro); GPO; NOS;
NOAA; Georgia Dept. of
Transportation

### 217
University of Georgia Libraries
Special Collections
Main Library
Athens, GA 30602
Tel. (404) 542-2972
Hours: 8–6, M–F; 9–6, Sa
Responsible Person: Willingham,
Robert M., Jr.
Special Strengths: Georgia & Southeast

(1660–1920)
Employees: Full Time    Part Time
Prof.        0        1
Non-Prof.    0        2
Holdings:
2000 Printed Maps
250 Manuscript Maps
15 Wall Maps
75 Books
50 Gazetteers
Chronological Coverage: 80% pre 1900;
20% post 1900
Map collection is cataloged 100%
Formats: Cards
Available to: Public, Students, Faculty
Average monthly use: 25
Copying Facilities: Copying machine,
Microform, Photographic reproduction
Equipment:
18 5-drawer cabinets
Hollinger Boxes
Square Footage: 600

### 218
Atlanta Public Library
Humanities Department
Margaret Mitchell Square
Atlanta, GA 30303-1083
Tel. (404) 688-4636
Responsible Person: Evans, David
Holdings:
1000 Printed Maps
40 Atlases
1 Globe
5 Wall Maps
380 Books
4 Gazetteers
Chronological Coverage:
100% post 1900
Available to: Public, Students, Faculty
Copying Facilities: Copying machine
Equipment:
5 vertical map cabinets
Square Footage: 500

### 219
Emory University
USGS Map Depository, Dept. of Geology
Atlanta, GA 30322
Tel. (404) 329-6491
Hours: 9–5, M–F
Responsible Person: Cramer, Howard R.,
Chair
Special Strengths: United States
Employees: Full Time    Part Time
Non-Prof.    0        1
Holdings:
50000 Printed Maps
4 Globes
100 Wall Maps
20 Raised Relief Maps
Chronological Coverage:
100% post 1900
Preservation methods: Chartex or
Fabric Mounting

Available to: Public, Students, Faculty
Average monthly use: 30
Interlibrary loan available
Equipment:
    Wooden cabinets
Square Footage: 780
Map Depositories: USGS (topo);
    USGS (geol)


220
Georgia Dept. of Archives & History
Surveyor General Section
Archives and Records Building
Atlanta, GA 30334
Tel. (404) 656-2367
Hours: 8–4:30, M–F
Responsible Person: Hemperley,
    Marion R.
Special Strengths: Georgia
Holdings:
    10000 Printed Maps
      500 Manuscript Maps
      400 Aerial Photographs
      100 Atlases
      100 Wall Maps
       25 Raised Relief Maps
      100 Books
Chronological Coverage: 50% pre 1900;
    50% post 1900
Map collection is cataloged 50%
Formats: Cards
Preservation methods: Encapsulation,
    Lamination, Deacidification
Available to: Public, Students, Faculty
Average monthly use: 80
Copying Facilities: Copying machine,
    Photographic reproduction, Photostatic
Equipment:
    1 vertical map cabinet
   24 16-drawer map files
Square Footage: 2000
Map Depositories: USGS (topo)


221
Georgia Geologic Survey
19 Martin Luther King, Jr. Dr. S.W.
Atlanta, GA 30334
Tel. (404) 656-3214
Hours: 8–4:30, M–F
Special Strengths: Georgia (Geology,
    Topography, Flooding)
Employees: Full Time    Part Time
    Prof.          1              1
Holdings:
    1000 Printed Maps
     100 Manuscript Maps
       5 Satellite Imagery
       2 Atlases
      10 Wall Maps
       4 Serial Titles
Chronological Coverage: 1% pre 1900;
    99% post 1900
Available to: Public, Students, Faculty
Average monthly use: 30
Copying Facilities: Copying machine,

Diazo printer
Equipment:
    20 5-drawer cabinets
     1 vertical map cabinet
Square Footage: 2250
Map Depositories: USGS (topo);
    USGS (geol)


222
Georgia Institute of Technology
Price Gilbert Memorial Library
Dept. of Government Documents & Maps
225 North Avenue
Atlanta, GA 30332
Tel. (404) 894-4538
Hours: 8–Midnight, M–Th; 8–6, F;
    9–6, Sa; 2–Midnight, Su
Responsible Person: Walker, Barbara J.
Special Strengths: Georgia,
    Southeastern U. S.
Special Collections: Joan Blaeu Grooten
    Atlas–9 folio volumes, Dutch Text
Employees: Full Time    Part Time
    Non-Prof.     1              6
Holdings:
    127000 Printed Maps
         5 Aerial Photographs
       900 Atlases
         4 Globes
        10 Wall Maps
        75 Raised Relief Maps
        10 Microforms
       500 Books
Chronological Coverage: 10% pre 1900;
    90% post 1900
Map collection is cataloged 98%
Classification: LC      Utility: OCLC
Formats: COM
Available to: Public, Students, Faculty
Circulates to: Public, Students, Faculty
Average annual circulation: Maps: 643
Interlibrary loan available
    Within University Center in Georgia
    only
Copying Facilities: Copying machine,
    Microform, Photographic reproduction
Equipment:
    57 5-drawer cabinets
     2 vertical map cabinets
     4 vertical files
Square Footage: 863
Map Depositories: USGS (topo);
    USGS (geol); DMA (topo); DMA
    (aero); DMA (hydro); GPO; NOS;
    NOAA, Georgia Dept. of Transportation


223
Georgia State University
Pullen Library
100 Decatur St., S.E.
Atlanta, GA 30303
Tel. (404) 658-2185
Hours: 8–10, M–Th; 8–8, F; 9–6, Sa;
    Noon–6, Su
Responsible Person: Christian, Gayle

Special Strengths: Georgia, Southeast
Special Collections: Sanborn Maps of
    Georgia (color microfilm)
Employees: Full Time    Part Time
    Prof.          0              1
    Non-Prof.      0              1
Holdings:
    8000 Printed Maps
     450 Atlases
       1 Globe
       8 Wall Maps
     100 Gazetteers
Chronological Coverage: 1% pre 1900;
    99% post 1900
Map collection is cataloged 80%
Classification: LC      Utility: OCLC
Formats: Cards, COM
Available to: Public, Students, Faculty
Copying Facilities: Copying machine
Equipment:
    8 5-drawer cabinets
    2 vertical map cabinets
Map Depositories: USGS (topo);
    USGS (geol); GPO; GA Dept. of
    Transportation


224
Augusta College, Reese Library
2500 Walton Way-10
Augusta, GA 30910
Tel. (404) 737-1745
Hours: 7:45–10:30, M–Th; 7:45–5, F;
    9:30–6, Sa; 2–10:30, Su
Responsible Person: McLean, Elfriede
Employees: Full Time    Part Time
    Prof.          0              2
    Non-Prof.      0              3
Holdings:
    887 Printed Maps
     55 Atlases
      1 Globe
      1 Wall Map
      2 Gazetteers
Chronological Coverage: 10% pre 1900;
    90% post 1900
Available to: Public, Students, Faculty
Circulates to: Public, Students, Faculty
Average annual circulation: Maps: 49
Copying Facilities: Copying machine,
    Photographic reproduction
Equipment:
    2 5-drawer cabinets
Map Depositories: GPO


225
West Georgia College
Irvine Sullivan Ingram Library
Map Collection
Carrollton, GA 30118
Tel. (404) 834-1370
Responsible Person: Ruskell, Virginia
Special Strengths: Southeast
Employees: Full Time    Part Time
    Prof.          0              1
    Non-Prof.      0              2

Holdings:
    11488 Printed Maps
      46 Atlases
       3 Globes
       2 Books
       1 Gazetteer
Chronological Coverage:
    100% post 1900
Map collection is cataloged 100%
Classification: LC    Utility: OCLC
Formats: Cards
Available to: Public, Students, Faculty
Circulates to: Students, Faculty
Average monthly use: 25
Average annual circulation: Maps: 854
Interlibrary loan available
Copying Facilities: Microform,
    Photographic reproduction
Equipment:
    21 5-drawer cabinets
      1 vertical map cabinet
      2 atlas stands
Square Footage: 1452
Map Depositories: USGS (topo)

### 226

Columbus College
Simon Schwob Memorial Library
Documents Section
Columbus, GA 31993
Tel. (404) 568-2042
Responsible Person: Posey, Merne H.
Special Strengths: Georgia
Employees: Full Time    Part Time
    Prof.        0          1
    Non-Prof.    0          2
Holdings:
    1131 Printed Maps
      25 Satellite Imagery
Chronological Coverage:
    100% post 1900
Map collection is cataloged 50%
Formats: Cards
Preservation methods: Encapsulation,
    Edging
Available to: Public, Students, Faculty
Average monthly use: 75
Copying Facilities: Copying machine,
    Microform
Equipment:
    2 5-drawer cabinets
Map Depositories: USGS (topo);
    USGS (geol); GPO

### 227

South Georgia College
Douglas, GA 31533
Tel. (912) 384-1100
Responsible Person: Kipp, Judy
Employees: Full Time    Part Time
    Prof.        0          1
    Non-Prof.    0          1
Holdings:
    16700 Printed Maps
Chronological Coverage: 1% pre 1900;

99% post 1900
Available to: Public, Students, Faculty
Circulates to: Public, Students, Faculty
Average annual circulation: Maps: 10
Interlibrary loan available
Copying Facilities: Copying machine
Equipment:
    20 5-drawer cabinets
Square Footage: 300
Map Depositories: USGS (topo)

### 228

Ocmulgee Regional Library
505 2nd Ave., P. O. Box 606
Eastman, GA 31023
Tel. (912) 374-4711
Hours: 9–6, M–F
Responsible Person: Whigham, Stephen
Special Strengths: Georgia (1870–1970)
Employees: Full Time    Part Time
    Prof.        0          2
    Non-Prof.    0          2
Holdings:
      25 Printed Maps
    1000 Manuscript Maps
      10 Aerial Photographs
      10 Satellite Imagery
      10 Atlases
       3 Globes
       5 Wall Maps
      25 Books
Chronological Coverage: 25% pre 1900;
    75% post 1900
Available to: Public, Students, Faculty
Circulates to: Public, Students, Faculty
Average monthly use: 5
Average annual circulation:
    Maps: 25; Books: 100
Interlibrary loan available
Copying Facilities: Copying machine,
    Microform
Square Footage: 50

### 229

Mercer University
Stetson Memorial Library
Macon, GA 31207
Tel. (912) 744-2960
Hours: 8–11, M–F
Responsible Person: Gotch, Julie
Special Strengths: Georgia
Holdings:
    1120 Printed Maps
       2 Satellite Imagery
    155 Atlases
       1 Globe
       4 Wall Maps
      20 Books
      15 Gazetteers
      10 Serial Titles
Chronological Coverage: 1% pre 1900;
    99% post 1900
Map collection is cataloged 99%
Classification: LC    Utility: OCLC
Formats: Cards

Available to: Public, Students, Faculty
Circulates to: Faculty
Average monthly use: 10
Average annual circulation: Maps: 5
Copying Facilities: Copying machine
Equipment:
    3 5-drawer cabinets
Square Footage: 36
Map Depositories: GPO

### 230

Southern Technical Institute
1112 Clay St.
Marietta, GA 30060
Tel. (404) 424-7275
Hours: 8–10, M–F; 2–6, Sa, Su
Responsible Person: Pattillo,
    John W.
Special Strengths: Georgia
Holdings:
    1630 Printed Maps
Chronological Coverage:
    100% post 1900
Available to: Public, Students, Faculty
Copying Facilities: Copying machine
Equipment:
    1 5-drawer cabinet
Square Footage: 15
Map Depositories: USGS (topo)

### 231

Georgia College
Russell Library, Special Collections
Milledgeville, GA 31061
Tel. (912) 453-5573
Hours: 9–11, 2–4, M–F
Responsible Person: Davis, Nancy
Special Strengths: Georgia (Historic,
    1790–present), Georgia (General
    Highway Maps, 1900–present)
Holdings:
    1834 Printed Maps
       7 Manuscript Maps
      32 Atlases
       1 Wall Map
      10 Books
      15 Gazetteers
Chronological Coverage: 15% pre 1900;
    85% post 1900
Preservation methods: Encapsulation,
    Deacidification
Available to: Public, Students, Faculty
Average monthly use: 30
Copying Facilities: Copying machine,
    Microform, Photographic reproduction
Equipment:
    2 5-drawer cabinets
Square Footage: 20

### 232

Chatham-Effingham-Liberty Regional
    Library
2002 Bull St.
Savannah, GA 31499

Tel. (912) 234-5127
Hours: 9–9, M–Th; 9–6, F; 10:30–6, Sa; 2–6, Su
Responsible Person: Driscoll, Alice, Head, Reference Dept.
Special Strengths: Georgia (Civil War)
Special Collections: Thomas Gamble Picture Collection
Employees: Full Time   Part Time
  Prof.     5         1
  Non-Prof.  1        3
Holdings:
  1180 Printed Maps
     2 Manuscript Maps
    53 Atlases
     1 Globe
     4 Wall Maps
     9 Gazetteers
Chronological Coverage: 3% pre 1900; 97% post 1900
Map collection is cataloged 5%
Classification: Dewey
Formats: COM, Accession list
Preservation methods: Lamination
Available to: Public
Circulates to: Public
Average monthly use: 175
Average annual circulation: Maps: 35
Interlibrary loan available
Copying Facilities: Copying machine, Microform
Equipment:
  2 5-drawer cabinets
  1 5-drawer vertical file
  1 atlas case
Square Footage: 48
Map Depositories: GPO; Savannah Metro Planning Commission

### 233
Georgia Historical Society
501 Whitaker St.
Savannah, GA 31499
Tel. (912) 944-2128
Hours: 10–5, M–F
Responsible Person: Bennett, Barbara
Special Strengths: Georgia (Colonial History)
Employees: Full Time   Part Time
  Prof.     0         1
  Non-Prof.  0        1
Holdings:
  1400 Printed Maps
    10 Aerial Photographs
    25 Atlases
    30 Wall Maps
    20 Books
     5 Gazetteers
     2 Serial Titles
Chronological Coverage: 80% pre 1900; 20% post 1900
Map collection is cataloged 30%
Formats: Cards
Preservation methods: Deacidification
Available to: Public, Students, Faculty
Equipment:

3 5-drawer cabinets
Map Depositories: USGS (topo)

### 234
Georgia Southern College Library
Statesboro, GA 30460
Tel. (912) 681-5645
Hours: 8–5, M–F
Responsible Person: Harrison, Orion, Head of Reference Department
Special Strengths: Georgia
Employees: Full Time   Part Time
  Non-Prof.    0        1
Holdings:
  2500 Printed Maps
    43 Atlases
     1 Globe
    30 Wall Maps
     1 Book
     2 Gazetteers
Chronological Coverage: 11% pre 1900; 89% post 1900
Available to: Public, Students, Faculty
Circulates to: Public, Students, Faculty
Average monthly use: 3
Copying Facilities: Copying machine
Equipment:
  13 5-drawer cabinets
Square Footage: 750
Map Depositories: USGS (topo); USGS (geol); GPO; NOS; NOAA; County Highway Maps of Georgia; US Census Maps

### 235
Valdosta State College Library
Government Documents
Valdosta, GA 31698
Tel. (912) 333-7149
Responsible Person: Zahner, Jane
Special Strengths: Southeast
Holdings:
  1085 Printed Maps
    20 Satellite Imagery
    42 Atlases
     2 Globes
     5 Wall Maps
     3 Books
    10 Gazetteers
Chronological Coverage: 10% pre 1900; 90% post 1900
Available to: Public, Students, Faculty
Circulates to: Students, Faculty
Average annual circulation: Maps: 35
Interlibrary loan available
Copying Facilities: Copying machine, Photographic reproduction
Equipment:
  5 5-drawer cabinets
Square Footage: 200
Map Depositories: USGS (topo); USGS (geol); DMA (topo); GPO

## Hawaii

### 236
Bernice P. Bishop Museum Library
Geography & Map Division
P. O. Box 19000-A
Honolulu, HI 96819
Tel. (808) 847-3511
Hours: 8–4, M–F
Responsible Person: Motteler, Lee S., Geographer
Special Strengths: Hawaii & Pacific Islands, Micronesia, Melanesia (Aerial photographs, 1940's), Hawaii & Pacific (Nautical charts, late 18th–early 19th century)
Special Collections: Hawaiian place name card catalog of approx. 20,000 names, accompanied by USGS 7.5 minute topographic maps with many of names added (ms. notation)
Employees: Full Time   Part Time
  Prof.      0        1
Holdings:
  20000 Printed Maps
   500 Manuscript Maps
  70000 Aerial Photographs
    450 Atlases
      8 Globes
     30 Wall Maps
     20 Raised Relief Maps
     10 Microforms
      1 Computer Tape
   1500 Books
    200 Gazetteers
      6 Serial Titles
Chronological Coverage: 10% pre 1900; 90% post 1900
Preservation methods: Encapsulation, Deacidification
Available to: Public
Average monthly use: 25
Copying Facilities: Copying machine, Photographic reproduction
Equipment:
  56 5-drawer cabinets
  1 vertical map cabinet
  4 pigeonhole cabinets
  1 upright cabinet
  Stereoscope
Square Footage: 900
Map Depositories: USGS (topo)

### 237
Hawaii Institute of Geophysics
Library Room 252
2525 Correa Road
Honolulu, HI 96822
Tel. (808) 948-7040
Hours: 7:30–5:45, M–Th; 7:30–4:30, F
Responsible Person: Price, Patricia
Special Strengths: Hawaii, Pacific Islands/Ocean
Holdings:
  8000 Printed Maps
    50 Atlases
     1 Globe

10 Microforms
Chronological Coverage: 1% pre 1900;
   99% post 1900
Available to: Public, Students, Faculty
Circulates to: Public, Students, Faculty
Average monthly use: 15
Average annual circulation: Maps: 100
Interlibrary loan available
   Available only to local libraries
Copying Facilities: Copying machine,
   Photographic reproduction
Equipment:
   9 5-drawer cabinets
   Wall rack w/ 75 hangers
Square Footage: 4000

238
Hawaii State Archives
Iolani Palace Grounds
Honolulu, HI 96813
Tel. (808) 548-2355
Hours: 7:45–4:30, M–F
Responsible Person: Itamura, Ruth S.,
   State Archivist
Special Strengths: Hawaiian Islands
   (1778–present)
Employees: Full Time   Part Time
   Prof.      0         1
Holdings:
   2025 Printed Maps
   1000 Aerial Photograghs
     60 Atlases
      5 Gazetteers
Chronological Coverage: 10% pre 1900;
   90% post 1900
Map collection is cataloged 85%
Classification: Local
Formats: Cards
Preservation methods: Encapsulation,
   Lamination, Chartex or Fabric
   Mounting
Available to: Public
Average monthly use: 5
Copying Facilities: Copying machine,
   Photographic reproduction
Equipment:
   6 5-drawer cabinets
   1 4-drawer flat file
   48 map canisters
Square Footage: 57

239
Hawaiian Historical Society
560 Kawaiahao St.
Honolulo, HI 96813
Tel. (808) 537-6271
Hours: 10–4, M–F
Responsible Person: Dunn, Barbara E.,
   Librarian & Executive
Special Strengths: Hawaii (19th century)
Employees: Full Time   Part Time
   Prof.      0         1
   Non-Prof.  0         1
Holdings:
   1000 Printed Maps

Chronological Coverage: 80% pre 1900;
   20% post 1900
Preservation methods: Encapsulation
Available to: Public, Students, Faculty
Copying Facilities: Copying machine,
   Photographic reproduction
Equipment:
   1 5-drawer cabinet

240
University of Hawaii, Manoa
Library-Map Collection
2550 The Mall
Honolulu, HI 96822
Tel. (808) 948-8539
Hours: 8:30–4:30, M–F
Responsible Person: Suzuki, Mabel,
   Library Technician
Employees: Full Time   Part Time
   Non-Prof.  1         1
Holdings:
   105000 Printed Maps
     4600 Aerial Photographs
       12 Atlases
        1 Globe
       50 Wall Maps
       20 Raised Relief Maps
       60 Gazetteers
        3 Serial Titles
Chronological Coverage: 1% pre 1900;
   99% post 1900
Map collection is cataloged 85%
Classification: LC      Utility: OCLC
Formats: Cards, COM
Preservation methods: Encapsulation
Available to: Public, Students, Faculty
Circulates to: Public, Students, Faculty
Average monthly use: 200
Average annual circulation: Maps: 500
Copying Facilities: Copying machine,
   Microform, Photographic reproduction
Equipment:
   92 5-drawer cabinets
   10 4-drawer file cabinets
   Zoom transfer scope, map-o-graph
Square Footage: 2306
Map Depositories: USGS (topo);
   USGS (geol); DMA (topo); DMA
   (aero); DMA (hydro); GPO; NOS;
   NOAA

**Idaho**
241
Boise State University, Library
Map Department
1910 University Dr.
Boise, ID 83725
Tel. (208) 385-3958
Hours: 7:30–10, M–F; 9–5, Sa
Responsible Person: Haacke, Don,
   Map Librarian
Special Strengths: Idaho (Aerial
   photography, Geology, Land Use),
   Pacific N.W., Intermountain West

Employees: Full Time   Part Time
   Non-Prof.  1         1
Holdings:
   103000 Printed Maps
    60000 Aerial Photographs
       30 Satellite Imagery
      239 Atlases
        3 Globes
       24 Wall Maps
       94 Raised Relief Maps
        7 Serial Titles
Chronological Coverage: 3% pre 1900;
   97% post 1900
Map collection is cataloged 33%
Classification: LC
Formats: Cards
Preservation methods: Encapsulation,
   Lamination, Chartex or Fabric
   Mounting, Edging
Available to: Public, Students, Faculty
Circulates to: Public, Students, Faculty
Average monthly use: 500
Average annual circulation:
   Maps: 16000
Interlibrary loan available
Copying Facilities: Copying machine
Equipment:
   34 5-drawer cabinets
    8 vertical map cabinets
    7 file cabinets
Square Footage: 3900
Map Depositories: USGS (topo);
   USGS (geol); GPO; NOAA

242
Idaho State Historical Society
610 N. Julia Davis Dr.
Boise, ID 83702
Tel. (208) 334-3356
Hours: 8–5, M–F
Responsible Person: Jones, Larry R.
Special Strengths: Idaho & Pacific
   Northwest (1800–present)
Employees: Full Time   Part Time
   Prof.      1         1
Holdings:
   8000 Printed maps
    500 Manuscript Maps
    100 Aerial Photographs
     10 Atlases
    100 Wall Maps
     20 Raised Relief Maps
     20 Books
     10 Gazetteers
Chronological Coverage: 15% pre 1900;
   85% post 1900
Preservation methods: Encapsulation
Available to: Public
Average monthly use: 50
Copying Facilities: Copying machine,
   Microform, Photographic reproduction
Equipment:
   8 5-drawer cabinets
   1 vertical map cabinet
   6 wood cabinets
Square Footage: 500

243
Idaho Falls Public Library
457 Broadway
Idaho Falls, ID 83402
Tel. (208) 529-1462
Hours: 9–9, M–Th; 9–5:30, F, Sa
Responsible Person: Anderson, Craig,
    Head of Reference Dept.
Special Strengths: Idaho (National
    Forests, Geology)
Holdings:
    894 Printed Maps
    40 Atlases
    3 Globes
    54 Books
    5 Gazetteers
    2 Serial Titles
Chronological Coverage: 2% pre 1900;
    98% post 1900
Available to: Public, Students, Faculty
Average monthly use: 250
Interlibrary loan available
Copying Facilities: Copying machine,
    Microform
Equipment:
    2 5-drawer cabinets
    Metal filing cabinets
Square Footage: 30


244
Idaho Geological Survey
University of Idaho
332 Morrill Hall
Moscow, ID 83843
Hours: 8–5, M–F
Responsible Person: Harmon, Elizabeth
Special Strengths: Idaho (Geology)
Employees: Full Time    Part Time
    Non-Prof.    0            2
Holdings:
    2200 Printed Maps
    6 Wall Maps
    400 Books
Chronological Coverage:
    100% post 1900
Available to: Public, Students, Faculty
Average monthly use: 40
Copying Facilities: Copying machine
Equipment:
    7 5-drawer cabinets
    1 8 shelf file table
    4 10 shelf cabinets
    Light table, Stereoscope
Square Footage: 200
Map Depositories: USGS (topo);
    USGS (geol)


245
University of Idaho Library
Map Section
Moscow, ID 83843
Tel. (208) 885-6344
Hours: 8–10, M–F; 9–5, Sa; 2–10, Su
Responsible Person: Baird, Dennis W.
Special Strengths: Idaho

Special Collections: Idaho & Pacific
    Northwest pre 1900 maps
Employees: Full Time    Part Time
    Prof.        0            1
    Non-Prof.    0            1
Holdings:
    126173 Printed Maps
    15 Manuscript Maps
    10000 Aerial Photographs
    100 Satellite Imagery
    800 Atlases
    1 Globe
    3 Wall Maps
    100 Raised Relief Maps
    500 Microforms
    300 Gazetteers
Chronological Coverage: 2% pre 1900;
    98% post 1900
Map collection is cataloged 25%
Classification: LC
Formats: Cards
Preservation methods: Encapsulation
Available to: Public, Students, Faculty
Average monthly use: 400
Copying Facilities: Copying machine,
    Microform, Photographic reproduction
Equipment:
    71 5-drawer cabinets
    6 vertical map cabinets
    5 file cabinets
Map Depositories: USGS (topo);
    USGS (geol); DMA (topo); DMA
    (aero); DMA (hydro); GPO; NOS;
    NOAA; Canada (topo); Canada (geol);
    USFS Northern Region


246
Idaho State University
Eli M. Oboler Library, Map Collection
Pocatello, ID 83209
Tel. (208) 236-3212
Responsible Person: Domitz, Gary
Employees: Full Time    Part Time
    Prof.        0            1
Holdings:
    42400 Printed Maps
    100 Atlases
    12 Raised Relief Maps
    200 Books
Chronological Coverage: 5% pre 1900;
    95% post 1900
Preservation methods: Lamination
Available to: Public, Students, Faculty
Circulates to: Public, Students, Faculty
Average monthly use: 32
Interlibrary loan available
Copying Facilities: Copying machine
Equipment:
    46 5-drawer cabinets
Square Footage: 560
Map Depositories: USGS (topo);
    USGS (geol); DMA (topo);
    GPO

247
Idaho State University
Geology Dept. Map Library
Pocatello, ID 83209
Tel. (208) 236-3365
Hours: 8–5, M–F
Responsible Person: Link, Paul
Special Strengths: Idaho, Utah,
    Wyoming
Employees: Full Time    Part Time
    Non-Prof.    0            1
Holdings:
    10000 Printed Maps
    5000 Aerial Photographs
    50 Atlases
    10 Wall Maps
    30 Raised Relief Maps
Chronological Coverage:
    100% post 1900
Formats: Cards
Available to: Students, Faculty
Circulates to: Students, Faculty
Average monthly use: 50
Average annual circulation: Maps: 150;
    Aerial Photographs: 50
Equipment:
    3 5-drawer cabinets
    10 vertical map cabinets


248
Pocatello Public Library
812 E. Clark
Pocatello, ID 83201
Hours: 10–9, M–Th; 10–6, F, Sa
Responsible Person: Wright, Janet K.
Special Strengths: Idaho
Holdings:
    1100 Printed Maps
    1 Aerial Photograph
    6 Satellite Imagery
    25 Atlases
    1 Globe
    1 Wall Map
    2 Raised Relief Maps
    6 Books
    10 Gazetteers
Chronological Coverage:
    100% post 1900
Available to: Public, Students
Copying Facilities: Copying machine
Equipment:
    1 9-drawer cabinet
Square Footage: 10


249
Ricks College
David O. McKay Learning Resources
    Center
Rexburg, ID 83440
Tel. (208) 356-1420
Hours: 7–10, M–F
Responsible Person: Reeser, Gale D.
Special Strengths: Western United
    States, Pacific N.W., Intermountain
    West

Holdings:
   13000 Printed Maps
     250 Atlases
       4 Globes
       5 Wall Maps
      15 Raised Relief Maps
      30 Gazetteers
       3 Serial Titles
Chronological Coverage: 10% pre 1900;
  90% post 1900
Map collection is cataloged 40%
Classification: LC     Utility: OCLC
Formats: Cards
Available to: Public, Students, Faculty
Circulates to: Public, Students, Faculty
Average monthly use: 60
Average annual circulation: Maps: 500
Interlibrary loan available
Copying Facilities: Copying machine
Equipment:
   10 5-drawer cabinets
    8 3-drawer cabinets
Square Footage: 625
Map Depositories: USGS (topo);
  DMA (topo); GPO

## Illinois

### 250
Aurora Public Library
One E. Benton St.
Aurora, IL 60506
Tel. (312) 896-9761
Hours: 9–9, M–F; 9–6, Sa
Responsible Person: Tutor, Kathryn
Holdings:
   1000 Printed Maps
      1 Aerial Photograph
     25 Atlases
      1 Globe
      2 Wall Maps
Chronological Coverage:
  100% post 1900
Available to: Public, Students
Circulates to: Public, Students
Average monthly use: 10
Average annual circulation: Maps: 174
Interlibrary loan available
  USGS topographic maps do not
  circulate
Copying Facilities: Copying machine
Equipment: 3 pamphlet file drawers
Square Footage: 12
Map Depositories: USGS (topo);
  Illinois Topographical maps

### 251
Southern Illinois University
Map Collection (Resource Room)
Department of Geography
Carbondale, IL 62901
Tel. (618) 453-3351
Special Strengths: Illinois, Mid-West
Employees: Full Time   Part Time
  Non-Prof.    0         1
Holdings:

  15000 Printed Maps
     50 Manuscript Maps
    250 Aerial Photographs
    150 Atlases
      1 Raised Relief Map
Chronological Coverage:
  100% post 1900
Available to: Students, Faculty
Circulates to: Students, Faculty
Average monthly use: 50
Copying Facilities: Copying machine
Equipment:
  20 5-drawer cabinets
Square Footage: 150

### 252
Southern Illinois University
Map Library
Morris Library, Science Division
Carbondale, IL 62901
Tel. (618) 453-2700
Hours: 7:45–11, M–Th; 7:45–9, F;
  11–6, Sa; 1–11, Su
Responsible Person: Ray, Jean M.,
  Map Librarian
Special Strengths: Southern Illinois,
  Southern Illinois (Aerial photography),
  Illinois (land ownership), Mississippi
  Valley
Special Collections: Sang Collection–
  64 early maps of N. America, esp.
  Mississippi Valley, 1584–1840
Employees: Full Time   Part Time
Prof.         0         1
Non-Prof.    0         4
Holdings:
 158000 Printed Maps
  47000 Aerial Photographs
    100 Satellite Imagery
   1000 Atlases
      6 Globes
     70 Wall Maps
    300 Raised Relief Maps
      3 Microforms
    800 Books
    200 Gazetteers
     25 Serial Titles
Chronological Coverage: 2% pre 1900;
  98% post 1900
Map collection is cataloged 95%
Classification: LC
Formats: Cards
Preservation methods: Encapsulation
Available to: Public, Students, Faculty
Circulates to: Public, Students, Faculty
Average monthly use: 200
Average annual circulation:
  Maps: 6745
Interlibrary loan available
Copying Facilities: Copying machine
Equipment:
  121 5-drawer cabinets
   14 4-, 5-drawer cabinets
    1 11-drawer cabinet
  Stereoscopic viewers, magnifying
  glasses, compasses, map measurer

Square Footage: 2800
Map Depositories: USGS (topo);
  USGS (geol); DMA (topo); DMA
  (aero); DMA (hydro); GPO; NOS;
  NOAA; Canada (topo); Canada (geol);
  IL Dept. of Transportation; IL State
  Geological Survey

### 253
Champaign Public Library &
  Information Center
505 S. Randolph
Champaign, IL 61820
Tel. (217) 356-7243
Hours: 9–9, M–F; 9–6, Sa; 2–6, Su
Responsible Person: Pinkston, Jane
Special Strengths: Illinois, National
  Parks, United States (Road Maps)
Employees: Full Time   Part Time
Non-Prof.    0         1
Holdings:
  2165 Printed Maps
    60 Atlases
     2 Wall Maps
    85 Books
     5 Gazetteers
Chronological Coverage: 1% pre 1900;
  99% post 1900
Available to: Public
Average monthly use: 1500
Average annual circulation:
  Maps: 1000
Interlibrary loan available
  Only folding maps circulate
Copying Facilities: Copying machine
Equipment:
  2 5-drawer cabinets
  2 vertical map cabinets
Square Footage: 62
Map Depositories: USGS (topo)

### 254
Illinois State Geological Survey Library
615 E. Peabody
Champaign, IL 61820
Tel. (217) 333-5110
Hours: 8–Noon, 1–5, M–F
Responsible Person: Krick, Mary
Special Strengths: Illinois, Geology
Special Collections: Original field
  notebooks from ISGS researchers
Holdings:
  10000 Printed Maps
  10000 Manuscript Maps
   7500 Aerial Photographs
Chronological Coverage: 5% pre 1900;
  95% post 1900
Map collection is cataloged 100%
Classification: LC
Formats: Cards
Preservation methods: Edging
Available to: Public
Average annual circulation:
  Maps: 1700; Aerial Photographs: 50
Copying Facilities: Copying machine,

Photographic reproduction
Equipment:
  37 5-drawer cabinets
  8 5-drawer cabinets
  1 rolled map case
Square Footage: 875
Map Depositories: USGS (topo)

255
Eastern Illinois University
Department of Geography & Geology
Geography & Geology Map Room
322 Science Building
Charleston, IL 61920
Tel. (217) 581-5400
Hours: By appointment
Responsible Person: Meyer, D. K.,
  Geography Coordinator
Special Collections: Lantern slides
  (paintings, some of maps)
Employees: Full Time     Part Time
  Non-Prof.     0           1
Holdings:
  8000 Printed Maps
  1500 Aerial Photographs
    8 Atlases
   18 Globes
  200 Wall Maps
   60 Raised Relief Maps
Chronological Coverage: 10% pre 1900;
  90% post 1900
Available to: Public, Students, Faculty
Circulates to: Public, Students, Faculty
Average monthly use: 1000
Copying Facilities: Copying machine,
  Dyeline, Photographic reproduction
Equipment:
  65 5-drawer cabinets
  1 vertical map cabinet
  4 5-drawer wood map cases
  4 6x8 wardrobe cabinets
  8 light tables; 35 stereoviewers
Square Footage: 570

256
Eastern Illinois University
Map Collection
Booth Library
Charleston, IL 61920
Tel. (217) 581-6072
Hours: 8–10, M–Th; 8–5, F; 9–5, Sa;
  2–10, Su
Responsible Person: Chen, Robert,
  Coordinator of Documents
Special Strengths: Illinios
Holdings:
  24558 Printed Maps
Chronological Coverage:
  100% post 1900
Map collection is cataloged 85%
Classification: LC     Utility: Will be
  OCLC
Formats: Cards
Available to: Public, Students, Faculty
Interlibrary loan available

Only depository maps are loaned
Copying Facilities: Copying machine
Equipment:
  28 5-drawer cabinets
Square Footage: 600
Map Depositories: USGS (topo);
  DMA (topo); GPO

257
Balzekas Museum of Lithuanian Culture
Map Collection
4012 Archer Ave.
Chicago, IL 60632
Tel. (312) 847-2441
Hours: 1–4, M–F
Responsible Person: Bakunas, Patricia
Special Strengths: Lithuania, Baltic
  States, Eastern Europe
Special Collections: Irene (Balzekas)
  Memorial Map Collection, 16th–19th
  century maps of Lithuania and
  Eastern Europe
Employees: Full Time     Part Time
  Prof.       0             1
Holdings:
  406 Printed Maps
    1 Manuscript Map
   12 Atlases
    2 Gazetteers
Chronological Coverage: 36% pre 1900;
  64% post 1900
Map collection is cataloged 100%
Classification: LC
Formats: Cards
Preservation methods: Encapsulation
Available to: Public, Students, Faculty
Average monthly use: 10
Copying Facilities: Copying machine
Equipment:
  1 5-drawer cabinet
Square Footage: 200

258
Chicago Historical Society Library
Clark Street at North Avenue
Chicago, IL 60614
Tel. (312) 642-4600
Hours: 9:30–4:30, T–Sa
Responsible Person: Dean, Grant T.
Special Strengths: Chicago (19th–20th
  century), Illinois (19th–20th century)
Employees: Full Time     Part Time
  Prof.       0             1
  Non-Prof.   0             1
Holdings:
  9000 Printed Maps
   500 Manuscript Maps
  1000 Aerial Photographs
   325 Atlases
    54 Globes
   300 Books
    50 Gazetteers
Chronological Coverage: 65% pre 1900;
  35% post 1900
Map collection is cataloged 40%
Classification: LC

Formats: Cards
Preservation methods: Encapsulation,
  Lamination, Chartex or Fabric
  Mounting, Edging, Deacidification
Available to: Public, Students, Faculty
Average monthly use: 10
Copying Facilities: Photographic
  reproduction

259
Chicago Public Library
Government Publications Department
425 N. Michigan Ave.
Chicago, IL 60611
Tel. (312) 269-3002
Hours: 9–7, M–Th; 9–6, F; 9–5, Sa
Responsible Person: Baumruk, Robert,
  Department Head
Employees: Full Time     Part Time
  Prof.       0             1
  Non-Prof.   0             2
Holdings:
  56215 Printed Maps
     25 Atlases
    100 Gazetteers
Chronological Coverage:
  100% post 1900
Available to: Public, Students, Faculty
Average monthly use: 25
Interlibrary loan available
  In library use only
Copying Facilities: Copying machine
Equipment:
  3 5-drawer cabinets
  36 vertical map cabinets
Square Footage: 500
Map Depositories: USGS (topo);
  USGS (geol); DMA (topo); DMA
  (aero); DMA (hydro); GPO

260
Chicago Public Library
Social Sciences & History Division
425 N. Michigan Ave.
Chicago, IL 60611
Tel. (312) 269-2830
Hours: 9–7, M–Th; 9–6, F; 9–5, Sa
Responsible Person: Mosser, Donald,
  Map Librarian
Holdings:
  55 Atlases
  25 Books
   3 Gazetteers
Chronological Coverage:
  100% post 1900
Available to: Public
Copying Facilities: Copying machine
Square Footage: 10

261
Illinois Department of Conservation
Room 100
160 N. LaSalle St.
Chicago, IL 60601

Tel. (312) 793-2070
Hours: 9–5, M–F
Special Strengths: Illinois
Special Collections: Illinois Lakes-
  depth & hydrology maps
Holdings:
  500 Manuscript Maps
Chronological Coverage:
  100% post 1900
Available to: Public, Students, Other
Copying Facilities: Copying machine

### 262

Illinois Institute of Technology
Documents Department Library
IIT Center
Chicago, IL 60616
Tel. (312) 567-6846
Hours: 8:30–10, M–Th; 8:30–5, F, Sa;
  2–10, Su
Responsible Person: Lom, J. A.
Employees: Full Time    Part Time
Prof.           0               1
Non-Prof.       0               1
Holdings:
  40000 Printed Maps
  20 Atlases
  1 Globe
  75 Books
  5 Gazetteers
Chronological Coverage:
  100% post 1900
Available to: Public, Students, Faculty
Copying Facilities: Copying machine,
  Microform, Photographic reproduction
Equipment:
  9 30-drawer units
Square Footage: 1000
Map Depositories: DMA (topo); GPO

### 263

Loyola University of Chicago
E. M. Cudahy Memorial Library
Map Collection
6525 N. Sheridan Road
Chicago, IL 60626
Tel. (312) 508-2637
Responsible Person: Fry, Roy,
  Coordinator, Public Services
Employees: Full Time    Part Time
Prof.           0               1
Holdings:
  700 Printed Maps
  40 Atlases
  30 Wall Maps
  5 Raised Relief Maps
  3 Gazetteers
Chronological Coverage:
  100% post 1900
Available to: Students, Faculty
Copying Facilities: Copying machine
Equipment:
  2 5-drawer cabinets
  1 vertical map cabinet
Map Depositories: USGS (topo);

GPO, CIA

### 264

Newberry Library
Map Section
60 W. Walton St.
Chicago, IL 60610
Tel. (312) 943-9090
Hours: 9–6, T–Sa
Responsible Person: Karrow,
  Robert W., Jr.
Special Strengths: Americas, Western
  Europe
Special Collections: Novacco (16th
  century maps printed in Italy); Ayer
  (Disc. & Explo. Americas), Graff
  (Trans-Mississippi West)
Employees: Full Time    Part Time
Prof.           1               0
Non-Prof.       0               1
Holdings:
  8000 Printed Maps
  5000 Manuscript Maps
  1600 Atlases
  2 Globes
  10 Wall Maps
  50 Microforms
  1200 Books
  400 Gazetteers
  70 Serial Titles
Chronological Coverage: 95% pre 1900;
  5% post 1900
Map collection is cataloged 40%
Classification: LC
Formats: Cards, Book Catalogs
Preservation methods: Encapsulation,
  Deacidification
Available to: Public
Average monthly use: 15
Copying Facilities: Copying machine,
  Microform, Photographic reproduction
Equipment:
  37 5-drawer cabinets
  Plan Variograph
Square Footage: 2390

### 265

Northeastern Illinois University
Reference Department
5500 N. St. Louis Ave.
Chicago, IL 60625
Tel. (312) 583-4050
Hours: 8–10, M–Th; 8–6, F
Responsible Person: Mistaras,
  Evangeline, Head Reference Librarian
Special Strengths: Illinois, Indiana,
  United States
Employees: Full Time    Part Time
Prof.           0               2
Non-Prof.       0               1
Holdings:
  1983 Printed Maps
  450 Atlases
  112 Books
Chronological Coverage:

100% post 1900
Map collection is cataloged 100%
Classification: LC      Utility: OCLC
Formats: Cards
Available to: Public, Students, Faculty
Circulates to: Public, Faculty
Average monthly use: 30
Average annual circulation: Maps: 25;
  Books:260
Interlibrary loan available
  USGS topographic maps do not
  circulate
Equipment:
  12 5-drawer cabinets
  8 vertical map cabinets
Square Footage: 92
Map Depositories: USGS (topo);
  USGS (geol); DMA (topo); DMA
  (hydro)

### 266

Rand McNally & Co.
Map Library
P. O. Box 7600
Chicago, IL 60680
Tel. (312) 673-9100
Hours: 8:30–4:30, M–F
Responsible Person: Rockey, Joseph
Special Strengths: United States,
  Canada, Gazetteers
Holdings:
  90000 Printed Maps
  300 Atlases
  8 Globes
  30 Raised Relief Maps
  1500 Books
  500 Gazetteers
  50 Serial Titles
Chronological Coverage:
  100% post 1900
Map collection is cataloged 95%
Formats: Cards
Average monthly use: 250
Interlibrary loan available
Copying Facilities: Copying machine,
  Photographic reproduction
Equipment:
  38 5-drawer cabinets
  1 vertical map cabinet
  Book Shelves
Square Footage: 2000

### 267

Swedish-American Archives of Greater
  Chicago
Swedish-American Historical Society
5125 N. Spaulding Ave.
Chicago, IL 60625
Tel. (312) 583-5722
Hours: 8:30–4:30, M–F
Responsible Person: Erickson, James,
  Executive Director
Special Strengths: Sweden
Employees: Full Time    Part Time
Prof.           0               2

Holdings:
  300 Printed Maps
Chronological Coverage: 5% pre 1900;
  95% post 1900
Available to: Public
Copying Facilities: Copying machine


**268**
University of Chicago Library
Map Collection
1100 E. 57th St.
Chicago, IL 60637
Tel. (312) 962-8761
Hours: 9–5, M–F; 9–Noon, Sa
Responsible Person: Zar, Kathleen,
  Map Librarian
Special Strengths: United States,
  Canada, W. Europe, Soviet Union,
  South Asia, Far East, (China, Japan)
Special Collections: Cities and towns;
  U. S. County Atlases (19th century);
  19th century street maps for
  W. European cities
Employees: Full Time    Part Time
  Prof.         0              1
  Non-Prof.     1              2
Holdings:
  275000 Printed Maps
    9500 Aerial Photographs
    1500 Atlases
       3 Globes
       5 Wall Maps
      32 Raised Relief Maps
     500 Books
     100 Gazetteers
      10 Serial Titles
Chronological Coverage: 25% pre 1900;
  75% post 1900
Preservation methods: Encapsulation
Available to: Public, Students, Faculty
Circulates to: Faculty
Average monthly use: 150
Interlibrary loan available
  Depending upon condition, format
Copying Facilities: Copying machine,
  Microform, Photographic reproduction
Equipment:
  96 5-drawer cabinets
  vertical files
  stereoviewers, light tables
Square Footage: 5005
Map Depositories: USGS (topo);
  USGS (geol); DMA (topo); DMA
  (aero); DMA (hydro); GPO; NOS;
  Canada (geol)


**269**
University of Illinois at Chicago
The University Library–Map Section
P. O. Box 8198 (801 S. Morgan St.)
Chicago, IL 60680
Tel. (312) 996-5277
Hours: 8:30–5, M–F
Responsible Person: Selmer, Marsha L.,
  Map Librarian

Special Strengths: Chicago (19th & late
  20th century); Illinois (19th & 20th
  century); United States; North
  Central States
Special Collections: Antiquarian Map
  Collection: Illinois, 19th cent.; Great
  Lakes Area 17th & 18th cent.;
  Eastern Europe & the Russian Empire,
  16th to 19th cent.; Aerial photomaps;
  Chicago, Northeastern Illinois
Employees: Full Time    Part Time
  Prof.         1              0
  Non-Prof.     1              2
Holdings:
  121630 Printed Maps
       1 Satellite Imagery
     589 Atlases
       2 Globes
       7 Raised Relief Maps
       2 Microforms
     136 Books
       2 Serial Titles
Chronological Coverage: 1% pre 1900;
  99% post 1900
Map collection is cataloged 99%
Classification: LC
Formats: Cards
Preservation methods: Encapsulation
Available to: Public, Students, Faculty
Circulates to: Students, Faculty
Average monthly use: 169
Average annual circulation:
  Maps: 2293
Interlibrary loan available
  In library use
Copying Facilities: Copying machine
Equipment:
  79 5-drawer cabinets
  Vertical files
  Light tables
Map Depositories: USGS (topo);
  USGS (geol); DMA (topo); DMA
  (aero); DMA (hydro)


**270**
Northern Illinois University
Map Library
Davis Hall 222
DeKalb, IL 60115
Tel. (815) 753-1367
Hours: 8–9, M–W; 8–5, Th, F
Responsible Person: Ridinger, Robert B.,
  Map Librarian
Special Strengths: Northern Illinois, all
  Illinois, North America (land use),
  socio-economic, geologic, imagery),
  South East Asia
Employees: Full Time    Part Time
  Prof.         1              0
  Non-Prof.     1              8
Holdings:
  174000 Printed Maps
     655 Aerial Photographs
    1575 Atlases
      18 Globes
     350 Wall Maps

      45 Raised Relief Maps
Chronological Coverage:
  100% post 1900
Map collection is cataloged 99%
Classification: LC       Utility: OCLC
Formats: Cards, LCS (circ. only)
Available to: Public, Students, Faculty
Circulates to: Public, Students, Faculty
Average monthly use: 900
Average annual circulation:
  Maps: 6800
Interlibrary loan available
Copying Facilities: Copying machine,
  Photographic reproduction
Equipment:
  130 5-drawer cabinets
  10 11-drawer cabinets
   1 8-drawer cabinet
Square Footage: 2800
Map Depositories: USGS (topo);
  USGS (geol); DMA (topo); DMA
  (aero); DMA (hydro); GPO; NOS;
  NOAA; Canada (topo)


**271**
Southern Illinois University,
  Edwardsville
Lovejoy Library, Map Library
Box 63
Edwardsville, IL 62062
Tel. (618) 692-2422
Hours: 8–11, M–Th; 8–5, F, Sa;
  11:30–10, Su
Responsible Person: Soloman, Marvin A.
Special Strengths: St. Louis Region,
  Illinois, Missouri
Employees: Full Time    Part Time
  Prof.         0              1
  Non-Prof.     0              1
Holdings:
  118000 Printed Maps
    6145 Aerial Photographs
     800 Atlases
       4 Wall Maps
       4 Raised Relief Maps
     200 Books
     200 Gazetteers
Chronological Coverage:
  100% post 1900
Map collection is cataloged 60%
Classification: LC
Formats: Cards
Preservation methods: Mending, Pam
  Bind
Available to: Public, Students, Faculty
Circulates to: Students, Faculty
Average monthly use: 500
Average annual circulation: Maps: 60
Interlibrary loan available
  Special permission
Copying Facilities: Copying machine
Equipment:
  74 5-drawer cabinets
   6 vertical map cabinets
Square Footage: 1200
Map Depositories: USGS (topo);

USGS (geol); DMA (aero); GPO;
NOAA

272
Gail Borden Public Library
200 N. Grove Ave.
Elgin, IL 60120
Tel. (312) 742-2411
Hours: 9–9, M–Th; 9–5:30, F, Sa;
2–5, Su
Responsible Person: Schneck, Ann,
Head, Adult Services Division
Special Strengths: Illinois
Employees: Full Time    Part Time
    Prof.         0           1
Holdings:
    4197 Printed Maps
      83 Atlases
       3 Globes
       1 Wall Map
Chronological Coverage: 1% pre 1900;
    99% post 1900
Available to: Public
Average monthly use: 500
Copying Facilities: Copying machine
Equipment:
    4 5-drawer cabinets
    3 3-drawer file cabinets
Square Footage: 50
Map Depositories: USGS (topo)

273
Principia College
Department of Earth Sciences
Elsah, IL 62028
Tel. (618) 374-2131
Responsible Person: Marshall, Fred,
    Chairman, Geology Department
Holdings:
    9800 Printed Maps
      50 Aerial Photographs
      50 Satellite Imagery
       3 Atlases
       3 Globes
       4 Wall Maps
       5 Raised Relief Maps
Equipment:
    5 5-drawer cabinets
    6 file cabinets
Map Depositories: USGS (topo);
    USGS (geol)

274
Northwestern University
Grant Memorial Library of Geology
Locy Hall, Room 101
Evanston, IL 60201
Tel. (312) 492-5525
Hours: 1–5, M–F
Responsible Person: Ayers, Janet,
    Geology Librarian
Employees: Full Time    Part Time
    Prof.         0           1
    Non-Prof.     0           2

Holdings:
    5380 Printed Maps
Chronological Coverage: 5% pre 1900;
    95% post 1900
Available to: Public, Students, Faculty
Average monthly use: 35
Average annual circulation: Maps: 88
Interlibrary loan available
Copying Facilities: Copying machine
Equipment:
    1 5-drawer cabinet
    6 vertical map cabinets
Map Depositories: USGS (geol)

275
Northwestern University
University Library, Map Collection
Evanston, IL 60201
Tel. (312) 492-7603
Hours: 10–12, 1–5, M–F; plus 7–10, T
Responsible Person: Fortney, Mary,
    Map Librarian
Employees: Full Time    Part Time
    Prof.         0           1
    Non-Prof.     1           1
Holdings:
    170104 Printed Maps
      1540 Aerial Photographs
        21 Satellite Imagery
         3 Globes
        27 Raised Relief Maps
         1 Microform
      1085 Books
        18 Serial Titles
Chronological Coverage: 3% pre 1900;
    97% post 1900
Map collection is cataloged 90%
Classification: LC
Formats: Cards
Preservation methods: Encapsulation,
    Edging
Available to: Public, Students, Faculty
Average monthly use: 180
Interlibrary loan available
    Special permission
Copying Facilities: Copying machine
Equipment:
    245 5-drawer cabinets
    Vertical files
Square Footage: 3740
Map Depositories: USGS (topo);
    DMA (topo); DMA (aero); DMA
    (hydro); NOS

276
Galesburg Public Library
40 E. Simmons St.
Galesburg, IL 61401
Tel. (309) 343-6118
Hours: 9–9, M–Th; 9–5, F, Sa
Responsible Person: Willenborg, Jane M.
Special Strengths: Illinois, Galesburg
    (1838–present)
Special Collections: Illinois county
    plat maps from mid-1800s

Employees: Full Time    Part Time
    Prof.         0           1
Holdings:
    69 Printed Maps
    456 Books
Chronological Coverage: 45% pre 1900;
    55% post 1900
Classification: LC
Formats: Cards
Preservation methods: Encapsulation
Available to: Public
Average monthly use: 10
Copying Facilities: Copying machine
Equipment:
    1 5-drawer cabinet
    7 vertical map cabinets
Square Footage: 23

277
Knox College Library
P. O. Box 500x
Galesburg, IL 61402
Tel. (309) 343-0112
Hours: 8–10, M–F
Responsible Person: Wilson, Douglas L.
Special Strengths: Middle West
    (pre 1900)
Special Collections: Edward C. Caldwell
    Collection
Holdings:
    550 Printed Maps
      1 Manuscript Map
     35 Atlases
     40 Books
     25 Gazetteers
Chronological Coverage: 95% pre 1900;
    5% post 1900
Map collection is cataloged 100%
Classification: LC    Utility: OCLC
Formats: Cards
Preservation methods: Encapsulation
Available to: Students, Faculty
Copying Facilities: Copying machine
Equipment:
    2 8-drawer cabinets
Square Footage: 30

278
Olivet Nazarene College
Benner Library
Box 592
Kankakee, IL 60901
Tel. (815) 939-5354
Hours: 8–10, M, T, Th; 8–6, 8:15–10, W;
    8–5, 7–9:30, F; 9–10, Sa
Responsible Person: Christensen,
    Lynette
Special Strengths: Illinois, Midwest
Employees: Full Time    Part Time
    Prof.         0           1
    Non-Prof.     0           1
Holdings:
    7500 Printed Maps
      45 Atlases
       1 Globe

6 Wall Maps
10 Gazetteers
Chronological Coverage:
    100% post 1900
Map collection is cataloged 100%
Formats: Cards
Available to: Public, Students, Faculty
Circulates to: Public, Students, Faculty
Interlibrary loan available
Copying Facilities: Copying machine
Equipment:
    9 5-drawer cabinets
    1 4-drawer filing cabinet
Square Footage: 150
Map Depositories: USGS (topo);
    USGS (geol)


279
Western Illinois University
University Map Library
Geography Department
Macomb, IL 61455
Tel. (309) 298-1171
Hours: 8–4:30, M–F
Responsible Person: Bergen, John V.,
    Professor of Geography
Special Strengths: United States,
    Illinois, Plat Books
Employees: Full Time     Part Time
Prof.            0              1
Non-Prof.        1              4
Holdings:
    150000 Printed Maps
    12000 Aerial Photographs
    3000 Atlases
    3 Globes
    500 Wall Maps
    30 Raised Relief Maps
    3500 Books
    200 Gazetteers
    50 Serial Titles
Map collection is cataloged 10%
Classification: Local, Local Handbook
Formats: Cards
Preservation methods: Lamination,
    Chartex or Fabric Mounting
Available to: Public, Students, Faculty
Circulates to: Public, Students, Faculty
Average annual circulation:
    Maps: 500; Books: 1000; Aerial
    Photographs: 100
Interlibrary loan available
    Replaceable maps
Copying Facilities: Copying machine,
    Photographic reproduction
Equipment:
    140 5-drawer cabinets
    12 vertical files
    Magnifier, Light or Tracing Tables,
    Stereoscopes
Square Footage: 4500
Map Depositories: USGS (topo);
    USGS (geol); DMA (topo); DMA
    (aero); DMA (hydro); NOS; Illinois
    DOT

280
Monmouth College
Hewes Library
Monmouth, IL 61462
Tel. (309) 457-2031
Hours: 8:30–12, M–Th; 8:30–10, F;
    9–5, Sa; 1–Midnight, Su
Responsible Person: Burhans, Skip,
    Reference/Gov. Docs. Librarian
Employees: Full Time     Part Time
Prof.            0              1
Non-Prof.        0              2
Holdings:
    46893 Printed Maps
    25 Atlases
    10 Books
    3 Gazetteers
Chronological Coverage:
    100% post 1900
Available to: Public, Students, Faculty
Average monthly use: 12
Average annual circulation: Maps: 125
Interlibrary loan available
Copying Facilities: Copying machine
Equipment:
    96 5-drawer cabinets
    4 vertical map cabinets
Square Footage: 250
Map Depositories: USGS (topo);
    USGS (geol)


281
Illinois State University
Map Room
Milner Library
Normal, IL 61761
Tel. (309) 438-3486
Hours: 8–10, M; 8–5, T–F
Responsible Person: Easton, William W.
Special Strengths: Illinois, Alaska,
    United States, Canada, Spain, Japan,
    Australia, Antarctica, Topography,
    Geology, Oceanography
Employees: Full Time     Part Time
Prof.            1              0
Non-Prof.        0              4
Holdings:
    275000 Printed Maps
    5 Manuscript Maps
    40800 Aerial Photographs
    15 Satellite Imagery
    3000 Atlases
    5 Globes
    30 Wall Maps
    10 Raised Relief Maps
    40 Microforms
    100 Books
    25 Gazetteers
    3 Serial Titles
Chronological Coverage: 5% pre 1900;
    95% post 1900
Map collection is cataloged 40%
Classification: LC
Formats: Computer Printout, Code
    Sheets
Available to: Public, Students, Faculty

Circulates to: Public, Students, Faculty
Average monthly use: 450
Average annual circulation:
    Maps: 3250; Aerial Photographs: 200
Interlibrary loan available
Copying Facilities: Copying machine,
    Map-O-Graph
Equipment:
    130 5-drawer cabinets
    16 10-drawer cabinets
    37 file cabinets
    Stereoscopes, Map-O-Graph
Square Footage: 2700
Map Depositories: USGS (topo);
    USGS (geol); DMA (topo); DMA
    (aero); DMA (hydro); GPO; NOS;
    NOAA; Canada (topo); Australia
    (topo); New Zealand (geol)


282
Oak Park Public Library
834 Lake St.
Oak Park, IL 60301
Tel. (312) 383-8200
Hours: 9–9, M–F; 9–5, Sa
Responsible Person: Keefe, Margaret
Holdings:
    3764 Printed Maps
Chronological Coverage:
    100% post 1900
Available to: Public
Average monthly use: 39
Average annual circulation: Maps: 6
Interlibrary loan available
    To libraries in the Suburban Library
    System
Copying Facilities: Coin-op photo copier
Equipment:
    1 6-drawer cabinet
    1 3-drawer cabinet
    1 10-drawer cabinet


283
Oak Lawn Public Library
9427 S. Raymond
Oaklawn, IL 60453
Tel. (312) 422-4990
Hours: 9–9, M–Th; 9–5, F, Sa
Responsible Person: Goodfellow, Bill
Special Strengths: Oak Lawn (1927–
    present; Plat/Real Estate), North-
    eastern Illinois
Holdings:
    600 Printed Maps
    12 Manuscript Maps
    3 Aerial Photographs
    65 Atlases
    1 Globe
    1 Wall Map
    30 Books
    5 Gazetteers
Chronological Coverage:
    100% post 1900
Available to: Public
Interlibrary loan available

In library use only
Copying Facilities: Copying machine
Equipment:
1 5-drawer cabinet
2 atlas cabinets

### 284
Illinois Valley Community College
Jacobs Library, Depository Library
R.R. #1
Oglesby, IL 61348
Tel. (815) 224-2720
Hours: 7:30–9:30, M–Th; 7:30–4:30, F
Responsible Person: Moyle, Evelyn,
Documents Librarian
Employees: Full Time    Part Time
Prof.         0           1
Non-Prof.     0           1
Holdings:
500 Printed Maps
50 Atlases
10 Gazetteers
Chronological Coverage:
100% post 1900
Map collection is cataloged 10%
Classification: SuDoc
Formats: Cards, COM
Available to: Public, Students, Faculty
Circulates to: Public, Students, Faculty
Average monthly use: 10
Average annual circulation: Maps: 20;
Books: 50
Copying Facilities: Copying machine
Equipment:
2 5-drawer cabinets
2 vertical map cabinets
Square Footage: 100
Map Depositories: USGS (geol);
DMA (aero); GPO

### 285
Palatine Public Library
Reference Department
500 N. Benton St.
Palatine, IL 60067
Tel. (312) 358-5881
Hours: 9–9, M–Th; 9–6, F; 9–5, Sa;
1–5, Su
Responsible Person: Burns, Mary
Frances, Head of Reference
Special Strengths: Illinois, Lake
Michigan (nautical charts)
Holdings:
1100 Printed Maps
40 Atlases
10 Books
Chronological Coverage:
100% post 1900
Preservation methods: Lamination
Available to: Public
Circulates to: Public
Interlibrary loan available
Copying Facilities: Copying machine
Equipment:
24 drawer map case

Atlas stand

### 286
Peoria Public Library
Reference & Business, Science &
Technology Departments
107 N.E. Monroe St.
Peoria, IL 61602
Tel. (309) 672-8844
Hours: 9–9, M–Th; 9–6, F, Sa (Closed
Sa in summer)
Responsible Person: Shrier, Jean
Special Strengths: Peoria, Illinois
Special Collections: Platbooks of
Illinois counties
Employees: Full Time    Part Time
Prof.         0           5
Holdings:
65322 Printed Maps
194 Atlases
3 Globes
3 Wall Maps
20 Books
Chronological Coverage: 5% pre 1900;
95% post 1900
Preservation methods: Lamination
Available to: Public, Students, Faculty
Copying Facilities: Copying machine,
Equipment:
34 5-drawer cabinets
Map Depositories: USGS (topo); GPO

### 287
Quincy Public Library
526 Jersey
Quincy, IL 62301
Tel. (217) 223-1309
Hours: Winter 9–9, M–F; 9–6, Sa;
1–5, Su. Summer 9–9, M; 9–6 T–Sa
Responsible Person: Albsmeyer, Betty,
Head Reference Librarian
Special Strengths: Illinois, Adams
County, Quincy
Employees: Full Time    Part Time
Prof.         0           1
Holdings:
548 Printed Maps
89 Atlases
1 Globe
4 Microforms
3 Gazetteers
Chronological Coverage: 10% pre 1900;
90% post 1900
Available to: Public
Circulates to: Public
Average monthly use: 4
Average annual circulation: Maps: 6;
Books: 5
Interlibrary loan available
Only road maps
Equipment:
1 5-drawer cabinet
1 vertical map cabinet
1 5-drawer file cabinet
Square Footage: 9

### 288
Augustana College
Department of Geography
Loring Map Library
Rock Island, IL 61201
Tel. (309) 794-7303
Hours: 8–5, M–F
Responsible Person: Moline,
Dr. Norman
Special Strengths: Sweden, Southeast
Asia
Special Collections: Scandinavia,
particularly Sweden
Employees: Full Time    Part Time
Prof.         0           1
Non-Prof.     0           2
Holdings:
65000 Printed Maps
100 Manuscript Maps
5200 Aerial Photographs
20 Satellite Imagery
100 Atlases
15 Globes
260 Wall Maps
250 Raised Relief Maps
55 Microforms
10 Books
5 Gazetteers
4 Serial Titles
Chronological Coverage: 1% pre 1900;
99% post 1900
Map collection is cataloged 60%
Classification: LC
Formats: Computer Printout
Available to: Public, Students, Faculty
Circulates to: Public, Students, Faculty
Average annual circulation:
Maps: 1000
Interlibrary loan available
DMA restrictions
Copying Facilities: Copying machine
Equipment:
59 5-drawer cabinets
2 wooden cabinets
Multiple format photo interpretation
station (FMA, Los Angeles)
Square Footage: 975
Map Depositories: USGS (topo);
USGS (geol); DMA (topo); DMA
(aero); DMA (hydro)

### 289
Illinois State Historical Library
Reference Department
Old State Capitol
Springfield, IL 62706
Tel. (217) 782-4836
Hours: 8:30–5, M–F
Responsible Person: Wilhelm, Diane,
Reference Librarian
Special Strengths: Illinois (Maps,
Atlases, Gazetteers, 1730–present),
U.S. (Civil War), U. S. (Antebellum)
Special Collections: 19th century
navigational guides including river
charts & gazetteers, 19th century

travel guides including gazetteers,
stage, steam boat, canal & railroad
routes
Holdings:
 1938 Printed Maps
  200 Manuscript Maps
  630 Atlases
  170 Books
  214 Gazetteers
    5 Serial Titles
Chronological Coverage: 60% pre 1900;
 40% post 1900
Map collection is cataloged 95%
Classification: Cutter
Formats: Cards
Preservation methods: Encapsulation
Available to: Public
Average monthly use: 15
Interlibrary loan available
 Only duplicate books are loaned
Copying Facilities: Copying machine,
 Photographic reproduction
Equipment:
 7 5-drawer cabinets
 31 standard library shelves
Square Footage: 71


### 290
Illinois State Library
Centennial Building
Springfield, IL 62756
Tel. (217) 782-5430
Hours: 8–4:30, M–F
Responsible Person: Sherwood,
 Arlyn
Special Strengths: Illinois
Special Collections: Illinois county
 highway maps (1937 to date); Illinois
 county atlases & maps (late 19th to
 early 20th century); Illinois official
 highway maps (1921 to date)
Employees: Full Time    Part Time
 Prof.        0         1
 Non-Prof.    0         1
Holdings:
 95000 Printed Maps
  2650 Atlases
     8 Wall Maps
     2 Raised Relief Maps
    15 Microforms
   135 Books
   330 Gazetteers
    85 Serial Titles
Chronological Coverage: 5% pre 1900;
 95% post 1900
Map collection is cataloged 40%
Classification: LC    Utility: OCLC
Formats: Cards, Online
Preservation methods: Encapsulation,
 Lamination, Deacidification
Available to: Public, Students, Faculty
Average monthly use: 30
Average annual circulation: Maps: 135
Interlibrary loan available
 Reference books do not circulate
Copying Facilities: Copying machine

Equipment:
 94 5-drawer cabinets
Square Footage: 1680
Map Depositories: USGS (topo); GPO
 Illinois documents


### 291
Governors State University
University Library
University Park, IL 60466
Tel. (312) 534-5000
Hours: 8:30–10, M–Th; 8:30–8, F;
 8:30–5, Sa
Responsible Person: Bate, Elaine
Employees: Full Time    Part Time
 Prof.        0         1
Holdings:
 900 Printed Maps
   2 Globes
  10 Wall Maps
 300 Books
   1 Serial Title
Chronological Coverage:
 100% post 1900
Map collection is cataloged 100%
Classification: LC    Utility: OCLC
Formats: Cards, Online
Available to: Public, Students, Faculty
Circulates to: Public, Students, Faculty
Copying Facilities: Copying machine
Equipment:
 4 5-drawer cabinets
Square Footage: 200
Map Depositories: GPO


### 292
University of Illinois
Geology Library, Map Room
223 Natural History Building
1301 W. Green St.
Urbana, IL 61801
Tel. (217) 333-1266
Hours: 8–5, M–F
Responsible Person: Ward, Dederick
Special Strengths: World (Geology)
Special Collections: Small collection of
 rare maps, mostly British
Holdings:
 34722 Printed Maps
Chronological Coverage: 10% pre 1900;
 90% post 1900
Map collection is cataloged 100%
Classification: LC    Utility: OCLC
Formats: Cards
Available to: Public, Students, Faculty
Circulates to: Public, Students, Faculty
Average monthly use: 120
Interlibrary loan available
Copying Facilities: Copying machine
Equipment:
 31 5-drawer cabinets
 9 vertical map cabinets
Square Footage: 79
Map Depositories: USGS (geol);
 Illinois Geological Survey


### 293
University of Illinois
Illinois Historical Survey
1408 W. Gregory Dr.
Urbana, IL 61801
Tel. (217) 333-1777
Hours: 9–5, M–F
Responsible Person: Hoffman, John,
 Librarian
Special Collections: Karpinsk Collection
 (photostats, 1600–1800); N. American
 Northwest Territory, Early
 Cartographers
 (1700–1800)
Employees: Full Time    Part Time
 Prof.        0         1
 Non-Prof.    1         1
Holdings:
 1800 Printed Maps
   10 Manuscript Maps
   40 Atlases
  100 Microforms
   30 Books
   10 Gazetteers
Chronological Coverage: 67% pre 1900;
 33% post 1900
Map collection is cataloged 99%
Classification: In-house
Formats: Cards
Preservation methods: Encapsulation,
 Lamination, Chartex or Fabric
 Mounting, Edging, Deacidification
Available to: Public, Students, Faculty
Average monthly use: 3
Copying Facilities: Copying machine,
 Microform, Photographic reproduction


### 294
University of Illinois
Map & Geography Library
418 University Library
1408 W. Gregory Dr.
Urbana, IL 61801
Tel. (217) 333-0827
Hours: 9–5, 7–10, M–Th; 9–5, F;
 1–4, Sa; 1–5, 7–10, Su
Responsible Person: Cobb, David A.
Special Strengths: Illinois, Midwest,
 United States, Canada, Europe, Latin
 America, Africa
Special Collections: Sanborn Fire
 Insurance maps of Illinois cities
 (28,000), 19th & 20th century county
 atlases of Midwestern states, Illinois
 aerial photography, NCIC microfiche
 data, Freeman collection of Early
 Maps of America, Lybyer collection
 of maps of the Near East, Schmidt
 collection of Lewis Evans maps,
 Cavagna collection of Italian maps
Employees: Full Time    Part Time
 Prof.        2         0
 Non-Prof.    1         8
Holdings:
 325208 Printed Maps
 144314 Aerial Photographs

1866 Atlases
8 Globes
60 Wall Maps
51 Raised Relief Maps
5706 Microforms
14795 Books
922 Gazetteers
815 Serial titles
Chronological Coverage: 15% pre 1900;
85% post 1900
Map collection is cataloged 90%
Classification: LC    Utility: OCLC
Formats: Cards, Online
Preservation methods: Encapsulation,
Chartex or Fabric Mounting,
Deacidification
Available to: Public, Students, Faculty
Circulates to: Public, Students, Faculty
Average monthly use: 1500
Average annual circulation:
Maps: 20000; Books: 5000
Interlibrary loan available
Except Sanborn's; pre 1900 imprints;
USGS 15' quadrangles
Copying Facilities: Copying machine,
Microform, Photographic reproduction
Equipment:
206 5-drawer cabinets
27 vertical map cabinets
3 atlas stands
1 microfilm cabinet
Vista Fiche Reader, Stereoscope,
Light table
Square Footage: 3738
Map Depositories: USGS (topo);
DMA (topo); DMA (aero); DMA
(hydro); GPO; NOS; NOAA; Canada
(topo); IL Dept. of Transportation;
Australia Division of National
Mapping, NCIC

## Indiana

### 295
Anderson College
Charles E. Wilson Library
Anderson, IN 46012
Tel. (317) 649-9071
Hours: 8–11, M–F; 9–5, Sa; 1:30–5,
8–11, Su
Responsible Person: Cruikshank, Renee
Employees: Full Time    Part Time
Prof.         0            1
Non-Prof.     0            1
Holdings:
2000 Printed Maps
93 Atlases
2 Globes
16 Books
1 Gazetteer
Chronological Coverage: 2% pre 1900;
98% post 1900
Available to: Students, Faculty
Circulates to: Students, Faculty
Copying Facilities: Copying machine
Equipment:
1 vertical map cabinet

Square Footage: 9

### 296
Anderson Public Library
32 W. 10th St.
Anderson, IN 46016
Tel. (317) 644-0938
Hours: 9–9, M–Th; 9–5:30, F, Sa;
1–5, Su
Responsible Person: Murphy, Tim
Special Strengths: Indiana
Employees: Full Time    Part Time
Prof.         0            1
Holdings:
414 Printed Maps
44 Atlases
2 Books
6 Gazetteers
Chronological Coverage: 10% pre 1900;
90% post 1900
Available to: Public
Average monthly use: 50
Copying Facilities: Copying machine
Equipment:
2 4-drawer file cabinets
Square Footage: 15
Map Depositories: GPO

### 297
Indiana University
Geography & Map Library
Kirkwood Hall, Room 301
Bloomington, IN 47401
Tel. (812) 335-1108
Hours: 8–5, M–F; 7 p.m.–10 p.m.,
Su–Th
Responsible Person: Seldin, Daniel T.,
Head
Special Strengths: Indiana
Special Collections: Sanborn Fire
Insurance Maps of Indiana, Census
Maps of Indiana, 1970 & 1980,
Alfred C. (Kinsey) Map Collection
Employees: Full Time    Part Time
Prof.         1            0
Non-Prof.     1            3
Holdings:
210000 Printed Maps
7000 Aerial Photographs
1700 Atlases
4 Globes
500 Wall Maps
500 Raised Relief Maps
8000 Microforms
12000 Books
200 Gazetteers
200 Serial Titles
Chronological Coverage: 15% pre 1900;
85% post 1900
Preservation methods: Encapsulation,
Chartex or Fabric Mounting
Available to: Public, Students, Faculty
Circulates to: Public, Students, Faculty
Average monthly use: 20
Average annual circulation: Maps: 100;

Books: 6000
Interlibrary loan available
Except rare & fragile items
Copying Facilities: Copying machine
Equipment:
103 5-drawer cabinets
1 8-drawer map case
1 16-drawer map case
Map-O-Graph, Lacy-Lucy,
2 Light tables
Square Footage: 3511
Map Depositories: USGS (topo);
DMA (topo); DMA (aero); DMA
(hydro); GPO; NOS; Indiana
Geological Survey

### 298
Indiana University
Geology Library
Geology Building, Room 601
Bloomington, IN 47405
Tel. (812) 335-7170
Hours: 8–11, M–Th; 8–5, F; 8–Noon, Sa
Responsible Person: Heiser, Lois, Head
Special Strengths: United States,
World, (Geology, Geophysics,
Hydrology)
Employees: Full Time    Part Time
Prof.         1            0
Non-Prof.     2            1
Holdings:
270000 Printed Maps
25 Aerial Photographs
300 Atlases
1 Globe
100 Wall Maps
100 Raised Relief Maps
3500 Microforms
Chronological Coverage: 10% pre 1900;
90% post 1900
Available to: Public, Students, Faculty
Circulates to: Public, Students, Faculty
Average monthly use: 75
Interlibrary loan available
Except fragile materials
Copying Facilities: Copying machine
Equipment:
9 5-drawer cabinets
15 vertical map cabinets
30 18-drawers
12 10-drawers
Square Footage: 840
Map Depositories: USGS (topo);
USGS (geol)

### 299
Indiana University
The Lilly Library
Bloomington, IN 47405
Tel. (812) 335-2452
Hours: 9–10, M–Th; 9–5, F; 9–Noon, Sa
Responsible Person: Cagle, William,
Lilly Librarian
Special Strengths: Indiana (19th
century), London (19th century),

Atlases (16th & 17th century,
Ptolemy, Ortelius)
Holdings:
500 Printed Maps
100 Manuscript Maps
200 Atlases
20 Wall Maps
100 Books
25 Gazetteers
Chronological Coverage: 99% pre 1900;
1% post 1900
Available to: Public, Students, Faculty
Average monthly use: 5
Average annual circulation: Maps: 50;
Books: 100
Copying Facilities: Copying machine,
Microform, Photographic reproduction

#### 300
Elkhart Public Library
300 S. Second St.
Elkhart, IN 46516
Tel. (219) 295-5669
Hours: 9–9, M–Th; 9–6, F, Sa
Responsible Person: Rhodes, Jeanine,
Reference Services
Special Strengths: United States
Employees: Full Time    Part Time
Non-Prof.      0              1
Holdings:
445 Printed Maps
38 Atlases
3 Wall Maps
3 Books
2 Gazetteers
Chronological Coverage: 5% pre 1900;
95% post 1900
Map collection is cataloged 100%
Classification: Dewey
Formats: Cards
Available to: Public, Students, Faculty
Circulates to: Public, Students, Faculty
Average monthly use: 20
Average annual circulation: Maps: 53
Interlibrary loan available
Copying Facilities: Copying machine,
Microform
Equipment:
2 10-drawer cabinets
2 atlas cases
Square Footage: 23

#### 301
Allen County Public Library
Business & Technology
900 Webster, P. O. Box 2270
Fort Wayne, IN 46801
Tel. (219) 424-7241
Hours: 9–9, M–Th; 9–6, F, Sa; 1–6, Su
Responsible Person: Rose, Linda
Special Strengths: Indiana, Kentucky,
Wisconsin, Illinois, Michigan, Ohio
Employees: Full Time    Part Time
Prof.          0              2
Holdings:

8849 Printed Maps
115 Atlases
3 Globes
150 Gazetteers
Chronological Coverage: 20% pre 1900;
80% post 1900
Available to: Public
Circulates to: Public
Average annual circulation: Maps: 20
Copying Facilities: Copying machine,
Microform
Equipment:
5 5-drawer cabinets
3 vertical map cabinets
Square Footage: 150
Map Depositories: USGS (topo)

#### 302
Gary Public Library
220 W. 5th Ave.
Gary, IN 46402
Tel. (219) 886-2484
Hours: 9–8, M–Th; 9–5, F, Sa
Responsible Person: Warrick, Lyle W.
Special Strengths: Indiana & Calumet
Region (1800–present), Great Lakes
Employees: Full Time    Part Time
Prof.          0              3
Non-Prof.      0              5
Holdings:
573 Printed Maps
60 Atlases
3 Wall Maps
Chronological Coverage: 25% pre 1900;
75% post 1900
Preservation methods: Lamination,
Chartex of Fabric Mounting
Available to: Public
Average monthly use: 10
Copying Facilities: Copying machine,
Microform
Equipment:
2 10-drawer cabinets
2 4-drawer cabinets
Square Footage: 25

#### 303
DePaul University
Roy O. West Library
Box 137
Greencastle, IN 46135
Tel. (317) 658-4514
Responsible Person: Bean, Cathie
Special Strengths: United States
Employees: Full Time    Part Time
Non-Prof.      1              1
Holdings:
100000 Printed Maps
Chronological Coverage:
100% post 1900
Available to: Public, Students, Faculty
Circulates to: Public, Students, Faculty
Copying Facilities: Copying machine
Equipment:
23 5-drawer cabinets

Square Footage: 288
Map Depositories: USGS (topo)

#### 304
Hanover College
Geology Map Library
Hanover, IN 47243
Tel. (812) 866-2151
Hours: 8–5, M–F
Responsible Person: Totten,
Dr. Stanley M.
Special Strengths: United States
Employees: Full Time    Part Time
Non-Prof.      0              1
Holdings:
20000 Printed Maps
Chronological Coverage: 1% pre 1900;
99% post 1900
Available to: Public, Students, Faculty
Circulates to: Public, Students, Faculty
Average monthly use: 10
Copying Facilities: Copying machine
Equipment:
15 5-drawer cabinets
7 file cabinets
Square Footage: 600
Map Depositories: USGS (topo);
USGS (geol)

#### 305
Indiana Historical Society Library
315 W. Ohio St.
Indianapolis, IN 46202
Tel. (317) 232-1879
Hours: 8:30–5, M–F; 8:30–4, Sa (Sept.
through May)
Responsible Person: Sharp, Linda
Carlson
Special Strengths: North America (pre
1800), Old Northwest & Indiana
Territory (pre 1800), Indiana
(1801–present)
Employees: Full Time    Part Time
Prof.          0              2
Holdings:
700 Printed Maps
100 Manuscript Maps
100 Atlases
50 Wall Maps
100 Books
50 Gazetteers
2 Serial Titles
Chronological Coverage: 95% pre 1900;
5% post 1900
Map collection is cataloged 15%
Classification: LC      Utility: OCLC
Formats: Cards
Preservation methods: Encapsulation
Available to: Public
Average monthly use: 5
Copying Facilities: Copying machine,
Microform, Photographic reproduction
Equipment:
2 5-drawer cabinets
2 10-drawer cabinets

Square Footage: 30

**306**
Indiana State Library
Indiana Division & Federal Documents
Collection
140 N. Senate Ave.
Indianapolis, IN 46204
Tel. (317) 232-3686
Hours: 8:15–5, M–F
Responsible Person: Flora, Doris
Special Strengths: Indiana (19th &
20th centuries)
Holdings:
91208 Printed Maps
420 Atlases
Chronological Coverage: 25% pre 1900;
75% post 1900
Map collection is cataloged 100%
Classification: Dewey    Utility: OCLC
Formats: Cards, COM
Available to: Public
Equipment:
74 5-drawer cabinets
Map Depositories: USGS (topo);
USGS (geol); DMA (topo); DMA
(aero); DMA (hydro); GPO

**307**
Indianapolis-Marion County Public
Library
Business, Science & Technology &
Social Science Dept.
Indianapolis, IN 46206
Tel. (317) 269-1741
Responsible Person: Leggett, Mark
Holdings:
500 Atlases
Chronological Coverage: 5% pre 1900;
95% post 1900
Available to: Public
Copying Facilities: Copying machine
Equipment:
2 5-drawer cabinets
8 vertical map cabinets
Princeton files

**308**
Ball State University
Department of Library Science
Map Collection
Muncie, IN 47306
Hours: 8–5, M–F
Responsible Person: Stout, Paul W.,
Map Librarian
Special Strengths: Indiana
Employees: Full Time    Part Time
Prof.          1          0
Non-Prof.      1          3
Holdings:
102691 Printed Maps
463 Manuscript Maps
528 Aerial Photographs
18 Satellite Imagery

1325 Atlases
2 Globes
21 Raised Relief Maps
393 Microforms
360 Books
181 Gazetteers
25 Serial Titles
Chronological Coverage: 1% pre 1900;
99% post 1900
Preservation methods: Encapsulation
Available to: Public, Students, Faculty
Circulates to: Students, Faculty
Average monthly use: 460
Average annual circulation:
Maps: 1500
Interlibrary loan available
Copying Facilities: Copying machine
Equipment:
64 5-drawer cabinets
2 vertical map cabinets
6 vertical file cabinets
560 pamphlet file boxes
Light table
Square Footage: 1650
Map Depositories: USGS (topo);
USGS (geol); DMA (topo); DMA
(aero); DMA (hydro); GPO; Indiana
Geological Survey

**309**
Ball State University
Dept. of Geography Map Collection
Dept. of Geography 350
Muncie, IN 47306
Tel: (317) 285-6275
Hours: 8:30–4:30, M–F
Responsible Person: Martin, Charles
Special Strengths: Indiana, Ohio,
Michigan, Wisconsin, Illinois
Employees: Full Time    Part Time
Prof.          0          1
Non-Prof.      0          1
Holdings:
10000 Printed Maps
6 Atlases
11 Globes
189 Wall Maps
226 Raised Relief Maps
1 Gazetteer
Chronological Coverage: 2% pre 1900;
98% post 1900
Available to: Students, Faculty
Circulates to: Students, Faculty
Average monthly use: 30
Equipment:
30 5-drawer cabinets
1 4-drawer office file case
Square Footage: 850

**310**
Indiana University Southeast Library
4201 Grant Line Rd.
New Albany, IN 47150
Tel. (812) 945-2731
Hours: 8–9, M–F

Responsible Person: Kenrick, Patrick J.
Special Strengths: Indiana, Kentucky
Employees: Full Time    Part Time
Non-Prof.      1          1
Holdings:
1000 Printed Maps
2 Wall Maps
50 Books
15 Gazetteers
Chronological Coverage:
100% post 1900
Available to: Public, Students, Faculty
Circulates to: Public, Students, Faculty
Average monthly use: 5
Average annual circulation: Maps: 2
Interlibrary loan available
Copying Facilities: Copying machine
Equipment:
3 5-drawer cabinets
1 vertical map cabinet
Square Footage: 50
Map Depositories: USGS (topo);
USGS (geol)

**311**
University of Notre Dame
Memorial Library
Microtext Reading Room
Notre Dame, IN 46556
Tel. (219) 239-6450
Hours: 8–11, M–Th; 8–10, F; 9–10, Sa
Responsible Person: Paidle, Pamela J.
Employees: Full Time    Part Time
Non-Prof.      1          12
Holdings:
140000 Printed Maps
Chronological Coverage:
100% post 1900
Available to: Public, Students, Faculty
Circulates to: Public, Students, Faculty
Average monthly use: 10
Average annual circulation: Maps: 150
Copying Facilities: Copying machine
Equipment:
57 5-drawer cabinets
Square Footage: 675
Map Depositories: USGS (topo);
USGS (geol); DMA (topo); DMA
(aero); DMA (hydro)

**312**
Earlham College
Wildman Science Library
Box 72
Richmond, IN 47374
Tel. (317) 962-6561
Hours: 8–11, M–Th; 8–10, F; 10–5, Sa;
12:30–11, Su
Responsible Person: Woolpy, Sara,
Science Librarian
Special Strengths: Indiana, Ohio,
Kentucky
Employees: Full Time    Part Time
Non-Prof.      0          3
Holdings:

9500 Printed Maps
  25 Atlases
   1 Globe
   2 Wall Maps
  25 Books
   5 Gazetteers
Chronological Coverage: 1% pre 1900;
  99% post 1900
Map collection is cataloged 100%
Classification: AGS
Formats: Cards
Available to: Public, Students, Faculty
Circulates to: Public, Students, Faculty
Average monthly use: 15
Average annual circulation:
  Maps: 175; Books: 30
Interlibrary loan available
Copying Facilities: Copying machine,
  Photographic reproduction
Equipment:
  16 5-drawer cabinets
   5 file cabinets
Square Footage: 350
Map Depositories: USGS (topo);
  USGS (geol)

### 313
Morrisson-Reeves Library
80 N. Sixth St.
Richmond, IN 47374
Tel. (317) 966-8291
Hours: 9–9, M–Th (9–5:30, July–
  August); 9–5:30, F, Sa
Responsible Person: McCafferty,
  Carol, Head Reference Librarian
Special Strengths: Wayne County,
  Indiana, Richmond, Indiana, Indiana
  (19th century atlases)
Holdings:
  1700 Printed Maps
   110 Atlases
     6 Gazetteers
Chronological Coverage: 5% pre 1900;
  95% post 1900
Map collection is cataloged 95%
Classification: Dewey
Formats: Cards
Preservation methods: Encapsulation,
  Deacidification
Available to: Public, Students
Circulates to: Public, Students
Copying Facilities: Copying machine,
  Microform, GPO

### 314
Indiana State University
Dept. of Geography & Geology
Map Library
Terre Haute, IN 47809
Tel. (812) 232-6311
Hours: 1–5, M–F
Responsible Person: Ellis, Ed, Curator
Special Strengths: United States
Employees: Full Time    Part Time
Non-Prof.      0          2

Holdings:
  160000 Printed Maps
   24000 Aerial Photographs
Chronological Coverage: 5% pre 1900;
  95% post 1900
Map collection is cataloged 50%
Formats: Cards
Available to: Students, Faculty
Circulates to: Students, Faculty
Average monthly use: 150
Equipment:
  86 5-drawer cabinets
  11 vertical map cabinets
Square Footage: 1080
Map Depositories: USGS (topo);
  USGS (geol)

### 315
Valparaiso University
Moellering Memorial Library, Map Library
Valparaiso, IN 46383
Tel. (219) 464-5364
Hours: 8–5, M–F
Responsible Person: Hess, Elmer B.,
  Documents/Map Librarian
Special Strengths: Indiana
Employees: Full Time    Part Time
Non-Prof.      0          2
Holdings:
  95000 Printed Maps
    2 Atlases
    1 Globe
  195 Gazetteers
Chronological Coverage: 100% post 1900
Available to: Public, Students, Faculty
Circulates to: Students, Faculty
Average monthly use: 20
Average annual circulation: Maps: 150
Copying Facilities: Copying machine
Equipment:
  11 5-drawer cabinets
  22 13-drawer wooden cabinets
Square Footage: 740
Map Depositories: USGS (topo);
  DMA (topo); DMA (hyrdo); GPO

### 316
Purdue University Libraries
Map Collection
Stewart Center, Room 279
West Lafayette, IN 47907
Tel. (317) 494-2906
Hours: 8–5, M–F
Responsible Person: Black, Anne,
  Library Assistant
Special Strengths: United States,
  Canada
Special Collections: Portugaliae
  Monumenta Cartographica (6 v.),
  Theatrum Orbis Terrarum—facsimile
  atlases (36 v.), Atlas Catalan de 1375,
  Le Grand Atlas (of William Blaeu,
  12 v.)—facsimile ed.
Employees: Full Time    Part Time
Non-Prof.      1          1

Holdings:
  118500 Printed Maps
    20 Manuscript Maps
   400 Atlases
     1 Globe
   75 Raised Relief Maps
   25 Books
  250 Gazetteers
Chronological Coverage: 1% pre 1900;
  99% post 1900
Preservation methods: Encapsulation
Available to: Public, Students, Faculty
Circulates to: Public, Students, Faculty
Average monthly use: 85
Average annual circulation:
  Maps: 4000; Books: 50
Interlibrary loan available
Copying Facilities: Copying machine,
  Photographic reproduction
Equipment:
  54 5-drawer cabinets
  Light table
Square Footage: 1640
Map Depositories: USGS (topo);
  DMA (topo); DMA (aero); DMA
  (hydro); GPO; Canada (topo)

### 317
Purdue University
Geosciences Map Room
Geosciences Building
West Lafayette, IN 47907
Tel. (317) 494-3259
Hours: 10:30–12:30, M–F
Responsible Person: Melhorn,
  Prof. Wilton
Special Strengths: United States
Special Collections: Indiana
  Geological Survey–Various Maps
Employees: Full Time    Part Time
Prof.          0          1
Non-Prof.    0          1
Holdings:
  30000 Printed Maps
   2000 Aerial Photographs
    50 Atlases
    20 Wall Maps
    82 Raised Relief Maps
Chronological Coverage: 5% pre 1900;
  95% post 1900
Map collection is cataloged 5%
Classification: Dewey    Utility: OCLC
Formats: Cards, Online
Preservation methods: Chartex or
  Fabric Mounting
Available to: Students, Faculty
Circulates to: Students, Faculty
Average monthly use: 20
Interlibrary loan available
Copying Facilities: Copying machine
Equipment:
  29 5-drawer cabinets
   3 vertical map cabinets
   1 universal tubefile
  11 filing cabinets

Square Footage: 720
Map Depositories: USGS (geol);
   Tenn. Division of Geology Geologic
   Map Series

## Iowa

### 318
Iowa Department of Transportation
   Library
800 Lincoln Way
Ames, IA 50010
Tel. (515) 239-1200
Hours: 8–4:30, M–F
Responsible Person: Zaletel, Hank
Special Strengths: Iowa (Highways;
   railroad series, 1975–; Iowa lakes;
   counties)
Holdings:
   750 Printed Maps
   2 Atlases
Chronological Coverage:
   100% post 1900
Map collection is cataloged 50%
Classification: Swank
Formats: Cards
Preservation methods: Encapsulation
Available to: Public
Average monthly use: 1
Average annual circulation: Books: 20
Copying Facilities: Copying machine,
   Photographic reproduction

### 319
Iowa State University
Library, Map Room
Ames, IA 50011
Tel. (515) 294-3956
Hours: 8–5, 7–10, M–Th; 8–5, F;
   2–6, Su
Responsible Person: Moody, Marilyn K.
Special Strengths: Iowa
Special Collections: Iowa State Planning
   Board, W.P.A. plans, charts, & maps
Employees: Full Time    Part Time
   Prof.         0           1
   Non-Prof.     1           3
Holdings:
   76659 Printed Maps
   20332 Aerial Photographs
   1048 Atlases
   9 Globes
   5 Wall Maps
   18 Raised Relief Maps
   250 Books
   50 Gazetteers
   30 Serial Titles
Chronological Coverage:
   100% post 1900
Map collection is cataloged 20%
Classification: LC
Formats: Computer Printout
Available to: Public, Students, Faculty
Circulates to: Public, Students, Faculty
Average monthly use: 258
Average annual circulation:

Maps: 1600; Books: 300
Interlibrary loan available
Copying Facilities: Copying machine
Equipment:
   73 5-drawer cabinets
   2 5-drawer files for Leitz viewer
Square Footage: 1500
Map Depositories: USGS (topo);
   USGS (geol); DMA (topo); GPO

### 320
University of Northern Iowa
Documents & Maps Library
Cedar Falls, IA 50613
Tel. (319) 273-6327
Hours: 7:30–5, M–F; 6 p.m.–9 p.m.,
   Su–Th
Responsible Person: Wilkinson,
   Patrick J.
Special Strengths: Iowa
Employees: Full Time    Part Time
   Prof.         0           1
   Non-Prof.     0           2
Holdings:
   30000 Printed Maps
   250 Aerial Photography
   75 Satellite Imagery
   25 Atlases
   5 Globes
   3 Wall Maps
   2 Raised Relief Maps
   14 Microforms
   300 Books
   10 Gazetteers
   1 Serial Title
Chronological Coverage: 10% pre 1900;
   90% post 1900
Map collection is cataloged 50%
Classification: LC
Formats: Cards
Preservation methods: Encapsulation,
   Lamination, Edging
Available to: Public, Students, Faculty
Circulates to: Students, Faculty
Average monthly use: 125
Average annual circulation:
   Maps: 650; Aerial Photographs: 15
Interlibrary loan available
Copying Facilities: Copying machine,
   Photographic reproduction
Equipment:
   33 5-drawer cabinets
   6 file cabinets
   1 microfilm cabinet
   Light table
Square Footage: 1350
Map Depositories: USGS (topo);
   USGS (geol); GPO; State of
   Iowa Docs.

### 321
Free Public Library
200 Pearl St.
Council Bluffs, IA 51501
Tel. (712) 323-7553

Hours: 9–9, M–Th; 9–6, F; 9–5, Sa;
   1–4:30, Su
Responsible Person: Smock, Mildred
Special Strengths: Iowa & surrounding
   states
Holdings:
   5000 Printed Maps
Chronological Coverage:
   100% post 1900
Available to: Public, Students
Circulates to: Public, Students
Copying Facilities: Copying machine,
Map Depositories: USGS (topo)

### 322
Drake University
Cowles Library
Government Publications Dept.
Des Moines, IA 50311
Tel. (515) 271-2814
Hours: 8–Midnight, M–Th; 8–10, F;
   8–8, Sa; 1–Midnight, Su
Responsible Person: Leonardo, James S.
Special Strengths: Iowa
Employees: Full Time    Part Time
   Non-Prof.     1           7
Holdings:
   2328 Printed Maps
   4 Atlases
   1 Globe
   3 Wall Maps
   28 Books
   71 Gazetteers
Chronological Coverage: 2% pre 1900;
   98% post 1900
Available to: Public, Students, Faculty
Average monthly use: 5
Copying Facilities: Copying machine
Equipment:
   2 5-drawer cabinets
Square Footage: 16
Map Depositories: USGS (topo);
   GPO; NOAA

### 323
Drake University
Geography-Geology Department
Harvey Ingham Hall, Room 110
Des Moines, IA 50311
Tel. (515) 271-2967
Hours: 9–5, M–F
Responsible Person: O'Brien, Dennis C.
Special Collections: USGS Geologic
   Folios
Employees: Full Time    Part Time
   Non-Prof.     0           1
Holdings:
   1000 Printed Maps
   200 Aerial Photographs
   400 Satellite Imagery
   1 Atlas
   3 Wall Maps
   2 Books
Chronological Coverage: 5% pre 1900;
   95% post 1900

Preservation methods: Lamination,
   Chartex or Fabric Mounting
Available to: Public, Students, Faculty
Average monthly use: 30
Copying Facilities: Copying machine
Equipment:
   4 5-drawer cabinets
   3 4-drawer files
   Mirror & pocket lens stereoscopes
Square Footage: 60
Map Depositories: USGS (geol)


324
Iowa Historical Library
Historical Building
East 12th & Grand
Des Moines, IA 50319
Tel. (515) 281-5472
Hours: 8–4, M–F
Responsible Person: Janssens,
   Soudabeh, Manuscript Librarian
Special Strengths: Iowa (1830–present)
Holdings:
   1100 Printed Maps
   125 Atlases
Chronological Coverage: 50% pre 1900;
   50% post 1900
Available to: Public, Students
Copying Facilities: Copying machine


325
State Archives of Iowa
E. 7th & Court Ave.
Des Moines, IA 50319
Tel. (515) 281-3007
Hours: 8–4:30, M–F
Responsible Person: McConnell,
   Edward N.
Special Strengths: Iowa (Original
   surveys, Railroads, Rivers & Parks,
   Aerial photos)
Special Collections: 20th Century
   Sanborn Fire Insurance Maps of Iowa
   (hard copy Fische), Original and WPA
   Copy Original Plats of Iowa (Surveys
   of Iowa)
Employees: Full Time    Part Time
Non-Prof.    0            1
Holdings:
   50 Printed Maps
   3500 Manuscript Maps
   1000 Aerial Photographs
   2 Atlases
   8209 Microforms
Chronological Coverage: 65% pre 1900;
   35% post 1900
Map collection is cataloged 85%
Preservation methods: Encapsulation
Available to: Public, Students, Faculty
Average monthly use: 20
Average annual circulation: Maps: 240;
   Aerial Photographs: 10
Copying Facilities: Copying machine,
   Microform; Photographic reproduction
Equipment:

16 5-drawer cabinets
Roller shelves
Square Footage: 300


326
Carnegie-Stout Public Library
11th & Bluff Sts.
Dubuque, IA 52001
Tel. (319) 583-9197
Hours: 9–9, M–Th; 9–5, Sa; 1–5, Su
   (Sept.–May)
Responsible Person: Dunn, Elizabeth
Special Strengths: Iowa, Illinois,
   Wisconsin
Holdings:
   600 Printed Maps
Chronological Coverage:
   100% post 1900
Available to: Public, Students, Faculty
Average monthly use: 5
Copying Facilities: Copying machine,
Equipment:
   2 5-drawer cabinets
Map Depositories: USGS (topo);
   GPO


327
Loras College
Wahlert Memorial Library
Dubuque, IA 52001
Tel. (319) 588-7125
Hours: 9–5, M–F
Responsible Person: Klein, Robert
Special Strengths: Iowa, Illinois,
   Wisconsin
Employees: Full Time    Part Time
Prof.        0            1
Holdings:
   3151 Printed Maps
   125 Atlases
Chronological Coverage:
   100% post 1900
Available to: Public, Students, Faculty
Copying Facilities: Copying machine
Equipment:
   3 5-drawer cabinets
Square Footage: 75
Map Depositories: USGS (topo);
   DMA (topo


328
Grinnell College
Burling Library
P. O. Box 805
Grinnell, IA 50112-0811
Tel. (515) 236-2521
Hours: 8–1 a.m., M–Th; 8–10, F;
   8–5, Sa; 1–1 a.m., Su
Responsible Person: Walker, Theresa P.
Special Strengths: Iowa
Employees: Full Time    Part Time
Prof.        0            1
Non-Prof.    0            1
Holdings:

1800 Printed Maps
150 Atlases
10 Gazetteers
Chronological Coverage: 10% pre 1900;
   90% post 1900
Available to: Public, Students, Faculty
Copying Facilities: Copying machine,
   Microform
Equipment:
   12 5-drawer cabinets
Square Footage: 300
Map Depositories: USGS (topo)


329
Iowa Geological Survey
123 N. Capitol St.
Iowa City, IA 52242
Tel. (319) 338-1173
Hours: 8–4:30, M–F
Responsible Person: Anderson, Ray
Special Strengths: Iowa (Geology,
   Water Resources, Coal Mines)
Employees: Full Time    Part Time
Prof.        0            5
Holdings:
   1600 Printed Maps
   200 Manuscript Maps
   10000 Aerial Photographs
   300 Satellite Imagery
   50 Atlases
   10 Wall Maps
   1000 Microforms
Chronological Coverage: 40% pre 1900;
   60% post 1900
Preservation methods: Encapsulation,
   Deacidification, Microfilm
Available to: Public, Students, Faculty
Average monthly use: 7
Interlibrary loan available
Copying Facilities: Copying machine;
   Ozalid
Equipment:
   20 5-drawer cabinets
   1 vertical map cabinet
   Stereo air photo viewers,
   Map-o-Graph, Microfilm readers
Square Footage: 590
Map Depositories: USGS (topo)


330
State Historical Society of Iowa Library
402 Iowa Ave.
Iowa City, IA 52240
Tel. (319) 353-4997
Hours: 8–4:30, M–F
Responsible Person: Kraft, Nancy E.
Special Strengths: Iowa (1850–present)
Special Collections: Sanborn Fire
   Insurance Maps of Iowa Cities &
   Towns (approx. 4500 microfiche)
Employees: Full Time    Part Time
Prof.        0            1
Non-Prof.    0            1
Holdings:
   1200 Printed Maps

400 Atlases
10 Wall Maps
4500 Microforms
10 Books
10 Gazetteers
3 Serial Titles
Chronological Coverage: 65% pre 1900;
35% post 1900
Map collection is cataloged 40%
Classification: LC      Utility: OCLC
Formats: Cards
Preservation methods: Encapsulation
Available to: Public, Students, Faculty
Copying Facilities: Copying machine,
Microform, Photographic reproduction
Equipment:
4 5-drawer cabinets
2 microfiche
Square Footage: 500

#### 331
University of Iowa Libraries
Special Collections Department
Map Collection
Iowa City, IA 52242
Tel. (319) 353-4467
Hours: 8–12, 1–5, M–F
Responsible Person: Green, Richard S.,
Map Librarian
Special Strengths: Iowa
Special Collections: Sanborn Fire
Insurance Maps of Cities in Iowa
(2200 maps & 4289 microfiche)
Employees: Full Time    Part Time
Prof.           1           0
Non-Prof.       0           3
Holdings:
99301 Printed Maps
96325 Aerial Photographs
60 Satellite Imagery
1971 Atlases
3 Globes
50 Wall Maps
36 Raised Relief Maps
2453 Microforms
1015 Books
347 Gazetteers
50 Serial Titles
Chronological Coverage: 1% pre 1900;
99% post 1900
Map collection is cataloged 85%
Classification: LC
Formats: Cards
Preservation methods: Encapsulation,
Edging
Available to: Public, Students, Faculty
Circulates to: Public, Students, Faculty
Average monthly use: 500
Average annual circulation: Maps: 500;
Books: 200; Aerial Photographs: 1500
Interlibrary loan available
Except rare items
Copying Facilities: Copying machine,
Microform, Photographic reproduction
Equipment:
123 5-drawer cabinets

20 4 & 5 drawer filing cabinets
Saltzman enlarger-reducer projector
2 folding mirror stereoscopes
Square Footage: 3468
Map Depositories: USGS (topo);
DMA (topo); DMA (aero); DMA
(hydro); GPO; NOS; Canada (topo)

#### 332
University of Iowa
Geology Library
Iowa City, IA 52242
Tel. (319) 353-4225
Hours: 8–10, M–Th; 8–5, F; 1–5, Sa;
1–5, 6–10, Su
Responsible Person: Zipp, Louis S.,
Geology Librarian
Special Strengths: North America
(Geology), United States
Employees: Full Time    Part Time
Prof.           1           0
Non-Prof.       1           4
Holdings:
81758 Printed Maps
1 Globe
Chronological Coverage: 10% pre 1900;
90% post 1900
Preservation methods: Lamination
Available to: Public, Students, Faculty
Average annual circulation:
Books: 4500
Interlibrary loan available
Copying Facilities: Copying machine
Equipment:
48 5-drawer cabinets
File cabinets
Map Depositories: USGS (topo);
USGS (geol); Canada (geol)

#### 333
University of Iowa
Office of the State Archaeologist
Documents Collection
317 Eastlawn
Iowa City, IA 52217
Tel. (319) 353-5177
Hours: 8–5, M–F
Responsible Person: Vondracek, Ruth
Special Strengths: Iowa (Archaeology)
Employees: Full Time    Part Time
Prof.           0           1
Holdings:
1800 Printed Maps
3 Wall Maps
Chronological Coverage:
100% post 1900
Average monthly use: 10
Copying Facilities: Copying machine
Equipment:
1 5-drawer cabinet
1 vertical map cabinet
Square Footage: 40

#### 334
Cornell College
Department of Geology
Mt. Vernon, IA 52314
Tel. (319) 895-8811
Responsible Person: Garvin, Paul,
Chair
Special Strengths: United States
Employees: Full Time    Part Time
Prof.           0           1
Non-Prof.       0           1
Holdings:
7000 Printed Maps
600 Aerial Photographs
20 Satellite Imagery
250 Atlases
2 Globes
12 Wall Maps
Chronological Coverage: 20% pre 1900;
80% post 1900
Available to: Students, Faculty
Average monthly use: 10
Equipment: 52 5-drawer cabinets
Square Footage: 800

#### 335
Ottomwa Public Library
129 N. Court
Ottomwa, IA 52501
Tel. (515) 682-7563
Hours: 9–6, M–W; 9–9, Th; 9–6, F, Sa
Responsible Person: Geib, Jerry
Special Strengths: Iowa
Employees: Full Time    Part Time
Prof.           0           2
Non-Prof.       0           1
Holdings:
320 Printed Maps
20 Atlases
1 Globe
3 Gazetteers
Chronological Coverage: 2% pre 1900;
98% post 1900
Map collection is cataloged 3%
Classification: Dewey
Formats: Cards
Available to: Public
Average monthly use: 10
Copying Facilities: Copying machine,
Microform
Equipment:
2 5-drawer cabinets
Square Footage: 15
Map Depositories: USGS (topo)

### Kansas
#### 336
Kansas Heritage Center
1000 Second Ave.
P. O. Box 1275
Dodge City, KS 67801
Tel. (316) 227-2823
Hours: 8–5, M–F
Responsible Person: Braddock, Betty,
Director

Special Strengths: Trans-Mississippi
  West (pre-1880), Kansas
Holdings:
  216 Printed Maps
  314 Aerial Photographs
  17 Atlases
  20 Wall Maps
  3 Raised Relief Maps
  10 Books
Chronological Coverage: 35% pre 1900;
  65% post 1900
Preservation methods: Encapsulation,
  Lamination, Chartex or Fabric
  Mounting
Available to: Public, Students, Faculty
Circulates to: Public, Students, Faculty
Average monthly use: 1
Average annual circulation: Maps: 6;
  Books: 4
Copying Facilities: Copying machine
Equipment:
  1 5-drawer cabinet
  1 vertical map cabinet
Square Footage: 20

### 337

Hutchinson Public Library
901 N. Main
Hutchinson, KS 67501
Tel. (316) 663-5441
Hours: 9–9, M–F; 9–6, Sa; 1–5, Su
Responsible Person: Mitchell, Marilyn
  Dean
Special Strengths: Kansas

| Employees: | Full Time | Part Time |
|---|---|---|
| Prof. | 0 | 1 |
| Non-Prof. | 0 | 4 |

Holdings:
  1405 Printed Maps
  38 Atlases
  110 Microforms
  33 Books
  2 Gazetteers
  405 Serial Titles
Chronological Coverage:
  100% post 1900
Available to: Public, Students
Average monthly use: 20
Copying Facilities: Copying machine,
  Microform
Equipment:
  2 5-drawer cabinets
Square Footage: 12
Map Depositories: USGS (topo)

### 338

University of Kansas Libraries
Kansas Collection
Lawrence, KS 66045
Tel. (913) 864-4274
Hours: 8–5, M–F; 9–1, Sa (during Fall
  & Spring semesters)
Responsible Person: Williams, Sheryl K.,
  Curator
Special Strengths: Kansas (1850–1930)

Special Collections: Sanborn Fire
  Insurance Maps of Kansas Towns

| Employees: | Full Time | Part Time |
|---|---|---|
| Prof. | 3 | 0 |
| Non-Prof. | 3 | 7 |

Holdings:
  9332 Printed Maps
Chronological Coverage: 60% pre 1900;
  40% post 1900
Map collection is cataloged 95%
Formats: Cards
Preservation methods: Encapsulation
Available to: Public, Students, Faculty
Average monthly use: 410
Average annual circulation:
  Maps: 1500
Copying Facilities: Copying machine,
  Microform, Photographic reproduction
Equipment:
  4 5-drawer cabinets
Square Footage: 1200

### 339

University of Kansas
Kenneth Spencer Research Library
Dept. of Special Collection
Historical Maps Collection
Lawrence, KS 66045-2800
Tel. (913) 864-4334
Hours: 8–6, M–F; 9–1, Sa (during Fall
  & Spring semesters)
Responsible Person: Mason, Alexandra.
  Spencer Librarian

| Employees: | Full Time | Part Time |
|---|---|---|
| Prof. | 0 | 1 |
| Non-Prof. | 0 | 2 |

Holdings:
  1050 Printed Maps
  357 Manuscript Maps
  200 Atlases
  3 Globes
  600 Books
  6 Serial Titles
Map collection is cataloged 75%
Classification: Other    Utility: OCLC
Formats: Cards, Book Catalog
Preservation methods: Encapsulation
Available to: Public, Students, Faculty
Average monthly use: 4
Copying Facilities: Copying machine,
  Microform, Photographic reproduction
Equipment:
  12 5-drawer cabinets
Square Footage: 550

### 340

University of Kansas
Spencer Research Library
KU Map Library
Lawrence, KS 66045
Tel. (913) 864-4420
Hours: 8–5, M–F; 9–1, Sa
Responsible Person: Koepp, Donna P.,
Special Strengths: Midwest, Kansas,
  Europe, East Asia, United States

| Employees: | Full Time | Part Time |
|---|---|---|
| Prof. | 1 | 0 |
| Non-Prof. | 0 | 3 |

Holdings:
  234000 Printed Maps
  200 Aerial Photographs
  1700 Atlases
  8 Globes
  10 Wall Maps
  25 Raised Relief Maps
  50 Microforms
  600 Books
  200 Gazetteers
  48 Serial Titles
Chronological Coverage: 5% pre 1900;
  95% post 1900
Map collection is cataloged 95%
Classification: Smith (local class.)
Formats: Cards
Preservation methods: Encapulation
Available to: Public, Students, Faculty
Circulates to: Public, Students, Faculty
Average monthly use: 170
Average annual circulation:
  Maps: 1283; Books: 264
Interlibrary loan available
Copying Facilities: Copying machine
Equipment:
  148 5-drawer cabinets
  Reducer/enlarger tracing machine
Square Footage: 3200
Map Depositories: USGS (topo);
  USGS (geol); DMA (topo)

### 341

Kansas State University Library
Map & Atlas Unit
Manhattan, KS 66506
Tel. (913) 532-6515
Hours: 8–5, M–F
Responsible Person: Johnson, John L.
Special Strengths: Great Plains

| Employees: | Full Time | Part Time |
|---|---|---|
| Prof. | 0 | 1 |
| Non-Prof. | 0 | 1 |

Holdings:
  80000 Printed Maps
  300 Aerial Photographs
  30 Satellite Imagery
  500 Atlases
  1 Globe
  3 Wall Maps
  300 Microforms
  40 Books
  2 Serial Titles
Chronological Coverage: 5% pre 1900;
  95% post 1900
Map collection is cataloged 50%
Classification: Modified LC
Formats: Cards
Available to: Public, Students, Faculty
Circulates to: Public, Students, Faculty
Average monthly use: 150
Average annual circulation:
  Maps: 2500
Interlibrary loan available

Landsat, Aerial photos & Atlases
are not available
Copying Facilities: Copying machine,
Microform
Equipment:
62 5-drawer cabinets
9 4-drawer cabinets
5 16 shelf units
Atlas cases
Square Footage: 1300
Map Depositories: USGS (topo);
USGS (geol); GPO

### 342

Kansas State University
Geography Department
Manhattan, KS 66506
Tel. (913) 532-6727
Responsible Person: Siddell, William R.
Holdings:
4000 Printed Maps
10000 Aerial Photographs
100 Satellite Imagery
12 Atlases
25 Globes
200 Wall Maps
6 Raised Relief Maps
1 Computer Tape
Chronological Coverage:
100% post 1900
Available to: Public, Students, Faculty
Circulates to: Public, Students, Faculty
Average annual circulation: Maps: 20
Equipment:
6 5-drawer cabinets
Stereoscopes
Square Footage: 300

### 343

Pittsburg State University
Leonard H. Axe Library
Pittsburg, KS 66762-9987
Tel. (316) 231-7000
Hours: 8–5, M–F
Responsible Person: Walter, Robert A.,
Government Documents
Employees: Full Time    Part Time
Prof.         1              1
Non-Prof.     0              3
Holdings:
1000 Printed Maps
30 Atlases
50 Microforms
100 Books
50 Gazetteers
Chronological Coverage:
100% post 1900
Available to: Public, Students, Faculty
Circulates to: Public, Students, Faculty
Average annual circulation: Maps: 100
Interlibrary loan available
Copying Facilities: Copying machine,
Microform
Equipment:
6 5-drawer cabinets

Square Footage: 50

### 344

Kansas Fish & Game Map File
RR #2, Box 54A
Pratt, KS 67124
Tel. (316) 672-5911
Hours: 8–5, M–F
Responsible Person: Eckhoff, Mark
Special Strengths: Kansas (Reservoirs,
State Lakes and Wildlife Areas)
Employees: Full Time    Part Time
Prof.         0              1
Holdings:
4000 Printed Maps
200 Aerial Photographs
Chronological Coverage:
100% post 1900
Map collection is cataloged 100%
Classification: Local
Preservation methods: Edging
Available to: Other
Average monthly use: 10
Copying Facilities: Copying machine

### 345

Kansas Dept. of Transportation
Bureau of Transportation Planning
State Office Building
Topeka, KS 66612
Tel. (913) 296-3841
Hours: 8–5, M–F
Responsible Person: Campbell, J. R.
Special Strengths: Kansas (Highways)
Holdings:
150000 Aerial Photographs
Chronological Coverage:
100% post 1900
Available to: Public
Copying Facilities: Copying machine,
Photographic reproduction

### 346

Kansas State Historical Society
Manuscripts, Maps & Photographs
Map Division
120 W. 10th, 1st Floor
Topeka, KS 66612
Tel. (913) 296-4793
Hours: 9–5, M–F
Responsible Person: Knecht, Bob,
Assistant Curator
Special Strengths: United States
(1750–present), Kansas (1800–present),
Great Plains (1800–present), The
West (1830–present)
Special Collections: Ado Hunnius
Collection of military and other maps,
1868–1898
Employees: Full Time    Part Time
Prof.         0              1
Holdings:
12996 Printed Maps
Chronological Coverage: 60% pre 1900;

40% post 1900
Classification: Local
Formats: Cards
Preservation methods: Encapsulation,
Deacidifcation, Japanese paper
Available to: Public, Students, Faculty
Average monthly use: 20
Copying Facilities: Copying machine,
Microform, Photographic reproduction
Equipment:
22 5-drawer cabinets
Square Footage: 284
Map Depositories: USGS (topo);
Kansas State Agencies

### 347

Kansas State Library
3rd Floor, State House
Topeka, KS 66612
Tel. (913) 296-3296
Hours: 8–5, M–F
Responsible Person: Galbraith, Marc
Holdings:
1700 Printed Maps
Chronological Coverage:
100% post 1900
Available to: Public, Students
Circulates to: Public
Average monthly use: 12
Copying Facilities: Copying machine,
4 file cabinets
Map Depositories: USGS (topo)

### 348

Wichita Public Library
Map Reference Section
223 S. Main St.
Wichita, KS 67202
Tel. (316) 262-0611
Hours: 8:30–9, M–Th; 8:30–5:30, F, Sa
Responsible Person: Vos, Larry A.
Special Strengths: Kansas
Employees: Full Time    Part Time
Prof.         0              1
Holdings:
21000 Printed Maps
120 Atlases
3 Globes
2 Raised Relief Maps
14 Books
85 Gazetteers
Chronological Coverage:
100% post 1900
Classification: LC    Utility: OCLC
Formats: Cards
Available to: Public, Students, Faculty
Circulates to: Public, Students, Faculty
Average monthly use: 100
Average annual circulation: Maps: 300
Copying Facilities: Copying machine
Equipment:
9 5-drawer cabinets
2 vertical map cabinets
Square Footage: 450
Map Depositories: USGS (topo)

349
Wichita State University
Ablah Library
Department of Special Collections
Wichita, KS 67208
Tel. (316) 689-3590
Hours: 8–5, M–F
Responsible Person: Kelly, Michael,
Curator
Special Strengths: Kansas/Great
Plains (1850–1920), Kansas (1870–
1900, Plat books)
Employees: Full Time    Part Time
Prof.           1              0
Non-Prof.    0              2
Holdings:
375 Printed Maps
135 Atlases
25 Books
Chronological Coverage: 95% pre 1900;
5% post 1900
Preservation methods: Encapsulation,
Deacidification
Available to: Public, Students, Faculty
Average monthly use: 5
Copying Facilities: Copying machine,
Microform, Photographic reproduction
Equipment:
4 5-drawer cabinets
Square Footage: 40

**Kentucky**

350
Berea College Department of Geology
Map Library
College Box 1105
Berea, KY 40404
Tel. (606) 986-9341
Hours: 8–5, M–F
Responsible Person: Lipchinsky, Z. L.
Special Strengths: Appalachia
Employees: Full Time    Part Time
Prof.           0              1
Holdings:
5000 Printed Maps
500 Aerial Photographs
2 Atlases
10 Globes
10 Wall Maps
20 Raised Relief Maps
Chronological Coverage: 10% pre 1900;
90% post 1900
Map collection is cataloged 100%
Classification: Local
Formats: Index sheets
Available to: Public, Students, Faculty
Circulates to: Public, Students, Faculty
Average monthly use: 5
Average annual circulation: Maps: 20
Interlibrary loan available
Copying Facilities: Copying machine
Equipment:
8 5-drawer cabinets
2 vertical map cabinets
1 flat desk type
Map Depositories: USGS (topo);

USGS (geol)

351
Western Kentucky University
Dept. of Special Collections
Kentucky Library
Bowling Green, KY 42101
Tel. (502) 745-2592
Hours: 8–4:30, M–F; 9–4:30, Sa
Responsible Person: Randy, Riley
Special Strengths: Kentucky (1780–
present), Mammoth Cave & Ohio
River Valley (Speleology)
Employees: Full Time    Part Time
Prof.           0              5
Non-Prof.    0              3
Holdings:
1000 Printed Maps
50 Manuscript Maps
7 Aerial Photographs
45 Atlases
2 Globes
2 Wall Maps
1 Raised Relief Map
25 Books
2 Gazetteers
1 Serial Title
Chronological Coverage: 35% pre 1900;
65% post 1900
Map collection is cataloged 85%
Formats: Cards
Preservation methods: Encapsulation,
Lamination, Chartex or Fabric
Mounting
Available to: Public, Students, Faculty
Average monthly use: 20
Interlibrary loan available
Photocopies only
Equipment:
5 5-drawer cabinets
Square Footage: 50

352
Western Kentucky University
Geography & Geology Dept.
Bowling Green, KY 42101
Tel. (502) 745-4555
Hours: 8–4:30, M–F
Responsible Person: Ahsan, Dr. S. R.
Special Strengths: Kentucky,
Tennessee
Special Collections: Students Manuscript
Maps of Kentucky
Employees: Full Time    Part Time
Prof.           0              2
Non-Prof.    0              2
Holdings:
4000 Printed Maps
1000 Manuscript Maps
4000 Aerial Photographs
400 Satellite Imagery
200 Atlases
50 Globes
600 Wall Maps

100 Raised Relief Maps
300 Microforms
100 Computer Tapes
200 Books
Chronological Coverage:
100% post 1900
Available to: Students, Faculty
Circulates to: Students, Faculty
Average monthly use: 100
Equipment:
40 5-drawer cabinets
60 vertical map cabinets
20 Aerial & Space Photo cabinets
Map-O-Graph, zoom stereoscope,
stereoscopes, map measurers
Square Footage: 1000

353
Western Kentucky University
Helm-Cravens Library
General Reference Room
Bowling Green, KY 42101
Tel. (502) 743-3951
Hours: 8—11, M–Th; 8–4:30, F;
9–4:30 Sa; 2–11, Su
Responsible Person: Leavy, Dr. Marvin,
Supervisor
Special Strengths: Kentucky
Employees: Full Time    Part Time
Prof.           3              0
Non-Prof.    1              0
Holdings:
900 Printed Maps
426 Atlases
4 Globes
4 Raised Relief Maps
100 Books
5 Gazetteers
20 Serial Titles
Chronological Coverage: 28% pre 1900;
72% post 1900
Available to: Public, Students, Faculty
Circulates to: Public, Students, Faculty
Interlibrary loan available
Reference materials excluded
Copying Facilities: Copying machine,
Microform
Equipment:
15 5-drawer cabinets
Square Footage: 200

354
Kentucky Dept. of Transportation
Division of Design Phototechnic Lab.
Kentucky State Office Building
Room 703
Frankfort, KY 40622
Tel. (402) 564-4900
Hours: 8–4:30, M–F
Responsible Person: Sames, Jim
Special Strengths: Kentucky
Employees: Full Time    Part Time
Prof.           4              0
Holdings:
80000 Printed Maps

200000 Aerial Photographs
100 Satellite Imagery
Chronological Coverage:
100% post 1900
Available to: Public
Average monthly use: 300
Copying Facilities: Copying machine,
Photographic reproduction
Equipment:
40 vertical map cabinets
Square Footage: 3000

355
Kentucky Historical Society Library
P. O. Box H
Frankfort, KY 40602
Tel. (502) 564-3016
Hours: 8–4:30, M–F
Responsible Person: Winter, Mary E.
Special Strengths: Kentucky and
individual Kentucky Counties (1784–
present), Southeast United States
(1750–present)
Employees: Full Time     Part Time
Prof.            1                0
Holdings:
900 Printed Maps
24 Manuscript Maps
6 Aerial Photographs
1 Satellite Imagery
30 Atlases
10 Wall Maps
Chronological Coverage: 75% pre 1900;
25% post 1900
Map collection is cataloged 60%
Classification: Chronological
Formats: Cards
Preservation methods: Encapsulation,
Deacidification
Available to: Public, Students, Faculty
Average monthly use: 30
Copying Facilities: Copying machine,
Microform, Photographic reproduction
Equipment:
22 5-drawer cabinets
Square Footage: 272

356
University of Kentucky Libraries
Map Collection
Lexington, KY 40506-0039
Tel. (606) 257-1853
Hours: 10–4:30, M–F
Responsible Person: Curtis, Gwen
Special Strengths: Kentucky
(1870–present)
Special Collections: Sanborn Insurance
Maps of Kentucky Cities
Employees: Full Time     Part Time
Non-Prof.      1                3
Holdings:
44600 Printed Maps
25075 Aerial Photographs
10 Satellite Imagery
780 Atlases

1 Globe
2 Wall Maps
21 Raised Relief Maps
8 Microforms
215 Books
250 Gazetteers
5 Serial Titles
Chronological Coverage: 20% pre 1900;
80% post 1900
Map collection is cataloged 10%
Classification: LC        Utility: OCLC
Formats: Cards
Available to: Public, Students, Faculty
Circulates to: Public, Students, Faculty
Average monthly use: 158
Average annual circulation: Maps: 410;
Books: 115; Aerial Photographs: 10
Interlibrary loan available
Copying Facilities: Copying machine,
Microform
Equipment:
41 5-drawer cabinets
8 filing cabinets
3 light tables
1 stereoscopic viewer
Map Depositories: DMA (topo); DMA
(aero); DMA (hydro); GPO; NOS;
KY Geological Survey

357
University of Kentucky
Pirtle Geology Library
100 Bowman Hall
Lexington, KY 40506
Tel. (606) 257-5730
Hours: 8–10, M–Th; 1–5, Sa, Su
Responsible Person: Spencer, Mary
Special Strengths: Kentucky (Geology)
Employees: Full Time     Part Time
Prof.            0                2
Non-Prof.      0                3
Holdings:
99815 Printed Maps
12 Satellite Imagery
36 Atlases
1 Globe
1 Wall Map
3 Gazetteers
30 Serial Titles
Chronological Coverage: 5% pre 1900;
95% post 1900
Map collection is cataloged 50%
Classification: In-house system
Formats: Cards
Preservation methods: Encapsulation,
Chartex or Fabric Mounting
Available to: Public, Students, Faculty
Average monthly use: 200
Average annual circulation:
Books: 23736
Copying Facilities: Copying machine,
Photographic reproduction
Equipment:
61 5-drawer cabinets
10 5-drawer vertical files
Square Footage: 1408

Map Depositories: USGS (topo);
USGS (geol); Canada (topo);
Canada (geol)

358
Filson Club, Inc.
118 W. Breckinridge St.
Louisville, KY 40203
Tel. (502) 582-3727
Hours: 9–5, M–F; 9–Noon, Sa
Responsible Person: Rush, Dorothy C.,
Librarian
Special Strengths: Kentucky
Special Collections: Filson Maps
of Kentucky
Employees: Full Time     Part Time
Prof.            2                0
Non-Prof.      2                1
Holdings:
1500 Printed Maps
50 Manuscript Maps
100 Aerial Photographs
100 Atlases
50 Gazetteers
Chronological Coverage: 60% pre 1900;
40% post 1900
Map collection is cataloged 80%
Classification: Dewey
Formats: Cards
Preservation methods: Encapsulation,
Chartex or Fabic Mounting
Available to: Public
Average monthly use: 100
Copying Facilities: Copying machine,
Photographic reproduction
Equipment:
5 5-drawer cabinets

359
U.S. Army Corps of Engineers
Louisville, Survey Branch
Louisville, KY 40201
Tel. (502) 582-5661
Hours: 8–4, M–F
Responsible Person: McClellan, Boyd K.
Special Strengths: Indiana, Ohio,
Illinois, Kentucky, (1895–present)
Special Collections: Ohio River,
Topographic Maps, Corps of
Engineers, 1911–1914
Employees: Full Time     Part Time
Prof.            4                1
Non-Prof.      15               1
Holdings:
85 Printed Maps
4000 Manuscript Maps
20000 Aerial Photographs
1 Globe
1750 Microforms
200 Books
Chronological Coverage: 5% pre 1900;
95% post 1900
Available to: Public
Average monthly use:15

Copying Facilities: Copying machine,
  Microform, Photographic reproduction,
  Blueprint
Equipment:
  29 5-drawer cabinets
  6 vertical map cabinets
  30 roller tray shelves
  Map-A-Graph, Stereo plotters with
    digitizing capability, Aerial film
Square Footage: 500

### 360

University of Louisville
Ekstrom Library, Reference Dept.
Louisville, KY 40292
Tel. (502) 588-6747
Hours: 8–11, M–Th; 8–6, F; 9–6, Sa;
  1–11, Su
Responsible Person: Ten Hoor, Joan,
  Reference Librarian
Special Strengths: Kentucky, Indiana
Employees: Full Time     Part Time
  Non-Prof.      0            1
Holdings:
  10860 Printed Maps
Chronological Coverage:
  100% post 1900
Available to: Public, Students, Faculty
Circulates to: Public, Students, Faculty
Interlibrary loan available
Copying Facilities: Copying machine
Equipment:
  11 5-drawer cabinets
  1 vertical map cabinet
  2 10-drawer units
  3-drawer filing cabinet
Map Depositories: USGS (topo);
  USGS (geol); DMA (topo)

### 361

Murray State University
Pogue Library, Special Collections
Murray, KY 42071
Tel. (502) 762-6152
Hours: 8–4:30, M–F
Responsible Person: Heim, Keith,
  Director
Special Strengths: Kentucky, Tennessee
Employees: Full Time     Part Time
  Prof.          1            0
  Non-Prof.      2            0
Holdings:
  19673 Printed Maps
  182 Atlases
    1 Globe
    4 Wall Maps
   24 Books
   16 Gazetteers
   77 Serial Titles
Chronological Coverage: 35% pre 1900;
  65% post 1900
Available to: Public, Students, Faculty
Copying Facilities: Copying machine,
  Microform, Photographic reproduction
Equipment:

56 5-drawer cabinets
  1 filing cabinet
Square Footage: 850
Map Depositories: GPO

## Louisiana

### 362

Centroplex Branch Library
120 St. Louis St.
P. O. Box 1471
Baton Rouge, LA 70821
Tel. (504) 389-4960
Hours: 8–6, M–Th; 8–5, F, Sa
Responsible Person: Marix, Elaine
Special Strengths: Baton Rouge,
  Louisiana
Employees: Full Time     Part Time
  Non-Prof.      1            0
Holdings:
  178 Printed Maps
    8 Manuscript Maps
   13 Aerial Photographs
Chronological Coverage: 40% pre 1900;
  60% post 1900
Available to: Public, Students
Average monthly use: 15
Copying Facilities: Copying machine
Equipment:
  8 5-drawer cabinets

### 363

Louisiana State Library
Louisiana Section
P. O. Box 131
Baton Rouge, LA 70821
Tel. (504) 343-4914
Hours: 8–4:30, M–F
Responsible Person: Callahan, Harriet
Special Strengths: Louisiana
Employees: Full Time     Part Time
  Prof.          0            1
Holdings:
  1600 Printed Maps
    50 Manuscript Maps
    15 Wall Maps
    14 Microforms
Chronological Coverage: 25% pre 1900;
  75% post 1900
Map collection is cataloged 30%
Classification: Subject Classification
Formats: Cards
Preservation methods: Encapsulation
Available to: Public
Circulates to: Public
Average monthly use: 10
Average annual circulation: Maps: 50
Interlibrary loan available
  Only Duplicates
Copying Facilities: Copying machine,
  Microform
Equipment:
  6 5-drawer cabinets
  3 horizontal cabinets
Square Footage: 150

### 364

Louisiana State University
School of Geoscience
Baton Rouge, LA 70803
Tel. (504) 388-6247
Hours: 8–12, 1–4:30, M–Th; 8–12, F
Responsible Person: Nelson, Joyce
Special Strengths: Louisiana (Aerial
  Photography), Latin America
Special Collections: Sanborn Fire
  Insurance Atlases for Louisiana
Employees: Full Time     Part Time
  Prof.          1            0
  Non-Prof.      0            5
Holdings:
  500000 Printed Maps
   60000 Aerial Photographs
     150 Atlases
      10 Globes
      18 Microforms
      50 Gazetteers
Chronological Coverage: 5% pre 1900;
  95% post 1900
Preservation methods: Lamination
Available to: Public, Students, Faculty
Circulates to: Students, Faculty
Average monthly use: 345
Average annual circulation:
  Maps: 5000
Interlibrary loan available
  Oil companies only
Copying Facilities: Copying machine
Equipment:
  150 5-drawer cabinets
   45 vertical map cabinets
    9 file cabinets
    1 aerial photo cabinet
  stereoscopes, light tables
Square Footage: 2700
Map Depositories: USGS (topo);
  USGS (geol); DMA (topo); DMA
  (hydro); NOS; NOAA

### 365

Southern University Library
Southern Branch P. O.
Baton Rouge, LA 70813
Tel. (504) 771-4990
Hours: 8–10, M–F; 8–5, Sa; 2–10, Su
Responsible Person: Zade, J. B.
Employees: Full Time     Part Time
  Prof.          2            0
Holdings:
  803 Printed Maps
   30 Atlases
    1 Globe
Chronological Coverage:
  100% post 1900
Classification: LC
Formats: Cards
Available to: Public, Students, Faculty
Interlibrary loan available
Equipment:
  3 5-drawer cabinets
Map Depositories: USGS (topo)

366
Northwestern State University
of Louisiana
Watson Library, Map Collection
Cammie G. Henry Research Center
Natchitoches, LA 71457
Tel. (318) 357-4585
Hours: 8–5:30, M–Th; 8–4:30, F
Responsible Person: Wells, Carol
Special Strengths: Louisiana
(1650–present)
Employees: Full Time    Part Time
Prof.         0            1
Non-Prof.   0            1
Holdings:
2001 Printed Maps
Chronological Coverage: 90% pre 1900;
10% post 1900
Preservation methods: Encapsulation,
Deacidification
Available to: Public, Students, Faculty
Copying Facilities: Copying machine
Equipment:
9 5-drawer cabinets
1 blueprint cabinet
Square Footage: 100

367
Historic New Orleans Collection
533 Royal St.
New Orleans, LA 70130
Tel. (504) 523-4662
Hours: 10–4:30, T–Sa
Responsible Person: Mahe, John A., II,
Curator
Special Strengths: New Orleans (1718–
present), Louisiana & Southeast
United States (1513–present)
Employees: Full Time    Part Time
Prof.         4            0
Holdings:
1000 Printed maps
130 Manuscript Maps
110 Aerial Photographs
2 Satellite Imagery
20 Atlases
4 Globes
40 Microforms
30 Books
6 Gazetteers
Chronological Coverage: 95% pre 1900;
5% post 1900
Map collection is cataloged 15%
Classification: LC
Formats: Cards
Preservation methods: Encapsulation,
Deacidification
Available to: Public, Students, Faculty
Average monthly use: 35
Copying Facilities: Copying machine,
Microform, Photographic reproduction
Equipment:
5 5-drawer cabinets
10 print cases
Square Footage: 60

368
Louisiana State Museum
Louisiana Historical Center
Cartographic Division
Old US Mint
400 Esplanade Ave.
New Orleans, LA 70116
Tel. (504) 568-8215
Hours: 8:45–4:45, M–F
Responsible Person: Castle, Joseph D.,
Curator of Maps
Special Strengths: North America
(1541–present), Louisiana (1540–
present), Gulf of Mexico–Outer
Continental Shelf (1590–present,
Geology)
Special Collections: Solis & Helen
Seiferth Cartographic Collection,
T. P. (Thompson) Collection, Gaspar
Cusachs Collection
Employees: Full Time    Part Time
Prof.         1            0
Non-Prof.   1            0
Holdings:
3300 Printed Maps
150 Manuscript Maps
21 Atlases
29 Wall Maps
14 Microforms
42 Books
5 Gazetteers
6 Serial Titles
Chronological Coverage: 85% pre 1900;
15% post 1900
Map collection is cataloged 70%
Classification: Museum Accession No.
Formats: Cards
Preservation methods: Encapsulation,
Chartex or Fabric Mounting,
Deacidification
Available to: Public, Students, Faculty
Average monthly use: 45
Copying Facilities: Copying machine,
Photographic reproduction
Equipment:
10 5-drawer cabinets
rolled map storage
Square Footage: 175

369
New Orleans Public Library
Business & Science Division
217 Loyola Ave.
New Orleans, LA 70140
Tel. (504) 596-2580
Hours: 10–6, T–Sa
Responsible Person: Bedikian,
Elizabeth, Head
Special Strengths: Louisiana,
Mississippi, Arkansas
Employees: Full Time    Part Time
Prof.         3            0
Non-Prof.   3            0
Holdings:
3000 Printed Maps
Chronological Coverage:

100% post 1900
Map collection is cataloged 10%
Formats: Cards
Available to: Public, Students
Average monthly use: 5
Copying Facilities: Copying machine,
Microform
Equipment:
1 5-drawer cabinet
Square Footage: 50
Map Depositories: USGS (geol); GPO

370
New Orleans Public Library
Louisiana Division
219 Loyola Ave.
New Orleans, LA 70140
Tel. (504) 596-2610
Hours: 10–6, T–Sa (Rare materials not
available after 5 or on Sa.)
Responsible Person: Everard, Wayne M.
Special Collections: New Orleans City
Archives Collection (Maps, Land
Surveys, Street Plans, 1700–present)
Employees: Full Time    Part Time
Prof.         3            1
Non-Prof.   3            0
Holdings:
2400 Printed Maps
400 Manuscript Maps
16700 Aerial Photographs
1 Satellite Imagery
118 Atlases
15 Wall Maps
12 Microforms
25 Books
Chronological Coverage: 10% pre 1900;
90% post 1900
Map collection is cataloged 75%
Classification: Internal
Formats: Cards
Available to: Public, Students, Faculty
Average monthly use: 50
Copying Facilities: Copying machine,
Microform
Equipment:
14 11-drawer cabinets
2 6-drawer cabinets
2 3-drawer cabinets
Square Footage: 150

371
Tulane University Library
U.S. Government Documents
New Orleans, LA 70118
Tel. (504) 865-5683
Hours: 8:30–10, M–Th; 10–5, Sa;
1–10, Su
Responsible Person: Heffner, Rose
Employees: Full Time    Part Time
Non-Prof.   4            0
Holdings:
13000 Printed Maps
100 Gazetteers
Chronological Coverage:

100% post 1900
Available to: Public, Students, Faculty
Circulates to: Faculty
Average annual circulation: Maps: 12
Interlibrary loan available
Copying Facilities: Copying machine
Equipment:
    10 5-drawer cabinets
    Book shelving for maps
Square Footage: 80
Map Depositories: USGS (topo); GPO

### 372
University of New Orleans
Earl K. Long Library
Government Documents
New Orleans, LA 70122
Tel. (504) 286-7276
Hours: 8–Midnight, M–Th; 8–10, F;
    9–6, Sa; 1–10, Su
Responsible Person: Skifsington, Frances
Special Strengths: Southern States
Employees: Full Time    Part Time
    Non-Prof.    0            5
Holdings:
    16000 Printed Maps
Chronological Coverage:
    100% post 1900
Available to: Public, Students, Faculty
Circulates to: Students, Faculty
Average monthly use: 50
Average annual circulation: Maps: 100
Interlibrary loan available
Copying Facilities: Copying machine
Equipment:
    26 5-drawer cabinets
    2 5-drawer oversized map cases
Map Depositories: USGS (topo);
    USGS (geol); GPO

### 373
Louisiana Tech University
Prescott Memorial Library
Government Documents Department
Ruston, LA 71272-0046
Tel. (318) 257-4962
Hours: 7:30–9, M–Th; 7:30–5, F
Responsible Person: Henson, Stephen
Employees: Full Time    Part Time
    Prof.        3            0
    Non-Prof.    0            8
Holdings:
    2200 Printed Maps
Chronological Coverage: 1% pre 1900;
    99% post 1900
Map collection is cataloged 100%
Classification: SuDocs & Local
Formats: Cards
Available to: Public, Students, Faculty
Interlibrary loan available
Copying Facilities: Copying machine
Equipment:
    8 5-drawer cabinets
    4 4-drawer vertical files
Square Footage: 500

Map Depositories: USGS (topo);
    USGS (geol); GPO

### 374
Louisiana State University
Shreveport Library
8515 Youree Dr.
Shreveport, LA 71115
Tel. (318) 797-5203
Hours: 8–9:30, M–F
Responsible Person: Parker, Malcolm G.
Special Strengths: Louisiana &
    neighboring states
Special Collections: Shreveport,
    Northwest Louisiana, Red River Valley
Employees: Full Time    Part Time
    Prof.        0            3
Holdings:
    500 Printed Maps
    4 Aerial Photographs
    35 Atlases
    1 Globe
    10 Wall Maps
    30 Books
    40 Gazetteers
Chronological Coverage: 2% pre 1900;
    98% post 1900
Map collection is cataloged 50%
Classification: Dewey    Utility: OCLC
Formats: Cards
Preservation methods: Encapsulation,
    Deacidification
Available to: Public
Average monthly use: 3
Average annual circulation:
    Books: 5
Copying Facilities: Copying machine
Equipment:
    9 5-drawer cabinets
    2 vertical map cabinets
Square Footage: 46
Map Depositories: USGS (topo)

## Maine
### 375
Maine Geological Survey
Station #22
Augusta, ME 04333
Tel. (207) 289-2801
Hours: 8–4, M–F
Responsible Person: Lepage, Carolyn
Special Strengths: Maine (Aerial
    photography, Geology)
Holdings:
    500 Printed Maps
    6000 Aerial Photographs
Chronological Coverage:
    100% post 1900
Formats: Index maps
Available to: Public
Average monthly use: 50
Copying Facilities: Diazo copies
Equipment:
    File cabinets
Square Footage: 100

### 376
Maine State Library
LMA Building/State House Station 64
Augusta, ME 04333
Tel. (207) 289-3561
Hours: 9–5, M, W, F; 9–9, T, Th;
    11–5, Sa (Winter: By appointment)
Responsible Person: Collins, Bonnie H.
Special Strengths: Maine (1750–1930)
Special Collections: Avery Collection–
    primarily Northern Maine (Mt.
    Katahdin Region), Baxter Collection
    (primarily Baxter State Park region)
Holdings:
    250 Printed Maps
    100 Manuscript Maps
    25 Atlases
    30 Wall Maps
    10 Books
    8 Gazetteers
Chronological Coverage: 75% pre 1900;
    25% post 1900
Classification: Index number
    TRS-80 microcomputer
Formats: Online, Computer
    Printout
Preservation methods: Encapsulation,
    Lamination, Chartex or Fabric
    Mounting, Deacidification
Available to: Public
Average monthly use: 5
Copying Facilities: Photographic
    reproduction
Equipment:
    1 5-drawer cabinet
    Special shelving
Square Footage: 206
Map Depositories: USGS (topo);
    USGS (geol); GPO

### 377
Bangor Public Library
145 Harlow St.
Bangor, ME 04401
Tel. (207) 947-8336
Hours: 9–9, M–F; 9–5, Sa
Responsible Person: Wight, Susan B.,
    Adult Services
Special Strengths: Maine
Holdings:
    300 Printed Maps
Chronological Coverage: 20% pre 1900;
    80% post 1900
Map collection is cataloged 100%
Classification: Dewey    Utility: OCLC
Formats: Cards
Available to: Public, Students
Copying Facilities: Copying machine
Equipment:
    Atlas cases
Map Depositories: USGS (topo)

### 378
Maine Maritime Museum
Hennessy Library/Archives

963 Washington St.
Bath, ME 04530
Tel. (207) 443-6311
Hours: 9–5, M–F
Responsible Person: Lipfert, Nathan,
  Assistant Curator
Special Strengths: World (Nautical
  charts, 19th cent.), Sayadahoc County,
  ME (19th cent.)
Special Collections: Personal chart
  collections of various shipmasters,
  Track charts of vessels of Sewall
  Fleet
Employees: Full Time     Part Time
  Prof.         0              1
Holdings:
  400 Printed Maps
  14 Atlases
  20 Wall Maps
  200 Books
  2 Gazetteers
Chronological Coverage: 90% pre 1900;
  10% post 1900
Available to: Public
Copying Facilities: Copying machine
Equipment:
  3 5-drawer cabinets
  Staff-built racks
Square Footage: 40


### 379

Bowdoin College Library
Brunswick, ME 04011
Tel. (207) 725-8731
Hours: 8:30–5, M–F
Responsible Person: Takagi, Elda G.
Employees: Full Time     Part Time
  Prof.         2              0
  Non-Prof.     0              1
Holdings:
  60000 Printed Maps
Chronological Coverage:
  100% post 1900
Map collection is cataloged 10%
Classification: LC
Formats: Cards
Available to: Public, Students, Faculty
Circulates to: Faculty
Average monthly use: 10
Average annual circulation: Maps: 4
Copying Facilities: Copying machine
Equipment:
  30 5-drawer cabinets
  1 vertical map cabinet
Map Depositories: USGS (topo);
  USGS (geol); DMA (topo); GPO


### 380

Maine Maritime Academy
Nutting Memorial Library
Castine, ME 04420
Tel. (207) 326-4311
Hours: 8–4, M–F
Responsible Person: Gilmore, Willard H.,
  Assistant Librarian

Special Strengths: Maine (Navigation
  charts)
Employees: Full Time     Part Time
  Prof.         1              0
Holdings:
  1178 Printed Maps
  1 Globe
  33 Wall Maps
Chronological Coverage:
  100% post 1900
Map collection is cataloged 10%
Classification: Other   Utility: OCLC
Formats: Cards
Available to: Public, Students, Faculty
Circulates to: Public, Students, Faculty
Interlibrary loan available
Copying Facilities: Copying machine
Equipment:
  3 5-drawer cabinets
Map Depositories: USGS (topo);
  DMA (topo); DMA (aero); DMA
  (hydro); GPO; NOS


### 381

University of Maine
Blake Library
Fort Kent, ME 04743
Tel. (207) 834-3162
Hours: 8–9, M–F
Responsible Person: Pittet, Marcel
Special Strengths: Maine
Employees: Full Time     Part Time
  Prof.         0              1
Holdings:
  200 Printed Maps
  5 Aerial Photographs
  1 Satellite Imagery
  20 Atlases
  1 Raised Relief Map
  2 Gazetteers
Chronological Coverage:
  100% post 1900
Available to: Public
Average monthly use: 5
Copying Facilities: Copying machine
Equipment:
  2 5-drawer cabinets
Square Footage: 75
Map Depositories: USGS (topo)


### 382

University of Maine at Orono
Fogler Library
Government Documents Dept.
Orono, ME 04469
Tel. (207) 581-1680
Hours: 8–4:30, M–F
Responsible Person: Wihbey,
  Francis R., Head
Special Strengths: New England,
  Canada, United States
Special Collections: USDA Soil
  Conservation Service Soil Surveys,
  USGS Open File Reports, U.S. Fish &
  Wildlife Service Ecological

Characterization of Coastal Maine,
  U.S. Census Bureau block, tract, &
  state maps
Employees: Full Time     Part Time
  Prof.         1              0
  Non-Prof.     4              3
Holdings:
  40500 Printed Maps
  380 Atlases
  2 Wall Maps
  13 Raised Relief Maps
  22200 Microforms
  7 Books
  260 Gazetteers
  9 Serial Titles
Chronological Coverage: 1% pre 1900;
  99% post 1900
Map collection is cataloged 4%
Formats: Cards
Available to: Public, Students, Faculty
Circulates to: Public, Students, Faculty
Average monthly use: 400
Average annual circulation: Maps: 100;
  Government Documents: 20000
Interlibrary loan available
Copying Facilities: Copying machine,
  Microform
Equipment:
  4 5-drawer cabinets
  8 vertical map cabinets
  1 10-drawer wooden map case
Square Footage: 400
Map Depositories: USGS (topo);
  USGS (geol); DMA (topo); DMA
  (aero); GPO; NOS; Canada (topo)


### 383

University of Maine at Orono
R. H. Fogler Library
Special Collections Department
Orono, ME 04469
Tel. (207) 581-1680
Hours: 8–4:30, M–F; 1–5, Su
Responsible Person: Flower, Eric S.,
  Head
Special Strengths: Maine
Employees: Full Time     Part Time
  Prof.         2              0
Holdings:
  2100 Printed Maps
  15 Wall Maps
  5 Books
Chronological Coverage: 27% pre 1900;
  73% post 1900
Map collection is cataloged 100%
Formats: Cards, Book Catalog
Preservation methods: Encapsulation
Available to: Public, Students, Faculty
Copying Facilities: Copying machine,
  Photographic reproduction
Equipment:
  3 5-drawer cabinets
Square Footage: 50
Map Depositories: Maine State
  Depository

### 384

Maine Historical Society
485 Congress St.
Portland, ME 04101
Tel. (207) 774-1822
Hours: 9–5, T, W, F; 9–8:30, Th;
 9–5, 2nd Sa of every month
Responsible Person: McCain,
 Margaret J., Librarian
Special Strengths: Maine (1600–1900)
Special Collections: Pejepscot
 Proprietors, Northeast Boundary,
 Kennebec Purchase, Waldo Purchase

Employees: Full Time     Part Time
Prof.          1              0

Holdings:
 500 Printed Maps
 170 Manuscript Maps
 70 Atlases
Chronological Coverage: 80% pre 1900;
 20% post 1900
Map collection is cataloged 85%
Classification: Boggs & Lewis
Formats: Cards
Available to: Public, Students, Faculty
Average monthly use: 20
Copying Facilities: Copying machine
Equipment:
 8 5-drawer cabinets
Square Footage: 150

### 385

Portland Public Library
5 Monument Square
Portland, ME 04101
Tel. (207) 773-4761
Hours: 9–6, M, W, F; 12–9, T, Th;
 9–5, Sa (except summer)
Responsible Person: Long, John

Employees: Full Time     Part Time
Prof.          0              1
Non-Prof.      0              1

Holdings:
 5000 Printed Maps
 120 Atlases
 1 Globe
 1 Wall Map
 2 Books
 150 Gazetteers
Chronological Coverage:
 100% post 1900
Available to: Public
Average monthly use: 15
Copying Facilities: Copying machine
Equipment:
 10 5-drawer cabinets
Square Footage: 200
Map Depositories: USGS (topo)

### 386

Colby College
Department of Geology, Map Library
Waterville, ME 04901
Tel. (207) 873-1131
Hours: 8–5, M–F

Responsible Person: Allen, Professor
 Donald B.
Special Strengths: Maine (Geology),
 Kentucky (Geology)

Employees: Full Time     Part Time
Prof.          1              0
Non-Prof.      0              1

Holdings:
 60000 Printed Maps
 2400 Aerial Photographs
 1 Satellite Imagery
 7 Atlases
 3 Globes
 100 Wall Maps
 12 Raised Relief Maps
 10 Microforms
 100 Books
 5 Gazetteers
 15 Serial Titles
Chronological Coverage: 2% pre 1900;
 98% post 1900
Available to: Public, Students, Faculty
Average monthly use: 10
Copying Facilities: Copying machine
Equipment:
 62 5-drawer cabinets
Square Footage: 900
Map Depositories: USGS (topo);
 USGS (geol)

## Maryland

### 387

Enoch Pratt Free Library
General Information Department
400 Cathedral St.
Baltimore, MD 21201
Tel. (301) 396-5472
Hours: 10–9, M–Th; 9–5, F, Sa; 1–5, Su
Responsible Person: Burke, Robert
Special Strengths: Great Britain,
 Canada, World (International Map of
 the World on the Millionth Scale)
Special Collections: Karpinsky
 Collection of photostat copies from
 French archives

Employees: Full Time     Part Time
Prof.          0              1
Non-Prof.      0              1

Holdings:
 101362 Printed Maps
 3 Globes
 8 Raised Relief Maps
Chronological Coverage: 10% pre 1900;
 90% post 1900
Map collection is cataloged 50%
Classification: Local
Formats: Cards
Available to: Public
Circulates to: Public
Average monthly use: 50
Interlibrary loan available
Copying Facilities: Photographic
 reproduction
Equipment:
 38 5-drawer cabinets
 14 vertical map cabinets

Map Depositories: USGS (topo);
 USGS (geol); DMA (topo); NOAA

### 388

Johns Hopkins University
Milton S. Eisenhower Library
Peabody Collection
17 E. Mount Vernon Pl.
Baltimore, MD 21202
Tel. (301) 659-8197
Hours: 9–5, M–Sa (Sept–May); 9–5,
 M–F (June–Aug)
Responsible Person: Hart, Lyn, Librarian
Special Strengths: Baltimore, Maryland,
 United States, Western Europe,
 (16th–19th cent.)

Employees: Full Time     Part Time
Prof.          2              1
Non-Prof.      4              2

Holdings:
 1633 Printed Maps
 9 Manuscript Maps
 200 Atlases
 1 Globe
 257 Books
 68 Gazetteers
 4 Serial Titles
Chronological Coverage: 98% pre 1900;
 2% post 1900
Map collection is cataloged 40%
Classification: Dewey
Formats: Cards
Preservation methods: Encapsulation
Available to: Public, Students, Faculty
Average monthly use: 10
Interlibrary loan available
 Books only
Copying Facilities: Copying machine,
 Photographic reproduction
Equipment:
 6 5-drawer cabinets
Square Footage: 29

### 389

Johns Hopkins University
Milton S. Eisenhower Library
Special Collection Division
John Work Garrett Library
4545 N. Charles St.
Baltimore, MD 21210
Tel. (301) 338-7641
Hours: 9–5, M–F
Responsible Person: Katz, Jane,
 John Work Garrett Librarian
Special Strengths: America (17th &
 18th cent.), World (16th & 17th cent.,
 Maritime Atlases)
Special Collections: Early maps of
 Maryland, 1635–1799

Employees: Full Time     Part Time
Prof.          1              0
Non-Prof.      0              1

Holdings:
 442 Printed Maps
 17 Manuscript Maps

35 Atlases
2 Globes
38 Books
Chronological Coverage: 98% pre 1900;
2% post 1900
Classification: Other    Utility: RLIN
Formats: Cards
Preservation methods: Encapsulation,
Lamination, Chartex or Fabric
Mounting, Edging, Deacidification
Available to: Public, Students, Faculty
Average monthly use: 2212
Copying Facilities: Copying machine,
Dyeline
Equipment:
1 5-drawer cabinet
Square Footage: 25

390
Johns Hopkins University
The Milton S. Eisenhower Library
Government Publications/Maps/Law
Department
Baltimore, MD 21218
Tel. (301) 338-8360
Hours: 8:30-5, M-F
Responsible Person: Gillispie, Jim,
Department Head
Special Strengths: United States
Employees: Full Time    Part Time
Prof.              2              0
Non-Prof.       3              1
Holdings:
183301 Printed Maps
25 Satellite Imagery
685 Atlases
1 Globe
200 Wall Maps
25 Raised Relief Maps
92 Books
221 Gazetteers
2 Serial Titles
Chronological Coverage: 20% pre 1900;
80% post 1900
Map collection is cataloged 80%
Classification: LC
Formats: Cards
Preservation methods: Encapsulation,
Lamination, Chartex or Fabric
Mounting, Edging, Deacidification
Available to: Public, Students, Faculty
Circulates to: Students, Faculty
Average annual circulation: Maps: 151
Interlibrary loan available
Very limited
Copying Facilities: Copying machine,
Photographic reproduction
Equipment:
35 5-drawer cabinets
1 vertical map cabinet
22 geology specimen cases
1 light table
Square Footage: 3432
Map Depositories: USGS (topo);
USGS (geol); GPO; MD Geological
Survey

391
Maryland Historical Society
Prints & Photographs Division
201 W. Monument St.
Baltimore, MD 21201
Tel. (301) 685-3750
Hours: 11-4:30, T-F; 9-4:30, Sa
Responsible Person: Baty, Laurie A.,
P & P Librarian
Special Strengths: Chesapeake Bay
(17th-20th cent.), Maryland
(17th-20th cent.), Baltimore
(19th cent.)
Special Collections: USGS 19th century
quadrangle maps for Maryland
Employees: Full Time    Part Time
Prof.              2              0
Non-Prof.       0              1
Holdings:
2500 Printed Maps
500 Manuscript Maps
85 Atlases
50 Wall Maps
1 Raised Relief Map
27 Books
3 Gazetteers
5 Serial Titles
Chronological Coverage: 80% pre 1900;
20% post 1900
Map collection is cataloged 80%
Formats: Cards
Preservation methods: Deacidification,
Japanese tissue
Available to: Public, Students, Faculty
Average monthly use: 5
Copying Facilities: Copying machine,
Photographic reproduction
Equipment:
15 5-drawer cabinets
Rolled storage ca. 90 maps
Square Footage: 487
Map Depositories: USGS (topo);
MD Department of Transportation

392
University of Maryland
Baltimore County
A. O. Kuhn Library & Gallery
5401 Wilkens Ave.
Catonsville, MD 21228
Tel. (301) 455-2358
Hours: 8-11, M-Th; 8-6, F; 10-4, Sa;
1-9, Su
Responsible Person: Stegall, Patricia
Special Strengths: Maryland
Employees: Full Time    Part Time
Prof.              0              1
Non-Prof.       0              1
Holdings:
4126 Printed Maps
2 Satellite Imagery
381 Atlases
2 Globes
1 Wall Map
10 Gazetteers
Chronological Coverage: 1% pre 1900;

99% post 1900
Map collection is cataloged 100%
Classification: LC
Formats: Cards
Available to: Public, Students, Faculty
Circulates to: Students, Faculty
Average annual circulation: Maps: 120
Copying Facilities: Copying machine
Equipment:
4 5-drawer cabinets
2 16-drawer map cabinets
Square Footage: 56
Map Depositories: USGS (topo);
MD Department of Transportation

393
University of Maryland
McKeldin Library, Documents/Maps
Room
College Park, MD 20742
Tel. (301) 454-3034
Hours: 8-11, M-Th; 8-6, F; 10-6, Sa;
Noon-11, Su
Responsible Person: Warren, Lola N.,
Acting Head
Employees: Full Time    Part Time
Prof.              0              2
Non-Prof.       0              3
Holdings:
70000 Printed Maps
75 Atlases
6 Wall Maps
50 Raised Relief Maps
20 Books
100 Gazetteers
Chronological Coverage: 5% pre 1900;
95% post 1900
Available to: Public, Students, Faculty
Average monthly use: 75
Copying Facilities: Copying machine
Equipment:
75 5-drawer cabinets
8 atlas cases
1 vertical file cabinet
Light table
Square Footage: 775
Map Depositories: USGS (topo);
DMA (topo); GPO

394
University of Maryland
McKeldin Library
Marylandia Department
College Park, MD 20742
Tel. (301) 454-3035
Hours: 8:30-5, M-F; 10-5, Sa
Responsible Person: Larson, Melanie
Special Strengths: Maryland (19th
cent.), Baltimore
Special Collections: Early maps of
Maryland, Sanborn Fire Insurance
Maps of Maryland Towns
Employees: Full Time    Part Time
Prof.              1              0
Non-Prof.       3              0

Holdings:
   2300 Printed Maps
      1 Manuscript Map
     10 Aerial Photographs
      1 Satellite Imagery
     50 Atlases
      4 Wall Maps
     15 Books
      5 Gazetteers
      1 Serial Title
Chronological Coverage: 40% pre 1900;
   60% post 1900
Map collection is cataloged 100%
Classification: In-house
Formats: Cards
Preservation methods: Lamination,
   Deacidification, Japanese tissue
Available to: Public, Students, Faculty
Average monthly use: 60
Copying Facilities: Copying machine,
   Photographic reproduction
Equipment:
   7 5-drawer cabinets
Square Footage: 40


### 395
Frostburg State College
Department of Geography
Frostburg, MD 21532
Tel. (301) 689-4369
Hours: 8–5, M–F
Responsible Person: Nizinski,
   William, Chair
Employees: Full Time    Part Time
   Prof.        2            0
   Non-Prof.    0            1
Holdings:
   3000 Printed Maps
      5 Atlases
     10 Globes
Chronological Coverage:
   100% post 1900
Formats: Cards
Preservation methods: Lamination
Available to: Public, Students, Faculty
Circulates to: Public, Students, Faculty
Average monthly use: 250
Average annual circulation: Maps: 200
Copying Facilities: Copying machine
Equipment:
   12 5-drawer cabinets
   Stereoscope, Map-A-Graph
Square Footage: 500


### 396
Frostburg State College Library
Document & Map Dept., Map Collection
Frostburg, MD 21532
Tel. (301) 689-4423
Hours: 8:30–10, M–Th; 8:30–5, F;
   1–5, Sa; 1–10, Su
Responsible Person: Davis, Harry O.,
   Document & Map Librarian
Special Strengths: Maryland &
   surrounding states, United States,

Canada, Latin America, Europe
Special Collections: Manuscript maps
   plus text for Potomac River Basin
   Demonstration Project in Georges
   Creek, Georges Creek Valley,
   Allegany County
Employees: Full Time    Part Time
   Prof.        0            1
   Non-Prof.    0            2
Holdings:
   30808 Printed Maps
       3 Globes
      30 Raised Relief Maps
       5 Books
      22 Gazetteers
Chronological Coverage: 1% pre 1900;
   99% post 1900
Map collection is cataloged 45%
Classification: LC
Formats: Cards
Preservation methods: Lamination
Available to: Public, Students, Faculty
Circulates to: Public, Students, Faculty
Average monthly use: 32
Average annual circulation: Maps: 350
Interlibrary loan available
Copying Facilities: Copying machine
Equipment:
   76 5-drawer cabinets
    1 vertical map cabinets
   Light table
Square Footage: 1350
Map Depositories: USGS (topo);
   DMA (topo); DMA (hydro); GPO


### 397
Maryland-Municipal Reference
   Rockville Library
99 Maryland Ave.
Rockville, MD 20854
Tel. (301) 279-1953
Hours: 9–9, M–Th; 9–5, F, Sa; 1–5, Su
Responsible Person: Burt, Patricia
Special Strengths: Maryland
   (1600's–present), Montgomery County
   (1950's–present)
Employees: Full Time    Part Time
   Prof.        2            0
Holdings:
   600 Printed Maps
Chronological Coverage: 30% pre 1900;
   70% post 1900
Available to: Public
Average monthly use: 50
Copying Facilities: Copying machine
Equipment:
   4 5-drawer cabinets
Square Footage: 24
Map Depositories: GPO


### 398
Salisbury State College
Blackwell Library
Salisbury, MD 21801
Tel. (301) 543-6130

Hours: 8–10, M–Th; 8–4, F
Responsible Person: Vail, Keith R.
Special Strengths: Middle Atlantic
   States
Employees: Full Time    Part Time
   Prof.        0            1
   Non-Prof.    0            1
Holdings:
   2000 Printed Maps
     40 Atlases
      3 Globes
      2 Wall Maps
      4 Raised Relief Maps
      5 Books
      4 Gazetteers
      4 Serial Titles
Chronological Coverage: 1% pre 1900;
   99% post 1900
Preservation methods: Lamination
Available to: Public, Students, Faculty
Circulates to: Students, Faculty
Average monthly use: 3
Average annual circulation: Maps: 20;
   Books: 12
Copying Facilities: Copying machine
Equipment:
   3 5-drawer cabinets
Square Footage: 100
Map Depositories: USGS (topo);
   GPO


### 399
Towson State University
Geography Map Library
Linthium Hall, Room 02
Towson, MD 21204
Tel. (301) 321-2963
Hours: 9–4, M–F
Responsible Person: Stevenson, Marshall
Special Strengths: Maryland (early
   1900's to present), Middle Atlantic
Employees: Full Time    Part Time
   Non-Prof.    0            3
Holdings:
   40000 Printed Maps
     300 Aerial Photographs
      30 Satellite Imagery
      75 Atlases
       5 Globes
     120 Wall Maps
     100 Raised Relief Maps
Chronological Coverage: 1% pre 1900;
   99% post 1900
Map collection is cataloged 100%
Classification: LC
Formats: Cards
Available to: Public, Students, Faculty
Average monthly use: 10
Average annual circulation: Maps: 100
Equipment:
   40 5-drawer cabinets
    2 vertical map cabinets
Map Depositories: USGS (geol);
   DMA (topo); DMA (aero); DMA
   (hydro); GPO

**Massachusetts**

### 400

Amherst College Library
Amherst, MA 01002
Tel. (413) 542-2319
Hours: 8:30–4:30, 6–9, M–F
Responsible Person: Merritt, Floyd S.
Special Strengths: United States
Employees: Full Time    Part Time
  Prof.         0          1
  Non-Prof.     0          1
Holdings:
  60000 Printed Maps
    485 Atlases
      4 Globes
    175 Wall Maps
      6 Raised Relief Maps
     25 Microforms
    155 Books
     65 Gazetteers
      3 Serial Titles
Chronological Coverage: 5% pre 1900;
  95% post 1900
Map collection is cataloged 5%
Classification: LC    Utility: OCLC
Formats: Cards, Online
Available to: Public, Students, Faculty
Average monthly use: 25
Copying Facilities: Copying machine,
  Microform
Equipment:
  33 5-drawer cabinets
  12 4-drawer cabinets
Square Footage: 784
Map Depositories: USGS (topo);
  USGS (geol); DMA (topo); GPO

### 401

University of Massachusetts
University Library, Map Collection
Amherst, MA 01003
Tel. (413) 545-2397
Hours: 8:30–5, M–F
Responsible Person: Shepard, Paul
Employees: Full Time    Part Time
  Non-Prof.     1          1
Holdings:
  103000 Printed Maps
     50 Wall Maps
Chronological Coverage: 1% pre 1900;
  99% post 1900
Preservation methods: Encapsulation
Available to: Public, Students, Faculty
Circulates to: Students, Faculty
Average monthly use: 250
Average annual circulation:
  Maps: 2000
Copying Facilities: Copying machine
Equipment:
  78 5-drawer cabinets
  15 3-drawer cabinets
Square Footage: 1100
Map Depositories: USGS (topo);
  USGS (geol); DMA (topo)

### 402

Boston Athenaeum
10½ Beacon St.
Boston, MA 02117
Tel. (617) 227-0270
Hours: 9–5:30, M–F; 9–4, Sa
  (October–May)
Special Strengths: Boston (1870–1930),
  New England (pre-1900)
Employees: Full Time    Part Time
  Prof.         0          4
Holdings:
  4000 Printed Maps
  1000 Atlases
     5 Globes
   100 Books
    50 Gazetteers
     1 Serial Title
Chronological Coverage: 75% pre 1900;
  25% post 1900
Map collection is cataloged 95%
Classification: LC    Utility: OCLC
Formats: Cards
Preservation methods: Encapsulation,
  Deacidification, Japanese paper
Average monthly use: 20
Copying Facilities: Copying machine,
  Photographic reproduction
Equipment:
  9 5-drawer cabinets
  Deep shelving for large flat books
Square Footage: 350
Map Depositories: USGS (topo)

### 403

Boston Public Library
666 Boylston St., Box 286
Boston, MA 02117
Tel. (617) 536-5400
Responsible Person: Waters, Mertin F.
Map Depositories: USGS (topo);
  USGS (geol); DMA (topo)

### 404

Boston University Geography Department
Map Library
48 Cummington St.
Boston, MA 02215
Tel. (617) 353-2525
Hours: Appointment Only
Responsible Person: McClennen, Eliza,
  Staff Cartographer
Holdings:
  3000 Printed Maps
     2 Globes
   110 Wall Maps
    12 Raised Relief Maps
Chronological Coverage: 5% pre 1900;
  95% post 1900
Available to: Students, Faculty
Average monthly use: 10
Average annual circulation: Maps: 50
Equipment:
  36 5-drawer cabinets
  Ceiling hooks for Wall Maps

1 light table
Square Footage: 568

### 405

Boston University
Geology Department
725 Commonwealth Ave.
Boston, MA 02215
Tel. (617) 353-2529
Hours: 8–4, M–F
Responsible Person: Stewart, John W.,
  Lab Curator
Special Strengths: New England
  (Geology)
Employees: Full Time    Part Time
  Non-Prof.     0          1
Holdings:
  9000 Printed Maps
   500 Aerial Photographs
     3 Atlases
     4 Globes
    60 Wall Maps
Chronological Coverage:
  100% post 1900
Map collection is cataloged 80%
Formats: Cards
Available to: Students, Faculty
Circulates to: Students, Faculty
Equipment:
  12 5-drawer cabinets

### 406

Bostonian Society Library
15 State St., 3rd Floor
Boston, MA 02109
Tel. (617) 242-5614
Hours: 9:30–4:30, M–F
Responsible Person: Leen, Mary,
  Librarian
Special Strengths: Boston (17th–20th
  cent.)
Employees: Full Time    Part Time
  Prof.         1          1
  Non-Prof.     1          0
Holdings:
  380 Printed Maps
   20 Manuscript Maps
   20 Aerial Photographs
   40 Atlases
   10 Books
    2 Gazetteers
Chronological Coverage: 80% pre 1900;
  20% post 1900
Available to: Public, Students, Faculty
Copying Facilities: Copying machine,
  Photographic reproduction
Equipment:
  2 5-drawer cabinets
Square Footage: 20

### 407

Massachusetts Historical Society
1154 Boylston St.
Boston, MA 02215

Tel. (617) 536-1608
Hours: 9–4:45, M–F
Responsible Person: Sparks, Robert V.,
Senior Assistant Librarian
Special Strengths: Massachusetts
(1750–1900), New England (1750–
1900), Boston (1750–1900)
Holdings:
5500 Printed Maps
600 Manuscript Maps
200 Atlases
75 Wall Maps
125 Books
30 Gazetteers
Chronological Coverage: 95% pre 1900;
5% post 1900
Map collection is cataloged 90%
Classification: In-house shelf list
Formats: Cards
Preservation methods: Encapsulation,
Chartex or Fabric Mounting,
Deacidification
Available to: Public, Students, Faculty
Average monthly use: 10
Copying Facilities: Copying machine,
Microform, Photographic reproduction
Equipment:
Custom made drawers & cabinets
Square Footage: 600

408
Massachusetts Secretary of State's Office
Archives Division
Room 55, State House
Boston, MA 02133
Tel. (617) 727-2816
Hours: 9–5, M–F
Special Strengths: Massachusetts
Special Collections: Massachusetts
towns, 17th–19th centuries
Employees: Full Time     Part Time
Prof.              1                  0
Non-Prof.          1                  0
Holdings:
500 Printed Maps
7000 Manuscript Maps
100 Aerial Photographs
100 Atlases
Chronological Coverage: 65% pre 1900;
35% post 1900
Map collection is cataloged 90%
Classification: Local
Formats: Cards
Preservation methods: Encapsulation,
Lamination, Chartex or Fabric
Mounting
Available to: Public
Average monthly use: 50
Copying Facilities: Copying machine,
Microform, Photographic reproduction
Equipment:
5 5-drawer cabinets
Archival storage cabinets
Square Footage: 150

409
Massachusetts State Library
341 State House
Boston, MA 02133
Tel. (617) 267-9400
Hours: 9–5, M–F
Responsible Person: Howitson, Brenda,
Chief of Special Collections
Special Strengths: Massachusetts
(pre-1900), New England (pre-1900)
Special Collections: Massachusetts
Railroad maps (manuscript), Panoramic
View maps–Massachusetts cities &
towns, Sanborn Insurance maps–
Massachusetts cities & towns
Employees: Full Time     Part Time
Prof.              1                  0
Non-Prof.          1                  1
Holdings:
15000 Printed Maps
200 Manuscript Maps
1000 Atlases
250 Books
Chronological Coverage: 70% pre 1900;
30% post 1900
Map collection is cataloged 100%
Classification: Other    Utility: OCLC
Formats: Cards
Preservation methods: Encapsulation
Available to: Public
Average monthly use: 75
Copying Facilities: Photographic
reproduction
Equipment:
50 5-drawer cabinets
1 vertical map cabinet
Square Footage: 200
Map Depositories: USGS (topo);
GPO; NOAA

410
University of Massachusetts, Boston
Dept. of Geography & Earth Science
Boston, MA 02115
Tel. (617) 929-8550
Responsible Person: Gelpke, Richard
Special Strengths: United States
Employees: Full Time     Part Time
Prof.              0                  2
Holdings:
30000 Printed Maps
100 Atlases
10 Globes
150 Wall Maps
20 Raised Relief Maps
5 Serial Titles
Chronological Coverage: 5% pre 1900;
95% post 1900
Available to: Students, Faculty
Copying Facilities: Copying machine
Equipment:
25 5-drawer cabinets
1 vertical map cabinet
Map Depositories: USGS (topo);
DMA (topo); DMA (aero); NOAA

411
Bridgewater State College
Maxwell Library
Bridgewater, MA 02324
Tel. (617) 697-1256
Hours: 7:45–11, M–Th; 7:45–5, F;
8:30–4, Sa; 1–10, Su
Responsible Person: McGowan,
Dr. Owen T. P.
Employees: Full Time     Part Time
Prof.              0                  1
Non-Prof.          0                  1
Holdings:
20599 Printed Maps
46 Satellite Imagery
203 Atlases
2 Globes
260 Wall Maps
1 Gazetteer
Chronological Coverage: 1% pre 1900;
99% post 1900
Available to: Public, Students, Faculty
Average monthly use: 10
Copying Facilities: Copying machine
Equipment:
58 5-drawer cabinets
2 vertical map cabinets
Open shelves
Square Footage: 800
Map Depositories: USGS (topo);
USGS (geol); DMA (topo); DMA
(aero)

412
Brookline Public Library
361 Washington St.
Brookline, MA 02146
Tel. (617) 734-0100
Hours: 12–9, M; 10–9, T–Th; 10–5:30, F,
Sa; 1–5, Su
Responsible Person: Abraham, Deborah,
Supervisor, Reference
Special Strengths: Brookline, MA
(1928–present)
Employees: Full Time     Part Time
Prof.              1                  0
Holdings:
1031 Printed Maps
10 Manuscript Maps
40 Atlases
2 Globes
1 Wall Map
2 Gazetteers
Chronological Coverage: 13% pre 1900;
87% post 1900
Map collection is cataloged 100%
Classification: Dewey
Formats: Cards
Preservation methods: Encapsulation,
Lamination, Chartex or Fabric
Mounting, Deacidification
Available to: Public
Average monthly use: 18
Copying Facilities: Copying machine

Equipment:
  1 vertical map cabinet
  1 6-drawer map cabinet
Square Footage: 18


### 413
Harvard College Library
Harvard Map Collection
Cambridge, MA 02138
Tel. (617) 495-2417
Hours: 9–1, 2–5, M–F
Responsible Person: Trout, Dr. Frank E.
Special Strengths: Comprehensive
  History & Science of Cartography,
  Gazetteers
Employees: Full Time    Part Time
  Prof.        1            0
  Non-Prof.    2            5
Holdings:
  500000 Printed Maps
  6100 Atlases
  1200 Wall Maps
  300 Microforms
  2900 Books
Chronological Coverage: 40% pre 1900;
  60% post 1900
Map collection is cataloged 100%
Classification: Modified LC & Harv.
Formats: Cards
Preservation methods: Encapsulation,
  Rice Paper Mounting
Available to: Public, Students, Faculty
Copying Facilities: Copying machine,
  Microform, Dyeline, Photographic
  reproduction
Equipment:
  452 5-drawer cabinets
Map Depositories: USGS (topo);
  DMA (topo); DMA (aero); DMA
  (hydro); GPO; NOS; NOAA


### 414
Harvard University
Geological Sciences Library
Map Collection
24 Oxford St.
Cambridge, MA 02138
Tel. (617) 495-2029
Hours: 9–5, M–F
Responsible Person: Wick, Constance S.,
  Librarian
Special Strengths: United States
  (Geology), New England (Geology)
Employees: Full Time    Part Time
  Prof.        0            1
  Non-Prof.    0            1
Holdings:
  15000 Printed Maps
  50 Atlases
  75 Wall Maps
  50 Books
Chronological Coverage: 5% pre 1900;
  95% post 1900
Map collection is cataloged 50%
Classification: LC

Formats: Cards
Preservation methods: Lamination,
  Chartex or Fabric Mounting
Available to: Public, Students, Faculty
Circulates to: Students, Faculty
Average monthly use: 50
Average annual circulation: Maps: 250
Copying Facilities: Copying machine
Equipment:
  54 5-drawer cabinets
Square Footage: 800
Map Depositories: USGS (geol)


### 415
Massachusetts Institute of Technology
Rotch Library
100 Massachusetts Ave., Room 7238
Cambridge, MA 02139
Tel. (617) 253-7054
Hours: 8:30–10, M–Th; 8:30–7, F;
  12–6, Sa; 2–10, Su
Responsible Person: Gregory, Rona
Special Strengths: Boston (Urban
  Planning)
Special Collections: Sanborn Fire
  Insurance Atlases of Great Boston
Holdings:
  1200 Printed Maps
  100 Aerial Photographs
  75 Atlases
  2 Globes
  2 Wall Maps
  350 Microforms
  3 Books
  2 Gazetteers
Chronological Coverage: 1% pre 1900;
  99% post 1900
Map collection is cataloged 20%
Classification: LC
Formats: Cards
Preservation methods: Encapsulation
Available to: Public, Students, Faculty
Circulates to: Students, Faculty
Average monthly use: 3
Average annual circulation: Maps: 20;
  Aerial Photographs: 10
Copying Facilities: Copying machine,
  Microform
Equipment:
  11 5-drawer cabinets
  2 4-drawer vertical files
Square Footage: 64
Map Depositories: GPO


### 416
Massachusetts Institute of Technology
Schwarz Memorial Map Room
Lindgren Library,
  Room 54-200
Cambridge, MA 02139
Tel. (617) 253-5679
Hours: 8:30–11, M–Th; 8:30–7, F;
  11–6, Sa; 1–11, Su
Responsible Person: Eaglesfield, Jean T.
Special Strengths: World (Geology)

Employees: Full Time    Part Time
  Prof.        1            0
  Non-Prof.    5            0
Holdings:
  10000 Printed Maps
  350 Atlases
  4 Globes
  300 Wall Maps
  100 Books
  1 Gazetteer
Chronological Coverage: 2% pre 1900;
  98% post 1900
Map Collection is cataloged 50%
Classification: LC
Formats: Cards
Available to: Public, Students, Faculty
Circulates to: Students, Faculty
Average monthly use: 5
Average annual circulation: Maps: 200;
  Books: 10000
Interlibrary loan available
Copying Facilities: Copying machine
Equipment:
  14 5-drawer cabinets
  10 vertical map cabinets
Square Footage: 710
Map Depositories: USGS (geol);
  DMA (hydro); GPO


### 417
Massachusetts Institute of Technology
Stein Club Map Room
14S-200
Cambridge, MA 02139
Tel. (617) 253-5651
Hours: 8:30–11, M–Th; 8:30–7, F;
  11–6, Sa; 1–11, Su
Responsible Person: Eaglesfield, Jean T.
Special Strengths: United States
Special Collections: Sky Survey
  Photographic plates (2000)
Employees: Full Time    Part Time
  Prof.        1            0
  Non-Prof.    0            1
Holdings:
  66000 Printed Maps
  50 Atlases
  3 Globes
  100 Books
  3 Gazetteers
  1 Serial Title
Chronological Coverage:
  100% post 1900
Available to: Public, Students, Faculty
Circulates to: Students, Faculty
Average monthly use: 50
Average annual circulation: Maps: 250;
  Books: 10
Interlibrary loan available
Copying Facilities: Copying machine,
  Photographic reproduction
Equipment:
  46 5-drawer cabinets
  Light table
Square Footage: 1546
Map Depositories: USGS (topo);
  DMA (topo)

418
Peabody Institute Library
Danvers Archival Center
15 Sylvan St.
Danvers, MA 01323
Tel. (617) 774-0554
Hours: 1–7:30, M; 9–12, 1–5, W–Th;
1–5, F
Responsible Person: Track, Richard,
Town Archivist
Special Strengths: Danvers, MA
(1830's–present)
Employees: Full Time    Part Time
Prof.            1            0
Holdings:
100 Printed Maps
500 Manuscript Maps
200 Aerial Photographs
10 Satellite Imagery
5 Atlases
2 Wall Maps
1 Raised Relief Map
Chronological Coverage: 70% pre 1900;
30% post 1900
Map collection is cataloged 3%
Formats: Cards
Preservation methods: Encapsulation,
Chartex or Fabric Mounting,
Deacidification
Available to: Public, Students
Average monthly use: 2
Copying Facilities: Copying machine,
Photographic reproduction
Equipment:
4 5-drawer cabinets

419
Museum of Our National Heritage
(Library)
33 Marrett Road
Lexington, MA 02173
Tel. (617) 861-6559
Hours: 10–4, M–F
Responsible Person: Silvestro, Dr.
Clement M., Director
Employees: Full Time    Part Time
Prof.            1            1
Holdings:
81 Printed Maps
11 Atlases
27 Books
2 Gazetteers
Chronological Coverage: 95% pre 1900;
5% post 1900
Classification: LC    Utility: RLIN
Formats: Cards
Preservation methods: Chartex or
Fabric Mounting, Deacidification,
Framed for display
Available to: Public
Average monthly use: 10
Interlibrary loan available
Collection is available to museums &
libraries
Copying Facilities: Copying machine
Equipment:

2 5-drawer cabinets
1 vertical map cabinet
Group of framed maps file
Library book type cases
Square Footage: 34

420
Pollard Memorial Library
401 Merrimack St.
Lowell, MA 10852
Tel. (617) 454-8821
Hours: 9–9, M; 9–5:30, T–F
Responsible Person: Hickey, Walter V.,
Special Collections
Special Strengths: Lowell, MA (Real
Estate), New England
Employees: Full Time    Part Time
Prof.            1            0
Holdings:
250 Printed Maps
5 Atlases
Chronological Coverage: 40% pre 1900;
60% post 1900
Preservation methods: Encapsulation
Available to: Public, Students, Faculty
Average monthly use: 25
Copying Facilities: Copying machine,
Microform
Equipment:
1 5-drawer cabinet
Map Depositories: USGS (topo)

421
University of Lowell–South Campus
O'Leary Library
Lowell, MA 02854
Tel. (617) 452-5000
Hours: 8–11, M–F
Responsible Person: Callahan, John,
Reference Librarian
Special Strengths: New England
Holdings:
500 Printed Maps
30 Atlases
1 Globe
5 Wall Maps
2 Gazetteers
Chronological Coverage:
100% post 1900
Available to: Public, Students, Faculty
Average monthly use: 10
Copying Facilities: Copying machine
Equipment:
2 5-drawer cabinets
1 vertical map cabinet
Map Depositories: USGS (topo);
DMA (topo); GPO

422
Tufts University
Wessell Library
Government Publications, Microforms
& Maps Department
Medford, MA 02155

Tel. (617) 628-5000
Hours: 9–10, M–F; 9–5, Sa; 10–10, Su;
Summer 9–5, M–F
Responsible Person: Heisser, David C. R.,
Documents Librarian
Special Strengths: United States
Employees: Full Time    Part Time
Prof.            2            0
Non-Prof.        1            1
Holdings:
99000 Printed Maps
Chronological Coverage: 5% pre 1900;
95% post 1900
Available to: Public, Students, Faculty
Circulates to: Students, Faculty
Average monthly use: 2122
Average annual circulation: Maps: 100
Equipment:
45 5-drawer cabinets
5 standard filing cabinets
Square Footage: 950
Map Depositories: USGS (topo);
USGS (geol); GPO

423
Merrimack Valley Textile Museum,
Library
800 Massachusetts Ave.
North Andover, MA 01845
Tel. (617) 686-0191
Hours: 10–4, T–F
Responsible Person: Sheriden, Chaire,
Librarian
Special Strengths: New England
(1840–1920, textile mfg. towns,
atlases/town plans), New England
1860–1920, textile mfg. towns, bird's
eye views), New England (1860–1900,
Mill towns & sites, surveyors' plans)
Special Collections: 1100 survey maps
of textile & other factory sites,
published for fire insurance purposes,
New England & New York State,
1870–1900
Employees: Full Time    Part Time
Prof.            1            2
Non-Prof.        2            0
Holdings:
1350 Printed Maps
135 Manuscript Maps
25 Aerial Photographs
70 Atlases
10 Wall Maps
6 Books
6 Gazetteers
Chronological Coverage: 75% pre 1900;
25% post 1900
Map collection is cataloged 80%
Classification: Local
Formats: Cards
Preservation methods: Encapsulation,
Deacidification
Available to: Public, Students, Faculty
Average monthly use: 5
Copying Facilities: Copying machine,
Photographic reproduction

Equipment:
  6 5-drawer cabinets
  5 atlas cases
  8 shelves
Square Footage: 55


424
Southeastern Massachusetts University
  Library
North Dartmouth, MA 02790
Tel. (617) 999-8679
Hours: 8:30–11, M–F; 9:30–5, Sa;
  2–9:30, Su
Responsible Person: Gibbs, Paige,
  Associate Reference Librarian
Special Strengths: United States
  (Nautical Charts), Massachusetts
Employees: Full Time    Part Time
  Prof.        0             1
  Non-Prof.    0             2
Holdings:
  6085 Printed Maps
   116 Atlases
     7 Books
     3 Gazetteers
Chronological Coverage: 2% pre 1900;
  98% post 1900
Available to: Public, Students, Faculty
Circulates to: Students, Faculty
Average monthly use: 150
Average annual circulation: Maps: 40;
  Books: 10
Interlibrary loan available
  Special Collections
Equipment:
  32 5-drawer cabinets
  1 vertical file cabinet
  Light table
Square Footage: 567
Map Depositories: USGS (topo);
  USGS (geol); DMA (topo); DMA
  (aero); DMA (hydro); GPO;
  NOS; NOAA


425
Forbes Library
20 West St.
Northampton, MA 01060
Tel. (413) 584-8399
Hours: 9–9, M–Th; 9–5, Sa
Responsible Person: Bisaillon,
  Blaise, Director
Special Strengths: Northampton
  (18th–19th cent.), Hampshire County
  (18th–19th cent.), Massachusetts
  (18th–19th cent.)
Employees: Full Time    Part Time
  Prof.        1             0
Holdings:
  1215 Printed Maps
    75 Atlases
     1 Globe
     7 Wall Maps
     4 Raised Relief Maps
     6 Books

  10 Gazetteers
   2 Serial Titles
Chronological Coverage: 50% pre 1900;
  50% post 1900
Map collection is cataloged 85%
Classification: Cutter   Utility: OCLC
Formats: Cards
Preservation methods: Chartex or
  Fabric Mounting, Edging,
  Deacidification
Available to: Public
Average monthly use: 30
Copying Facilities: Copying machine
Equipment:
  6 5-drawer cabinets
Map Depositories: USGS (topo)


426
Smith College Map Library
Department of Geology
Burton Hall
Northampton, MA 01063
Tel. (413) 584-2700
Hours: 8–4, M–F
Responsible Person: Newton, Robert M.
Special Strengths: United States
Employees: Full Time    Part Time
  Non-Prof.    0             3
Holdings:
  75000 Printed Maps
    500 Manuscript Maps
     50 Wall Maps
     25 Raised Relief Maps
    200 Gazetteers
Chronological Coverage: 1% pre 1900;
  99% post 1900
Available to: Public, Students, Faculty
Circulates to: Students, Faculty
Average monthly use: 10
Average annual circulation: Maps: 200
Copying Facilities: Copying machine
Equipment:
  32 5-drawer cabinets
  10 18-drawer cabinets
   5 11-drawer cabinets
Square Footage: 1000
Map Depositories: USGS (topo);
  USGS (geol)


427
Essex Institute
James Duncan Phillips Library
Salem, MA 01970
Tel. (617) 744-3390
Hours: 9–4:30, M–F
Responsible Person: Ritchie, Mary M.,
  Assistant Librarian
Special Strengths: Essex County, MA
  (19th cent.), New England (19th cent.),
  U.S. (19th cent.)
Employees: Full Time    Part Time
  Prof.        0             2
  Non-Prof.    0             1
Holdings:
  1200 Printed Maps

  150 Manuscript Maps
  150 Atlases
  150 Wall Maps
   20 Books
   20 Gazetteers
Chronological Coverage: 90% pre 1900;
  10% post 1900
Classification: Dewey
Formats: Cards
Preservation methods: Encapsulation,
  Deacidification
Available to: Public
Average monthly use: 5
Copying Facilities: Copying machine
Equipment:
  5 5-drawer cabinets
  Regular shelves


428
Peabody Museum of Salem
Phillips Library
East India Square
Salem, MA 01970
Tel. (617) 745-1876
Hours: 10–4:30, M–F
Responsible Person: Trinkaus-Randall,
  Gregor, Librarian
Special Strengths: Globes (19th cent.),
  World (17th–20th cent., Nautical
  Charts)
Special Collections: Nautical Charts
Employees: Full Time    Part Time
  Non-Prof.    0             1
Holdings:
  5200 Printed Maps
    25 Manuscript Maps
   150 Atlases
    12 Globes
    65 Books
     2 Gazetteers
     6 Serial Titles
Chronological Coverage: 90% pre 1900;
  10% post 1900
Map collection is cataloged 90%
Formats: Cards
Available to: Public
Average monthly use: 1
Copying Facilities: Copying machine,
  Photographic reproduction
Equipment:
  22 5-drawer cabinets
Square Footage: 144


429
Salem State College Library
352 Lafayette St.
Salem, MA 01970
Tel. (617) 745-0556
Hours: 9–4, M–F
Responsible Person: Macnutt, Glenn
Special Strengths: United States
Employees: Full Time    Part Time
  Prof.        0             1
  Non-Prof.    0             1
Holdings:

71000 Printed Maps
Chronological Coverage:
  100% post 1900
Available to: Public
Average monthly use: 30
Copying Facilities: Copying machine
Equipment:
  18 5-drawer cabinets
Square Footage: 800
Map Depositories: USGS (topo);
  USGS (geol)


### 430

Mount Holyoke College
Geology Map Room
Clapp Laboratory, Room 303
South Hadley, MA 01075
Tel. (413) 538-2134
Hours: By appointment
Responsible Person: Davis, P. Tom,
  Assistant Professor
Special Strengths: United States
Employees: Full Time    Part Time
Non-Prof.      0           5
Holdings:
  50000 Printed Maps
    500 Aerial Photographs
     50 Wall Maps
Chronological Coverage: 1% pre 1900;
  99% post 1900
Available to: Public, Students, Faculty
Circulates to: Students, Faculty
Average monthly use: 10
Average annual circulation: Maps: 100
Copying Facilities: Copying machine,
  Photographic reproduction
Equipment:
  3 5-drawer cabinets
  2 vertical map cabinets
  7 file cabinets
  4-drawer files
  Stereoscopes, Dark room
Square Footage: 450
Map Depositories: USGS (topo);
  USGS (geol)


### 431

City Library
220 State Street
Springfield, MA 01103
Tel. (413) 739-3871
Hours: 9-9, M-Th; 9-5, F, Sa
Responsible Person: Wilson, Reginald
Special Strengths: Springfield, New
  England, United States
Special Collections: Springfield
  Central Inc.–Maps & Renderings
Employees: Full Time    Part Time
Prof.        12           0
Non-Prof.     2           0
Holdings:
  1000 Printed Maps
     7 Manuscript Maps
    30 Atlases
     1 Globe

   10 Wall Maps
    5 Raised Relief Maps
    5 Microforms
    2 Gazetteers
Chronological Coverage: 5% pre 1900;
  95% post 1900
Map collection is cataloged 95%
Classification: Dewey
Formats: Cards
Preservation methods: Encapsulation,
  Chartex or Fabric Mounting,
  Deacidification
Available to: Public
Circulates to: Public
Interlibrary loan available
Copying Facilities: Copying machine
Equipment:
  1 vertical map cabinet
  Stack shelves
Map Depositories: USGS (topo);
  USGS (geol); GPO


### 432

Watertown Free Public Library
123 Main St.
Watertown, MA 02172
Tel. (617) 924-5390
Hours: 9-5, M, F, Sa; 1-9, T, Th
Responsible Person: Mack, Forrest
Special Strengths: Watertown, MA
  (1830–present)
Employees: Full Time    Part Time
Prof.         0           1
Holdings:
  800 Printed Maps
   30 Manuscript Maps
   50 Aerial Photographs
   40 Atlases
    2 Globes
   10 Wall Maps
    1 Microform
    2 Gazetteers
Chronological Coverage: 20% pre 1900;
  80% post 1900
Map collection is cataloged 40%
Classification: LC   Utility: OCLC
Formats: Cards
Preservation methods: Encapsulation,
  Deacidification
Available to: Public
Average monthly use: 50
Copying Facilities: Copying machine,
  Microform
Equipment:
  2 5-drawer cabinets
  1 vertical map cabinet
  Hangers
Square Footage: 60


### 433

Babson College
Great Map Museum
Wellesley, MA 02157
Tel. (617) 235-7158
Hours: 10-5, Daily

Responsible Person: Smith, Dirk,
  Curator
Special Collections: Largest relief
  model of U.S. in the world (60'x35')
  set on a curve with natural vegetation
  colors, as if seeing U.S. from 700 miles
  in space
Employees: Full Time    Part Time
Prof.         1           0
Non-Prof.     0           4
Holdings:
  50 Printed Maps
   3 Globes
  12 Wall Maps
   4 Raised Relief Maps
Chronological Coverage: 90% pre 1900;
  10% post 1900
Available to: Public, Students, Faculty
Equipment:
  1 vertical map cabinet


### 434

Wellesley College
Geology Department
Science Center
Wellesley, MA 02181
Tel. (617) 235-0320
Hours: By appointment
Responsible Person: Gordon, Martha
Employees: Full Time    Part Time
Non-Prof.     0           2
Holdings:
  8700 Printed Maps
Chronological Coverage:
  100% post 1900
Available to: Public, Students, Faculty
Average monthly use: 10
Copying Facilities: Copying machine
Equipment:
  58 5-drawer cabinets
   2 vertical map cabinets
  Open shelves
Square Footage: 800
Map Depositories: USGS (topo);
  USGS (geol); DMA (topo); DMA
  (aero)


### 435

Williams College
Department of Geology
Williamstown, MA 01267
Tel. (413) 597-2221
Hours: 9-4, M-F
Employees: Full Time    Part Time
Non-Prof.     0           1
Holdings:
  50000 Printed Maps
      5 Atlases
      2 Globes
     35 Wall Maps
     20 Raised Relief Maps
      5 Gazetteers
Chronological Coverage:
  100% post 1900
Available to: Students, Faculty

Interlibrary loan available
Copying Facilities: Copying machine
Equipment:
  8 5-drawer cabinets
  367 other flat drawers
Square Footage: 450
Map Depositories: USGS (topo);
  USGS (geol); Canada (geol)

### 436
Woods Hole Oceanographic Institution
Data Library, McLean Laboratory
Quissett Campus
Woods Hole, MA 02543
Tel. (617) 548-1400
Hours: 8–5, M–F
Responsible Person: Dunkle, William M.
Special Strengths: World Oceans,
  Coastal Land Regions, Historical
  Charts & Maps for the New England
  Region
Employees: Full Time   Part Time
  Prof.     2        0
  Non-Prof.  0       1
Holdings:
  50000 Printed Maps
    200 Manuscript Maps
    500 Aerial Photographs
    100 Satellite Imagery
   1000 Atlases
      3 Globes
     30 Wall Maps
     75 Raised Relief Maps
    100 Microforms
   1000 Computer Tapes
    100 Books
     30 Gazetteers
     50 Serial Titles
Chronological Coverage: 5% pre 1900;
  95% post 1900
Map collection is cataloged 90%
Classification: AGS
Formats: Cards
Preservation methods: Encapsulation
Available to: Public, Students, Faculty
Circulates to: Students, Faculty
Average monthly use: 60
Average annual circulation:
  Maps: 2000; Books: 600
Copying Facilities: Copying machine,
  Microform, Photographic reproduction,
  Ozalid
Equipment:
  60 5-drawer cabinets
  100 vertical map cabinets
  Special shelves for some charts
  Standard 35mm & Microfiche Viewers
Square Footage: 5000
Map Depositories: USGS (topo);
  USGS (geol); DMA (topo); DMA
  (aero); DMA (hydro); NOS; NOAA;
  Canada (topo); Canada (geol)

### 437
American Antiquarian Society

185 Salisbury St.
Worcester, MA 01609
Tel. (617) 755-5221
Hours: 9–5, M–F
Responsible Person: Bumgardner,
  Georgia B.
Special Strengths: New England,
  Massachusetts, Worcester, MA
Employees: Full Time   Part Time
  Non-Prof.   0       1
Holdings:
  10000 Printed Maps
    100 Manuscript Maps
    450 Atlases
      4 Globes
    200 Books
    150 Gazetteers
      7 Serial Titles
Preservation methods: Deacidification
Available to: Public, Faculty
Average monthly use: 5
Copying Facilities: Copying machine,
  Microform, Photographic reproduction
  Photostat
Equipment:
  6 5-drawer cabinets
  15 7-drawer cabinets

### 438
Clark University
Guy H. Burnham Map & Aerial
  Photograph Library
Worcester, MA 01610
Tel. (617) 793-7322
Hours: 8:45–4:45, M–F
Responsible Person: Johnson, Jenny,
  Map & Geography Librarian
Special Strengths: New England,
  Africa, Central America
Special Collections: William Libbey
  Slide Collection (a collection of
  14,000 turn-of-the-century glass
  lantern slides)
Employees: Full Time   Part Time
  Prof.     0        1
  Non-Prof.  0       6
Holdings:
  139000 Printed Maps
    7300 Aerial Photographs
      30 Satellite Imagery
     525 Atlases
      11 Globes
     160 Wall Maps
      45 Raised Relief Maps
      35 Microforms
     200 Books
     225 Gazetteers
      47 Serial Titles
Chronological Coverage: 15% pre 1900;
  85% post 1900
Map collection is cataloged 15%
Classification: LC    Utility: OCLC
Formats: Cards, Online
Preservation methods: Encapsulation
Available to: Public, Students, Faculty
Circulates to: Public, Students, Faculty

Average monthly use: 140
Average annual circulation: Maps: 980;
  Books: 150; Aerial Photographs: 38
Interlibrary loan available
  Except atlases, reference books, wall
  maps, aerial photos
Copying Facilities: Copying machine,
  Photograph reproduction
Equipment:
  133 5-drawer cabinets
  12 vertical file cabinets
  Light table, Stereoscopes,
  Pantograph, magnifiers
Square Footage: 6300
Map Depositories: USGS (topo);
  USGS (geol); DMA (topo); US
  Forest Service

## Michigan
### 439
Albion College
Stockwell Memorial Library
602 E. Cass St.
Albion, MI 49224
Tel. (517) 629-5511
Hours: 8–11, M–F; 9–12, Sa; 1–12, Su
Responsible Person: Kenz, William G.
Special Strengths: Michigan
Employees: Full Time   Part Time
  Prof.     0        1
  Non-Prof.  0       2
Holdings:
  2000 Printed Maps
    30 Atlases
     1 Wall Map
    20 Books
    11 Gazetteers
Chronological Coverage:
  100% post 1900
Map collection is cataloged 5%
Classification: LC    Utility: OCLC
Formats: Cards
Available to: Public, Students, Faculty
Average monthly use: 10
Interlibrary loan available
  Photocopy only
Copying Facilities: Copying machine
Equipment:
  2 5-drawer cabinets
  1 vertical map cabinet
Square Footage: 800
Map Depositories: USGS (topo);
  USGS (geol); DMA (topo); GPO

### 440
Grand Valley State College
Zumberge Library
Allendale, MI 49401
Tel. (616) 895-7611
Responsible Person: Beasecker, Robert
Special Strengths: United States,
  Michigan
Employees: Full Time   Part Time
  Prof.     1        0
  Non-Prof.  0       1

Holdings:
46400 Printed Maps
3 Microforms
Chronological Coverage:
100% post 1900
Available to: Public, Students, Faculty
Copying Facilities: Copying machine,
Tracing table
Equipment:
24 5-drawer cabinets
2 4-drawer file cabinets
Square Footage: 100
Map Depositories: USGS (topo); NOS

441
Alma College Library
Map & Atlas Area
Alma, MI 48801
Tel. (517) 463-7227
Hours: 8–11, M–Th; 8–9, F; 9–9, Sa;
1–11, Su
Responsible Person: Dollard, Peter,
Library Director
Special Strengths: Michigan, United
States
Employees: Full Time     Part Time
Prof.            0              4
Non-Prof.      0             17
Holdings:
1600 Printed Maps
83 Atlases
Chronological Coverage: 5% pre 1900;
95% post 1900
Classification: LC
Formats: Cards
Available to: Public, Students, Faculty
Circulates to: Public, Students, Faculty
Interlibrary loan available
Copying Facilities: Copying machine
Equipment:
1 5-drawer cabinet
1 vertical map cabinet
1 6-drawer unit
1 20-drawer map case
Square Footage: 40
Map Depositories: USGS (topo)

442
Michigan Historical Collections
University of Michigan
Bentley Historical Library
1150 Beal Ave.
Ann Arbor, MI 48109-2113
Tel. (313) 764-3482
Hours: 8:30–5, M–F; 9–12:30, Sa
(May–Sept.)
Responsible Person: Coombs, Leonard A.
Special Strengths: Michigan, Great
Lakes
Employees: Full Time     Part Time
Prof.            0              1
Holdings:
2000 Printed Maps
1500 Manuscript Maps

100 Aerial Photographs
225 Atlases
5 Microforms
20 Books
10 Gazetteers
Chronological Coverage: 75% pre 1900;
25% post 1900
Classification: Local
Formats: Cards
Preservation methods: Encapsulation,
Lamination, Deacidification
Available to: Public, Students, Faculty
Average monthly use: 25
Copying Facilities: Copying machine,
Microform, Photographic reproduction,
Photostat
Equipment:
12 5-drawer cabinets

443
University at Michigan
Hatcher Graduate Library, Map Room
Ann Arbor, MI 48109
Tel. (313) 764-0407
Hours: 1–5, M–F; 6:30–9:30, M–F
(school year)
Responsible Person: Bergen, Kathleen
Special Collections: 7500 Lantern
Slides (Maps & Views)
Employees: Full Time     Part Time
Non-Prof.      1              4
Holdings:
260000 Printed Maps
2000 Aerial Photographs
6070 Atlases
3 Globes
50 Raised Relief Maps
Chronological Coverage: 6% pre 1900;
94% post 1900
Map collection is cataloged 100%
Classification: LC     Utility: RLIN
Formats: Cards
Preservation methods: Encapsulation,
Lamination, Chartex or Fabric
Mounting, Deacidification
Available to: Public, Students, Faculty
Average monthly use: 150
Copying Facilities: Copying machine,
Photographic reproduction
Equipment:
248 5-drawer cabinets
16 vertical map cabinets
1 light table, 1 planimeter,
1 Map-O-Graph
Square Footage: 4000
Map Depositories: USGS (topo);
USGS (geol); DMA (topo); DMA
(aero); DMA (hydro); GPO; NOS;
NOAA

444
Ferris State College
901 S. State St.
Big Rapids, MI 49307
Tel. (616) 796-0461

Responsible Person: Dickinson,
Raymond B., Documents Librarian
Special Strengths: Michigan
Special Collections: Plat Maps for
Michigan Counties, College Campus
Maps for Michigan Colleges
Employees: Full Time     Part Time
Prof.            1              0
Holdings:
3000 Printed Maps
30 Aerial Photographs
50 Atlases
2 Globes
1500 Microforms
Chronological Coverage:
100% post 1900
Map collection is cataloged 30%
Classification: Other
Preservation methods: Lamination
Available to: Public, Students, Faculty
Circulates to: Public, Students, Faculty
Average monthly use: 10
Average annual circulation: Maps: 30
Interlibrary loan available
Copying Facilities: Copying machine
Equipment:
3 5-drawer cabinets
4 filing cabinets
Square Footage: 50

445
Baldwin Public Library
300 W. Merrill
Birmingham, MI 48012
Tel. (313) 647-1700
Hours: 9:30–9, M–Th; 9:30–5:30, F, Sa
Responsible Person: Moffet, James
Special Strengths: Michigan, Oakland
County
Special Collections: Historical Atlases
of Oakland County, Michigan
Employees: Full Time     Part Time
Prof.            1              0
Non-Prof.      1              0
Holdings:
3000 Printed Maps
20 Atlases
2 Globes
8 Wall Maps
2 Gazetteers
Chronological Coverage: 5% pre 1900;
95% post 1900
Available to: Public, Students
Circulates to: Public, Students
Copying Facilities: Copying machine
Equipment:
2 vertical map cabinets
2 atlas cases
Square Footage: 20

446
Detroit Public Library
History & Travel Dept., Map Room
5201 Woodward Ave.
Detroit, MI 48202

Tel. (313) 833-1445
Special Collections: Sanborn Fire
    Insurance maps of Michigan
Employees: Full Time    Part Time
    Prof.            1              3
    Non-Prof.     0              1
Holdings:
    161318 Printed Maps
        25 Aerial Photographs
      3658 Atlases
        13 Globes
          3 Raised Relief Maps
          5 Microforms
      2170 Books
        25 Serial Titles
Chronological Coverage:  15% pre 1900;
    85% post 1900
Map collection is cataloged 90%
Classification: Dewey
Available to: Public, Students, Faculty
Average monthly use: 200
Interlibrary loan available
Copying Facilities: Copying machine,
    Microform, Photographic reproduction
Map Depositories: USGS (topo);
    USGS (geol); DMA (topo); DMA
    (aero); DMA (hydro); GPO; NOS;
    Canada (geol)


447
Wayne State University
G. Flint Purdy Library
Reference Department
Detroit, MI 48202
Tel. (313) 577-4040
Special Strengths: United States
Employees: Full Time    Part Time
    Non-Prof.     0              1
Holdings:
    42000 Printed Maps
        20 Aerial Photographs
          4 Globes
        15 Raised Relief Maps
        80 Books
          5 Gazetteers
Chronological Coverage:  5% pre 1900;
    95% post 1900
Formats: Cards
Available to: Public, Students, Faculty
Circulates to: Faculty
Average monthly use: 35
Copying Facilities: Copying machine
Equipment:
    21 5-drawer cabinets
    11 vertical map cabinets
      3 Plan files
      4 standard file cabinets
Square Footage: 1600
Map Depositories: USGS (topo);
    GPO


448
Michigan State University
Map Library
East Lansing, MI 48824

Tel. (517) 353-4593
Hours: 8–10:45, M–F, Noon–10:45,
    Sa, Su
Responsible Person: Rivera, Diana H.
Special Strengths: Michigan, United
    States, Canada, Africa, Latin America
Employees: Full Time    Part Time
    Prof.            0              1
    Non-Prof.     0              2
Holdings:
    137730 Printed Maps
      2280 Atlases
          3 Globes
        10 Wall Maps
        50 Books
      250 Gazetteers
          7 Serial Titles
Chronological Coverage:  5% pre 1900;
    95% post 1900
Classification: AGS      Utility: OCLC
Formats: Cards
Available to: Public, Students, Faculty
Circulates to: Faculty, Other
Average annual circulation:
    Maps: 5500; Books: 3000
Interlibrary loan available
    Limited
Copying Facilities: Copying machine,
    Microform, Photographic reproduction
Equipment:
    2 vertical files
Map Depositories: USGS (topo);
    DMA (topo); DMA (aero); DMA
    (hydro); GPO; Canada (topo)


449
Flint Public Library
General Reference
1026 E. Kearsley
Flint, MI 48502
Tel. (313) 232-7111
Hours: 9–9, M–Th; 9–6, F, Sa
Responsible Person: Field, Judith J.
Special Strengths: Michigan
Employees: Full Time    Part Time
    Prof.            0              7
    Non-Prof.     0             12
Holdings:
    800 Printed Maps
      50 Atlases
      15 Gazetteers
Chronological Coverage:
    100% post 1900
Available to: Public
Circulates to: Public
Equipment:
    6 5-drawer cabinets
    2 vertical map cabinets
Map Depositories: GPO


450
Michigan Technological University
Map Library
Government Documents Department
Houghton, MI 49931

Tel. (906) 487-2599
Responsible Person: Hawthorne,
    June, Head
Special Strengths: United States
Special Collections: USBM mine maps
    of Michigan
Holdings:
    98000 Printed Maps
      150 Atlases
Chronological Coverage:
    100% post 1900
Available to: Public, Students, Faculty
Copying Facilities: Photographic
    reproduction
Map Depositories: USGS (topo);
    USGS (geol); DMA (topo); GPO


451
Kalamazoo Public Library
315 S. Rose St.
Kalamazoo, MI 49007-5270
Tel. (616) 342-9837
Hours: 9–9, M–F; 9–6, Sa; 1–5, Su
    (except July & August)
Special Strengths: United States
    (major cities)
Employees: Full Time    Part Time
    Prof.            1              0
    Non-Prof.     1              0
Holdings:
    600 Printed Maps
        1 Satellite Imagery
      65 Atlases
        2 Wall Maps
        4 Gazetteers
Chronological Coverage:
    100% post 1900
Available to: Public, Students
Copying Facilities: Photographic
    reproduction
Equipment:
    12-drawer map case
Map Depositories: USGS (topo)


452
Western Michigan University
Map Library, Waldo Library
Kalamazoo, MI 49008
Tel. (616) 383-5952
Hours: 8–11:30, M–Th; 8–6, F; 9–6, Sa;
    12–11:30, Su
Responsible Person: McDonnell,
    Michael, Reference Librarian
Special Collections: United States
    Soil Surveys
Employees: Full Time    Part Time
    Prof.            0              1
    Non-Prof.     0             10
Holdings:
    165000 Printed Maps
      200 Atlases
Chronological Coverage:  2% pre 1900;
    98% post 1900
Available to: Public, Students, Faculty

Average monthly use: 150
Copying Facilities: Copying machine
Equipment:
  4 5-drawer cabinets
  2 vertical map cabinets
Map Depositories: USGS (topo);
  USGS (geol); Canada (geol);
  State & Foreign Geological Survey
  Map series

### 453
Western Michigan University
Physical Sciences Library
Kalamazoo, MI 49008
Tel. (616) 383-4943
Hours: 8–11:30, M–F
Responsible Person: Sichel, Beatrice,
  Head
Special Strengths: United States
Special Collections: United States
  geology
Employees: Full Time    Part Time
  Prof.          1              0
  Non-Prof.   3              0
Holdings:
  2397 Printed Maps
Chronological Coverage:
  100% post 1900
Map collection is cataloged 100%
Classification: LC
Formats: Cards
Available to: Public, Students, Faculty
Circulates to: Public, Students, Faculty
Copying Facilities: Copying machine
Equipment:
  9 5-drawer cabinets
Map Depositories: USGS (geol)

### 454
Michigan Department of State
State Archives, Michigan History Div.
3405 N. Logan
Lansing, MI 48918
Tel. (517) 373-0512
Hours: 8–12, 1–5, M–F
Responsible Person: Barnett, LeRoy,
  Reference Archivist
Special Strengths: Michigan (19th–
  20th cent.)
Special Collections: Rural Property
  Inventories of Northern Michigan,
  1935–1940
Employees: Full Time    Part Time
  Prof.          0              1
Holdings:
  300 Printed Maps
  500000 Manuscript Maps
  30 Atlases
  50 Wall Maps
  5 Microforms
  2 Books
  1 Gazetteer
Chronological Coverage: 10% pre 1900;
  90% post 1900
Classification: In-house

Formats: Cards
Available to: Public
Average monthly use: 4
Copying Facilities: Copying machine,
  Photographic reproduction
Equipment:
  20 5-drawer cabinets
  53 Solander horizontal files
Square Footage: 250

### 455
Macomb County Library
16480 Hall Road
Mt. Clemens, MI 48044
Tel. (313) 469-5300
Hours: 9–9, M, W; 1–9, T, Th; 9–5,
  F, Sa; 1–5, Su (Sept–May)
Responsible Person: Burgeson, Diane
Special Strengths: Michigan
Employees: Full Time    Part Time
  Prof.          1              0
Holdings:
  1266 Printed Maps
    2 Aerial Photographs
  225 Atlases
    4 Wall Maps
    4 Books
  25 Gazetteers
Chronological Coverage: 1% pre 1900;
  99% post 1900
Map collection is cataloged 100%
Classification: Dewey   Utility: OCLC
Formats: Cards, COM, Online
Preservation methods: Lamination
Available to: Public
Circulates to: Public
Interlibrary loan available
  Reference atlases & books do not
  circulate
Copying Facilities: Copying machine,
  Microform
Equipment:
  4 5-drawer cabinets
  2 vertical map cabinets
Map Depositories: GPO

### 456
Central Michigan University
Charles V. Park Library
Map Collection
Mt. Pleasant, MI 48859
Tel. (517) 774-3414
Hours: 8–Midnight, M–Th; 8–10, F;
  9–10, Sa; Noon–Midnight, Su
Responsible Person: Shirley, David B.,
  Map Librarian
Employees: Full Time    Part Time
  Prof.          0              1
  Non-Prof.   0              1
Holdings:
  25839 Printed Maps
    4 Satellite Imagery
  71 Atlases
    3 Wall Maps
  26 Books

  139 Gazetteers
    3 Serial Titles
Chronological Coverage:
  100% post 1900
Map collection is cataloged 100%
Classification: LC      Utility: OCLC
Formats: Cards
Preservation methods: Lamination,
  Edging
Available to: Public, Students, Faculty
Average monthly use: 70
Copying Facilities: Copying machine,
  Microform, Photographic reproduction
Equipment:
  50 5-drawer cabinets
  8 file cabinets
Square Footage: 1800
Map Depositories: USGS (topo);
  USGS (geol); DMA (topo); GPO

### 457
Avon Township Public Library
Adult Services
210 W. University Dr.
Rochester, MI 48063
Tel. (313) 651-1426
Hours: 9:30–9, M–Th; 9:30–5:30, F;
  9:30–5, Sa; 1–5, Su
Responsible Person: Satterthwarte,
  Diane
Special Strengths: United States,
  Oakland County & Rochester area
Employees: Full Time    Part Time
  Prof.          0              1
  Non-Prof.   0              1
Holdings:
  1500 Printed Maps
  35 Atlases
    3 Wall Maps
  20 Books
    3 Gazetteers
Chronological Coverage: 2% pre 1900;
  98% post 1900
Available to: Public
Circulates to: Public
Copying Facilities: Copying machine
Equipment:
  1 vertical map cabinet
  Atlas case

### 458
Eastern Michigan University
Center of Educational Resources
Map Library
Ypsilanti, MI 48197
Tel. (313) 487-3191
Hours: 8:30–5, M–F; 6–9:30, M–Th
Responsible Person: Hansen, Joanne
Employees: Full Time    Part Time
  Prof.          0              4
  Non-Prof.   0              1
Holdings:
  37705 Printed maps
  2000 Aerial Photographs
  1000 Atlases

2 Globes
8 Raised Relief Maps
300 Books
5 Serial Titles
Chronological Coverage: 3% pre 1900;
97% post 1900
Classification: Local
Available to: Public, Students, Faculty
Average monthly use: 350
Copying Facilities: Copying machine
Map Depositories: USGS (topo);
USGS (geol); DMA (topo); NOS

## Minnesota

459
Bemidji State University
Geography Department Map Library
Roy P. Meyer Memorial Map Library
Bemidji, MN 56601
Tel. (218) 755-2000
Hours: 8–4:30, M–F
Responsible Person: Smith, Peter C.
Special Strengths: Minnesota
Employees: Full Time    Part Time
Non-Prof.       0              1
Holdings:
22000 Printed Maps
3 Manuscript Maps
104000 Aerial Photographs
6 Satellite Imagery
30 Atlases
5 Globes
95 Wall Maps
260 Raised Relief Maps
13 Books
2 Gazetteers
Chronological Coverage: 1% pre 1900;
99% post 1900
Map collection is cataloged 95%
Formats: Cards
Available to: Public, Students, Faculty
Circulates to: Public, Students, Faculty
Average monthly use: 70
Copying Facilities: Copying machine,
Photographic reproduction
Equipment:
41 5-drawer cabinets
2 vertical map cabinets
10 vertical filing cabinets
Numonics digitizer
Kelsh stereo plotter
Square Footage: 1100
Map Depositories: USGS (topo);
USGS (geol); DMA (topo); DMA
(aero)

460
St. John's University
Alcuin Library
Collegeville, MN 56321
Tel. (612) 363-2117
Hours: 8–Midnight, M–F
Responsible Person: Carol P. Johnson
Special Strengths: Illinois

Employees: Full Time    Part Time
Prof.           0              1
Non-Prof.       0              1
Holdings:
14000 Printed Maps
50 Atlases
100 Gazetteers
Chronological Coverage: 1% pre 1900;
99% post 1900
Map collection is cataloged 95%
Classification: SuDocs   Utility: OCLC
Formats: Cards
Available to: Public, Students, Faculty
Average monthly use: 5
Copying Facilities: Copying machine,
Microform
Equipment:
14 5-drawer cabinets
5 vertical map cabinets
Square Footage: 462
Map Depositories: DMA (topo); GPO

461
Duluth Public Library
520 W. Superior St.
Duluth, MN 55802
Tel. (218) 723-3802
Responsible Person: O'Neil, Denise,
Federal Documents Librarian
Special Strengths: United States,
Northeastern Minnesota, Great
Lakes (Nautical)
Employees: Full Time    Part Time
Prof.           1              0
Non-Prof.       0              2
Chronological Coverage: 1% pre 1900;
99% post 1900
Map collection is cataloged 1%
Classification: Dewey
Formats: COM, Online
Available to: Public
Circulates to: Public
Average monthly use: 75
Average annual circulation: Maps: 50
Interlibrary loan available
Copying Facilities: Copying machine
Equipment: 16 5-drawer cabinets
Map Depositories: USGS (topo); GPO

462
University of Minnesota, Duluth
Map Library
Dept. of Sociology-Anthropology-
Geography
Duluth, MN 55812
Tel. (218) 726-7293
Responsible Person: Levine, Gordon L.
Special Strengths: Upper Midwest,
Minnesota, Duluth, Canada
Employees: Full Time    Part Time
Prof.           0              1
Non-Prof.       0              1
Holdings:
30000 Printed Maps
1000 Aerial Photographs

40 Atlases
400 Wall Maps
50 Raised Relief Maps
100 Books
50 Gazetteers
Chronological Coverage: 1% pre 1900;
99% post 1900
Map collection is cataloged 20%
Classification: LC
Formats: Cards
Available to: Public, Students, Faculty
Circulates to: Public, Students, Faculty
Average monthly use: 100
Average annual circulation: Maps: 400
Copying Facilities: Copying machine,
Photographic reproduction
Equipment:
34 5-drawer cabinets
Square Footage: 400
Map Depositories: USGS (topo);
NOAA

463
Dakota County Library System
1340 Wescott Rd.
Eagan, MN
Tel. (612) 452-9600
Responsible Person: Ahlgren, Dorothy
Special Strengths: Minnesota, Dakota
County
Holdings:
2225 Printed Maps
40 Atlases
4 Globes
3 Wall Maps
3 Books
10 Gazetteers
Chronological Coverage: 8% pre 1900;
92% post 1900
Map collection is cataloged 10%
Classification: Local
Formats: Cards
Preservation methods: Lamination
Available to: Public, Students
Circulates to: Public, Students
Average monthly use: 25
Average annual circulation: Maps: 600;
Books: 200
Copying Facilities: Copying machine
Equipment:
1 5-drawer cabinet
1 vertical map cabinet
3 atlas cases
1 atlas range
Square Footage: 84

464
Mankato State University
Memorial Library, Map Library
M.S.U. Box 19
Mankato, MN 56001
Tel. (507) 389-6201
Hours: 7:45–11:45, M–Th; 7:45–4:30, F;
10–5, Sa; 1–11:45, Su
Responsible Person: Amling, Russell K.,

Map Librarian
Special Strengths: Minnesota, United
States
Employees: Full Time    Part Time
  Prof.       1           0
  Non-Prof.   0           8
Holdings:
  74736 Printed Maps
  18000 Aerial Photographs
    685 Atlases
      7 Globes
     30 Wall Maps
     50 Raised Relief Maps
     20 Microforms
    100 Gazetteers
Chronological Coverage: 10% pre 1900;
  90% post 1900
Map collection is cataloged 100%
Classification: LC    Utility: OCLC
Formats: Online
Available to: Public, Students, Faculty
Circulates to: Public, Students, Faculty
Interlibrary loan available
Copying Facilities: Copying machine,
  Microform, Photographic reproduction
Equipment:
  17 5-drawer cabinets
  1 vertical map cabinet
  4-drawer file cabinet
  3 oversize (5-drawer cabinets)
Square Footage: 2730
Map Depositories: USGS (topo);
  USGS (geol); DMA (topo); DMA
  (hydro); GPO; NOS; NOAA


### 465
Far Eastern Research Library
5812 Knox Avenue South
Minneapolis, MN 55419
Tel. (612) 926-6887
Hours: 9–5, M–F
Responsible Person: Cavanaugh,
  Dr. Jerome, Director
Special Strengths: China (1910–
  present), Taiwan (1920–1945)
Employees: Full Time    Part Time
  Prof.       3           0
  Non-Prof.   1           1
Holdings:
  150 Printed Maps
   10 Manuscript Maps
   15 Atlases
    5 Wall Maps
   35 Books
  120 Gazetteers
    5 Serial Titles
Chronological Coverage: 2% pre 1900;
  98% post 1900
Map collection is cataloged 100%
Classification: Local
Formats: Cards, Online
Preservation methods: Chartex or
  Fabric Mounting
Available to: Public
Average monthly use: 15
Copying Facilities: Copying machine

Square Footage: 10


### 466
Minneapolis Public Library
History Department
300 Nicollet Mall
Minneapolis, MN 55401
Tel. (612) 372-6500
Hours: 9–9, M–Th; 9–5:30, F, Sa
Responsible Person: Bruce, Robert,
  Department Head
Employees: Full Time    Part Time
  Prof.       1           0
Available to: Public
Circulates to: Public
Copying Facilities: Copying machine
Equipment:
  25 5-drawer cabinets
   3 vertical map cabinets
Square Footage: 146
Map Depositories: USGS (topo)


### 467
University of Minnesota
James Ford Bell Library
472 Wilson Library
309 19th Avenue South
Minneapolis, MN 55455
Tel. (612) 373-2888
Hours: 8–5, M–F
Responsible Person: Parker, John,
  Curator
Special Strengths: World (1400–1800,
  Geographical exploration)
Employees: Full Time    Part Time
  Prof.       2           0
  Non-Prof.   0           2
Holdings:
  200 Printed Maps
  100 Manuscript Maps
  150 Atlases
Map collection is cataloged 90%
Classification: Dewey    Utility: RLIN
Formats: Cards, Printed Cat.
Available to: Public, Students, Faculty
Copying Facilities: Copying machine,
  Microform, Photographic reproduction
Equipment:
  Specially built map cabinets


### 468
University of Minnesota
Wilson Library, Map Library
309 19th Ave. S.
Minneapolis, MN 55455
Tel. (612) 373-2825
Hours: 9–5, M, T, Th, F; 1–8, W
Responsible Person: Treude, Mai,
  Map Librarian
Special Strengths: Minnesota (Aerial
  photographs, 1930–present)
Employees: Full Time    Part Time
  Prof.       1           0
  Non-Prof.   1           1

Holdings:
  214377 Printed Maps
  154519 Aerial Photographs
       3 Globes
      25 Raised Relief Maps
    3930 Books
      33 Serial Titles
Chronological Coverage: 20% pre 1900;
  80% post 1900
Map collection is cataloged 100%
Classification: LC
Formats: Cards
Preservation methods: Encapsulation,
  Lamination
Available to: Public, Students, Faculty
Circulates to: Faculty
Average annual circulation:
  All combined: 4200
Interlibrary loan available
  Maps do not circulate
Copying Facilities: Copying machine
Equipment:
  172 5-drawer cabinets
  Stereoscopes
Square Footage: 8916
Map Depositories: USGS (topo);
  DMA (topo); DMA (aero); DMA
  (hydro); NOS; Canada (topo)


### 469
University of Minnesota
Winchell Library of Geology
204 Pillsbury Hall
310 Pillsbury Drive SE
Minneapolis, MN 55455
Tel. (612) 373-4052
Hours: 8–4:30, M–F
Responsible Person: Dvorzak, Marie,
  Head, Geology Library
Special Strengths: Minnesota
  (Geology), United States (Geology)
Employees: Full Time    Part Time
  Prof.       0           1
  Non-Prof.   0           1
Holdings:
  75000 Printed Maps
     35 Atlases
Chronological Coverage: 2% pre 1900;
  98% post 1900
Available to: Public, Students,
  Faculty
Circulates to: Students, Faculty
Average monthly use: 20
Average annual circulation:
  Maps: 1000
Interlibrary loan available
  Special permission only
Copying Facilities: Copying
  machine
Equipment:
  15 5-drawer cabinets
  Lane specimen cabinets
  ('rock' cabinets)
Map Depositories: USGS (geol)

**470**
Moorhead State University
Livingston Lord Library
Documents Department
Moorhead, MN 56560
Tel. (218) 236-2922
Hours: 7:45–10:45, M–Th; 7:45–4:15, F;
 10–4:45, Sa; 1–10:45, Su
Responsible Person: Weikert, Karen Ann
Special Strengths: Minnesota
Employees: Full Time    Part Time
 Prof.        0          1
 Non-Prof.    0          2
Holdings:
 4000 Printed Maps
  180 Atlases
    2 Globes
    1 Raised Relief Map
 1200 Books
   30 Gazetteers
   10 Serial Titles
Chronological Coverage: 100% post 1900
Map collection is cataloged 5%
Classification: LC    Utility: OCLC
Formats: Cards, Online
Available to: Public, Students, Faculty
Circulates to: Students, Faculty
Average monthly use: 20
Average annual circulation: Maps: 35
Copying Facilities: Copying machine
Equipment:
 3 5-drawer cabinets
 1 3-drawer file cabinet
Square Footage: 92
Map Depositories: GPO

**471**
Carleton College
Geology Map Library
Northfield, MN 55057
Tel. (507) 663-4401
Hours: 1:30–4:30, M–F
Responsible Person: Vick, Timothy
Special Strengths: United States
 (Geology)
Employees: Full Time    Part Time
 Non-Prof.    0          5
Holdings:
 200000 Printed Maps
     2 Atlases
   200 Wall Maps
    20 Raised Relief Maps
Chronological Coverage: 5% pre 1900;
 95% post 1900
Preservation methods: Chartex or
 Fabric Mounting
Available to: Public, Students, Faculty
Circulates to: Students, Faculty
Average monthly use: 20
Average annual circulation: Maps: 100
Equipment:
 75 5-drawer cabinets
 Zoom transfer scope, stereo viewers
Square Footage: 1500
Map Depositories: USGS (topo);
 USGS (geol); DMA (topo)

**472**
St. Cloud State University
Learning Resources
St. Cloud, MN 56301
Tel. (612) 255-2022
Hours: 7:45–11, M–Th; 7:45–4, F;
 9–5, Sa; 2–10, Su
Responsible Person: Busse,
 Laurence R., Government Documents
Special Strengths: Central States
Employees: Full Time    Part Time
 Prof.        1          1
 Non-Prof.    1         10
Holdings:
 80000 Printed Maps
  2000 Aerial Photographs
   250 Atlases
   250 Wall Maps
Chronological Coverage: 10% pre 1900;
 90% post 1900
Available to: Public, Students, Faculty
Circulates to: Public, Students, Faculty
Average monthly use: 500
Average annual circulation:
 Maps: 6000
Copying Facilities: Copying machine,
 Microform
Equipment:
 20 5-drawer cabinets
Square Footage: 3000
Map Depositories: USGS (topo);
 USGS (geol); GPO

**473**
Macalester College Library
1600 Grand Ave.
St. Paul, MN 55105
Tel. (612) 696-6546
Responsible Person: Feldick, Peggy R.,
 Reference Librarian
Special Strengths: Minnesota
Employees: Full Time    Part Time
 Prof.        1          1
 Non-Prof.    0          4
Holdings:
 990 Printed Maps
 200 Atlases
   1 Globe
   2 Wall Maps
  50 Books
  10 Gazetteers
   2 Serial Titles
Chronological Coverage:
 100% post 1900
Available to: Public, Students, Faculty
Circulates to: Students, Faculty
Average monthly use: 5
Average annual circulation: Maps: 25
Copying Facilities: Copying machine
Equipment:
 3 5-drawer cabinets
 1 vertical map cabinet
Square Footage: 75

**474**
Minnesota Historical Society

Map Library
690 Cedar St.
St. Paul, MN 55101
Tel. (612) 296-4543
Hours: 8:30–5, M–Sa
Responsible Person: Walstrom, Jon L.,
 Map Librarian
Employees: Full Time    Part Time
 Prof.        1          0
Special Strengths: Minnesota
 (1800–present)
Holdings:
 30000 Printed Maps
    50 Aerial Photographs
  1150 Atlases
   160 Wall Maps
   140 Books
    10 Gazetteers
Chronological Coverage: 50% pre 1900;
 50% post 1900
Preservation methods: Encapsulation,
 Deacidification
Available to: Public, Students
Average monthly use: 65
Copying Facilities: Copying machine,
 Photographic reproduction
Equipment:
 6 5-drawer cabinets
 6 10-drawer units
 8 geol. sample cases
Square Footage: 750
Map Depositories: USGS (topo)

**475**
Ramsey County Public Library
2180 N. Hamline Ave.
St. Paul, MN 55113
Tel. (612) 631-0494
Hours: 9:30–9, M–Sa; 1–5, Su
Responsible Person: Cartwright, John
Special Strengths: Ramsey Co., MN
 (1910, Atlas, History), Minnesota
 (Land Use)
Employees: Full Time    Part Time
 Prof.        6          9
Holdings:
 500 Printed Maps
  30 Atlases
   1 Globe
   1 Wall Map
   1 Gazetteer
Chronological Coverage:
 100% post 1900
Map collection is cataloged 20%
Classification: Dewey    Utility: OCLC
Formats: COM
Available to: Public, Students, Faculty
Circulates to: Public, Students, Faculty
Average monthly use: 50
Average annual circulation:
 Maps: 1000; Books: 50
Interlibrary loan available
 Materials less than one year old are
 not available
Copying Facilities: Copying machine,
 Microform

Equipment:
Atlas stand
Square Footage: 30


476
U.S. Army Corps of Engineers
Map Files
1135 U.S. Post Office & Custom House
St. Paul, MN 55101
Tel. (612) 725-7992
Hours: 8–4:30, M, T, Th
Responsible Person: Hageman,
Marianne D.
Special Strengths: Minnesota (Aerial
photography, Area river systems),
Wisconsin (Aerial photography, Area
river systems), North Dakota (Aerial
photography, Area river systems)
Employees: Full Time    Part Time
Prof.            0            1
Non-Prof.        0            2
Holdings:
37000 Printed Maps
1096 Aerial Photographs
30000 Microforms
Chronological Coverage: 4% pre 1900;
96% post 1900
Preservation methods: Edging
Available to: Public
Average monthly use: 30
Average annual circulation: Maps: 400;
Aerial Photographs: 500
Interlibrary loan available
Special permission only
Copying Facilities: Copying machine,
Microform
Equipment:
36 5-drawer cabinets
56 vertical map cabinets
1 3-drawer map cabinet
Square Footage: 142


477
University of Minnesota
Minnesota Geological Survey Library
2642 University Ave.
St. Paul, MN 55114-1057
Tel. (612) 373-3372
Hours: 8–4:30, M–F
Responsible Person: Swanson, Lynn,
Senior Library Assistant
Special Strengths: Minnesota, Geology
Employees: Full Time    Part Time
Prof.            1            0
Holdings:
3000 Printed Maps
30 Manuscript Maps
3000 Aerial Photographs
22 Atlases
10 Books
5 Gazetteers
30 Serial Titles
Chronological Coverage: 5% pre 1900;
95% post 1900
Map collection is cataloged 60%

Classification: In-House System
Formats: Cards
Available to: Public, Students, Faculty
Average monthly use: 40
Average annual circulation: Maps: 250;
Books: 5; Aerial Photographs: 50
Copying Facilities: Copying machine
Equipment:
6 5-drawer cabinets
1 vertical map cabinet
shelves
Square Footage: 15
Map Depositories: USGS (topo);
USGS (geol)


478
Gustavus Adolphus College
Department of Geography
St. Peter, MN 56082
Tel. (507) 931-7312
Hours: 8–5, M–F
Responsible Person: Moline, Robert
Special Strengths: Upper Midwest,
Southwest California, Western Europe
Employees: Full Time    Part Time
Prof.            0            1
Non-Prof.        0            1
Holdings:
50000 Printed Maps
4000 Aerial Photographs
Chronological Coverage: 5% pre 1900;
95% post 1900
Available to: Public, Students, Faculty
Circulates to: Public, Students, Faculty
Average annual circulation: Maps: 100
Equipment:
30 5-drawer cabinets
Square Footage: 750
Map Depositories: USGS (topo);
USGS (geol); DMA (topo); DMA
(aero); DMA (hydro)


**Mississippi**
479
Mississippi University for Women
Fant Memorial Library
Columbus, MS 39701
Tel. (601) 329-4750
Hours: 8–10, M–Th; 8–6, F; 10:30–4:30,
Sa; 2–10, Su
Responsible Person: Payne, Dr. David L.,
Director of Library
Special Strengths: United States
Holdings:
5634 Printed Maps
34 Manuscript Maps
27 Satellite Imagery
1 Globe
11462 Microforms
42 Books
3 Gazetteers
1 Serial Title
Chronological Coverage: 3% pre 1900;
97% post 1900
Classification: Dewey

Formats: Cards
Available to: Public
Average monthly use: 20
Copying Facilities: Copying machine,
Microform
Equipment:
2 5-drawer cabinets
2 atlas cases
Map Depositories: GPO


480
University of Southern Mississippi
Cook Memorial Library
Box 5053
Hattiesburg, MS 39401
Tel. (601) 266-4252
Hours: 8–11, M–F
Responsible Person: Odom, Mac
Employees: Full Time    Part Time
Prof.            0            1
Non-Prof.        0            1
Holdings:
1300 Printed Maps
5 Atlases
4 Wall Maps
3 Gazetteers
Chronological Coverage:
100% post 1900
Available to: Public, Students, Faculty
Circulates to: Public, Students, Faculty
Average monthly use: 1
Average annual circulation: Maps: 5
Interlibrary loan available
Copying Facilities: Copying machine
Equipment:
36 5-drawer cabinets
4 filing cabinets
Map Depositories: DMA (topo); DMA
(aero); DMA (hydro)


481
Jackson Metropolitan Library
Reference Department
301 N. State St.
Jackson, MS 39201
Tel. (601) 944-1120
Hours: 8:30–9, M–Th; 8:30–6, F;
8:30–5, Sa
Responsible Person: Landon, Rosemary
Special Strengths: United States (street
maps), Foreign cities (street maps),
Mississippi
Employees: Full Time    Part Time
Prof.            4            0
Non-Prof.        1            2
Holdings:
650 Printed Maps
25 Atlases
1 Globe
4 Wall Maps
50 Books
5 Gazetteers
Chronological Coverage: 10% pre 1900;
90% post 1900
Map collection is cataloged 75%

Classification: Dewey
Formats: Cards
Available to: Public, Students
Average monthly use: 10
Copying Facilities: Copying machine
Equipment:
   2 5-drawer cabinets
Square Footage: 8

### 482
Mississippi Bureau of Geology Library
2525 N. West St.
P. O. Box 5348
Jackson, MS 39216
Tel. (601) 354-6228
Hours: 8–5, M–F
Responsible Person: Wooley, Carolyn,
   Librarian
Special Strengths: Mississippi, Alabama,
   Tennessee, Louisiana, Arkansas

| Employees: | Full Time | Part Time |
|---|---|---|
| Prof. | 1 | 0 |
| Non-Prof. | 0 | 1 |

Holdings:
  13000 Printed Maps
    950 Atlases
      5 Globes
      3 Raised Relief Maps
    300 Books
    275 Gazetteers
      5 Serial Titles
Chronological Coverage: 5% pre 1900;
   95% post 1900
Map collection is cataloged 95%
Classification: LC
Formats: Cards
Preservation methods: Encapsulation
Available to: Public, Students, Faculty
Circulates to: Public, Students, Faculty
Average monthly use: 75
Average annual circulation: Maps: 125;
   Books: 2500
Interlibrary loan available
Copying Facilities: Copying machine,
   Microform
Equipment:
   118 5-drawer cabinets
   2 vertical map cabinets
   Light table
Square Footage: 2280
Map Depositories: USGS (topo);
   USGS (geol); DMA (topo); GPO;
   NOS; NOAA

### 483
Mississippi Department of Archives
   & History
Special Collections Section
P. O. Box 571
Jackson, MS 39205
Tel. (601) 359-1424
Hours: 8–5, M–F; 8:30–4:30, Sa
Responsible Person: McBee,
   Martha W.
Special Strengths: Mississippi

| Employees: | Full Time | Part Time |
|---|---|---|
| Prof. | 1 | 0 |

Holdings:
  7000 Printed Maps
  2500 Aerial Photographs
     9 Microforms
Chronological Coverage: 45% pre 1900;
   55% post 1900
Map collection is cataloged 100%
Formats: Cards
Preservation methods: Encapsulation,
   Lamination, Deacidification
Available to: Public
Average monthly use: 30
Copying Facilities: Copying machine,
   Microform, Photographic reproduction
Equipment:
   15 5-drawer cabinets
Square Footage: 225

### 484
Mississippi Research & Development
   Center
Information Services Division
3325 Ridgewood Rd.
Jackson, MS 39235
Tel. (601) 982-6314
Hours: 8–5, M–F
Responsible Person: Moore, Marilyn
Special Strengths: Mississippi
Holdings:
  3000 Printed Maps
   500 Aerial Photographs
    23 Satellite Imagery
     2 Atlases
    10 Wall Maps
   300 Microforms
     5 Computer Tapes
    10 Books
Chronological Coverage:
   100% post 1900
Map collection is cataloged 1%
Classification: LC   Utility: OCLC
Formats: Online
Available to: Public, Students, Faculty
Circulates to: Faculty
Average monthly use: 10
Average annual circulation: Maps: 300
Copying Facilities: Copying machine,
   Microfiche printer
Equipment:
   6 5-drawer cabinets
   Microfiche printer, Digitizer, Color
   graphics terminal, Matrix camera

### 485
Mississippi State University
Mitchell Memorial Library
P. O. Drawer 5408
Mississippi State, MS 39762
Tel. (601) 325-3060
Hours: 8–11:30, M–Th; 8–5, F; 9–6, Sa;
   2–11:30, Su
Responsible Person: Downey, Mary
Special Strengths: United States

| Employees: | Full Time | Part Time |
|---|---|---|
| Prof. | 3 | 1 |
| Non-Prof. | 0 | 13 |

Holdings:
  12000 Printed Maps
    200 Aerial Photographs
    400 Atlases
      6 Globes
      7 Gazetteers
Chronological Coverage: 10% pre 1900;
   90% post 1900
Map collection is cataloged 5%
Classification: LC   Utility: OCLC
Formats: Cards
Available to: Public, Students, Faculty
Circulates to: Public, Students, Faculty
Average monthly use: 25
Interlibrary loan available
Copying Facilities: Copying machine
Equipment: 54 5-drawer cabinets
Square Footage: 2000
Map Depositories: USGS (topo)

### 486
University of Mississippi
Williams Library
University, MS 38677
Tel. (601) 232-7091
Hours: 8–8, M; 8–4:30, T–F; 10–12, Sa
Responsible Person: Mills, D. Annie E.
Special Strengths: United States,
   World

| Employees: | Full Time | Part Time |
|---|---|---|
| Prof. | 1 | 0 |
| Non-Prof. | 2 | 11 |

Holdings:
  45000 Printed Maps
Chronological Coverage: 25% pre 1900;
   75% post 1900
Classification: SuDocs
Formats: Cards
Available to: Public, Students, Faculty
Interlibrary loan available
Copying Facilities: Copying machine
Equipment:
   40 5-drawer cabinets
Square Footage: 562
Map Depositories: USGS (topo);
   DMA (aero)

## Missouri
### 487
Southeast Missouri State University
Kent Library, Map Collection
Cape Girardeay, MO 63701
Tel. (314) 651-2243
Hours: 8–5, M–F
Responsible Person: Willingham,
   J. Robert
Special Strengths: Missouri &
   adjacent states

| Employees: | Full Time | Part Time |
|---|---|---|
| Prof. | 1 | 0 |

Holdings:
  1000 Printed Maps

75 Aerial Photographs
200 Atlases
1 Globe
Chronological Coverage:
100% post 1900
Available to: Public, Students, Faculty
Average monthly use: 20
Copying Facilities: Copying machine
Equipment:
3 5-drawer cabinets
1 vertical map cabinet
Square Footage: 50
Map Depositories: USGS (topo);
GPO; NOAA

488
State Historical Society of Missouri
Map Collection
1020 Lowry
Columbia, MO 65201
Tel. (314) 882-7083
Hours: 8–4:30, M–F
Responsible Person: Brownlee,
Dr. Richard S.
Special Strengths: Louisiana Purchase,
Missouri (1700–present)
Special Collections: Missouri County
Atlases, Aerial Photographs for
Missouri Counties
Employees: Full Time     Part Time
Prof.              0                 5
Holdings:
1600 Printed Maps
35000 Aerial Photographs
430 Atlases
26 Microforms
45 Books
10 Gazetteers
Chronological Coverage: 60% pre 1900;
40% post 1900
Map collection is cataloged 80%
Formats: Cards
Preservation methods: Lamination,
Chartex or Fabric Mounting,
Deacidification
Available to: Public, Students, Faculty
Average monthly use: 5
Copying Facilities: Copying machine,
Photographic reproduction
Equipment:
20 5-drawer cabinets
8 vertical map cabinets
6 oversize map cabinets
Square Footage: 270
Map Depositories: USGS (topo);
USGS (geol); State of Missouri
government agencies

489
University of Missouri
Geography, History & Philosophy Library
3833 Ellis Library
Columbia, MO 65201-5149
Tel. (314) 882-6824
Hours: 8–5, M–Th; 8–4, F

Responsible Person: Edwards, Anne G.
Special Collections: Sanborn Fire
Insurance Maps of Missouri
Employees: Full Time     Part Time
Prof.              1                 0
Non-Prof.      0                 1
Holdings:
32000 Printed Maps
1 Globe
1 Wall Map
Chronological Coverage: 5% pre 1900;
95% post 1900
Available to: Public, Students, Faculty
Circulates to: Students, Faculty
Average monthly use: 10
Average annual circulation: Maps: 25
Copying Facilities: Copying machine
Equipment:
35 5-drawer cabinets
Hanging folders
Map Depositories: USGS (topo);
DMA (topo)

490
University of Missouri
Geology Library
201 Geology Building
Columbia, MO 65211
Tel. (314) 882-4860
Hours: 8–12, 1–5, M–F
Responsible Person: Heidlage, Robert
Employees: Full Time     Part Time
Prof.              0                 1
Holdings:
100000 Printed Maps
2500 Aerial Photographs
Chronological Coverage: 5% pre 1900;
95% post 1900
Available to: Public, Students, Faculty
Circulates to: Public, Students, Faculty
Interlibrary loan available
Depending on physical condition
Copying Facilities: Copying machine,
Microform
Equipment:
60 5-drawer cabinets
10 vertical map cabinets
Large cabinets
Square Footage: 780
Map Depositories: USGS (topo);
USGS (geol); Canada (geol); Geol.
Surveys of S. Africa, India, Gr. Britain,
Australia

491
University of Missouri, Columbia
Dept. of Geography, Map Collection
10 Stewart Hall
Columbia, MO 65211
Tel. (314) 882-8370
Hours: 8–5, M–F
Responsible Person: Schroeder,
Walter A., Chairman
Special Strengths: Missouri
Holdings:

4200 Printed Maps
200 Aerial Photographs
166 Atlases
4 Globes
480 Wall Maps
20 Raised Relief Maps
1382 Microforms
20 Books
80 Gazetteers
Chronological Coverage: 2% pre 1900;
98% post 1900
Map collection is cataloged 95%
Formats: Cards
Available to: Public, Students, Faculty
Circulates to: Public, Students, Faculty
Average monthly use: 120
Average annual circulation: Maps: 100
Copying Facilities: Copying machine,
Photographic reproduction
Equipment: 13 5-drawer cabinets

492
Kansas City Public Library
Map Room
311 E. 12th St.
Kansas City, MO 64106
Tel. (816) 221-2685
Hours: 9–5, M–Sa
Responsible Person: Fuhri, Fiona,
Reference Coordinator
Special Strengths: Missouri
Employees: Full Time     Part Time
Prof.              0                 1
Non-Prof.      0                 2
Holdings:
62000 Printed Maps
1000 Atlases
50 Books
Chronological Coverage: 2% pre 1900;
98% post 1900
Map collection is cataloged 2%
Classification: SuDocs
Formats: Cards
Available to: Public
Average monthly use: 20
Interlibrary loan available
USGS topos not loaned
Copying Facilities: Copying machine
Equipment:
18 5-drawer cabinets
32 11-drawer cabinets
Square Footage: 675
Map Depositories: USGS (topo);
GPO; Missouri State Agencies

493
Linda Hall Library
5109 Cherry St.
Kansas City, MO 64110
Tel. (816) 363-4600
Hours: 9–8:30, M; 9–5, T–F; 10–4, Sa
Responsible Person: Cox, Bruce B.,
Documents Librarian
Special Strengths: Unites States
(Geology)

Employees: Full Time    Part Time
Prof.       1        0
Non-Prof.    0        1
Holdings:
   62000 Printed Maps
     200 Atlases
Chronological Coverage:
   100% post 1900
Map collection is cataloged 1%
Classification: LC
Formats: Cards
Available to: Public, Students, Faculty
Average monthly use: 30
Average annual circulation: Maps:
   590
Copying Facilities: Copying machine,
   Microform, Photographic reproduction
Equipment:
   72 5-drawer cabinets
   13 file cabinets
Square Footage: 2358
Map Depositories: USGS (topo);
   USGS (geol)

### 494

University of Missouri, Kansas City
Dept. of Geosciences, Map Library
300 Geology-Physics Building
5100 Rockhill Rd.
Kansas City, MO 64110
Tel. (816) 276-1334
Hours: 9–5, M–F
Responsible Person: Gaebel, Dr. Ed.,
   Chairman
Special Strengths: Mid Continent
Employees: Full Time    Part Time
Non-Prof.    0        1
Holdings:
   500 Printed Maps
   300 Aerial Photographs
    20 Satellite Imagery
    10 Atlases
    20 Globes
   125 Wall Maps
    20 Raised Relief Maps
    20 Books
Chronological Coverage:
   100% post 1900
Map collection is cataloged 80%
Formats: Cards
Available to: Students, Faculty
Average monthly use: 50
Copying Facilities: Copying machine
Equipment:
   8 5-drawer cabinets
   Wall maps rack

### 495

Missouri Dept. of Natural Resources
Division of Geology & Land Survey
Geological Library
1111 Fairgrounds Rd.
Rolla, MO 65401
Tel. (314) 364-1752
Hours: 8–5, M–F

Responsible Person: Cussins, Marcia,
   Librarian
Special Strengths: Missouri
Special Collections: Unpublished aerial
   geologic maps, Structural maps,
   Economic geology maps, Unpublished
   cave maps; Rare, out-of-print geologic
   maps published by the Missouri
   Geological Survey
Employees: Full Time    Part Time
Prof.       1        1
Holdings:
    1000 Printed Maps
   12000 Manuscript Maps
   75000 Aerial Photographs
     220 Atlases
    3100 Microforms
      30 Serial Titles
Chronological Coverage: 5% pre 1900;
   95% post 1900
Map collection is cataloged 90%
Classification: Dewey
Formats: Cards, Computer Printout
   lists
Available to: Public, Students, Faculty
Average monthly use: 130
Interlibrary loan available
   Except archival originals
Copying Facilities: Microform,
   Photocopy
Equipment:
   10 5-drawer cabinets
Map Depositories: USGS (topo);
   USGS (geol)

### 496

Missouri Dept. of Natural Resources
Division of Geology & Land Survey
Land Survey Repository
111 Fairgrounds Rd.
Rolla MO 65401
Tel. (314) 364-1752
Hours: 8–5, M–F
Responsible Person: McDermott,
   Jack C., Chief of Land Records
Special Strengths: Missouri (Land
   Survey maps, notes & related
   information)
Special Collections: Collection of
   Unpublished Survey Information
Employees: Full Time    Part Time
Prof.       2        0
Non-Prof.    0        2
Holdings:
     150 Printed Maps
     150 Manuscript Maps
    1000 Aerial Photographs
     215 Atlases
   250000 Microforms
     200 Books
       6 Serial Titles
Chronological Coverage: 25% pre 1900;
   75% post 1900
Map collection is cataloged 75%
Formats: Cards, Printed Catalog
Preservation methods: Microfilm

Available to: Public, Students
Circulates to: Public, Students
Average annual circulation:
   Maps: 1000
Interlibrary loan available
Copying Facilities: Copying machine,
   Microform
Equipment:
   12 5-drawer cabinets
   File cabinets
   Vertical files

### 497

University of Missouri, Rolla
Curtis Laws Wilson Library
Rolla, MO 65401-0249
Tel. (314) 341-4007
Hours: 8–Midnight, M–Th; 8–10, F;
   8–5, Sa; 2–Midnight, Su
Responsible Person: Parson, Kathy
Special Strengths: Missouri
Employees: Full Time    Part Time
Prof.       0        1
Non-Prof.    0        1
Holdings:
   1500 Printed Maps
    100 Aerial Photographs
    100 Atlases
      1 Globe
     50 Books
     10 Gazetteers
Chronological Coverage: 25% pre 1900;
   75% post 1900
Available to: Public, Students, Faculty
Circulates to: Public, Students, Faculty
Average monthly use: 10
Average annual circulation: Maps: 30;
   Books: 60
Interlibrary loan available
Copying Facilities: Copying machine
Equipment:
   21 5-drawer cabinets
   14 vertical map cabinets
    3 atlas cases
Square Footage: 900
Map Depositories: GPO

### 498

University of Missouri, Rolla
Dept. of Geology & Geophysics Library
Rolla, MO 65401
Tel. (314) 341-4669
Hours: 8–5, M–F
Responsible Person: Spreng, A. C.
Special Strengths: United States,
   Missouri (1900–present)
Employees: Full Time    Part Time
Prof.       0        1
Non-Prof.    0        1
Holdings:
   5000 Printed Maps
     50 Manuscript Maps
   2000 Aerial Photographs
     10 Satellite Imagery
     10 Atlases

2 Globes
10 Wall Maps
10 Raised Relief Maps
1 Gazetteer
Chronological Coverage:
100% post 1900
Preservation methods: Chartex or
Fabric Mounting
Available to: Public, Students, Faculty
Circulates to: Students, Faculty
Average monthly use: 50
Average annual circulation: Maps: 500
Interlibrary loan available
No photos
Copying Facilities: Copying machine
Equipment:
8 5-drawer cabinets
Enlarger/Reducer
Map Depositories: USGS (topo);
USGS (geol); DMA (topo); DMA
(hydro); NOAA


499
Southwest Missouri State University
Dept. of Geosciences, Map Library
901 S. National
Springfield, MO 65804-0089
Tel. (417) 836-5800
Hours: 8–5, M–F
Responsible Person: Rafferty,
Milton, Head
Special Strengths: Ozark Region
Employees: Full Time    Part Time
Non-Prof.    0         4
Holdings:
2000 Printed Maps
5000 Aerial Photographs
12 Atlases
24 Globes
250 Wall Maps
5 Raised Relief Maps
Chronological Coverage:
100% post 1900
Available to: Students, Faculty
Circulates to: Faculty
Copying Facilities: Copying machine
Equipment:
2 5-drawer cabinets
10 wall cabinets
Square Footage: 900


500
Southwest Missouri State University
Duane G. Meyer Library
Map Collection
Box 175
Springfield, MO 65804-0095
Tel. (417) 836-5104
Hours: 8–10, M–Th; 8–5, F; 10–3, Sa;
2–7, Su
Responsible Person: Coombs, James A.,
Map Librarian
Special Strengths: Ozark Plateau
(1820–present), United States

Employees: Full Time    Part Time
Prof.        1          0
Non-Prof.    0          6
Holdings:
86357 Printed Maps
33022 Aerial Photographs
1 Satellite Imagery
776 Atlases
2 Globes
113 Wall Maps
6 Raised Relief Maps
154 Microforms
129 Books
3 Gazetteers
18 Serial Titles
Chronological Coverage: 8% pre 1900;
92% post 1900
Map collection is cataloged 10%
Classification: LC    Utility: OCLC
Formats: Cards
Available to: Public, Students, Faculty
Circulates to: Public, Students, Faculty
Average monthly use: 125
Average annual circulation: Maps: 1000;
Books: 100; Aerial Photographs: 15
Interlibrary loan available
Copying Facilities: Copying machine,
Microform
Equipment:
60 5-drawer cabinets
7 3-drawer, 9 4-drawer cabinets
Vertical file cabinets
4 light tables, 1 enlarging/reducing
projector, 1 stereoscope
Square Footage: 2237
Map Depositories: USGS (topo);
USGS (geol); DMA (topo); DMA
(aero); DMA (hydro); GPO: MO State
Agencies' Maps


501
Missouri Botanical Garden Library
P. O. Box 299
St. Louis, MO 63166
Tel. (314) 577-5155
Hours: 8:30–5, M–F
Responsible Person: Mykrantz,
Barbara L., Archivist
Special Strengths: Africa (16th cent.–
present), South America, Central
America, Tropical areas of World
(Vegetation & Soil), United States
Surveys of West–19th cent.
Employees: Full Time    Part Time
Prof.        0          1
Holdings:
6773 Printed Maps
4 Manuscript Maps
2 Satellite Imagery
378 Atlases
1866 Books
225 Gazetteers
2 Serial Titles
Chronological Coverage: 10% pre 1900;
90% post 1900
Map collection is cataloged 1%
Classification: LC    Utility: OCLC

Formats: Cards
Preservation methods: Encapsulation,
Neutral paper
Available to: Public, Students, Faculty
Average monthly use: 25
Interlibrary loan available
Copying Facilities: Copying machine
Equipment:
11 5-drawer cabinets
Square Footage: 98


502
Missouri Historical Society
Research Library & Archives
Jefferson Memorial Building/Forest Park
St. Louis, MO 63112-1099
Tel. (314) 361-1424
Hours: 9:30–4:45, T–F
Responsible Person: Klein, Stephanie A.,
Librarian-Archivist
Special Strengths: St. Louis (1800–
present), Missouri (1800–present)
Holdings:
2000 Printed Maps
200 Atlases
Chronological Coverage: 50% pre 1900;
50% post 1900
Map collection is cataloged 75%
Classification: Local
Formats: Cards
Available to: Public
Copying Facilities: Copying machine,
Photographic reproduction
Equipment:
9 5-drawer cabinets


503
Saint Louis University
Pius XII Memorial Library
3655 W. Pine Blvd.
St. Louis, MO 63108
Tel. (314) 658-3105
Hours: 8:30–5, M–F
Responsible Person: Waide, John
Special Strengths: Missouri (1925–
present), Illinois (1925–present)
Employees: Full Time    Part Time
Prof.        1          0
Non-Prof.    0          3
Holdings:
100000 Printed Maps
500 Aerial Photographs
100 Satellite Imagery
200 Atlases
3 Wall Maps
100 Books
Chronological Coverage:
100% post 1900
Available to: Public, Students, Faculty
Average monthly use: 20
Copying Facilities: Copying machine
Equipment:
10 vertical map cabinets
15 10-drawer cabinets
22 5-drawer cabinets

Square Footage: 1000
Map Depositories: USGS (topo);
    USGS (geol); GPO


### 504
St. Louis Public Library
1301 Olive St.
St. Louis, MO 63103
Tel. (314) 241-2288
Hours: 9–9, M; 9–5, T–Sa
Responsible Person: Molobeck, Noel C.
Special Strengths: United States,
    Missouri, St. Louis
Employees: Full Time    Part Time
    Prof.        3            0
Holdings:
    106678 Printed Maps
    325 Atlases
    1 Globe
    525 Books
    5 Serial Titles
Chronological Coverage: 25% pre 1900;
    75% post 1900
Map collection is cataloged 50%
Classification: LC
Formats: Cards
Preservation methods: Lamination,
    Chartex or Fabric Mounting
Available to: Public
Circulates to: Public, Students, Faculty
Average monthly use: 110
Average annual circulation: Maps: 25
Copying Facilities: Photographic
    reproduction, Photostat
Equipment:
    6 vertical map cabinets
    13 vertical cases
    58 flat folio cases
    216 metal drawers
Square Footage: 2530
Map Depositories: USGS (topo);
    USGS (geol); DMA (topo); DMA
    (aero); DMA (hydro)


### 505
Washington University
Earth & Planetary Sciences Library
St. Louis, MO 63130
Tel. (314) 889-5406
Hours: 8:30–9, M–Th; 9–Noon, Sa
Responsible Person: Hartwig, Deborah
Special Strengths: Missouri (Geology)
Employees: Full Time    Part Time
    Prof.        1            0
    Non-Prof.    1            2
Holdings:
    76716 Printed Maps
    45 Atlases
    1 Globe
    3 Raised Relief Maps
Chronological Coverage:
    100% post 1900
Available to: Public, Students, Faculty
Average monthly use: 150
Copying Facilities: Copying machine

Equipment:
    63 5-drawer cabinets
    7 vertical map cabinets
    8 vertical file cabinets
    22 oversize map drawers
Square Footage: 700
Map Depositories: USGS (topo);
    USGS (geol); DMA (topo); DMA
    (aero); DMA (hydro); GPO


### 506
Washington University
Regional Planetary Image Facility
Campus Box 1169
St. Louis, MO 63130
Tel. (314) 889-5679
Hours: 8:30–4:30, M–F
Responsible Person: Weiss, Betty,
    Librarian
Special Strengths: Earth, Moon, Planets
    and their satellites
Employees: Full Time    Part Time
    Prof.        6            0
    Non-Prof.    0            9
Holdings:
    1500 Printed Maps
    5000 Aerial Photographs
    500000 Satellite Imagery
    25 Atlases
    14 Globes
    5000 Microforms
    750 Computer Tapes
Chronological Coverage:
    100% post 1900
Map collection is catlaoged 100%
Formats: Cards, Computer Printout
Available to: Public, Students, Faculty
Average monthly use: 40
Copying Facilities: Copying machine,
    Photographic reproduction
Equipment:
    12 5-drawer cabinets
    File Cabinets
    Compact Shelving
    Digitizer/Mini Computer System
    run by VAX-11/750
Map Depositories: USGS (topo);
    USGS (geol)


### 507
Central Missouri State University
Geography Dept., Map Library
Wood 4
Warrensburg, MO 64093
Tel. (816) 429-4048
Hours: 8–5, M–F
Responsible Person: Daniels, David D.
Special Strengths: Missouri, North
    America
Employees: Full Time    Part Time
    Prof.        0            1
    Non-Prof.    0            4
Holdings:
    30000 Printed Maps
    18075 Aerial Photographs

    3750 Satellite Imagery
    50 Atlases
    43 Globes
    300 Wall Maps
    30 Raised Relief Maps
    5000 Books
    30 Gazetteers
Chronological Coverage: 5% pre 1900;
    95% post 1900
Map collection is cataloged 100%
Classification: AGS
Formats: Cards
Preservation methods: Lamination,
    Chartex or Fabric Mounting, Edging
Available to: Public, Students, Faculty
Circulates to: Public, Students, Faculty
Average monthly use: 120
Copying Facilities: Copying machine,
    Photographic reproduction
Equipment:
    29 5-drawer cabinets
    8 various sized map drawers
    Stereoscopes, enlarging/reducing
    projector, light tables
Square Footage: 930
Map Depositories: DMA (topo); DMA
    (hydro)


## Montana
### 508
Eastern Montana College Library*
1500 N. 30th St.
Billings, MT 59101
Tel. (406) 657-2320
Responsible Person: Hause, Aaron,
    Documents, Serials & Maps
Map Depositories: USGS (topo); GPO


### 509
Montana State University
Roland R. Renne Library
Documents Department
Bozeman, MT 59717-0022
Tel. (406) 994-3430
Responsible Person: Stephens, Marian G.,
    Documents Librarian
Special Strengths: Montana
Holdings:
    3000 Printed Maps
    1 Globe
    2 Wall Maps
    1 Raised Relief Map
Chronological Coverage:
    100% post 1900
Formats: Cards
Preservation methods: Lamination
Available to: Public, Students, Faculty
Copying Facilities: Copying machine
Equipment:
    6 5-drawer cabinets
Square Footage: 54
Map Depositories: USGS (topo);
    USGS (geol); GPO

510
Montana State University*
Earth Sciences Dept. Map Library
Traphagen Hall, Room 7
Bozeman, MT 59715
Tel. (406) 994-3331
Responsible Person: Taylor, Robert
Holdings:
  50000 Printed Maps
Available to: Public, Students, Faculty
Map Depositories: USGS (topo);
  USGS (geol); DMA (topo)

511
Montana Tech Library
Documents Division
Butte, MT 59701
Tel. (406) 496-4286
Hours: 7:30–11:30, M–Th; 7:30–5, F;
  9–5, Sa; 12:30–11:30, Su
Responsible Person: Jolley, Kea
Special Strengths: Montana (Geology
  & Mineral Resources)
Employees: Full Time    Part Time
  Prof.          0            1
  Non-Prof.      0            3
Holdings:
  100000 Printed Maps
  25 Atlases
  2 Globes
  3 Wall Maps
  20 Raised Relief Maps
  30 Books
  30 Gazetteers
Chronological Coverage: 10% pre 1900;
  90% post 1900
Available to: Public, Students, Faculty
Circulates to: Students, Faculty
Interlibrary loan available
Copying Facilities: Copying machine,
  Microform
Equipment:
  22 5-drawer cabinets
Map Depositories: USGS (topo);
  USGS (geol); DMA (topo); DMA
  (hydro); GPO

512
Montana Dept. of Commerce
Census & Economic Information Center
1424 9th Ave.
Helena, MT 59620-0401
Tel. (406) 444-3707
Hours: 8–12, 1–5, M–F
Responsible Person: Roberts, Patricia,
  Program Manager
Special Strengths: Montana (Census,
  Land Use)
Special Collections: Montana Census
  Maps Microfiche, Mylar Masters
Holdings:
  2805 Printed Maps
  1 Atlas
  120 Microforms
Chronological Coverage:

100% post 1900
Copying Facilities: Microform, Census
  Maps for fee
Equipment:
  3 5-drawer cabinets
Square Footage: 36

513
Montana Historical Society Library
225 N. Roberts St.
Helena, MT 59620
Tel. (406) 444-2681
Hours: 8–5, M–F; 9–5, Sa
Responsible Person: Clark, Robert M.,
  Librarian
Special Strengths: Montana (1850–
  present)
Special Collections: Montana State
  Agencies, Sanborn Fire Insurance
  Maps for Montana
Employees: Full Time    Part Time
  Prof.          0            3
  Non-Prof.      0            1
Holdings:
  6000 Printed Maps
  350 Manuscript Maps
  125 Atlases
  1 Globe
  18 Wall Maps
  1 Raised Relief Map
  14 Microforms
  50 Books
  5 Gazetteers
  2 Serial Titles
Chronological Coverage: 45% pre 1900;
  55% post 1900
Map collection is cataloged 95%
Formats: Cards, Microfiche of Cards
Preservation methods: Encapsulation,
  Deacidification, Dry Cleaning
Available to: Public
Average monthly use: 50
Interlibrary loan available
  Except microfilm maps
Copying Facilities: Copying machine,
  Photographic reproduction
Equipment:
  20 5-drawer cabinets
  1 3-drawer file cabinet
  3 6-drawer wooden cabinets
  USGS Land area & slope indicator
Square Footage: 340
Map Depositories: USGS (topo);
  MT State Agencies

514
City County Library of Missoula
301 E. Main
Missoula, MT 59802
Tel. (406) 721-2665
Hours: 12–9, M–Th; 10–6, F, Sa
Responsible Person: Stevens, Vaun,
  Reference Librarian
Special Strengths: Western Montana

Employees: Full Time    Part Time
  Prof.          0            1
  Non-Prof.      0            2
Holdings:
  2000 Printed Maps
  57 Atlases
  1 Globe
  1 Wall Map
  1 Raised Relief Map
  15 Books
  1 Gazetteer
Chronological Coverage: 5% pre 1900;
  95% post 1900
Available to: Public, Students, Faculty
Circulates to: Public, Students
Average monthly use: 50
Average annual circulation: Maps: 50
Copying Facilities: Copying machine
Equipment:
  1 vertical map cabinet
  1 12-drawer cabinet
Square Footage: 30

515
University of Montana
Map Collection, Documents Division
Maureen & Mike Mansfield Library
Missoula, MT 59812
Tel. (406) 243-4564
Hours: 8–5, M–F
Responsible Person: Piquette,
  Constance M.
Special Strengths: Montana
Special Collections: Montana Historical
  Maps & the Exploration of the West;
  USGS Open-File Reports of Montana
  & Adjacent Area
Employees: Full Time    Part Time
  Prof.          1            0
  Non-Prof.      0            1
Holdings:
  83000 Printed Maps
  25 Manuscript Maps
  10 Satellite Imagery
  261 Atlases
  3 Globes
  10 Wall Maps
  10 Raised Relief Maps
  300 Microforms
  25 Books
  50 Gazetteers
Chronological Coverage: 20% pre 1900;
  80% post 1900
Map collection is cataloged 95%
Classification: LC
Formats: Cards
Preservation methods: Encapsulation,
  Chartex or Fabric Mounting
Available to: Public, Students, Faculty
Circulates to: Public, Students, Faculty
Average monthly use: 200
Average annual circulation: Maps: 150
Interlibrary loan available
Copying Facilities: Copying machine,
  Microform, Photographic reproduction
Equipment: 22 5-drawer cabinets

17 vertical map cabinets
3 wooden 10-drawer cabinets
3 4-drawer cabinets
1 light table
Square Footage: 5500
Map Depositories: USGS (topo);
  USGS (geol); DMA (topo); DMA
  (aero); DMA (hydro); GPO; MT State
  Agencies

## Nebraska

### 516
Midland Lutheran College
Geology Department
Fremont, NE 68025
Tel. (402) 721-5480
Hours: By appointment
Responsible Person: Carlson, Gary A.
Special Strengths: United States
Special Collections: Powell, Hayden &
  King 19th century surveys, USGS
  Geologic Folios
Holdings:
  5000 Printed Maps
   300 Aerial Photographs
    30 Satellite Imagery
     3 Atlases
    10 Globes
     5 Wall Maps
    20 Raised Relief Maps
    20 Books
Chronological Coverage: 5% pre 1900;
  95% post 1900
Map collection is cataloged 60%
Formats: Cards
Preservation methods: Lamination
Available to: Faculty
Circulates to: Public, Students, Faculty
Average monthly use: 2
Copying Facilities: Copying machine
Equipment:
  10 5-drawer cabinets
  Stereoscopes
Map Depositories: USGS (topo)

### 517
Kearney State College
Calvin T. Ryan Library
Kearney, NE 68849
Tel. (308) 234-8542
Hours: 7:30–11, M–Th; 7:30–5, F;
  10–5, Sa; 2–11, Su
Responsible Person: Keith, Diana J.,
  Government Documents
Special Strengths: Nebraska
Employees: Full Time    Part Time
  Non-Prof.    1          2
Holdings:
  1171 Printed Maps
     1 Satellite Imagery
    80 Atlases
    28 Wall Maps
    24 Books
    10 Gazetteers
Chronological Coverage: 1% pre 1900;

99% post 1900
Map collection is cataloged 70%
Classification: SuDocs   Utility: OCLC
Formats: Cards
Available to: Public, Students, Faculty
Circulates to: Public, Students, Faculty
Average annual circulation: Maps: 50;
  Books: 5
Interlibrary loan available
Copying Facilities: Copying machine,
  Microform
Equipment:
  3 5-drawer cabinets
  2 4-drawer cabinets
  2 atlas stands
Square Footage: 60
Map Depositories: GPO

### 518
Kearney State College
Geography Map Library
Dept. of Geography
Kearney, NE 68849
Tel. (308) 234-8356
Hours: 9–5, M–F
Responsible Person: Bennett, Gordon E.
Special Strengths: Nebraska
Special Collections: Nebraska Aerial
  Photos from 1930's
Employees: Full Time    Part Time
  Prof.        0           1
Holdings:
   9000 Printed Maps
     50 Manuscript Maps
  70000 Aerial Photographs
     50 Satellite Imagery
     50 Atlases
     20 Globes
    100 Wall Maps
    100 Raised Relief Maps
     30 Books
     10 Gazetteers
      3 Serial Titles
Chronological Coverage: 10% pre 1900;
  90% post 1900
Map collection is cataloged 30%
Formats: Cards, Index maps
Available to: Public, Students, Faculty
Circulates to: Public, Students
Average monthly use: 5
Average annual circulation: Maps: 100;
  Books: 10; Aerial Photographs: 50
Interlibrary loan available
Copying Facilities: Copying machine
Equipment:
  14 5-drawer cabinets
   2 vertical map cabinets
  11 42-drawer cabinets
  Stereo viewers, Parrallax bars,
  Scales, Protractors
Square Footage: 800

### 519
Nebraska State Historical Society
  Library

1500 R St., Box 82554
Lincoln, NE 68506
Tel. (402) 471-4750
Hours: 8–5, M–Sa
Responsible Person: Reinert, Ann,
  Library Dept. Head
Special Strengths: Nebraska (1854–
  present), United States (1810–present)
Special Collections: Sanborn Fire
  Insurance Maps of Nebraska Towns,
  State Department of Roads printed
  maps
Employees: Full Time    Part Time
  Prof.        4           0
  Non-Prof.    4           0
Holdings:
  3000 Printed Maps
    40 Manuscript Maps
   400 Atlases
    10 Books
    20 Gazetteers
Chronological Coverage: 60% pre 1900;
  40% post 1900
Map collection is cataloged 99%
Formats: Cards
Preservation methods: Encapsulation
Available to: Public, Students, Faculty
Average monthly use: 12
Copying Facilities: Copying machine,
  Photographic reproduction
Equipment:
  6 5-drawer cabinets
  1 vertical map cabinet
Square Footage: 36

### 520
University of Nebraska, Lincoln
C. Y. Thompson Library, East Campus
Lincoln, NE 68583-2802
Tel. (402) 472-2802
Responsible Person: Schreiner, Lyle
Employees: Full Time    Part Time
  Non-Prof.    1           1
Holdings:
  600 Printed Maps
   27 Atlases
    1 Globe
    4 Books
    1 Gazetteer
Chronological Coverage: 5% pre 1900;
  95% post 1900
Available to: Public, Students, Faculty
Average monthly use: 5
Interlibrary loan available
Copying Facilities: Copying machine,
  Microform
Equipment:
  2 5-drawer cabinets
  1 3-drawer map cabinet
Square Footage: 33
Map Depositories: USDA Forest
  Service; US Soil Survey Maps (50
  states)

521
University of Nebraska, Lincoln
Geology Library
303 Morrill Hall
Lincoln, NE 68588-0410
Tel. (402) 472-3628
Hours: 8–5, 7–10, M–Th; 8–5, F;
 9–12, Sa
Responsible Person: Adams, Agnes
Employees: Full Time    Part Time
 Prof.          1              0
 Non-Prof.   1              3
Holdings: 70000 Printed Maps
Chronological Coverage: 2% pre 1900;
 98% post 1900
Classification: LC    Utility: OCLC
Formats: Cards
Available to: Public, Students, Faculty
Circulates to: Public, Students, Faculty
Interlibrary loan available
Copying Facilities: Copying machine
Map Depositories: USGS (topo);
 USGS (geol)


522
University of Nebraska, Lincoln
University Archives/Special Coll. Div.
308 Love Library
Lincoln, NE 68588
Tel. (402) 472-2531
Hours: 8–5, M–F
Responsible Person: Svoboda, Joseph G.,
 Head
Holdings:
 800 Printed Maps
 100 Manuscript Maps
 100 Atlases
Chronological Coverage: 80% pre 1900;
 20% post 1900
Available to: Public, Students, Faculty
Average monthly use: 5
Copying Facilities: Copying machine,
 Microform, Photographic reproduction
Equipment:
 10 5-drawer cabinets
Square Footage: 100


523
University of Nebraska, Lincoln
University Libraries
Love Library Map Collection
Lincoln, NE 68588-0410
Tel. (402) 472-2525
Hours: 8–5, M–F
Responsible Person: Moreland, Virginia
Special Strengths: Nebraska, Kansas
Employees: Full Time    Part Time
 Prof.          0              1
 Non-Prof.   0              1
Holdings:
 30000 Printed Maps
 2 Globes
 20 Wall Maps
Chronological Coverage: 1% pre 1900;
 99% post 1900

Available to: Public, Students, Faculty
Circulates to: Students, Faculty
Interlibrary loan available
 Fragile condition do not circulate
Copying Facilities: Copying machine,
 Microform
Equipment:
 57 5-drawer cabinets
Square Footage: 1056
Map Depositories: DMA (topo); DMA
 (aero); DMA (hydro); GPO


524
Omaha Public Library
215 S. 15th St.
Omaha, NE 68102
Tel. (402) 444-4825
Hours: 9–8:30, M–F; 9–5:30, Sa
Responsible Person: Heenan, Thomas,
 History Librarian
Special Strengths: Omaha, Nebraska
Holdings:
 1800 Printed Maps
 200 Atlases
 75 Gazetteers
Chronological Coverage: 10% pre 1900;
 90% post 1900
Preservation methods: Encapsulation,
 Chartex or Fabric Mounting
Available to: Public
Copying Facilities: Copying machine
Equipment:
 1 5-drawer cabinet
 4 vertical map cabinets


525
Omaha Public Library
Business/Science/Technology
215 S. 15 St.
Omaha, NE 68102
Tel. (402) 444-4817
Hours: 9–8:30, M–F; 9–5:30, Sa
Responsible Person: Davenport, Janet,
 Documents Librarian
Special Strengths: United States
Employees: Full Time    Part Time
 Non-Prof.   0              3
Holdings:
 51250 Printed Maps
Chronological Coverage: 1% pre 1900;
 99% post 1900
Available to: Public, Students, Faculty
Average monthly use: 50
Copying Facilities: Copying machine
Equipment:
 40 5-drawer cabinets
 4 atlas stands
Square Footage: 310
Map Depositories: USGS (topo); GPO


526
University of Nebraska Libraries, Omaha
Reference Department
Omaha, NE 68182

Tel. (402) 554-2611
Hours: 7–11, M–Th; 7–6, F; 9–5, Sa;
 1–10, Su
Responsible Person: Hill, John
Special Strengths: Northern Great
 Plains
Special Collections: Afghanistan maps
 & atlases
Employees: Full Time    Part Time
 Prof.          1              0
 Non-Prof.   0              1
Holdings:
 12000 Printed Maps
 300 Atlases
 1 Globe
 6 Wall Maps
 50 Books
 25 Gazetteers
Chronological Coverage:
 100% post 1900
Map collection is cataloged 5%
Classification: LC    Utility: OCLC
Formats: Cards
Available to: Public, Students
Circulates to: Public, Students
Average monthly use: 100
Copying Facilities: Copying machine
Equipment:
 25 5-drawer cabinets
 2 vertical map cabinets
Square Footage: 200
Map Depositories: USGS (topo); GPO


527
University of Nebraska, Omaha
Department of Geography-Geology
Omaha, NE 68162
Tel. (402) 553-2726
Responsible Person: Peake, Dr. Jeffrey
Special Strengths: Upper Midwest
 (Landsat Imagery), Nebraska, Middle
 East
Holdings:
 15000 Printed Maps
 400 Aerial Photographs
 500 Satellite Imagery
 10 Atlases
 2 Globes
 200 Wall Maps
 150 Raised Relief Maps
 4 Microforms
 100 Computer Tapes
Chronological Coverage: 1% pre 1900;
 99% post 1900
Map collection is cataloged 30%
Available to: Public, Students, Faculty
Average monthly use: 5
Average annual circulation: Maps: 50;
 Aerial Photographs: 30
Interlibrary loan available
 No tapes
Equipment:
 30 5-drawer cabinets
 2 vertical map cabinets
 Light tables, 4 zoom transfer scopes
Square Footage: 1000

## Nevada

**528**
Nevada State Library
401 N. Carson St.
Capitol Complex
Carson City, NV 89710
Tel. (702) 885-5160
Hours: 8–5, M–F
Responsible Person: Andersen, Valerie
Special Strengths: Nevada, California
Holdings:
    4000 Printed Maps
    25 Atlases
    1 Globe
    20 Wall Maps
Chronological Coverage:
    100% post 1900
Available to: Public
Copying Facilities: Copying machine
Equipment:
    5 5-drawer cabinets
    1 vertical map cabinet
Map Depositories: USGS (topo);
    NV State Agency Pub.

**529**
Clark County Library
Reference Department
1401 E. Flamingo Rd.
Las Vegas, NV 89109
Tel. (702) 733-7810
Hours: 9–9, M–Th; 9–5, F, Sa; 1–5, Su
Responsible Person: Honsa, Vlasta,
    Assistant Administrator
Special Strengths: Nevada, United
    States
Employees: Full Time    Part Time
    Prof.        2            0
    Non-Prof.    1            0
Holdings:
    1870 Printed Maps
    7 Aerial Photographs
    105 Atlases
    1 Globe
    4 Wall Maps
    121 Microforms
    3 Gazetteers
Chronological Coverage: 5% pre 1900;
    95% post 1900
Preservation methods: Lamination,
    Edging
Available to: Public
Average monthly use: 200
Copying Facilities: Copying machine,
    Microform
Equipment:
    2 5-drawer cabinets
    vertical files,
    pamphlet boxes

**530**
University of Nevada
Department of Geoscience
Las Vegas, NV 89154
Tel. (702) 739-3262
Responsible Person: Weide, Dr. David L.
Special Strengths: Western United
    States
Employees: Full Time    Part Time
    Non-Prof.    0            1
Holdings:
    15000 Printed Maps
    4000 Aerial Photographs
    250 Wall Maps
    75 Raised Relief Maps
Chronological Coverage:
    100% post 1900
Available to: Public, Students, Faculty
Circulates to: Students, Faculty
Average monthly use: 30
Average annual circulation: Maps: 500
Copying Facilities: Copying machine
Equipment:
    10 5-drawer cabinets
    2 vertical map cabinets
    shelf racks
    Bausch & Lomb Stereozoom transfer
    scope
Square Footage: 600

**531**
University of Nevada, Las Vegas
James R. Dickinson Library
Documents Area
4505 Maryland Parkway
Las Vegas, NV 89154
Tel. (702) 739-3409
Hours: 8–9, M–Th; 8–5, F; 9:30–6, Sa;
    Noon–8, Su (shorter in Sum.)
Responsible Person: Brown, Alice,
    Documents Librarian
Holdings:
    4000 Printed Maps
    40 Atlases
    1 Globe
    5 Raised Relief Maps
Chronological Coverage: 5% pre 1900;
    95% post 1900
Available to: Public, Students, Faculty
Average monthly use: 200
Interlibrary loan available
Copying Facilities: Copying machine
Equipment:
    6 5-drawer cabinets
    2 vertical map cabinets
    1 4-drawer cabinet
Square Footage: 240
Map Depositories: USGS (topo);
    DMA (topo)

**532**
Nevada Bureau of Mines & Geology
Open Files Section
Room 311 SEM, University of Nevada
Reno, NV 89557-0088
Tel. (702) 784-6691
Hours: 8–4:30, M–F
Responsible Person: Weimer-McMillion,
    Becky
Special Strengths: Nevada (Geology,
Claim Maps, Underground Geology,
& Mine Workings; late 1800's to
present)
Special Collections: Nevada NCIC
    State affiliate for maps and air
    photo/imagery info.
Employees: Full Time    Part Time
    Prof.        1            0
    Non-Prof.    0            1
Holdings:
    10000 Printed Maps
    100000 Aerial Photographs
    1 Raised Relief Map
    500 Microforms
    10 Books
Chronological Coverage: 5% pre 1900;
    95% post 1900
Available to: Public
Average monthly use: 50
Copying Facilities: Copying machine,
    Microform, Dyeline
Equipment:
    17 5-drawer cabinets
    File drawers for storing air photos
    Minolta Reader/Printed (microfiche
    & film), stereo glasses
Square Footage: 1536
Map Depositories: USGS (topo);
    NOAA

**533**
Nevada Historical Society
1650 N. Virginia St.
Reno, NV 89503
Tel. (702) 789-0190
Hours: 10–5, W–Su
Responsible Person: Mortensen, Lee,
    Research Librarian
Special Strengths: Nevada (Mining,
    Plats & Townsite)
Employees: Full Time    Part Time
    Prof.        0            1
Holdings:
    3000 Printed Maps
    500 Manuscript Maps
    30 Aerial Photographs
    50 Atlases
Chronological Coverage: 25% pre 1900;
    75% post 1900
Map collection is cataloged 75%
Classification: Local
Formats: Cards
Preservation methods: Chartex or
    Fabric Mounting, Deacidification
Available to: Public
Average monthly use: 50
Copying Facilities: Copying machine,
    Photographic reproduction
Equipment:
    3 5-drawer cabinets
    5 vertical map cabinets
    3 3-drawer units
    1 16-drawer wooden case
Square Footage: 300

534
University of Nevada Library
Government Publications Department
Reno, NV 89557
Tel. (702) 784-6579
Hours: 8–8, M–Th; 8–5, F
Responsible Person: Totton, Kathryn
Special Strengths: Nevada (Census),
United States (Census)
Holdings:
1000 Printed Maps
10 Satellite Imagery
2 Atlases
1000 Microforms
100 Gazetteers
Chronological Coverage: 2% pre 1900;
98% post 1900
Available to: Public, Students, Faculty
Circulates to: Public, Students, Faculty
Average monthly use: 15
Average annual circulation: Maps: 25
Interlibrary loan available
Copying Facilities: Microform
Equipment: Boxes
Map Depositories: GPO

535
University of Nevada
Geography Department
William D. Phillips Memorial Map
Library
Reno, NV 89557
Tel. (702) 784-6968
Responsible Person: Kramer, Terrill J.
Employees: Full Time    Part Time
Prof.          1           0
Non-Prof.      0           1
Holdings:
15000 Printed Maps
500 Aerial Photographs
4 Atlases
350 Wall Maps
50 Raised Relief Maps
Chronological Coverage: 5% pre 1900;
95% post 1900
Available to: Public, Students, Faculty
Equipment:
Boxed storage
8 stereoscopes, 2 polar planimeters,
misc. scales
Square Footage: 600

536
University of Nevada, Reno
Mines Library, Map Collection
Reno, NV 89557
Tel. (702) 784-6596
Hours: 8–5, M–F
Responsible Person: Newman, Linda,
Map Librarian
Special Strengths: Nevada (topographic
& geological)
Employees: Full Time    Part Time
Prof.          0           1
Non-Prof.      0           3

Holdings:
97400 Printed Maps
15 Atlases
1 Globe
15 Wall Maps
2 Raised Relief Maps
1850 Microforms
46 Books
8 Gazetteers
7 Serial Titles
Chronological Coverage: 5% pre 1900;
95% post 1900
Map collection is cataloged 5%
Formats: Cards
Preservation methods: Encapsulation,
Magic mend tape
Available to: Public, Students, Faculty
Circulates to: Public, Students, Faculty
Average monthly use: 510
Average annual circulation:
Maps: 2500
Interlibrary loan available
Except certain historical items &
reference works
Copying Facilities: Copying machine
Equipment:
83 5-drawer cabinets
18 4-drawer metal cabinets
Light table
Square Footage: 2000
Map Depositories: USGS (topo);
USGS (geol); DMA (topo); DMA
(aero); DMA (hydro); GPO

537
Washoe County Library
301 S. Center St.
Reno, NV 89505
Tel. (702) 785-4010
Hours: 10–8, M–W; 12–6, Th, F;
1–5, Sa, Su
Responsible Person: McDonald, John
Special Strengths: Nevada, Reno and
Washoe County
Employees: Full Time    Part Time
Prof.          0           1
Non-Prof.      0           1
Holdings:
1780 Printed Maps
115 Atlases
1 Globe
6 Wall Maps
15 Raised Relief Maps
12 Books
14 Gazetteers
Chronological Coverage: 7% pre 1900;
93% post 1900
Preservation methods: Lamination
Available to: Public
Average monthly use: 200
Copying Facilities: Copying machine,
Microform
Equipment:
2 5-drawer cabinets
2 vertical map cabinets

Atlas Stand
Square Footage: 75

**New Hampshire**
538
New Hampshire Dept. of Public Works
& Highways, Planning & Econ. Div.
John O. Morton Building
Hazen Dr.
Concord, NH 03301
Hours: 8–4, M–F
Special Strengths: New Hampshire
(Public Highways)
Holdings:
5000 Aerial Photographs
Chronological Coverage:
100% post 1900
Available to: Public
Average annual circulation: 300
Copying Facilities: Print Machine
Equipment:
16 10-drawer flat files
Square Footage: 160

539
New Hampshire Historical Society
30 Park St.
Concord, NH 03301
Tel. (603) 225-3381
Hours: 9–4:30, M–Sa
Responsible Person: Copeley, William
Special Strengths: New Hampshire
(1750–1900)
Employees: Full Time    Part Time
Prof.          1           0
Holdings:
500 Printed Maps
500 Manuscript Maps
40 Atlases
40 Wall Maps
20 Books
20 Gazetteers
Chronological Coverage: 80% pre 1900;
20% post 1900
Map collection is cataloged 100%
Classification: Dewey
Formats: Cards
Preservation methods: Encapsulation,
Chartex or Fabric Mounting,
Deacidification, Acid-Free Tape
Available to: Public
Average monthly use: 20
Copying Facilities: Copying machine,
Photographic reproduction
Equipment:
6 5-drawer cabinets
Square Footage: 100

540
New Hampshire State Library
20 Park St.
Concord, NH 03301
Tel. (603) 271-2394
Hours: 8–4:30, M–F

Special Strengths: New Hampshire
Holdings:
   1500 Printed Maps
     50 Atlases
     22 Wall Maps
      5 Microforms
     35 Gazetteers
Chronological Coverage: 10% pre 1900;
   90% post 1900
Classification: Dewey   Utility: OCLC
Formats: Cards
Preservation methods: Lamination
Available to: Public
Average monthly use: 20
Copying Facilities: Copying machine,
   Microform
Equipment:
   18 5-drawer cabinets
Square Footage: 512
Map Depositories: USGS (topo)

### 541

University of New Hampshire
Durham Library
Durham, NH 03824
Tel. (603) 862-1777
Hours: 8–Midnight, M–F
Responsible Person: Adomovich, Frank
Employees: Full Time    Part Time
  Prof.        1           0
  Non-Prof.    3           0
Holdings:
   60000 Printed Maps
      10 Gazetteers
Chronological Coverage: 5% pre 1900;
   95% post 1900
Map collection is cataloged 15%
Classification: LC   Utility: OCLC
Formats: Cards
Preservation methods: Lamination,
   Deacidification
Available to: Public, Students, Faculty
Average monthly use: 100
Copying Facilities: Copying machine,
   Dyeline
Equipment:
   50 5-drawer cabinets
Square Footage: 500
Map Depositories: USGS (topo);
   USGS (geol); GPO

### 542

Dartmouth College
Library Map Room
Baker Library
Hanover, NH 03755
Tel. (603) 646-2579
Hours: 8–4:30, M–F
Responsible Person: Berthelsen,
   John F., Map Curator
Special Strengths: New England,
   Polar/Arctic, USSR, Central America
Special Collections: Stefansson (Polar-
   Arctic), Karpinski, Scavenious

Employees: Full Time    Part Time
  Prof.        1           0
Holdings:
   128500 Printed Maps
     500 Manuscript Maps
     350 Aerial Photographs
      25 Satellite Imagery
   2900 Atlases
      25 Globes
     225 Wall Maps
     300 Raised Relief Maps
     250 Books
     200 Gazetteers
      15 Serial Titles
Chronological Coverage: 12% pre 1900;
   88% post 1900
Map collection is cataloged 95%
Classification: LC   Utility: OCLC
Formats: Cards
Preservation methods: Encapsulation
Available to: Public, Students, Faculty
Circulates to: Faculty
Average monthly use: 400
Average annual circulation: Maps: 300;
   Books: 1000; Aerial Photographs: 10
Interlibrary loan available
   Except manuscripts, rare materials
Copying Facilities: Copying machine
Equipment:
   115 5-drawer cabinets
   12 vertical map cabinets
   Stereo-pair lamp, light table
Square Footage: 4000
Map Depositories: USGS (topo);
   USGS (geol); DMA (topo); DMA
   (aero); DMA (hydro); GPO; NOS;
   NOAA; Canada (topo); Canada (geol)

### 543

New England College
Danforth Library
Henniker, NH 03242
Tel. (603) 428-2344
Hours: 8–Midnight, M–F
Responsible Person: VanWeelden, Kathy
Special Strengths: New England
Special Collections: White Mountain
   Topographic Series
Employees: Full Time    Part Time
  Prof.        1           0
Holdings:
   500 Printed Maps
    30 Atlases
     2 Globes
    15 Raised Relief Maps
    30 Books
    10 Gazetteers
Chronological Coverage:
   100% post 1900
Available to: Public, Students, Faculty
Circulates to: Public, Students, Faculty
Average monthly use: 1
Interlibrary loan available
Copying Facilities: Copying machine,
   Microform
Equipment: 2 5-drawer cabinets

Square Footage: 40
Map Depositories: USGS (topo)

### 544

Keene State College
Map Depository
Department of Geography
Keene, NH 03431
Tel. (603) 352-1909
Responsible Person: Bayr, Klaus J.
Special Strengths: United States
Employees: Full Time    Part Time
  Non-Prof.    0          1
Holdings:
   20000 Printed Maps
Chronological Coverage:
   100% post 1900
Map collection is cataloged 100%
Classification: Local
Formats: Cards
Available to: Public, Students, Faculty
Circulates to: Public, Students, Faculty
Average monthly use: 80
Average annual circulation:
   Maps: 3000
Equipment:
   26 12-drawer cabinets
Square Footage: 150
Map Depositories: USGS (topo);
   USGS (geol)

### 545

Manchester City Library
405 Pine St.
Carpenter Memorial Building
Manchester, NH 03104
Tel. (603) 624-6550
Hours: 9–9, M, T, Th; 9–5:30, W, F;
   9–5,                    Sa
Responsible Person: Carter, Michael
Special Strengths: New Hampshire,
   City of Manchester, New England
Employees: Full Time    Part Time
  Prof.        1           0
Holdings:
   1000 Printed Maps
     12 Manuscript Maps
     75 Aerial Photographs
     50 Atlases
      6 Globes
      6 Wall Maps
Chronological Coverage: 5% pre 1900;
   95% post 1900
Available to: Public
Copying Facilities: Copying machine
Equipment:
   1 5-drawer cabinet
   1 vertical map cabinet
Map Depositories: USGS (topo);
   USGS (geol); GPO

### 546

Manchester Historic Association
129 Amherst St.

Manchester, NH 03104
Tel. (603) 622-7531
Responsible Person: Engle, Helen
Special Strengths: Manchester (1835–present)
Special Collections: Bird's Eye View maps of Manchester; Amoskeag Manufacturing Co., Amoskeag Industries

Employees: Full Time    Part Time
Prof.          2             0

Holdings:
    2500 Printed Maps
    100 Manuscript Maps
    2 Globes
    5 Wall Maps
Chronological Coverage: 75% pre 1900; 25% post 1900
Preservation methods: Encapsulation, Chartex or Fabric Mounting, Deacidification
Available to: Public, Students, Faculty
Average monthly use: 10
Equipment:
    5 5-drawer cabinets
    1 vertical map cabinet
    Custom built storage units

### 547
Saint Anselm College
Geisel Library
Manchester, NH 03102
Tel. (603) 669-1030
Hours: 8–Midnight, M–Th; 8–9, F; 9–5, Sa; 1–Midnight, Su
Responsible Person: Gannon, Barbara C.
Special Strengths: New Hampshire

Employees: Full Time    Part Time
Prof.          1             0

Holdings:
    400 Printed Maps
    45 Atlases
    1 Globe
    3 Wall Maps
Chronological Coverage:
    100% post 1900
Map collection is cataloged 100%
Classification: LC
Formats: Cards
Available to: Public, Students, Faculty
Circulates to: Public, Students, Faculty
Average monthly use: 35
Average annual circulation: Maps: 200
Interlibrary loan available
Copying Facilities: Copying machine
Equipment:
    1 5-drawer cabinet
Square Footage: 100
Map Depositories: USGS (topo)

## New Jersey
### 548
Atlantic City Free Public Library
Illinois & Pacific Aves.
Atlantic City, NJ 08401

Tel. (609) 345-2269
Responsible Person: Nee, Paul, Adult Services Librarian
Special Strengths: Atlantic City (1872–present)
Holdings:
    400 Printed Maps
Preservation methods: Encapsulation, Deacidification
Available to: Public
Average monthly use: 10
Equipment:
    Vertical files

### 549
Rutgers University
Camden A. & S. Library
Camden, NJ 08102
Tel. (609) 757-6034
Hours: 8–10:30, M–F
Responsible Person: Mount, Jack D.
Special Strengths: Camden County, NJ; New Jersey
Special Collections: Geologic Atlas of the United States

Employees: Full Time    Part Time
Prof.          1             0

Holdings:
    2500 Printed Maps
    35 Atlases
    1 Globe
    5 Wall Maps
    2 Books
    5 Gazetteers
Chronological Coverage: 5% pre 1900; 95% post 1900
Available to: Public, Students, Faculty
Copying Facilities: Copying machine
Equipment:
    5 5-drawer cabinets
    1 5-drawer file cabinet
Square Footage: 150
Map Depositories: GPO

### 550
East Brunswick New Jersey Library
2 Jean Walling Civic Center
East Brunswick, NJ 08816
Tel. (201) 390-6767
Hours: 9–9, M–Th; 9–5, F; 10–5, Sa; 1–5, Su
Responsible Person: Stone, Jason R.
Special Strengths: New Jersey

Employees: Full Time    Part Time
Prof.          1             0

Holdings:
    820 Printed Maps
    38 Atlases
    1 Globe
    1 Wall Map
    35 Microforms
    3 Books
    10 Gazetteers
Chronological Coverage: 1% pre 1900; 99% post 1900

Preservation methods: Lamination
Available to: Public, Students
Average monthly use: 40
Copying Facilities: Copying machine, Microform
Equipment:
    2 5-drawer cabinets
    1 vertical map cabinet
Square Footage: 15
Map Depositories: GPO

### 551
East Orange Public Library
21 S. Arlington Ave.
East Orange, NJ 07018
Tel. (201) 266-5612
Hours: 9–9, M, T, Th; 9–6, W; 10–6, F; 9–5, Sa; 1–5, Su
Responsible Person: Starkey, J. Robert
Special Strengths: East Orange, New Jersey

Employees: Full Time    Part Time
Prof.          0             1

Holdings:
    1800 Printed Maps
    70 Atlases
    3 Globes
    10 Wall Maps
    1 Raised Relief Map
    25 Books
    4 Gazetteers
Chronological Coverage: 1% pre 1900; 99% post 1900
Map collection is cataloged 10%
Classification: Dewey
Formats: Cards
Available to: Public
Circulates to: Public
Interlibrary loan available
Equipment:
    1 atlas stand
    2 vertical files
Square Footage: 18

### 552
Johnson Free Public Library
275 Moore St.
Hackensack, NJ 07601
Tel. (201) 343-4169
Hours: 9–9, M–Th; 9–5, F, Sa
Responsible Person: Goerner, Richard, Map Librarian
Special Strengths: New Jersey, Berger County & Hackensack, (1860–1920)

Employees: Full Time    Part Time
Prof.          1             0

Holdings:
    3985 Printed Maps
    2 Aerial Photographs
    118 Atlases
    1 Globe
    2 Wall Maps
    11 Gazetteers
Chronological Coverage: 50% pre 1900; 50% post 1900

Classification: Dewey
Formats: Cards
Preservation methods: Lamination
Available to: Public, Students, Faculty
Copying Facilities: Copying machine,
  Microform
Equipment:
  1 5-drawer cabinet
  2 vertical map cabinets
  10 open shelving
Square Footage: 40

553
Irvington Public Library
Civic Square
Irvington, NJ 07111
Tel. (201) 372-6400
Hours: 9–9, M, T, Th; 9–5:30, W, Sa;
  9–5, Su
Special Strengths: Essex County, New
  Jersey, Irvington, United States
Employees: Full Time    Part Time
  Non-Prof.    0    1
Holdings:
  3500 Printed Maps
    2 Manuscript Maps
    25 Atlases
    1 Globe
    6 Wall Maps
    2 Books
    3 Gazetteers
Chronological Coverage: 1% pre 1900;
  99% post 1900
Available to: Public, Students
Circulates to: Public, Students
Average annual circulation: Maps: 10;
  Books: 20
Interlibrary loan available
Copying Facilities: Microform,
  Photographic reproduction
Equipment:
  1 5-drawer cabinet
  1 vertical map cabinet
Square Footage: 18
Map Depositories: GPO

554
Jersey City Public Library
New Jersey Reference Section
472 Jersey Ave.
Jersey City, NJ 07302
Tel. (201) 547-4503
Hours: 9–5, M–F; 10–5, Sa
Responsible Person: Doherty, Joan F.
Special Strengths: Hudson County, NJ
  (1700–present); New Jersey
Employees: Full Time    Part Time
  Prof.    2    0
  Non-Prof.    1    0
Holdings:
  500 Printed Maps
    10 Manuscript Maps
    30 Aerial Photographs
    5 Satellite Imagery
    50 Atlases

5 Wall Maps
5 Microforms
10 Books
3 Gazetteers
Chronological Coverage: 50% pre 1900;
  50% post 1900
Map collection is cataloged 60%
Classification: Dewey
Formats: Cards
Preservation methods: Encapsulation,
  Lamination
Available to: Public
Average monthly use: 50
Copying Facilities: Copying machine
Equipment:
  2 5-drawer cabinets
  1 vertical map cabinet
  Rolled map containers
Square Footage: 50
Map Depositories: USGS (topo)

555
Hammond Incorporated
Editorial Department Library
515 Valley St.
Maplewood, NJ 07040
Tel. (201) 763-6000
Hours: 9–5, M–F
Responsible Person: Dupuy, Ernest J.,
  Librarian
Special Strengths: U.S., World (partial),
  World (political), World (demography),
  Canada (road maps), Latin America
  (road maps)
Employees: Full Time    Part Time
  Prof.    1    0
Holdings:
  13000 Printed Maps
    750 Atlases
    4 Globes
    16 Raised Relief Maps
  7000 Books
  1000 Gazetteers
Chronological Coverage: 1% pre 1900;
  99% post 1900
Copying Facilities: Copying machine,
  Photographic reproduction
Equipment:
  20 5-drawer cabinets
  12 vertical files
  3 periodical cabinets
  1 Lucikon Map Enlarger

556
Rutgers University Libraries
Department of Special Collections/
  Archives
New Brunswick, NJ 08903
Tel. (201) 932-7006
Hours: School Year: 9–5, M, T, Th, F;
  9–9, W; 12–6, Sa
Responsible Person: Becker, Ronald,
  Curator of Manuscripts
Special Strengths: New Jersey
  (1750–1950)

Special Collections: USGS Topographic
  maps for New Jersey on microfilm
Employees: Full Time    Part Time
  Prof.    0    1
Holdings:
  2500 Printed Maps
    300 Manuscript Maps
    60 Atlases
    10 Wall Maps
    10 Raised Relief Maps
    5 Books
    10 Gazetteers
Chronological Coverage: 65% pre 1900;
  35% post 1900
Map collection is cataloged 10%
Classification: LC
Formats: Cards
Preservation methods: Encapsulation
Available to: Public, Students, Faculty
Average monthly use: 25
Copying Facilities: Copying machine
Equipment:
  17 5-drawer cabinets
  Cardboard tubes
Square Footage: 800

557
New Jersey Historical Society Library
230 Broadway
Newark, NJ 07104
Tel. (201) 483-3939
Hours: 9:30–4:15, M–Sa
Responsible Person: Irwin, Barbara,
  Library Director
Special Strengths: New Jersey
  (pre-1900)
Employees: Full Time    Part Time
  Prof.    4    1
  Non-Prof.    1    0
Holdings:
  1300 Printed Maps
  2000 Manuscript Maps
    200 Atlases
    2 Globes
    100 Books
    10 Gazetteers
Chronological Coverage: 90% pre 1900;
  10% post 1900
Map collection is cataloged 85%
Formats: Cards
Preservation methods: Encapsulation,
  Edging, Deacidifcation, Cleaning,
  Matting
Available to: Public, Students, Faculty
Copying Facilities: Copying machine
Equipment: 12 5-drawer cabinets

558
Rutgers University
John Cotton Dana Library
185 University Ave.
Newark, NJ 07102
Tel. (201) 648-5901
Hours: 8–11, M–Th; 8–6, F; 10–6, Sa;
  Noon–8, Su

Responsible Person: McSweeney, Linda
Employees: Full Time    Part Time
    Prof.           0              1
    Non-Prof.    0              1
Holdings:
    800 Printed Maps
    275 Atlases
      1 Globe
      3 Wall Maps
    150 Books
      50 Gazetteers
      12 Serial Titles
Chronological Coverage:
    100% post 1900
Map collection is cataloged 5%
Classification: LC      Utility: RLIN
Formats: Cards, COM
Available to: Public, Students, Faculty
Average monthly use: 20
Copying Facilities: Copying machine
Equipment:
    3 5-drawer cabinets
    1 vertical map cabinet
Square Footage: 600
Map Depositories: USGS (topo); GPO


559
Rutgers University
Library of Science & Medicine
Piscataway, NJ 08854
Tel. (201) 932-2895
Hours: 8 a.m.–1 a.m., M–Th; 8–9, F;
    10–6, Sa; Noon–1 a.m., Su
Responsible Person: Goodman, Susan
Special Strengths: New Jersey
    (1890-present), Geology
Employees: Full Time    Part Time
    Prof.           0              1
    Non-Prof.    0              1
Holdings:
    100000 Printed Maps
        200 Aerial Photographs
        190 Atlases
          4 Raised Relief Maps
          80 Books
        120 Gazetteers
Chronological Coverage:
    100% post 1900
Map collection is cataloged 1%
Classification: LC      Utility: RLIN
Formats: Cards
Available to: Public, Students, Faculty
Copying Facilities: Copying machine
Equipment:
    43 5-drawer cabinets
    1 5-drawer lateral file
    1 5-drawer filing cabinet
Square Footage: 900
Map Depositories: USGS (topo);
    USGS (geol); DMA (topo); DMA
    (aero); DMA (hydro); GPO


560
Princeton University Library
The Richard Halliburton Map Collection

Princeton, NJ 08544
Tel. (609) 452-3214
Hours: 9–4, M–F
Responsible Person: Spellman,
    Lawrence E., Curator
Special Strengths: New Jersey
    (Colonial era to present), U.S., Europe
    (Guides), North America (Guides)
Special Collections: Sanborn Fire
    Insurance Maps of most New Jersey
    cities from 1885–1935
Employees: Full Time    Part Time
    Prof.           1              0
    Non-Prof.    0              4
Holdings:
    230000 Printed Maps
      1000 Aerial Photographs
        100 Satellite Imagery
        400 Atlases
          26 Globes
            5 Wall Maps
          75 Raised Relief Maps
      2000 Books
        150 Gazetteers
          40 Serial Titles
Chronological Coverage: 3% pre 1900;
    97% post 1900
Available to: Public, Students, Faculty
Circulates to: Students, Faculty
Average monthly use: 300
Average annual circulation:
    Maps: 1400; Books: 200
Interlibrary loan available
    Only reproductions
Copying Facilities: Copying machine,
    Microform, Photographic reproduction,
    Tracing (light) table
Equipment:
    140 5-drawer cabinets
    5 filing cabinets
    Magnifiers, Stereo Viewer,
    Light table
Square Footage: 3000
Map Depositories: USGS (topo);
    DMA (topo); DMA (aero); DMA
    (hydro); NOS; NOAA


561
Princeton University
Geology Library, Map Collection
Guyot Hall
Princeton, NJ 08544
Tel. (609) 351-2525
Hours: 9–5, M–F
Responsible Person: Gaspari-Bridges,
    Patricia A.
Special Strengths: United States
    (Geology)
Special Collections: (Color;
    paper/slides), USGS Geologic Folio
    Atlases, United States Selected
    Landsat Series
Employees: Full Time    Part Time
    Prof.           1              0
    Non-Prof.    0              4

Holdings:
    127000 Printed Maps
        500 Aerial Photographs
        200 Satellite Imagery
          50 Atlases
            7 Globes
          10 Wall Maps
          20 Raised Relief Maps
        300 Microforms
        100 Books
          25 Gazetteers
          10 Serial Titles
Chronological Coverage: 1% pre 1900;
    99% post 1900
Classification: LC
Formats: Computer Printout
Preservation methods: Encapsulation,
    Lamination, Chartex or Fabric
    Mounting, Deacidification
Available to: Public, Students, Faculty
Circulates to: Faculty
Average monthly use: 50
Average annual circulation: Maps: 100
Copying Facilities: Copying machine
Equipment:
    11 5-drawer cabinets
    72 10-drawer cabinets
    Light tables
Square Footage: 4000
Map Depositories: USGS (topo);
    USGS (geol); Canada (geol)


562
New Jersey Geological Survey
CN 029
Trenton, NJ 08625
Tel. (609) 292-2576
Hours: 8–4:30, M–F
Responsible Person: Graff, William P.
Special Strengths: New Jersey (Geology)
Employees: Full Time    Part Time
    Non-Prof.    0              1
Holdings:
    2500 Printed Maps
      150 Manuscript Maps
    10000 Aerial Photographs
      15 Atlases
      100 Microforms
Chronological Coverage: 35% pre 1900;
    65% post 1900
Available to: Public
Average monthly use: 5
Copying Facilities: Copying machine
Equipment:
    15 5-drawer cabinets
    2 vertical map cabinets
    Bausch & Lomb Stereoscope
Square Footage: 250
Map Depositories: USGS (topo)


563
New Jersey State Library
New Jersey Reference Services
185 W. State St.

Trenton, NJ 08625-0520
Tel. (609) 292-6274
Hours: 8:30–4:30, M–F; 9–5, Sa
Special Strengths: New Jersey
Holdings:
   500 Printed Maps
   125 Atlases
   75 Wall Maps
Chronological Coverage: 75% pre 1900;
   25% post 1900
Map collection is cataloged 50%
Classification: Other   Utility: OCLC
Formats: Cards
Available to: Public
Copying Facilities: Copying machine
Equipment:
   10 5-drawer cabinets
   1 vertical map cabinet
Map Depositories: USGS (topo)

### 564
West Orange Public Library
46 Mt. Pleasant Ave.
West Orange, NJ 07052
Tel. (201) 736-0198
Hours: 10–5, T, Th, F; 9–9, M, W;
   9–5, Sa; 9–1, Su
Responsible Person: Cushing, Margaret,
   Reference Librarian
Special Strengths: West Oranges &
   Oranges (1875–present)
Employees: Full Time   Part Time
Prof.       1       1
Holdings:
   500 Printed Maps
   40 Atlases
   1 Globe
   3 Wall Maps
   3 Raised Relief Maps
   8 Books
   6 Gazetteers
   2 Serial Titles
Chronological Coverage: 5% pre 1900;
   95% post 1900
Map collection is cataloged 10%
Classification: Dewey
Formats: Cards
Available to: Public, Students
Average monthly use: 100
Copying Facilities: Copying machine
Equipment:
   1 5-drawer cabinet
   1 vertical map cabinet
Square Footage: 10

### 565
Motor Bus Society, Inc., Library
P. O. Box 7058
West Trenton, NJ 08628
Hours: By mail inquiry or special
   appointment only
**Responsible Person: Hoschek, John P.,**
   VP, Library & Research
**Special Strengths: United States**
   (1923–present), Canada (1923–present)

Employees: Full Time   Part Time
Prof.       0       1
Holdings:
   5000 Printed Maps
Chronological Coverage:
   100% post 1900
Available to: Public
Copying Facilities: Copying machine
Equipment:
   5-drawer files

## New Mexico
### 566
Albuquerque Public Library
501 Copper, NW
Albuquerque, NM 87102
Tel. (505) 766-7720
Hours: 9–9, M–Th; 9–5:30, F, Sa
Responsible Person: Shelton,
   M. Perlinda
Special Strengths: New Mexico
Employees: Full Time   Part Time
Prof.       0       1
Non-Prof.   0       1
Holdings:
   700 Printed Maps
   31 Atlases
   2 Globes
   2 Wall Maps
   11 Microforms
   32 Books
   3 Gazetteers
Chronological Coverage:
   100% post 1900
Available to: Public
Average monthly use: 50
Copying Facilities: Copying machine
Equipment:
   1 5-drawer cabinet
   6 vertical file cabinets
Square Footage: 50

### 567
University of New Mexico
Department of Geology, Map Collection
Northrup Hall
Albuquerque, NM 87131
Tel. (505) 277-4204
Hours: By appointment
Responsible Person: Wells,
   Dr. Stephen G.
Special Strengths: New Mexico,
   Southwest
Employees: Full Time   Part Time
Prof.       1       0
Non-Prof.   0       1
Holdings:
   7500 Printed Maps
   10 Wall Maps
Chronological Coverage: 5% pre 1900;
   95% post 1900
Map collection is cataloged 40%
Formats: Inventory list
Preservation methods: Edging
Available to: Students, Faculty

Circulates to: Students, Faculty
Average monthly use: 6
Average annual circulation: Maps: 100
Equipment:
   18 5-drawer cabinets
   9 filing cabinets
   Stereoscopes, Parallax bars
Square Footage: 150
Map Depositories: USGS (geol)

### 568
University of New Mexico
General Library Map Room
Albuquerque, NM 87131
Hours: 8:30–4, M–F
Responsible Person: Rex, Heather,
   Map Specialist
Special Strengths: Western United
   States, New Mexico (1779–present),
   Albuquerque/Bernalillo County
   (Aerial photography, 1970–present)
Special Collections: Some 19th cent.
   Survey Maps for New Mexico, Sanborn
   Fire Insurance Maps of New Mexico
   Towns, New Mexico Road Maps from
   1910, Albuquerque & Bernalillo County
   Zone Atlas Maps & Air Photos
Employees: Full Time   Part Time
Non-Prof.   1       4
Holdings:
   107000 Printed Maps
   50 Manuscript Maps
   6800 Aerial Photographs
   30 Satellite Imagery
   800 Atlases
   3 Globes
   87 Wall Maps
   40 Raised Relief Maps
   150 Microforms
   400 Books
   200 Gazetteers
   10 Serial Titles
Chronological Coverage: 1% pre 1900;
   99% post 1900
Preservation methods: Encapsulation,
   Edging
Available to: Public, Students, Faculty
Circulates to: Public, Students, Faculty
Average monthly use: 200
Average annual circulation: Maps: 500;
   Aerial Photographs: 20
Interlibrary loan available
   Books/Atlases do not circulate
Copying Facilities: Copying machine,
   Microform, Photographic reproduction
Equipment:
   111 5-drawer cabinets
   18 rock-a-file drawers
   Light table, magnifying glass,
   Scale conversion rulers
Square Footage: 3800
Map Depositories: USGS (topo);
   USGS (geol); DMA (topo); DMA
   (aero); DMA (hydro); GPO; NOS;
   NOAA; U.S. Forest Service; U.S.
   Bureau of Land Managment

569
New Mexico State University Library
Map Collection
P.O. Box 3475
Las Cruces, NM 88003
Tel. (505) 646-3238
Hours: 8–5, M–F
Responsible Person: Myers, Christine B.,
  Special Collections
Special Strengths: New Mexico
  Southwestern United States
Employees: Full Time     Part Time
  Prof.          1              0
  Non-Prof.      1              1
Holdings:
  35000 Printed Maps
      5 Manuscript Maps
    300 Atlases
      3 Globes
     12 Wall Maps
     48 Raised Relief Maps
     25 Books
     50 Gazetteers
Chronological Coverage: 1% pre 1900;
  99% post 1900
Map collection is cataloged 75%
Classification: LC     Utility: OCLC
Formats: Cards
Preservation methods: Encapsulation,
  Lamination, Chartex of Fabric
  Mounting
Available to: Public, Students, Faculty
Circulates to: Public, Students, Faculty
Average monthly use: 200
Average annual circulation: Maps: 100
Interlibrary loan available
  Special permission required
Copying Facilities: Copying machine,
  Microform, Photographic reproduction
Equipment:
  39 5-drawer vertical cabinets
   3 5-drawer vertical cabinets
   4 4-drawer vertical cabinets
Square Footage: 1000
Map Depositories: USGS (topo);
  USGS (geol); DMA (topo); DMA
  (aero); DMA (hydro)


570
New Mexico Highlands University
Donnelly Library
Las Vegas, NM 87701
Tel. (505) 425-7511
Hours: 8–10, M–Th; 8–11, F; 8–5, Sa;
  2–10, Su
Responsible Person: Jaggers, Karen,
  Associate Librarian
Special Strengths: New Mexico
  (Geology)
Employees: Full Time     Part Time
  Prof.          1              0
  Non-Prof.      1              1
Holdings:
  11700 Printed Maps
      2 Aerial Photographs
    116 Satellite Imagery
    171 Atlases
      1 Globe
      1 Wall Map
     12 Raised Relief Maps
     32 Books
      1 Gazetteer
Chronological Coverage: 1% pre 1900;
  99% post 1900
Available to: Public, Students, Faculty
Average monthly use: 40
Copying Facilities: Copying machine,
  Microform
Equipment:
  12 5-drawer cabinets
   3 vertical map cabinets
Square Footage: 375
Map Depositories: USGS (topo);
  USGS (geol); GPO


571
Eastern New Mexico University
Golden Library
Portales, NM 88130
Tel. (505) 562-2624
Hours: 7:30–11:30, M–F
Responsible Person: Richter, Edward A.,
  Reference
Special Strengths: New Mexico,
  Southwest
Employees: Full Time     Part Time
  Prof.          0              2
  Non-Prof.      0              2
Holdings:
  6514 Printed Maps
    10 Aerial Photographs
    50 Satellite Imagery
   195 Atlases
     1 Globe
    80 Wall Maps
    78 Raised Relief Maps
    65 Books
   110 Gazetteers
Chronological Coverage: 2% pre 1900;
  98% post 1900
Map collection is cataloged 35%
Classification: LC     Utility: OCLC
Formats: Cards
Preservation methods: Lamination,
  Edging
Available to: Public, Students, Faculty
Copying Facilities: Copying machine,
  Photographic reproduction
Equipment:
  24 5-drawer cabinets
   8 vertical map cabinets
Square Footage: 600
Map Depositories: USGS (topo);
  DMA (topo); DMA (aero); DMA
  (hydro); GPO


572
Museum of New Mexico
History Library
P. O. Box 2087
Santa Fe, NM 87503
Tel. (505) 827-6470
Hours: 1–5, M–F
Responsible Person: Romero, Orlando,
  Research Librarian
Special Strengths: New Mexico
  (19th century)
Employees: Full Time     Part Time
  Prof.          1              0
Holdings:
  3000 Printed Maps
    50 Manuscript Maps
   100 Atlases
    50 Books
    10 Gazetteers
Chronological Coverage: 90% pre 1900;
  10% post 1900
Map collection is cataloged 95%
Classification: LC
Formats: Cards
Preservation methods: Encapsulation
Available to: Public
Average monthly use: 50
Copying Facilities: Reproduction
  arranged
Equipment:
  12 5-drawer cabinets
Square Footage: 400


573
Museum of New Mexico
Laboratory of Anthropology–Library
P. O. Box 2087
Santa Fe, NM 87503
Tel. (505) 827-8941
Hours: 9–12, 1–5, M–F
Responsible Person: Holt, Laura,
  Librarian
Special Strengths: New Mexico
Special Collections: Forest Atlas of
  the National Forests of the United
  States (1909), 10 folios
Employees: Full Time     Part Time
  Prof.          1              0
Holdings:
  2500 Printed Maps
    50 Aerial Photographs
    50 Atlases
     2 Raised Relief Maps
    20 Books
    35 Gazetteers
Chronological Coverage: 1% pre 1900;
  99% post 1900
Map collection is cataloged 95%
Formats: Cards
Available to: Public
Average monthly use: 1
Copying Facilities: Copying machine
Equipment:
  5 5-drawer cabinets
Square Footage: 48
Map Depositories: USGS (topo)


574
Museum of New Mexico
Laboratory of Anthropology–

Survey Room
P.O. Box 2087
Santa Fe, NM 87503
Tel. (505) 827-8941
Hours: 9–4, M–F
Responsible Person: Jackson, Marsha
Special Strengths: New Mexico
  (Archaeological sites)
Special Collections: Archaeological
  sites in the state of New Mexico
  (ca. 50,000)
Employees: Full Time    Part Time
  Prof.         7              0
  Non-Prof.     0              1
Holdings:
  40000 Printed Maps
  40000 Manuscript Maps
  10000 Aerial Photographs
  20 Wall Maps
Chronological Coverage:
  100% post 1900
Map collection is cataloged 100%
Preservation methods: Edging
  Acid free folders
Average monthly use: 40
Copying Facilities: Copying machine
Equipment:
  4 5-drawer cabinets
  2 vertical map cabinets
  22 file cabinets
  12 shelves, 2 vaults
  1 mirror stereoscope
  1 digitizer, 1 Light table
Square Footage: 500

### 575

New Mexico State Library
325 Don Gaspar
Santa Fe, NM 87503
Tel. (505) 827-3823
Hours: 8–5, M–F
Special Strengths: New Mexico
Employees: Full Time    Part Time
  Prof.         0              6
Holdings:
  4000 Printed Maps
  30 Atlases
  2 Wall Maps
  10 Raised Relief Maps
  25 Books
  5 Gazetteers
Chronological Coverage: 5% pre 1900;
  95% post 1900
Available to: Public, Students, Faculty
Average monthly use: 50
Copying Facilities: Copying machine,
  Microform
Equipment:
  8 5-drawer cabinets
  3 atlas cases
Square Footage: 28
Map Depositories: USGS (topo);
  USGS (geol); GPO

### 576

New Mexico State Record Center
  & Archives
404 Montezuma
Santa Fe, NM 87503
Tel. (505) 827-8860
Hours: 8–5, M–F
Responsible Person: Smith-Gonzales,
  Sherry
Special Strengths: New Mexico
  (Military Exploration of New Mexico)
Special Collections: Surveyor General
  Land Grant Maps of New Mexico
  (manuscripts)
Employees: Full Time    Part Time
  Prof.         4              0
  Non-Prof.     1              0
Holdings:
  2000 Printed Maps
  100 Manuscript Maps
  12 Aerial Photographs
  6 Atlases
  1 Wall Map
  24 Raised Relief Maps
  20 Books
  12 Gazetteers
Chronological Coverage: 70% pre 1900;
  30% post 1900
Available to: Public, Students, Faculty
Average monthly use: 30
Copying Facilities: Copying machine
Equipment: 5 5-drawer cabinets
Square Footage: 30

### 577

Western New Mexico University
Miller Library
Silver City, NM 88062
Tel. (505) 538-6731
Responsible Person: Baumwart, May
Special Strengths: New Mexico
Employees: Full Time    Part Time
  Prof.         1              0
  Non-Prof.     0              1
Holdings:
  600 Printed Maps
  6 Satellite Imagery
  42 Atlases
  2 Globes
  4 Wall Maps
  1 Raised Relief Map
  21 Books
  4 Gazetteers
Chronological Coverage: 10% pre 1900;
  90% post 1900
Available to: Public, Students, Faculty
Average monthly use: 30
Interlibrary loan available
  Building use only
Copying Facilities: Copying machine,
  Microform
Equipment:
  2 5-drawer cabinets
  2 rolled holders
Square Footage: 100
Map Depositories: USGS (topo);

GPO

### 578

New Mexico Bureau of Mines & Mineral
  Resources
Information, Resource & Service Center
Campus Station
Socorro, NM 87801
Tel. (505) 835-5420
Hours: 8–5, M–F
Responsible Person: Menzie, David,
  Manager/Geologist
Special Strengths: New Mexico
  (Mine Maps, Geology)
Employees: Full Time    Part Time
  Prof.         1              2
  Non-Prof.     1              4
Holdings:
  300 Printed Maps
  150 Manuscript Maps
  5 Wall Maps
Chronological Coverage: 5% pre 1900;
  95% post 1900
Map collection is cataloged 50%
Classification: LC    Utility: OCLC
Formats: Cards, Online
Available to: Public, Students, Faculty
Copying Facilities: Copying machine,
  Microform, Blueline
Equipment:
  2 5-drawer cabinets
  1 vertical map cabinet
  2 filing cabinets
Square Footage: 30

### 579

New Mexico Institute of Mining &
  Technology
Martin Speare Memorial Library
Campus Station
Socorro, NM 87801
Tel. (505) 835-5615
Hours: 8–11, M–Th; 8–5, F; 10–8, Sa;
  10–11, Su
Responsible Person: Reynolds, Betty,
  Director
Special Strengths: Geology
Employees: Full Time    Part Time
  Prof.         1              0
  Non-Prof.     1              0
Holdings:
  5075 Printed Maps
  76 Atlases
  2 Globes
  5 Wall Maps
  5 Gazetteers
Chronological Coverage: 5% pre 1900;
  95% post 1900
Map collection is cataloged 10%
Classification: LC    Utility: OCLC
Available to: Public, Students, Faculty
Circulates to: Public, Students, Faculty
Average monthly use: 25
Average annual circulation: Maps: 10
Interlibrary loan available

Copying Facilities: Copying machine
Equipment:
   4 5-drawer cabinets
Square Footage: 400

## 580

Kit Carson Memorial Foundation
Research Library & Archives
P.O. Box B
Taos, NM 87571
Tel. (505) 758-4741
Hours: By appointment
Responsible Person: Bayer, Jack,
   Director
Special Strengths: New Mexico, Trans
   Mississippi West

| Employees: | Full Time | Part Time |
|---|---|---|
| Prof. | 4 | 0 |
| Non-Prof. | 0 | 3 |

Holdings:
   533 Printed Maps
   200 Manusript Maps
    30 Aerial Photographs
    10 Atlases
     8 Raised Relief Maps
     5 Books
Chronological Coverage: 25% pre 1900;
   75% post 1900
Map collection is cataloged 100%
Formats: Cards
Available to: Public, Students, Faculty
Average monthly use: 10
Copying Facilities: Copying machine
Equipment:
   1 5-drawer cabinet
   Light table, Stereoscope
Square Footage: 140

## New York

### 581

Albany Institute of History & Art
McKinney Library
125 Washington Ave.
Albany, NY 12210
Tel. (518) 463-4478
Hours: 8:30–4, M–F
Responsible Person: Severson, Daryl J.
Special Strengths: New York State
   (1695–present), Albany City & County

| Employees: | Full Time | Part Time |
|---|---|---|
| Prof. | 1 | 0 |

Holdings:
   225 Printed Maps
    25 Manuscript Maps
Chronological Coverage: 90% pre 1900;
   10% post 1900
Map collection is cataloged 100%
Formats: Cards
Preservation methods: Encapsulation,
   Deacidification
Available to: Public
Average monthly use: 10
Copying Facilities: Copying machine,
   Photographic reproduction
Equipment:

3 5-drawer cabinets

### 582

New York State Dept. of Transportation
Map Information Unit
State Campus Bldg., Room 105
Albany, NY 12232
Tel. (518) 457-3555
Hours: 8:30–4:40, M–F
Responsible Person: Hein, Paul
Special Strengths: New York State
   (Planimetric & Topographic Base
   Maps, Aerial photography 1968–
   present)
Special Collections: Federal Aid/-
   Functional Classification Highway
   Maps, Official New York State Base
   Maps, Highway Reference Marker
   Maps

| Employees: | Full Time | Part Time |
|---|---|---|
| Prof. | 3 | 0 |
| Non-Prof. | 1 | 0 |

Holdings:
    4000 Printed Maps
    4000 Manuscript Maps
  100000 Aerial Photographs
     25 Satellite Imagery
     20 Raised Relief Maps
     50 Books
      5 Gazetteers
Chronological Coverage: 1% pre 1900;
   99% post 1900
Map collection is cataloged 90%
Formats: Cards, Computer Printout
Available to: Public
Average monthly use: 1000
Average annual circulation:
   Maps: 2500; Aerial Photographs: 75
Equipment:
   71 5-drawer cabinets
   2 vertical map cabinets
   20 map shelves
   Mirror stereoscopes, Light tables,
   Zoom-transfer scope, projectors
Square Footage: 2240
Map Depositories: NOS

### 583

New York State Geological Survey
Cartographic Unit
Albany, NY 12230
Tel. (518) 473-8057
Hours: 8:30–4, M–F
Responsible Person: Skiba, John B.
Special Strengths: New York State

| Employees: | Full Time | Part Time |
|---|---|---|
| Prof. | 1 | 1 |

Holdings:
   1000 Printed Maps
    500 Aerial Photographs
      1 Atlas
      1 Globe
      4 Wall Maps
      1 Raised Relief Map
      5 Books

Chronological Coverage:
   100% post 1900
Available to: Faculty
Circulates to: Faculty
Average monthly use: 10
Average annual circulation: Maps: 400;
   Aerial Photographs: 100
Equipment:
   24 5-drawer cabinets
   Stereoscope
Square Footage: 50

### 584

New York State Library
Manuscripts & Special Collections
Cultural Education Center
Albany, NY 12230
Tel. (518) 474-4461
Hours: 9–5, M–F
Responsible Person: Corsaro, James,
   Senior Librarian
Special Strengths: New York (1650–
   present), New York (1860–1910,
   County Atlases), World (1750–1920,
   Atlases), New York (1780–1850,
   Cadastral)
Special Collections: James Hall
   Papers-Maps (19th cent.–geological)

| Employees: | Full Time | Part Time |
|---|---|---|
| Prof. | 4 | 0 |
| Non-Prof. | 3 | 0 |

Holdings:
  160000 Printed Maps
    5000 Manuscript Maps
     50 Aerial Photographs
    1100 Atlases
      3 Globes
     20 Wall Maps
     50 Raised Relief Maps
    650 Books
     15 Gazetteers
     15 Serial Titles
Chronological Coverage: 35% pre 1900;
   65% post 1900
Map collection is cataloged 60%
Classification: Dewey
Formats: Cards, Lists
Preservation methods: Encapsulation,
   Lamination, Deacidification, Binding
   restoration
Available to: Public, Students, Faculty
Average monthly use: 200
Average annual circulation: Books: 30
Interlibrary loan available
   Books only
Copying Facilities: Copying machine,
   Microform, Photostat
Equipment:
   350 5-drawer cabinets
   4 vertical map cabinets
   30 oversize map files
   Rolled maps on shelves
Map Depositories: USGS (topo);
   USGS (geol); DMA (topo); DMA
   (aero); DMA (hydro); GPO; NOS;
   NOAA; Canada (topo); Canada (geol);

NY Dept. of Transportation; Various state & foreign geol. surveys

### 585
State University of New York, Albany
Government Publications
University Library
Albany, NY 12222
Tel. (518) 457-3347
Hours: 9–10, M–F
Responsible Person: Lee, Tae Moon
Special Strengths: United States
Employees: Full Time     Part Time
Prof.              0              3
Non-Prof.       0              1
Holdings:
   8000 Printed Maps
   200 Atlases
Chronological Coverage:
   100% post 1900
Map collection is cataloged 5%
Classification: LC    Utility: OCLC
Formats: Cards
Available to: Public, Students, Faculty
Copying Facilities: Copying machine
Equipment:
   22 5-drawer cabinets
   16 file cabinets
Map Depositories: USGS (topo);
   USGS (geol); DMA (topo); GPO

### 586
Alfred University Geology Map Library
Department of Geology
Alfred, NY 14802
Tel. (607) 871-2203
Responsible Person: Davis, Dr. R.
   Laurence
Special Strengths: New York,
   Pennsylvania, West Virginia
Employees: Full Time     Part Time
Non-Prof.       0              1
Holdings:
   7000 Printed Maps
   100 Aerial Photographs
   25 Atlases
   2 Globes
   30 Raised Relief Maps
   50 Books
   5000 Serial Titles
Chronological Coverage: 5% pre 1900;
   95% post 1900
Map collection is cataloged 100%
Classification: Local
Formats: Cards
Available to: Public, Students, Faculty
Circulates to: Students, Faculty
Average monthly use: 10
Copying Facilities: Copying machine
Equipment:
   4 5-drawer cabinets
   10 file cabinets
   Zoom transferscope
Square Footage: 500
Map Depositories: USGS (topo);

USGS (geol)

### 587
Adirondack Museum Library
Blue Mountain Lake, NY 12812
Tel. (518) 352-7311
Hours: By appointment
Responsible Person:  Pepper, Jerold
Special Strengths: Adirondack Park
Employees: Full Time     Part Time
Prof.              1              1
Holdings:
   1043 Printed Maps
   189 Manuscript Maps
   2 Satellite Imagery
   22 Atlases
   9 Books
   19 Gazetteers
Chronological Coverage:  35% pre 1900;
   65% post 1900
Map collection is cataloged 99%
Formats: Cards
Preservation methods: Encapsulation,
   Deacidification
Available to: Public, Students, Faculty
Copying Facilities: Photographic
   reproduction
Equipment:
   6 5-drawer cabinets
   Vault
Square Footage: 100

### 588
Brooklyn Public Library
History Division, Map Collection
Grand Army Plaza
Brooklyn, NY 11238
Tel. (212) 780-7794
Hours: 9–8, M–Th; 10–6, Sa; 1–5, Su
Responsible Person: Yoshinaga, Tsugio
Special Strengths: Brooklyn
   (pre-1900–present)
Special Collections: New York State
   County Atlases, Historic City Plans
   & Views
Employees: Full Time     Part Time
Prof.              1              0
Non-Prof.       2              0
Holdings:
   80000 Printed Maps
   50 Aerial Photographs
   100 Satellite Imagery
   850 Atlases
   1 Globe
   6 Wall Maps
   15 Raised Relief Maps
   500 Books
   300 Gazetteers
   5 Serial Titles
Chronological Coverage: 10% pre 1900;
   90% post 1900
Classification: Dewey
Formats: Cards, COM
Preservation methods: Encapsulation,
   Lamination, Deacidification

Available to: Public, Students, Faculty
Circulates to: Public, Students, Faculty
Copying Facilities: Copying machine
Equipment:
   68 5-drawer cabinets
   12 vertical map cabinets
Square Footage: 825
Map Depositories: USGS (topo);
   DMA (topo)

### 589
Pratt Institute Library
200 Willoughby Ave.
Brooklyn, NY 11205
Tel. (212) 636-3686
Hours: 9–5, M–F
Responsible Person: McSweeney,
   Josephine
Special Strengths: Brooklyn, New York
   City
Holdings:
   500 Printed Maps
   40 Atlases
   1 Wall Map
   10 Books
   4 Gazetteers
Chronological Coverage:
   100% post 1900
Available to: Students, Faculty
Average monthly use: 50
Copying Facilities: Copying machine
Equipment:
   6 5-drawer cabinets
   1 vertical map cabinet
Map Depositories: USGS (topo)

### 590
Buffalo & Erie County Public Library
Lafayette Square
Buffalo, NY 14203
Tel. (716) 856-7525
Hours: 9–6, T, W, F, Sa; 9–9, M, Th
Responsible Person: Willet, Ruth
Special Strengths: Buffalo, New York,
   Western New York
Employees: Full Time     Part Time
Prof.              0              1
Non-Prof.       0              2
Holdings:
   100000 Printed Maps
   6 Aerial Photographs
   2 Satellite Imagery
   12 Wall Maps
   16 Raised Relief Maps
   21 Serial Titles
Chronological Coverage: 25% pre 1900;
   75% post 1900
Map collection is cataloged 25%
Formats: Cards
Preservation methods: Lamination
Available to: Public, Students, Faculty
Circulates to: Public
Copying Facilities: Copying machine
Equipment:
   3 vertical map cabinets

2 vertical files
Map Depositories: USGS (topo);
   USGS (geol); DMA (topo); DMA
   (aero); DMA (hydro); GPO

### 591
State University of New York, Buffalo
University Libraries
Science & Engineering Library
Map Collection
Buffalo, NY 14260
Tel. (716) 636-2946
Hours: 8–11, M–F; 12–11, Sa, Su
Responsible Person: Woodson, Ernest L.
Special Strengths: New York State,
   Canada, Erie County, NY (aerial
   photos)
Employees: Full Time    Part Time
   Prof.        0           1
   Non-Prof.    0           1
Holdings:
   200000 Printed Maps
     3000 Aerial Photographs
      100 Satellite Imagery
     1000 Atlases
        1 Globe
       10 Wall Maps
       50 Raised Relief Maps
      500 Microforms
        1 Computer Tape
      150 Books
       10 Gazetteers
Chronological Coverage: 15% pre 1900;
   85% post 1900
Preservation methods: Encapsulation,
   Edging
Available to: Public, Students, Faculty
Circulates to: Public, Students, Faculty
Average monthly use: 1000
Average annual circulation: Maps: 600;
   Aerial Photographs: 200
Interlibrary loan available
Copying Facilities: Copying machine,
   Microform
Equipment:
   75 5-drawer cabinets
   30 5-drawer file cabinets
   Mirror stereoscope
   Zoom-transfer scope
Square Footage: 2900
Map Depositories: USGS (topo);
   USGS (geol); DMA (topo); DMA
   (aero); DMA (hydro); GPO; NOS;
   NOAA; Canada (topo); Canada (geol)

### 592
New York State Historical Association
P. O. Box 800 Lake Road
Cooperstown, NY 13326
Tel. (607) 547-2509
Hours: 9–5, M–F
Responsible Person: Clark, Sara J.
Special Strengths: New York Counties
   (19th cent. atlases), New York (Canals
   & Waterways)

Employees: Full Time    Part Time
   Prof.        1           0
Holdings:
   384 Printed Maps
    16 Manuscript Maps
   100 Atlases
    10 Raised Relief Maps
     1 Microform
    10 Books
    15 Gazetteers
Chronological Coverage: 65% pre 1900;
   35% post 1900
Map collection is cataloged 95%
Classification: Dewey
Formats: Cards
Available to: Public
Average monthly use: 5
Copying Facilities: Copying machine,
   Photographic reproduction
Equipment:
   2 5-drawer cabinets
Square Footage: 200

### 593
State University College at Cortland
Dept. of Geology, Map Collection
Cortland, NY 13045
Tel. (607) 753-2815
Hours: 9–5, M–F
Responsible Person: Bugh, Dr. James E.
Special Strengths: New York
Employees: Full Time    Part Time
   Non-Prof.    0           2
Holdings:
   10000 Printed Maps
     100 Manuscript Maps
     500 Aerial Photographs
       1 Globe
      50 Wall Maps
      50 Raised Relief Maps
Chronological Coverage: 5% pre 1900;
   95% post 1900
Map collection is cataloged 75%
Formats: Cards
Preservation methods: Chartex or
   Fabric Mounting
Available to: Public, Students, Faculty
Circulates to: Public, Students, Faculty
Average monthly use: 10
Copying Facilities: Copying machine
Equipment:
   25 5-drawer cabinets
Square Footage: 750

### 594
State University College at Fredonia
Daniel A. Reed Library
Fredonia, NY 14063
Tel. (716) 673-3183
Hours: 8:30–5, M–F
Responsible Person: Moran, John,
   Head, Public Services
Special Strengths: Chautauqua &
   Cattaraugus Counties, New York
   (maps & aerial photos); Western New

York (Holland Land Co. Microform
   Records)
Holdings:
    185 Printed Maps
   2005 Aerial Photographs
    210 Atlases
      6 Globes
     40 Wall Maps
      5 Raised Relief Maps
     16 Microforms
    150 Books
     20 Gazetteers
      1 Serial Title
Chronological Coverage: 15% pre 1900;
   85% post 1900
Map collection is cataloged 100%
Classification: LC    Utility: OCLC
Formats: Cards
Available to: Public, Students, Faculty
Copying Facilities: Copying machine,
   Microform, Photographic reproduction
Equipment:
   2 10-drawer map cabinets
   1 atlas case

### 595
State University College at Geneseo
Milne Library
Geneseo, NY 14454
Tel. (716) 245-5591
Hours: 8–11, M–Th; 8–10, F; 9–9, Sa;
   Noon–11, Su
Responsible Person: Stapley, Polly
Special Strengths: New York State,
   especially Genesee Valley Region
Employees: Full Time    Part Time
   Prof.        0           1
   Non-Prof.    0           1
Holdings:
   4000 Printed Maps
    250 Atlases
     10 Wall Maps
     20 Books
     10 Gazetteers
Chronological Coverage: 1% pre 1900;
   99% post 1900
Map collection is cataloged 50%
Classification: Local system
Formats: Cards
Available to: Public, Students, Faculty
Circulates to: Public, Students, Faculty
Average monthly use: 30
Copying Facilities: Copying machine
Equipment:
   8 5-drawer cabinets
Square Footage: 50
Map Depositories: USGS (topo)

### 596
Hobart & William Smith Colleges
Warren Hunting Smith Library
Geneva, NY 14456
Tel. (315) 789-5500
Hours: 8:30–11:30, M–Th; 8:30–10,
   F, Sa; 10–11:30, Su

Responsible Person: Thompson, Gary B.
Special Strengths: New York,
Pennsylvania
Employees: Full Time    Part Time
    Non-Prof.    0          1
Holdings:
    5498 Printed Maps
        10 Manuscript Maps
        141 Atlases
        10 Wall Maps
        10 Raised Relief Maps
        684 Books
        20 Gazetteers
        4 Serial Titles
Chronological Coverage: 5% pre 1900;
    95% post 1900
Map collection is cataloged 95%
Formats: Cards
Preservation methods: Deacidification
Available to: Public, Students, Faculty
Circulates to: Public, Students, Faculty
Average annual circulation: Maps: 100
Interlibrary loan available
    Books only
Copying Facilities: Copying machine
Equipment:
    6 5-drawer cabinets
    5 vertical map cabinets
Map Depositories: USGS (topo);
    USGS (geol)

### 597

Long Island University–
C. W. Post Campus
Government Documents Department
Greenvale, NY 11548
Tel. (516) 299-2842
Hours: 9–8, M–Th; 9–5, F; 10–5, Sa;
    1–6, Su
Responsible Person: Yukawa, Masako
Special Strengths: United States
Employees: Full Time    Part Time
    Prof.       2          0
    Non-Prof.   2          6
Holdings:
    2000 Printed Maps
        20 Aerial Photographs
        50 Atlases
        5 Wall Maps
        2 Books
        26 Gazetteers
Chronological Coverage:
    100% post 1900
Available to: Public, Students, Faculty
Circulates to: Faculty
Average monthly use: 10
Average annual circulation: Maps: 100;
    Aerial Photographs: 5
Interlibrary loan available
    In-house use only
Copying Facilities: Copying machine,
    Microform
Equipment:
    6 5-drawer cabinets
Square Footage: 27

### 598

Hofstra University Library
Hempstead, NY 11550
Tel. (516) 560-5972
Hours: 9–9, M, T; 9–5, W–F; 12–5,
    Sa, Su
Responsible Person: Jennings, Vincent,
    Documents & Map Librarian
Special Strengths: United States
Employees: Full Time    Part Time
    Prof.       0          1
    Non-Prof.   0          1
Holdings:
    50000 Printed Maps
        1 Serial Title
Chronological Coverage:
    100% post 1900
Available to: Public, Students, Faculty
Average monthly use: 20
Copying Facilities: Copying machine
Equipment:
    36 5-drawer cabinets
Square Footage: 500
Map Depositories: USGS (topo);
    GPO

### 599

Franklin D. Roosevelt Library
259 Albany Post Road
Hyde Park, NY 12538
Tel. (914) 229-8114
Hours: 9–5, M–F
Responsible Person: Griffith, Sheryl,
    Acting Librarian
Special Strengths: Hudson River Valley
    (18th–20th cent.), F. D. Roosevelt
    Family Properties (plans & blueprints)
Employees: Full Time    Part Time
    Prof.       0          1
    Non-Prof.   0          1
Holdings:
    600 Printed Maps
    200 Manuscript Maps
        15 Atlases
Chronological Coverage: 15% pre 1900;
    85% post 1900
Formats: Typescript finding aid
Preservation methods: Encapsulation
Available to: Public
Copying Facilities: Copying machine,
    Microform, Photographic reproduction
Equipment:
    41 3-drawer cabinets
Square Footage: 1975

### 600

Cornell University
John M. Olin Library
Dept. of Maps, Microtexts, Newspapers
Ithaca, NY 14853
Tel. (607) 256-5258
Hours: 8–10, M–Th; 8–6, F; 9–6, Sa;
    1–10, Su
Responsible Person: Berthelsen,

Barbara, Map Librarian
Special Strengths: New York, China
Special Collections: Echols (S.E. Asia),
    Hartmann (emphasis on Vietnam),
    Wason (China–East Asia), Jared
    (Sparks)—Manuscript maps of the
    American Revolution
Employees: Full Time    Part Time
    Prof.       1          0
    Non-Prof.   1          2
Holdings:
    154000 Printed Maps
        860 Atlases
        10 Globes
        25 Raised Relief Maps
        3 Microforms
        730 Books
        210 Gazetteers
        4 Serial Titles
Chronological Coverage: 2% pre 1900;
    98% post 1900
Map collection is cataloged 90%
Classification: LC    Utility: RLIN
Formats: Cards
Preservation methods: Encapsulation,
    Chartex or Fabric Mounting
Available to: Public, Students, Faculty
Circulates to: Students, Faculty
Average annual circulation:
    Maps: 1300
Copying Facilities: Copying machine,
    Microform, Photographic reproduction
Equipment:
    231 5-drawer cabinets
    3 rolled map cases
    1 light table
Square Footage: 3143
Map Depositories: USGS (topo);
    USGS (geol); DMA (topo); DMA
    (aero); DMA (hydro); GPO

### 601

Cornell University
Resource Information Laboratory
Box 22 Roberts Hall
Ithaca, NY 14853
Tel. (607) 256-6520
Hours: 8–5, M–F
Responsible Person: Hardy, Dr. Ernest E.
Special Strengths: New York State
    (Aerial photography & remote sensing
    imagery)
Special Collections: U.S. Fish & Wildlife
    Wetlands Maps, about 400 special
    studies in New York State Agricultural
    Districts, New York State Land Use &
    Natural Resources Inventory
Employees: Full Time    Part Time
    Prof.       5          2
    Non-Prof.   0          2
Holdings:
    3000 Printed Maps
    4000 Aerial Photographs
Chronological Coverage:
    100% post 1900

Map collection is cataloged 100%
Formats: Cards
Preservation methods: Lamination,
  Air Conditioning for Photos
Available to: Public, Students, Faculty
Average monthly use: 20
Copying Facilities: Copying machine,
  Diazo
Equipment:
  35 5-drawer cabinets
  21 4-drawer file cabinets
  37 roll files
  Zoom transfer scope
  Zoom stereo scope, special projectors
Square Footage: 2400


### 602

Spacecraft Planetary Imaging Facility
Cornell University
317 Space Sciences Building
Ithaca, NY 14853
Tel. (607) 256-3833
Hours: 9–4:30, M–F
Responsible Person: Dermott, Margaret
Special Strengths: Mars (Geology,
  Topographic), Moon (Geology,
  Topographic)
Employees: Full Time    Part Time
  Prof.         1           0
  Non-Prof.     2           0
Holdings:
    500 Printed Maps
  100000 Satellite Imagery
      2 Atlases
      9 Globes
   3500 Computer Tapes
      6 Books
Chronological Coverage:
  100% post 1900
Map collection is cataloged 100%
Formats: Online, Computer Printout
Available to: Public, Students, Faculty
Average monthly use: 15
Equipment:
  9 5-drawer cabinets
  2 vertical map cabinets
  Map racks
  Light tables, rollers for viewing SIR-A
  rolls, digitizing tablet
Square Footage: 90
Map Depositories: USGS planetary
  maps/mosaics from Astrogeologic Br.


### 603

Queens Borough Public Library
History, Travel, Biography Division
89-11 Merrick Blvd.
Jamaica, NY 11432
Tel. (212) 990-0762
Hours: 10–9, M–F; 10–5:30, Sa;
  12–5, Su
Responsible Person: Hammer, Deborah,
  Division Head
Special Strengths: New York State,
  United States

Special Collections: Historical Maps
  of New York
Employees: Full Time    Part Time
  Prof.         6           0
  Non-Prof.     3           0
Holdings:
   7044 Printed Maps
      2 Satellite Imagery
    556 Atlases
      1 Globe
      3 Wall Maps
     30 Raised Relief Maps
     20 Books
      4 Gazetteers
Chronological Coverage: 25% pre 1900;
  75% post 1900
Map collection is cataloged 75%
Classification: Numerical
  Utility: OCLC
Formats: Cards, COM
Available to: Public, Students
Circulates to: Public, Students
Average monthly use: 90
Average annual circulation: Maps: 200;
  Books: 900
Interlibrary loan available
  Circulating Atlases Only
Copying Facilities: Copying machine
Equipment:
  10 5-drawer cabinets
  10 4-drawer file cabinets
  3 open shelf map cases
Square Footage: 94


### 604

York College Library
Jamaica, NY 11451
Tel. (212) 969-4015
Hours: 9–9, M–Th; 9–5, F; 10–2, Sa;
  10–1, Su
Responsible Person: Di Russo, Ben
Special Strengths: Lunar, Planetary,
  United States (Geology)
Employees: Full Time    Part Time
  Prof.         0           2
  Non-Prof.     0           1
Holdings:
   2697 Printed Maps
     59 Aerial Photographs
    242 Satellite Imagery
     89 Atlases
    144 Books
      3 Gazetteers
Chronological Coverage:
  100% post 1900
Map collection is cataloged 18%
Classification: LC    Utility: OCLC
Formats: Cards, Indexes & Guides
Available to: Public, Students, Faculty
Circulates to: Students, Faculty
Copying Facilities: Copying machine
Equipment:
  2 5-drawer cabinets
  1 vertical map cabinet
  5 atlas stands
Map Depositories: USGS (topo);

USGS (geol)


### 605

State University of New York College,
  New Paltz
Map Repository, Wooster Science Bldg.
New Paltz, NY 12561
Tel. (914) 257-2167
Hours: 8:30–4, M–F
Responsible Person: Egemeier,
  Dr. Stephen
Special Strengths: United States
Employees: Full Time    Part Time
  Prof.         0           1
  Non-Prof.     0           4
Holdings:
  10000 Printed Maps
    500 Aerial Photographs
    100 Satellite Imagery
     25 Wall Maps
     25 Raised Relief Maps
    200 Microforms
      2 Gazetteers
Chronological Coverage: 5% pre 1900;
  95% post 1900
Preservation methods: Chartex or
  Fabric Mounting
Available to: Public, Students, Faculty
Circulates to: Students, Faculty
Average monthly use: 4
Average annual circulation: Maps: 100
Copying Facilities: Copying machine
Equipment:
  25 5-drawer cabinets
  File cabinets for GQ collection
  Microfilm & microfiche readers
Square Footage: 500
Map Depositories: USGS (topo);
  USGS (geol)


### 606

Columbia University Libraries
Lehman Library, Map Room
420 W. 118t St.
New York, NY 10027
Tel. (212) 280-5002
Responsible Person: May, Bryan,
  Head, Documents Service
Employees: Full Time    Part Time
  Non-Prof.     0           1
Holdings:
  185000 Printed Maps
     300 Atlases
       5 Globes
      10 Wall Maps
      10 Raised Relief Maps
      50 Gazetteers
Chronological Coverage: 10% pre 1900;
  90% post 1900
Available to: Students, Faculty
Average monthly use: 20
Equipment:
  204 5-drawer cabinets
Square Footage: 4000
Map Depositories: USGS (topo);

USGS (geol); DMA (topo); DMA
(aero); DMA (hydro); GPO; NOAA;
Canada (topo)


607
Explorers Club
James B. Ford Library
The Edmund Hillary Map Room
46 E. 70th St.
New York, NY 10024
Tel. (212) 628-8383
Hours: By appointment
Holdings:
  1500 Printed Maps
    50 Atlases
    50 Books
    25 Gazetteers
  100 Serial Titles
Chronological Coverage: 10% pre 1900;
  90% post 1900
Preservation methods: Encapsulation
Available to: Public
Copying Facilities: Copying machine
Equipment:
  10 5-drawer cabinets


608
Hispanic Society of America
613 W. 155th St.
New York, NY 10032
Tel. (212) 926-2234
Hours: 1–4:30, T–F; 10–4:30, Sa
Responsible Person: Dufour, Lydia A.,
  Associate Curator
Special Strengths: Spain (pre-1900),
  Portugal (pre-1900), Latin America
  (pre-1900), Globes (17th–18th cent.)
Employees: Full Time    Part Time
  Prof.          1             0
  Non-Prof.      1             0
Holdings:
  1400 Printed Maps
    8 Atlases
    30 Globes
    7 Wall Maps
    1 Raised Relief Map
Chronological Coverage: 95% pre 1900;
  5% post 1900
Classification: Local
Available to: Public
Average monthly use: 1
Average annual circulation: Maps: 30
Copying Facilities: Photographic
  reproduction
Equipment:
  3 12-drawer metal cabinets
  10 oak cabinets
Square Footage: 200


609
Hunter College
Dept. of Geology & Geography
695 Park Ave.
New York, NY 10021

Tel. (212) 570-5290
Responsible Person: Clark, Dr. Keith
Holdings:
  1000 Printed Maps
    300 Aerial Photographs
    50 Atlases
    10 Globes
    50 Wall Maps
    20 Raised Relief Maps
    20 Computer Tapes
Chronological Coverage:
  100% post 1900
Available to: Students, Faculty
Circulates to: Students, Faculty
Average monthly use: 5
Copying Facilities: Copying machine
Equipment:
  16 5-drawer cabinets
  Zoom transfer scope,
  Various stereoscopes
Map Depositories: DMA (topo); DMA
(hydro)


610
New York Historical Society Library
170 Central Park West
New York, NY 10024
Tel. (212) 873-3400
Hours: 10–5, T–Sa
Responsible Person: Richards, Katherine
Special Collections: Erskine-Dewitt
  manuscript maps of Revolutionary
  areas
Holdings:
  30000 Printed Maps
  1000 Manuscript Maps
  1100 Atlases
    3 Globes
    2 Wall Maps
    2 Raised Relief Maps
  200 Gazetteers
Chronological Coverage: 90% pre 1900;
  10% post 1900
Map collection is cataloged 5%
Formats: Cards
Available to: Public, Students, Faculty
Copying Facilities: Microform,
  Photographic reproduction
Equipment:
  35 5-drawer cabinets


611
New York Public Library
The Research Libraries, Map Division
Fifth Avenue & 42nd St.
New York, NY 10018
Tel. (212) 930-0587
Hours: 10–6, M, W, F, Sa; 10–9, T
Responsible Person: Hudson, Alice C.,
  Chief
Special Strengths: New York City
  (19th–20th cent.); Midwest & East
  United States (County Atlases,
  19th–20th cent.); United States
Special Collections: Cloth Maps,

Christmas Card Maps, Antiquarian
Dealers Catalogs, Commercial
Dealers/Publishers Catalogs, Official
Government Catalogs
Employees: Full Time    Part Time
  Prof.          4             0
  Non-Prof.      0             2
Holdings:
  355402 Printed Maps
    50 Manuscript Maps
  10745 Atlases
    6 Globes
    23 Raised Relief Maps
  120 Microforms
  2927 Books
  475 Gazetteers
  84 Serial Titles
Chronological Coverage: 40% pre 1900;
  60% post 1900
Map collection is cataloged 97%
Classification: Geographic
  Utility: RLIN
Formats: Cards, Online
Preservation methods: Encapsulation,
  Deacidification
Available to: Public
Average monthly use: 760
Interlibrary loan available
  Photocopies
Copying Facilities: Copying machine,
  Dyeline, Photostatic 35mm
Equipment:
  224 5-drawer cabinets
  23 drop front storage boxes
  Light table, magnifying glasses
Square Footage: 4200
Map Depositories: USGS (topo);
  USGS (geol); DMA (topo); DMA
  (aero); DMA (hydro); GPO; NOS;
  NOAA


612
United Nations
Map Collection
Dag Hammarskjold Library
New York, NY 10017
Tel. (212) 754-7425
Hours: 9–5:30, M–F
Responsible Person: Dulka, Michael
Special Strengths: World (Gazetteers)
Employees: Full Time    Part Time
  Prof.          1             0
  Non-Prof.      1             0
Holdings:
  80000 Printed maps
    100 Manuscript Maps
  1500 Atlases
    3 Globes
    20 Wall Maps
    20 Raised Relief Maps
  1500 Books
  1500 Gazetteers
    20 Serial Titles
Chronological Coverage: 1% pre 1900;
  99% post 1900
Preservation methods: Lamination

Average monthly use: 300
Copying Facilities: Copying machine
Equipment:
   78 5-drawer cabinets
   7 vertical file units
   1 light table
Square Footage: 2100
Map Depositories: Gt. Brit. Directorate
   of Overseas Surveys

### 613
State University College at Oneonta
James M. Milne Library
Map Collection
Oneonta, NY 13820
Tel. (607) 431-3454
Hours: 8–4:30, M–F
Responsible Person: Ice, Dian Carolyn,
   Map Librarian
Employees: Full Time    Part Time
   Prof.        1            0
   Non-Prof.    0            1
Holdings:
   19782 Printed Maps
      10 Satellite Imagery
      16 Atlases
      17 Wall Maps
       2 Raised Relief Maps
     103 Microforms
      98 Books
      60 Gazetteers
       2 Serial Titles
Chronological Coverage: 1% pre 1900;
   99% post 1900
Map collection is cataloged 100%
Classification: LC    Utility: OCLC
Formats: Cards
Available to: Public, Students, Faculty
Circulates to: Students, Faculty
Average monthly use: 5
Average annual circulation: Maps: 38
Copying Facilities: Microform,
   IBM photocopiers
Equipment:
   32 5-drawer cabinets
Square Footage: 1129
Map Depositories: DMA (topo); DMA
   (aero); DMA (hydro); GPO; NOS;
   USGS (land use/land cover)

### 614
Lamont-Doherty Geological Observatory
   of Columbia University
Palisades, NY 10964
Tel. (914) 359-2900
Hours: 9–5, M–F
Responsible Person: Klimley, Susan
Special Strengths: World (1960–present),
   Geology
Employees: Full Time    Part Time
   Prof.        0            1
   Non-Prof.    0            1
Holdings:
   5000 Printed Maps
Chronological Coverage:

100% post 1900
Preservation methods: Encapsulation
Circulates to: Students, Faculty
Average monthly use: 5
Average annual circulation: Maps: 60
Interlibrary loan available
Copying Facilities: Copying machine
Equipment:
   6 3-drawer blue print cabinets
Square Footage: 200
Map Depositories: USGS (geol)

### 615
State University College of Arts
   & Sciences, Potsdam
Crumb Library
Potsdam, NY 13676
Tel. (315) 267-2486
Hours: 8–11, M–Th; 8–9, F; 10–11,
   Sa, Su
Responsible Person: Eldbloom,
   Nancy C., Documents & Map Librarian
Special Strengths: New York State
Employees: Full Time    Part Time
   Prof.        1            0
   Non-Prof.    0            2
Holdings:
   4300 Printed Maps
Chronological Coverage: 2% pre 1900;
   98% post 1900
Map collection is cataloged 5%
Classification: LC    Utility: OCLC
Formats: Cards
Available to: Public, Students, Faculty
Circulates to: Public, Students, Faculty
Interlibrary loan available
Copying Facilities: Copying machine
Equipment:
   11 10-drawer cabinets
Square Footage: 250
Map Depositories: USGS (topo);
   USGS (geol); GPO

### 616
State University College of Arts
   & Science, Potsdam
Geography Department
Potsdam, NY 13676
Tel. (315) 267-2213
Responsible Person: Rawden, Fiske
Special Strengths: Northern New York
Employees: Full Time    Part Time
   Prof.        0            1
Holdings:
   3000 Printed Maps
     400 Aerial Photographs
      10 Atlases
       3 Globes
      50 Wall Maps
      18 Raised Relief Maps
      12 Gazetteers
Chronological Coverage:
   100% post 1900
Available to: Students, Faculty
Copying Facilities: Copying machine,

Photographic reproduction
Equipment:
   12 5-drawer cabinets

### 617
Vassar College Library
Special Collections
Poughkeepsie, NY 12601
Tel. (914) 452-7000
Hours: 8:30–Noon, 1–5, M–F
Responsible Person: Browar, Lisa,
   Curator
Special Collections: Lasker Atlas
   Collection of Antique Atlases
   (1572–1778)
Employees: Full Time    Part Time
   Prof.        1            0
Holdings:
   200 Printed Maps
    40 Atlases
Chronological Coverage: 85% pre 1900;
   15% post 1900
Available to: Public, Students, Faculty
Average monthly use: 1
Copying Facilities: Copying machine
Equipment:
   4 5-drawer cabinets

### 618
Vassar College
Geology Map Library
Poughkeepsie, NY 12601
Tel. (914) 452-7000
Hours: 7:30–5, M–F
Special Strengths: United States
Special Collections: Hayden Surveys–
   exploration of the American West
Employees: Full Time    Part Time
   Non-Prof.    0            4
Holdings:
   20000 Printed Maps
     100 Aerial Photographs
      25 Satellite Imagery
     100 Atlases
       5 Globes
      25 Wall Maps
      10 Raised Relief Maps
Chronological Coverage: 5% pre 1900;
   95% post 1900
Available to: Public, Students, Faculty
Average monthly use: 50
Copying Facilities: Copying machine
Equipment:
   25 5-drawer cabinets
   1 vertical map cabinet
   9 wood sectional shelves
Map Depositories: USGS (topo);
   USGS (geol); DMA (topo); DMA
   (aero)

### 619
S.U.N.Y. at Stony Brook
Earth & Space Sciences Library
Map Room

Stony Brook, NY 11794-2199
Tel. (516) 246-3616
Hours: 8:30–10, M–Th; 8:30–5, F;
  1–5, Sa; 2–10, Su
Responsible Person: Walcott, Rosalind
Special Strengths: Geology
Employees: Full Time    Part Time
  Prof.        1          0
  Non-Prof.    3          0
Holdings:
  3000 Printed Maps
    10 Satellite Imagery
    50 Atlases
    10 Wall Maps
     2 Raised Relief Maps
   100 Books
     5 Gazetteers
    15 Serial Titles
Chronological Coverage:
  100% post 1900
Map collection is cataloged 30%
Classification: LC    Utility: OCLC
Formats: Cards
Available to: Public, Students, Faculty
Circulates to: Students, Faculty
Average monthly use: 20
Average annual circulation: Maps: 50;
  Books:50
Interlibrary loan available
  Only if suitable for mailing
Copying Facilities: Copying machine,
  Microform
Equipment:
  17 5-drawer cabinets
  5 filing cabinets
Square Footage: 1600
Map Depositories: USGS (geol)

### 620

State University of New York at Stony
  Brook
Melville Library, Map Collection
Stony Brook, NY 11794
Tel. (516) 246-5975
Hours: 8:30–Midnight, M–Th;
  8:30–10, F; 10–6, Sa; 2–Midnight, Su
Responsible Person: Shupe, Barbara,
  Map Librarian
Special Strengths: Long Island,
  New York
Employees: Full Time    Part Time
  Prof.        1          0
  Non-Prof.    0         14
Holdings:
  87500 Printed Maps
   300 Aerial Photographs
    50 Satellite Imagery
   457 Atlases
     5 Globes
    10 Wall Maps
    35 Microforms
   211 Books
   239 Gazetteers
     8 Serial Titles
Chronological Coverage: 1% pre 1900;
  99% post 1900

Preservation methods: Lamination
Available to: Public, Students, Faculty
Circulates to: Students, Faculty
Average monthly use: 280
Interlibrary loan available
  2 week loan period
Copying Facilities: Copying machine
Equipment:
  144 5-drawer cabinets
  5 file cabinets
  4 atlas cases
  4 drafting tables
  1 light table
Square Footage: 960
Map Depositories: USGS (topo);
  USGS (geol); DMA (topo); DMA
  (aero); DMA (hydro); GPO; NOS;
  NOAA

### 621

Canal Museum Library
318 Erie Blvd. East
Syracuse, NY 13202
Tel. (315) 471-0593
Hours: 9–5, M–F
Responsible Person: Waswloh, Todd S.,
  Librarian/Archivist
Special Strengths: New York
  (1833–1920), Canals
Employees: Full Time    Part Time
  Prof.        1          0
Holdings:
  1000 Printed Maps
  6000 Manuscript Maps
   100 Aerial Photographs
    30 Atlases
    20 Wall Maps
    50 Books
Chronological Coverage: 80% pre 1900;
  20% post 1900
Available to: Public, Students, Faculty
Average monthly use: 1
Copying Facilities: Copying machine,
  Photographic reproduction
Equipment:
  9 5-drawer cabinets
  1 3-drawer cabinet
Square Footage: 431

### 622

Syracuse University Libraries
  Map Collection
E. S. Bird Library
Syracuse, NY 13210
Tel. (315) 423-2575
Hours: 8–10, M–Th; 8–6, F; 10–6, Sa;
  10–10, Su
Responsible Person: Waltz, Mary Anne
Special Strengths: New York, United
  States
Employees: Full Time    Part Time
  Prof.        1          0
  Non-Prof.    1          2
Holdings:
  135000 Printed Maps

     5 Aerial Photographs
   100 Satellite Imagery
  1500 Atlases
     5 Globes
    25 Wall Maps
    20 Raised Relief Maps
   200 Microforms
   100 Computer Tapes
   100 Books
   150 Gazetteers
    30 Serial Titles
Chronological Coverage: 2% pre 1900;
  98% post 1900
Map collection is cataloged 65%
Classification: LC    Utility: OCLC
Formats: Cards, COM, Online
Preservation methods: Encapsulation,
  Edging
Available to: Public, Students, Faculty
Circulates to: Public, Students, Faculty
Average monthly use: 300
Average annual circulation:
  Maps: 1500; Books: 450
Interlibrary loan available
  Pre-1900 materials, encapsulated
  materials
Copying Facilities: Copying machine,
  Microform, Color copies
Equipment:
  114 5-drawer cabinets
  24 vertical map cabinets
  1 Hamilton-Calumet file
  4 Ulrich planfiles
  Mileage gauge, light table
Square Footage: 2550
Map Depositories: USGS (topo);
  USGS (geol); DMA (topo); DMA
  (aero); GPO

### 623

Troy Public Library
Reference Department
100 Second St.
Troy, NY 12180
Tel. (518) 274-7071
Hours: 9–9, M–Th; 9–5, F, Sa
Responsible Person: Gamache, Ellen,
  Head
Special Strengths: Troy & Rensselaer
  County (Historical Maps)
Employees: Full Time    Part Time
  Prof.        0          1
Holdings:
  2000 Printed Maps
    25 Atlases
     3 Globes
Chronological Coverage: 20% pre 1900;
  80% post 1900
Available to: Public
Circulates to: Public
Average monthly use: 10
Average annual circulation: Maps: 100
Interlibrary loan available
  Local maps
Copying Facilities: Copying machine
Equipment:
  2 5-drawer cabinets

3 vertical map cabinets
Map Depositories: GPO

### 624
United States Military Academy Library
West Point, NY 10996
Tel. (914) 938-2954
Hours: 8–4:30, M–F
Responsible Person: Capps, Marie T.,
 Maps & Manuscripts Librarian
Special Strengths: U.S. Military History,
 U.S. Western Expansion, Civil War
Special Collections: Gilmer Maps,
 Confederate States of America Maps
Employees: Full Time    Part Time
 Prof.        1         0
Holdings:
 2000 Printed Maps
  100 Manuscript Maps
  200 Aerial Photographs
   1 Globe
  20 Wall Maps
   5 Raised Relief Maps
Chronological Coverage: 70% pre 1900;
 30% post 1900
Map collection is cataloged 70%
Classification: Dewey   Utility: OCLC
Formats: Cards
Preservation methods: Encapsulation,
 Deacidification, Mending
Available to: Public, Students, Faculty
Average monthly use: 15
Copying Facilities: Copying machine,
 Photographic reproduction
Equipment:
 15 5-drawer cabinets
 1 vertical map cabinet

## North Carolina
### 625
Gardner-Webb College Library
P. O. Box 836
Boiling Springs, NC 28017
Tel. (704) 434-2361
Hours: 7:45–Midnight, M–Th; 7:45–5, F;
 9–5, Sa; 6–10, Su
Responsible Person: Bowles, David
Special Strengths: North Carolina
Employees: Full Time    Part Time
 Prof.        0         3
Holdings:
 493 Printed Maps
  1 Raised Relief Map
Chronological Coverage:
 100% post 1900
Preservation methods: Lamination
Available to: Public, Students, Faculty
Circulates to: Faculty
Average monthly use: 15
Copying Facilities: Copying machine
Equipment:
 1 12-drawer cabinet
Square Footage: 20
Map Depositories: USGS (topo)

### 626
Appalachian State University
Map Library
Rankin Hall
Boone, NC 28608
Tel. (704) 262-3000
Hours: 8–5, M–F
Responsible Person: Stillwell,
 Dr. H. Daniel
Employees: Full Time    Part Time
 Prof.        0         1
 Non-Prof.    0         3
Holdings:
 75000 Printed Maps
 11450 Aerial Photographs
  250 Satellite Imagery
  800 Atlases
   20 Globes
  300 Wall Maps
  100 Raised Relief Maps
  200 Books
  300 Gazetteers
  200 Serial Titles
Chronological Coverage: 2% pre 1900;
 98% post 1900
Available to: Public, Students, Faculty
Circulates to: Public, Students, Faculty
Average monthly use: 150
Average annual circulation: Maps: 150
Interlibrary loan available
Copying Facilities: Copying machine,
 Photographic reproduction
Equipment:
 80 5-drawer cabinets
 Mirror stereoscopes
 pocket stereoscopes
Square Footage: 1232
Map Depositories: USGS (topo);
 USGS (geol); DMA (topo); DMA
 (aero); DMA (hydro)

### 627
Campbell University
Carrie Rich Memorial Library
Map Collection
Buies Creek, NC 27506
Tel. (919) 893-4111
Responsible Person: Dickerson, Karen,
 Reference Librarian
Special Strengths: Southeast
Holdings:
 14000 Printed Maps
   50 Atlases
   1 Globe
   2 Wall Maps
   1 Raised Relief Map
   30 Books
   5 Gazetteers
Chronological Coverage:
 100% post 1900
Available to: Public, Students, Faculty
Average monthly use: 30
Average annual circulation: Maps: 100;
 Books: 300
Interlibrary loan available
Copying Facilities: Copying machine

Equipment:
 2 5-drawer cabinets
 1 vertical map cabinet
 Book shelves
Square Footage: 238
Map Depositories: USGS (topo);
 USGS (geol)

### 628
University of North Carolina at Chapel
 Hill
North Carolina Collection
Wilson Library (024-A)
Chapel Hill, NC 27514
Tel. (919) 962-1172
Hours: 8–5, M–F
Responsible Person: Cotten, Alice R.,
 Assistant Curator
Special Strengths: North Carolina
Employees: Full Time    Part Time
 Prof.        1         0
 Non-Prof.    0         1
Holdings:
 4250 Printed Maps
Chronological Coverage: 50% pre 1900;
 50% post 1900
Map collection is cataloged 98%
Classification: Dewey   Utility: OCLC
Formats: Cards
Preservation methods: Lamination,
 Deacidification
Available to: Public, Students, Faculty
Average monthly use: 50
Average annual circulation:
 Maps: 2000
Copying Facilities: Copying machine,
 Photographic reproduction
Equipment:
 15 5-drawer cabinets
Square Footage: 600

### 629
University of North Carolina at Chapel
 Hill
Watson Library (024-A), Maps Collection
Chapel Hill, NC 27514
Tel. (919) 962-3028
Hours: 8–5, M–F
Responsible Person: Poe, Celia D.,
 Map Librarian
Special Strengths: North Carolina,
 Southeastern United States, Latin
 America, Eastern Africa, Eastern
 Europe
Special Collections: Historical maps
 of Southeastern United States
Employees: Full Time    Part Time
 Prof.        1         0
 Non-Prof.    0         2
Holdings:
 92000 Printed Maps
   5 Satellite Imagery
 1175 Atlases
   2 Globes
   75 Wall Maps

120 Raised Relief Maps
8 Microforms
600 Books
310 Gazetteers
12 Serial Titles
Chronological Coverage: 6% pre 1900;
94% post 1900
Map collection is cataloged 1%
Classification: LC
Formats: Cards, COM
Available to: Public, Students, Faculty
Circulates to: Public, Students, Faculty
Average monthly use: 85
Interlibrary loan available
Copying Facilities: Copying machine,
Microform, Photographic reproduction
Equipment:
39 5-drawer cabinets
5 10-drawer cabinets
2 vertical files
Square Footage: 2900
Map Depositories: USGS (topo);
USGS (geol); DMA (topo); DMA
(aero); DMA (hydro); NOS

630
University of North Carolina
Geology Library
Mitchell Hall 029-A
Chapel Hill, NC 27514
Tel. (919) 962-2386
Hours: 8–5, M–F
Responsible Person: Sheaves, Miriam L.
Special Strengths: North Carolina
(Geology), Southeastern United States
(Geology)
Employees: Full Time    Part Time
Prof.          1            0
Non-Prof.      0            1
Holdings:
104000 Printed Maps
10 Manuscript Maps
20 Satellite Imagery
320 Atlases
3 Globes
106 Microforms
600 Books
200 Gazetteers
700 Serial Titles
Chronological Coverage: 2% pre 1900;
98% post 1900
Map collection is cataloged 100%
Classification: LC
Formats: Cards
Available to: Public, Students, Faculty
Circulates to: Public, Students, Faculty
Average monthly use: 1000
Average annual circulation: Maps: 490;
Books:9990
Interlibrary loan available
Copying Facilities: Copying machine
Equipment:
62 5-drawer cabinets
Kaile Projector
Square Footage: 696
Map Depositories: USGS (topo);

USGS (geol)

631
University of North Carolina
John N. Couch Library
301 Coker Hall 010-A, Dept. of Biology
Chapel Hill, NC 27514
Tel. (919) 962-3783
Hours: 8–5, M–F
Responsible Person: Burk, William R.,
Botany Librarian
Special Strengths: North Carolina
Employees: Full Time    Part Time
Prof.          1            0
Non-Prof.      1            1
Holdings:
1462 Printed Maps
25 Atlases
4 Wall Maps
3 Gazetteers
Chronological Coverage:
100% post 1900
Map collection is cataloged 100%
Formats: Cards
Available to: Public, Students, Faculty
Circulates to: Public, Students, Faculty
Average monthly use: 12
Average annual circulation: Maps: 131
Interlibrary loan available
Copying Facilities: Copying machine,
Photographic reproduction
Equipment:
2 5-drawer cabinets
Square Footage: 1120
Map Depositories: USGS (topo)

632
Public Library of Charlotte &
Mecklenburg County
310 N. Tryon St.
Charlotte, NC 28202
Tel. (704) 374-2798
Hours: 9–9, M–F; 9–6, Sa; 2–6, Su
(Sept.–May)
Responsible Person: Brice, Bill
Special Strengths: North Carolina
Employees: Full Time    Part Time
Prof.          1            0
Holdings:
7500 Printed Maps
10 Aerial Photographs
55 Atlases
5 Wall Maps
25 Books
5 Gazetteers
Chronological Coverage: 1% pre 1900;
99% post 1900
Available to: Public, Students, Faculty
Circulates to: Public, Students, Faculty
Average monthly use: 60
Average annual circulation: Maps: 250
Copying Facilities: Copying machine
Equipment:
2 5-drawer cabinets
1 vertical map cabinet

2 horizontal cabinets
Map Depositories: GPO

633
University of North Carolina at Charlotte
Atkins Library, Documents Department
Charlotte, NC 28223
Tel. (704) 597-2243
Hours: 8–11, M–Th; 8–6, F; 10–6, Sa;
2–11, Su
Responsible Person: Davis, Beverly
Employees: Full Time    Part Time
Prof.          1            0
Non-Prof.      3            0
Holdings:
24001 Printed Maps
Chronological Coverage:
100% post 1900
Preservation methods: Encapsulation
Available to: Public, Students, Faculty
Average monthly use: 55
Copying Facilities: Copying machine
Equipment:
24 5-drawer cabinets
Map Depositories: USGS (topo);
USGS (geol); GPO

634
Western Carolina University
Hunter Library, Map Room
Cullowhee, NC 28273
Tel. (704) 227-7362
Hours: 9–5, M–F
Responsible Person: Oser, Anita K.
Special Strengths: North Carolina,
Jamaica, Swaziland, Nepal
Employees: Full Time    Part Time
Prof.          0            1
Non-Prof.      0            3
Holdings:
57447 Printed Maps
498 Satellite Imagery
280 Atlases
3 Globes
6 Wall Maps
1 Raised Relief Map
31 Books
3 Gazetteers
Chronological Coverage: 1% pre 1900;
99% post 1900
Map collection is cataloged 5%
Classification: LC    Utility: OCLC
Formats: Cards
Preservation methods: Encapsulation,
Lamination
Available to: Public, Students, Faculty
Circulates to: Public, Students, Faculty
Average monthly use: 100
Average annual circulation:
Maps:1930
Interlibrary loan available
Copying Facilities: Copying machine,
Microform
Equipment:
34 5-drawer cabinets

Double face wood book shelves
Light table
Square Footage: 4400
Map Depositories: USGS (topo);
  USGS (geol); DMA (topo); DMA
  (aero); GPO

635
Duke University
Perkins Library
Public Documents & Maps Department
Durham, NC 27706
Tel. (919) 684-2380
Hours: 8–5, 7–10, M–Th; 8–5, F;
  9–5, Sa; 2–10, Su
Responsible Person: Eisenbeis, Kathleen
Employees: Full Time    Part Time
  Prof.          1          0
  Non-Prof.      1          0
Holdings:
  62100 Printed Maps
    100 Aerial Photographs
    50 Atlases
    1 Globe
    10 Wall Maps
    35 Raised Relief Maps
    2 Microforms
    170 Books
    30 Gazetteers
Chronological Coverage: 1% pre 1900;
  99% post 1900
Preservation methods: Lamination
Available to: Public, Students, Faculty
Circulates to: Students, Faculty
Interlibrary loan available
Copying Facilities: Copying machine
Equipment:
  78 5-drawer cabinet
Square Footage: 943
Map Depositories: USGS (topo);
  USGS (geol); DMA (topo); GPO

636
Cumberland County Public Library
N. C. Reference Department
P. O. Box 1720
Fayetteville, NC 28302
Tel. (919) 483-1580
Hours: 9–9, M–Th; 9–6, F, Sa; 2–6, Su
Responsible Person: Hall, Cynthia A.
Special Strengths: North Carolina
  (Colonial–present)
Employees: Full Time    Part Time
  Prof.          2          0
Holdings:
  2000 Printed Maps
    5 Atlases
    1 Globe
    1 Wall Map
    50 Books
    15 Gazetteers
Chronological Coverage: 50% pre 1900;
  50% post 1900
Map collection is cataloged 75%
Classification: Dewey

Formats: COM
Available to: Public, Students, Faculty
Average monthly use: 20
Copying Facilities: Photographic
  reproduction
Equipment:
  2 5-drawer cabinets

637
Greensboro Public Library
201 N. Greene St.
P. O. Drawer x-4
Greensboro, NC 27402
Tel. (919) 373-2471
Hours: 9–9, M–Th; 9–6, F, Sa; 2–6, Su
Responsible Person: Windham, Shirley L.,
  Head, Reference
Special Strengths: Greensboro, Guilford
  County, North Carolina
Employees: Full Time    Part Time
  Prof.          0          2
Holdings:
  1340 Printed Maps
    1 Aerial Photograph
    180 Atlases
    1 Globe
    34 Wall Maps
    1 Raised Relief Map
    7 Books
    2 Gazetteers
Chronological Coverage: 5% pre 1900;
  95% post 1900
Map collection is cataloged 8%
Classification: Dewey   Utility: OCLC
Formats: Cards, Online
Preservation methods: Lamination,
  Chartex or Fabric Mounting,
  Deacidification
Available to: Public
Copying Facilities: Copying machine
Equipment:
  2 5-drawer cabinets

638
Guilford College Library
5800 W. Friendly Ave.
Greensboro, NC 27410
Tel. (919) 292-5511
Special Strengths: North Carolina
  (Geology)
Special Collections: Geological
  Survey maps of North Carolina
Holdings:
  700 Printed Maps
    120 Atlases
    2 Globes
    10 Raised Relief Maps
    25 Books
    5 Gazetteers
    4 Serial Titles
Chronological Coverage:
  100% post 1900
Map collection is cataloged 100%
Classification: LC
Formats: Cards

Available to: Public, Students, Faculty
Copying Facilities: Copying machine
Equipment:
  2 5-drawer cabinets
Square Footage: 9

639
University of North Carolina
  at Greensboro
Jackson Library–Reference Dept.
Greensboro, NC 27412
Tel. (919) 379-5419
Hours: 8–10, M–Th; 8–5, F; 1–4, Sa;
  1–9, Su
Responsible Person: Ryckman, Nancy
Special Strengths: North Carolina
Employees: Full Time    Part Time
  Prof.          0          1
  Non-Prof.      0          1
Holdings:
  5000 Printed Maps
    200 Atlases
    4 Globes
    10 Wall Maps
    5 Gazetteers
    153 Serial Titles
Chronological Coverage: 1% pre 1900;
  99% post 1900
Map collection is cataloged 60%
Classification: Local
Formats: Cards
Available to: Public, Students, Faculty
Circulates to: Students, Faculty
Average monthly use: 20
Average annual circulation: Maps: 10
Copying Facilities: Copying machine
Equipment:
  9 5-drawer cabinets
  1 vertical map cabinet
  Wall shelving
Square Footage: 460
Map Depositories: USGS (topo);
  DMA (topo); GPO

640
East Carolina University
Map Library, Dept. of Geology
Greenville, NC 27834
Tel. (919) 757-6016
Hours: By appointment
Responsible Person: Otte, Lee J.
Special Strengths: United States
Employees: Full Time    Part Time
  Prof.          0          1
Holdings:
  5000 Printed Maps
    100 Wall Maps
Chronological Coverage:
  100% post 1900
Map collection is cataloged 100%
Formats: Cards
Available to: Students, Faculty
Average monthly use: 6
Copying Facilities: Copying machine
Equipment:

5 5-drawer cabinets
6 4-drawer file cabinets
Square Footage: 100
Map Depositories: USGS (geol)


### 641

North Carolina Geological Survey
P. O. Box 27687
Raleigh, NC 27611
Tel. (919) 733-2423
Hours: 8–5, M–F
Responsible Person: Flynt, B. J. Jr.
Special Strengths: North Carolina
 (Geology)
Special Collections: Select North
 Carolina folios from Geologic Atlas of
 the United States (USGS) 1897–1931
Employees: Full Time     Part Time
 Prof.         2              0
Holdings:
 20000 Printed Maps
 15000 Aerial Photographs
Chronological Coverage: 2% pre 1900;
 98% post 1900
Available to: Public, Students, Faculty
Average monthly use: 100
Average annual circulation: Maps: 400
Copying Facilities: Copying machine,
 Microform, Dyeline, Photographic
 reproduction
Equipment:
 24 5-drawer cabinets
Square Footage: 600


### 642

North Carolina State Archives
109 E. Jones St.
Raleigh, NC 27611
Tel. (919) 733-3952
Hours: 8–5:30, T–F; 8:30–5:30, Sa
Special Strengths: North Carolina
 (16th–20th cent.)
Special Collections: North Carolina
 Railroad Company records, Sanborn
 Fire Insurance Maps of North Carolina
 Towns, Swamp Land Surveys, Civil
 War campaign maps
Employees: Full Time     Part Time
 Prof.         5              0
 Non-Prof.     2              1
Holdings:
 4000 Printed Maps
Chronological Coverage: 75% pre 1900;
 25% post 1900
Map collection is cataloged 98%
Formats: Cards
Preservation methods: Encapsulation,
 Lamination, Deacidification
Available to: Public
Copying Facilities: Photographic
 reproduction, Photostat
Equipment:
 23 5-drawer cabinets
Square Footage: 270


### 643

North Carolina State Museum of Natural
 History
Brimley Memorial Library
Southeastern Maps Collection
102 N. Salisbury St.
Raleigh, NC 27611
Tel. (919) 733-7450
Hours: 9–5, M–Sa; 1–5, Su
Responsible Person: Cooper, Dr. John E.
Special Strengths: Southeastern United
 States
Holdings:
 5000 Printed Maps
 200 Aerial Photographs
 15 Atlases
 1 Raised Relief Map
 50 Books
Available to: Public, Students, Faculty
Interlibrary loan available
Copying Facilities: Copying machine
Equipment:
 6 5-drawer cabinets
Map Depositories: USGS (topo)


### 644

North Carolina State University
D. H. Hill Library, Documents Dept.
Box 7111
Raleigh, NC 27695-7111
Tel. (919) 737-3280
Hours: 8–10, M–F
Responsible Person: Newman, Lisa A.
Employees: Full Time     Part Time
 Prof.         0              1
 Non-Prof.     0              1
Holdings:
 8250 Printed Maps
 1 Globe
 3 Wall Maps
Chronological Coverage: 1% pre 1900;
 99% post 1900
Available to: Public, Students, Faculty
Average monthly use: 180
Copying Facilities: Copying machine
Equipment:
 13 5-drawer cabinets
 6 11-drawer, 1 25-drawer
 2 file cabinets
 3 atlas cases
Square Footage: 160
Map Depositories: USGS (topo);
 USGS (geol); DMA (aero); DMA
 (hydro); GPO; NOS


### 645

Catawba College
Corriher-Linn-Black Library
2300 W. Innes St.
Salisbury, NC 28144
Tel. (704) 637-4448
Hours: 8–9:30, M–Th; 8–5, F;
 1:30–9:30, Su
Responsible Person: Sell, Dr. Betty
Special Strengths: North Carolina &

neighboring states
Employees: Full Time     Part Time
 Prof.         0              4
 Non-Prof.     0              2
Holdings:
 5039 Printed Maps
 123 Aerial Photographs
 61 Satellite Imagery
 81 Atlases
 2 Wall Maps
 1185 Microforms
 145 Books
 7 Gazetteers
 3 Serial Titles
Chronological Coverage:
 100% post 1900
Map collection is cataloged 3%
Classification: Dewey
Formats: Cards
Available to: Public, Students, Faculty
Circulates to: Students, Faculty
Average monthly use: 60
Average annual circulation: Maps: 20;
 Aerial Photographs: 5
Interlibrary loan available
Copying Facilities: Copying machine,
 Microform, Photographic reproduction
Equipment:
 3 5-drawer cabinets
 2 vertical map cabinets
 7 shelf atlas stand
Square Footage: 175
Map Depositories: USGS (topo);
 USGS (geol); GPO


### 646

Rowan Public Library
Edith M. Clark History Room
201 W. Fisher St.
Salisbury, NC 28144
Tel. (704) 633-5578
Hours: 9–9, M–F; 9–5, Sa; 1–5, Su
Responsible Person: Young, Beth
Special Strengths: North Carolina
 (Rowan County, 1750–1900)
Special Collections: Maps of Salisbury–
 Rowan County from the time the
 county was formed in 1753
Employees: Full Time     Part Time
 Prof.         0              1
 Non-Prof.     1              0
Holdings:
 322 Printed Maps
 6 Atlases
 10 Books
 14 Gazetteers
Chronological Coverage: 75% pre 1900;
 25% post 1900
Preservation methods: Lamination,
 Edging
Available to: Public
Copying Facilities: Copying machine
Equipment:
 2 5-drawer cabinets
Square Footage: 10

647
Mitchell Community College Library
W. Bread St.
Statesville, NC 28677
Tel. (704) 873-2201
Hours: 8–10, M–Th; 8–5, F; 1–5, Su
Responsible Person: Bradwhas, Marcia,
  Director LRC
Special Strengths: North Carolina
Holdings:
  625 Printed Maps
Chronological Coverage:
  100% post 1900
Available to: Public, Students, Faculty
Average monthly use: 10
Copying Facilities: Copying machine
Equipment:
  1 5-drawer cabinet
Square Footage: 8
Map Depositories: USGS (topo);
  USGS (geol)


648
Cape Fear Technical Institute Library
411 North Front St.
Wilmington, NC 28403-3993
Tel. (919) 343-0481
Hours: 8–10, M–F
Responsible Person: McGough,
  Willie B., Jr.
Holdings:
  500 Printed Maps
  10 Manuscript Maps
  50 Aerial Photographs
  20 Satellite Imagery
  20 Atlases
  3 Globes
  6 Wall Maps
  20 Raised Relief Maps
  10 Books
  10 Gazetteers
  10 Serial Titles
Chronological Coverage: 1% pre 1900;
  99% post 1900
Map collection is cataloged 50%
Formats: Cards
Available to: Public, Students, Faculty
Average monthly use: 25
Copying Facilities: Copying machine
Equipment:
  4 5-drawer cabinets
Square Footage: 50


649
University of North Carolina, Wilmington
Randall Library
601 S. College Rd.
Wilmington, NC 28403-3298
Tel. (919) 791-4330
Hours: 7:45–Midnight, M–Th; 7:45–6, F;
  10–6, Sa; 1–Midnight, Su
Responsible Person: Manerfeld, Arlene,
  Documents Librarian
Special Strengths: North Carolina &
  surrounding states

| Employees: | Full Time | Part Time |
|---|---|---|
| Prof. | 1 | 0 |
| Non-Prof. | 1 | 1 |

Holdings:
  1850 Printed maps
Chronological Coverage:
  100% post 1900
Available to: Public, Students, Faculty
Average monthly use: 25
Copying Facilities: Copying machine,
  Microform
Equipment:
  4 5-drawer cabinets
Square Footage: 40
Map Depositories: USGS (topo);
  USGS (geol)


650
Wake Forest University
Z. Smith Reynolds Library
Box 7777, Reynolds Station
Winston-Salem, NC 27109
Tel. (919) 761-5828
Hours: 9–11, M–F; 9–5, Sa; 1–11, Su
Responsible Person: Giles, Patricia,
  Head, Reference Dept.
Special Strengths: Southeast

| Employees: | Full Time | Part Time |
|---|---|---|
| Prof. | 3 | 0 |
| Non-Prof. | 0 | 12 |

Holdings:
  5000 Printed Maps
  50 Atlases
  1 Globe
  6 Wall Maps
  10 Gazetteers
Chronological Coverage: 1% pre 1900;
  99% post 1900
Map collection is cataloged 3%
Classification: Own system
  Utility: OCLC
Formats: Cards
Available to: Public, Students, Faculty
Average monthly use: 12
Copying Facilities: Copying machine
Equipment:
  8 5-drawer cabinets
Map Depositories: USGS (topo)


**North Dakota**
651
State Historical Society of ND
State Archives & Historical Research
  Library
North Dakota Heritage Center
Bismarck, ND 58505-0179
Tel. (701) 224-2668
Hours: 8–5, M–F
Responsible Person: Gray, David P.
Special Strengths: Dakota Territory
  (1870–1889), North Dakota (1889–
  present)

| Employees: | Full Time | Part Time |
|---|---|---|
| Prof. | 1 | 0 |

Holdings:
  3000 Printed Maps

  250 Manuscript Maps
  10000 Aerial Photographs
  400 Satellite Imagery
  240 Atlases
  50 Wall Maps
  12 Microforms
  10 Books
Chronological Coverage: 20% pre 1900;
  80% post 1900
Map collection is cataloged 25%
Classification: Dewey   Utility: OCLC
Formats: Cards
Preservation methods: Encapsulation,
  Deacidification
Available to: Public, Students, Faculty
Average monthly use: 40
Interlibrary loan available
Copying Facilities: Copying machine
Equipment:
  180 5-drawer cabinets
Square Footage: 100
Map Depositories: ND Highway Dept.
  Maps


652
North Dakota State University Library
Fargo, ND 58105
Tel. (701) 237-8886
Hours: 8–10, M–F
Responsible Person: Buck, Aileen,
  Map Librarian
Special Strengths: North Dakota

| Employees: | Full Time | Part Time |
|---|---|---|
| Prof. | 0 | 1 |
| Non-Prof. | 0 | 1 |

Holdings:
  70000 Printed Maps
  160 Atlases
  2 Globes
  2 Wall Maps
  5 Raised Relief Maps
  5 Books
  5 Gazetteers
  5 Serial Titles
Chronological Coverage:
  100% post 1900
Map collection is cataloged 95%
Classification: Local
Formats: Cards
Available to: Public, Students, Faculty
Average monthly use: 200
Copying Facilities: Copying machine
Equipment:
  24 vertical map cabinets
  1 light table
Square Footage: 1524
Map Depositories: USGS (topo);
  DMA (topo)


653
University of North Dakota
Department of Geography
Grand Forks, NC 58202
Tel. (701) 777-4246
Hours: 8:30–4, M–F

Responsible Person: Chang, Kang-tsung, Chair
Employees: Full Time    Part Time
Non-Prof.    0         1
Holdings:
  40000 Printed Maps
    200 Aerial Photographs
     50 Satellite Imagery
     30 Atlases
     20 Globes
    150 Wall Maps
Chronological Coverage: 10% pre 1900; 90% post 1900
Map collection is cataloged 50%
Classification: Local
Formats: Cards
Available to: Public, Students, Faculty
Average monthly use: 5
Copying Facilities: Copying machine
Equipment:
  20 5-drawer cabinets
Square Footage: 140
Map Depositories: DMA (topo); DMA (aero); DMA (hydro)

### 654

University of North Dakota
Geology Library
326 Leonard Hall
Grand Forks, ND 58202
Tel. (701) 777-3221
Hours: 8–12, 1–4:30, M–F
Responsible Person: Gilbert, Holly
Special Strengths: North America (Geology)
Employees: Full Time    Part Time
Prof.       0         1
Non-Prof.   0         2
Holdings:
  95125 Printed Maps
  42610 Aerial Photographs
    239 Atlases
     21 Wall Maps
     21 Raised Relief Maps
      5 Books
      1 Gazetteer
Chronological Coverage: 100% post 1900
Map collection is cataloged 50%
Classification: Other    Utility: OCLC
Formats: Cards
Available to: Public, Students, Faculty
Circulates to: Public, Students, Faculty
Average annual circulation: Maps: 840; Aerial Photographs: 900
Copying Facilities: Copying machine
Equipment:
  62 5-drawer cabinets
  3 vertical map cabinets
  8 8-drawer cabinets
Map Depositories: USGS (topo); USGS (geol); GPO; Canada (geol)

### 655

Minot State College
Earth Science Department

Minot, ND 58201
Tel. (701) 857-3000
Hours: 8–5, M–F
Responsible Person: Martin, DeWayne
Special Strengths: Northern Midwest
Employees: Full Time    Part Time
Prof.       0         1
Non-Prof.   0         2
Holdings:
  30000 Printed Maps
    800 Aerial Photographs
    400 Satellite Imagery
     40 Wall Maps
Chronological Coverage: 100% post 1900
Preservation methods: Edging
Available to: Public, Students, Faculty
Circulates to: Public, Students, Faculty
Average monthly use: 200
Average annual circulation: Maps: 400
Equipment:
  3 5-drawer cabinets
  10 vertical map cabinets
  Map-o-graph enlarger
Map Depositories: USGS (topo); USGS (geol)

### 656

Minot State College
Memorial Library
Minot, ND 58701
Tel. (701) 857-3200
Responsible Person: Clark, George
Special Strengths: Midwest, North Dakota, Dakota Territory (19th cent.)
Employees: Full Time    Part Time
Prof.       0         2
Non-Prof.   0         2
Holdings:
  36500 Printed Maps
   1000 Aerial Photographs
    300 Satellite Imagery
    160 Atlases
      4 Globes
     10 Wall Maps
     20 Raised Relief Maps
    100 Books
      1 Gazetteer
      1 Serial Title
Chronological Coverage: 1% pre 1900; 99% post 1900
Available to: Public, Students, Faculty
Circulates to: Public, Students, Faculty
Average monthly use: 50
Average annual circulation: Maps: 600
Copying Facilities: Copying machine
Equipment:
  5 5-drawer cabinets
  7 vertical files
  9 custom built cabinets
Square Footage: 972
Map Depositories: USGS (topo); USGS (geol)

## Ohio

### 657

Akron-Summit County Public Library
Science & Technology Department
55 S. Main St.
Akron, OH 44326
Tel. (216) 762-7621
Hours: 9–9, M–Th; 9–6, F; 9–5, Sa
Responsible Person: McKnight, Joyce
Special Strengths: United States
Employees: Full Time    Part Time
Prof.       0         6
Non-Prof.   0         4
Holdings:
  36000 Printed Maps
Chronological Coverage: 100% post 1900
Preservation methods: Lamination
Available to: Public
Average monthly use: 45
Copying Facilities: Copying machine
Equipment:
  28 5-drawer cabinets
Square Footage: 72
Map Depositories: USGS (topo)

### 658

Ohio University
Map Collection
Athens, OH 45701
Tel. (614) 594-5240
Hours: 8–Midnight, M–F; 10–10, Sa; Noon–Midnight, Su
Responsible Person: Foster, Theodore S.
Special Strengths: Southeast Asia, Indonesia, Africa
Employees: Full Time    Part Time
Prof.       1         1
Non-Prof.   0         6
Holdings:
  129360 Printed Maps
      16 Manuscript Maps
    6030 Aerial Photographs
       6 Satellite Imagery
    1208 Atlases
       4 Globes
      60 Wall Maps
       3 Raised Relief Maps
      28 Microforms
      40 Books
     163 Gazetteers
       6 Serial Titles
Chronological Coverage: 15% pre 1900; 85% post 1900
Map collection is cataloged 30%
Classification: LC    Utility: OCLC
Formats: Cards
Preservation methods: Edging
Available to: Public, Students, Faculty
Circulates to: Public, Students, Faculty
Average monthly use: 300
Average annual circulation: Maps: 2600; Books: 30
Interlibrary loan available
Copying Facilities: Copying machine, Microform, Photographic reproduction

Equipment:
  22 5-drawer cabinets
  Atlas cases
  Light table
Square Footage: 3000
Map Depositories: USGS (topo);
  USGS (geol); DMA (topo); DMA
  (aero); DMA (hydro); GPO

### 659

Barberton Public Library
602 W. Park Ave.
Barberton, OH 44203
Tel. (216) 745-1194
Hours: 10–9, M–F; 10–6, Sa
Responsible Person: Kirbawy, Barbara,
  Director
Special Strengths: Ohio (1800–present)
Holdings:
  448 Printed Maps
  87 Atlases
  2 Globes
  10 Wall Maps
  1 Raised Relief Map
  4 Gazetteers
Chronological Coverage: 5% pre 1900;
  95% post 1900
Preservation methods: Encapsulation
Available to: Public
Circulates to: Public
Interlibrary loan available
Copying Facilities: Copying machine
Equipment:
  1 5-drawer cabinet

### 660

Bowling Green State University
Map Library
Bowling Green, OH 43402
Tel. (419) 372-2156
Hours: 9–5, M, W, Th; 9–10, T;
  6–10, Su
Responsible Person: Collins, Evron
Special Strengths: Ohio
Employees: Full Time    Part Time
  Prof.        1           0
  Non-Prof.    3           0
Holdings:
  40500 Printed Maps
  2000 Aerial Photographs
  300 Atlases
  4 Globes
  2 Raised Relief Maps
  200 Books
  100 Gazetteers
  5 Serial Titles
Chronological Coverage: 1% pre 1900;
  99% post 1900
Preservation methods: Encapsulation,
  Archival tape
Available to: Public, Students, Faculty
Circulates to: Public Students, Faculty
Average monthly use: 200
Average annual circulation:
  Maps: 1200

Interlibrary loan available
Copying Facilities: Copying machine,
  Photographic reproduction
Equipment:
  36 5-drawer cabinets
  9 vertical map cabinets
  3 wooden cases
Square Footage: 250
Map Depositories: USGS (topo);
  USGS (geol); DMA (topo); DMA
  (aero); GPO; NOS; Canada (topo);
  Canada (geol)

### 661

Stark County District Library
715 Market Ave., North
Canton, OH 44702
Tel. (216) 452-0665
Hours: 9–9, M–Th; 9–5, F, Sa
Responsible Person: Renner, Mary Ann,
  Head, Reference Dept.
Special Strengths: Ohio (historical
  atlases)
Employees: Full Time    Part Time
  Prof.        2           0
  Non-Prof.    2           1
Holdings:
  1000 Printed Maps
  250 Aerial Photographs
  140 Atlases
  1 Globe
  2 Wall Maps
  20 Books
  5 Gazetteers
  2 Serial Titles
Chronological Coverage: 15% pre 1900;
  85% post 1900
Map collection is cataloged 14%
Classification: Dewey    Utility: OCLC
Formats: Cards
Preservation methods: Lamination
Available to: Public, Students
Circulates to: Public, Students
Average monthly use: 600
Average annual circulation: Maps: 60
Interlibrary loan available
Copying Facilities: Copying machine,
  Microform
Equipment:
  1 vertical map cabinet
  1 10-drawer map cabinet
  1 5-drawer atlas stand

### 662

Public Library of Cincinnati & Hamilton
  County
Map Collection, History Department
800 Vine St.
Cincinnati, OH 45202-2071
Tel. (513) 369-6909
Hours: 9–9, M–F; 9–6, Sa
Responsible Person: Neely, Gardiner,
  Map Librarian
Special Strengths: Cincinnati &
  Hamilton County (19th cent.); Ohio

& surrounding states (19th cent.
  atlases)
Employees: Full Time    Part Time
  Prof.        0           1
  Non-Prof.    1           0
Holdings:
  137951 Printed Maps
  125 Aerial Photographs
  1250 Atlases
  3 Globes
  10 Raised Relief Maps
  10 Microforms
  250 Books
  500 Gazetteers
  20 Serial Titles
Chronological Coverage: 10% pre 1900;
  90% post 1900
Preservation methods: Lamination,
  Chartex or Fabric Mounting
Available to: Public, Students, Faculty
Circulates to: Public, Students, Faculty
Copying Facilities: Copying machine,
  Microform
Equipment:
  78 5-drawer cabinets
  21 vertical file cabinets
Square Footage: 1400
Map Depositories: USGS (topo);
  USGS (geol); DMA (topo); DMA
  (aero); DMA (hydro); GPO

### 663

University of Cincinnati
University Libraries
103 Old Tech ML 13
Cincinnati, OH 45221
Tel. (513) 475-4332
Responsible Person: Spohn, Richard
Employees: Full Time    Part Time
  Non-Prof.    1           3
Holdings:
  110000 Printed Maps
  2500 Aerial Photographs
  250 Wall Maps
  6 Raised Relief Maps
Chronological Coverage:
  100% post 1900
Map collection is cataloged 60%
Formats: Cards
Available to: Public, Students, Faculty
Circulates to: Students, Faculty
Copying Facilities: Copying machine
Equipment:
  70 5-drawer cabinets
  2 vertical map cabinets
  7 4-drawer file cabinets
Square Footage: 1200
Map Depositories: USGS (topo);
  USGS (geol); DMA (topo); DMA
  (aero); GPO; Canada (geol)

### 664

Case Western Reserve
Special Materials Collection
Sears Library

10900 Euclid Ave.
Cleveland, OH 44106
Tel. (216) 368-6602
Hours: 8–12, M–Th; 8–5, F; 9–5:30 Sa
Responsible Person: Smiley, Gladys M.
Employees: Full Time    Part Time
  Prof.          0            1
  Non-Prof.      0            1
Holdings:
  50000 Printed Maps
Chronological Coverage:
  100% post 1900
Available to: Students, Faculty
Circulates to: Students
Equipment:
  69 5-drawer cabinets
Map Depositories: USGS (topo);
  USGS (geol); DMA (topo)

## 665

Cleveland Public Library
Map Collection
325 Superior Avenue
Cleveland, OH 44114-1271
Tel. (216) 623-2880
Hours: 9–6, M–Sa
Responsible Person: Farrell, Maureen,
  Head of Map Collection
Special Strengths: Ohio (1800–present),
  United States
Special Collections: Ohio County
  Atlases, Ohio Sanborn and Hopkins
  Plat Maps (bound volumes and
  microfilm 1886–1972), London Maps,
  1750–1850
Employees: Full Time    Part Time
  Prof.          0            1
  Non-Prof.      1            2
Holdings:
  111275 Printed Maps
     18 Aerial Photographs
      1 Satellite Imagery
   1170 Atlases
      3 Globes
      6 Wall Maps
      7 Raised Relief Maps
     97 Microforms
    658 Books
    334 Gazetteers
     37 Serial Titles
Chronological Coverage: 10% pre 1900;
  90% post 1900
Map collection is cataloged 5%
Classification: LC    Utility: OCLC
Formats: Cards, Online
Preservation methods: Encapsulation,
  Deacidification
Available to: Public
Average monthly use: 470
Interlibrary loan available
  Depending upon physical condition
Copying Facilities: Copying machine,
  Photographic reproduction
Equipment:
  85 5-drawer cabinets
  14 vertical map cabinets

Square Footage: 2998
Map Depositories: USGS (topo);
  USGS (geol); DMA (topo); DMA
  (aero); DMA (hydro); GPO; NOS

## 666

Western Reserve Historical Society
History Library
10825 East Blvd.
Cleveland, OH 44106
Tel. (216) 721-5722
Hours: 9–5, T–Sa
Responsible Person: Pike, Kermit J.
Employees: Full Time    Part Time
  Prof.          0            5
Holdings:
  3000 Printed Maps
  1000 Aerial Photographs
   600 Atlases
     3 Globes
   160 Books
    40 Gazetteers
Chronological Coverage: 75% pre 1900;
  25% post 1900
Map collection is cataloged 90%
Classification: In-house
Formats: Cards
Available to: Public
Average monthly use: 30
Copying Facilities: Copying machine,
  Microform, Photographic reproduction
Equipment:
  20 5-drawer cabinets
   2 vertical map cabinets
  40 map boxes
  15 shelves

## 667

Ohio Department of Natural Resources
Division of Geological Survey
Building B, Fountain Square
Columbus, OH 43224
Tel. (614) 265-6605
Hours: 8–5, M–F
Responsible Person: Hackathorn,
  Merrianne
Special Strengths: Ohio
Employees: Full Time    Part Time
  Prof.          0            1
Holdings:
  2000 Printed Maps
   100 Manuscript Maps
  1000 Aerial Photographs
     2 Atlases
     5 Wall Maps
     2 Raised Relief Maps
     6 Books
Chronological Coverage: 10% pre 1900;
  90% post 1900
Preservation methods: Lamination,
  Chartex or Fabric Mounting
Available to: Public, Students, Faculty
Average monthly use: 50
Copying Facilities: Copying machine
Equipment:

30 5-drawer cabinets
 6 vertical map cabinets
18 multiple drawer wooden map
cabinets
Map Depositories: USGS (topo)

## 668

Ohio Historical Society
Library, Archives-Library Division
1982 Velma Ave.
Columbus, OH 43211
Tel. (614) 466-1500
Hours: 9–5, T–Sa
Responsible Person: Gutgesell, Stephen
Special Strengths: Ohio
Employees: Full Time    Part Time
  Prof.          0            1
Holdings:
  14000 Printed Maps
   1000 Manuscript Maps
    500 Aerial Photographs
    500 Atlases
     15 Books
     40 Gazetteers
Chronological Coverage: 55% pre 1900;
  45% post 1900
Map collection is cataloged 75%
Classification: In-house system
  Utility: OCLC
Formats: Cards
Preservation methods: Encapsulation,
  Lamination, Deacidification,
  Dry and Solvent cleaning
Available to: Public, Students, Faculty
Average annual circulation: Maps: 375
Copying Facilities: Copying machine,
  Microform, Photographic reproduction
Equipment:
  17 5-drawer cabinets
Square Footage: 325
Map Depositories: Ohio State
  Documents

## 669

Ohio State University
Map Library
1858 Neil Avenue Mall
Columbus, OH 43210
Tel. (614) 422-2393
Hours: 8:30–5:30, M–F
Responsible Person: Schoyer, George
Employees: Full Time    Part Time
  Prof.          0            1
  Non-Prof.      0            2
Holdings:
  118461 Printed Maps
      30 Satellite Imagery
     835 Atlases
       1 Globe
      12 Wall Maps
      10 Raised Relief Maps
     452 Books
     248 Gazetteers
      10 Serial Titles
Chronological Coverage: 10% pre 1900;

90% post 1900
Preservation methods: Encapsulation
Available to: Public, Students, Faculty
Circulates to: Public, Students, Faculty
Average monthly use: 250
Average annual circulation: Maps: 53
Interlibrary loan available
Copying Facilities: Copying machine
Equipment:
    122 5-drawer cabinets
    2 vertical file cabinets
Square Footage: 1944
Map Depositories: USGS (topo);
    DMA (topo); DMA (aero); DMA
    (hydro); GPO; NOS; Canada (topo)

### 670

Public Library of Columbus
Biography, History & Travel Division
28 S. Hamilton Rd.
Columbus, OH 43213
Tel. (614) 222-7154
Hours: 9–9, M–Th; 9–6, F, Sa
Responsible Person: Newman, John,
    Division Head
Special Strengths: Ohio, Columbus
Special Collections: Plat Books of Ohio
    Counties (current); Sanborn Fire
    Insurance Maps of Columbus, 1923–,
    Historical Maps of Ohio, 1922–present
Holdings:
    2000 Printed Maps
    160 Atlases
    10 Gazetteers
Chronological Coverage: 33% pre 1900;
    67% post 1900
Available to: Public
Circulates to: Public
Copying Facilities: Copying machine
Equipment:
    2 15-drawer cabinets
Map Depositories: USGS (topo);
    Ohio Dept. of Natural Resources

### 671

State Library of Ohio
Documents Department
65 S. Front St.
Columbus, OH 43215
Tel. (614) 462-7051
Hours: 8–5, M–Th; 9–5, F
Responsible Person: Hordusky, Clyde,
    Documents Specialist
Employees: Full Time    Part Time
Prof.           0              1
Holdings:
    33000 Printed Maps
Chronological Coverage:
    100% post 1900
Available to: Public
Circulates to: Public
Equipment:
    12 11-drawer blueprint cases
Map Depositories: USGS (topo); GPO

### 672

Dayton & Montgomery County Public
    Library
215 East Third St.
Dayton, OH 45402
Tel. (513) 224-1651
Hours: 9–9, M–F; 9–6, Sa
Responsible Person: Buck, Jeremy R.
Special Strengths: United States,
    Dayton & Montgomery County
Holdings:
    22200 Printed Maps
    150 Aerial Photographs
    425 Atlases
    1 Globe
    32 Wall Maps
    5 Raised Relief Maps
    75 Books
    15 Gazetteers
Chronological Coverage: 1% pre 1900;
    99% post 1900
Preservation methods: Encapsulation
Available to: Public, Students, Faculty
Circulates to: Public, Students, Faculty
Average monthly use: 200
Average annual circulation: Maps: 100
Copying Facilities: Photographic
    reproduction
Equipment:
    53 5-drawer cabinets
    7 file drawers
Square Footage: 405
Map Depositories: USGS (topo)

### 673

Dayton Museum of Natural History
2629 Ridge Ave.
Dayton, OH 45414
Tel. (513) 275-7431
Hours: 9–6, M–F
Responsible Person: Morse, Diana,
    Curator of Geology
Special Strengths: Ohio & adjoining
    states, United States, Moon, Mars,
    Mercury
Employees: Full Time    Part Time
Prof.           1              0
Non-Prof.       0              1
Holdings:
    10000 Printed Maps
    15 Manuscript Maps
    13 Aerial Photographs
    3 Satellite Imagery
    16 Atlases
    3 Globes
    8 Wall Maps
    2 Raised Relief Maps
    1 Gazetteer
Chronological Coverage: 100% post 1900
Map collection is cataloged 90%
Formats: Cards, Indexes
Preservation methods: Chartex of
    Fabric Mounting
Available to: Public, Students
Average monthly use: 25
Equipment:

4 5-drawer cabinets
File boxes & shelves
Map Depositories: USGS (topo);
    USGS (geol)

### 674

Wright State University Library
Colonel Glenn Highway
Dayton, OH 45435
Tel. (513) 873-2925
Hours: 8–9, M–Th; 8–5, F; 9–5, Sa;
    1–9, Su
Special Strengths: United States
Employees: Full Time    Part Time
Prof.           1              0
Non-Prof.       0              1
Holdings:
    29000 Printed Maps
Available to: Public, Students, Faculty
Circulates to: Students, Faculty
Copying Facilities: Copying machine
Equipment:
    22 5-drawer cabinets
    7 4-drawer cabinets
Map Depositories: USGS (topo);
    USGS (geol); GPO

### 675

Denison University
Dept. of Geology-Geography
Map Library
Granville, OH 43023
Tel. (614) 587-6487
Hours: 8:30–4:30, M–F
Responsible Person: Malcuit, Robert J.,
    Chairperson
Employees: Full Time    Part Time
Non-Prof.       0              2
Holdings:
    50000 Printed Maps
Chronological Coverage:
    100% post 1900
Map collection is cataloged 100%
Available to: Public, Students, Faculty
Circulates to: Public, Students, Faculty
Copying Facilities: Copying machine
Equipment:
    3 5-drawer cabinets
Square Footage: 200
Map Depositories: USGS (topo);
    USGS (geol)

### 676

Kent State University
Map Library
406 McGilvrey Hall
Kent, OH 44242
Tel. (216) 672-2017
Hours: 8–12, 1–5, M–F
Responsible Person: Canan, Julia,
    Map Library Supervisor
Special Collections: Sanborn Fire
    Insurance Maps of Ohio cities &
    towns

Employees: Full Time   Part Time
Non-Prof.   1   1
Holdings:
   200000 Printed Maps
    1400 Atlases
      85 Raised Relief Maps
     250 Gazetteers
Chronological Coverage: 5% pre 1900
   95% post 1900
Available to: Public, Students, Faculty
Circulates to: Public, Students, Faculty
Average monthly use: 50
Interlibrary loan available
Copying Facilities: Copying machine
Equipment:
   172 5-drawer cabinets
    5 vertical map cabinets
    3 15-drawer cabinets
    1 light table
Map Depositories: USGS (topo);
   USGS (geol); DMA (topo); DMA
   (aero); NOAA

### 677
Lakewood Public Library
15425 Detroit Ave.
Lakewood, OH 44107
Tel. (216) 226-8275
Hours: 9–9, M–F; 9–6, Sa
Responsible Person: Culp, Carol Ann
Special Strengths: Ohio, United States
Employees: Full Time   Part Time
Prof.   3   1
Non-Prof.   2   3
Holdings:
   450 Printed Maps
    2 Satellite Imagery
   257 Atlases
    1 Globe
    1 Wall Map
    46 Books
    11 Gazetteers
Chronological Coverage: 40% pre 1900;
   60% post 1900
Map collection is cataloged 90%
Classification: Dewey   Utility: OCLC
Formats: Cards, Online
Available to: Public
Copying Facilities: Copying machine,
   Microform
Equipment:
   2 5-drawer cabinets
   2 atlas cases
Square Footage: 24

### 678
Miami University
Brill Science Library
Oxford, OH 45056
Tel. (513) 529-7526
Hours: 8–5, 6:30–10, M–Th; 8–5, F;
   1–5, 6:30–10, Su
Responsible Person: Blazek, Inka,
   Library Assistant II
Special Strengths: Ohio, Indiana,

Wyoming
Special Collections: United States
   Geologic Atlas-Folios
Employees: Full Time   Part Time
Prof.   1   0
Non-Prof.   0   2
Holdings:
   70000 Printed Maps
    100 Aerial Photographs
     50 Atlases
      1 Globe
     10 Microforms
    150 Books
     50 Gazetteers
Chronological Coverage: 5% pre 1900;
   95% post 1900
Available to: Public, Students, Faculty
Average monthly use: 200
Copying Facilities: Copying machine
Equipment:
   28 5-drawer cabinets
   15 vertical map cabinets
   16 filing cabinets
   Light table
Map Depositories: USGS (topo);
   USGS (geol); DMA (topo); DMA
   (aero); DMA (hydro); GPO

### 679
Warder Public Library
Reference Department
137 E. High St.
P. O. Box 1080
Springfield, OH 45501-1080
Tel. (513) 323-8616
Hours: 9–9, M–F; 9–6, Sa; 1–5, Su
Responsible Person: Snow, Christine,
   Reference Librarian
Special Strengths: Ohio
Employees: Full Time   Part Time
Prof.   0   4
Non-Prof.   0   5
Holdings:
   1000 Printed Maps
Chronological Coverage:
   100% post 1900
Available to: Public
Copying Facilities: Copying machine
Equipment:
   3 5-drawer cabinets
   1 vertical map cabinet

### 680
Wittenberg University
Department of Geology
Springfield, OH 45501
Tel. (513) 327-7335
Hours: 9–4:30, M–F
Responsible Person: Morris, R. W.,
   Chairman
Special Strengths: Ohio, United States
Employees: Full Time   Part Time
Non-Prof.   0   3
Holdings:
   11197 Printed Maps

   1726 Aerial Photographs
    448 Atlases
      4 Globes
      6 Wall Maps
    102 Raised Relief Maps
Chronological Coverage: 20% pre 1900;
   80% post 1900
Map collection is cataloged 80%
Formats: Cards
Available to: Public, Students, Faculty
Average monthly use: 15
Copying Facilities: Copying machine
Equipment:
   21 5-drawer cabinets
    5 vertical map cabinets
    1 wooden cabinet
   Stereoscopes, Lacy-Lucy to
   enlarge & reduce maps
Square Footage: 147
Map Depositories: USGS (topo);
   USGS (geol)

### 681
Toledo-Lucas County Public Library
325 Michigan St.
Toledo, Oh 43624
Tel. (419) 255-7055
Hours: 9–9, M–Th; 9–5:30, F, Sa
Responsible Person: Christian, Donna,
   Manuscripts & Maps
Special Strengths: United States,
   Toledo, Ohio
Employees: Full Time   Part Time
Prof.   0   3
Holdings:
   43000 Printed Maps
    200 Atlases
     20 Gazetteers
Chronological Coverage: 5% pre 1900;
   95% post 1900
Map collection is cataloged 5%
Classification: Local
Formats: Cards
Preservation methods: Encapsulation
Available to: Public
Circulates to: Public
Interlibrary loan available
Copying Facilities: Copying machine
Equipment:
   Open shelves
   1 10-drawer map case
   4 wood cabinets
Map Depositories: USGS (topo);
   DMA (topo); GPO

### 682
University of Toledo
Wm. S. Carlson Library, Map Collection
2801 W. Bancroft St.
Toledo, OH 43606
Tel. (419) 537-2865
Hours: 8–5, M–F
Responsible Person: McLean, G. Robert
Special Strengths: United States,
   Europe

Employees: Full Time    Part Time
    Prof.        1          0
    Non-Prof.    0          3
Holdings:
    124000 Printed Maps
    75 Aerial Photographs
    69 Atlases
    3 Globes
    4 Wall Maps
    10 Raised Relief Maps
    217 Microforms
    150 Books
    125 Gazetteers
    2 Serial Titles
Chronological Coverage: 1% pre 1900;
    99% post 1900
Map collection is cataloged 45%
Classification: LC    Utility: OCLC
Formats: Cards
Preservation methods: Lamination
Available to: Public, Students, Faculty
Average monthly use: 122
Average annual circulation:
    Maps: 3000
Copying Facilities: Copying machine,
    Microform; Photographic reproduction
Equipment:
    98 5-drawer cabinets
    5 4-drawer file cabinets
    Microfiche Reader
Square Footage: 2025
Map Depositories: USGS (topo);
    USGS (geol); DMA (topo); DMA
    (aero); DMA (hydro); GPO; NOS;
    NOAA

684
Public Library of Youngstown &
    Mahoning County
Science & Industry Department
305 Wick Ave.
Youngstown, OH 44503
Tel. (216) 744-8636
Hours: 9–5:30, M–F
Responsible Person: Cole, Orin
Special Strengths: Ohio
Holdings: 2200 Printed Maps
Chronological Coverage:
    100% post 1900
Available to: Public
Interlibrary loan available
    Photocopies only
Copying Facilities: Copying machine
Equipment:
    3 5-drawer cabinets
Map Depositories: USGS (topo)


## Oklahoma

685
East Central University
Linscheid Library, Map Collection
Ada, OK 74820
Tel. (405) 332-8000
Hours: 2–4, M–F, by appointment
Responsible Person: Aldridge, Betsy
Special Strengths: Oklahoma (esp.
    Southeast)
Special Collections: Oklahoma aerial
    photography, 1940–1960; Oklahoma
    land maps used by Admire Realtor Co.,
    1940–1960
Employees: Full Time    Part Time
    Prof.        0          1
    Non-Prof.    0          1
Holdings:
    1435 Printed Maps
    1200 Aerial Photographs
    50 Satellite Imagery
    75 Atlases
    1 Globe
    30 Wall Maps
    1 Raised Relief Map
    120000 Microforms
    50 Books
    10 Gazetteers
    5 Serial Titles
Chronological Coverage: 5% pre 1900;
    95% post 1900
Map collection is cataloged 20%
Classification: LC    Utility: OCLC
Formats: Cards
Preservation methods: Lamination
Available to: Public, Students, Faculty
Circulates to: Public, Students, Faculty
Interlibrary loan available
    Condition of material
Copying Facilities: Copying machine
Equipment:
    Steel file cabinets
    Wooden atlas racks
Square Footage: 70
Map Depositories: USGS (topo);

USGS (geol); DMA (topo); DMA
(aero); GPO

686
Central State University Library
100 N. University
Edmond, OK 73034
Tel. (405) 341-2980
Hours: 7:30–11, M–Th; 7:30–5, F;
    10–6,, Sa; 2–11, Su
Responsible Person: Buckallew, Fritz A.
Special Strengths: Oklahoma
    (pre-Statehood)
Employees: Full Time    Part Time
    Prof.        0          1
Holdings:
    33114 Printed Maps
    50 Manuscript Maps
    50 Aerial Photographs
    50 Satellite Imagery
    50 Raised Relief Maps
Chronological Coverage: 3% pre 1900;
    97% post 1900
Map collection is cataloged 20%
Classification: Smith    Utility: OCLC
Formats: Cards, Online
Preservation methods: Encapsulation
Available to: Public, Students, Faculty
Average monthly use: 35
Interlibrary loan available
Copying Facilities: Copying machine
Equipment:
    44 5-drawer cabinets
Square Footage: 480
Map Depositories: USGS (topo)

687
University of Oklahoma
Geology Library
830 Van Vleet Oval
Room 103
Norman, OK 73019
Tel. (405) 325-6451
Hours: 8–5, 7–10, M–Th; 8–5, F;
    10–2, Sa; 2–5, Su
Responsible Person: Kidd, Claren M.
Special Strengths: Oklahoma (Geology)
Employees: Full Time    Part Time
    Prof.        0          2
    Non-Prof.    0          1
Holdings:
    150000 Printed Maps
    200 Atlases
    1 Globe
    6 Wall Maps
    2 Raised Relief Maps
    200 Books
    12 Gazetteers
    2 Serial Titles
Chronological Coverage: 1% pre 1900;
    99% post 1900
Map collection is cataloged 60%
Formats: Cards
Preservation methods: Encapsulation
Available to: Public, Students, Faculty

683
Otterbein College
Courtright Memorial Library
Westerville, OH 43081
Tel. (614) 890-3000
Hours: 7:45–10, M–Th; 7:45–5, F;
    10–5, Sa; 2–10, Su
Responsible Person: Becker, John,
    Director
Employees: Full Time    Part Time
    Prof.        7          1
    Non-Prof.    0          20
Holdings:
    400 Printed Maps
    3 Globes
    4 Gazetteers
Chronological Coverage: 1% pre 1900;
    99% post 1900
Available to: Public, Students, Faculty
Circulates to: Students, Faculty
Average monthly use: 6
Average annual circulation: Maps: 23
Interlibrary loan available
Copying Facilities: Copying machine
Equipment:
    4 5-drawer cabinets
Square Footage: 50

Circulates to: Public, Students, Faculty
Average monthly use: 40
Average annual circulation:
  Maps: 1500; Books: 60
Interlibrary loan available
Copying Facilities: Copying machine,
  Photographic reproduction
Equipment:
  90 5-drawer cabinets
Square Footage: 1440
Map Depositories: USGS (topo);
  USGS (geol); DMA (topo); U.S. State
  & Int'l geological survey map series

### 688
Metropolitan Library System
Documents Department
131 N. W. 3rd
Oklahoma City, OK 73102
Tel. (405) 235-0571
Hours: 9–6, M, W, Th; 9–9, T; 9–5, F, Sa
Responsible Person: Durham, Marge
Special Strengths: United States
Holdings:
  50000 Printed Maps
Available to: Public, Students, Faculty
Circulates to: Public, Students, Faculty
Copying Facilities: Copying machine
Equipment:
  Horizontal shelves
  10 25-drawer map cabinets
Map Depositories: USGS (topo);
  USGS (geol); GPO

### 689
Oklahoma Department of Libraries
Archives Division
200 NE 18th
Oklahoma City, OK 73105
Tel. (405) 521-2502
Hours: 8–5, M–F
Responsible Person: Clark, Robert L., Jr.,
  Director
Special Strengths: Oklahoma
Special Collections: U.S. General Land
  Office Field Notes, BLM Survey,
  1870–1910, Oklahoma 1937 Tax
  Commission Land Ownership,
  Oklahoma aerial photographs,
  1939–1957, Oklahoma Dept. of
  Highways maps
Employees: Full Time    Part Time
  Prof.        1           0
  Non-Prof.    1           0
Holdings:
  3000 Printed Maps
  2000 Manuscript Maps
    66 Aerial Photographs
    15 Wall Maps
   236 Books
Chronological Coverage: 5% pre 1900;
  95% post 1900
Map collection is cataloged 95%
Classification: Internal
Formats: Cards, Written Index

Preservation methods: Encapsulation,
  Deacidification, Paper Repair
Available to: Public, Students, Faculty
Average monthly use: 80
Copying Facilities: Copying machine,
  Microform
Equipment:
  87 5-drawer cabinets
  Shelves
Square Footage: 900

### 690
Oklahoma Historical Society
Research Library
Oklahoma City, OK 73105
Tel. (405) 521-2491
Hours: 9–9, M–F
Responsible Person: Shoemaker,
  Edward C.
Special Strengths: Indian Territory &
  Oklahoma (1880–early 1900's)
Employees: Full Time    Part Time
  Prof.        1           0
Holdings:
  300 Printed Maps
   30 Atlases
   15 Books
   10 Gazetteers
Chronological Coverage: 55% pre 1900;
  45% post 1900
Preservation methods: Encapsulation
Available to: Public, Students, Faculty
Average monthly use: 5
Copying Facilities: Copying machine
Equipment:
  3 5-drawer cabinets
Square Footage: 10

### 691
Oklahoma State University
Edmon Low Library, Map Room
Box 12927, Capitol Station
Stillwater, OK 74078
Tel. (405) 624-6311
Hours: 8–5, M–F
Responsible Person: Richardson, Bill
Special Strengths: Oklahoma
Special Collections: Oklahoma aerial
  photographs
Employees: Full Time    Part Time
  Non-Prof.    1           6
Holdings:
  162303 Printed Maps
   64048 Aerial Photographs
       5 Globes
     128 Wall Maps
       1 Raised Relief Map
     190 Books
       2 Gazetteers
       2 Serial Titles
Chronological Coverage: 5% pre 1900;
  95% post 1900
Map collection is cataloged 50%
Classification: LC
Formats: Cards

Preservation methods: Encapsulation,
  Chartex or Fabric Mounting
Available to: Public, Students, Faculty
Circulates to: Public, Students, Faculty
Average monthly use: 241
Average annual circulation:
  Maps: 4232; Aerial Photographs: 235
Copying Facilities: Copying machine
Equipment:
  83 5-drawer cabinets
  24 vertical map cabinets
   1 5-drawer wooden cabinet
   1 light table
Square Footage: 1716
Map Depositories: USGS (topo);
  USGS (geol); DMA (topo); GPO

### 692
Tulsa City-County Library
Business & Technology Department
400 Civic Center
Tulsa, OK 74103
Tel. (918) 592-7988
Hours: 9–9, M–Th; 9–5, F, Sa; 1–5, Su
Responsible Person: Ecker, Tomese
Special Collections: General Land
  Office Plat Maps
Employees: Full Time    Part Time
  Prof.        1           0
Holdings:
  50000 Printed Maps
    250 Aerial Photographs
     10 Atlases
Chronological Coverage: 5% pre 1900;
  95% post 1900
Available to: Public
Average monthly use: 350
Interlibrary loan available
Copying Facilities: Copying machine
Equipment:
  43 5-drawer cabinets
  40 file cabinets
Square Footage: 800
Map Depositories: USGS (topo);
  USGS (geol); GPO

### 693
University of Tulsa
McFarlin Library, Government Documents
600 S. College
Tulsa, OK 74104
Tel. (918) 592-6000
Hours: 7:30–Midnight, M–Th;
  7:30–10, F; 10–8, Sa; 1–Midnight, Su
Responsible Person: Nobles, Steve
Employees: Full Time    Part Time
  Prof.        1           0
  Non-Prof.    1           1
Holdings:
  20000 Printed Maps
      1 Atlas
      1 Globe
      6 Books
      2 Gazetteers
Chronological Coverage:

100% post 1900
Map collection is cataloged 1%
Classification: Dewey
Formats: Cards
Available to: Public, Students, Faculty
Interlibrary loan available
Copying Facilities: Copying machine,
  Microform
Equipment:
  12 5-drawer cabinets
Square Footage: 64
Map Depositories: GPO

## Oregon

### 694
Southern Oregon State College
Map Collection
Ashland, OR 97520
Tel. (503) 482-6445
Hours: 8–5, M–F
Responsible Person: Otness, Harold M.
Special Strengths: Oregon
Employees: Full Time    Part Time
  Prof.         0            1
Holdings:
  26700 Printed Maps
    300 Aerial Photographs
    100 Atlases
      1 Globe
    100 Gazetteers
Chronological Coverage:
  100% post 1900
Map collection is cataloged 5%
Classification: LC
Formats: Cards
Available to: Public, Students, Faculty
Circulates to: Students, Faculty
Average monthly use: Maps: 500
Interlibrary loan available
Copying Facilities: Copying machine
Equipment:
  24 5-drawer cabinets
  1 wood cabinet open side
  3 4-drawer cabinets
Square Footage: 640
Map Depositories: USGS (topo)

### 695
Central Oregon Community College
  Library
NW College Way
Bend, OR 97701
Tel. (503) 382-6112
Hours: 8–9, M–Th; 8–4, F; 3–9, Su
Responsible Person: Fogg, Larry
Special Strengths: Oregon, Central
  Oregon (city street maps, 1900–1920)
Employees: Full Time    Part Time
  Non-Prof.     0            2
Holdings:
  3000 Printed Maps
    50 Atlases
     1 Globe
     1 Wall Map
    20 Raised Relief Maps

Chronological Coverage: 5% pre 1900;
  95% post 1900
Available to: Public, Students, Faculty
Copying Facilities: Copying machine,
  Microform
Equipment:
  2 5-drawer cabinets
  1 vertical map cabinet
  shelving for rolled maps
Square Footage: 400
Map Depositories: USGS (topo)

### 696
Oregon State University
William Jasper Kerr Library, Map Room
Corvallis, OR 97331
Tel. (503) 754-2971
Hours: 10–Noon, 1–5, M–F; 7–9, M–Th;
  10–2, Sa
Responsible Person: Perry, Joanne M.,
  Map Librarian
Special Strengths: Oregon (Geology),
  Oregon (National Forest Maps)
Special Collections: Metsker County
  Atlases for Oregon, Sanborn Fire
  Insurance Maps for Oregon
Employees: Full Time    Part Time
  Prof.         1            0
  Non-Prof.     0            3
Holdings:
  142450 Printed Maps
   11086 Aerial Photographs
     588 Atlases
       4 Globes
      47 Wall Maps
      35 Raised Relief Maps
     520 Books
       3 Serial Titles
Chronological Coverage: 1% pre 1900;
  99% post 1900
Map collection is cataloged 65%
Classification: LC    Utility: OCLC
Formats: Cards
Preservation methods: Encapsulation,
  Lamination, Chartex or Fabric
  Mounting, Edging
Available to: Public, Students, Faculty
Circulates to: Public Students, Faculty
Average monthly use: 380
Average annual circulation:
  Maps: 1500
Interlibrary loan available
  Depends on condition, age, &
  availability of material
Copying Facilities: Copying machine,
  Reader-printers
Equipment:
  110 5-drawer cabinets
  19 vertical map cabinets
  18 shelves (wooden)
  Stereoscope, pantograph, planimeter,
  distance wheels, 2 light tables
Square Footage: 3457
Map Depositories: USGS (topo);
  USGS (geol); DMA (topo); DMA
  (aero); DMA (hydro); GPO; NOS;

NOAA; OR Dept. of Trans.

### 697
University of Oregon
Map Library
165 Condon Hall
Eugene, OR 97403
Tel. (503) 686-3051
Hours: 8–9, M–Th; 8–5, F; Noon–5, Su
Responsible Person: Stark, Peter L.,
  Map Librarian
Special Strengths: Pacific Northwest,
  Oregon (aerial photographs, 1936–)
Employees: Full Time    Part Time
  Prof.         1            0
  Non-Prof.     0            8
Holdings:
  220789 Printed Maps
  333388 Aerial Photographs
      80 Satellite Imagery
    2508 Atlases
       3 Globes
     574 Wall Maps
     254 Raised Relief Maps
     778 Microforms
     676 Books
     200 Gazetteers
       7 Serial Titles
Chronological Coverage: 5% pre 1900;
  95% post 1900
Map collection is cataloged 95%
Classification: LC
Formats: Cards
Preservation methods: Encapsulation,
  Lamination, Chartex or Fabric
  Mounting, Edging
Available to: Public, Students, Faculty
Circulates to: Students, Faculty
Average monthly use: 625
Average annual circulation:
  Maps: 11000; Aerial Photographs:
  9000; Slides: 4000
Interlibrary loan available
  Non-circulating: Historical & valuable
  maps, all books & atlases
Copying Facilities: Copying machine
Equipment:
  86 5-drawer cabinets
  11 vertical map cabinets
  76 filing cabinets
  6 mirror stereoscopes,
  1 microfiche reader
Square Footage: 2314
Map Depositories: USGS (topo);
  USGS (geol); DMA (topo); DMA
  (aero); DMA (hydro); GPO; NOS;
  NOAA; OR Depts. of Trans., Geol.
  & Min Ind., Forestry, Water

### 698
Oregon Institute of Technology Library
Map Section
Oretech Branch P. O.
Klamath Falls, OR 97601
Tel. (503) 882-6321

Hours: 7:30–10, M–Th; 7:30–5, F;
  8–5, Sa; 6–10, Su
Responsible Person: Weber, Robert
Special Strengths: Oregon
Employees: Full Time    Part Time
  Prof.         0            2
Holdings:
  1447 Printed Maps
    30 Atlases
     1 Globe
     2 Wall Maps
    23 Raised Relief Maps
Chronological Coverage:
  100% post 1900
Map collection is cataloged 100%
Formats: Cards
Available to: Public, Students, Faculty
Circulates to: Public, Students, Faculty
Average monthly use: 60
Average annual circulation:
  Maps: 1100
Interlibrary loan available
Copying Facilities: Copying machine
Equipment:
  2 5-drawer cabinets
  2 12-drawer map cabinets
Square Footage: 80
Map Depositories: USGS (topo)

### 699
Eastern Oregon State College
Walter M. Pierce Library
La Grande, OR 97850
Tel. (503) 963-1540
Hours: 7:30–10, M–Th; 7:30–5, F;
  1–5, Sa; 7–11, Su
Responsible Person: Anderson, Verl A.
Special Strengths: Oregon, Washington,
  Idaho
Employees: Full Time    Part Time
  Prof.         0            1
  Non-Prof.     0            2
Holdings:
  3500 Printed Maps
  43000 Aerial Photographs
    20 Satellite Imagery
    40 Atlases
     1 Globe
     2 Wall Maps
    15 Raised Relief Maps
    35 Books
     6 Gazetteers
     8 Serial Titles
Chronological Coverage:
  100% post 1900
Map collection is cataloged 25%
Classification: LC
Formats: Cards
Available to: Public, Students, Faculty
Circulates to: Public, Students, Faculty
Average monthly use: 50
Average annual circulation: Maps: 250;
  Aerial Photographs: 15
Interlibrary loan available
  Reference material
Copying Facilities: Copying machine

Equipment:
  6 5-drawer cabinets
  File cabinets
Square Footage: 350
Map Depositories: USGS (topo);
  USGS (geol); GPO

### 700
Library Association of Portland
Literature & History Department
801 SW 10th
Portland, OR 97205
Tel. (503) 223-7201
Hours: 10–9, T–Th; 10–5:30, F, Sa
Responsible Person: Kahl, Barbara
Special Strengths: Oregon, Pacific,
  Northwest
Holdings:
  85548 Printed Maps
    706 Aerial Photographs
    300 Atlases
      1 Globe
     20 Wall Maps
     23 Raised Relief Maps
      1 Microform
    300 Books
    300 Gazetteers
Chronological Coverage: 5% pre 1900;
  95% post 1900
Preservation methods: Encapsulation
Available to: Public, Students, Faculty
Copying Facilities: Copying machine,
  Microform
Equipment:
  12 5-drawer cabinets
  2 vertical files
  4 8-drawer map cabinets
Map Depositories: USGS (topo);
  DMA (topo); DMA (aero); DMA
  (hydro); GPO

### 701
Oregon Dept. of Geology & Mineral
  Industries Library
1005 St. Office Building
1400 SW 6th Ave.
Portland, OR 97201
Tel. (503) 229-5580
Hours: 8:30–12, 1–4:30, M–F
Responsible Person: Nevendorf, Klaus
Special Strengths: Oregon (Geology)
Holdings:
  5500 Printed Maps
Chronological Coverage:
  100% post 1900
Available to: Public, Students, Faculty
Average monthly use: 30
Equipment:
  2 vertical map cabinets
Map Depositories: USGS (geol)

### 702
Oregon Historical Society Library
Maps Department

1230 S.W. Park Ave.
Portland, OR 97205
Tel. (503) 222-1721
Hours: 10–4:45, M–Sa
Responsible Person: Winroth, Elizabeth
Special Strengths: Oregon, Pacific
  Northwest, North Pacific (exploration
  & history); Alaska (exploration &
  history), Siberia (exploration &
  history)
Special Collections: Pacific Northwest
  maritime & overland explorations,
  Western exploration, North America
  pre 1850
Employees: Full Time    Part Time
  Prof.         1            0
Holdings:
  15000 Printed Maps
    50 Manuscript Maps
   110 Atlases
     1 Globe
    17 Raised Relief Maps
  7300 Microforms
    33 Books
    17 Gazetteers
    15 Serial Titles
Chronological Coverage: 20% pre 1900;
  80% post 1900
Map collection is cataloged 1%
Classification: LC    Utility: OCLC
Formats: Cards
Preservation methods: Encapsulation,
  Chartex or Fabric Mounting,
  Edging, Deacidification
Available to: Public
Average monthly use: 60
Copying Facilities: Copying machine,
  Photographic reproduction
Equipment:
  21 5-drawer cabinets
  Custom map cabinets
Square Footage: 680
Map Depositories: USGS (topo);
  Oregon State Depts.

### 703
Portland State University Library
Social Sciences Division
P. O. Box 1151
Portland, OR 97207
Tel. (503) 229-4904
Hours: 8–10, M–F
Responsible Person: de Graaff, Jerome
Employees: Full Time    Part Time
  Non-Prof.     0            1
Holdings:
  13334 Printed Maps
Chronological Coverage:
  100% post 1900
Classification: LC
Formats: Cards
Preservation methods: Encapsulation
Available to: Public, Students, Faculty
Circulates to: Students, Faculty
Interlibrary loan available
Copying Facilities: Copying machine,

Microform
Map Depositories: USGS (topo);
DMA (topo); DMA (aero); DMA
(hydro); GPO; NOS; NOAA

704
Oregon State Library
Documents Section
State Library Building
Salem, OR 97130
Tel. (503) 378-4239
Hours: 11–5, M–F
Responsible Person: Myers, Dick
Employees: Full Time    Part Time
Prof.        0              1
Holdings:
  30000 Printed Maps
     50 Atlases
    500 Microforms
    250 Gazetteers
Chronological Coverage:
  100% post 1900
Available to: Public
Average monthly use: 20
Average annual circulation:
  Maps: 1000
Interlibrary loan available
Copying Facilities: Copying machine,
  Microform
Equipment:
  30 5-drawer cabinets
Map Depositories: USGS (topo);
  USGS (geol); DMA (topo); DMA
  (aero); DMA (hydro); GPO

**Pennsylvania**
705
Moravian College
Reeves Library
Bethlehem, PA 18018
Tel. (215) 861-1440
Hours: 8–Midnight, S–Th; 8–10, F;
  10–10, Sa
Responsible Person: Gerencher, Dr.
  Joseph
Special Strengths: Middle Atlantic
  States, World
Employees: Full Time    Part Time
Prof.        1              0
Holdings:
  20000 Printed Maps
     10 Aerial Photographs
     10 Satellite Imagery
     50 Atlases
      3 Globes
     30 Wall Maps
     80 Raised Relief Maps
      5 Books
      5 Gazetteers
     10 Serial Titles
Chronological Coverage: 5% pre 1900;
  95% post 1900
Available to: Public, Students, Faculty
Circulates to: Public, Students, Faculty
Average monthly use: 5

Average annual circulation: Maps: 100
  Books: 10
Copying Facilities: Copying machine,
  Microform
Equipment:
  5 5-drawer cabinets
  3 vertical map cabinets
  Open drawers
  7 stacks of 30 drawers
Square Footage: 180
Map Depositories: USGS (topo);
  DMA (topo)

706
Bryn Mawr College
Department of Geology
New Gulph Rd.
Bryn Mawr, PA 19010
Tel. (215) 645-5111
Hours: 9–5, M–F
Responsible Person: Crawford, Maria
  Luisa
Special Strengths: World (Geology)
Employees: Full Time    Part Time
Non-Prof.     0              1
Holdings:
  100150 Printed Maps
     10 Atlases
      3 Globes
     15 Wall Maps
     10 Raised Relief Maps
Chronological Coverage:
  100% post 1900
Map collection is cataloged 10%
Formats: Cards
Preservation methods: Lamination,
  Chartex or Fabric Mounting
Available to: Public, Students, Faculty
Average monthly use: 10
Copying Facilities: Copying machine
Equipment:
  Wooden shelves
  8-drawer cabinets
Square Footage: 1000
Map Depositories: USGS (topo);
  USGS (geol); DMA (topo); GPO

707
Clarion University
Carlson Library
Clarion, PA 16214
Tel. (814) 226-2303
Hours: 8–10, M–Th; 8–5, F; 11–5, Sa;
  2–10, Su
Responsible Person: Mager, John G.
Special Strengths: Pennsylvania,
  Clarion County
Employees: Full Time    Part Time
Prof.        0              1
Non-Prof.    0              2
Holdings:
  1500 Printed Maps
    45 Atlases
     2 Globes
     1 Wall Map

  65 Books
  15 Gazetteers
   5 Serial Titles
Chronological Coverage: 1% pre 1900;
  99% post 1900
Map collection is cataloged 95%
Classification: LC    Utility: OCLC
Formats: Cards
Available to: Public, Students, Faculty
Circulates to: Public, Students, Faculty
Interlibrary loan available
Copying Facilities: Copying machine
Equipment:
  8 5-drawer cabinets
Square Footage: 300

708
Gettysburg College
Musselman Library
Gettysburg, PA 17325
Tel. (717) 334-3131
Hours: 8:30–5, M–F
Responsible Person: Hedrick, David,
  A-V Librarian
Special Collections: Stuckenberg Map
  Collection (15th–18th cent. maps &
  atlases of Europe)
Employees: Full Time    Part Time
Prof.        0              1
Non-Prof.    0              3
Holdings:
  100 Atlases
    2 Globes
Chronological Coverage: 67% pre 1900;
  33% post 1900
Map collection is cataloged 20%
Classification: LC    Utility: OCLC
Formats: Cards, COM
Preservation methods: Encapsulation
Available to: Public, Students, Faculty
Circulates to: Students, Faculty
Average monthly use: 2
Copying Facilities: Copying machine,
  Photographic reproduction
Equipment:
  4 5-drawer cabinets

709
Pennsylvania Geologic Survey Library
Dept. of Environmental Resources
P. O. Box 2357
101 S. 2nd St.
Harrisburg, PA 17120
Tel (717) 787-8077
Hours: 8–4, M–F
Special Strengths: Pennsylvania
  (Geology)
Employees: Full Time    Part Time
Prof.        1              0
Non-Prof.    1              0
Holdings:
  8500 Printed Maps
  1300 **Manuscript Maps**
  9700 **Aerial Photographs**
  1500 Satellite Imagery

20 Atlases
1 Globe
30 Wall Maps
50 Raised Relief Maps
5000 Microforms
6000 Books
16 Gazetteers
97 Serial Titles
Chronological Coverage: 7% pre 1900;
93% post 1900
Available to: Public, Students, Faculty
Average monthly use: 60
Copying Facilities: Copying machine
Equipment:
75 5-drawer cabinets
5-drawer vertical files
Square Footage: 500
Map Depositories: USGS (topo);
USGS (geol)

### 710
Pennsylvania Historical & Museum
Commission
Division of Archives & Manuscripts
Box 1026
Harrisburg, PA 17108-1026
Tel. (717) 783-9898
Hours: 8:30–4:45, M–F
Responsible Person: Ries, Linda A.,
Associate Archivist
Special Strengths: Pennsylvania
(1683–present)
Special Collections: Manuscript
Group II, The Map Collection
Employees: Full Time    Part Time
Prof.          0             1
Non-Prof.   0             1
Holdings:
735 Printed Maps
150 Manuscript Maps
600 Aerial Photographs
15 Atlases
300 Wall Maps
10 Raised Relief Maps
Chronological Coverage: 65% pre 1900;
35% post 1900
Map collection is cataloged 100%
Classification: Numerical
Formats: Published guide
Preservation methods: Encapsulation,
Lamination, Chartex or Fabric
Mounting, Deacidification
Available to: Public, Students, Faculty
Average monthly use: 12
Copying Facilities: Photographic
reproduction
Equipment:
35 5-drawer cabinets
Acid-free storage containers
Square Footage: 312
Map Depositories: USGS (topo)

### 711
State Library of Pennsylvania
Map Collection

Box 1601
Harrisburg, PA 17105
Tel. (717) 783-5954
Hours: 8:30–5, M–F
Responsible Person: Tilden, Elwyn
Special Strengths: Pennsylvania
Employees: Full Time    Part Time
Prof.          0             1
Non-Prof.   0             1
Holdings:
13000 Printed Maps
175 Atlases
2 Globes
2 Wall Maps
6 Raised Relief Maps
15 Gazetteers
2 Serial Titles
Chronological Coverage: 10% pre 1900;
90% post 1900
Map collection is cataloged 20%
Classification: Dewey   Utility: OCLC
Formats: Cards
Available to: Public, Students
Average monthly use: 30
Copying Facilities: Copying machine,
Microform, Photographic reproduction
Equipment:
3 vertical map cabinets
7 10-drawer map cabinets
Square Footage: 300

### 712
Indiana University of Pennsylvania
Department of Geography
Map & Image Library
16 Leonard Hall
Indiana, PA 15705
Tel. (412) 357-2250
Hours: 10–4, M–F
Responsible Person: Stephens, John
Special Strengths: Pennsylvania,
Middle Atlantic Region, United States,
Canada, Central America, Caribbean
Special Collections: Digital cartographic
& imagery data (e.g., terrain models,
census DIME files, & LANDSAT
data), Cartographic & image-
processing software (available on-line
through Library's computing facilities)
Employees: Full Time    Part Time
Prof.          0             2
Non-Prof.   0             2
Holdings:
15000 Printed Maps
100 Manuscript Maps
5200 Aerial Photographs
150 Satellite Imagery
75 Atlases
20 Globes
120 Wall Maps
250 Raised Relief Maps
15 Computer Tapes
80 Books
100 Gazetteers
10 Serial Titles
Chronological Coverage: 2% pre 1900;

98% post 1900
Formats: Cards
Preservation methods: Chartex or
Fabric Mounting
Available to: Public, Students, Faculty
Circulates to: Students, Faculty
Average monthly use: 150
Copying Facilities: Copying machine
Equipment:
15 5-drawer cabinets
8 vertical map cabinets
Map-o-graph, reflecting projector,
Zoom transfer scope, light table
Square Footage: 1100
Map Depositories: USGS (topo);
NOAA

### 713
Indiana University of Pennsylvania
Geoscience Map Library
114 Walsh Hall
Indiana, PA 15705
Tel. (412) 357-2379
Hours: 9–2:15, M–F
Special Strengths: Pennsylvania
Employees: Full Time    Part Time
Prof.          0             6
Non-Prof.   0             2
Holdings:
1400 Printed Maps
30 Aerial Photographs
10 Satellite Imagery
20 Wall Maps
15 Raised Relief Maps
Chronological Coverage: 2% pre 1900;
98% post 1900
Map collection is cataloged 100%
Formats: Cards
Preservation methods: Lamination,
Chartex or Fabric Mounting, Edging
Available to: Students, Faculty
Circulates to: Faculty
Average monthly use: 150
Equipment:
3 5-drawer cabinets
2 vertical map cabinets
Square Footage: 120

### 714
Kutztown University
Rohrbach Library, Map Collection
Kutztown, PA 19530
Tel. (215) 683-4480
Hours: 7:45–11, M–Th; 7:45–5, F;
11–5, Sa; 2–11, Su
Responsible Person: Sprankle, Anita T.
Special Strengths: Pennsylvania
Employees: Full Time    Part Time
Prof.          0             1
Non-Prof.   0             1
Holdings:
13250 Printed Maps
400 Aerial Photographs
10 Satellite Imagery
4 Globes

1 Wall Map
500 Raised Relief Maps
50 Microforms
Chronological Coverage: 1% pre 1900;
99% post 1900
Map collection is cataloged 100%
Classification: Boggs-Lewis
Utility: OCLC
Formats: Cards
Available to: Public, Students, Faculty
Circulates to: Public, Students, Faculty
Average monthly use: 150
Average annual circulation: Maps: 275
Copying Facilities: Copying machine
Equipment:
32 5-drawer cabinets
2 vertical map cabinets
4 bins for raised relief maps
Square Footage: 1488
Map Depositories: USGS (topo)

715
Bucknell University
Ellen Clarke Bertrand Library
Lewisburg, PA 17837
Tel. (717) 524-1462
Hours: 7:45–Midnight, M–Th;
7:45–10, F; 9–10, Sa;
Noon–Midnight, Su
Responsible Person: Peroni, Patricia A.
Special Strengths: Pennsylvania
Employees: Full Time    Part Time
Prof.           0            1
Non-Prof.       0            1
Holdings:
3110 Printed Maps
1 Globe
Chronological Coverage: 1% pre 1900;
99% post 1900
Map collection is cataloged 100%
Classification: LC    Utility: OCLC
Formats: Cards
Available to: Public, Students, Faculty
Circulates to: Public, Students, Faculty
Average monthly use: 50
Average annual circulation: Maps: 100
Interlibrary loan available
Copying Facilities: Copying machine
Equipment:
12 5-drawer cabinets
2 file cabinets
Square Footage: 200
Map Depositories: USGS (topo);
USGS (geol); GPO

716
New Castle Public Library
207 E. North St.
New Castle, PA 16102
Tel. (412) 658-6659
Hours: 8:30–9, M–Th; 8:30–5:30, F–Su
Responsible Person: Morelli, M. A.,
Librarian
Special Strengths: Pennsylvania,
Ohio

Employees: Full Time    Part Time
Prof.           1            0
Holdings:
1500 Printed Maps
45 Aerial Photographs
Chronological Coverage: 5% pre 1900;
95% post 1900
Map collection is cataloged 100%
Formats: Cards
Available to: Public
Circulates to: Public
Average annual circulation: Maps: 150
Interlibrary loan available
Local district libraries only
Copying Facilities: Copying machine,
Microform
Equipment: 3 5-drawer cabinets
Square Footage: 7
Map Depositories: USGS (topo)

717
American Philosophical Society Library
105 S. 5th St.
Philadelphia, PA 19106-3386
Tel. (215) 627-0706
Hours: 9–5, M–F
Responsible Person: Stephens,
Hildegard
Special Strengths: North America
(18th & 19th cent.)
Employees: Full Time    Part Time
Prof.           0            1
Holdings:
1200 Printed Maps
92 Manuscript Maps
2300 Aerial Photographs
2 Globes
10 Wall Maps
100 Books
150 Gazetteers
Chronological Coverage: 90% pre 1900;
10% post 1900
Map collection is cataloged 90%
Classification: Boggs
Formats: Cards
Preservation methods: Lamination,
Deacidification
Available to: Public, Students, Faculty
Copying Facilities: Photographic
reproduction
Equipment:
14 5-drawer cabinets
Wide shelf stacks
Square Footage: 60

718
Free Library of Philadelphia
Map Collection
Logan Square
Philadelphia, PA 19103-1157
Tel. (215) 686-5397
Hours: 9–5, M–F
Responsible Person: Boardman, Richard
Special Strengths: Pennsylvania,
Philadelphia, United States,

Cartobibliographies
Special Collections: Kelso Collection
of Jansson-Visscher Maps,
Philadelphia Ward Atlases,
Pennsylvania County Atlases
Employees: Full Time    Part Time
Prof.           1            0
Non-Prof.       1            0
Holdings:
130000 Printed Maps
10 Manuscript Maps
500 Aerial Photographs
6 Satellite Imagery
2800 Atlases
15 Globes
15 Raised Relief Maps
800 Books
300 Gazetteers
25 Serial Titles
Chronological Coverage: 20% pre 1900;
80% post 1900
Map collection is cataloged 15%
Classification: Local
Formats: Cards
Preservation methods: Encapsulation,
Lamination, Deacidification
Available to: Public, Students
Copying Facilities: Copying machine,
Microform
Equipment:
116 5-drawer cabinets
Light table
Map Depositories: USGS (topo);
USGS (geol); DMA (topo); DMA
(aero); GPO

719
Temple University
Samuel Paley Library, Map Unit
Philadelphia, PA 19122
Tel. (215) 787-8213
Hours: 9–9, M–F; 9–5, Sa; 12–8, Su
Responsible Person: Ginsburgs, Ida G.
Special Strengths: Eastern United
States
Employees: Full Time    Part Time
Prof.           0            1
Non-Prof.       0            1
Holdings:
61835 Printed Maps
676 Atlases
1 Globe
20 Wall Maps
215 Gazetteers
6 Serial Titles
Chronological Coverage: 5% pre 1900;
95% post 1900
Map collection is cataloged 20%
Classification: AGS
Formats: Cards
Available to: Public, Students, Faculty
Circulates to: Faculty
Interlibrary loan available
Library use only
Copying Facilities: Copying machine
Equipment:

25 5-drawer cabinets
6 4-drawer filing cabinets
20 drawer 5″ deep cabinets
Square Footage: 1680
Map Depositories: USGS (topo);
  USGS (geol); DMA (topo); GPO

### 720
University of Pennsylvania
Geology Map Library
Hayden Hall
Philadelphia, PA 19104
Tel. (215) 898-5724
Responsible Person: Faul, Carol
Special Strengths: United States,
  Canada, World
Employees: Full Time    Part Time
  Prof.           0              1
  Non-Prof.       0              4
Holdings:
  95000 Printed Maps
     10 Atlases
      5 Globes
     20 Wall Maps
     20 Books
Chronological Coverage: 3% pre 1900;
  97% post 1900
Preservation methods: Chartex or
  Fabric Mounting
Average monthly use: 50
Copying Facilities: Copying machine
Equipment:
  50 5-drawer cabinets
  Open shelving
  6 wood drawers
  Map enlarger
Square Footage: 10000
Map Depositories: USGS (topo);
  USGS (geol); DMA (topo); DMA
  (aero); DMA (hydro); NOS; NOAA;
  Canada (topo); Canada (geol)

### 721
Carnegie Library of Pittsburgh
Science & Technology Department
4400 Forbes Ave.
Pittsburgh, PA 15213
Tel. (412) 621-7300
Hours: 9–9, M–F
Responsible Person: Brosky,
  Catherine M.
Special Strengths: United States
  (Geology)
Employees: Full Time    Part Time
  Prof.           9              0
  Non-Prof.      12              0
Holdings:
  70900 Printed Maps
    300 Microforms
    250 Books
      2 Serial Titles
Chronological Coverage: 5% pre 1900;
  95% post 1900
Available to: Public, Students, Faculty
Average monthly use: 50

Copying Facilities: Copying machine
Equipment:
  2 vertical map cabinets
Map Depositories: USGS (topo);
  USGS (geol)

### 722
Historical Society of Western
  Pennsylvania
Archives Department
4338 Bigelow Blvd.
Pittsburgh, PA 15213
Tel. (412) 681-5533
Hours: 9:30–4:30, T–Sa
Responsible Person: Reid, Ruth S.,
  Archivist
Special Strengths: Western Pennsylvania
  (1790–1876, Land Ownership)
Employees: Full Time    Part Time
  Prof.           1              0
Holdings:
  1430 Printed Maps
     4 Manuscript Maps
    10 Aerial Photographs
   125 Atlases
     6 Wall Maps
     1 Raised Relief Map
    24 Books
    24 Gazetteers
     3 Serial Titles
Chronological Coverage: 80% pre 1900;
  20% post 1900
Map collection is cataloged 99%
Formats: Cards
Preservation methods: Cleaning,
  Repairing
Available to: Public, Students, Faculty
Average monthly use: 40
Copying Facilities: Copying machine
Equipment:
  3 5-drawer cabinets
  1 4-drawer cabinet
Square Footage: 219

### 723
University of Pittsburgh
G-8 Hillman Library, Map Collection
Pittsburgh, PA 15260
Tel. (412) 624-4449
Hours: 8:30–9, M–F; 8:30–4:45, Sa;
  Noon–9, Su
Responsible Person: Aiken, Jean R.
Employees: Full Time    Part Time
  Prof.           0              1
  Non-Prof.       0              1
Holdings:
  76380 Printed Maps
Map collection is cataloged 30%
Formats: Cards
Available to: Public, Students, Faculty
Circulates to: Students, Faculty
Copying Facilities: Copying machine,
  Microform
Equipment:
  227 5-drawer cabinets

Map Depositories: USGS (topo);
  DMA (topo); DMA (aero); DMA
  (hydro); GPO; NOAA

### 724
Shippensburg University
Ezra Lehman Memorial Library
Shippensburg, PA 17257
Tel. (717) 532-1634
Hours: 8–11, M–F; 8–4:30, F; 9–5, Sa;
  1–10, Su
Responsible Person: Warkentin,
  Katherine
Special Strengths: Pennsylvania
Employees: Full Time    Part Time
  Prof.           0              1
  Non-Prof.       0              1
Holdings:
  2500 Printed Maps
Chronological Coverage:
  100% post 1900
Available to: Public, Students, Faculty
Copying Facilities: Copying machine,
  Microform
Equipment:
  8 5-drawer cabinets
Map Depositories: USGS (topo);
  GPO

### 725
Slippery Rock University
Geography & Environment Studies Dept.
DMATC Map Depository
107 Spotts World Culture Building
Slippery Rock, PA 16057
Tel. (412) 794-7310
Hours: 8–5, M–F
Responsible Person: Rizza, Dr. Paul F.
Special Strengths: Europe, United
  States
Employees: Full Time    Part Time
  Non-Prof.       0              1
Holdings:
  20000 Printed Maps
     50 Manuscript Maps
    245 Aerial Photographs
     32 Atlases
    300 Wall Maps
     25 Raised Relief Maps
      8 Gazetteers
Chronological Coverage: 1% pre 1900;
  99% post 1900
Map collection is cataloged 99%
Formats: Cards
Available to: Public, Students, Faculty
Circulates to: Public, Students, Faculty
Average monthly use: 10
Average annual circulation: Maps: 500
Equipment:
  24 5-drawer cabinets
   2 12-drawer cabinets
Map Depositories: USGS (topo);
  DMA (topo)

726
Swarthmore College Library
U.S. Documents Collection
Swarthmore, PA 19081
Tel. (215) 447-7493
Hours: 8:15–10, M–F
Responsible Person: Williamson,
  Susan G.
Special Strengths: Northeast
Employees: Full Time    Part Time
  Prof.        1           0
  Non-Prof.    0           2
Holdings:
  7020 Printed Maps
  3510 Aerial Photographs
    20 Books
     3 Gazetteers
Chronological Coverage:
  100% post 1900
Available to: Public, Students, Faculty
Average monthly use: 5
Copying Facilities: Copying machine
Equipment:
  4 5-drawer cabinets
Square Footage: 20
Map Depositories: USGS (topo);
  GPO


727
Pennsylvania State University
Pattee Library, Maps Section
University Park, PA 16802
Tel. (814) 863-0094
Hours: 7:45–Midnight, M–Th; 7:45–9,
  F, Sa; 12–12, Su
Responsible Person: Proehl, Karl H.
Special Strengths: Pennsylvania,
  United States, Europe
Special Collections: Warrantee
  Township Maps of Pennsylvania,
  Sanborn Fire Insurance Maps for
  Pennsylvania towns & cities,
  Pennsylvania County Boundary Maps
  1790–1878
Employees: Full Time    Part Time
  Prof.        1           0
  Non-Prof.    2          12
Holdings:
  274000 Printed Maps
      32 Aerial Photographs
      28 Satellite Imagery
    2935 Atlases
       8 Globes
      14 Wall Maps
     126 Raised Relief Maps
      82 Books
     512 Gazetteers
      22 Serial Titles
Chronological Coverage: 1% pre 1900;
  99% post 1900
Map collection is cataloged 60%
Classification: LC
Formats: Cards, Online
Preservation methods: Encapsulation,
  Lamination
Available to: Public, Students, Faculty

Circulates to: Public, Students, Faculty
Average monthly use: 1560
Average annual circulation:
  Maps: 3575
Interlibrary loan available
Copying Facilities: Copying machine,
  Microform
Equipment:
  161 5-drawer cabinets
   11 vertical map cabinets
Square Footage: 5400
Map Depositories: USGS (topo);
  DMA (topo); DMA (aero); DMA
  (hydro); GPO; NOS; Canada (topo);
  Australia Dept. of Resources &
  Energy (geol)


728
Pennsylvania State University
Earth & Mineral Sciences Library
105 Deike Building
University Park, PA 16802
Tel. (814) 865-9517
Hours: 8–11, M–F; 8–9, Sa; 12–11, Su
Responsible Person: McWilliams,
  Emilie T., Librarian
Special Strengths: Pennsylvania
  (Geology), Rocky Mountains, Eastern
  United States
Special Collections: Pennsylvania Second
  Geol. Survey (pre 1900), Pennsylvania
  Grand Atlas (pre 1900)
Employees: Full Time    Part Time
  Prof.        1           0
  Non-Prof.    4          12
Holdings:
  21000 Printed Maps
    136 Satellite Imagery
    150 Atlases
      1 Globe
      1 Wall Map
      1 Raised Relief Map
   2000 Microforms
     16 Books
     15 Gazetteers
    120 Serial Titles
Chronological Coverage: 1% pre 1900;
  99% post 1900
Preservation methods: Encapsulation,
  Lamination
Available to: Public, Students, Faculty
Circulates to: Public, Students, Faculty
Average monthly use: 20
Average annual circulation:
  Maps: 1000
Interlibrary loan available
Copying Facilities: Copying machine
Equipment:
  50 5-drawer cabinets
   1 vertical map cabinet
  Light table
Map Depositories: USGS (geol),
  Canada (geol)

729
West Chester University
Francis Harvey Green Library
West Chester, PA 19383
Tel. (215) 436-8102
Hours: 9–5, M–F
Responsible Person: Burns Duffy,
  Mary Ann
Special Strengths: Pennsylvania,
  Chester County
Employees: Full Time    Part Time
  Prof.        1           0
  Non-Prof.    1           0
Holdings:
  4468 Printed Maps
     1 Manuscript Map
   200 Aerial Photographs
     3 Satellite Imagery
   255 Atlases
     2 Globes
    10 Wall Maps
    12 Raised Relief Maps
   381 Books
    76 Gazetteers
     5 Serial Titles
Chronological Coverage: 3% pre 1900;
  97% post 1900
Map collection is cataloged 100%
Classification: LC    Utility: OCLC
Formats: Cards
Available to: Public
Circulates to: Public, Students, Faculty
Average monthly use: 120
Average annual circulation: Maps: 20
Interlibrary loan available
Copying Facilities: Copying machine
Equipment:
  12 5-drawer cabinets
   1 light table
Square Footage: 980
Map Depositories: USGS (topo);
  DMA (topo); GPO


**Puerto Rico**
730
University of Puerto Rico
General Library, Documents Room
Rio Piedras, PR 00931
Tel. (809) 764-0000
Hours: 7:30–7, M–W; 7:30–5, Th, F;
  8–Midnight, Sa
Responsible Person: Reyes, Angeles M.
Special Strengths: World
Employees: Full Time    Part Time
  Prof.        0           1
Holdings:
  17057 Printed Maps
     55 Atlases
      1 Globe
     20 Books
     20 Gazetteers
Chronological Coverage:
  100% post 1900
Available to: Public, Students, Faculty
Average monthly use: 2
Average annual circulation: Maps: 25;

Books: 5
Equipment:
28 5-drawer cabinets
Square Footage: 400
Map Depositories: USGS (topo);
USGS (geol); DMA (topo); DMA
(aero); DMA (hydro); GPO; NOS;
NOAA; Canada (topo); Canada (geol)

## Rhode Island

### 731
University of Rhode Island
University Library
Kingston, RI 02881
Tel. (401) 792-2594
Hours: 8:30–4:30, M–F
Responsible Person: Maslyn, David C.
Special Strengths: Rhode Island
Employees: Full Time     Part Time
Prof.              1                0
Non-Prof.       1                0
Holdings:
15000 Printed Maps
10 Atlases
7 Wall Maps
25 Gazetteers
Chronological Coverage: 1% pre 1900;
99% post 1900
Preservation methods: Chartex or
Fabric Mounting, Deacidification
Available to: Public, Students, Faculty
Average monthly use: 2
Copying Facilities: Copying machine,
Photographic reproduction
Equipment:
6 5-drawer cabinets
10 vertical map cabinets
1 oversize plan hold architect cabinet
Light table
Square Footage: 225
Map Depositories: DMA (topo); DMA
(aero); DMA (hydro)

### 732
Brown University
John Carter Brown Library
Box 1894
Providence, RI 02912
Tel. (401) 863-2725
Hours: 8:30–5, M–F; 9–Noon, Sa
(academic year); 9–5, M–F (otherwise)
Responsible Person: Danforth, Susan L.,
Curator of Maps
Special Strengths: North America (to
1800), West Indies (to ca. 1835), South
America (to ca. 1835)
Employees: Full Time     Part Time
Prof.              1                0
Non-Prof.       0                1
Holdings:
3700 Printed Maps
500 Manuscript Maps
2000 Books
Chronological Coverage: 95% pre 1900;
5% post 1900

Map collection is cataloged 100%
Formats: Cards
Available to: Public, Students, Faculty
Copying Facilities: Photographic
reproduction
Equipment:
15 5-drawer cabinets
Square Footage: 500

### 733
Brown University
Map Collection (Sciences)
Sciences Library, Box I
Providence, RI 02912
Tel. (401) 863-3333
Hours: 9–5, M–F
Responsible Person: Galkowski,
Patricia E.
Special Strengths: United States
(Geology)
Employees: Full Time     Part Time
Prof.              0                1
Non-Prof.       0                1
Holdings:
70000 Printed Maps
2 Globes
2 Wall Maps
Chronological Coverage:
100% post 1900
Map collection is cataloged 30%
Classification: LC     Utility: RLIN
Formats: Cards
Available to: Public, Students, Faculty
Circulates to: Faculty
Average annual circulation: Maps: 1
Copying Facilities: Copying machine,
Photographic reproduction
Equipment:
50 5-drawer cabinets
9 3-drawer, 12 10-drawer cabinets
16 4-drawer cabinets
Square Footage: 1750
Map Depositories: USGS (topo);
USGS (geol)

### 734
Providence Public Library
150 Empire St.
Providence, RI 02903
Tel. (401) 521-8705
Hours: 9:30–9, M–Th; 9:30–5:30, F, Sa
Special Strengths: Rhode Island
(1600–present), New England, New
York
Employees: Full Time     Part Time
Prof.              1                0
Non-Prof.       0                1
Holdings:
4500 Printed Maps
50 Aerial Photographs
10 Satellite Imagery
60 Atlases
2 Globes
2 Wall Maps
140 Gazetteers

Chronological Coverage: 40% pre 1900;
60% post 1900
Map collection is cataloged 25%
Classification: Subject Headings
Formats: Cards
Preservation methods: Encapsulation,
Lamination, Chartex or Fabric
Mounting
Available to: Public
Copying Facilities: Copying machine
Equipment:
14 5-drawer cabinets
2 4-drawer cabinets
Square Footage: 1450
Map Depositories: USGS (topo);
GPO

### 735
Rhode Island Historical Society Library
121 Hope St.
Providence, RI 02906
Tel. (401) 331-8575
Hours: 12–9, M; 9–6, T–Th (Winter),
9–6, W–Sa (Summer)
Responsible Person: Taylor, Maureen,
Graphics Curator
Special Strengths: Rhode Island
Employees: Full Time     Part Time
Prof.              2                0
Holdings:
1417 Printed Maps
900 Manuscript Maps
300 Aerial Photographs
127 Atlases
Chronological Coverage: 70% pre 1900;
30% post 1900
Map collection is cataloged 30%
Classification: LC
Available to: Public, Students, Faculty
Average monthly use: 35
Copying Facilities: Copying machine,
Photographic reproduction
Equipment:
12 5-drawer cabinets

## South Carolina
### 736
Charleston County Library
404 King St.
Chaleston, SC 29403
Tel. (803) 723-1645
Hours: 9:30–9, M–Th; 9:30–6, F, Sa;
2–6, Su
Responsible Person: Finn, Prudence,
Reference Librarian
Special Strengths: Charleston SC,
Charleston County, South Carolina
Employees: Full Time     Part Time
Prof.              0                1
Holdings:
700 Printed Maps
77 Atlases
3 Wall Maps
12 Books
6 Gazetteers

Chronological Coverage: 40% pre 1900;
 60% post 1900
Available to: Public
Average monthly use: 25
Copying Facilities: Copying machine,
 Microform
Equipment:
 2 5-drawer cabinets
 2 vertical map cabinets
Square Footage: 45

### 737
Citadel
Chemistry/Geology Dept. Library
Charleston, SC 29409
Tel. (803) 792-5041
Hours: 8–4, M–F
Responsible Person: May, Prof. J. P.
Special Strengths: South Carolina
Employees: Full Time     Part Time
 Non-Prof.      0           1
Holdings:
 3000 Printed Maps
Chronological Coverage:
 100% post 1900
Available to: Public, Students, Faculty
Average monthly use: 2
Interlibrary loan available
Equipment:
 5 5-drawer cabinets
Square Footage: 20
Map Depositories: USGS (topo);
 USGS (geol)

### 738
Clemson University
Robert Muldrow Cooper Library
Clemson, SC 29631
Tel. (803) 656-3024
Hours: 8–10, M–Th; 8–5, F; 10–6, Sa;
 1–10, Su
Responsible Person: Harris, Maureen,
 Head, Public Documents
Special Strengths: United States
Employees: Full Time     Part Time
 Prof.          1           0
 Non-Prof.      4           5
Holdings:
 30000 Printed Maps
 20 Satellite Imagery
 40 Atlases
 5 Raised Relief Maps
 15 Books
 5 Gazetteers
 25 Serial Titles
Chronological Coverage:
 100% post 1900
Map collection is cataloged 50%
Classification: LC
Formats: Cards
Available to: Public, Students, Faculty
Circulates to: Public, Students, Faculty
Average monthly use: 10
Interlibrary loan available
Copying Facilities: Copying machine

Equipment:
 30 5-drawer cabinets
Map Depositories: USGS (geol);
 DMA (topo); DMA (aero); DMA
 (hydro); GPO; NOS

### 739
South Carolina Dept. of Archives &
 History
1430 Senate St., P. O. Box 11,669
Columbia, SC 29211
Tel. (803) 758-5816
Hours: 9–9, M–F; 9–6, Sa; 1–9, Su
Responsible Person: Lesser, Charles H.,
 Assistant Director
Special Strengths: South Carolina
 (Plats for Land Grants), South
 Carolina & Adjacent States (Surveys
 of Boundary Lines)
Employees: Full Time     Part Time
 Prof.          2           0
 Non-Prof.      2           0
Holdings:
 400 Printed Maps
 150000 Manuscript Maps
 15 Atlases
 50 Wall Maps
 250 Microforms
 25 Books
 5 Gazetteers
Chronological Coverage: 95% pre 1900;
 5% post 1900
Classification: SPINDEX software
Formats: Cards, COM
Preservation methods: Encapsulation,
 Lamination, Deacidification
Available to: Public, Students, Faculty
Average monthly use: 600
Copying Facilities: Copying machine,
 Microform, Photographic reproduction
Equipment:
 2 5-drawer cabinets
 Archival storage boxes,
 Black light for faded MSS.

### 740
University of South Carolina
Map Library
Columbia, SC 29208
Tel. (803) 777-2802
Hours: 8:30–5, M–F
Responsible Person: McQuillan,
 David C., Map Librarian
Special Strengths: South Carolina &
 Columbia (1786–present), U S. &
 Southwest U.S.
Employees: Full Time     Part Time
 Prof.          1           0
 Non-Prof.      0           3
Holdings:
 180000 Printed Maps
 60000 Aerial Photographs
 1500 Atlases
 3 Globes
 73 Raised Relief Maps

100 Books
276 Gazetteers
Chronological Coverage: 5% pre 1900;
 95% post 1900
Map collection is cataloged 40%
Classification: LC
Formats: Cards
Available to: Public, Students, Faculty
Average monthly use: 100
Copying Facilities: Toshiba Fax Copier
Equipment:
 127 5-drawer cabinets
 31 4-drawer cabinets
 4 stereo viewers, 2 "330" scale
 planimeters, light table
Square Footage: 3300
Map Depositories: USGS (topo);
 USGS (geol); DMA (topo); DMA
 (aero); DMA (hydro); GPO

### 741
University of South Carolina
South Caroliniana Library
Columbia, SC 29208
Tel. (803) 777-3132
Hours: 8:30–5, M, W, F; 8:30–8, T, Th;
 9–5, Sa
Responsible Person: Richardson,
 Eleanor M.
Special Strengths: South Carolina
Special Collections: Kendall Collection
Employees: Full Time     Part Time
 Prof.          0           1
Holdings:
 1186 Printed maps
 43 Manuscript Maps
 26 Aerial Photographs
 30 Atlases
 9 Books
 1 Gazetteer
Chronological Coverage: 70% pre 1900;
 30% post 1900
Map collection is cataloged 100%
Preservation methods: Chartex or
 Fabric Mounting
Available to: Public, Students, Faculty
Interlibrary loan available
 Books only
Copying Facilities: Copying machine,
 Microform, Photographic reproduction
Equipment:
 4 5-drawer cabinets
Square Footage: 50

### 742
USC Coastal Carolina College
Kimbel Library
P. O. Box 1954
Conway, SC 29526
Tel. (803) 347-3161
Hours: 8–9, M–Th; 8–5, F; 12–4, Sa;
 2–9, Su
Responsible Person: Bull, Mary R.,
 Public Service Librarian
Special Strengths: North Carolina,

South Carolina
Employees: Full Time     Part Time
Non-Prof.     6              10
Holdings:
   2600 Printed Maps
    100 Atlases
     50 Books
      5 Gazetteers
Chronological Coverage:
   100% post 1900
Available to: Public, Students, Faculty
Circulates to: Faculty
Average monthly use: 5
Average annual circulation: Maps: 40;
   Books: 75
Interlibrary loan available
   Photocopies only
Copying Facilities: Copying machine,
   Microform
Equipment:
   6 5-drawer cabinets
Square Footage: 60
Map Depositories: USGS (topo)


### 743
Furman University
Geology Department
Greenville, SC 29613
Employees: Full Time     Part Time
Non-Prof.     0              5
Holdings:
   18000 Printed Maps
Chronological Coverage:
   100% post 1900
Map collection is cataloged 75%
Available to: Public, Students, Faculty
Circulates to: Public, Students, Faculty
Average monthly use: 5
Copying Facilities: Copying machine
Equipment:
   15 5-drawer cabinets
Map Depositories: USGS (topo);
   USGS (geol)


### 744
Greenville County Library
General Reference Collection
300 College St.
Greenville, SC 29601
Tel. (803) 242-5000
Hours: 9–9, M–F; 9–6, Sa; 2–6, Su
Responsible Person: Freeman, Larry
Special Strengths: Atlantic Seaboard
   (Colonial History)
Employees: Full Time     Part Time
Prof.         2              1
Holdings:
   1200 Printed Maps
    12 Atlases
    15 Wall Maps
     2 Raised Relief Maps
     4 Gazetteers
Chronological Coverage: 40% pre 1900;
   60% post 1900
Map collection is cataloged 50%

Classification: Local    Utility: OCLC
Available to: Public
Average monthly use: 15
Copying Facilities: Copying machine
Equipment:
   4 5-drawer cabinets
   1 file cabinet
Square Footage: 65


### 745
Greenville County Library
Local Information & History Collection
300 College St.
Greenville, SC 29601
Tel. (803) 242-5000
Hours: 9–9, M–F; 9–6, Sa; 2–6, Su
Responsible Person: Freeman, Larry
Special Strengths: North Carolina,
   South Carolina, Georgia, United States
Employees: Full Time     Part Time
Non-Prof.     1              0
Holdings:
   809 Printed Maps
   116 Atlases
    10 Raised Relief Maps
     4 Books
     8 Gazetteers
Chronological Coverage: 15% pre 1900;
   85% post 1900
Map collection is cataloged 45%
Classification: Dewey    Utility: OCLC
Formats: COM
Available to: Public, Students
Circulates to: Public, Students
Average monthly use: 40
Average annual circulation: Maps: 275
Copying Facilities: Copying machine
Equipment:
   1 9-drawer map case
   1 wooden atlas stand
Square Footage: 50


## South Dakota
### 746
Alexander Mitchell Public Library
519 S. Kline St.
Aberdeen, SD 57401
Tel. (605) 225-4186
Hours: 9–6, M–F
Responsible Person: Olsen, Janus,
   Director
Special Strengths: Pre-Dakota Territory,
   Dakota Territory, North & South
   Dakota Maps (1820–present)
Employees: Full Time     Part Time
Prof.         0              2
Non-Prof.     0              2
Holdings:
   596 Printed Maps
    12 Manuscript Maps
    29 Atlases
     2 Globes
    11 Wall Maps
   100 Books
     1 Gazetteer

Chronological Coverage: 45% pre 1900;
   55% post 1900
Map collection is cataloged 40%
Classification: Dewey
Formats: Cards
Preservation methods: Encapsulation,
   Deacidification
Available to: Public
Copying Facilities: Photocopy Sharpafax
Equipment:
   1 5-drawer cabinet
   12 vertical map cabinets
Square Footage: 1560


### 747
South Dakota State University
H. M. Briggs Library, Documents Dept.
Brookings, SD 57007
Tel. (605) 688-5106
Hours: 7:45–11:30, M–Th; 7:45–9, F;
   10–5, Sa; 1–11:30, Su
Responsible Person: Kim, B. J.,
   Documents Librarian
Special Strengths: United States
Employees: Full Time     Part Time
Prof.         1              0
Non-Prof.     1              5
Holdings:
   65000 Printed Maps
    100 Atlases
    100 Books
     32 Serial Titles
Chronological Coverage: 1% pre 1900;
   99% post 1900
Map collection is cataloged 1%
Classification: LC     Utility: OCLC
Formats: Cards
Available to: Public, Students, Faculty
Circulates to: Public, Students, Faculty
Average annual circulation:
   Maps: 1700
Interlibrary loan available
Copying Facilities: Copying machine
Equipment:
   48 5-drawer cabinets
Square Footage: 500
Map Depositories: USGS (topo);
   DMA (topo); DMA (aero); GPO


### 748
South Dakota State Archives
State Library & Archives
800 N. Illinois St.
Pierre, SD 57501
Tel. (605) 773-3173
Hours: 8–5, M–F
Responsible Person: Hibpshman, Larry,
   State Archivist
Special Strengths: South Dakota &
   adjacent (Survey plats ca. 1860–1920;
   highways, railroads, 1880–1970)
Special Collections: South Dakota
   Commissioner of School & Public
   Lands boundary, reservation, land
   survey plats & field notes, ca. 1860–

**1920**
Employees: Full Time    Part Time
   Prof.       2          0
   Non-Prof.   1          0
Holdings:
   100 Printed Maps
   1000 Manuscript Maps
   500 Aerial Photographs
   1000 Microforms
Chronological Coverage: 10% pre 1900;
   90% post 1900
Preservation methods: Encapsulation,
   Deacidification
Available to: Public, Students, Faculty
Interlibrary loan available
   Within South Dakota only
Copying Facilities: Copying machine,
   Microform
Equipment:
   5 5-drawer cabinets
   1 galvanized steel roll case
Square Footage: 45
Map Depositories: Maps & related
   materials from SD agencies

**749**
South Dakota State Historical Society
   & Historical Resource Center
Memorial Building
Pierre, SD 57501
Tel. (605) 773-4370
Hours: 8–5, M–F
Responsible Person: Evetts, Rosemary,
   Head of Center
Special Strengths: South Dakota
   (1860–present)
Holdings:
   8000 Printed Maps
   55 Atlases
   2 Wall Maps
Chronological Coverage: 20% pre 1900;
   80% post 1900
Map collection is cataloged 2%
Classification: National Archives
Formats: Cards
Available to: Public, Students, Faculty
Average monthly use: 10
Copying Facilities: Copying machine
Equipment:
   8 5-drawer cabinets
   1 vertical map cabinets
Square Footage: 30

**750**
South Dakota School of Mines &
   Technology
Dept. of Geology & Geological Engineering
Rapid City, SD 57701
Tel. (605) 394-2461
Hours: 8–5, M–F
Special Strengths: South Dakota &
   adjacent states (geology & mining)
Employees: Full Time    Part Time
   Non-Prof.   0          1

Holdings:
   2500 Printed Maps
   500 Manuscript Maps
   1000 Aerial Photographs
   100 Satellite Imagery
Chronological Coverage: 30% pre 1900;
   70% post 1900
Formats: Cards
Available to: Public, Students, Faculty
Average monthly use: 10
Interlibrary loan available
Copying Facilities: Copying machine
Equipment:
   9 24 tray cabinets
Square Footage: 500
Map Depositories: USGS (topo);
   USGS (geol)

**751**
South Dakota School of Mines &
   Technology
Devereaux Library
Map Collection
500 E. St. Joseph St.
Rapid City, SD 57701
Tel. (605) 394-2419
Hours: 8–4, M–F
Responsible Person: McCauley, Philip F.
Special Strengths: Eastern Wyoming &
   Western South Dakota Black Hills
   area (Geology), Iowa, Minnesota,
   Montana, North Dakota, Nebraska,
   Wyoming
Employees: Full Time    Part Time
   Prof.       0          1
   Non-Prof.   0          1
Holdings:
   8000 Printed Maps
   5 Aerial Photographs
   3 Satellite Imagery
   60 Atlases
   1 Globe
   12 Wall Maps
   25 Microforms
   200 Books
   3 Gazetteers
   5 Serial Titles
Chronological Coverage: 10% pre 1900;
   90% post 1900
Map collection is cataloged 100%
Classification: LC    Utility: OCLC
Formats: Cards
Preservation methods: Lamination
Available to: Public, Students, Faculty
Circulates to: Public, Students, Faculty
Average monthly use: 100
Interlibrary loan available
   Reference items do not circulate
Copying Facilities: Copying machine,
   Photographic reproduction
Equipment:
   6 5-drawer cabinets
Square Footage: 700
Map Depositories: USGS (topo);
   USGS (geol); GPO

**752**
EROS Data Center
Data Management Section
Sioux Falls, SD 57198
Tel. (605) 594-6594
Hours: 7:30–4:15, M–F
Responsible Person: Smith, Tim
Special Strengths: United States
Employees: Full Time    Part Time
   Prof.       1          0
Holdings:
   60000 Printed Maps
   5200000 Aerial Photographs
   602000 Satellite Imagery
   1 Globe
Chronological Coverage:
   100% post 1900
Average monthly use: 20
   Hanging files
Square Footage: 6450
Map Depositories: USGS (topo);
   DMA (topo)

**753**
Black Hills State College
Case Library for Western Historical
   Studies
1200 University Ave.
Spearfish, SD 57783
Tel. (605) 642-6833
Hours: 8–12, 1–5, M–F
Responsible Person: Jones, Dora Ann,
   Special Collections
Employees: Full Time    Part Time
   Prof.       1          0
   Non-Prof.   0          3
Holdings:
   2000 Printed Maps
   1020 Aerial Photographs
   91 Atlases
   7 Wall Maps
   10 Books
   1 Serial Title
Chronological Coverage: 5% pre 1900;
   95% post 1900
Available to: Public, Students, Faculty
Copying Facilities: Copying machine
Equipment:
   5 5-drawer cabinets
   1 vertical map cabinet
   1 10-drawer, 2 7-drawer cabinets
   1 6-drawer map case
Square Footage: 35

**754**
University of South Dakota
I. D. Weeks Library, Map Collection
Vermillion, SD 57069
Tel. (605) 677-5371
Hours: 8–5, M–F
Responsible Person: Van Balen, John
Special Strengths: South Dakota
   (Hydrology, Geology), Upper Great
   Plains (1730–1889)

Employees: Full Time    Part Time
  Prof.            0             1
  Non-Prof.        0             1
Holdings:
  25000 Printed Maps
    250 Manuscript Maps
     50 Aerial Photographs
    300 Atlases
      5 Globes
     15 Wall Maps
     50 Microforms
      1 Computer Tape
     25 Books
     15 Gazetteers
      2 Serial Titles
Chronological Coverage: 1% pre 1900;
  99% post 1900
Map collection is cataloged 90%
Classification: LC    Utility: OCLC
Formats: Cards
Preservation methods: Encapsulation
Available to: Public, Students, Faculty
Circulates to: Public, Students, Faculty
Average monthly use: 10
Average annual circulation: Maps: 75
Interlibrary loan available
Copying Facilities: Copying machine,
  Microform, Photographic reproduction
Equipment:
  6 5-drawer cabinets
  2 vertical map cabinets
Map Depositories: USGS (topo);
  USGS (geol); GPO; Canada (geol);
  Gr. Brit., Australia (Geology); Various
  state surveys

**Tennessee**
### 755
Chattanooga-Hamilton County
  Bicentennial Library
Local History & Genealogy Dept.
1001 Broad St.
Chattanooga, TN 37402
Tel. (615) 757-5317
Hours: 9–9, M–Th; 9–6, F, Sa
Responsible Person: Swann, Clara W.
Special Strengths: Chattanooga,
  Hamilton County, Tennessee, Georgia
Employees: Full Time    Part Time
  Prof.            1             0
  Non-Prof.        3             1
Holdings:
  600 Printed Maps
   17 Aerial Photographs
    8 Atlases
    3 Raised Relief Maps
    5 Gazetteers
Chronological Coverage: 50% pre 1900;
  50% post 1900
Classification: Local
Formats: Cards
Available to: Public
Average monthly use: 1521
Equipment:
  4 5-drawer cabinets
  1 vertical map cabinet

2 oversize 5-drawer cabinets

### 756
Austin Peay State University
Felix G. Woodward Library
Box 4595
601 E. College St.
Hours: 8–10:30, M–Th; 8–4:30, F;
  9–5, Sa; 1–10:30, Su
Responsible Person: May, Anne C.,
  Head, Information Services
Special Strengths: Tennessee
Employees: Full Time    Part Time
  Prof.            1             0
  Non-Prof.        1             0
Holdings:
  1154 Printed maps
    50 Atlases
     1 Globe
     2 Wall Maps
    50 Books
     8 Serial Titles
Chronological Coverage: 5% pre 1900;
  95% post 1900
Preservation methods: Lamination
Available to: Public, Students, Faculty
Copying Facilities: Copying machine,
  Microform, Photographic reproduction
Equipment:
  8 5-drawer cabinets
  Light table
Map Depositories: USGS (topo);
  GPO

### 757
Tennessee Tech
Department of Earth Sciences Library
Box 5062, T. T. U.
Cookeville, TN 38505
Tel. (615) 528-3121
Responsible Person: Finch,
  Dr. Richard C.
Special Strengths: Southeastern
  United States
Employees: Full Time    Part Time
  Non-Prof.        0             1
Holdings:
  46000 Printed Maps
Chronological Coverage: 1% pre 1900;
  99% post 1900
Available to: Students, Faculty
Circulates to: Students, Faculty
Interlibrary loan available
Equipment:
  31 5-drawer cabinets
  30 file drawers
  Light tables, reducing/enlarging
  viewer

### 758
Tennessee Technical University
Jere Whitson Memorial Library
Cookeville, TN 38501
Tel. (615) 528-3217

Hours: 8–10, M–F
Responsible Person: Moore, Jean
Special Strengths: United States
Employees: Full Time    Part Time
  Prof.            0             1
  Non-Prof.        0             2
Holdings:
  30000 Printed Maps
     87 Atlases
Chronological Coverage:
  100% post 1900
Available to: Public, Students, Faculty
Average monthly use: 500
Copying Facilities: Copying machine,
  Microform
Equipment:
  22 5-drawer cabinets
  3 vertical map cabinets
Map Depositories: USGS (topo);
  USGS (geol); GPO

### 759
Carson-Newman College
Map Library, Dept. of Geology
Jefferson, City, TN 37760
Tel. (615) 475-9061
Hours: 8–5, M–F
Responsible Person: Freels,
  Dr. Edward T.
Special Strengths: Eastern United
  States, Tennessee (Geology)
Employees: Full Time    Part Time
  Non-Prof.        0             1
Holdings:
  12000 Printed Maps
     70 Raised Relief Maps
Chronological Coverage:
  100% post 1900
Available to: Public, Students, Faculty
Circulates to: Students, Faculty
Average monthly use: 15
Average annual circulation: Maps: 150
Copying Facilities: Copying machine
Equipment:
  1 vertical map cabinet
  25 4-drawer oversize cabinets
Square Footage: 350
Map Depositories: USGS (topo)

### 760
East Tennessee State University
Sherrod Library, Map Collection
Box 22, 450A
Johnson City, TN 37614
Tel. (615) 929-5334
Hours: 8–10:30, M–Th; 8–4:30, F;
  9–5, Sa; 1–10:30, Su
Responsible Person: Patrick, Stephen
Special Strengths: Tennessee
Employees: Full Time    Part Time
  Prof.            0             1
  Non-Prof.        0             2
Holdings:
  50000 Printed Maps
     10 Raised Relief Maps

Chronological Coverage:
100% post 1900
Available to: Public, Students, Faculty
Average monthly use: 50
Copying Facilities: Copying machine,
Microform
Equipment:
38 5-drawer cabinets
2 4-drawer file cabinets
4 5-drawer file cabinets
Square Footage: 600
Map Depositories: USGS (topo);
USGS (geol); DMA (topo); GPO;
TN Dept. of Conserv. Div. of Geology

761
Knox County Public Library System
500 W. Church St.
Knoxville, TN 37902
Tel. (615) 523-6937
Hours: 9–8:30, M, T; 9–5:30, W–F;
1–5, Su
Responsible Person: Whisman, Tom
Special Strengths: Tennessee, Knoxville
Employees: Full Time    Part Time
Non-Prof.       1          0
Holdings:
2500 Printed Maps
100 Atlases
1 Globe
3 Wall Maps
25 Books
9 Gazetteers
Chronological Coverage:
100% post 1900
Available to: Public
Circulates to: Public
Interlibrary loan available
Copying Facilities: Copying machine,
Microform
Equipment:
1 5-drawer cabinet
Square Footage: 100
Map Depositories: Metro Planning
Commission (Knox County)

762
University of Tennessee Knoxville
James D. Hoskins Library (Main)
Reference/Documents Department
Knoxville, TN 37996-1000
Tel. (615) 974-4171
Hours: 8–Midnight, M–Th; 8–10, F;
9–6, Sa; 1–Midnight, Su
Responsible Person: Bassett, Robert J.,
Head
Special Strengths: Tennessee
Employees: Full Time    Part Time
Non-Prof.       2          6
Holdings:
800 Printed Maps
200 Atlases
1 Wall Map
15 Books
10 Gazetteers

Chronological Coverage: 5% pre 1900;
95% post 1900
Map collection is cataloged 99%
Classification: LC    Utility: OCLC
Formats: Cards
Available to: Public, Students, Faculty
Circulates to: Students, Faculty
Average monthly use: 35
Average annual circulation: Maps: 30
Copying Facilities: Copying machine
Equipment:
2 5-drawer cabinets
1 vertical map cabinet
Square Footage: 125

763
University of Tennessee Library
Special Collections
Knoxville, TN 37999-1000
Tel. (615) 974-4480
Hours: 9–5:30, M–F
Responsible Person: Dobson, John,
Curator
Special Strengths: Tennessee
(18th & 19th cent. maps)
Employees: Full Time    Part Time
Prof.           1          0
Non-Prof.       2          2
Holdings:
6646 Printed Maps
Chronological Coverage: 16% pre 1900;
Classification: Local
Formats: Cards
Preservation methods: Encapsulation
Available to: Public, Students, Faculty
Average monthly use: 50
Copying Facilities: Copying machine,
Photographic reproduction
Equipment:
10 5-drawer cabinets
Open shelves
Square Footage: 148

764
University of Tennessee
Dept. of Geography, Map Library
Knoxville, TN 37996
Tel. (615) 974-2418
Hours: 9–12, 1–4, Daily
Responsible Person: Brinkman,
Leonard W.
Special Strengths: United States
Employees: Full Time    Part Time
Prof.           0          1
Non-Prof.       0          4
Holdings:
250000 Printed Maps
100 Atlases
250 Raised Relief Maps
50 Books
100 Gazetteers
Chronological Coverage: 10% pre 1900;
90% post 1900
Preservation methods: Encapsulation
Available to: Public, Students, Faculty

Circulates to: Public, Students, Faculty
Average monthly use: 50
Average annual circulation:
Maps: 1500; Books: 20
Copying Facilities: Copying machine,
Photographic reproduction
Equipment:
187 5-drawer cabinets
5 file cabinets, 1 folio cabinet,
1 atlas cabinet
Square Footage: 1350
Map Depositories: USGS (topo);
USGS (geol); DMA (topo); DMA
(aero); DMA (hydro); NOAA

765
Memphis State University Libraries
Map Library, Govt. Documents Dept.
Memphis, TN 38152
Tel. (901) 454-2296
Hours: 8–10, M–Th; 8–5, F; 1–6, Sa, Su
Responsible Person: Wedig, Eric M.
Special Strengths: Tennessee,
Southeast
Employees: Full Time    Part Time
Prof.           2          0
Non-Prof.       1          0
Holdings:
23327 Printed Maps
275 Atlases
2 Globes
50 Books
120 Gazetteers
Chronological Coverage: 2% pre 1900;
98% post 1900
Available to: Public, Students, Faculty
Circulates to: Public, Students, Faculty
Average monthly use: 35
Average annual circulation: Maps: 100
Interlibrary loan available
Copying Facilities: Copying machine,
Microform
Equipment:
69 5-drawer cabinets
Square Footage: 1300
Map Depositories: USGS (topo);
DMA (topo); GPO

766
Memphis State University
Brister Library
Mississippi Valley Collection (Special
Collections)
Memphis, TN 38152
Tel. (901) 454-2210
Hours: 8–4:30, M–F
Responsible Person: Terreo, John,
Special Collections Librarian
Special Strengths: Tennessee
(1900–1960's)
Employees: Full Time    Part Time
Prof.           1          0
Non-Prof.       2          0
Holdings:
300 Printed Maps

2 Wall Maps
Chronological Coverage: 20% pre 1900;
  80% post 1900
Available to: Public, Students, Faculty
Average monthly use: 4
Copying Facilities: Copying machine
Equipment:
  4 5-drawer cabinets
Square Footage: 25

### 767
Memphis State University
Engineering Library
Memphis, TN 38152
Tel. (901) 454-2179
Hours: 8–9, M–Th; 8–4:30, F; 9–1, Sa;
  1–5, Su
Responsible Person: Ward, Suzanne,
  Librarian
Special Strengths: Tennessee (Geology),
  Mid-South Region
Employees: Full Time    Part Time
  Prof.           1              0
  Non-Prof.       1              6
Holdings:
  6066 Printed Maps
  100 Aerial Photographs
  15 Atlases
  1 Wall Map
  25 Books
Chronological Coverage: 3% pre 1900;
  97% post 1900
Map collection is cataloged 20%
Classification: LC    Utility: OCLC
Formats: Cards
Available to: Public, Students, Faculty
Circulates to: Students, Faculty
Average monthly use: 10
Average annual circulation: Maps: 33;
  Books: 9856
Copying Facilities: Copying machine,
  Microform
Equipment:
  12 5-drawer cabinets
  4 vertical map cabinets
Square Footage: 378
Map Depositories: USGS (topo)

### 768
Memphis/Shelby County Public Library
  & Information Center
1850 Peabody Ave.
Memphis, TN 38104
Tel. (901) 725-8876
Hours: 9–9, M–Th; 9–6, F, Sa; 1–5, Su
Holdings:
  69439 Printed Maps
Chronological Coverage:
  100% post 1900
Available to: Public, Students, Faculty
Copying Facilities: Copying machine,
  Microform
Equipment:
  30 1-drawer cabinets
  15 14-drawer cabinets

5 15-drawer
Map Depositories: USGS (topo)

### 769
Public Library of Nashville/Davidson Co.,
Map Collection, Reference Dept.
222 8th Ave. No.
Nashville, TN 37203
Tel. (615) 244-4700
Hours: 9–7, M–F; 9–5, Sa; 2–5, Su
Responsible Person: Lawrence, David C.
Special Strengths: United States
Employees: Full Time    Part Time
  Prof.           1              0
  Non-Prof.       0              2
Holdings:
  550 Printed Maps
  10 Manuscript Maps
  50 Atlases
  1 Globe
  3 Wall Maps
  50 Books
  10 Gazetteers
  5 Serial Titles
Chronological Coverage: 10% pre 1900;
  90% post 1900
Map collection is cataloged 100%
Formats: Cards
Available to: Public, Students, Faculty
Circulates to: Public, Students, Faculty
Average monthly use: 50
Average annual circulation: Maps: 100
Interlibrary loan available
Copying Facilities: Copying machine
Equipment:
  4 5-drawer cabinets
  4 vertical map cabinets
Square Footage: 50

### 770
Tennessee State Library & Archives
403 Seventh Ave. N.
Nashville, TN 37219
Tel. (615) 741-2764
Hours: 8–4:30, M–Sa
Responsible Person: Bell, Marylin,
  Reference Archivist
Special Strengths: Tennesse, United
  States
Employees: Full Time    Part Time
  Prof.           0              6
  Non-Prof.       0              4
Holdings:
  8300 Printed Maps
  100 Atlases
  100 Gazetteers
  3 Serial Titles
Chronological Coverage: 7% pre 1900;
  93% post 1900
Map collection is cataloged 44%
Classification: LC    Utility: OCLC
Formats: Cards
Preservation methods: Encapsulation,
  Lamination, Deacidification
Available to: Public

Average monthly use: 140
Interlibrary loan available
  Photocopies only
Copying Facilities: Copying machine,
  Microform, Photographic reproduction
Equipment:
  81 5-drawer cabinets
Map Depositories: USGS (topo)

### 771
Vanderbilt University Library
Science Library—Map Room
419 21st Ave. South
Nashville, TN 37240-0007
Tel. (615) 322-2775
Responsible Person: Robinson, Cris,
  Library Assistant
Special Strengths: Tennessee,
  Southeastern States
Employees: Full Time    Part Time
  Non-Prof.       0              1
Holdings:
  100000 Printed Maps
  2 Globes
  30 Wall Maps
  50 Raised Relief Maps
Chronological Coverage: 5% pre 1900;
  95% post 1900
Available to: Public, Students, Faculty
Circulates to: Students, Faculty
Average monthly use: 15
Average annual circulation:
  Maps: 1200
Copying Facilities: Copying machine
Equipment:
  40 5-drawer cabinets
  12 file cabinets
  Light table
Square Footage: 1200
Map Depositories: USGS (topo);
  USGS (geol); GPO; NOAA

## Texas
### 772
Sul Ross State University
Alpine, TX 79830
Tel. (915) 837-8121
Responsible Person: Spears, Norman,
  Librarian
Special Strengths: Texas, Big Bend
Holdings:
  4317 Printed Maps
  12 Atlases
  1 Globe
Chronological Coverage:
  100% post 1900
Classification: Dewey
Formats: Cards
Available to: Public, Students, Faculty
Copying Facilities: Copying machine

### 773
University of Texas at Arlington Library
Cartographic History Library

P. O. Box 19497
Arlington, TX 77019
Tel. (817) 273-3393
Hours: 8–5, M–F; 10–2, Sa
Responsible Person: Colley,
   Dr. Charles C., Director
Special Strengths: World (1493–early
   20th cent.); Texas & Gulf of Mexico
   (16th cent.–19th cent.)
Special Collections: Works of great
   cartographers of Europe and the New
   World, Emphasis on mapping and
   exploration of the American West,
   Mexican boundaries, Mexican War,
   1846–48
Employees: Full Time    Part Time
Prof.           4             0
Non-Prof.     0             1
Holdings:
   4000 Printed Maps
     50 Manuscript Maps
   300 Atlases
     3 Globes
     30 Wall Maps
   1500 Books
     6 Serial Titles
Chronological Coverage: 50% pre 1900;
   50% post 1900
Map collection is cataloged 90%
Classification: LC
Formats: Cards
Preservation methods: Encapsulation,
   Deacidification
Available to: Public, Students, Faculty
Average monthly use: 40
Copying Facilities: Photographic
   reproduction
Equipment:
   18 5-drawer cabinets
   12 vertical map cabinets
   35mm slide index of maps
Square Footage: 3750


774
University of Texas at Arlington Library
Documents Department
P. O. Box 19497
Arlington, TX 76019
Tel. (817) 273-3391
Hours: 8–10, M–Th; 8–5, F; 10–6, Sa;
   1–9, Su
Responsible Person: Morris, Pamela A.
Special Strengths: Texas, United States
Special Collections: The Cartographic
   History Library, Special Collections
   Division
Employees: Full Time    Part Time
Prof.           2             0
Non-Prof.     3             6
Holdings:
   8451 Printed Maps
Chronological Coverage: 2% pre 1900;
   98% post 1900
Map collection is cataloged 40%
Classification: LC    Utility: OCLC
Formats: Cards, Online

Available to: Public, Students, Faculty
Interlibrary loan available
   Library use only
Copying Facilities: Copying machine,
   Miocroform
Equipment:
   18 5-drawer cabinets
   7 vertical map cabinets
   1 atlas case
Map Depositories: GPO


775
Austin Public Library
Austin History Center
P. O. Box 2287
Austin, TX 78768
Tel. (512) 472-5433
Hours: 9–8:45, M–Th; 9–5:45, F, Sa;
   12–5:45, Su
Responsible Person: Warren, Karen
Special Strengths: Austin/Travis
   County, Texas
Employees: Full Time    Part Time
Non-Prof.     0             1
Holdings:
   742 Printed Maps
   150 Aerial Photographs
     20 Books
Chronological Coverage: 10% pre 1900;
   90% post 1900
Map collection is cataloged 60%
Classification: Other   Utility: OCLC
Formats: Cards
Preservation methods: Encapsulation
Available to: Public
Average monthly use: 2122
Interlibrary loan available
Copying Facilities: Copying machine,
   Photographic reproduction
Equipment:
   10 5-drawer cabinets
Square Footage: 40


776
Texas State Library
State Archives Division
Box 12927, Capitol Station
Austin, TX 78711
Tel. (512) 475-2445
Hours: 8–5, M–F
Responsible Person: Saegert, Laura
Special Strengths: Texas, portions of
   United States and Mexico
Holdings:
   3500 Printed Maps
     19 Manuscript Maps
   200 Aerial Photographs
     25 Atlases
     10 Wall Maps
     20 Books
     8 Gazetteers
Chronological Coverage: 66% pre 1900;
   34% post 1900
Map collection is cataloged 50%
Formats: Cards

Preservation methods: Encapsulation,
   Lamination, Deacidification
Available to: Public, Students, Faculty
Average monthly use: 20
Copying Facilities: Copying machine
Equipment:
   12 5-drawer cabinets
Square Footage: 75


777
University of Texas at Austin
Department of Geography
Austin, TX 78712
Tel. (512) 471-5116
Hours: 8–5, M–F
Responsible Person: Holz, Robert K.
Special Strengths: Texas (remote
   sensing), Latin America, Europe
Special Collections: Latin American
   Flat Maps
Employees: Full Time    Part Time
Prof.           0             1
Non-Prof.     0             1
Holdings:
   5000 Printed Maps
   2500 Aerial Photographs
   250 Satellite Imagery
   150 Atlases
     30 Globes
   250 Wall Maps
     25 Raised Relief Maps
     40 Computer Tapes
     50 Books
Chronological Coverage: 10% pre 1900;
   90% post 1900
Available to: Students, Faculty
Circulates to: Students, Faculty
Average monthly use: 50
Average annual circulation: Maps: 300;
   Books: 100; Aerial Photographs: 100
Copying Facilities: Copying machine
Equipment:
   30 5-drawer cabinets
   Zoom-Transfer scope, Motorized
   light table, Saltzman vertical reflector
Square Footage: 800


778
University of Texas at Austin
Perry-Castaneda Library
Map Collection
PCL 1306
Austin, TX 78712
Tel. (512) 471-5944
Hours: 8–Midnight, M–F; 9–Midnight,
   Sa; Noon–Midnight, Su
Responsible Person: Tongate, John,
   Head, Reference Services
Special Strengths: Comprehensive
   World coverage, United States
Special Collections: Tax plat maps of
   Austin & Travis County, Texas
Employees: Full Time    Part Time
Prof.           0             1
Non-Prof.     0             2

Holdings:
   172000 Printed Maps
     300 Atlases
       2 Globes
      20 Wall Maps
      28 Raised Relief Maps
      32 Microforms
      30 Books
     160 Gazetteers
       2 Serial Titles
Chronological Coverage: 1% pre 1900;
  99% post 1900
Map collection is cataloged 30%
Classification: LC   Utility: OCLC
Formats: Cards
Preservation methods: Encapsulation,
  Edging
Available to: Public, Students, Faculty
Circulates to: Public, Students, Faculty
Average annual circulation: Maps: 955;
  Books: 25
Copying Facilities: Copying machine,
  Microform
Equipment:
  110 5-drawer cabinets
  8 vertical files
  Light table
Square Footage: 6910
Map Depositories: USGS (topo);
  DMA (topo); DMA (aero); DMA
  (hydro); GPO; NOS; NOAA

### 779

University of Texas at Austin
Walters Geology Library
Tobin International Geological Map
  Collection
Austin, TX 78712
Tel. (512) 471-1257
Hours: 8–5, M–F
Responsible Person: Pintozzi,
  Chestalene, Geology Librarian
Special Strengths: Texas (Geology),
  Southwestern United States (Geology)
Employees: Full Time   Part Time
Prof.        0           1
Non-Prof.    0           1
Holdings:
  30000 Printed Maps
     4 Atlases
     1 Globe
    10 Wall Maps
Chronological Coverage: 5% pre 1900;
  95% post 1900
Preservation methods: Encapsulation,
  Edging
Available to: Public, Students, Faculty
Circulates to: Public, Students, Faculty
Average monthly use: 200
Average annual circulation:
  Maps: 2000
Copying Facilities: Copying machine
Equipment:
  32 5-drawer cabinets
  20 vertical map cabinets
  6 filing cabinets

Square Footage: 1184
Map Depositories: USGS (geol)

### 780

Lamar University
Gray Library
Box 10021 University Station
Beaumont, TX 77710
Tel. (409) 838-8261
Hours: 7:30–11, M–Th; 7:30–4:30, F;
  8–5, Sa; 2–11, Su
Responsible Person: Holland, Marty,
  Head, Government Docs.
Employees: Full Time   Part Time
Prof.        0           1
Non-Prof.    0           1
Holdings:
  6542 Printed Maps
   400 Atlases
     1 Globe
     2 Serial Titles
Chronological Coverage: 1% pre 1900;
  99% post 1900
Map collection is cataloged 3%
Classification: LC   Utility: OCLC
Formats: Cards
Available to: Public, Students, Faculty
Average monthly use: 6
Copying Facilities: Copying machine,
  Microform
Equipment:
  16 5-drawer cabinets
  1 vertical map cabinet
Map Depositories: GPO

### 781

Arnulfo L. Oliveira Memorial Library
1825 May St.
Brownsville, TX 78520
Tel. (512) 544-8221
Hours: 7:30–10, M–Th; 7:30–6, F;
  8–5, Sa; 2–9, Su
Responsible Person: Sandberg, Diane
  McNamara
Special Strengths: South Texas
  (Historical), United States (Road Maps)
Holdings:
  528 Printed Maps
    2 Aerial Photographs
   25 Atlases
    1 Globe
    4 Wall Maps
   11 Books
    9 Gazetteers
Chronological Coverage: 5% pre 1900;
  95% post 1900
Preservation methods: Lamination
Available to: Public, Students, Faculty
Copying Facilities: Copying machine
Equipment:
  2 5-drawer cabinets
Square Footage: 50

### 782

Texas A & M University
Sterling C. Evans Library
Map Department
College Station, TX 77843
Tel. (409) 845-1024
Hours: 8–11, M–Th; 8–8, F; 9–6, Sa;
  12–11, Su
Special Strengths: Texas (Geology,
  Soils, Petroleum)
Employees: Full Time   Part Time
Prof.        0           2
Non-Prof.    2           6
Holdings:
  82608 Printed Maps
  1100 Aerial Photographs
   100 Atlases
    10 Globes
   500 Wall Maps
     8 Raised Relief Maps
     4 Microforms
   300 Books
   200 Gazetteers
     6 Serial Titles
Chronological Coverage: 5% pre 1900;
  95% post 1900
Map collection is cataloged 100%
Classification: LC   Utility: OCLC
Formats: Cards
Preservation methods: Encapsulation,
  Lamination, Edging, Deacidification
Available to: Public, Students, Faculty
Circulates to: Public, Students, Faculty
Average monthly use: 900
Average annual circulation:
  Maps: 5538; Aerial Photographs: 100
Interlibrary loan available
  Depending on condition of material
Copying Facilities: Copying machine
Equipment:
  116 5-drawer cabinets
  10 vertical files
  Pocket & mirror stereoscopes,
  Light table
Square Footage: 2782
Map Depositories: USGS (topo);
  USGS (geol); DMA (topo); DMA
  (aero); DMA (hydro); GPO; NOS;
  NOAA

### 783

Dallas Public Library
Government Publications Division,
  Map Collection
1515 Young St.
Dallas, TX 75201
Tel. (214) 749-4168
Hours: 9–9, M–Th; 9–5, Sa; 1–5, Su
Responsible Person:  Rathvon, David
Special Strengths: Texas
Employees: Full Time   Part Time
Prof.        1           0
Non-Prof.    0           3
Holdings:
  21900 Printed Maps
   870 Aerial Photographs

217 Atlases
  2 Globes
  5 Wall Maps
  1 Raised Relief Map
229 Microforms
156 Books
176 Gazetteers
 25 Serial Titles
Chronological Coverage:
  100% post 1900
Map collection is cataloged 10%
Classification: LC    Utility: OCLC
Formats: COM, Online
Preservation methods: Encapsulation
Available to: Public
Average monthly use: 280
Interlibrary loan available
Copying Facilities: Copying machine,
  Microform
Equipment:
  68 5-drawer cabinets
  22 3-drawer vertical cabinets
  3 5-drawer oversize cabinets
  Light table
Map Depositories: USGS (topo); GPO

### 784
Southern Methodist University
Science Engineering Library
Edwin J. Foscue Map Library
Dallas, TX 75275
Tel. (214) 692-2285
Hours: 8–4:30, M–F
Responsible Person: Fouts, Dorothy
Special Strengths: Texas (Geology)
Employees: Full Time    Part Time
Non-Prof.    1            2
Holdings:
  180000 Printed Maps
   3500 Aerial Photographs
    225 Atlases
      1 Globe
     10 Wall Maps
    330 Books
    220 Gazetteers
     10 Serial Titles
Chronological Coverage: 1% pre 1900;
  99% post 1900
Map collection is cataloged 99%
Classification: LC
Formats: Cards
Preservation methods: Encapsulation
Available to: Public, Students, Faculty
Circulates to: Students, Faculty
Average monthly use: 50
Average annual circulation: Maps: 325
Interlibrary loan available
  Rare maps & atlases do not circulate
Copying Facilities: Copying machine
Equipment:
  102 5-drawer cabinets
  1 vertical map cabinet
Square Footage: 2016
Map Depositories: USGS (topo);
  USGS (geol); DMA (topo); DMA
  (aero); DMA (hydro); GPO; NOS;
  NOAA

### 785
North Texas State University Library
Box 5188 NT Station
Denton, TX 76203
Tel. (817) 565-2870
Hours: 8–5, M–F
Responsible Person: Kelly, Melody S.,
  Documents Librarian
Special Strengths: Texas
Employees: Full Time    Part Time
Prof.        2            0
Non-Prof.    4            5
Holdings:
  12833 Printed Maps
      1 Globe
Chronological Coverage:
  100% post 1900
Map collection is cataloged 95%
Classification: LC    Utility: OCLC
Formats: Cards, Online
Preservation methods: Encapsulation,
  Lamination
Available to: Public, Students, Faculty
Average monthly use: 15
Interlibrary loan available
  Library use only
Copying Facilities: Copying machine,
  Microform
Equipment:
  36 5-drawer cabinets
  Light table
Square Footage: 364
Map Depositories: USGS (topo);
  GPO

### 786
University of Texas at El Paso Library
El Paso, TX 79968-0582
Tel. (915) 747-5685
Hours: 8–10, M–Th; 8–5, F; 10–6, Sa;
  1–10, Su
Responsible Person: Lohrman, Fred,
  Maps Assistant
Special Strengths: Southwest, Mexico
Special Collections: Mexico
  Topographic & Geologic (1:50,000 &
  1:250,000) Maps
Employees: Full Time    Part Time
Prof.        1            0
Non-Prof.    0            2
Holdings:
  76689 Printed Maps
     40 Manuscript Maps
    100 Aerial Photographs
    100 Satellite Imagery
     50 Atlases
      5 Globes
      4 Wall Maps
     10 Raised Relief Maps
    100 Books
    200 Gazetteers
      2 Serial Titles
Chronological Coverage: 6% pre 1900;
  94% post 1900
Map collection is cataloged 100%
Classification: T. R. Smith System

Formats: Cards
Preservation methods: Encapsulation,
  Lamination, Deacidification
Available to: Public, Students, Faculty
Circulates to: Students, Faculty
Average monthly use: 85
Average annual circulation: Maps: 921;
  Aerial Photographs: 10
**Interlibrary loan available**
  **Except historical maps, fragile maps, &
  reference maps**
Copying Facilities: Copying machine,
  Microform
Equipment:
  81 5-drawer cabinets
  Light table
Square Footage: 1600
Map Depositories: USGS (topo);
  USGS (geol); DMA (topo); GPO;
  NOAA

### 787
Amon Carter Museum
P. O. Box 2365
Fort Worth, TX 76113
Tel. (817) 738-1933
Hours: 10–5, M–F
Responsible Person: Tyler, Ron
Special Strengths: American West
  (1810–1900)
Special Collections: Extensive
  collection of 19th cent. (American)
  city views
Holdings:
  100 Printed Maps
  300 Books
    3 Serial Titles
Chronological Coverage: 90% pre 1900;
10% post 1900
Map collection is cataloged 90%
Classification: Dewey
Formats: Cards, Computer Printout,
  Registrar's records
Preservation methods: Deacidification
Available to: Public, Faculty
Copying Facilities: Copying machine,
  Microform, Photographic reproduction
Equipment:
  1 vertical map cabinet

### 788
Amoco Production Company
  (International)
Library Information Center
P. O. Box 4381
Houston, TX 77210
Tel. (713) 931-2781
Hours: 7–4:15, M–F
Responsible Person: Johansen,
  Priscilla P., Map Librarian
Special Strengths: Africa, Middle East,
  Central America, South America,
  Australia
Employees: Full Time    Part Time
Prof.        1            0

Holdings:
   11000 Printed Maps
     49 Atlases
Chronological Coverage:
   100% post 1900
Map collection is cataloged 70%
Classification: Modified LC
Formats: Online, Computer Printout
Available to: Public
Circulates to: Public
Average monthly use: 25
Average annual circulation:
   Maps: 1000
Copying Facilities: Copying machine,
   Slides of maps
Equipment:
   15 vertical map cabinets
Square Footage: 600

### 789

Lunar & Planetary Institute
Planetary Image Center
3303 NASA Rd. 1
Houston, TX 77058
Tel. (713) 486-2172
Hours: 8–5, M–F
Responsible Person: Weber, Ron
Special Strengths: Caribbean
Special Collections: Planetary
   photography
Holdings:
    3000 Printed Maps
  275000 Aerial Photographs
     20 Atlases
     10 Globes
Chronological Coverage:
   100% post 1900
Formats: Computer Printout
Available to: Public, Students, Faculty
Copying Facilities: Copying machine
Map Depositories: USGS Planetary
   Maps

### 790

Rice University
Fondren Library
Govt. Document & Microforms Dept.
P. O. Box 1892
Houston, TX 77251-1892
Tel. (713) 527-8101
Hours: 8–5, M–F
Responsible Person: Kile, Barbara
Employees: Full Time   Part Time
  Prof.     1        0
  Non-Prof.  3        0
Holdings:
  15352 Printed Maps
     1 Globe
Map collection is cataloged 60%
Classification: LC   Utility: OCLC
Formats: Cards
Available to: Public, Students, Faculty
Circulates to: Public, Students, Faculty
Interlibrary loan available
Copying Facilities: Copying machine

Map Depositories: USGS (topo);
   USGS (geol); DMA (topo); GPO

### 791

University of Houston Libraries
4800 Calhoun Blvd.
Houston, TX 77004
Tel. (713) 749-1163
Hours: 7:30–10, M–Th; 7:30–6, F;
   9–5, Sa: 12–8, Su
Responsible Person: Meyers, Judy
Special Strengths: Southwest
Employees: Full Time   Part Time
  Prof.     1        0
  Non-Prof.  0        1
Holdings:
  30000 Printed Maps
   1000 Atlases
    30 Wall Maps
    15 Books
Chronological Coverage: 2% pre 1900;
   98% post 1900
Map collection is cataloged 3%
Classification: LC   Utility: OCLC
Formats: Online
Preservation methods: Chartex or
   Fabric Mounting
Available to: Public, Students, Faculty
Average monthly use: 100
Interlibrary loan available
Copying Facilities: Copying machine,
   Color, enlarging
Equipment:
   110 5-drawer cabinets
   16 file cabinets
Square Footage: 2000
Map Depositories: USGS (topo);
   USGS (geol); DMA (topo); DMA
   (aero); DMA (hydro); GPO; NOAA

### 792

Sam Houston State University Library
Information Services
Humboldt, TX 77341
Tel. (409) 294-1614
Responsible Person: Holder, Ann H.
Special Strengths: Texas, Louisiana,
   Oklahoma, Arkansas, New Mexico
Employees: Full Time   Part Time
  Prof.     0        1
  Non-Prof.  0        3
Holdings:
  7937 Printed Maps
   110 Atlases
     1 Globe
     8 Books
     6 Gazetteers
    43 Serial Titles
Chronological Coverage:
   100% post 1900
Available to: Public, Students, Faculty
Copying Facilities: Copying machine
Map Depositories: USGS (topo)

### 793

Texas A & I University
Department of Geosciences
Campus Box 164
Kingsville, TX 78363
Tel. (512) 595-3310
Hours: 8–12, 1–5, M–F
Responsible Person: Russell,
   Dr. John L.
Special Strengths: South Texas,
   Northern Mexico
Holdings:
  30000 Printed Maps
    400 Aerial Photographs
     25 Atlases
     20 Globes
    350 Wall Maps
Chronological Coverage:
   100% post 1900
Available to: Public, Students, Faculty
Interlibrary loan available
Copying Facilities: Copying machine
Map Depositories: USGS (topo);
   USGS (geol); DMA (topo)

### 794

San Jacinto Museum of History
   Association
3800 Park Road 1836
La Porte, TX 77571
Tel. (713) 479-2421
Hours: 10–5, M–F, by appointment only
Responsible Person: Atkins, Winston,
   Librarian
Special Strengths: Texas (pre-1900),
   Central America (pre-1900)
Special Collections: Texas & New
   Spain prior to 1900
Holdings:
   500 Printed Maps
Chronological Coverage: 95% pre 1900;
   5% post 1900
Map collection is cataloged 100%
Formats: Cards
Available to: Public
Copying Facilities: Copying machine,
   Photographic reproduction
Equipment:
   2 5-drawer cabinets

### 795

Texas Tech University Library
Map Collection
Lubbock, TX 79409
Tel. (806) 742-2236
Responsible Person: Geyer, Barbara,
   Map Librarian
Special Strengths: High Plains
   (Geology), Rocky Mountains
Employees: Full Time   Part Time
  Prof.     0        1
  Non-Prof.  0        1
Holdings:
  6000 Printed Maps
   350 Atlases

2 Globes
3 Wall Maps
1 Raised Relief Map
150 Gazetteers
Chronological Coverage:
100% post 1900
Map collection is cataloged 10%
Classification: LC    Utility: OCLC
Formats: Cards, Online
Preservation methods: Encapsulation,
Lamination, Chartex or Fabric
Mounting
Available to: Public, Students, Faculty
Circulates to: Students, Faculty
Interlibrary loan available
Copying Facilities: Copying machine,
Microform
Equipment:
12 5-drawer cabinets
Atlas cases, Filing cabinets
Square Footage: 650

796
Midland County Public Library
301 W. Missouri
Midland, TX 79701
Tel. (915) 683-2708
Hours: 9–9, M–Th; 9–6, F, Sa;
Summer: 9–9, M; 9–6, T–Sa
Responsible Person: Wegner, Sandra,
Special Collections
Special Strengths: West Texas,
Permian basin
Holdings:
7623 Printed Maps
Chronological Coverage:
100% post 1900
Available to: Public
Copying Facilities: Copying machine
Map Depositories: USGS (topo)

797
Stephen F. Austin State University
Library
SFA Box 13055
Nacogdoches, TX 75962
Tel. (409) 569-4217
Hours: 8–10, M–F
Responsible Person: Bennett, Betty,
Documents/Map Librarian
Holdings:
12000 Printed Maps
150 Atlases
1 Globe
66 Gazetteers
Chronological Coverage:
100% post 1900
Classification: USGS Topo # System
Formats: 1 Card Retrieval
Available to: Public Students, Faculty
Copying Facilities: Copying machine
Map Depositories: USGS (topo);
USGS (geol); DMA (topo)

798
University of Texas at Dallas
McDermott Library
Government Documents/Maps Office
P. O. Box 830643
Richardson, TX 75083-0643
Tel. (214) 690-2918
Hours: 9–6, M–Th; 9–5, F; 10–3, Sa;
2–7, Su
Responsible Person: Allen, Mary Martha
Special Strengths: Texas, Louisiana,
Arkansas, Utah, Colorado, Arizona,
Nevada, California, New Mexico,
Oklahoma
Employees: Full Time    Part Time
Prof.          2              0
Non-Prof.    1              2
Holdings:
19700 Printed Maps
200 Aerial Photographs
100 Atlases
123 Wall Maps
3 Raised Relief Maps
10000 Microforms
3 Books
5 Gazetteers
Chronological Coverage: 1% pre 1900;
99% post 1900
Map collection is cataloged 66%
Classification: LC
Formats: Cards
Available to: Public, Students, Faculty
Circulates to: Students, Faculty
Average monthly use: 25
Average annual circulation: Maps: 80
Copying Facilities: Copying machine,
Microform
Equipment:
32 5-drawer cabinets
3 vertical map cabinets
Square Footage: 300
Map Depositories: USGS (topo);
GPO

799
San Antonio Conservation Society
107 King William St.
San Antonio, TX 78204
Tel. (512) 224-6163
Hours: 10–3, M & T
Responsible Person: Jones, Marianna C.,
Librarian
Special Strengths: San Antonio,
Texas
Employees: Full Time    Part Time
Prof.          0              1
Non-Prof.    0              15
Holdings:
182 Printed maps
4 Atlases
5 Wall Maps
Chronological Coverage: 35% pre 1900;
65% post 1900
Map collection is cataloged 100%
Formats: Cards
Preservation methods: Encapsulation,

Lamination, Chartex or Fabric
Mounting
Available to: Public, Students, Faculty
Average monthly use: 5
Copying Facilities: Copying machine
Equipment:
3 5-drawer cabinets
Square Footage: 24

800
Trinity University
Elizabeth Coates Maddux Library
715 Stadium Dr.
San Antonio, TX 78284
Tel. (512) 736-7429
Hours: 8–5, M–F
Responsible Person: MacKay, Jane M.
Holdings:
600 Printed Maps
100 Atlases
1 Globe
50 Gazetteers
Chronological Coverage:
100% post 1900
Available to: Public, Students, Faculty
Copying Facilities: Copying machine
Map Depositories: USGS (topo)

801
Baylor University
Box 6307
Waco, TX 76706
Tel (817) 755-2111
Hours: 9–5, M–F
Responsible Person: Olbrich, William,
Documents Librarian
Special Strengths: Yucatan Peninsula
Holdings:
5000 Printed Maps
50 Atlases
55 Gazetters
Chronological Coverage:
100% post 1900
Available to: Public Students, Faculty
Interlibrary loan available
Copying Facilities: Copying machine
Map Depositories: USGS (topo);
DMA (topo)

802
Baylor University
Department of Geology
Waco, TX 76706
Tel. (817) 755-2361
Hours: 8–5, M–F
Responsible Person: Allen, Pete
Employees: Full Time    Part Time
Non-Prof.    0              1
Holdings:
16000 Printed Maps
2000 Aerial Photographs
Chronological Coverage: 2% pre 1900;
98% post 1900
Available to: Students, Faculty

Circulates to: Students
Average monthly use: 200
Average annual circulation: Maps: 500
Copying Facilities: Copying machine
Equipment:
  20 5-drawer cabinets
  20 3-drawer file cabinets
Square Footage: 700
Map Depositories: USGS (topo);
  USGS (geol)

### 803
Baylor University
The Texas Collection
P. O. Box 6396
Waco, TX 76706
Tel. (817) 755-1268
Hours: 9–5, 7–10, M–Th; 9–5, F;
  9–Noon, Sa; Summers: 9–5, M–F
Responsible Person: Keeth, Kent,
  Director
Special Strengths: Texas (1650–1860),
  Texas (20th cent.; County land patents
  & land ownership)
Special Collections: J. P. Bryan
  Collection (1650s–1900), William A.
  Blakley Collection (1820–1890),
  Frances Poage Map Collection (post
  1860)
Employees: Full Time    Part Time
  Prof.         0          2
  Non-Prof.     0          1
Holdings:
  8500 Printed Maps
    50 Atlases
     3 Globes
    37 Books
Chronological Coverage: 20% pre 1900;
  80% post 1900
Available to: Public, Students, Faculty
Copying Facilities: Copying machine,
  Microform, Photographic reproduction
Equipment:
  8 5-drawer cabinets

### Utah
### 804
Southern Utah State College Library
Special Collections Room
Li 214 D
Cedar City, UT 84720
Tel. (801) 586-7945
Hours: 9–4, M–F
Responsible Person: Cooper, Inez S.
Special Strengths: Utah (1842–present)
Special Collections: William Rees
  (Palmer) & Kate Vilate Isom Palmer
  Western History Collection
Employees: Full Time    Part Time
  Prof.         0          1
  Non-Prof.     0          3
Holdings:
  300 Printed Maps
    6 Wall Maps
Chronological Coverage: 90% pre 1900;

10% post 1900
Map collection is cataloged 50%
Classification: Local
Preservation methods: Encapsulation,
  Lamination, Chartex or Fabric
  Mounting
Available to: Public, Students, Faculty
Average annual circulation: Maps: 75
Equipment:
  4 5-drawer cabinets

### 805
Utah State University
Merrill Library
UMC 30
Logan, UT 84322
Tel. (801) 750-2682
Hours: 8–10, M–Th; 8–5, F
Responsible Person: Weiss, Stephen C.
Special Strengths: Utah, The West,
  United States
Employees: Full Time    Part Time
  Prof.         3          0
  Non-Prof.     1          0
Holdings:
  53707 Printed Maps
  24400 Aerial Photographs
    210 Atlases
      1 Globe
     63 Wall Maps
      7 Raised Relief Maps
     12 Books
      6 Gazetteers
Chronological Coverage: 10% pre 1900;
  90% post 1900
Map collection is cataloged 15%
Classification: LC    Utility: OCLC
Formats: Cards, Online
Preservation methods: Chartex or
  Fabric Mounting
Available to: Public, Students, Faculty
Average monthly use: 200
Copying Facilities: Copying machine
Equipment:
  90 5-drawer cabinets
Square Footage: 2124
Map Depositories: USGS (topo);
  USGS (geol); DMA (topo); DMA
  (hydro); GPO; NOS; NOAA

### 806
U. S. Forest Service
Engineering, R–4
Technical Information Center
324 25th St., Room 3006
Ogden, UT 84401
Tel. (801) 625-5487
Hours: 7:45–4:15, M–F
Responsible Person: Rhees, Linda M.
Special Strengths: California, Idaho,
  Nevada, Utah, Wyoming, Surveying
  plats, notes
Special Collections: Map layers and
  source material used to produce R-4
  forest maps

Employees: Full Time    Part Time
  Non-Prof.     2          5
Holdings:
  5000 Printed Maps
Chronological Coverage: 10% pre 1900;
  90% post 1900
Map collection is cataloged 25%
Classification: USFS Filing System
Formats: Computer Printout
Available to: Public
Copying Facilities: Copying machine,
  Microform
Equipment:
  42 5-drawer cabinets
  6 Plan Hold Files
Square Footage: 400

### 807
Weber County Library
2464 Jefferson Ave.
Ogden, UT 84401
Tel. (801) 399-8517
Hours: 10–9, M–Th; 10–6, F, Sa
Responsible Person: Petterson, Mary
Employees: Full Time    Part Time
  Prof.         3          1
  Non-Prof.     0          4
Holdings:
  2000 Printed Maps
    26 Atlases
     2 Globes
   250 Wall Maps
    30 Raised Relief Maps
     2 Books
     5 Gazetteers
Chronological Coverage: 2% pre 1900;
  98% post 1900
Classification: Dewey
Formats: Online
Preservation methods: Chartex or
  Fabric Mounting
Available to: Public
Circulates to: Public, Students
Interlibrary loan available
  Only wall and vertical file maps
Copying Facilities: Copying machine
Equipment:
  1 5-drawer cabinet
  1 vertical map cabinet

### 808
Brigham Young University
Geography Department, Map Collection
690 SWKT
Provo, UT 84602
Tel. (801) 378-3851
Hours: 8–5, M–F
Responsible Person: Nielsen, B. Kelly
Special Strengths: Utah, The West
Employees: Full Time    Part Time
  Prof.         2          0
  Non-Prof.     0          4
Holdings:
  27300 Printed Maps
   1550 Manuscript Maps

42400 Aerial Photographs
   21 Satellite Imagery
   46 Atlases
   12 Globes
  256 Wall Maps
   75 Raised Relief Maps
    6 Microforms
    3 Computer Tapes
  100 Books
    1 Gazetteer
    6 Serial Titles
Chronological Coverage: 3% pre 1900;
  97% post 1900
Map collection is cataloged 5%
Classification: Dewey
Formats: Cards, Index sheets
Preservation methods: Encapsulation,
  Lamination, Chartex or Fabric
  Mounting, Edging, Deacidification
Available to: Students, Faculty
Circulates to: Public, Students, Faculty
Average monthly use: 200
Average annual circulation:
  Maps: 22000; Books: 300; Aerial
  Photographs: 20000
Copying Facilities: Copying machine,
  Dyeline, Photographic reproduction
Equipment:
  21 5-drawer cabinets
  8 vertical map cabinets
  5 rolled map cabinets
  4 wooden cabinets
  Map measurer, stereoscopes,
  magnifying lens, viewing tables
Square Footage: 3500

### 809

Brigham Young University
Harold B. Lee Library, Map Collection
1354 HBLL
Provo, UT 84602
Tel. (801) 378-4482
Hours: 8–10, M–Th; 8–6, F; 9–6, Sa
Responsible Person: Moffat, Riley,
  Map & Geography Librarian
Special Strengths: Utah (1850–present),
  United States, United States
  (Gazetteers, 1800–present)
Employees: Full Time    Part Time
Prof.         1            1
Non-Prof.    0            1
Holdings:
  144549 Printed Maps
    1000 Aerial Photographs
    4868 Atlases
      15 Globes
      10 Wall Maps
     100 Raised Relief Maps
     200 Microforms
       5 Serial Titles
Chronological Coverage: 5% pre 1900;
  95% post 1900
Map collection is cataloged 50%
Classification: LC    Utiliy: RLIN
Formats: Cards
Preservation methods: Encapsulation,

Lamination, Chartex or Fabric
Mounting, Deacidification,
Wetmounting
Available to: Public, Students, Faculty
Circulates to: Students, Faculty
Average monthly use: 500
Average annual circulation:
  Maps: 2500; Books: 250
Interlibrary loan available
  No series maps, out-of-print maps
  & atlases or folio atlases
Copying Facilities: Copying machine,
  Microform, Photographic reproduction
Equipment:
  135 5-drawer cabinets
  23 vertical map cabinets
  Map-o-graph
Square Footage: 2500
Map Depositories: USGS (topo);
  USGS (geol); DMA (topo); DMA
  (aero); DMA (hydro); GPO; 20 geol.
  series; UNESCO, PAIGH

### 810

Latter Day Saints Genealogical Dept.
  Library
Map Collection
50 E. N. Temple
Salt Lake City, UT 84150
Tel. (801) 531-3416
Hours: 8–9, M–F; 8–5, Sa
Responsible Person: Roach, Delbert
Special Strengths: United States, World
Employees: Full Time    Part Time
Prof.         1            0
Holdings:
  8500 Printed Maps
   500 Atlases
   100 Microforms
    50 Booobks
   500 Gazetteers
Chronological Coverage: 50% pre 1900;
  50% post 1900
Map collection is cataloged 100%
Classification: AGS
Formats: COM, Online, Computer
  Printout
Preservation methods: Encapsulation,
  Chartex or Fabric Mounting
Available to: Public
Average monthly use: 2500
Copying Facilities: Copying machine,
  Photographic reproduction
Equipment:
  6 5-drawer cabinets
Square Footage: 200

### 811

Salt Lake City Public Library
209 E. 5th South
Salt Lake City, UT 84111
Tel. (801) 363-5733
Hours: 9–9, M–F; 9–6, Sa; 1–5, Su
  (October–April)
Responsible Person: Peters, Sharon

Special Strengths: U.S., Canada
Special Collections: USGS Folios
  1–200, Stansbury Expedition Maps
Employees: Full Time    Part Time
Prof.         1            0
Non-Prof.    0            1
Holdings:
  9034 Printed Maps
    4 Satellite Imagery
   90 Atlases
    1 Globe
    6 Wall Maps
    3 Raised Relief Maps
    1 Microform
   37 Gazetteers
Chronological Coverage: 1% pre 1900;
  99% post 1900
Preservation methods: Encapsulation
Available to: Public
Circulates to: Public
Average annual circulation:
  Maps:: 2000
Interlibrary loan available
Copying Facilities: Copying machine,
  Microform
Equipment:
  2 5-drawer cabinets
  4 4-drawer cabinets
Map Depositories: USGS (topo)

### 812

Salt Lake County Whitmore Br.
2197 E. 7000 South
Salt Lake City, UT 84121
Tel. (801) 943-4636
Hours: 11–9, M–F
Responsible Person: Ellefsen, Dave
Special Strengths: Utah
Employees: Full Time    Part Time
Prof.         1            0
Non-Prof.    0            1
Holdings:
  1500 Pinted Maps
    75 Atlases
     1 Globe
   110 Wall Maps
     5 Gazetteers
Chronological Coverage: 10% pre 1900;
  90% post 1900
Map collection is cataloged 15%
Classification: Dewey   Utility: OCLC
Formats: Online
Preservation methods: Lamination
Available to: Public
Circulates to: Public
Average monthly use: 50
Average annual circulation: Maps: 100;
  Books: 150
Interlibrary loan available
Copying Facilities: Copying machine,
  Microform
Equipment:
  Atlas–5 shelf
  Pamphlet boxes

813
USDA-ASCS Aerial Photography Field
  Office
2222 West 2300 South
Salt Lake City, UT 84119
Tel. (801) 524-5846
Hours: 7–5:30, M–F
Responsible Person: Wall, Louis,
  Customer Service
Special Strengths: United States
  (Aerial photographs, 1940–present)
Employees: Full Time    Part Time
  Non-Prof.    1           1
Holdings:
  58000 Printed Maps
  11000000 Aerial Photographs
Chronological Coverage:
  100% post 1900
Available to: Public, Students, Faculty
Copying Facilities: Photographic
  reproduction
Equipment:
  58 5-drawer cabinets
  Stereoscopes, Zoom transfer scopes,
    Film tables
Map Depositories: USGS (topo)


814
University of Utah
Science & Engineering Library
Map Collection
158 Marriott Library
Salt Lake City, UT 84112
Tel. (801) 581-7533
Hours: 7:30–11, M–Th; 7:30–6, F;
  11–6, Sa; 11–11, Su
Responsible Person: Cox, Barbara
Special Strengths: Intermountain
  Coast, Western U.S. (Geology), Near
  East
Employees: Full Time    Part Time
  Non-Prof.    0           1
Holdings:
  120000 Printed Maps
  1000 Aerial Photographs
  110 Satellite Imagery
  800 Atlases
  3 Globes
  4 Wall Maps
  15 Raised Relief Maps
  3 Computer Tapes
  20 Books
  60 Gazetteers
Chronological Coverage: 2% pre 1900;
  98% post 1900
Classification: LC    Utility: OCLC
Formats: Cards
Preservation methods: Encapsulation,
  Lamination, Chartex or Fabric
  Mounting, Edging
Available to: Public, Students, Faculty
Circulates to: Public, Students, Faculty
Average annual circulation: Maps: 800
Interlibrary loan available
Copying Facilities: Copying machine
Equipment:

96 5-drawer cabinets
1 vertical map cabinet
3 14-drawer file cabinets
Light table
Square Footage: 1600
Map Depositories: USGS (topo);
  USGS (geol); DMA (topo)


815
Utah Dept. of Transportation
Community Relations Division
4501 S. 2700 West
Salt Lake City, UT 84119
Tel. (801) 965-4104
Responsible Person: Krogman, Jacquie,
  Office Specialist
Special Strengths: Utah
Employees: Full Time    Part Time
  Non-Prof.    1           0
Holdings:
  8000 Printed Maps
  1000 Wall Maps
Chronological Coverage:
  100% post 1900
Classification: Local
Formats: Booklet
Available to: Public, Students, Faculty
Average monthly use: 200
Equipment:
  8 10-drawer units


816
Utah Geological & Mineral Survey
  Library
606 Blackhawk Way
Salt Lake City, UT 84108
Tel. (801) 581-6831
Hours: 8–5, M–F
Responsible Person: Yonatani, Mage,
  Librarian
Special Strengths: Utah
Employees: Full Time    Part Time
  Non-Prof.    1           1
Holdings:
  400 Printed Maps
  100 Manuscript Maps
  300 Aerial Photographs
  2 Atlases
  1 Wall Map
  12 Raised Relief Maps
  200 Microforms
Chronological Coverage: 5% pre 1900;
  95% post 1900
Map collection is cataloged 80%
Formats: Cards
Available to: Public
Average monthly use: 50
Copying Facilities: Copying machine
Equipment:
  8 5-drawer cabinets
  6 5-drawer filing cabinets
Square Footage: 100
Map Depositories: USGS (topo)

817
Utah State Historical Map Library
300 Rio Grande
Salt Lake City, UT 84101
Tel. (801) 533-5808
Hours: 9–5, M–F
Responsible Person: Whetstone, Susan
Special Strengths: Utah
Special Collections: Francis Marion
  Bishop maps of Colorado River
Employees: Full Time    Part Time
  Prof.        1           0
Holdings:
  18000 Printed Maps
  1000 Manuscript Maps
  300 Aerial Photographs
  6 Atlases
  10 Wall Maps
  12 Raised Relief Maps
  700 Microforms
  100 Books
Chronological Coverage: 40% pre 1900;
  60% post 1900
Preservation methods: Encapsulation,
  Deacidification
Available to: Public, Students, Faculty
Average monthly use: 15
Copying Facilities: Copying machine,
  Photographic reproduction
Equipment:
  8 5-drawer cabinets
  2 vertical map cabinets
  4 open ended cases
  1 13-drawer case
  Microfilm reader


**Vermont**
818
University of Vermont
Bailey/Howe Library
Map Room
Burlington, VT 05405
Tel. (802) 656-2020
Hours: 10:30–4, 7–10, M–Th; 10:30–4,
  F; 1–5, Sa, Su
Responsible Person: Clark, Suzanne M.
Special Strengths: Canada (20th cent.)
Employees: Full Time    Part Time
  Prof.        1           0
  Non-Prof.    1           1
Holdings:
  155000 Printed Maps
  600 Aerial Photographs
  375 Atlases
  1 Globe
  11 Raised Relief Maps
  32 Microforms
  50 Books
  270 Gazetteers
  6 Serial Titles
Chronological Coverage: 5% pre 1900;
  95% post 1900
Map collection is cataloged 95%
Classification: AGS    Utility: OCLC
Formats: Cards
Available to: Public, Students, Faculty

Circulates to: Students, Faculty
Average monthly use: 260
Average annual circulation: Maps: 200
Copying Facilities: Copying machine
Equipment:
  77 5-drawer cabinets
  5 vertical map cabinets
  Pull-out atlas shelves
  Stereoscope, Light table
Square Footage: 2334
Map Depositories: USGS (topo);
  USGS (geol); DMA (topo); DMA
  (aero); DMA (hydro); GPO; NOS;
  NOAA; Canada (topo)


### 819

University of Vermont
Department of Geography
Burlington, VT 05405-0114
Tel. (802) 656-3060
Hours: 8–4:30, M–F
Special Strengths: Vermont
Holdings:
  5000 Printed Maps
  500 Manuscript Maps
  5000 Aerial Photographs
  2000 Satellite Imagery
  5 Atlases
  3 Globes
  100 Wall Maps
  30 Raised Relief Maps
  20 Computer Tapes
Chronological Coverage:
  100% post 1900
Available to: Public, Students, Faculty
Circulates to: Public, Students, Faculty
Average monthly use: 50
Average annual circulation:
  Maps: 1000; Aerial Photographs: 300
Copying Facilities: Copying machine
Equipment:
  15 5-drawer cabinets


### 820

University of Vermont
Department of Special Collections
Bailey/Howe Library
Burlington, VT 05401
Tel. (802) 656-2138
Hours: 8:30–9, M–Th; 8:30–5, F
Responsible Person: Buechler, John,
  Head
Special Strengths: Vermont
Special Collections: Sanborn Fire
  Insurance City Maps for Vermont,
  Vermont Manuscript & Early Printed
  Maps
Employees: Full Time   Part Time
  Prof.        3           0
  Non-Prof.    1           3
Holdings:
  900 Printed Maps
  300 Manuscript Maps
  70 Atlases
  3 Globes

75 Wall Maps
10 Books
20 Gazetteers
Chronological Coverage: 65% pre 1900;
  35% post 1900
Map collection is cataloged 90%
Formats: Cards
Preservation methods: Encapsulation,
  Chartex or Fabric Mounting,
  Deacidification
Available to: Public, Students, Faculty
Average monthly use: 30
Copying Facilities: Copying machine
Equipment:
  15 5-drawer cabinets
Square Footage: 70


### 821

Middlebury College
Department of Geography
Science Center 402
Middlebury, VT 05753
Tel. (802) 388-3711
Hours: By appointment
Responsible Person: Churchill, Prof.
  Robert
Special Strengths: United States,
  South Asia, East Asia
Employees: Full Time   Part Time
  Non-Prof.    0           1
Holdings:
  200000 Printed Maps
  500 Aerial Photographs
  5 Globes
  200 Wall Maps
  50 Raised Relief Maps
Chronological Coverage:
  100% post 1900
Available to: Public, Students, Faculty
Circulates to: Public, Students, Faculty
Average monthly use: 20
Average annual circulation: Maps: 400
Copying Facilities: Copying machine,
  Dyeline
Equipment:
  100 5-drawer cabinets
  5 vertical files
Square Footage: 400
Map Depositories: USGS (topo);
  USGS (geol); DMA (topo)


### 822

Vermont Department of Forests, Parks
  & Recreation
Heritage II
79 River St.
Montpelier, VT 05602
Tel. (802) 828-3471
Hours: 8–4:30, M–F
Responsible Person: Greene, Norman
Special Strengths: Vermont (Aerial
  Photos 1939–1979); Vermont (Original
  Grants, Boundaries)
Employees: Full Time   Part Time
  Non-Prof.    0           2

Holdings:
  1200 Manuscript Maps
  31383 Aerial Photographs
Chronological Coverage: 5% pre 1900;
  95% post 1900
Available to: Public
Average monthly use: 10
Copying Facilities: Copying machine
Equipment:
  7 5-drawer cabinets
  Reflecting & magnifying stereoscopes
Square Footage: 60


### 823

Vermont Department of Libraries
Law & Document Unit
Montpelier, VT 05602
Tel. (802) 828-3268
Hours: 7:45–4:30, M–F
Responsible Person: Tamburello,
  Paula
Special Strengths: Vermont
Special Collections: Vermont Highway
  Department Maps; Vermont Serial
  Photos, USGS Maps of Vermont,
  Beer's 19th-cent. County Atlases of
  Vermont
Employees: Full Time   Part Time
  Prof.        4           1
Holdings:
  50 Printed Maps
  1650 Aerial Photographs
  5 Atlases
Chronological Coverage: 20% pre 1900;
  80% post 1900
Available to: Public
Average monthly use: 25
Copying Facilities: Copying machine
Equipment:
  3 5-drawer cabinets
  Atlas case
Square Footage: 100
Map Depositories: USGS (topo)


### 824

Vermont Historical Society
Pavilion Building
109 State St.
Montpelier, VT 05602
Tel. (802) 828-2291
Hours: 8–4:30, M–F
Responsible Person: Brigham, Mary Pat
Special Strengths: Vermont, New
  England, Eastern New York, Eastern
  Canada
Special Collections: James (Wilson)
  Globes
Employees: Full Time   Part Time
  Prof.        1           1
  Non-Prof.    0           2
Holdings:
  1000 Printed Maps
  300 Manuscript Maps
  60 Atlases
  3 Globes

50 Books
30 Gazetteers
Chronological Coverage: 80% pre 1900;
20% post 1900
Map collection is cataloged 90%
Classification: Dewey
Formats: Cards
Preservation methods: Encapsulation,
Deacidification
Available to: Public
Average monthly use: 50
Copying Facilities: Copying machine
Equipment:
16 5-drawer cabinets
Square Footage: 30

### 825

Vermont State Geologist's Library
Geologist Office, Agency of Env. Conserv.
State Office Building Post Office
Montpelier, VT 05602
Tel. (802) 828-3365
Hours: 8–5, M–F
Responsible Person: Ratte, Dr. Charles A.
Special Strengths: Vermont (Geology)
Employees: Full Time    Part Time
Prof.          0              1
Holdings:
185 Printed Maps
2700 Aerial Photographs
2 Raised Relief Maps
10 Microforms
1 Book
1 Gazetteer
1 Serial Title
Chronological Coverage:
100% post 1900
Map collection is cataloged 95%
Classification: Local
Formats: Lists
Preservation methods: Edging
Available to: Public, Students, Faculty
Circulates to: Students, Faculty
Average monthly use: 5
Average annual circulation: Maps: 20;
Books: 2; Aerial Photographs: 5
Copying Facilities: Copying machine
Equipment:
7 5-drawer cabinets
Vertical cardboard map tube file
Stereoscope
Square Footage: 50
Map Depositories: USGS (topo);
USGS (geol)

### 826

Norwich University Library
South Main Street
Northfield, VT 05663
Tel. (802) 485-5011
Responsible Person: Painter,
Jacqueline S., Documents
Librarian
Special Strengths: New England, New
York, United States

Employees: Full Time    Part Time
Prof.          0              1
Non-Prof.      0              1
Holdings:
1570 Printed Maps
26 Atlases
3 Globes
1 Wall Map
52 Books
6 Serial Titles
Chronological Coverage:
100% post 1900
Available to: Public, Students, Faculty
Equipment:
2 10-drawer cabinets
Copying Facilities: Copying machine
Square Footage: 100
Map Depositories: USGS (topo);
USGS (geol); GPO

### 827

Norwich University
Earth Science Dept., Earth Science
Library
Northfield, VT 05663
Tel. (802) 485-5011
Hours: 8–5, M–F
Responsible Person: Larsen, Frederick
Special Strengths: New England,
Northeast
Employees: Full Time    Part Time
Prof.          0              1
Non-Prof.      0              1
Holdings:
2000 Printed Maps
24 Aerial Photographs
12 Satellite Imagery
3 Atlases
2 Globes
24 Wall Maps
166 Raised Relief Maps
Chronological Coverage: 2% pre 1900;
98% post 1900
Available to: Public, Students, Faculty
Average monthly use: 25
Interlibrary loan available
Copying Facilities: Copying machine
Equipment:
6 5-drawer cabinets
4-drawer, 13-drawer cabinets
12-drawer cabinet
2 stereoscopes
Square Footage: 400

### 828

Shelburne Museum Research Library
Route 7
Shelburne, VT 05482
Tel. (802) 985-3344
Special Strengths: Vermont
Special Collections: Vermont Birds
Eye Views
Holdings:
80 Printed Maps
5 Manuscript Maps

2 Globes
10 Wall Maps
Chronological Coverage: 80% pre 1900;
20% post 1900
Map collection is cataloged 85%
Classification: In-house
Formats: Museum catalog books
Preservation methods: Acid free storage
Copying Facilities: Copying machine,
Photographic reproduction

## Virginia

### 829

U. S. Government Printing Office Library
5236 Eisenhower Ave.
Alexandria, VA 22304
Tel. (703) 557-1409
Hours: 8–4, M–F
Responsible Person: Baldwin, Gil
Special Strengths: United States
(Federal government issued only)
Employees: Full Time    Part Time
Prof.          2              0
Chronological Coverage:
100% post 1900
Map collection is cataloged 100%
Classification: SuDocs   Utility: OCLC
Available to: Public
Copying Facilities: Microform
Map Depositories: GPO

### 830

Arlington County Dept. of Libraries
Virginiana Collection
1015 N. Quincy St.
Arlington, VA 22201
Tel. (703) 527-4777
Hours: 9–10, M–Th; 9–5, F, Sa; 1–9, Su
Responsible Person: Collins, Sara,
Virginiana Librarian
Special Strengths: Arlington County
(1876–1930)
Employees: Full Time    Part Time
Prof.          1              0
Holdings:
700 Printed Maps
6 Aerial Photographs
1 Satellite Imagery
9 Atlases
10 Wall Maps
2 Raised Relief Maps
1500 Microforms
3 Books
6 Gazetteers
Chronological Coverage: 10% pre 1900;
90% post 1900
Map collection is cataloged 15%
Formats: Cards
Preservation methods: Encapsulation,
Deacidification
Available to: Public, Students
Average monthly use: 50
Copying Facilities: Copying machine
Equipment:
3 5-drawer cabinets

Hanging blue print stands
Square Footage: 30

### 831

Virginia Tech
Geology Library
3040 Derring Hall
Blacksburg, VA 24061
Tel. (703) 961-6101
Hours: 8–10, M–Th; 8–5, F; 10–2, Su
Responsible Person: Crissinger, John D.
Special Strengths: Virginia (Aerial
  photographs, Geology)
Employees: Full Time    Part Time
  Prof.          0          1
  Non-Prof.      0          1
Holdings:
  15000 Printed Maps
  33500 Aerial Photographs
  50 Atlases
  35 Wall Maps
  25 Raised Relief Maps
Chronological Coverage: 1% pre 1900;
  99% post 1900
Available to: Public, Students, Faculty
Circulates to: Public, Students, Faculty
Average annual circulation: Maps: 700;
  Aerial Photographs: 100
Interlibrary loan available
Copying Facilities: Copying machine
Equipment:
  23 5-drawer cabinets
  11 file cabinets
  15 shelves
Square Footage: 400
Map Depositories: USGS (geol);
  Canada (geol); Va Div. of Min.
  Resources

### 832

Virginia Tech
Newman Library, Map Collection
Blacksburg, VA 24061
Tel. (703) 961-6101
Hours: 8–9, M–Th; 8–5, F
Responsible Person: Crissinger, John D.
Special Strengths: Virginia
Employees: Full Time    Part Time
  Prof.          0          1
  Non-Prof.      0          3
Holdings:
  115000 Printed Maps
  41 Raised Relief Maps
Chronological Coverage: 5% pre 1900;
  95% post 1900
Available to: Public, Students, Faculty
Average Annual Circulation:
  Maps: 16500
Interlibrary loan available
Copying Facilities: Copying machine
Equipment:
  131 5-drawer cabinets
Square Footage: 1500
Map Depositories: USGS (topo);
  DMA (topo); DMA (aero); DMA

(hydro); GPO; Canada (topo)

### 833

Virginia Tech
Newman Library, Special Collections
Blacksburg, VA 24061
Tel. (703) 961-6308
Hours: 9–4:30, M–F
Responsible Person: McMullen, Glenn
Special Strengths: Virginia (Civil War
  Battlefields, Coal Mines, Railroads)
Employees: Full Time    Part Time
  Prof.          0          2
Holdings:
  450 Printed Maps
  50 Manuscript Maps
  20 Atlases
  2 Wall Maps
  20 Gazetteers
Chronological Coverage: 50% pre 1900;
  50% post 1900
Map collection is cataloged 50%
Classification: LC
Formats: Cards
Preservation methods: Encapsulation
Available to: Public, Students, Faculty
Average monthly use: 5
Equipment:
  2 5-drawer cabinets
Square Footage: 25

### 834

University of Virginia
Alderman Library, Dept. of Rare Books
Charlottesville, VA 22901
Tel. (804) 924-3026
Hours: 9–5, M–F; 9–1, Sa
Responsible Person: Runge, William,
  Curator American History
Special Strengths: Virginia (1860–
  1930), North America (18th cent.)
Special Collections: McGregor Collection
  of 18th century maps of North America
  (150 items)
Employees: Full Time    Part Time
  Non-Prof.      0          1
Holdings:
  3800 Printed Maps
  50 Manuscript Maps
  500 Aerial Photographs
  200 Atlases
  2 Wall Maps
  50 Books
  15 Gazetteers
  5 Serial titles
Chronological Coverage: 30% pre 1900;
  70% post 1900
Map collection is cataloged 80%
Classification: LC
Formats: Cards
Preservation methods: Encapsulation
Available to: Public, Students, Faculty
Average monthly use: 20
Average annual circulation: Maps: 100;
  Books: 100; Aerial Photographs: 4

Copying Facilities: Copying machine,
  Photographic reproduction
Equipment:
  25 5-drawer cabinets
Square Footage: 300

### 835

University of Virginia
Alderman Library, Govt. Documents
Charlottesville, VA 22901
Tel. (804) 924-3026
Responsible Person: Newsome, Walter
Employees: Full Time    Part Time
  Prof.          0          1
  Non-Prof.      0          2
Holdings:
  200000 Printed Maps
  90 Atlases
  250 Gazetteers
Chronological Coverage:
  100% post 1900
Available to: Public, Students, Faculty
Circulates to: Public, Students, Faculty
Interlibrary loan available
  In-state only
Copying Facilities: Copying machine
Equipment:
  90 5-drawer cabinets
Square Footage: 1100
Map Depositories: USGS (topo);
  USGS (geol); DMA (topo); DMA
  (aero); DMA (hydro); GPO

### 836

University of Virginia
Department of Environmental Sciences
Clark Hall
Charlottesville, VA 22903
Tel. (804) 924-7761
Holdings:
  12000 Printed Maps
Chronological Coverage:
  100% post 1900
Available to: Public, Students, Faculty
Circulates to: Public, Students, Faculty
Copying Facilities: Copying machine
Equipment:
  20 5-drawer cabinets
Map Depositories: USGS (topo

### 837

Chesapeake Public Library
300 Cedar Road
Chesapeake, VA 23320
Tel. (804) 547-6591
Hours: 9–9, M–Th; 9–5, F, Sa; 1–5, Su
Responsible Person: Edmondson,
  Ernestine, Head/Reference
Employees: Full Time    Part Time
  Non-Prof.      0          1
Holdings:
  3000 Printed Maps
  66 Aerial Photographs
  75 Atlases

2 Globes
1 Wall Map


### 838
George Mason University
Fenwick Library, Audiovisual Library
4400 University Dr.
Fairfax, VA 22030
Tel. (703) 323-2605
Hours: 7:30–Midnight, M–Th; 7:30–6,
  F; 9–5, Sa; 1–9, Su
Responsible Person: Major, Linda M.,
  Librarian Assistant
Employees: Full Time    Part Time
  Prof.        1         0
  Non-Prof.    1         1
Holdings:
  80000 Printed Maps
    200 Aerial Photographs
    30 Atlases
    1 Globe
Chronological Coverage: 1% pre 1900;
  99% post 1900
Available to: Public, Students, Faculty
Copying Facilities: Copying machine
Equipment:
  38 5-drawer cabinets
Square Footage: 600
Map Depositories: USGS (topo)


### 839
Virginia Institute of Marine Science
  Library
Gloucester Point, VA 23062
Tel. (804) 642-2111
Hours: 8–4:30, M–F
Responsible Person: Barrick, Susan,
  Librarian
Special Strengths: Chesapeake Bay &
  East Coast (Nautical charts), Virginia
Employees: Full Time    Part Time
  Prof.        0         2
Holdings:
  2500 Printed Maps
    50 Atlases
    50 Books
    10 Gazetteers
Chronological Coverage: 1% pre 1900;
  99% post 1900
Available to: Public, Students, Faculty
Circulates to: Students, Faculty
Copying Facilities: Copying machine
Equipment:
  5 5-drawer cabinets
  2 atlas cabinets
Map Depositories: USGS (topo);
  NOS


### 840
Hampden–Sydney College
Eggleston Library
Hampden–Sydney, VA 23943
Tel. (804) 223-4381
Hours: 8–10, M–F

Responsible Person: Zoellner, Alan F.
Special Strengths: Virginia
Employees: Full Time    Part Time
  Prof.        0         1
  Non-Prof.    0         2
Holdings:
  873 Printed Maps
Chronological Coverage:
  100% post 1900
Available to: Public, Students, Faculty
Average monthly use: 5
Copying Facilities: Copying machine
Equipment:
  1 5-drawer cabinet
Square Footage: 9
Map Depositories: USGS (topo)


### 841
James Madison University Library
Harrisonburg, VA 22807
Tel. (703) 433-6267
Hours: 8–Midnight, M–Th; 9–6, Sa;
  Noon–Midnight, Su
Responsible Person: Miller, Gordon W.
Special Strengths: Virginia, Shenandoah
  Valley
Employees: Full Time    Part Time
  Prof.        0         1
  Non-Prof.    0         1
Holdings:
  2850 Printed Maps
    100 Atlases
    1 Globe
    200 Books
    10 Gazetteers
    17 Serial Titles
Chronological Coverage: 5% pre 1900;
  95% post 1900
Preservation methods: Lamination
Available to: Public, Students, Faculty
Average monthly use: 15
Average annual circulation: Maps: 400
Copying Facilities: Copying machine,
  Microform
Equipment:
  3 5-drawer cabinets
Square Footage: 60
Map Depositories: USGS (topo)


### 842
Virginia Military Institute
Department of Civil Engineering
Lexington, VA 24450
Tel. (703) 463-6331
Hours: By appointment
Special Strengths: Virginia
Holdings:
  850 Printed maps
Chronological Coverage:
  100% post 1900
Available to: Public, Students, Faculty
Average monthly use: 10
Equipment:
  4 5-drawer cabinets
Square Footage: 100

Map Depositories: USGS (topo)


### 843
Lynchburg College
Knight-Capron Library
Lynchburg, VA 24501
Tel. (804) 522-8206
Hours: 9–5, M–F
Responsible Person: Beckel, Deborah
Special Strengths: Virginia (19th cent.),
  Maryland (17th–19th cent.), Virginia
  (18th–20th cent., Iron Furnaces)
Special Collections: John D. Capron
  Map Collection
Holdings:
  150 Printed Maps
    20 Gazetteers
Chronological Coverage: 80% pre 1900;
  20% post 1900
Available to: Public, Students, Faculty
Interlibrary loan available
  Photocopies only
Copying Facilities: Copying machine,
  Microform
Equipment:
  2 5-drawer cabinets
Square Footage: 20


### 844
Christopher Newport College
Captain John Smith Library
50 Shore Line
Newport News, VA 23606
Tel. (804) 599-7132
Hours: 8–10:30, M–Th; 8–4:45, F
Responsible Person: Treacy, Hugh J.,
  Reference/Instruction
Special Strengths: Virginia
Employees: Full Time    Part Time
  Non-Prof.    0         1
Holdings:
  1381 Printed Maps
Chronological Coverage:
  100% post 1900
Available to: Public, Students, Faculty
Copying Facilities: Copying machine
Equipment:
  1 vertical map cabinet
Square Footage: 8
Map Depositories: USGS (topo)


### 845
Mariners' Museum
Newport News, VA 23606
Tel. (804) 595-0368
Hours: 9–5, M–Sa
Responsible Person: Crew, Roger T., Jr.,
  Archivist
Employees: Full Time    Part Time
  Prof.        2         0
  Non-Prof.    2         0
Holdings:
  1655 Printed Maps
Chronological Coverage: 75% pre 1900;

25% post 1900
Map collection is cataloged 100%
Classification: Local
Formats: Cards
Preservation methods: Encapsulation,
 Chartex or Fabric Mounting
Available to: Public
Average monthly use: 10
Copying Facilities: Copying machine,
 Photographic reproduction
Equipment:
 9 5-drawer cabinets
Square Footage: 216

### 846
Norfolk Public Library
301 E. City Hall Ave.
Norfolk, VA 23510
Tel. (804) 441-2887
Hours: 9–5, M–F
Responsible Person: Barnes, Cynthia
Employees: Full Time     Part Time
 Prof.          1          0
 Non-Prof.      1          0
Holdings:
 4320 Printed Maps
 181 Aerial Photographs
 99 Atlases
 1 Globe
 3 Wall Maps
 10 Books
 28 Gazetteers
Chronological Coverage: 5% pre 1900;
 95% post 1900
Preservation methods: Encapsulation
Available to: Public
Average monthly use: 20
Copying Facilities: Copying machine,
 Photographic reproduction
Equipment:
 6 5-drawer cabinets
 1 5-drawer filing cabinet
 2 filing cabinet drawers
Square Footage: 36
Map Depositories: GPO

### 847
Old Dominion University
Government Publications
Hampton Blvd.
Norfolk, VA 23508
Tel. (804) 440-4168
Hours: 8–9, M–Th; 8–5, F; 9–5, Sa;
 1–5, Su
Responsible Person: Amerski, Audrey
Special Strengths: Virginia (Geology),
 South Carolina, North Carolina,
 Maryland, Chesapeake Bay
Employees: Full Time     Part Time
 Prof.          1          0
 Non-Prof.      0          1
Holdings:
 6026 Printed Maps
 1042 Aerial Photographs
 32 Satellite Imagery

617 Atlases
 1 Globe
 1 Wall Map
 25 Microforms
 40 Books
 55 Gazetteers
Chronological Coverage: 2% pre 1900;
 98% post 1900
Map collection is cataloged 30%
Classification: GPO
Formats: Cards
Available to: Public, Students, Faculty
Circulates to: Students, Faculty
Average monthly use: 25
Average annual circulation: Maps: 100;
 Aerial Photographs: 25
Interlibrary loan available
Copying Facilities: Copying machine,
 Microform
Equipment:
 1 vertical map cabinet
 8 10-drawer cabinets
 2 11-drawer cabinets
Square Footage: 144
Map Depositories: USGS (geol);
 GPO

### 848
U.S. Army Corps of Engineers
Norfolk District
803 Front St.
Norfolk, VA 23510
Tel. (804) 441-3562
Hours: 7–4:30, M–F
Responsible Person: Killam, Lane
Employees: Full Time     Part Time
 Prof.          1          0
 Non-Prof.      0          1
Holdings:
 90000 Printed Maps
Chronological Coverage: 20% pre 1900;
 80% post 1900
Available to: Public, Students, Faculty
Copying Facilities: Diazo

### 849
Radford University
Geography Department, Map Collection
P. O. Box 5811
Radford, VA 24142
Tel. (703) 731-5254
Hours: 8–5, M–F
Responsible Person: Kuennecke,
 Dr. Berad H.
Special Strengths: Virginia, Eastern
 United States
Employees: Full Time     Part Time
 Prof.          1          0
 Non-Prof.      2          0
Holdings:
 20000 Printed Maps
 5000 Aerial Photographs
 900 Satellite Imagery
 25 Globes
 120 Wall Maps

18 Raised Relief Maps
Chronological Coverage:
 100% post 1900
Map collection is cataloged 50%
Formats: Cards
Available to: Public, Students, Faculty
Circulates to: Public, Students, Faculty
Average monthly use: 50
Average annual circulation:
 Maps: 8000; Aerial Photographs: 200
Equipment:
 7 5-drawer cabinets
 Stereoscopes
Square Footage: 400
Map Depositories: USGS (topo)

### 850
U. S. Geological Survey Library, Reston
950 National Center
Reston, VA 22092
Tel. (703) 860-6671
Hours: 7:15–4:15, M–F
Responsible Person: Chappell, Barbara,
 Chief of Reference
Special Strengths: World & Other
 (1830–present, Geology & Earth
 Sciences), United States
Employees: Full Time     Part Time
 Prof.          3          1
 Non-Prof.      0          2
Holdings:
 290000 Printed Maps
 1000 Manuscript Maps
 600 Atlases
 7 Globes
 30 Wall Maps
 200 Raised Relief Maps
 50 Microforms
 1000 Books
 300 Gazetteers
 50 Serial Titles
Chronological Coverage: 2% pre 1900;
 98% post 1900
Map collection is cataloged 15%
Classification: USGS   Utility: OCLC
Formats: Cards
Preservation methods: Chartex or
 Fabric Mounting, Edging
Available to: Public, Students, Faculty
Average annual circulation:
 Maps: 2400
Interlibrary loan available
 Open file reports do not circulate
Copying Facilities: Copying machine,
 Microform
Equipment:
 650 5-drawer cabinets
Square Footage: 9700
Map Depositories: USGS (topo);
 USGS (geol); DMA (aero); GPO;
 NOAA; Canada (geol)

### 851
Richmond Public Library
Map File–Literature & History

101 E. Franklin St.
Richmond, VA 23219
Tel. (804) 780-4672
Hours: 9–9, M–F; 9–5, Sa; 2–6, Su
Responsible Person: Sanderson,
    James W.
Special Strengths: Virginia
Employees: Full Time    Part Time
    Prof.        0            1
Holdings:
    1500 Printed Maps
        1 Aerial Photograph
        1 Globe
        1 Wall Map
Chronological Coverage:
    100% post 1900
Available to: Public
Average monthly use: 30
Copying Facilities: Copying machine
Equipment:
    1 vertical map cabinet
    2 cabinets designed for VA Geological
    Survey Maps
Square Footage: 11


                852
Virginia Historical Society
P. O. Box 7311
Richmond, VA 23221
Tel. (804) 358-4901
Hours: 9–4:45, M–Sa
Responsible Person: Cole, Howson W.
Special Strengths: Virginia (1497–
    present)
Employees: Full Time    Part Time
    Prof.        0            1
    Non-Prof.    0            1
Holdings:
    5500 Printed Maps
        10 Manuscript Maps
        1 Aerial Photograph
        75 Atlases
        1 Globe
        1 Wall Map
        30 Books
        2 Gazetteers
        1 Serial Title
Chronological Coverage: 80% pre 1900;
    20% post 1900
Map collection is cataloged 90%
Classification: LC
Formats: Cards
Preservation methods: Lamination,
    Deacidification
Available to: Public, Students, Faculty
Average monthly use: 15
Copying Facilities: Copying machine,
    Photographic reproduction
Equipment:
    15 5-drawer cabinets
Square Footage: 77


                853
Virginia State Library
Archives & Branch Division

Archives Branch Map Collection
12th & Capitol Streets
Richmond, VA 23219-3491
Tel. (804) 786-2306
Hours: 8:15–5, M–Sa
Responsible Person: Gonzales,
    Anthony J.
Special Strengths: Virginia,
    Southeast
Special Collections: Sanborn Fire
    Insurance Maps (ca. 2000), Board of
    Public Works, Manuscript maps (ca.
    400) relating to 19th cent. Virginia
    internal improvements (roads, canals,
    railroads)
Employees: Full Time    Part Time
    Prof.        0            1
Holdings:
    85528 Printed Maps
        15 Atlases
        1 Globe
        10 Wall Maps
        1 Raised Relief map
        1 Microform
        18 Books
        2 Gazetteers
Chronological Coverage: 75% pre 1900;
    25% post 1900
Map collection is cataloged 90%
Classification: Dewey
Formats: Cards
Preservation methods: Lamination,
    Deacidification
Available to: Public
Average monthly use: 60
Average annual circulation:
    Maps: 1800
Copying Facilities: Copying machine,
    Photographic reproduction
Equipment:
    120 5-drawer cabinets
Square Footage: 480
Map Depositories: USGS (topo);
    USGS (geol)


                854
Roanoke City Public Library
Virginia Room
706 S. Jefferson St.
Roanoke, VA 24106
Tel. (703) 981-2073
Hours: 9–5, M–Sa
Responsible Person: Tuckwiller,
    Alice Carol
Employees: Full Time    Part Time
    Prof.        1            0
    Non-Prof.    0            1
Holdings:
    692 Printed Maps
        4 Aerial Photographs
        1 Atlas
        4 Wall Maps
Chronological Coverage: 12% pre 1900;
    88% post 1900
Preservation methods: Encapsulation
Available to: Public

Average monthly use: 2
Copying Facilities: Copying machine
Equipment:
    2 5-drawer cabinets


                855
College of William & Mary
Earl Gregg Swem Library
Williamsburg, VA 23185
Tel. (804) 253-4407
Hours: 8–Midnight, M–F; 9–6, Sa;
    1–Midnight, Su
Responsible Person: Moore, Del,
    Reference Coordinator
Special Collections: The John Womack
    (Wright) Collection of Maps, 1699–
    1918, of Belgium, France, Holland,
    Germany and Italy (200 maps)
Employees: Full Time    Part Time
    Prof.        0            3
Holdings:
    2700 Printed Maps
        25 Manuscript Maps
        60 Atlases
        2 Globes
        3 Wall Maps
Chronological Coverage: 30% pre 1900;
    70% post 1900
Map collection is cataloged 95%
Formats: Cards
Preservation methods: Encapsulation,
    Deacidification
Available to: Public, Students, Faculty
Copying Facilities: Copying machine,
    Microform
Equipment:
    10 5-drawer cabinets
    1 vertical map cabinet
Square Footage: 135
Map Depositories: USGS (topo);
    USGS (geol); GPO


                856
Colonial Williamsburg Foundation
Williamsburg, VA 23185
Tel. (804) 299-1000
Hours: 9–5, M–F
Responsible Person: Pritchard,
    Margaret B., Map Curator
Special Strengths: Colonial America
    (17th & 18th cent.)
Employees: Full Time    Part Time
    Prof.        1            0
Holdings:
    700 Printed Maps
        2 Manuscript Maps
        10 Atlases
        5 Globes
        20 Wall Maps
Chronological Coverage: 90% pre 1900;
    10% post 1900
Map collection is cataloged 80%
Formats: Cards
Preservation methods: Encapsulation,
    Deacidification

Available to: Students, Faculty
Average monthly use: 1
Copying Facilities: Copying machine
Equipment:
  2 5-drawer cabinets

857
Colonial Williamsburg Foundation
The Research Center
P. O. Box C, Francis & S. Henry Sts.
Williamsburg, VA 23187
Tel. (804) 229-1000
Hours: 8:30–5, M–F; 9–1, Sa
Responsible Person: Ingram, Dr. John E.
Special Strengths: Virginia (1600–1900)
Special Collections: U.S. Geodetic
  Survey Maps–Virginia, Rochambeau
  Maps (photocopies), Wood Maps of
  Virginia (photocopies)
Employees: Full Time    Part Time
  Prof.        0          1
  Non-Prof.    0          3
Holdings:
  1000 Printed Maps
    20 Manuscript Maps
     5 Aerial Photographs
   200 Microforms
   200 Books
    10 Gazetteers
Chronological Coverage: 90% pre 1900;
  10% post 1900
Map collection is cataloged 90%
Formats: Cards
Preservation methods: Encapsulation,
  Deacidification
Available to: Public, Students, Faculty
Average monthly use: 10
Copying Facilities: Copying machine,
  Photographic reproduction
Equipment:
  6 5-drawer cabinets
Square Footage: 50

858
University of Virginia
Clinch Valley College
John Cook Wyllie Library
Wise, VA 24293
Tel. (703) 328-2431
Hours: 8–10, M–Th; 8–4:30, F; 1–5, Sa;
  1:30–10, Su
Responsible Person: Gibson, Neva
Special Strengths: Virginia (Geology),
  Tennessee (Geology), Kentucky
  (Geology), North Carolina (Geology)
Employees: Full Time    Part Time
  Prof.        0          1
Holdings:
  2748 Printed Maps
    52 Atlases
     1 Globe
     1 Wall Map
    11 Raised Relief maps
    75 Books
     5 Gazetteers
     6 Serial titles

Chronological Coverage: 2% pre 1900;
  98% post 1900
Available to: Public, Students, Faculty
Average monthly use: 5
Copying Facilities: Copying machine
Equipment:
  4 5-drawer cabinets
Square Footage: 9
Map Depositories: USGS (topo);
  USGS (geol)

## Washington
859
Western Washington University
Dept. of Geography & Regional Planning
Map Library
Bellingham, WA 98247
Tel. (206) 676-3272
Hours: 9–4, M, T, Th, F; 9–4, 6–8, W
Responsible Person: Collins, Janet,
  Map Curator
Special Strengths: Pacific Northwest,
  Alaska, Canada, Pacific Rim
Special Collections: Washington State
  Department of Natural Resources–
  Orthophoto series of Washington
  State
Employees: Full Time    Part Time
  Prof.        1          0
  Non-Prof.    0          9
Holdings:
  172000 Printed Maps
   20600 Aerial Photographs
     45 Satellite Imagery
    670 Atlases
     55 Globes
    391 Wall Maps
     50 Raised Relief Maps
    410 Microforms
    500 Books
    167 Gazetteers
      9 Serial Titles
Chronological Coverage: 5% pre 1900;
  95% post 1900
Map collection is cataloged 95%
Classification: LC
Formats: Cards
Preservation methods: Encapsulation,
  Lamination, Chartex or Fabric
  Mounting, Edging
Available to: Public, Students, Faculty
Average monthly use: 500
Copying Facilities: Copying machine
Equipment:
  251 5-drawer cabinets
  9 vertical file cabinets
  Light tables, drafting tables,
  Stereoscopes, Map-o-graph, planimeter
Square Footage: 3000
Map Depositories: USGS (topo);
  USGS (geol); DMA (topo); DMA
  (aero); DMA (hydro); NOS; NOAA;
  Canada (topo); WA State Dept. of
  Natural Resources

860
Eastern Washington University
J. F. Kennedy Memorial Library
Archives & Special Collections
Cheney, WA 99004
Tel. (509) 359-2261
Hours: 7:30–5, 6–9, M–F
Responsible Person: Rea, Jay W.
Special Strengths: Pacific Northwest
  (1810–1940)
Employees: Full Time    Part Time
  Prof.        1          0
  Non-Prof.    1          0
Holdings:
  11694 Printed maps
     8 Manuscript Maps
    62 Atlases
     1 Globe
     9 Wall Maps
     1 Raised Relief Map
   1930 Books
    22 Gazetteers
Chronological Coverage: 1% pre 1900;
  99% post 1900
Preservation methods: Encapsulation,
  Lamination, Chartex or Fabric
  Mounting
Available to: Public, Students, Faculty
Average monthly use: 10
Average annual circulation: Maps: 233
Copying Facilities: Copying machine,
  Microform
Equipment:
  5 5-drawer cabinets
  Special shelving
Square Footage: 70
Map Depositories: GPO

861
Central Washington University Library
Documents Department
Ellensburg, WA 98926
Tel. (509) 963-1541
Hours: 8–10, M–Th; 8–5, F; 9–5, Sa;
  1–10, Su
Responsible Person: Hartman, Ruth D.
Special Strengths: Washington,
  Oregon, Idaho
Employees: Full Time    Part Time
  Prof.        1          0
  Non-Prof.    1          2
Holdings:
  70000 Printed Maps
    175 Atlases
     3 Globes
     5 Wall Maps
    25 Raised Relief Maps
    50 Books
   150 Gazetteers
Chronological Coverage: 5% pre 1900;
  95% post 1900
Classification: LC    Utility: OCLC
Formats: Cards
Preservation methods: Lamination
Available to: Public, Students, Faculty
Circulates to: Public, Students, Faculty

Average monthly use: 300
Average annual circulation:
Maps: 4798
Interlibrary loan available
Except heavily used maps
Copying Facilities: Copying machine,
Microform
Equipment:
48 5-drawer cabinets
1 vertical map cabinet
Square Footage: 660
Map Depositories: USGS (topo);
USGS (geol); DMA (topo); DMA
(aero); DMA (hydro); GPO; NOS;
NOAA

862
Evergreen State College Library
Olympia, WA 98505
Tel. (206) 866-6000
Hours: 8:45–10:45, M–Th; 8:45–6:45,
F; 11–6:45, Sa, Su
Responsible Person: Stilson, Malcolm,
Head of Reference
Special Strengths: Washington

| Employees: | Full Time | Part Time |
|---|---|---|
| Prof. | 0 | 2 |
| Non-Prof. | 0 | 2 |

Holdings:
409 Printed Maps
150 Atlases
1 Globe
188 Wall Maps
95 Books
50 Gazetteers
5 Serial Titles
Chronological Coverage: 15% pre 1900;
85% post 1900
Available to: Public, Students, Faculty
Circulates to: Public, Students, Faculty
Average monthly use: 15
Average annual circulation: Maps: 55;
Books: 120
Interlibrary loan available
Rare maps do not circulate
Copying Facilities: Copying machine,
Microform, Photographic reproduction
Equipment:
2 5-drawer cabinets
2 vertical map cabinets
Square Footage: 100
Map Depositories: USGS (topo);
USGS (geol); DMA (topo); DMA
(aero); GPO

863
Washington Dept. of Natural Resources,
Photos, Map & Reports
QW-21
Olympia, WA 98504
Tel. (206) 753-5338
Hours: 8–4:30, M–F
Special Strengths: Washington
(Orthophotos & aerial photos)

| Employees: Full Time | Part Time |
|---|---|
| Non-Prof. 4 | 0 |

Holdings:
1500 Printed Maps
500 Manuscript Maps
350000 Aerial Photographs
Chronological Coverage:
100% post 1900
Map collection is cataloged 100%
Classification: Public Land Survey
Formats: Index Maps
Preservation methods: Lamination
Available to: Public
Copying Facilities: Copying machine,
Photographic reproduction
Equipment:
50 5-drawer cabinets
2 vertical map cabinets
Stereoscopes, Microfiche viewers
Square Footage: 2300

864
Washington State Dept. of Natural
Resources
Division of Geology & Earth Resources
Library P4-12
Olympia, WA 98504
Tel. (206) 459-6373
Hours: 8–4:30, M–F
Responsible Person: Manson, Connie
Special Strengths: Washington

| Employees: | Full Time | Part Time |
|---|---|---|
| Prof. | 1 | 0 |
| Non-Prof. | 0 | 1 |

Holdings:
5000 Printed Maps
250 Manuscript Maps
Chronological Coverage: 1% pre 1900;
99% post 1900
Equipment:
4 5-drawer cabinets
Map Depositories: USGS (topo)

865
Washington State Library
Documents Section
AJ-11
Olympia, WA 98504
Tel. (206) 753-4057
Hours: 8–5, M–F
Responsible Person: Bregent, Ann

| Employees: | Full Time | Part Time |
|---|---|---|
| Prof. | 1 | 0 |

Holdings:
15000 Printed Maps
100 Atlases
25000 Microforms
200 Gazetteers
Chronological Coverage:
100% post 1900
Available to: Public
Average monthly use: 50
Copying Facilities: Copying machine,
Microform
Equipment: 10 5-drawer cabinets

Square Footage: 750
Map Depositories: USGS (topo); GPO

866
Washington State University
Department of Geology Map Library
Pullman, WA 99164-2812
Tel. (509) 335-3009
Hours: 8–5, M–F
Responsible Person: Hooper,
Dr. Peter R.
Special Strengths: Washington,
Oregon, Idaho, Montana

| Employees: | Full Time | Part Time |
|---|---|---|
| Prof. | 0 | 1 |
| Non-Prof. | 0 | 1 |

Holdings:
10000 Printed Maps
12 Manuscript Maps
30 Aerial Photographs
12 Atlases
100 Wall Maps
24 Raised Relief Maps
75 Books
8 Serial Titles
Chronological Coverage: 3% pre 1900;
97% post 1900
Map collection is cataloged 80%
Classification: Alpha & numerical
Formats: Cards
Available to: Public, Students, Faculty
Circulates to: Public, Students, Faculty
Average monthly use: 15
Equipment:
25 5-drawer cabinets
3 vertical map cabinets
12 file cabinets
2 mirror stereoscopes
Square Footage: 525
Map Depositories: USGS (geol)

867
Washington State University
Owen Science & Engineering Library
Pullman, WA 99164-3200
Tel. (509) 335-2671
Hours: 8–Midnight, M–F
Responsible Person: Roberts, Betty,
Head
Holdings: 30000 Printed Maps
Available to: Public, Students, Faculty
Circulates to: Public, Students, Faculty
Interlibrary loan available
Copying Facilities: Copying machine
Equipment:
16 5-drawer cabinets
7 vertical map cabinets
Map Depositories: USGS (topo);
USGS (geol)

868
Renton Public Library
100 Cedar River
Renton, WA 98055

Tel. (206) 235-2612
Hours: 9–9, M–Th; 10–6, F, Sa
Responsible Person: Petersen, Clark
Special Strengths: Washington
Employees: Full Time    Part Time
    Non-Prof.    0          1
Holdings:
    5171 Printed Maps
     195 Atlases
       3 Globes
       1 Raised Relief Map
Chronological Coverage:
    100% post 1900
Available to: Public, Students, Faculty
Circulates to: Public
Average annual circulation: Maps: 166;
    Books: 600
Copying Facilities: Copying Machine
Equipment:
    2 5-drawer cabinets
    2 vertical map cabinets
Square Footage: 100

### 869
Seattle Public Library
History Department,
Map Collection
1000 Fourth Ave.
Seattle, WA 98104
Tel. (206) 625-4894
Hours: 9–9, M–W; 12–9, Th; 9–6, F, Sa;
    1–5, Su
Responsible Person: Henry, Marjorie R.,
    Map Librarian
Special Strengths: Seattle (1855–
    present), King County (1855–present),
    Washington (1855–present), Kroll,
    Metsker (1920–present, Atlases;
    Seattle & environs, Washington
    Counties)
Special Collections: Washington County
    plat maps (1905–1983), Seattle Ward
    maps (1910–1915), Seattle-King
    County street maps (1875–present),
    U.S. Forest Service Maps–Washington
    (1923–1984), Nautical Charts–Puget
    Sound Area (1931–1984)
Employees: Full Time    Part Time
    Prof.        0          1
    Non-Prof.    0          2
Holdings:
    71709 Printed Maps
      850 Atlases
        3 Globes
       12 Wall Maps
       30 Raised Relief Maps
      131 Books
      150 Gazetteers
       12 Serial Titles
Chronological Coverage: 2% pre 1900;
    98% post 1900
Map collection is cataloged 98%
Classification: AGS
Formats: Cards, COM
Preservation methods: Lamination,
    Chartex or Fabric Mounting

Available to: Public
Circulates to: Public
Average monthly use: 1300
Average annual circulation:
    Maps: 8000
Copying Facilities: Copying machine
Equipment:
    40 5-drawer cabinets
     4 vertical map cabinets
     1 8-drawer, 1 19-drawer cabinet
     7 12-drawer, 1 10-drawer cabinets
Square Footage: 852
Map Depositories: USGS (topo);
    USGS (geol); DMA (topo); DMA
    (aero); DMA (hydro); GPO; NOS;
    U.S. FS (Pacific NW); BLN
    (Washington)

### 870
University of Washington Libraries
Map Section FM-25
Seattle, WA 98195
Tel. (206) 543-9392
Hours: 7:30–5:30, M–F
Responsible Person: Hiller, Steve
Special Strengths: Washington
Employees: Full Time    Part Time
    Prof.        1          0
    Non-Prof.    0          4
Holdings:
    201889 Printed Maps
     39352 Aerial Photographs
        17 Satellite Imagery
      1506 Atlases
         4 Serial Titles
Chronological Coverage: 1% pre 1900;
    99% post 1900
Preservation methods: Encapsulation,
    Deacidification
Available to: Public, Students, Faculty
Circulates to: Students, Faculty
Average monthly use: 1000
Interlibrary loan available
Copying Facilities: Copying machine,
    Microform, Photographic reproduction
Equipment:
    166 5-drawer cabinets
     30 vertical file cabinets
     98 sections stack shelves
    Stereoscopes, light table
Square Footage: 7000
Map Depositories: USGS (topo);
    USGS (geol); DMA (topo); DMA
    (aero); DMA (hydro); GPO; NOS;
    NOAA; Canada (geol); WA State
    Dept. of Natural Resources

### 871
University of Washington Libraries
Pacific Northwest Collection
Suzzallo Library FM-25
Seattle, WA 98195
Tel. (206) 543-1929
Hours: 10–5, M–F; 1–5, Sa
Responsible Person: Rockerson, Carla

Special Strengths: Washington (1909–
    1929, Fire Insurance maps), Western
    Pacific (1750–1900, Explorers
    routes-atlases), Seattle (Plat atlases,
    1900–present)
Employees: Full Time    Part Time
    Prof.        2          0
    Non-Prof.    1          3
Holdings:
    2695 Printed Maps
      12 Gazetteers
Chronological Coverage: 50% pre 1900;
    50% post 1900
Map collection is cataloged 50%
Classification: Dewey
Formats: Cards
Preservation methods: Encapsulation,
    Deacidification
Available to: Public, Students, Faculty
Copying Facilities: Microform, Dyeline,
    Photographic reproduction
Equipment:
    21 5-drawer cabinets

### 872
Spokane Public Library
Information Services
West 906 Maine Ave.
Spokane, WA 99201
Tel. (509) 838-3361
Hours: 9–9, M, T, Th; 1–6, W; 9–6,
    F, Sa
Responsible Person: Verd, Tom W.,
    Head, Information Services
Special Collections: Northwest History
    Collection (original)
Holdings:
    8500 Printed Maps
     250 Gazetteers
Chronological Coverage: 2% pre 1900;
    98% post 1900
Classification: SuDocs
Formats: Cards
Available to: Public, Students, Faculty
Average monthly use: 300
Interlibrary loan available
    Except topographic quadrangles
Copying Facilities: Copying machine,
    Microform
Equipment:
    5 5-drawer cabinets
    2 vertical cabinets
Map Depositories: USGS (topo);
    USGS (geol); DMA (topo); DMA
    (aero); DMA (hydro); GPO

### 873
Pacific Lutheran University
R. A. Mortvedt Library, Reference Dept.
S. 121st & Park Ave.
Tacoma, WA 98447
Tel. (206) 535-7500
Hours: 7:30–12, M–Th; 7:30–11, F;
    10–11, Sa; 11–12, Su
Responsible Person: McDonald, Susan

Holdings:
   5000 Printed Maps
Available to: Public, Students, Faculty
Copying Facilities: Copying machine
Equipment:
   5 5-drawer cabinets
Map Depositories: USGS (topo);
   USGS (geol); NOS


874
Tacoma Public Library
Special Collections
1102 Tacoma Ave. South
Tacoma, WA 98402
Tel. (206) 591-5622
Hours: 9–9, M–Th; 9–6, F, Sa
Responsible Person: Reese, Gary Fuller
Special Strengths: Pacific Northwest
   (1850–present)
Holdings:
   35000 Printed Maps
      350 Aerial Photographs
      250 Atlases
        5 Globes
      100 Wall Maps
        5 Raised Relief Maps
      250 Books
      100 Gazetteers
Chronological Coverage: 20% pre 1900;
   80% post 1900
Map collection is cataloged 5%
Classification: Dewey
Formats: Cards
Preservation methods: Lamination
Available to: Public
Average monthly use: 150
Copying Facilities: Copying machine
Equipment:
   12 5-drawer cabinets
   Folded maps on shelves
Square Footage: 550
Map Depositories: USGS (topo)


875
University of Puget Sound
Department of Geology
Tacoma, WA 98416
Tel. (206) 756-3129
Hours: 9–5, M–F
Responsible Person: Lauther, Stewart,
   Chairman
Employees: Full Time    Part Time
   Non-Prof.     0            1
Holdings:
   30000 Printed Maps
      500 Aerial Photographs
Preservation methods: Chartex or
   Fabric Mounting, Edging
Available to: Public, Students, Faculty
Circulates to: Students, Faculty
Average monthly use: 12
Average annual circulation: Maps: 150
Interlibrary loan available
Copying Facilities: Copying machine
Equipment:

25 12-drawer cabinets
 5 10-drawer cabinets
Stereoscopes
Square Footage: 300
Map Depositories: USGS (topo)


876
Washington State Historical Society
315 N. Stadium Way
Tacoma, WA 98403
Tel. (206) 593-2830
Hours: 9:30–5, T–Sa
Special Strengths: Pacific Northwest
   (19th & 20th cent.)
Special Collections: Allen Collection
Holdings:
   1313 Printed Maps
    235 Aerial Photographs
     17 Atlases
      8 Gazetteers
Chronological Coverage: 66% pre 1900;
   34% post 1900
Map collection is cataloged 75%
Formats: Cards
Available to: Public, Students
Copying Facilities: Copying machine
Equipment:
   5 5-drawer cabinets
   1 vertical map cabinet
Square Footage: 60


877
Whitman College
Penrose Memorial Library
345 Boyer
Walla Walla, WA 99362
Tel. (509) 527-5191
Hours: 8–Midnight, M–Th; 8–9, F, Sa;
   11–Midnight, Su
Responsible Person: Sparks, Marilyn
Special Collections: Pacific Northwest
   Collection (Regional Historical
   Material)
Employees: Full Time    Part Time
   Prof.          0            1
   Non-Prof.     0            2
Holdings:
   30000 Printed Maps
    2618 Aerial Photographs
     266 Atlases
       1 Globe
       3 Raised Relief Maps
      80 Books
Chronological Coverage: 8% pre 1900;
   92% post 1900
Map collection is cataloged 10%
Formats: Cards
Preservation methods: Encapsulation
Available to: Public, Students, Faculty
Circulates to: Students, Faculty
Interlibrary loan available
Copying Facilities: Copying machine,
   Microform
Equipment:
   1 5-drawer cabinets

7 vertical map cabinets
Map Depositories: USGS (topo);
   USGS (geol); DMA (topo); GPO


West Virginia
878
National Mine Health & Safety Academy
Average monthly use: 10
Copying Facilities: Copying machine
Equipment:
   3 5-drawer cabinets
Square Footage: 40
Map Depositories: USGS (topo)
   Leslie E., Chief
Special Strengths: United States
   (Mining)
Employees: Full Time    Part Time
   Prof.          0            1
   Non-Prof.     0            1
Holdings:
   2200 Printed Maps
     47 Atlases
      3 Gazetteers
Chronological Coverage:
   100% post 1900
Classification: In-House
Available to: Public, Students, Faculty
Average monthly use: 10
Copying Facilities: Copying machine
Equipment:
   3 5-drawer cabinets
Square Footage: 40
Map Depositories: USGS (topo)


879
National Park Service
Harpers Ferry Center Library
Harpers Ferry, WV 25425
Tel. (304) 535-6371
Hours: 8–4:30, M–F
Responsible Person: Nathanson, David
Special Strengths: United States (Civil
   War Battles), United States (Economic
   & Social Atlases), All States &
   Territories (Parks, Monuments, etc.,
   20th cent.)
Employees: Full Time    Part Time
   Prof.          1            1
   Non-Prof.     1            2
Holdings:
    175 Printed Maps
     25 Atlases
   10000 Microforms
     50 Books
      6 Gazetteers
      1 Serial Title
Chronological Coverage: 50% pre 1900;
   50% post 1900
Preservation methods: Encapsulation
Average monthly use: 150
Copying Facilities: Copying machine
Equipment:
   2 5-drawer cabinets
   2 microfilm cabinets
Square Footage: 50

### 880

West Virginia State College
Drain-Jordan Library
Institute, WV 25112
Tel. (304) 766-3116
Hours: 8–10, M–Th; 8–7, (8–5 in summer)
  F; 11–3, Sa; 1–5, Su
Responsible Person: Scott, John E.,
  Director
Employees: Full Time    Part Time
  Prof.        1            0
  Non-Prof.    2            0
Holdings:
  400 Printed Maps
   50 Atlases
Chronological Coverage: 2% pre 1900;
  98% post 1900
Classification: LC    Utility: OCLC
Formats: Cards
Available to: Public, Students, Faculty
Circulates to: Public, Students, Faculty
Copying Facilities: Microform,
  Photographic reproduction
Equipment:
  4 lg. 18th cent. cabinets
Map Depositories: USGS (topo);
  GPO

### 881

West Virginia Geological & Economic
  Survey
P. O. Box 879
Morgantown, WV 26507
Tel. (304) 594-2331
Hours: 8–5, M–F
Special Strengths: West Virginia
  (Geology)
Employees: Full Time    Part Time
  Prof.        0            1
Holdings:
  1500 Printed Maps
  20000 Aerial Photographs
   100 Satellite Imagery
     1 Raised Relief Map
     1 Book
     1 Gazetteer
Chronological Coverage: 5% pre 1900;
  95% post 1900
Available to: Public, Students, Faculty
Equipment:
  100 5-drawer cabinets
  1 vertical map cabinet
Map Depositories: USGS (topo)

### 882

West Virginia University Library
West Virginia & Regional History
  Collection
Colson Hall
Morgantown, WV 26506
Tel. (304) 293-4040
Hours: 8–5, M–F; 9–5, Sa
Responsible Person: Parkinson,
  George P., Curator
Special Strengths: West Virginia

Special Collections: Sanborn Fire
  Insurance Maps of West Virginia
  Towns, West Virginia Geological
  Survey Maps
Employees: Full Time    Part Time
  Prof.        3            0
  Non-Prof.    5            5
Holdings:
  5000 Printed Maps
  1000 Manuscript Maps
  5000 Aerial Photographs
   50 Atlases
    10 Microforms
    50 Books
     5 Gazetteers
Chronological Coverage: 30% pre 1900;
  70% post 1900
Map collection is cataloged 100%
Formats: Cards
Preservation methods: Encapsulation
Available to: Public, Students, Faculty
Average monthly use: 50
Average annual circulation: Books: 200
Copying Facilities: Copying machine,
  Microform, Photographic reproduction
Equipment:
  20 5-drawer cabinets
Square Footage: 200
Map Depositories: West Virginia
  Geological Survey

### 883

West Virginia University Library
Map Collection
P. O. Box 6069
Morgantown, WV 26506-6069
Tel. (304) 293-3640
Hours: 8–Midnight, M–Th; 8–11, F;
  9–6, Sa; 1–11, Su
Responsible Person: Brown, Joe J.
Special Strengths: West Virginia,
  Appalachia
Employees: Full Time    Part Time
  Prof.        1            0
  Non-Prof.    0            1
Holdings:
  44930 Printed Maps
      1 Gazetteer
Chronological Coverage:
  100% post 1900
Available to: Public, Students, Faculty
Circulates to: Public, Students, Faculty
Average monthly use: 150
Average annual circulation: Maps: 350
Interlibrary loan available
Copying Facilities: Copying machine
Equipment:
  10 12-drawer oversize mayo cases
Square Footage: 300
Map Depositories: USGS (topo);
  USGS (geol); GPO

### 884

Shepherd College
Ruth Scaroborough Library

Shepherdstown, WV 25443
Tel. (304) 876-6775
Employees: Full Time    Part Time
  Prof.        0            1
  Non-Prof.    0            2
Holdings:
  800 Printed Maps
   24 Atlases
    3 Globes
   74 Books
    3 Gazetteers
Chronological Coverage: 3% pre 1900;
  97% post 1900
Available to: Public, Students, Faculty
Average monthly use: 3
Average annual circulation:
  Books: 20000
Copying Facilities: Copying machine,
  Microform
Equipment:
  2 5-drawer cabinets
Map Depositories: GPO

## Wisconsin

### 885

Lawrence University
Seeley G. Mudd Library
Appleton, WI 54912
Tel. (414) 735-6750
Hours: 8–4, M–F
Responsible Person: Ribbens, Lois
Employees: Full Time    Part Time
  Prof.        0            1
  Non-Prof.    0            1
Holdings:
  1000 Printed Maps
   40 Atlases
   10 Gazetteers
Chronological Coverage: 5% pre 1900;
  95% post 1900
Available to: Public, Students, Faculty
Average monthly use: 2
Copying Facilities: Copying machine
Equipment:
  3 vertical map cabinets
Square Footage: 200
Map Depositories: USGS (topo);
  DMA (topo)

### 886

Beloit College
Colonel Robert Morse Library
731 College St.
Beloit, WI 53511
Tel. (608) 365-3391
Hours: 8:30–11, M–Th; 8:30–8, F, Sa;
  1–11, Su
Responsible Person: Zimmerman,
  Roxy A.
Employees: Full Time    Part Time
  Prof.        0            1
  Non-Prof.    0            3
Holdings:
  102212 Printed Maps
   290 Atlases

50 Books
Chronological Coverage:
   100% post 1900
Available to: Public, Students, Faculty
Circulates to: Students, Faculty
Average monthly use: 30
Average annual circulation: Maps: 100;
   Books: 20000
Copying Facilities: Copying machine,
   Microform
Equipment:
   47 5-drawer cabinets
   8 vertical map cabinets
   21 3-drawer cabinets
Square Footage: 715
Map Depositories: USGS (topo);
   USGS (geol); DMA (topo); GPO

### 887
University of Wisconsin, Eau Claire
Simpson Geographic Research Center
Department of Geography
Eau Claire, WI 54701
Tel. (715) 836-3244
Hours: 9–5, M–F
Responsible Person: Cahow, Dr. Adam
Special Strengths: USA, Canada
Employees: Full Time   Part Time
Prof.       0           1
Non-Prof.   0           3
Holdings:
   120000 Printed Maps
     4000 Aerial Photographs
     200 Satellite Imagery
     100 Atlases
      20 Globes
     500 Wall Maps
     100 Raised Relief Maps
     500 Books
     100 Gazetteers
      20 Serial Titles
Chronological Coverage:
   100% post 1900
Preservation methods: Lamination,
   Chartex or Fabric Mounting
Available to: Public, Students, Faculty
Circulates to: Public, Students, Faculty
Average monthly use: 500
Average annual circulation:
   Maps: 2000; Books: 1000; Aerial
   Photographs: 500; Article Reprints:
   1500
Equipment:
   125 5-drawer cabinets
   15 filing cabinets
   Kelsh Plotter
Square Footage: 2000
Map Depositories: USGS (topo);
   USGS (geol); DMA (topo); Canada
   (topo)

### 888
University of Wisconsin, Green Bay
Government Publications Department
Library Learning Center

Green Bay, WI 54301-7001
Tel. (414) 465-2333
Hours: 8–11:30, M–Th; 8–8, F; 9–6, Sa;
   1–11:30, Su
Responsible Person: Pletcher, Kathy
Special Strengths: Wisconsin (19th &
   20th cent.), North East Wisconsin
   (19th cent.)
Employees: Full Time   Part Time
Prof.       0           1
Non-Prof.   0           3
Holdings:
   45000 Printed Maps
     300 Atlases
       1 Globe
       4 Wall Maps
       1 Raised Relief Map
      44 Microforms
      50 Gazetteers
Chronological Coverage: 10% pre 1900;
   90% post 1900
Map collection is cataloged 85%
Classification: LC    Utility: OCLC
Formats: Cards
Preservation methods: Encapsulation,
   Edging
Available to: Public, Students, Faculty
Average annual circulation:
   Maps: 2680
Copying Facilities: Copying machine,
   Microform
Equipment:
   58 5-drawer cabinets
   4 vertical map cabinets
Square Footage: 500
Map Depositories: USGS (topo);
   USGS (geol); DMA (topo); DMA
   (aero); GPO; Canada (topo)

### 889
University of Wisconsin, LaCrosse
Geography Department Map Library
207 Cowley
LaCrosse, WI 54601
Tel. (608) 785-8333
Hours: 8–5, M–F
Responsible Person: Holder, Dr. Virgil
Special Strengths: Wisconsin
Employees: Full Time   Part Time
Non-Prof.   0           1
Holdings:
   11000 Printed Maps
    3500 Aerial Photographs
    1500 Satellite Imagery
      40 Atlases
      30 Globes
     250 Wall Maps
      35 Raised Relief Maps
      10 Books
       2 Gazetteers
Chronological Coverage: 5% pre 1900;
   95% post 1900
Preservation methods: Encapsulation,
   Chartex or Fabric Mounting, Edging
Available to: Public, Students, Faculty
Copying Facilities: Copying machine,

Photographic reproduction
Equipment:
   64 5-drawer cabinets
   40 vertical map cabinets
Square Footage: 900
Map Depositories: USGS (topo);
   USGS (geol); DMA (topo); DMA
   (aero); DMA (hydro)

### 890
University of Wisconsin, LaCrosse
Murphy Library
1631 Pine St.
LaCrosse, WI 54601
Tel. (608) 785-8513
Hours: 8–5, 6:30–9:30, M–F; 8–12,
   1–5, Sa; 1–5, 6:30–9:30, Su
Responsible Person: Sechrest, Sandra
Special Strengths: Wisconsin
Employees: Full Time   Part Time
Prof.       0           2
Non-Prof.   0          11
Holdings:
   2300 Printed Maps
     12 Manuscript Maps
    100 Aerial Photographs
    570 Atlases
      4 Globes
     40 Wall Maps
      3 Raised Relief Maps
    380 Microforms
   2100 Books
     55 Gazetteers
Chronological Coverage: 10% pre 1900;
   90% post 1900
Map collection is cataloged 20%
Formats: Cards
Preservation methods: Encapsulation,
   Chartex or Fabric Mounting, Edging,
   Deacidification
Available to: Public, Students, Faculty
Circulates to: Public, Students
Average annual circulation: Maps: 20;
   Books: 320
Interlibrary loan available
Copying Facilities: Copying machine
Equipment:
   8 5-drawer cabinets
   1 vertical map cabinet
   6 atlas cases
Square Footage: 240
Map Depositories: USGS (topo);
   GPO

### 891
State Historical Society of Wisconsin
Map Collection
816 State St.
Madison, WI 53706
Tel. (608) 262-5867
Hours: 8–5, M–F; 9–4, Sa
Responsible Person: Edmonds, Michael,
   Special Collections Librarian
Special Strengths: Wisconsin (19th
   cent.), North Central States (18th–

19th cent.), Wisconsin and adjacent states (19th cent. county atlases)
Special Collections: European atlases (16th–19th cent.); Wisconsin land-ownership maps & atlases, Wisconsin bird's eye views, Wisconsin state & local government unpublished administrative maps
Employees: Full Time    Part Time
Prof.            0            1
Non-Prof.        0            1
Holdings:
  23000 Printed Maps
   2000 Manuscript Maps
   2500 Atlases
      1 Globe
     70 Wall Maps
      3 Raised Relief Maps
     25 Microforms
    500 Books
     12 Gazetteers
      8 Serial Titles
Chronological Coverage: 80% pre 1900; 20% post 1900
Map collection is cataloged 88%
Classification: Expanded Cutter
Formats: Cards
Preservation methods: Encapsulation, Deacidification
Available to: Public
Average monthly use: 90
Average annual circulation:
  Maps: 4000
Copying Facilities: Copying machine, Microform; Photographic reproduction
Equipment:
  91 5-drawer cabinets
  Archives Boxes
Square Footage: 2700
Map Depositories: USGS (topo)

892
University of Wisconsin, Madison
Arthur M. Robinson Map Library
310 Science Hall
550 N. Park St.
Madison, WI 53706
Tel. (608) 262-1471
Hours: 8–12, 1–5, M–F
Responsible Person: Galneder, Mary
Special Strengths: Wisconsin, Wisconsin (Air photos 1930s–1960s)
Employees: Full Time    Part Time
Prof.            1            0
Non-Prof.        0            5
Holdings:
  207500 Printed Maps
  133500 Aerial Photographs
      11 Globes
    1002 Wall Maps
     248 Raised Relief Maps
     750 Books
Chronological Coverage: 3% pre 1900; 97% post 1900
Map collection is cataloged 100%
Classification: LC

Formats: Cards
Preservation methods: Encapsulation, Lamination, Chartex or Fabric Mounting, Deacidification
Available to: Public, Students, Faculty
Circulates to: Public, Students, Faculty
Interlibrary loan available
  Depends on condition of material
Copying Facilities: Copying machine, Microform, Photographic reproduction, PMT
Map Depositories: USGS (topo); USGS (geol); DMA (topo); DMA (aero); DMA (hydro); GPO; NOS; Canada (topo)

893
University of Wisconsin, Madison
Geological & Natural History Survey
1815 University Ave.
Madison, WI 53706
Tel. (608) 262-1705
Special Strengths: Wisconsin, United States
Employees: Full Time    Part Time
Non-Prof.        0            1
Holdings:
  1200 Printed Maps
  1600 Manuscript Maps
Preservation methods: Lamination

894
University of Wisconsin Center
Manitowoc Library
705 Viebahn St.
Manitowoc, WI 54220
Tel. (414) 683-4718
Hours: 8–4:30, M–F
Responsible Person: Bjerke, Robert A.
Special Strengths: Wisconsin, Great Lakes (Nautical Charts)
Employees: Full Time    Part Time
Prof.            1            0
Holdings:
  1750 Printed Maps
Chronological Coverage:
  100% post 1900
Available to: Public, Students, Faculty
Circulates to: Students, Faculty
Average monthly use: 1
Average annual circulation: Maps: 10
Interlibrary loan available
Copying Facilities: Copying machine
Equipment:
  2 5-drawer cabinets
Square Footage: 10
Map Depositories: USGS (topo)

895
Milwaukee Public Library
814 W. Wisconsin Ave.
Milwaukee, WI 53233
Tel. (414) 278-3000
Hours: 8:30–9, M–Th; 8:30–5:30, F, Sa

Responsible Person: Gordon, Carol, Map Librarian
Special Strengths: Wisconsin, Milwaukee, Great Lakes Region, Great Lakes (Nautical charts, 1900–present)
Special Collections: The Local History Department contains historical maps & atlases of local, state & regional interest & a collection of over 1,000 Great Lakes nautical charts.
Employees: Full Time    Part Time
Prof.            1            0
Holdings:
  120000 Printed Maps
    2500 Atlases
       2 Globes
      50 Wall Maps
      20 Raised Relief Maps
     500 Books
     150 Gazetteers
      33 Serial Titles
Chronological Coverage: 20% pre 1900; 80% post 1900
Map collection is cataloged 50%
Classification: Dewey   Utility: OCLC
Formats: Cards
Preservation methods: Encapsulation
Available to: Public
Interlibrary loan available
  Each item is evaluated individually.
Copying Facilities: Copying machine, Microform
Equipment:
  44 5-drawer cabinets
   2 vertical map cabinets
  15 9-drawer, 6 11-drawer cabinets
   3 10-drawer 1″ cases
Map Depositories: USGS (topo); USGS (geol); DMA (topo); DMA (aero); DMA (hydro); GPO

896
Milwaukee Public Library
Local History Room, Special Collections
814 W. Wisconsin
Milwaukee, WI 53233
Tel. (414) 278-3074
Responsible Person: Woehrmann, Paul, Local History Librarian
Special Strengths: Great Lakes (Nautical Charts), Wisconsin (Historical Platbooks, Sanborn fire insurance atlases)
Employees: Full Time    Part Time
Prof.            0            2
Non-Prof.        0            1
Holdings:
  2500 Printed Maps
   342 Atlases
    10 Globes
     1 Wall Map
    25 Computer Tapes
    30 Gazetteers
Chronological Coverage: 50% pre 1900; 50% post 1900

Map collection is cataloged 65%
Classification: Dewey    Utility: OCLC
Formats: Cards
Preservation methods: Encapsulation
Available to: Public
Copying Facilities: Copying machine
Equipment:
   14 5-drawer cabinets

897
University of Wisconsin
Milwaukee Library
American Geographical Society Map
   Collection
P. O. Box 399
Milwaukee, WI 53211
Tel. (414) 963-7775
Hours: 8–5, M–F; 8–12, Sa
Responsible Person: Baruth, Christopher,
   Map & Imagery Librarian
Employees: Full Time    Part Time
   Prof.          1                2
   Non-Prof.    0                5
Holdings:
   400000 Printed Maps
   98000 Satellite Imagery
   6000 Atlases
   65 Globes
   200 Wall Maps
   100 Raised Relief Maps
   1500 Books
   300 Gazetteers
Chronological Coverage: 3% pre 1900;
   97% post 1900
Map collection is cataloged 100%
Classification: AGS    Utility: OCLC
Formats: Cards
Preservation methods: Encapsulation,
   Deacidification
Available to: Public, Students, Faculty
Interlibrary loan available
   Rare & fragile materials not sent
Copying Facilities: Copying machine,
   Photographic reproduction
Equipment:
   548 5-drawer cabinets
   2 vertical map cabinets
Square Footage: 6000
Map Depositories: USGS (topo);
   USGS (geol); DMA (topo); DMA
   (aero); DMA (hydro); GPO; NOS;
   NOAA; Canada (topo); Norway,
   Sweden, New Zealand, Australia,
   Finland, Germany

898
University of Wisconsin, Milwaukee
Map Library
Room 385, Sabin Hall
Milwaukee, WI 53201
Tel. (414) 963-4871
Hours: 9:30–7:30, M–F
Responsible Person: Flannery, James
   John
Special Strengths: United States,

Wisconsin
Employees: Full Time    Part Time
   Non-Prof.     0            4
Holdings:
   160000 Printed Maps
   1500 Aerial Photographs
   20 Satellite Imagery
   10 Atlases
   3 Globes
   800 Wall Maps
   15 Raised Relief Maps
   60 Books
Chronological Coverage: 3% pre 1900;
   97% post 1900
Map Collection is cataloged 85%
Classification: LC    Utility: OCLC
Formats: Cards
Available to: Public, Students, Faculty
Circulates to: Public, Students, Faculty
Average monthly use: 400
Copying Facilities: Copying machine
Equipment:
   46 5-drawer cabinets
   18 vertical map cabinets
   26 special vertical two door cabinets
   Zoom transferscope, electronic
   planimeters
Square Footage: 5400
Map Depositories: USGS (topo);
   USGS (geol); DMA (topo); DMA
   (aero); DMA (hydro); NOS

899
University of Wisconsin, Oshkosh
Department of Geology
Oshkosh, WI 54901
Tel. (414) 424-4460
Hours: By appointment
Special Strengths: Wisconsin, Illinois,
   Minnesota, Iowa, Michigan, Indiana
Holdings:
   39125 Printed Maps
   20 Wall Maps
   5 Raised Relief Maps
Chronological Coverage:
   100% post 1900
Available to: Public, Students, Faculty
Circulates to: Public, Students, Faculty
Average monthly use: 4
Average annual circulation: Maps: 50
Equipment:
   28 5-drawer cabinets
   4 filing cabinets
Square Footage: 288
Map Depositories: USGS (topo)

900
University of Wisconsin, Oshkosh
Dept. of Geography & Urban Studies
Oshkosh, WI 54901
Tel. (414) 424-4242
Responsible Person: Bruyer, Dr. D.
Special Strengths: Wisconsin
Holdings:
   20500 Printed Maps

4600 Aerial Photographs
   25 Atlases
   3 Globes
   340 Wall Maps
   160 Raised Relief Maps
Available to: Students, Faculty
Average monthly use: 10
Copying Facilities: Copying machine
Equipment:
   37 5-drawer cabinets
   1 28-drawer wood cabinet
   Parallax box, Stereoscope
Square Footage: 504

901
University of Wisconsin, Oshkosh
Polk Library
Oshkosh, WI 54901
Tel. (414) 424-3347
Hours: 7:45–10, M–Th; 7:45–4:30, F;
   1:30–5, Sa; 1:30–10, Su
Responsible Person: Krueger, Gerald J.
Employees: Full Time    Part Time
   Prof.          1                2
   Non-Prof.    1                8
Holdings:
   1500 Printed Maps
   50 Atlases
Chronological Coverage:
   100% post 1900
Available to: Public, Students, Faculty
Circulates to: Students, Faculty
Average monthly use: 2
Average annual circulation: Maps: 15
Interlibrary loan available
Copying Facilities: Copying machine,
   Photographic reproduction
Equipment:
   8 5-drawer cabinets
Map Depositories: USGS (topo);
   USGS (geol); DMA (topo); DMA
   (aero); DMA (hydro); GPO

902
University of Wisconsin, Platteville
Karrmann Library
Platteville, WI 53818
Tel. (608) 342-1758
Hours: 7:45–Midnight, M–Th;
   7:45–10, F; 9–5, Sa
Responsible Person: Hohenstein,
   Margaret
Special Strengths: Wisconsin &
   surrounding states
Employees: Full Time    Part Time
   Prof.          0                1
   Non-Prof.    0                2
Holdings:
   30523 Printed Maps
Chronological Coverage:
   100% post 1900
Available to: Public, Students, Faculty
Circulates to: Public, Students, Faculty
Average annual circulation: Maps:100
Interlibrary loan available

Copying Facilities: Copying machine, Microform
Equipment:
Princeton files, Light table
Square Footage: 200
Map Depositories: USGS (topo); USGS (geol); DMA (topo); DMA (aero); DMA (hydro); GPO

### 903

Racine Public Library, Adult Service
75 7th St.
Racine, WI 53403
Tel. (414) 636-9241
Hours: 9–9, M–F; 9–5:30, Sa
Responsible Person: Hartman, Jill
Special Strengths: United States
Employees: Full Time    Part Time
Prof.        0             6
Holdings:
1130 Printed Maps
5 Wall Maps
135 Gazetteers
Chronological Coverage:
100% post 1900
Available to: Public
Copying Facilities: Copying machine
Equipment:
3 5-drawer cabinets
15′ linear shelving
Map Depositories: GPO

### 904

University of Wisconsin, Stevens Point
Map Library
Geography-Geology Department
Stevens Point, WI 54481
Tel. (715) 346-2629
Hours: 9–4, M–Th; 10–2, F
Responsible Person: McKinney, William M.
Special Strengths: Wisconsin
Employees: Full Time    Part Time
Prof.        0             2
Non-Prof.    0            10
Holdings:
98000 Printed Maps
33 Aerial Photographs
45 Atlases
1 Globe
20 Books
25 Gazetteers
Chronological Coverage: 1% pre 1900; 99% post 1900
Preservation methods: Lamination
Available to: Public, Students, Faculty
Circulates to: Public, Students, Faculty
Average monthly use: 60
Average annual circulation:
Maps: 1000
Equipment:
73 5-drawer cabinets
10 filing cabinets
Square Footage: 1062
Map Depositories: USGS (topo);

USGS (geol)

### 905

University of Wisconsin, Superior
Jim Dan Hill Library
Reference & Research Department
Superior, WI 54880
Tel. (715) 394-8341
Hours: 7:45–10, M–Th; 7:45–5, F; 10–4, Sa; 6–10, Su
Responsible Person: Greve, Edward F.
Special Strengths: Wisconsin
Employees: Full Time    Part Time
Prof.        0             1
Non-Prof.    0             3
Holdings:
1500 Printed Maps
150 Atlases
15 Gazetteers
Chronological Coverage:
100% post 1900
Available to: Students, Faculty
Average monthly use: 4
Equipment:
4 10-drawer cabinets

### 906

University of Wisconsin, Whitewater
Department of Geography Map Library
Upham Hall Room 7
Whitewater, WI 53190
Tel. (414) 472-1071
Responsible Person: Botts, Howard
Special Strengths: Wisconsin, United States
Special Collections: Geological folios
Employees: Full Time    Part Time
Non-Prof.                  2
Holdings:
16491 Printed Maps
1975 Aerial Photographs
36 Atlases
21 Globes
337 Wall Maps
3 Raised Relief Maps
74 Gazetteers
Chronological Coverage: 5% pre 1900; 95% post 1900
Preservation methods: Lamination, Chartex or Fabric Mounting
Available to: Students, Faculty
Circulates to: Students, Faculty
Average monthly use: 5
Equipment:
23 5-drawer cabinets
1 vertical map cabinet
10 8-drawer cabinets
1 6-drawer cabinet
Square Footage: 1500

### 907

University of Wisconsin, Whitewater
Documents & Research Collections
Whitewater, WI 53190

Tel. (414) 472-4671
Hours: 8–9, M–Th; 8–5, F
Responsible Person: Peterson, Amy K., Head
Employees: Full Time    Part Time
Prof.        0             2
Non-Prof.    0             3
Holdings:
4400 Printed Maps
126 Gazetteers
Chronological Coverage:
100% post 1900
Available to: Public, Students, Faculty
Circulates to: Public, Students, Faculty
Average monthly use: 6
Copying Facilities: Copying machine, Microform
Square Footage: 175
Map Depositories: DMA (topo); GPO

## Wyoming

### 908

Casper College
Goodstein Foundation Library
125 College Dr.
Casper, WY 82601
Tel. (307) 268-2269
Hours: 7:30–10, M–Th; 7:30–4:30, F; 2:30–10, Su
Responsible Person: Malone, Rose Mary, Western History Library
Special Strengths: Wyoming
Holdings:
3573 Printed Maps
4 Manuscript Maps
8 Aerial Photographs
1 Satellite Imagery
74 Atlases
2 Globes
6 Wall Maps
3 Raised Relief Maps
31 Books
2 Serial Titles
Chronological Coverage: 1% pre 1900; 99% post 1900
Map collection is cataloged 100%
Classification: LC
Formats: Cards
Preservation methods: Encapsulation, Lamination, Chartex or Fabric Mounting
Available to: Public, Students, Faculty
Copying Facilities: Copying machine, Microform
Equipment:
3 5-drawer cabinets
5 vertical map cabinets
Map Depositories: USGS (topo); USGS (geol)

### 909

Natrona County Public Library
307 E. 2nd St.
Casper, WY 82601

Tel. (307) 237-4935
Hours: 9–9, M–W; 9–6, Th–Sa; 2–6, Su
Responsible Person: Nowak, Kathleen,
Earth Sciences Librarian
Special Strengths: Wyoming (Geology)
Special Collections: State Geological
Survey Maps from North Dakota,
South Dakota, Montana, Colorado
& Idaho
Employees: Full Time    Part Time
Prof.           1              0
Holdings:
6400 Printed Maps
500 Aerial Photographs
25 Atlases
1 Globe
3 Wall Maps
1 Raised Relief Map
48 Books
2 Gazetteers
Chronological Coverage: 1% pre 1900;
99% post 1900
Available to: Public
Average monthly use: 20
Average annual circulation: Maps: 200;
Books: 100
Copying Facilities: Copying machine
Equipment:
4 vertical map cabinets
1 8-drawer cabinet
2 light tables
Square Footage: 250
Map Depositories: USGS (topo)

### 910
Wyoming State Archives
Museums & Historical Department
Historical Research & Publication Div.
Barrett Building
Cheyenne, WY 82002
Tel. (307) 777-7518
Hours: 8–5, M–F
Responsible Person: Roberts, Phil,
Documents Supervisor
Special Strengths: Wyoming (1869–
1950)
Special Collections: Wyoming Territorial
Maps (1869–1890)
Employees: Full Time    Part Time
Prof.           1              2
Non-Prof.     0              1
Holdings:
1200 Printed Maps
100 Manuscript Maps
50 Atlases
35 Wall Maps
2 Raised Relief Maps
30 Gazetteers
Chronological Coverage: 40% pre 1900;
60% post 1900
Classification: In-house system
Formats: Cards
Preservation methods: Encapsulation,
Deacidification
Available to: Public
Average monthly use: 25

Copying Facilities: Copying machine,
Photographic reproduction
Equipment:
5 5-drawer cabinets
Square Footage: 150

### 911
Wyoming State Library
Government Publications Depository
Supreme Court & Library Building
Cheyenne, WY 82002
Tel. (307) 777-7281
Hours: 8–5, M–F
Responsible Person: Frobom,
Jerome B., Head
Special Strengths: Wyoming
Employees: Full Time    Part Time
Prof.           1              0
Non-Prof.     1              0
Holdings:
2000 Printed Maps
Chronological Coverage:
100% post 1900
Available to: Public, Students
Circulates to: Public
Average monthly use: 6
Average annual circulation: Maps: 75
Interlibrary loan available
Copying Facilities: Copying machine
Equipment:
5 5-drawer cabinets
1 vertical map cabinet
Square Footage: 120
Map Depositories: GPO

### 912
Campbell County Public Library*
2101 4J Rd.
Gillette, WY 82716
Tel. (307) 682-3223
Responsible Person: Cook, Lucy
Holdings:
1000 Printed Maps
Chronological Coverage:
100% post 1900
Available to: Public
Map Depositories: USGS (topo);
GPO

### 913
Fremont County Library
451 N. 2nd
Lander, WY 82520
Tel. (307) 332-5194
Hours: 9–9, M–Th; 9–5, 7–9, F; 10–5, Sa
Responsible Person: Behringer, Ken
Special Strengths: Wyoming
Employees: Full Time    Part Time
Prof.           1              1
Holdings:
1500 Printed Maps
Chronological Coverage: 1% pre 1900;
99% post 1900
Available to: Public

Copying Facilities: Copying machine
Equipment:
1 5-drawer cabinet
Square Footage: 30

### 914
Geological Survey of Wyoming
Box 300B, University Station
Laramie, WY 82071
Tel. (307) 742-2054
Hours: 8–5, M–F
Responsible Person: Glass, Gary B.
Special Strengths: Wyoming (Geology
& Mineral Resources), Wyoming
(Geology), Wyoming (Photography,
1940's–1980's, High, Low & Satellite)
Employees: Full Time    Part Time
Non-Prof.     0              1
Holdings:
1500 Printed Maps
Chronological Coverage: 2% pre 1900;
98% post 1900
Map collection is cataloged 50%
Classification: In-house
Formats: Cards, Maps
Available to: Public, Students, Faculty
Circulates to: Public, Students, Faculty
Average monthly use: 20
Interlibrary loan available
Only on extraordinary occasions
Copying Facilities: Copying machine,
Microform, Ozalid (blueline)
Equipment:
10 5-drawer cabinets
3 vertical map cabinets
10 4-drawer file cabinets
Microfilm viewer
Square Footage: 200
Map Depositories: USGS (topo);
USGS (geol)

### 915
University of Wyoming
Department of Geography
Laramie, WY 82071
Tel. (303) 766-3311
Responsible Person: Brown,
Dr. Robert H.
Special Strengths: United States
Holdings:
5000 Printed Maps
20 Manuscript Maps
1000 Aerial Photographs
200 Wall Maps
Chronological Coverage:
100% post 1900
Available to: Students, Faculty
Average monthly use: 1
Average annual circulation: Maps: 10;
Aerial photographs: 20
Equipment:
12 5-drawer cabinets
Rolled wall map holder
2 mirror stereoscopes
2 light tables, planimeters,

Map measurers
Square Footage: 136

916
University of Wyoming
Geology Library
P. O. Box 3006, University Station
Laramie, WY 82071
Tel. (307) 766-3374
Hours: 8–10, M–Th; 8–5, F; 9–4, Sa;
12–10, Su
Special Strengths: Rocky Mountain
Area (Geology, Geophysics,
Geomorphology)
Employees: Full Time    Part Time
Prof.          0              1
Non-Prof.    3              1
Holdings:
20000 Printed Maps
12 Atlases
2 Globes
8 Wall Maps
4 Books
Chronological Coverage: 3% pre 1900;
97% post 1900
Map collection is cataloged 100%
Classification: In-house
Formats: Cards
Preservation methods: Edging
Available to: Public, Students, Faculty
Circulates to: Public, Students, Faculty
Average monthly use: 75
Average annual circulation: Maps: 900
Interlibrary loan available
Copying Facilities: Copying machine
Equipment:
6 5-drawer cabinets
Square Footage: 260
Map Depositories: USGS (topo);
USGS (geol); Canada (geol); WY
Geological Survey

917
University of Wyoming
Map Collection, Coe Library
University Station, Box 3334
Laramie, WY 82071
Tel. (307) 766-2174
Hours: 8–20, M–Th; 8–5, F; 9:30–4:30,
Sa; 1–9, Su
Responsible Person: Walsh, Jim,
Maps/Documents Librarian

Special Strengths: Wyoming (1800–),
West (1800–), Rocky Mountain Region
(1800–)
Special Collections: Sanborn Fire
Insurance Maps (Wyoming–paper;
Alaska, Idaho, Nevada, New Mexico,
Utah–microfilm)
Employees: Full Time    Part Time
Prof.             2                 0
Non-Prof.       3                 4
Holdings:
97010 Printed Maps
5 Satellite Imagery
68 Atlases
2 Globes
13 Wall Maps
19 Raised Relief Maps
43 Microforms
125 Books
296 Gazetteers
41 Serial Titles
Chronological Coverage: 3% pre 1900;
97% post 1900
Map collection is cataloged 3%
Classification: LC
Formats: Cards
Preservation methods: Encapsulation
Available to: Public, Students, Faculty
Circulates to: Public, Students, Faculty
Average monthly use: 125
Average annual circulation: Maps: 800
Interlibrary loan available
Pre-1900 maps
Copying Facilities: Copying machine,
Microform
Equipment:
60 5-drawer cabinets
4 Steel cabinets
Book shelves
Light table
Square Footage: 1667
Map Depositories: USGS (topo);
USGS (geol); DMA (topo); DMA
(aero); DMA (hydro); GPO; NOS;
NOAA; Geological Survey of Wyoming

918
Central Wyoming College
Learning Resources Center
2660 Peck Ave.
Riverton, WY 82501
Tel. (307) 856-9291

Hours: 8–5, 6–9, M–Th; 8–5, F;
1–5, Su
Special Strengths: Wyoming
Holdings:
1600 Printed Maps
100 Aerial Photographs
20 Atlases
1 Globe
Chronological Coverage:
100% post 1900
Available to: Public, Students, Faculty
Interlibrary loan available
Copying Facilities: Copying machine
Equipment:
2 5-drawer cabinets
Map Depositories: USGS (topo)

919
Sheridan College
Griffith Memorial Library
Sheridan, WY 82801
Tel. (307) 674-6446
Hours: 7:45–9:30, M–Th; 7:45–5, F;
11:30–4:30, Sa; 3–8, Su
Responsible Person: Mydland, Karen
Special Strengths: Colorado, Idaho,
Montana, North Dakota, South Dakota,
Utah, Wyoming
Special Collections: USGS Geologic
Atlases for region
Employees: Full Time    Part Time
Non-Prof.       1                 0
Holdings:
8500 Printed Maps
76 Atlases
1 Globe
9 Raised Relief Maps
4 Gazetteers
Chronological Coverage:
100% post 1900
Available to: Public, Students, Faculty
Circulates to: Public, Students, Faculty
Average monthly use: 12
Average annual circulation: Maps: 85
Interlibrary loan available
Except Atlases & Reference books
Copying Facilities: Copying machine,
Microform
Equipment:
5 5-drawer cabinets
Square Footage: 28
Map Depositories: USGS (topo);
GPO

# Sources for Cartographic Information

## A. U. S. Geological Survey Depositories

*The U. S. Geological Survey was established in 1879 to consolidate federal mapping programs and to provide basic mapping needs for the nation. Its original goal of providing basic topographical coverage for the nation has been greatly expanded and USGS products now include natural resource mapping, aerial photography, satellite imagery, and others, as well as topographic mapping. Listed below are those map reference libraries designated as official recipients for USGS products. Users of this volume are encouraged to contact individual libraries regarding their collections since many have limited depositories (i.e., geologic maps only, topographic maps only for their state or region, etc.)*

### Alabama

The University of Alabama
Department of Anthropology
P. O. Box 6135
University, AL 35486

Department of Geography
U. A. Map Library
Box 1982, Farrah Hall
University, AL 35486

Dept. of Geography–Geology
Jacksonville State University
Jacksonville, AL 36265

Special Collections Department
Ralph Brown Draughon Library
Auburn University
Auburn, AL 36849

### Alaska

Matanuska-Susitna Community College
University of Alaska
P. O. Box 899
Palmer, AK 99645

University of Alaska
Elmer E. Rasmuson Library
310 Tanana Dr.
Fairbanks, AK 99701

Institute of Marine Science
University of Alaska
Fairbanks, AK 99701

Library
Geophysical Institute
University of Alaska
Fairbanks, AK 99701

Librarian
Ketchikan Public Library
629 Dock St.
Ketchikan, AK 99901

### Arizona

Library & Archives
3rd Floor Capitol
Phoenix, AZ 85007

Map Collection
Daniel E. Noble Library
Arizona State University
Tempe, AZ 85287

University of Arizona
University Library
Map Collection
Tucson, AZ 85721

Library
Northern Arizona University
Government Documents, Box 6022
Flagstaff, AZ 86011

Director of Learning Resources
Yavapai College
Prescott, AZ 86301

### Arkansas

Magale Library
Southern State College
Southern Arkansas University
Magnolia, AR 71753

University of Central Arkansas
Geography Department
Old Main, Room M36
Conway, AR 72032

Dean B. Ellis Library
Arkansas Room
P. O. Box 2040
State University, AR 72467

Arkansas College
Batesville, AR 72501

Mullins Library
Reference Department
University of Arkansas
Fayetteville, AR 72701

### California

UCLA Map Library
University of California
Los Angeles, CA 90024

Geology–Geophysics Library
4697 Geology Bldg., Map Room
UCLA
Los Angeles, CA 90024

California State University–Los Angeles
Dept. of Geography & Urban Studies
5151 State University Dr.
Los Angeles, CA 90032

Los Angeles Public Library
Acquisitions/Serials
361 S. Anderson St.
Los Angeles, CA 90033

Documents Librarian
Long Beach Public Library
101 Pacific Ave.
Long Beach, CA 90802

Documents Librarian
Pasadena Public Library
285 E. Walnut St.
Pasadena, CA 91101

Acquisitions Department, 1–32
Millikan Memorial Library
California Institute of Technology
Pasadena, CA 91125

Geology Library
California Institute of Technology
Pasadena, CA 91125

Geography Map Library
Department of Geography
California State University
Northridge, CA 91330

Governments Publications
Honnold Library
Claremont College
Claremont, CA 91711

Pomona Public Library
TSD–Documents
625 S. Garer Ave.
Pomona, CA 91766

Library Serials Unit
California State Poly University
3801 Temple Ave.
Pomona, CA 91768

L. A. County Public Library
Special Materials Unit
8800 Valley Blvd.
Rosemead, CA 91770

Map Section, C-075 P
Central University Library
University of California, San Diego
La Jolla, CA 92093

Serials Records Acquisitions Department
Library C-075A
University of California, San Diego
La Jolla, CA 92093

San Diego Public Library
Science & Industry Section
820 "E" St.
San Diego, CA 92101

Map Collection
University Library
San Diego State University
San Diego, CA 92182

Palm Springs Public Library
300 S. Sunrise Way
Palm Springs, CA 92262

Irvine Map Library
Armacost Library
University of Redlands
Redlands, CA 92373

University of California
Government Sciences Library
P. O. Box 5900
Riverside, CA 92517

University of California
Physical Sciences Library
P. O. Box 5900
Riverside, CA 92517

Museum Scientist
Dept. of Earth Sciences
University of California
Riverside, CA 92521

William T. Boyce Library
Fullerton College
321 E. Chapman Ave.
Fullerton, CA 92634

Library–Documents Section
California State University
P. O. Box 4150
Fullerton, CA 92634

Cartography Laboratory
Department of Geography
California State University
Fullerton, CA 92634

Map Collection Library
University of California, Irvine
Irvine, CA 92664

Map & Imagery Laboratory
Library
University of California
Santa Barbara, CA 93106

Librarian
West Hills College
300 Cherry Lane
Coalinga, CA 93210

Library
West Hills College
457 C St.
Lemoore, CA 93245

Documents & Maps Department
California Polytechnic State
University Library
San Luis Obispo, CA 93407

Map Librarian
Henry Madden Library
California State University
Fresno, CA 93740

Map Depository
Sunnyvale Public Library
665 W. Olive Ave.
Sunnyvale, CA 94086

Documents Department
San Francisco Public Library
Civic Center
San Francisco, CA 94102

Mechanics Institute Library
57 Post St.
San Francisco, CA 94104

Josephine D. Randall
Junior Museum
199 Museum Way
San Francisco, CA 94114

Library
California Academy of Science
Golden Gate Park
San Francisco, CA 94110

San Francisco State University
Geography Department Map Library
1600 Holloway Ave.
San Francisco, CA 94132

Palo Alto City Library
1213 Newell Road
Palo Alto, CA 94303

Government Documents Department
Federal Division
Stanford University Libraries
Stanford, CA 94305

Branner Earth Sciences Library
School of Earth Sciences
Stanford University
Stanford, CA 94305

Central Map Collection
General Reference Department
Stanford University Library
Stanford, CA 94305

Reference Libraries
Alameda Free Library
1433 Oak St.
Alameda, CA 94501

Library
Diablo Valley College
Pleasant Hill, CA 64523

Documents Librarian
Contra Costa County Library
1750 Oak Park Blvd.
4 Pleasant Hill, CA 94523

Reference Department
California State University Library
25800 Hillary St.
Hayward, CA 94541

JFK Library
Reference Department
505 Santa Clara St.
Vallejo, CA 94590

History & Literature Department
Oakland Public Library
125 14th St.
Oakland, CA 94612

Merritt College Library
12500 Campus Dr.
Oakland, CA 94619

Map Room
General Library
University of California
Berkeley, CA 94720

Earth Sciences Library
University of California
230 Earth Sciences Bldg.
Berkeley, CA 94720

Documents Librarian
Richmond Public Library
Richmond, CA 94804

Contra Costa College
2600 Mission Bell Dr.
San Pablo, CA 94806

Department of Geography Library
Cabrillo College
6500 Soquel Dr.
Aptos, CA 95003

Map Librarian
Cupertino Library
10400 Torre Ave.
Cupertino, CA 95014

City Librarian
Santa Clara Public Library
2635 Homestead Rd.
Santa Clara, CA 95051

University of Santa Clara
Orradre Library
Documents Department
Santa Clara, CA 95053

University Library
Map Collection
University of California
Santa Cruz, CA 95064

Stockton Public Library
605 N. El Dorado
Stockton, CA 95202

Goleman Library
San Joaquin Delta College
5151 Pacific Ave.
Stockton, CA 95202

Documents Department
Library
Humboldt State University
Arcata, CA 95521

Map Collection University Library
University of California, Davis
Davis, CA 95616

Library
Dept. of Water Science & Engineering
University of California
Davis, CA 95616

Government Publications
California State Library
P. O. Box 2037
Sacramento, CA 95809

California State University Library
Social Science Reference Department
200 Jed Smith Dr.
Sacramento, CA 95819

University Library
Library—Maps
California State University, Chico
Chico, CA 95929

## Colorado

Documents Division
Denver Public Library
1357 Broadway
Denver, CO 80203

Map Library
Campus Box 184
University of Colorado
Boulder, CO 80309

Earth Science Library
Campus Box 184
University of Colorado
Boulder, CO 80309

Colorado School of Mines
Arthur Lakes Library
Map Room
Golden, CO 80401

The Libraries
Colorado State University
Fort Collins, CO 90523

Map Service, Acquisitions
James A. Michener Library
University of Northern Colorado
Greeley, CO 80609

Learning Resources Center
Pikes Peak Community College
5675 S. Academy Blvd.
Colorado Springs, CO 80906

Map Collection–Library
University of Colorado
Colorado Springs, CO 80933

Southern Colorado State College
Pueblo, CO 81001

Western State College of Colorado
Division of Natural Sciences &
  Mathematics
Geology Department
Gunnison, CO 81230

Fort Lewis College Library
Durango, CO 81301

Technical Library
Bendix-Grand Junction Operations
P. O. Box 1569
Grand Junction, CO 81501

Tutt Library
Colorado College
Colorado Springs, CO 80903

## Connecticut

Hartford Public Library
Reference & General Reading Dept.
500 Main Street
Hartford, CT 06103

Map Room
University of Connecticut Library
Storrs, CT 06268

Wesleyan University
Department of Earth & Environmental
  Science
Middletown, CT 06457

Connecticut State Library
231 Capital Ave.
Hartford, CT 06115

Free Public Library
133 Elm St.
New Haven, CT 06510

Geology Library
Yale University
210 Whitney Ave., POB 6666
New Haven, CT 06511

Reference Map Librarian
South Connecticut State College
501 Crescent St.
New Haven, CT 06515

Librarian
Peabody Museum of Natural History
Yale University
New Haven, CT 06520

Yale University Library
Map Collection
Box 1603A
New Haven, CT 06520

Bridgeport Public Library
925 Broad St.
Technology & Business Department
Bridgeport, CT 06603

The Ferguson Library
Stamford Public Library
96 Broad St.
Stamford, CT 06901

**Delaware**

Newark Free Library
750 E. Delaware Ave.
Newark, DE 19711

Government Documents
Morris Library
University of Delaware
Newark, DE 19711

Wilmington Institute Free Library &
    New Castle County Free Library
Wilmington, DE 19801

**District of Columbia**

The Public Library
Documents Desk
902 "G" St., N. W.
Washington, DC 20001

Map Library
Metro Washington Council of
    Governments
1875 Eye St., Suite 200
Washington, DC 20006

National Geographic Society
Cartographic Department
17th & M Streets
Washington, DC 20036

George Washington University
Library, Serial Department
Washington, DC 20052

Library of Congress
Geography & Map Division
Washington, DC 20540

Library of Congress
Exchange & Gifts Division
First Street SE Stop 303
Washington, DC 20540

**Florida**

Reference Maps Librarian
University of North Florida
St. Johns Bluff Rd., Box 17605
Jacksonville, FL 32216

Maps Division
R. M. Strozier Library
Florida State University
Tallahassee, FL 32306

John C. Pace Library
University of West Florida
Pensacola, FL 32504

Map Librarian
University of Florida Libraries
Gainesville, FL 32611

Documents Librarian
Dupont–Ball Library
Stetson University
Deland, FL 32720

Library
Seminole Junior College
Sanford, FL 32771

Mills Memorial Library
Rollins College
Winter Park, FL 32789

Orlando Public Library
Business/Sci/Tech/Dept.
10 North Rosalind
Orlando, FL 32801

Florida Collection
Miami–Dade Public Library
One Biscayne blvd.
Miami, FL 33132

Documents Section
Florida International University Library
Tamiami Trail
Miami, FL 33199

Library
Documents Division
Florida Atlantic University
Boca Raton, FL 33432

Government Documents Department
Library
University of South Florida
Tampa, FL 33620

**Georgia**

Southern Technical Institute
534 Clay Street
Marietta, GA 30060

West Georgia College
Carrollton, GA 30118

Emory University
Department of Geology
Atlanta, GA 30222

Library, Reference Department
Georgia State University
104 Decatur St., S.E.
Atlanta, GA 30303

Map Library
W. R. Pullen Library
Georgia State University
104 Decatur St., S.E.
Atlanta, GA 30303

Gift & Exchange Librarian
Price Gilbert Memorial Library
Georgia Institute of Technology
Atlanta, GA 30332

Georgia Southern College Library
Statesboro, GA 30458

The E. Louise Patten Library
Piedmont College
Demorest, GA 30535

Map Room
University of Georgia
Science Library
Athens, GA 30602

Library
South Georgia College
Douglas, GA 31533

Library
Valdosta State College
Valdosta, GA 31698

Government Documents
Simon Schwob Memorial Library
Columbus College
Columbus, GA 31907

**Hawaii**

University of Hawaii at Hilo
Library, Government Documents Dept.
Hilo Campus P. O. Box 1357
Hilo, HI 96720

University of Hawaii Library
Map Collection
2550 The Mall
Honolulu, HI 96822

**Idaho**

Department of Geology
Idaho State University
Pocatello, ID 83201

Pocatello Public Library
Pocatello, ID 83201

Documents Division
Idaho State University Library
Pocatello, ID 83209

Documents Department
Learning Resources Center
Ricks College
Rexburg, ID 83440

Boise State University Library
1910 College Blvd.
Boise, ID 83725

Boise State University Library
Documents Division
Boise, ID 83725

Documents Librarian
University of Idaho
Moscow, ID 83483

**Illinois**

Northern Illinois University
Map Library—Room 222
William Morris Davis Hall
De Kalb, IL 60115

Adult Services
Gail Borden Public Library
200 N. Grove Ave.
Elgin, IL 60120

Map Curator
The University Library
Northwestern University
Evanston, IL 60201

Public Library
Aurora, IL 60506

Field Museum of Natural History
Roosevelt Road & Lake Shore Drive
Chicago, IL 60605

Government Publications Department
Chicago Public Library
425 N. Michian Ave.
Chicago, IL 60611

The John Crerar Library
35 W. 33rd St.
Chicago, IL 60626

Loyola University of Chicago
6525 N. Sheridan Rd.
Chicago, IL 60626

Map Librarian
University of Chicago
1100 E. 57th St.
Chicago, IL 60680

University of Illinois at Chicago Circle
P. O. Box 8198
Library—Map Section
Chicago, IL 60680

Benner Library & Resource Center
Olivet Nazarene College
P. O. Box 592
Kankakee, IL 60901

Augustana College Library
3500 7th Ave.
Rock Island, IL 61201

Loring Map Library
Augustana College
639 38th St.
Rock Island, IL 61201

Department of Geology
Knox College
Galesburg, IL 61401

Map Library
Department of Geography
Western Illinois University
Macomb, IL 61455

Documents Librarian
Monmouth College
Monmouth, IL 61462

Peoria Public Library
107 N. E. Monroe
Peoria, IL 61602

Milner Library Map Room
Illinois State University
Normal, IL 61761

Map & Geography Library
418 University Library
University of Illinois
1408 W. Gregory Dr.
Urbana, IL 61801

University of Illinois
Library
Urbana, IL 61801

Booth Library
Eastern Illinois University
Charleston, IL 61920

Geography Department
Eastern Illinois University
322 Science Building
Charleston, IL 61920

Map Library
Lovejoy Library
Southern Illinois University
Edwardsville, IL 62025

Southern Illinois University
Department of Earth Science
Geography & Planning
Edwardsville, IL 62026

Department of Geology
Principia College
Elsah, IL 62028

Illinois State Library
Documents Unit
Centennial Building
Springfield, IL 62756

Map Room
Science Library
Southern Illinois University
Carbondale, Il 62901

**Indiana**

Prevo Science Library
Science Center
Depauw University
Greencastle, IN 46135

Library—Documents Department
Depauw University
Box 137
Greencastle, IN 46135

University Library
Serials
815 West Michigan St.
Indianapolis, IN 46202

Indiana State Library, Serials
140 N. Senate Ave.
Indianapolis, IN 46204

Moellering Library, Map Room
Valparaiso University
Valparaiso, IN 46383

Library
Indiana University
The NW Campus
3400 Broadway
Gary, IN 46408

Microtext Reading Room
Memorial Library
University of Notre Dame
Notre Dame, IN 46556

Allen County Public Library
900 Webster St.
P. O. Box 2270
Fort Wayne, IN 46801

Walter E. Helmke Library
Indiana University
Purdue University
Fort Wayne, IN 46805

Indiana University Southeast Library
4201 Grant Line Rd.
Box 679
IVS Library/Reference
New Albany, IN 47150

Hanover College
Geology Department
Map Library
Hanover, IN 47243

Map Collection
Department of Library Service
Ball State University
Muncie, IN 47306

Department of Geology
Earlham College
Richmond, IN 47374

Map Library
Wildman Science Library
Box E-72 Earlham College
Richmond, IN 47374

Documents Department
Indiana University Library
Bloomington, IN 46405

Geography & Map Library
Indiana University
Kirkwood Hall 3076405
Bloomington, IN 47405

Geology–Geography Department
Indiana State University
Terre Haute, IN 47809

Map Collection—Geography Department
Purdue University Libraries
Stewart Center
West Lafayette, IN 47907

Library
St. Joseph's College
Rensselaer, IN 47978

## Iowa

Iowa State University
University Library
Map Librarian
Ames, IA 50010

Library, Government Documents
Grinnell College
Grinnell, IA 50112

Government Publications Department
Cowles Library
Drake University
Des Moines, IA 50311

State Library
Division of State Library Comm. of
   Historical Building
Des Moines, IA 50319

Library
Government Documents & Maps
University of Northern Iowa
Cedar Falls, IA 50613

Public Library
Council Bluffs, IA 51501

Wahlert Memorial Library
Loras College
1450 Alta Vista
Dubuque, IA 52001

Carnegie–Stout Free Public Library
Dubuque, IA 52001

University of Iowa
Geology Department
Iowa City, IA 52242

University of Iowa Libraries
Map Collection
Iowa City, IA 52242

Geology Library
University of Iowa
136 Trowbridge
Iowa City, IA 52242

Ottumwa Public Library
125 N. Court St.
Ottumwa, IA 52501

## Kansas

University of Kansas
Spencer Research Library
Lawrence, KS 66045

Library
Documents Division
Kansas State University
Manhattan, KS 66506

State Libraries of Kansas
3rd Floor State House Building
Topeka, KS 66506

Wichita Public Library
223 S. Main
Wichita, KS 67202

Hutchinson Public Library
901 N. Main St.
Hutchinson, KS 67501

## Kentucky

Library Reference Department
Belknap Campus
University of Louisville
Louisville, KY 40208

Dept. of Geology & Geography
Berea College
C.P.O. 1105
Berea, KY 40403

Geology Library
100 Bowman Hall
University of Kentucky
Lexington, KY 40506

Library
North Kentucky University
Highland Heights, KY 41076

## Louisiana

Tulane University Documents Dept.
Howard Tilton Memorial Library
New Orleans, LA 70118

Federal Documents
Earl K. Long Library
University of New Orleans
New Orleans, LA 70122

New Orleans Public Library
Business & Science Division
New Orleans, LA 70140

Map Room School of Geoscience
Louisiana State University
University Station
313 Geology Building
Baton Rouge, LA 70803

Magale Library
Centenary College
Shreveport, LA 71104

Prescott Memorial Library
Louisiana Tech University
Ruston, LA 71272

## Maine

Bowdoin College
Library
Brunswick, ME 04011

University of Maine
College Ave.
Gorham, ME 04038

Public Library
Portland, ME 04101

Bates College Library
Lewistown, ME 04240

Maine State Library
Cultural Building
Station #64
Augusta, ME 04333

Bangor Public Library
Periodical Department
145 Harlow St.
Bangor, ME 04401

Tri-State Regional Document Depository
Raymond H. Fogler Library
University of Maine
Orono, ME 04473

Department of Geography
University of Maine
Ft. Kent, ME 04743

Colby College
Department of Geology
Waterville, ME 04901

Department of Geology
University of Maine
Preble Hall
Farmington, ME 04938

## Maryland

Documents Map Room
McKeldin Library
University of Maryland
College Park, MD 20742

Documents Librarian
Enoch Pratt Free Library
400 Cathedral St.
Baltimore, MD 21201

Maryland Historical Society
201 W. Monument St.
Prints & Photographs Department
Baltimore, MD 21201

Johns Hopkins University
Milton E. Eisenhower Library
Map Room
Baltimore, MD 21218

Johns Hopkins University
Government Publications/Map Dept.
34th & Charles Streets
Baltimore, MD 21218

University of Maryland Library
5401 Wilkins Ave.
Baltimore, MD 21228

Frostburg State College Library
Map Collection
Frostburg, MD 21532

Jerome Frampton Library
Frostburg State College
Frostburg, MD 21533

Blackwell Library
Salisbury State College
Salisbury, MD 21801

**Massachusetts**

Serials Department
University of Massachusetts Library
Amherst, MA 01002

Amherst College Library
Amherst, MA 01002

Forbes Library
20 West St.
Northampton, MA 01063

Smith College
Department of Geology
Clark Science Center
Northampton, MA 01063

Department of Geology
Mt. Holyoke College
South Hadley, MA 01075

Documents Section
City Library
220 State St.
Springfield, MA 01103

Documents Librarian
Williams College Library
Williamstown, MA 01267

Department of Geology
Williams College
Williamstown, MA 01267

Free Public Library
Technology Division
Worcester, MA 01608

Map Curator
Graduate School of Geography
Clark University
Worcester, MA 01610

Goddard Library
Clark University
Worcester, MA 01610

Haverhill Public Library
99 Main St.
Haverhill, MA 01830

Lowell City Library
401 Merrimack St.
Lowell, MA 01852

University of Lowell
Reference Department
O'Leary Library South Campus
Lowell, MA 01854

Map Curator
The Library
Salem State College
Salem, MA 01970

Boston Athenaeum
10½ Beacon St.
Boston, MA 02108

Boston Public Library
Map Section
Boston, MA 02117

Documents Division
Joseph P. Healey Library
University of Massachusetts–Boston
Boston, MA 02125

Massachusetts State Library
442 State House
Boston, MA 02133

Department of Geological Sciences
Map Room, Geological Museum
Oxford St.
Cambridge, MA 02138

Map Room
Harvard University
Cambridge, MA 02138

Gordon McKay Library
Division of Engrg. Applied Physics
Harvard University
Pierce Hall
Boston, MA 02138

Geological Sciences Library
Harvard University
24 Oxford St.
Boston, MA 02138

Library
Museum of Comparative Zoology
Harvard University
Boston, MA 02138

MIT Libraries
Serial Journal Room 14 F-210
Massachusetts Institute of Technology
Cambridge, MA 02139

Tufts University
Geology Department
Lane Hall
Medford, MA 02155

Babson College
Map & Globe Museum
Babson Park, MA 02157

Department of Geology
Wellesley College
Wellesley, MA 02181

Bridgewater State College
Library
Bridgewater, MA 02324

Massachusetts Maritime Academy
Division of State Colleges
Buzzards Bay, MA 02532

Woods Hole Oceanographic Institute
Data Library McLean Laboratory
Quisset Campus
Woods Hole, MA 02543

Free Public Library
Box C-902
New Bedford, MA 02740

**Michigan**

Map Room
825 Harlan Hatcher Graduate Library
University of Michigan
Ann Arbor, MI 48109

Eastern Michigan University
University Library
Map Library
Ypsilanti, MI 48197

Wayne State University
G. Flint Purdy Library
Detroit, MI 48202

History & Travel Department
Detroit Public Library
5201 Woodward Ave.
Detroit, MI 48202

Monteith Library
Alma College
Alma, MI 48801

Michigan State University
Library, Documents Department
East Lansing, MI 48859

Central Michigan University
Geography Department
Moore Hall
Mt. Pleasant, MI 48859

Central Michigan University
Library—Documents Department
Mt. Pleasant, MI 48859

Western Michigan University
Waldo Library
Map Library
Kalamazoo, MI 49008

Map Department
James White Library
Andrews University
Berrien Springs, MI 49104

Stockwell Memorial Library
Albion College
602 E. Cass St.
Albion, MI 49224

Department of Geology
Grand Valley State College
College Landing
Allendale, MI 49401

Grand Rapids Public Library
Michigan Room
60 Library Plaza N.E.
Grand Rapids, MI 49503

Documents & Map Department
Olson Library
Northern Michigan University
Marquette, MI 49855

Michigan Technological University
Library, Map Librarian
Houghton, MI 49931

**Minnesota**

Geology Map Library
Geology Department
Carleton College
Northfield, MN 55057

Map Library
Minnesota Historical Library
690 Cedar St.
St. Paul, MN 55101

Winchell Library of Geology
201 Pill Hl
310 Pillsbury SE
University of Minnesota
Minneapolis, MN 55455

Map Library
S 76 Wilson Library
University of Minnesota
Minneapolis, MN 55455

Documents Librarian
Duluth Public Library
520 W. Superior St.
Duluth, MN 55802

University of Minnesota
Duluth Campus Library
Duluth, MN 55812

Map Library
Department of Geography
University of Minnesota
Duluth, MN 55812

Memorial Library
Mankato State College
Box 19
Mankato, MN 56001

Department of Geography
Gustavus Adolphus College
St. Peter, MN 56082

Map Section
Learning Resources Services
St. Cloud State University
St. Cloud, MN 56301

Bemidji State College
Department of Geography
Bemidji, MN 56301

**Mississippi**

The Library
Documents Department
University of Mississippi
University, MS 38677

Department of Geology
University of Southern Mississippi
Southern Station, Box 5051
Hattiesburg, MS 39406

University of Southern Mississippi
Box 5053
Hattiesburg, MS 39401

Acquisitions Department
Mitchell Memorial Library
Mississippi State University
State College, MS 39762

**Missouri**

St. Louis Public Library
1301 Olive St.
St. Louis, MO 63103

St. Louis University
Pius XII Memorial Library
3655 W. Pine
Serial Department
St. Louis, MO 63108

Earth & Planetary Science Library
Washington University
St. Louis, MO 63130

Mercantile Library
Box 633
St. Louis, MO 63188

Depository Librarian
S. E. Missouri State University
Cape Girardeau, MO 63701

Kansas City Public Library
Documents Division
311 E. 12th St.
Kansas City, MO 64106

Linda Hall Library
Documents Division
5109 Cherry St.
Kansas City, MO 64110

Geology Library
201 Geology Building
University of Missouri
Columbia, MO 65201

Library Documents
University of Missouri
Columbia, MO 65201

Library—Document Section
University of Missouri—Rolla
Rolla, MO 65401

Department of Geology
University of Missouri—Rolla
Rolla, MO 65401

Map Collection
Southwest Missouri State University
Library
Springfield, MO 65804

**Montana**

Eastern Montana College
Documents
Billings, MT 59101

Lewistown Carnegie Public Library
701 W. Main
Lewistown, MT 59457

Montana Historical Society Library
225 N. Roberts St.
Helena, MT 59601

Montana College of Mineral Science
  & Technology
Pork St.
Butte MT 59701

Department of Earth Sciences
Montana State University
Bozeman, MT 59715

Documents Librarian
Montana State University
Bozeman, MT 59717

Montana State University
Department of Earth Sciences
Bozeman, MT 59717

Department of Geology
University of Montana
Missoula, MT 59812

Mansfield Library
Documents Division
University of Montana
Missoula, MT 59812

**Nebraska**

Midland College Library
Fremont, NE 68025

Omaha Public Library
215 S. 15th St.
Omaha, NE 68102

University Library, Documents
University of Nebraska at Omaha
60th & Dodge Street
Omaha, NE 68182

University of Nebraska Libraries
Acquisition Department
Serials Section
Lincoln, NE 68588

**Nevada**

Documents Librarian
University of Nevada, Las Vegas
4505 Maryland Parkway
Las Vegas, NV 89154

Getchnell Library
University of Nevada—Reno
Reno, NV 89557

Nevada State Library
Documents Desk
401 N. Carson
Carson City, NV 89701

**New Hampshire**

Nashua Public Library
2 Court St.
Nashua, NH 03060

Geisel Library
Saint Anselm's College
Manchester, NH 03102

New England College
Henniker, NH 03242

State Library
Concord, NH 03301

Department of Geography
Map Repository
Keene State College
Keene, NH 03431

Baker Library—Map Room
Dartmouth College
Hanover, NH 03755

Serials Section
Baker Library
Dartmouth College
Hanover, NH 03755

Dartmouth College
Department of Earth Sciences
Hanover, NH 03755

Department of Earth Science
University of New Hampshire
James Hall
Durham, HN 03824

University of New Hampshire
Library–Map Room
Durham, NH 03824

**New Jersey**

Plainfield Public Library
8th Street at Park Avenue
Plainfield, NJ 07060

Dana Library, Reference Department
Rutgers University
185 University Ave.
Newark, NJ 07102

Newark Public Library
U. S. Documents Division
5 Washington St.
Newark, NJ 07102

Public Library
Government Documents Division
Science & Technology Department
11 S. Broad St.
Elizabeth, NJ 07202

Free Public Library
Documents Division
472 Jersey Ave.
Jersey City, NJ 07302

Map Curator
Monmouth County Library
State Highway No. 35
Shrewsbury, NJ 07701

Burlington County Library
Mt. Holly, NJ 08060

Documents Department
Stockton State College Library
Pomona, NJ 08240

Documents Division
Firestone Library
Princeton University
Princeton, NJ 08544

Geology Library
Gayot Hall
Princeton Univeristy
Princeton, NJ 08544

Documents Librarian
New Jersey State Library
185 W. State St.
Trenton, NJ 08625

Delaware River Basin Comm. Library
P. O. Box 7360 Mines Library
Trenton, NJ 08628

Government Publications
Rutgers University
Library of Science & Medicine
Piscataway, NJ 08854

**New Mexico**

Department of Geology
University of New Mexico
Albuquerque, NM 87106

University of New Mexico Library
Map Coordinator
Albuquerque, NM 87131

Map Room, General Library
University of New Mexico
Albuquerque, NM 87131

New Mexico State Library
325 Don Gaspar Ave.
Santa Fe, NM 87503

Lab of Anthropology Library
Museum of New Mexico
P. O. Box 2087
Santa Fe, NM 87503

Donnelly Library
New Mexico Highlands University
Las Vegas, NM 87701

New Mexico Bureau of Mines & Mineral
  Resources
Campus Station
Socorro, MN 87801

Map Collection, Special Collection
New Mexico State University Library
Box 3475
Las Cruces, NM 88003

**New York**

School of Visual Arts
209 E. 23rd St.
New York, NY 10010

New York Public Library
Grand Central Station
P. O. Box 2233
New York, NY 10017

New York Public Library
Grand Central Station
P. O. Box 2221
New York, NY 10017

New York Public Library–Div M
Grand Central Station
P. O. Box 2238
New York, NY 10017

Government Documents Division
Hunter College Library
695 Park Ave.
New York, NY 10021

Hunter College
Department of Geology & Geography
695 Park Ave.
New York, NY 10021

Library–Serials Unit
American Museum of Natural History
Central Park West at 79th Street
New York, NY 10024

Columbia University Map Room
Herbert Lehman Library
420 W. 118th St.
New York, NY 10027

Documents Service Center
Columbia University Libraries
420 W. 118th St., Room 327
New York, NY 10027

The Wollman Library
Barnard College
Columbia University
New York, NY 10027

Columbia University
Department of Geology
556 Schermerhorn Hall
New York, NY 10027

Department of Earth & Planetary Science
College of the City of New York
Convent Avenue & 138th Street
New York, NY 10031

Lamont–Doherty Geol. Observer of
   Columbia University
Palisades, NY 10964

Pratt Institute Library
Reference Department
200 Willoughby Ave.
Brooklyn, NY 11205

Brooklyn College
Department of Geology
Bedford Avenue & Avenue H
Brooklyn, NY 11210

Brooklyn Public Library
History Division
Grand Army Plaza
Brooklyn, NY 11238

Geology Department
Queens College
Flushing, NY 11367

Queens College
Department of Earth & Environmental
   Sciences
Flushing, NY 11367

Acquisitions Librarian
York College
City College of New York
150 14 Jamaica Ave.
Jamaica, NY 11432

Documents Librarian
Hofstra University
Hempstead Long Island, NY 11550

Main Library
Documents Section
State University of New York
Stony Brook, NY 11794

Library, Serials Department
Rensselaer Polytechnic Institute
Troy, NY 12181

State University of New York
University Library
Government Publications Department
1400 Washington Ave.
Albany, NY 12222

New York State Library
Government Documents Unit
Empire State Plaza
Albany, NY 12230

New York State Museum & Science
   Service Library
State Education Building Annex
Albany, NY 12234

Schaffer Library
Union College
Schenectady, NY 12308

Geology Map Depository
Sojourner Truth Library
State University College
New Paltz, NY 12561

Vassar College Library
Poughkeepsie, NY 12601

Vassar College
Department of Geology & Geography
Box 373
Poughkeepsie, NY 12601

Feinberg Library
State University College
Plattsburgh, NY 12901

Syracuse University
Bird Library
Geography, Area Studies
Syracuse, NY 13210

Hamilton College Library
Serials Department
Clinton, NY 13323

Utica Public Library
303 Genessee St.
Utica, NY 13501

State University College
Crumb Library
Potsdam, NY 13676

Science Library
Harpur College of State University
   of New York
Binghamton, NY 13901

Buffalo & Erie County Public Library
Documents Division
Lafayette Square
Buffalo, NY 14203

State University Coll. at Buffalo
Department of Geography
1300 Elmwood Ave.
Buffalo, NY 14222

State University of New York at Buffalo
University Libraries
Buffalo, NY 14260

Drake Memorial Library
State University of New York
Brockport, NY 14420

State University College
Milne Library
Geneseo, NY 14454

Hobart & Wm. Smith Colleges Library
Geneva, NY 14456

University of Rochester Map Center
Rush Rhees Library
University of Rochester
Rochester, NY 14627

Herrick Memorial Library
Alfred University
Alfred, NY 14802

Alfred University
Geology Department Library
245 Science Center
Alfred, NY 14802

College of Ceramics Library
Alfred University
Alfred, NY 14802

Cornell University Libraries
Serials Department
Ithaca, NY 14853

Cornell University Library
Map Library
Ithaca, NY 14853

## North Carolina

Wake Forest University Library
Z. Smith Reynolds Library
Box 7777, Reynolds Station
Winston-Salem, NC 27109

Jackson Library
University of North Carolina
Greensboro, NC 27412

Map Division
Carrie Rich Memorial Library
Campbell College
Buies Creek, NC 27506

Geology Library
Mitchell Hall 029A
University of North Carolina
Chapel Hill, NC 27514

Library
Health Affairs
University of North Carolina
Chapel Hill, NC 27514

John N. Couch Library
Department of Botany
University of North Carolina
Chapel Hill, NC 27514

North Carolina State Museum
Box 27647
Raleigh, NC 27611

Documents Librarian
The D. H. Hill Library
North Carolina State University
Raleigh, NC 27650

Department Library
N. C. S. J./M. E. & A. S.
Box 5068
214 Withers Hall
Raleigh, NC 27650

Documents Librarian
Duke University Library
Durham, NC 27706

Geology Department
East Carolina University
P. O. Box 2751
Greenville, NC 27834

Department of Geography
East Carolina University
Greenville, NC 27834

Serials & Documents Librarian
Gardner–Webb College Library
P. O. Box 836
Boiling Springs, NC 28017

Library
Catawba College
Salisbury, NC 28144

University of North Carolina
Library, Documents Section
Charlotte, NC 28223

Documents Librarian
University of North Carolina
Wilmington, NC 28406

Map Library
Geography Department
Appalachian State University
Boone, NC 28607

Mitchell Community College
Learning Resources
Statesville, NC 28677

Mitchell Community College
Library
West Bradd St.
Statesville, NC 28677

Western Carolina University
Reference Librarian
Cullowhee, NC 28723

## North Dakota

Map Collection
Library
North Dakota State University
Fargo, ND 58105

Geology Library
326 Leonard Hall
University of North Dakota
Grand Forks, ND 58202

University of North Dakota
Geology Library
University Station
Grand Forks, ND 58202

Division of Science
Minot State College
Minot, ND 58701

## Ohio

Ohio Wesleyan University Library
Acquisitions Department
Delaware, OH 43015

Ohio Wesleyan University
New Science Building
90 S. Henry St.
Delaware, OH 43015

Ohio Wesleyan University
Geography–Geology Department
Map Library
Delaware, OH 43015

Chalmers Memorial Library
Kenyon College
Gambier, OH 43022

Wm. Howard Doane Library
Geology Maps Division
Denison University
Granville, OH 43023

Serials Division
1858 Neil Ave.
Columbus, OH 43210

Orton Memorial Library
Ohio State University
155 S. Oval Drive
Columbus, OH 43210

Columbus & Ohio Division
Public Library
28 South Hamilton Rd.
Columbus, OH 43213

State Library of Ohio
Documents Section
65 S. Front St.
Columbus, OH 43215

Department of Geology
Seismographic Station
Bowling Green State Univesity
Bowling Green, OH 43402

Bowling Green State University
Map Library
Bowling Green, OH 43403

University of Toledo Library
Government Documents Division
Toledo, OH 43606

Toledo Public Library
Science & Technology Department
325 Michigan St.
Toledo, OH 43624

Sears Library, Geology Collection
10900 Euclid Ave.
Case Western Reserve University
Cleveland, OH 44106

Map Collection
Cleveland Public Library
325 Superior Ave.
Cleveland, OH 44114

Cleveland State University Library
Map Collection
1860 E. 22nd St.
Cleveland, OH 44115

Department of Geology
Kent State University
Kent, OH 44240

Map Library
406 McGilvrey Hall
Kent State University
Kent, OH 44242

Akron Public Library
55 S. Main St.
Akron, OH 44326

The Public Library of Youngstown &
  Mahoning County
305 Wick Ave.
Science & Industry Division
Youngstown, OH 44503

Science Library
Miami University
Oxford, OH 45056

Map Library
The Public Library
8th & Vine Streets
Cincinnati, OH 45202

University of Cincinnati
Geology/Geography Library
103 Old Tech Building
Cincinnati, OH 45221

University of Cincinnati Library
Documents
Cincinnati, OH 45221

Department of Earth Sciences
Antioch College
Yellow Springs, OH 45387

Olive Kettering Library
Antioch College
Yellow Springs, OH 45387

Dayton Public Library
215 E. 3rd St.
Dayton, OH 45402

Dayton Museum of Natural History
2629 Ridge Ave.
Dayton, OH 45414

Reference Department
Wright State University
Dayton, OH 45431

Department of Geology
Wittenberg University
Springfield, OH 45501

Warder Memorial Library
Reference Department
137 E. High St.
Springfield, OH 45501

Serials Librarian, Thomas Library
Wittenberg University
Springfield, OH 45501

Wittenberg University
Department of Geology
Springfield, OH 45501

Map Librarian, Ohio University
Athens, OH 45701

Nelsonville Public Library
Athens Branch
65 N. Court St.
Athens, OH 45701

Office of Librarian
Marietta College
Marietta, OH 45750

## Oklahoma

Geology Library
University of Oklahoma
830 Van Vleet Oval, Room 103
Norman, OK 73019

Map Department
Central State University
Edmond, OK 73034

Department of Geography
University of Oklahoma
Norman, OK 73069

Metropolitan Library System
Documents Department
131 N.W. Third
Oklahoma City, OK 73102

Oklahoma Historical Society
Historical Building
Oklahoma City, OK 73105

Museum of the Great Plains
P. O. Box 68
Lawton, OK 73502

Map Collection
Edmon Low Library
Oklahoma State University
Stillwater, OK 74078

Tulsa City–County Library
Business & Technology Department
400 Civic Center
Tulsa, OK 74103

## Oregon

Portland State University
Library–Serial Documents Division
P. O. Box 1151
Portland, OR 97207

Oregon State Library
Documents Section
State Library Building
Salem, OR 97310

Oregon State University Library
Documents Division
Corvallis, OR 97331

Oregon State University
Map Library
Corvallis, OR 97331

Department of Social Science
Western Oregon State College
Monmouth, OR 97361

Map Room, 165 Cordon Hall
University of Oregon
Eugene, OR 97403

Library
Southern Oregon State College
Ashland, OR 97520

Southern Oregon State College
Department of Geography
Ashland, OR 97520

Librarian
Oregon Institute of Technology
Oretech Branch P. O.
Klamath Falls, OR 97601

Library
Central Oregon Community College
NW College Way
Bend, OR 97701

Reference Librarian
Walter M. Pierce Library
Eastern Oregon College
Lagrande, OR 97850

## Pennsylvania

Government Documents Section
Carnegie Library of Pittsburgh
4400 Forbes Ave.
Pittsburgh, PA 15213

Northland Public Library
300 Cumberland Road
Pittsburgh, PA 15273

University of Pittsburgh
Documents Office, G-8
Hillman Library
Pittsburgh, PA 15260

Reference Department
Indiana University of Pennsylvania
Rhodes R. Stabley Library
Indiana, PA 15701

Cambria County Library
248 Main St.
Johnstown, PA 15901

Reference Librarian
New Castle Public Library
106 E. North St.
New Castle, PA 16101

Geography Department, Map Library
Clarion State College
Clarion, PA 16214

Allegheny College
Department of Geology
Meadville, PA 16335

Warren Public Library
205 Market St.
P. O. Box 489
Warren, PA 16365

Edinboro State College
Department of Earth Sciences
Edinboro, PA 16444

Baron-Forness Library
Edinboro State College
Edinboro, PA 16444

Edinboro State College
Department of Geography
Edinboro, PA 16444

Library
Juniata College
Huntingdon, PA 16652

Earth & Mineral Sciences Library
105 Deike Building
University Park, PA 16802

Reference Department
Pattee Library
Pennsylvania State University
University Park, PA 16802

Map Section
Patte library
Pennsylvania State University
University Park, PA 16802

Dickinson College Library
Carlisle, Pa 17013

Map Collection, General Library
State Library of Pennsylvania
Box 1601
Harrisburg, PA 17105

Shippensburg State College
Ezra Lehman Memorial Library
Shippensburg, PA 17257

Map Collection
Department of Geography
Millersville State College
Millersville, PA 17551

Geoscience Department
Lock Haven State College
Lock Haven, PA 17745

Bucknell University
Ellen Clarke Bertrand Library
Lewisburg, PA 17837

Linderman Library No. 30
Lehigh University
Bethlehem, PA 18105

Library
Moravian College
Bethlehem, PA 18018

Department of Geology
Lafayette College
Easton, PA 18042

Lafayette College
Skillman Library
Acquisitions Department
Easton, PA 18042

ESSC Library
Documents Department
East Stroudsburg State College
East Stroudsburg, PA 18301

Librarian
Public Library
Scranton, PA 18503

Reference Librarian
Osterhout Free Library
71 S. Franklin
Wilkes-Barre, PA 18701

Geology Department Library
Bryn Mawr College
Bryn Mawr, PA 19010

Geology Department
Bryn Mawr College
Park Hall
Bryn Mawr, PA 19010

Reference Department
Swarthmore College Library
Swarthmore, PA 19081

Map Collection
Free Library of Philadelphia
Logan Square
Philadelphia, PA 19103

Geology Map Library
Hayden Hall
University of Pennsylvania
Philadelphia, PA 19104

Temple University Library
Documents Room
Philadelphia, PA 19122

LaSalle College
Department of Geology
Philadelphia, PA 19141

Francis Harvey Green Library
Documents & Maps Librarian
West Chester State College
West Chester, PA 19380

Map Librarian
Kutztown State College
Rohrbach Library
Kutztown, PA 19530

Documents Librarian
Kutztown State College
Kutztown, PA 19530

**Rhode Island**

Reference Department
Providence Public Library
150 Empire St.
Providence, RI 02903

Brown University Library
Documents Division
Providence, RI 02912

**South Carolina**

Map Library
University of South Carolina
Columbia, SC 29208

Daniel Library
The Citadel
Serials & Documents
Charleston, SC 29409

Geology Department
Furman University
Greenville, SC 29613

**South Dakota**

Documents Department
H. M. Briggs Library
South Dakota State University
Brookings, SD 57007

Gifts & Exchange (Geology)
I. D. Weeks Library
University of South Dakota
Vermillion, SD 57069

South Dakota School of Mines
  & Technology
Devereaux Library
Rapid City, SD 57701

**Tennessee**

Felix G. Woodward Library
Austin Peay State University
Clarksville, TN 37040

Joint University Libraries
Science Library—Map Room
Nashville, TN 37203

Tennessee State Library
State Library Section
403 7th Ave. North
Nashville, TN 37219

Map Library
East Tennessee State University
Johnson City, TN 37614

Carson–Newman College
Map Library
Department of Geology
Jefferson City, TN 37760

Map Library
Department of Geography
University of Tennessee
Knoxville, TN 37996

Memphis Public Library &
Information Center
Document Section
1850 Peabody Ave.
Memphis, TN 38104

Government Publications Department
Memphis Public Library
1850 Peabody Ave.
Memphis, TN 38104

Engineering Library
Memphis State University
Memphis, TN 38152

Physical Science Department
University of Tennessee—Martin
Martin, TN 38237

Documents Librarian
Jere Whitson Memorial Library
Tennessee Technological University
Cookeville, TN 38501

**Texas**
Senior Reference Librarian
University of Texas–Dallas
P. O. Box 643
Richardson, TX 75080

Dallas Public Library
Map Librarian
1515 Young St.
Dallas, TX 75201

Dallas Seismic Observatory
Southern Methodist University
Dallas, TX 75275

Map Library
Southern Methodist University
Science/Engineering Library
Dallas, TX 75275

Library–Documents Department
Stephen F. Austin State University
Nacogdoches, TX 75961

Department of Geology
University of Texas–Arlington
Box 19049
Arlington, TX 76019

Fort Worth Public Library
300 Taylor St.
Fort Worth, TX 76102

North Texas State University
Library
Documents Department
Denton, TX 76203

Department of Geology
Baylor University
Waco, TX 76703

Baylor University Library
Documents Department
Box 6307 B.U. Station
Waco, TX 76703

William Marsh Rice University
Fondren Library–Gifts & Exchange
P. O. Box 1892
Houston, TX 77001

Houston Public Library
500 McKinney Ave.
Government Documents Section
Houston, TX 77002

University of Houston Libraries
Gifts & Exchange Section
4800 Calhoun Blvd.
Houston, TX 77004

Social Science Librarian
Sam Houston State University
Huntsville, TX 77340

Sam Houston State University
Department of Geography
P. O. Box 2148
Huntsville, TX 77341

Rosenberg Library
2310 Sealy
Galveston, TX 77550

Lamar University Library
Government Documents
Box 10021
Lamar University Station
Beaumont, TX 77710

Department of Geology
Box 10031
Lamar University
Beaumont, TX 77710

Department of Geology
Texas A & M University
College Station, TX 77840

Map Librarian
Sterling C. Evans Library
Texas A & M University
College Station, TX 77843

Documents Librarian, Map Collection
Trinity University Library
715 Stadium Dr.
San Antonio, TX 78284

Geology Library
University of Texas at Austin
Geology Building 302
Austin, TX 78712

Central Serials Record
General Libraries
University of Texas at Austin
Austin, TX 78712

Library, Documents Department
Texas Tech. University
P. O. Box 4079
Lubbock, TX 79409

Midland Public Library
301 W. Missouri
P. O. Boc 1191
Midland, TX 79702

Technical Department
Midland Public Library
301 W. Missouri
P. O. Box 1191
Midland, TX 79702

Geology Department
Sul Ross State University
Alpine, TX 79830

Sul Ross State University Library
Alpine, TX 79830

The Library Annex—Maps Section
University of Texas at El Paso
El Paso, TX 79968

**Utah**
Map Section
Salt Lake City Public Library
209 E. 5th South
Salt Lake City, UT 84111

University of Utah
Government Documents Library
Salt Lake City, UT 84112

Salt Lake City
Public Library
209 E. 5th South
Salt Lake City, UT 84112

Utah State University
Merrill Library
Learning Resources Program
Documents UMC 30
Logan, UT 84332

Department of Geology
Utah State University
Logan, UT 84322

Documents Department
Stewart Library 2901
Weber State College
Ogden, UT 84408

Documents & Map Section
Lee Library
Brigham Young University
Provo, UT 84602

Library
Southern Utah State College
Cedar City, UT 84720

**Vermont**

Guy W. Bailey Library—Map Room
University of Vermont
Burlington, VT 05405

Vermont Department of Libraries
Law & Document Unit
Montpelier, VT 05602

Government Documents Librarian
Henry Prescott Chaplin Library
Norwich University
Northfield, VT 05663

Norwich University
Department of Earth Science
Northfield, VT 05663

Middlebury College
Map Library, Department of Geography
Warner Science Hall
Middlebury, VT 05753

**Virginia**

Fenwick Library
George Mason University
4400 University Dr.
Fairfax, VA 22030

Madison College Library
Harrisonburg, VA 22801

Madison Memorial Library
James Madison University
Harrisonburg, VA 22807

Bridgewater College Library
Bridgewater, VA 22812

Public Documents
Alderman Library
University of Virginia
Charlottesville, VA 22901

University of Virginia
Department of Environmental Sciences
Clark Hall
Charlottesville, VA 22903

Virginia Institute of Marine Science
Gloucester Point, VA 23062

Acquisitions Department
Earl Gregg Swem Library
College of William & Mary
Williamsburg, VA 23185

Federal Documents Librarian
Virginia State Library
11th & Capitol Streets
Richmond, VA 23219

Documents Librarian
Chesapeake Public Library
300 Cedar Rd.
Chesapeake, VA 23320

University Library
Documents Department
Old Dominion University
Norfolk, VA 23508

Chaptain John Smith Library
Christopher Newport College
50 Shoe Lane
Newport News, VA 23606

Hampden–Sidney College
Library
Hampden Sidney, VA 23943

Virginia Polytechnic
Institute & State University Library
Blacksburg, VA 24061

Geology Library
Department of Geological Sciences
Virginia Polytechnic Institute and State
   University
Blacksburg, VA 24061

Radford University
Department of Geography
Radford, VA 24142

John Cook Wyllie Library
Clinch Valley College of The University
   of Virginia
Wise, VA 24293

Department of Geology
Virginia Military Institute
Lexington, VA 24450

**Washington**

Bellevue Public Library
11501 Main St.
Bellevue, WA 98004

Documents Librarian
Seattle Public Library
1000 4th Ave.
Seattle, WA 98104

Engineering Library F H 15
Engineering Library Building
University of Washington
Seattle, WA 98105

Map Section
University of Washington Libraries
FM 025
Seattle, WA 98195

Map Section
University of Washington Libraries
FM-25
Seattle, WA 98105

Department of Geology
Western Washington University
Haggard Hall
Bellingham, WA 98225

Western Washington University
Map Library
Arntzen Hall 101
Bellingham, WA 98225

Tacoma Public Library
Business & Technology Department
Tacoma, WA 98402

University of Puget Sound
Department of Geology
Tacoma, WA 98416

Reference Support Services
Robert A. L. Mortvedt Library
Pacific Lutheran University
Tacoma, WA 98447

Documents Center
Washington State Library
Olympia, WA 98504

Library, Documents Section
Central Washington University
Ellensburg, WA 98926

Washington State University
Department of Geology
Pullman, WA 99163

The Science & Engineering Library
Washington State University
Pullman, WA 99164

Washington Water Research Center
Washington State University
Albrook Hydraulics Lab 202-B
Pullman, WA 99164

Reference Department
Spokane Public Library
West 906 Main Ave.
Spokane, WA 99201

Document Librarian
Penrose Memorial Library
Whitman College
Walla Walla, WA 99362

**Wisconsin**

Parkside Library
University of Wisconsin—Parkside
Kenosha, WI 53141

Map Librarian
AGS Collection
University of Wisconsin
Golda Meir Library POB 399
Milwaukee, WI 53201

The University of Wisconsin—Milwaukee
Department of Geography
Map Library
Milwaukee, WI 53211

Milwaukee Public Library
Documents
814 W. Wisconsin Ave.
Milwaukee, WI 53233

Reference Librarian
Beloit College Libraries
Beloit, WI 53511

Map Library, Science Hall
University of Wisconsin
550 N. Park St.
Madison, WI 53706

Wisconsin State Historical Society
Manuscripts & Maps Section
816 State St.
Madison, WI 53706

Karrmann Library
Government Publications
University of Wisconsin—Platteville
Plateville, WI 53818

University of Wisconsin Center
Manitowoc County
705 Viebahn St.
Manitowoc, WI 54220

Government Publications Department
Library Learning Center
University of Wisconsin–Green Bay
Green Bay, WI 54302

Department of Geography
University of Wisconsin
Stevens Point, WI 54481

Library–Documents
Wisconsin State University
La Crosse WI 54601

University of Wisconsin—La Crosse
Murphy Library
1631 Pine St.
La Crosse, WI 54601

Simpson Geography Research Center
Department of Geography
University of Wisconsin–Eau Claire
Eau Claire, WI 54701

Department of Geology
University of Wisconsin—Oshkosh
Oshkosh, WI 54901

Government Documents
Seeley G. Mudd Library
Lawrence University
Appleton, WI 54911

## West Virginia

Library
West Virginia State College
Institute, WV 25112

Learning Resource Center
Mesa Academy
Airport Road
Beckley, WV 25801

Library, Map Room
West Virginia University
Morgantown, WV 26506

West Virginia University Library
Reference Department
Morgantown, WV 26506

## Wyoming

Wyoming State Library
Supreme Court & State Library Building
Cheyenne, WY 82002

Librarian
Coe Library
University of Wyoming
P. O. Box 3334, University Station
Laramie, WY 82071

Central Wyoming College
Library
Riverton, WY 82501

Western History Librarian
Casper College
125 College Dr.
Casper, WY 82601

Natrona County Public Library
307 E. Second St.
Casper, WY 82601

Information Services Librarian
George Amos Memorial Library
412 S. Gillette Ave.
Gillette, WY 82716

Librarian
Griffith Memorial Library
Sheridan College
Sheridan, WY 82801

# B. Defense Mapping Agency Depositories

*The Defense Mapping Agency provides the basic mapping for the military forces under the Department of Defense. Their depository program began after World War II when the Army Map Service, as it was then called, distributed thousands of captured maps to many libraries and academic departments. The program continued to grow with annual shipments of surplus maps to a select group of libraries. Currently, this program is being merged with those depositories of the Government Printing Office and the U.S. Geological Survey. Those libraries below are members of the "old" depository program and will surely expand in the future with the reorganization of the Federal mapping distribution program.*

## Alabama

Special Collections Department
Ralph Brown Draughon Library
Auburn University
Auburn, AL 36849

The University of Alabama
Department of Geography
P. O. Box 1982
University, AL 35486

Department of Geography
College Station
University of North Alabama
Florence, AL 35630

Library
Auburn University at Montgomery
Montgomery, AL 36117

## Arizona

Map Collection, University Library
Arizona State University
Tempe, AZ 85281

University of Arizona
Tucson, AZ 85721

## Arkansas

Government Documents
University Libraries
University of Arkansas
Fayetteville, AR 72701

## California

Department of Geography
California State University
Fullerton, CA 92634

Marine Geology Library, MS99
USGS, Pacific Branch
345 Middlefield Rd.
Menlo Park, CA 94025

California State College
5800 State College Parkway
San Bernardino, CA 92407

Library
California State College
Stanislaus
800 Monte Vista Ave.
Turlock, CA 95380

Library–Maps
California State University
Chico, CA 95929

Library
California State University
Fresno, CA 93740

Department of Geography
California State University
1250 Bellflower Blvd.
Long Beach, CA 90840

Department of Geography & Urban
  Studies
California State University
5151 State University Drive
Los Angeles, CA 90032

Department of Geography
Map Library
California State University
18111 Nordhoff St.
Northridge, CA 91330

The Honnold Library
The Claremont Colleges
Claremont, CA 91711

Earth Sciences Department
Los Angeles City College
855 N. Vermont Ave.
Los Angeles, CA 90029

Map Room, History Department
Los Angeles Public Library
630 W. 5th St.
Los Angeles, CA 90071

History & Literature Department
The Oakland Public Library
125 14th St.
Oakland, CA 94612

Government Publications
Map Collection
University Library

San Diego State University
San Diego, CA 92182

San Francisco State University
Government Documents Department
1630 Holloway Ave.
San Francisco, CA 94132

Central Map Collection
Cecil H. Green Library
Stanford University Library
Stanford, CA 94305

Map Room
General Library
University of California
Berkeley, CA 94720

Map Collection
Shields Library
University of California
Davis, CA 95616

UCLA Map Library
Social Sciences Building
University of California
Los Angeles, CA 90024

Government Publications Department
University of California Library
P. O. Box 5900
Riverside, CA 92507

Map Section–C-075P
University Library
University of California, San Diego
La Jolla, CA 92093

Map & Imagery Collection Library
University of California
Santa Barbara, CA 93106

University Library
Map Collection
University of California
Santa Cruz, CA 95064

Catalog Department
Doheny Memorial Library, USC
University Park
Los Angeles, CA 90007

Map Collection
University Library
Humboldt State University
Arcata, CA 95501

## Colorado

Map Room
Arthur Lakes Library
Colorado School of Mines
Golden, CO 80401

Libraries
Colorado State University
Fort Collins, CO 80523

Denver Public Library
Government Publications Department
1357 Broadway
Denver, CO 80203

Fountain Valley School
Colorado Springs, CO 80911

Earth Science Library
Campus Box 184
University of Colorado
Boulder, CO 80309

Department of Geography
University of Denver
Denver, CO 80210

## Connecticut

Department of Geography
Central Connecticut State College
New Britain, CT 06050

Hartford Public Library
Reference Department
500 Main St.
Hartford, CT 06103

Reference Department
Hilton C. Buley Library
Southern Connecticut State College
501 Crescent St.
New Haven, CT 06515

Map Room
Library, U-5
University of Connecticut
Storrs, CT 06268

Map Room
Science Library
Wesleyan University
Middletown, CT 06457

Map Collection
Yale University Library
Box 1603A Yale Station
New Haven, CT 06520

## Delaware

Map Department
University of Delaware Library
Newark, DE 19711

## District of Columbia

Consortium of Universities
  of the Metro Area
G. Washington University Library
2130 H St., N.W.
Washington, DC 20052

Geography & Map Division
Library of Congress
Washington, DC 20052

National Geographic Society
Cartographic Division–Map Library
17th & M Streets, N.W.
Washington, DC 20036

**Florida**

Florida Atlantic University Library
Collection Development Department
Boca Raton, FL 33432

Map Division
R. M. Strozier Library
Florida State University
Tallahassee, FL 32306

Map Library–Library East
University of Florida Libraries
University of Florida
Gainesville, FL 32611

Department of Geography
University of Miami
Box 24–8152–University Branch
Coral Gables, FL 33124

University of South Florida
Documents Library
Tampa, FL 33620

Library–Reference Department
University of North Florida
P. O. Box 17605
Jacksonville, FL 32216

**Georgia**

Price Gilbert Memorial Library
Georgia Institute of Technology
Atlanta, GA 30332

Map Collection
Science Library
University of Georgia Libraries
Athens, GA 30602

**Hawaii**

Map Librarian, Hamilton Library
University of Hawaii
2550 The Mall
Honolulu, HI 96822

Pacific Scientific Information Center
Bernice P. Bishop Museum
P. O. Box 19000-A
Honolulu, HI 96819

**Idaho**

Idaho State University Library
Pocatello, ID 83843

University of Idaho Library
Social Sciences
Moscow, ID 83843

**Illinois**

Department of Geography
Augustana College
Rock Island, IL 61201

Eastern Illinois University
Booth Library
Serials Dept., Map Section
Charleston, IL 61920

The James S. Kemper Library
Illinois Institute of Technology
3300 South Federal St.
Chicago, IL 60616

Map Library
Illinois State University
Normal, IL 61761

Illinois Valley Community
College Library
R.R. #1
Oglesby, IL 61348

Map Library
Room 222, Davis Hall
University of Northern Illinois
DeKalb, IL 60115

Map Collection
The University Library
Northwestern University
Evanston, IL 60201

Science Division
Morris Library
Southern Illinois University
Carbondale, IL 62901

Lovejoy Library
Box 63
Southern Illinois University
Edwardsville, IL 62026

Map Library
J. Regenstein Library
University of Chicago
1100 E. 57th St.
Chicago, IL 60637

The Library, Map Section
University of Illinois at Chicago Circle
P. O. Box 8198
Chicago, IL 60680

Map & Geography Library
University of Illinois Library
University of Illinois
Urbana, IL 61801

Map–Geography Library
Department of Geography
Western Illinois University
Macomb, IL 61455

Illinois State Library
Centennial Building
Springfield, IL 62706

**Indiana**

Map Collection
Department of Library Service
Ball State University
Muncie, IN 47306

Geography & Map Library
Indiana University
Kirkwood Hall
Bloomington, IN 47405

Map Collection
Purdue University Libraries
Stewart Center
West Lafayette, IN 47907

Geography & Geology Dept.
Indiana State University
Terre Haute, IN 47809

Microtext Reading Room
Memorial Library
University of Notre Dame
Notre Dame, IN 46556

Map Librarian
Moellering Library
Valparaiso University
Valparaiso, IN 46383

**Iowa**

Government Publications Department
Iowa State University Library
Iowa State University
Ames, IA 50011

Map Collection
University of Iowa Libraries
Iowa City, IA 52242

Loras College
Library
14th & Alta Vista Streets
Dubuque, IA 52001

**Kansas**

Kansas University Map Library
Spenser Research Library
University of Kansas
Lawrence, KS 66045

**Kentucky**

Map Department, MIK Library
University of Kentucky
Lexington, KY 40506

Reference Department
University of Louisville
Library
Belknap Campus
Louisville, KY 40208

**Louisiana**

School of Geoscience
Louisiana State University
Baton Rouge, LA 70803

Southern University Library
Southern Branch P. O.
Baton Rouge, LA 70813

U. S. Government Documents
Tulane University Library
New Orleans, LA 70118

**Maine**

Bowdoin College Library
Brunswick, ME 04011

Nutting Memorial Library
Maine Maritime Academy
Castine, ME 04421

Government Documents Department
Raymond H. Fogler Library
University of Maine
Orono, ME 04473

**Maryland**

Enoch Pratt Free Library
General Information Department
400 Cathedral Avenue
Baltimore, MD 21201

Geography Department
Frostburg College
Frostburg, MD 21532

Department of Geography &
   Environmental Planning
Towson State University
Towson, MD 21204

Documents/Maps Room
McKeldin Library
University of Maryland
College Park, MD 20742

**Massachusetts**

Amherst College Library
Amherst, MA 01002

Boston Public Library
Copley Square
Boston, MA 02117

Boston State College
Department of Regional Studies
625 Huntington Ave.
Boston, MA 02115

Clement C. Maxwell Library
Bridgewater State College
Bridgewater, MA 02324

Map Library
Graduate School of Geography
Clark University
Worcester, MA 01610

Harvard Map Collection
Harvard College Library
Cambridge, MA 02138

Stein Club Map Room
Room 14S-100
Massachusetts Institute of Technology
Cambridge, MA 02139

Capt. C. H. Hurley Library
Massachusetts Maritime Academy
Taylor's Point
Buzzards Bay, MA 02532

Department of Geology
Smith College
Northampton, MA 01060

Southeastern Massachusetts University
Library Communications Center
P. O. Box 6, Old Westport Rd.
North Dartmouth, MA 02747

University of Massachusetts Library
Amherst, MA 01002

Department of Geology
Wellesley College
Wellesley, MA 02181

Woods Hole Oceanographic Institute
Data Library, McLean Laboratory
Quissett Campus
Woods Hole, MA 02543

**Minnesota**

Department of Geography
Gustavus Adolphus College
St. Peter, MN 56082

Map Library
Memorial Library
Mankato State College
Mankato, MN 56001

Alcuin Library
St. John's University
Collegeville, MN 56321

Map Division
O. M. Wilson University of Minnesota
Minneapolis, MN 55455

**Mississippi**

Mississippi State University Library
P. O. Drawer 5408
Mississippi State, MS 39762

Documents Department
University of Mississippi Library
University, MS 38677

University of Southern Mississippi
Southern Station, Box 5053
Hattiesburg, MS 39406-5053

**Missouri**

Geography Department
Wood Building, Room 6
Central Missouri State University
Warrensburg, MO 64093

St. Louis Public Library
1301 Olive St.
St. Louis, MO 63103

Map Collection
Box 175, Library
Southwest Missouri State University
901 S. National Ave.
Springfield, MO 65804-0095

3B33 Ellis Library
University of Missouri
Columbia, MO 65201

Department of Geology & Geophysics
University of Missouri
Rolla, MO 65401

Earth & Planetary Sciences Library
Washington University
St. Louis, MO 63130

**Montana**

Library of Montana College of Mineral
   Science & Technology
Butte, MT 59701

Department of Earth Sciences
Montana State University
Bozeman, MT 59715

Documents Division
University of Montana Library
Missoula, MT 59812

**Nebraska**

Documents
207 Love Library
University of Nebraska
Lincoln, NE 68588-0410

**Nevada**

Mines Library
University of Nevada
Reno, NV 89557

**New Hampshire**

Dartmouth College Library
Hanover, NH 03755

**New Jersey**

Map Division
Princeton University Library
Princeton, NJ 08540

Government Documents Department
Library of Science & Medicine
Rutgers University
Piscataway, NJ 08903

Department of Geography
Trenton State College
Trenton, NJ 08625

**New Mexico**

Documents Department
Golden Library
Eastern New Mexico University
Portales, NM 88130

Special Collections Librarian
New Mexico State University
Box 3475
Las Cruces, NM 88003

Map Room, Zimmerman Library
University of New Mexico
Albuquerque, NM 87131

**New York**

Brooklyn Public Library
Ingersoll Bldg., Grand Army Plaza
History Division
Brooklyn, NY 11238

Documents Division
Buffalo and Erie County Public Library
Lafayette Square
Buffalo, NY 14203

Department of Geography
Colgate University
Hamilton, NY 13346

Columbia University, Map Room
International Affairs Library
420 W. 118th St.
New York, NY 10027

Cornell University Libraries
Ithaca, NY 14853

Hofstra University Library
1000 Fulton Ave.
Hempstead, NY 11550

Map Division
The New York Public Library
Fifth Avenue & 42nd St.
New York, NY 10018

New York State Library
Manuscripts & Special Collections
Cultural Education Center
Albany, NY 12230

Hunter College of the City University
   of New York
Department of Geology & Geography
695 Park Avenue
New York, NY 10021

Acquisitions Department Library
Rensselaer Polytechnic Institute
Troy, NY 12181

James M. Milne Library
State University College
Oneonta, NY 13820

SUNY at Binghamton Library
Binghamton, NY 13901

Map Collection
Science & Engineering Library
SUNY at Buffalo
Amherst, NY 14226

Main Library, Map Library
SUNY at Stony Brook
Stony Brook, NY 11794

Area Studies, Bird Library
Syracuse University
Syracuse, NY 13210

Department of Geology & Geography
Vassar College
Poughkeepsie, NY 12601

**North Carolina**

Geography Department
Appalachian State University
Boone, NC 28608

LLRC
Cape Fear Technical Institute
411 North Front St.
Wilmington, NC 28401

Public Documents Department
William R. Perkins Library
Duke University
Durham, NC 27706

Department of Geography
East Carolina University
P. O. Box 2723
Greenville, NC 27834

James E. Shepard Memorial Library
North Carolina Central University
Durham, NC 27707

Documents Department
D. H. Hill Library
North Carolina State University
Box 5007
Raleigh, NC 27650

Map Collection
University of North Carolina Library
Chapel Hill, NC 27514

Documents Department
J. M. Atkins Library
University of North Carolina
UNCC Station
Charlotte, NC 28223

Hunter Library
Western Carolina University
Cullowhee, NC 29723

**North Dakota**

Library
North Dakota State University
Fargo, ND 58102

Department of Geography
University of North Dakota
Grand Forks, ND 58202

**Ohio**

Map Library
Bowling Green State University
Bowling Green, OH 43403

Map Collection
Cleveland Public Library
325 Superior Ave.
Cleveland, OH 44114

Map Library Supervisor
406 McGilvrey Hall
Kent State University
Kent, OH 44242

Science Library
Miami University
Oxford, OH 45056

Map Library
The Ohio State University
1858 Neil Ave.
Columbus, OH 43210

Ohio University Library
Athens, OH 45701

Public Library of Cincinnati & Hamilton
   County
800 Vine St.
Cincinnati, OH 45202

Geography Department
100 Swift Hall
University of Cincinnati
Cincinnati, OH 45221

University of Toledo Libraries
University of Toledo
Toledo, OH 43606

**Oklahoma**

Documents Department
Oklahoma State University Library
Stillwater, OK 74078

Geology Library
830 Van Vleet Oval, Room 103
The University of Oklahoma
Norman, OK 73019

McFarlin Library
University of Tulsa
600 S. College
Tulsa, OK 74104

## Oregon

The Library Association of Portland
Multnomah County Library
801 S.W. 10th Ave.
Portland, OR 97205

William Jasper Kerr Library
Oregon State University
Corvallis, OR 97331

Portland State University Library
P. O. Box 1151
Portland, OR 97207

Map Librarian, Map Library
University of Oregon
Eugene, OR 97403

## Pennsylvania

Department of Geology
Bryn Mawr College
Bryn Mawr, PA 19010

The Free Library of Philadelphia
Map Collection
Logan Square
Philadelphia, PA 19103

Department of Geography
Map Collection
Millersville State College

Department of Earth Sciences
Moravian College
Bethlehem, PA 18018

Pattee Library, Maps Section
The Pennsylvania State University
University Park, PA 16802

Department of Geography
Slippery Rock State College
Slippery Rock, PA 16057

Geology Map Library
Hayden Hall
University of Pennsylvania
Philadelphia, PA 19104

Map Librarian
G-8 Hillman Hall
University of Pittsburgh
Pittsburgh, PA 15260

Document & Map Librarian
Library
West Chester State College
West Chester, PA 19380

## Puerto Rico

University of Puerto Rico
General Library
Documents & Maps Room
Rio Piedras, Puerto Rico 00931

## Rhode Island

Documents Department
Brown University
Providence, RI 02912

Special Collections Librarian
University of Rhode Island
Kingston, RI 02881

## South Carolina

Robert Muldrow Cooper Library
Public Documents Unit
Clemson, SC 29361

Map Library
University of South Carolina
Columbia, SC 29208

## South Dakota

Documents Department
H. M. Briggs Library
South Dakota State University
Brookings, SD 57007

## Tennessee

Sherrod Library
East Tennessee State University
Johnson City, TN 37601

The Map Library
J. W. Brister Library
Memphis State University
Memphis, TN 38152

Map Library
Department of Geography
University of Tennessee
Knoxville, TN 37916

## Texas

Baylor University Library
Box 6307
Waco, TX 76706

Prairie View A & M University Library
P. O. Drawer T
Prairie View, TX 77445

Reference/Collection Development Dept.
Fondren Library
Rice University
P. O. Box 1892
Houston, TX 77001

Science Engineering Library
Southern Methodist University
Dallas, TX 75272

University of Houston Libraries
Map Collection
4800 Calhoun Blvd.
Houston, TX 77004

Geography–Geology Department
Texas A & I University
Kingsville, TX 78363

Texas A & M University
University Library, Map Room
College Station, TX 77843

Texas A & M University
Texas Maritime Academy
P. O. Box 1675
Galveston, TX 77553

Documents Collection
University of Texas
The General Library PCL 2.403
Austin, TX 78712

Marine Science Institute
Geophysics Laboratory
700 The Strand
Galveston, TX 77550

The Library Annex–Map Section
Documents & Maps Library
The University of Texas
El Paso, TX 79968

Department of Geoscience (Geog)
West Texas State University
Canyon, TX 79016

## Utah

Map Collection
1354 HBLL
Brigham Young University
Provo, UT 84602

159 Mariott Library
University of Utah
Salt Lake City, UT 84112

Utah State University
Merrill Library & Learning Resources
  Program
Logan, UT 84332

## Vermont

Middlebury College
410 Warner Science Hall
Middlebury, VT 05753

Map Librarian
Bailey/Howe Library
University of Vermont
Burlington, VT 05405

## Virginia

University Libraries
Virginia Polytechnic Institute

State University
Blacksburg, VA 24060

Virginia State Library
Richmond, VA 23219

Public Documents
Alderman Library
University of Virginia
Charlottesville, VA 22901

**Washington**

Central Washington University
Documents Department
Library
Ellensburg, WA 98926

Seattle Public Library
1000 Fourth Ave.
Seattle, WA 98104

Owen Science & Engineering Library
Serial Record
Washington State University
Pullman, WA 99164

Map Library
Western Washington University
Bellingham, WA 98225

Penrose Memorial Library
Whitman College
345 Boyer Ave.
Walla Walla, WA 99362

Map Section
University of Washington
Libraries, Room 25
Seattle, WA 98195

**West Virginia**

West Virginia University Library
Morgantown, WV 26506-6069

**Wisconsin**

Beloit College Libraries
Beloit, WI 53511

Seeley G. Mudd Library
Periodicals Department
Lawrence University
Appleton, WI 54911

American Geographical Society Collection
  of The University of Wisconsin
Milwaukee Library
P. O. Box 399
Milwaukee, WI 53201

Milwaukee Public Library
814 W. Wisconsin Ave.
Milwaukee, WI 53233

Map Library–Science Hall
University of Wisconsin
550 N. Park St.
Madison, WI 53706

University of Wisconsin
Library–Government Publications
Green Bay, WI 54302

Geography Department, Map Library
Sabin Hall, Room 385
University of Wisconsin
Milwaukee, WI 53201

Documents Division
Polk Library
The University of Wisconsin
Oshkosh, WI 54901

Karrmann Library
University of Wisconsin
Platteville, WI 53818

Geography/Geology Department
University of Wisconsin
Stevens Point, WI 54481

Documents & Research Collections
University of Wisconsin
Whitewater, WI 53190

**Wyoming**

COE Library, Documents Division
University of Wyoming
Box 3334, University Station
Laramie, WY 82071

# C. National Cartographic Information Centers & Affiliates

*The National Cartographic Information Center (NCIC) was formed in 1973 to coordinate the cartographic information gathering activities of the federal government. It soon expanded to include the four regional mapping centers and their state affiliates. These centers and affiliates have up-to-date information on the availability of cartographic products for their respective areas and are designated public service units.*

National Cartographic Information Center
U. S. Geological Survey
507 National Center
Reston, Virginia 22092
(703) 860-6045

Eastern Mapping Center
National Cartographic Information Center
U. S. Geological Survey
536 National Center
Reston, Virginia 22092
(703) 860-6336

Mid-Continent Mapping Center
National Cartographic Information Center
U. S. Geological Survey
1400 Independence Road
Rolla, Missouri 65401
(314) 341-0851

National Space Technology Laboratories
National Cartographic Information Center
U. S. Geological Survey
Building 3101
NSTL Station, Mississippi 39529
(601) 688-3544

Rocky Mountain Mapping Center
National Cartographic Information Center
U. S. Geological Survey
Stop 504, Box 25046, Federal Center
Denver, Colorado 80225
(303) 236-5829

Western Mapping Center
National Cartographic Information Center
U. S. Geological Survey
345 Middlefield Road
Menlo Park, California 94025
(415) 323-8111 ext. 2427

Alaska Office
National Cartographic Information Center
U. S. Geological Survey
4232 University Drive
Anchorage, Alaska 99508-4664
(907) 271-4159

EROS Data Center
U. S. Geological Survey
Sioux Falls, South Dakota 57198
(605) 594-6507

NCIC FEDERAL AFFILIATES

Tennessee Valley Authority
200 Baney Building
311 Broad Street
Chattanooga, Tennessee 37401
(615) 751-MAPS

NCIC STATE AFFILIATES

## Alabama

Geological Survey of Alabama
420 Hackberry Lane
P. O. Box O, University Station
University of Alabama 35486
(205) 349-2852

## Arizona

Arizona State Land Department
Information Resources Division
1624 West Adams, Room 302
Phoenix, Arizona 85007
(602) 255-4061

Arizona State Library
Dept. of Archives and Records
Map Services
1700 West Washington
Phoenix, Arizona 85007
(602) 255-4046

## Arkansas

Arkansas Geological Commission
Vardelle Parham Geology Center
3815 West Roosevelt Road
Little Rock, Arkansas 72204
(501) 371-1488

## California

Map and Imagery Laboratory Library
Library, University of California
Santa Barbara, California 93106
(805) 961-2779

Map Information Office
State of California
1416 9th Street
P. O. Box 388
Sacramento, California 95802
(916) 445-9259

## Connecticut

Natural Resources Center
Dept. of Environmental Protection
165 Capitol Avenue
Room 553
Hartford, Connecticut 06106
(203) 566-3540

*Satellite Office*

University of Connecticut Library
Map Library, Level 4
Storrs, Connecticut 06268
(203) 486-4589

## Delaware

Delaware Geological Survey
University of Delaware
101 Penny Hall
Newark, Delaware 19716
(302) 451-2833

## Georgia

Office of Research and Information
Department of Community Affairs
40 Marietta Street, N.W., Suite 800
Atlanta, Georgia 30303
(404) 656-2900

## Hawaii

Department of Planning and Economic
  Development
Kamamalu Building
250 South King St.
Honolulu, Hawaii 96813
(808) 548-3047

## Idaho

Idaho State Historical Library
325 West State
Boise, Idaho 83702
(208) 334-3356

## Illinois

(User Services)
  University of Illinois at Urbana-
    Champaign
  Map & Geography Library
  1407 West Gregory Drive
  Urbana, Illinois 61801
  (217) 333-0827

(Data Acquisition)
  Illinois State Geological Survey
  615 East Peabody Drive
  Champaign, Illinois 61820
  (217) 344-1481

## Kentucky

Director and State Geologist
Kentucky Geological Survey
311 Breckinridge Hall
University of Kentucky
Lexington, Kentucky 40506
(606) 257-3196

## Louisiana

Office of Public Works
Department of Transportation and
  Development
P. O. Box 94245 Capitol Station
Baton Rouge, Louisiana 70804-9245
(504) 342-7773

## Maryland

Maryland Geological Survey
The Rotunda, Suite 440
711 West 40th Street
Baltimore, Maryland 21211
(301) 338-7212

## Massachusetts

University of Massachusetts
Director/Coordinator
Cartographic Information Research

Services
102D Hasbrouck Laboratory
Amherst, Massachusetts 01003
(413) 545-0359

## Michigan

Division of Land Resource Programs
Michigan Department of Natural
  Resources
Steven T. Mason Building, Box 30028
Lansing, Michigan 48909
(517) 373-3328

## Minnesota

Minnesota State Planning Agency
Land Management Information Center
Room LL65, Metro Square Building
7th & Robert Streets
Saint Paul, Minnesota 55101
(612) 297-2490

## Mississippi

Geographic Information Systems Division
Mississippi Research and Development
  Center
3825 Ridgewood Road
Jackson, Mississippi 39211
(601) 982-6606

## Missouri

Missouri Department of Natural
  Resources
Division of Geology and Land Survey
P. O. Box 250
Rolla, Missouri 65401
(314) 364-1752

## Montana

Montana Bureau of Mines and Geology
Montana Tech
Main Hall, Room 200
Butte, Montana 59701
(406) 496-4167

## Nebraska

Director and State Geologist
Conservation and Survey Division
University of Nebraska
Lincoln, Nebraska 68508
(402) 472-3471

## Nevada

Nevada Bureau of Mines and Geology
University of Nevada, Reno
Reno, Nevada 89557-0088
(702) 784-6691

## New Hampshire

Documents Librarian
Documents Department
Dimond Library
University of New Hampshire
Durham, New Hampshire 03824

(603) 862-1777

**New Jersey**

Department of Environmental Protection
New Jersey Geological Survey
CN-029
Trenton, New Jersey 08625
(609) 292-2576

**New Mexico**

University of New Mexico
Technology Applications Center
2500 Central Avenue, S.E.
Albuquerque, N. M. 87131
(505) 277-3622

**North Carolina**

Chief, Geological Survey Section
Division of Land Resources, DNRCD
P. O. Box 27687
Raleigh, North Carolina 27611
(919) 733-2423

**North Dakota**

North Dakota State Water Commission
State Office Building
209 East Boulevard
Bismarck, North Dakota 58501
(701) 224-2750

**Ohio**

Ohio Dept. of Natural Resources
Division of Soil and Water
Conservation Division
Remote Sensing Center
Fountain Square, Building E
Columbus, Ohio 43224
(614) 265-6610

**Oregon**

Oregon State Library
Public Services
Salem, Oregon 97310
(503) 378-4502

University of Oregon
Geography Dept., Map Library
165 Condon Hall
Eugene, Oregon 97403
(503) 686-3051

**Pennsylvania**

Department of Environmental Resources
Bureau of Topographic and Geological
    Survey
P. O. Box 2357
Harrisburg, Pennsylvania 17120
(717) 787-2169

**Rhode Island**

Rhode Island Cartographic Information
    Center
Marine Resources Building
University of Rhode Island
Narragansett, Rhode Island 02882
(401) 792-6539

**South Carolina**

South Carolina Land Resources
    Conservation Commission
2221 Devine Street, Suite 222
Columbia, South Carolina 29205
(803) 758-2823

**Tennessee**

Tennessee Division of Geology
701 Broadway
Nashville, Tennessee 37203
(615) 742-6696

**Texas**

Texas Natural Resources Information
    System
P. O. Box 13087
Austin, Texas 78711
(512) 475-3321

**Utah**

Utah Geological and Mineral Survey
606 Black Hawk Way
Research Park

Salt Lake City, Utah 84108-1280
(801) 581-6831

**Virginia**

Department of Conservation and
    Economic Development
Division of Mineral Resources
Natural Resources Building
Box 3667
Charlottesville, Virginia 22903
(804) 293-5121

**Washington**

(User Services)
    Washington State Library
    Information Services Division
    Olympia, Washington 98504
    (206) 753-4027

(Data Acquisitions)
    Division of Management Services
    Photos, Maps and Reports Section
    2165 Capitol Way
    Olympia, Washington 98504
    (206) 753-5338

**West Virginia**

West Virginia Geological and
    Economic Survey
West Virginia Cartographic Center
P. O. Box 879
Morgantown, West Virginia 26505
(304) 594-2331

**Wisconsin**

State Cartographer's Office
144 Science Hall
550 North Park Street
Madison, Wisconsin 53706
(608) 262-3065

**Wyoming**

State Engineer
Barrett Building
Cheyenne, Wyoming 82002
(307) 777-7354

# D. State Information Resources

*Each state has a multitude of agencies that create, disseminate and use cartographic information in a variety of formats. Listed below is an address file for each state compiled by the U. S. Geological Survey.*

**Alabama**

Alabama Bureau of Publicity &
    Information
532 S. Perry St.
Montgomery, AL 36130
(205) 261-4169
1-800-ALABAMA (Out-of-State, except

Alaska & Hawaii)
800-392-8096 (In-State)

State of Alabama Highway Department
Bureau of State Planning
11 S. Union St., Room 313
Montgomery, AL 36130

(205) 832-5354 Bureau Chief
(205) 832-6128 Map Room 110

Geological Survey of Alabama
P. O. Drawer O
University, AL 35486
(205) 349-2852

NCIC State Affiliate

Alabama Department of Aeronautics
11 S. Union St.
State Highway Building
Montgomery, AL 36130
(205) 832-6290

Alabama Department of Conservation
& Natural Resources
Division of State Parks
64 N. Union St.
Montgomery, AL 36130
(205) 832-6323

## Alaska

Division of Tourism
Alaska Department of Commerce &
Economic Development
Pouch E
Juneau, AK 99811
(907) 465-2010

Department of Natural Resources
Division of Geological & Geophysical
Surveys
Pouch 7-028
Anchorage, AK 99510
(907) 276-2653

Division of Mining
Mines Information Office
794 University Ave., Basement
Fairbanks, AK 99701
(907) 474-7062

Alaska Department of Transportation &
Public Facilities
Division of Design & Construction
Pouch 6900
411 Aviation Dr.
Anchorage, AK 99502
(907) 266-1500

Department of Natural Resources
Division of Technical Services
Pouch 7035
Anchorage, AK 99510
(907) 786-2291

Department of Natural Resources
Division of Land & Water Management
Pouch 7-005
Anchorage, AK 99510
(907) 265-4355

Alaska Department of Transportation
& Public Facilities
Bridge Design
P. O. Box 1467
Juneau, AK 99802
(907) 789-0841

## American Samoa

Office of Tourism
Government of American Samoa
P. O. Box 1147
Pago Pago, American Samoa 96799

## Arizona

Arizona Highways
2039 W. Lewis Ave.
Phoenix, AZ 85009
(602) 258-6641

Arizona State Land Department
Information Resources Division
1624 W. Adams, Room 302
Phoenix, AZ 85007
(902) 255-4061
NCIC State Affiliate

Arizona Office of Economic Planning
and Development
1700 W. Washington, Room 505
Phoenix, AZ 85007
(602) 255-5371

Arizona Bureau of Geology & Mineral
Technology
845 N. Park Ave.
Tucson, AZ 85719
(602) 626-2733

Arizona State Office of Tourism
3507 N. Central Ave.
Suite 506
Phoenix, AZ 85012
(602) 255-3618

Arizona Department of Transportation
206 S. 17th Ave., Room 181A
Phoenix, AZ 85007
(602) 261-7325

Arizona Department of Transportation
Aeronautics Division
1801 W. Jefferson, Room 426M
Phoenix, AZ 85007
(602) 261-7691

## Arkansas

Arkansas State Highway &
Transportation Department
Map Sales, Room 203
9500 New Benton Highway
P. O. Box 2261
Little Rock, AR 72203
(501) 569-2444

Arkansas Geological Commission
3815 W. Roosevelt Rd.
Vardelle Parham Geology Center
Little Rock, AR 72204
(501) 371-1488 or 371-1646
NCIC State Affiliate

Arkansas Division of Aeronautics
Adams Field–Old Terminal Building
Little Rock, AR 72202
(501) 376-6781

## California

California Department of Transportation
1120 N St.
P. O. Box 1499
Sacramento, CA 95807
(916) 445-4616
(916) 324-6732 (Map Orders)

California Department of Conservation
Division of Mines & Geology
1416 9th St., Room 1341
Sacramento, CA 95814
(916) 445-0514

California Department of Transportation
Division of Aeronautics
1120 N St.
Sacramento, CA 95814
(916) 322-3090

California Department of Water
Resources
Map Information Office
Division of Planning
P. O. Box 388
Sacramento, CA 95802
(916) 445-9259

## Colorado

State Cartographer
Colorado Division of Local Government
1313 Sherman St., Room 520
Denver, CO 80203
(303) 866-3004

Colorado Geological Survey
Department of Natural Resources
1313 Sherman St., Room 715
Denver, CO 80203
(303) 866-2611

Report Preparation Section
Division of Transportation Planning
Colorado Department of Highways
4201 E. Arkansas Ave.
Denver, CO 80222
(303) 757-9523

## Connecticut

Division of Tourism
Connecticut Department of Economic
Development
210 Washington St.
Hartford, CT 06106
(203) 566-3385

Connecticut Department of
Transportation
24 Wolcott Hill Rd.
P. O. Drawer "A"
Wethersfield, CT 06109
(203) 566-2410

Department of Environmental Protection
Natural Resources Center
State Office Building, Room 553
Hartford, CT 06106
(203) 566-3540
NCIC State Affiliate

Connecticut Department of
 Transportation
Bureau of Aeronautics
24 Wolcott Hill Rd.
Wethersfield, CT 06109
(203) 566-3076

Connecticut Geological & Natural
 History Survey
Department of Environmental Protection
State Office Building, Room 561
Hartford, CT 06106
(203) 566-3540

## Delaware

Delaware Department of Transportation
Office of Planning & Programming
P. O. Box 778
Highways Administration Building
Dover, DE 19903
(302) 736-4346

Delaware Geological Survey
University of Delaware
101 Penny Hall
Newark, DE 19716
(302) 451-2833
NCIC State Affiliate

Delaware Development Office
P. O. Box 1401
99 Kings Highway
Dover, DE 19903
(302) 736-4271

## District of Columbia

Department of Public Works
Office of Policy & Planning
415 12th St., N.W.
Room 519
Washington, D. C. 20004
Office: (202) 727-5764
Map Distribution Info: (202) 727-5764

## Florida

Division of Tourism
Florida Department of Commerce
107 W. Gaines St., Room 505
Tallahassee, FL 32301
(904) 488-5606
(904) 487-1462 (for maps, brochures,
 travel information)

Department of Transportation
Haydon Burns Building
605 Suwannee St.
Tallahassee, FL 32301

Department of Natural Resources
Bureau of Geology
903 W. Tennessee St.
Tallahassee, FL 32301
(904) 488-4191

Florida Department of Natural Resources
Division of Recreation & Parks
3900 Commonwealth Blvd.
Tallahassee, FL 32303
(904) 488-6131

## Georgia

Office of Research & Evaluation
Department of Community Affairs
40 Marietta St., N.W.
Eighth Floor
Atlanta, GA 30303
(404) 656-2900
NCIC State Affiliate

Georgia Department of Transportation
Map Sales Unit
2 Capitol Square
Atlanta, GA 30334
(404) 656-5336

Georgia Department of Transportation
Planning Data Services
Cartographic Branch
5025 New Peachtree Rd. N.E.
Chamblee, GA 30341
(404) 393-7370

## Guam

Department of Land Management
Government of Guam
P. O. Box 2950
Agana, Guam, U.S.A. 96910
(671) 472-8851

Department of Public Works
Government of Guam
P. O. Box 2950
Agana, Guam U.S.A. 96910
(671) 646-5831 Ext. 278

Guam Visitors Bureau
Bayview Plaza
1220 Pale San Vitores Rd.
P. O. Box 3520
Tamuning, Guam U.S.A. 96911
(671) 646-5278

Bureau of Planning
Government of Guam
P. O. Box 2950
Agana, Guam U.S.A. 96910
(671) 646-5278

## Hawaii

Hawaii Visitors Bureau
2270 Kalakaua Ave., Suite 801
Honolulu, HI 96815
(808) 923-1811

Hawaii Department of Transportation
869 Punchbowl St.
Honolulu, HI 96813
(808) 548-4719

Department of Land & Natural Resources
Division of Water & Land Development
P. O. Box 373
Honolulu, HI 96809
(808) 548-7539

Department of Planning & Economic
 Development
Kamamalu Building
250 S. King St.
Honolulu, HI 96813
(808) 548-3047
NCIC State Affiliate

## Idaho

Idaho Division of Economic & Community
 Affairs
State Capitol Building, Room 108
Boise, ID 83720
(208) 334-4714

Idaho Bureau of Mines & Geology
Room 332 Morrill Hall
University of Idaho
Moscow, ID 83843
(208) 885-7991

Idaho Transportation Department
Management Services Section
P. O. Box 7129
Boise, ID 83707
(208) 334-2569

Idaho State Historical Library
325 W. State
Boise, ID 83702
(208) 334-3356
NCIC State Affiliate

Idaho Department of Fish & Game
P. O. Box 25
Boise, ID 83707
(208) 334-3700

## Illinois

Illinois Department of Transportation
2300 S. Dirksen Pkwy.
Springfield, IL 62764
(217) 782-7820

Illinois Office of Tourism
Department of Commerce & Community
 Affairs
2209 W. Main St.
Marion, IL 62959
(618) 997-4371

Illinois Office of Tourism
Department of Commerce & Community
 Affairs

620 E. Adams St.
Springfield, IL 62701
(217) 782-7139

Illinois Department of Conservation
160 N. LaSalle St.
Chicago, IL 60601
(312) 793-2070

Illinois Division of Aeronautics
Capital Airport
One Langhorne Bond Dr.
Springfield, IL 62706
(217) 753-4400

Illinois Tourist Information Center
310 South Michigan Ave., Suite 108
Chicago, IL 60604
(312) 793-2094

Illinois State Geological Survey
Natural Resources Building
615 E. Peabody Dr.
Champaign, IL 61820
(217) 344-1481
NCIC State Affiliate
(Data Acquisition)

University of Illinois at
   Urbana-Champaign
Map & Geography Library
1408 W. Gregory Dr.
Urbana, IL 61801
(217) 333-0827
NCIC State Affiliate
(User Services)

**Indiana**

Indiana Department of Commerce
Tourism Division
1 N. Capitol, Suite 700
Indianapolis, IN 46204-2243
(317) 232-8860

Indiana Department of Highways
Public Information Office
1106 State Office Building
100 N. Senate Ave.
Indianapolis, IN 46204
(317) 232-5115

Division of State Parks
Indiana Department of Natural Resources
616 State Office Building
Indianapolis, IN 46204
(317) 232-4124

Aeronautics Commission of Indiana
100 N. Senate Ave.
Indianapolis, IN 46204
(317) 232-3794

Publications Section
Indiana Geological Survey
611 N. Walnut Grove
Bloomington, IN 47405

(812) 335-7636

Division of Water
Indiana Department of Natural Resources
605 State Office Building
Indianapolis, IN 46204
(317) 232-4180

**Iowa**

Tourism
Iowa Development Commission
600 E. Court Ave.
Des Moines, IA 50306
(515) 281-3100

Iowa Conservation Commission
Wallace State Office Building
Des Moines, IA 50319
(515) 281-5145

Planning & Research Division
Iowa Department of Transportation
800 Lincoln Way
Ames, IA 50010
(515) 239-1661

Iowa Aeronautics Division
Department of Transportation
Des Moines Municipal Airport
Des Moines, IA 50321
(515) 281-4280

Iowa Geological Survey
123 N. Capitol St.
Iowa City, IA 52242
(319) 338-1173

**Kansas**

Travel & Tourism Division
Kansas Department of Economic
   Development
503 Kansas Ave., 6th Floor
Topeka, KS 66603
(913) 296-2009

Kansas Geological Survey
Raymond C. Moore Hall
1930 Constant Ave., Campus West
University of Kansas
Lawrence, KS 66044
(913) 864-3965

Bureau of Transportation Planning
Kansas Department of Transportation
State Office Building
Topeka, KS 66612
(913) 296-3841

Kansas Fish & Game Commission
Box 54A, RR2
Pratt, KS 67124
(316) 672-5911

Kansas Aviation Division
Department of Transportation
7th Floor, State Office Building

Topeka, KS 66612
(913) 296-2553

**Kentucky**

Kentucky Department of Travel
   Development
Capitol Plaza Tower, 22nd Floor
Frankfort, KY 40601
(502) 564-4930

Chief Drainage Engineer
Kentucky Transportation Cabinet
6th Floor, State Office Building
Frankfort, KY 40622
(502) 564-3280

Kentucky Geological Survey, NCIC
311 Breckinridge Hall
University of Kentucky
Lexington, KY 40506
(606) 257-3196
ATTN: NCIC Coordinator
NCIC State Affiliate

Division of Mass Transportation
7th Floor, State Office Building
Frankfort, KY 40622
(502) 564-7433

**Louisiana**

Louisiana Geological Survey
Box G, University Station
Baton Rouge, LA 70893
(504) 342-6754

Louisiana Office of Tourism
P. O. Box 44291, Capitol Station
Baton Rouge, LA 70804
(504) 925-3860

Louisiana Department of Transportation
   & Development
Office of Aviation & Public Transportation
P. O. Box 44245, Capitol Station
Baton Rouge, LA 70804
(504) 925-7742

Office of Public Works
Department of Transportation &
   Development
P. O. Box 44155, Capitol Station
Baton Rouge, LA 70804
(504) 342-7580
NCIC State Affiliate

**Maine**

State Development Office
Executive Department
State House Station #59
193 State St.
Augusta, ME 04333
(207) 289-2656

Maine Division of Aeronautics
Department of Transportation

State Airport
Augusta, ME 04330
(207) 289-3185

Maine Geological Survey
Department of Conservation
Ray Building
State House, Station 22
Augusta, ME 04333
(207) 289-2801

State Planning Office
Executive Department
State House, Station 38
Augusta, ME 04333
(207) 289-3261

Land Use Regulation Commission
Department of Conservation
State House, Station 22
Augusta, ME 04333
(207) 289-2631

## Maryland

Maryland Forest & Park Services
Department of Natural Resources
Tawes State Office Building
Annapolis, MD 21401
(301) 269-3761, 3776

Maryland Department of Economic &
    Community Development
Office of Tourist Development
1748 Forest Dr.
Annapolis, MD 21401
(301) 269-3517

Maryland Geological Survey
The Rotunda
711 W. 40th St.
Suite 440
Baltimore, MD 21211
(301) 338-7066
(General Public Information)
(301) 338-7212
NCIC State Affiliate

Maryland Department of Transportation
P. O. Box 8755
Baltimore-Washington International
    Airport, MD 21240
(301) 859-7311

Office of General Aviation Service
Maryland State Aviation Administration
Baltimore-Washington International
    Airport, MD 21240
(301) 859-7064

Maryland State Highway Administration
Cartographic Section
2323 W. Joppa Rd.
Brooklandville, MD 21022
(301) 321-3518

## Massachusetts

Massachusetts Department of Commerce
    and Development
100 Cambridge St.
Boston, MA 02202
(617) 727-3218

Massachusetts Department of Public
    Works
Photogrammetric Section
100 Nashua St.
Boston, MA 02114
(617) 727-8287

Executive Office of Transportation &
    Construction
10 Park Plaza
Boston, MA 02116-3969
(617) 973-7000

Secretary of the Commonwealth
Citizen Information Service
1 Ashburton Place, 16th Floor
Boston, MA 02108
(617) 727-7030

Massachusetts State Archives
State House, Room 55
Boston, MA 02133
(617) 727-2816

Department of Fisheries & Wildlife
Route 135
Westboro, MA 01581
(617) 366-4479

Massachusetts Aeronautics Commission
Boston-Logan Airport
East Boston, MA 02128
(617) 727-5350

Massachusetts Turnpike Authority
State Transportation Building
10 Park Plaza
Suite 5170
Boston, MA 02116
(617) 973-7300

University of Massachusetts
Remote Sensing Center
102D Hasbrouck
Amherst, MA 01003
(413) 545-0359
NCIC State Affiliate

State Geologist
Department of Environmental Quality
    Engineering
Division Waterways
1 Winter St., 7th Floor
Boston, MA 02108
(617) 292-5690

Department of Environmental
    Management
Division of Forest & Parks

100 Cambridge St.
Boston, MA 02202
(617) 727-3180

## Michigan

Travel Bureau
Michigan Department of Commerce
P. O. Box 30226
Lansing, MI 48909
(517) 373-1195
(800) 292-2520 (within Michigan)
(800) 248-5700 (from CT, DC, DE, IL,
    IN, IA, KY, MA, MD, MN, MO, NC,
    NH, NJ, NY, OH, PA, RI, SD, TN,
    VT, VA, WV, WI)

Michigan Department of Transportation
Transportation Building
425 W. Ottawa
P. O. Box 30050
Lansing, MI 48909
(517) 373-2090

Michigan Aeronautics Commission
Aviation Information
Capital City Airport
Lansing, MI 48906
(517) 373-2146

Michigan Department of Natural
    Resources
Division of Land Resource Programs
Mason Building, 7th Floor
P. O. Box 30028
Lansing, MI 48909
(517) 373-3328
NCIC State Affiliate

## Minnesota

Minnesota State Planning Agency
Land Management Information Center
Room LL65, Metro Square Building
7th & Robert Streets
St. Paul, MN 55101
(612) 297-2490
NCIC State Affiliate

Office of Tourism
Department of Energy & Economic
    Development
240 Bremer Building
419 N. Robert St.
St. Paul, MN 55101
(612) 296-5029
(800) 652-9747 (within Minnesota)
(800) 328-1461 (nationwide)

Minnesota Department of Natural
    Resources
Division of Parks & Recreation
Box 39, Centennial Building
St. Paul, MN 55155
(612) 296-4776

Aeronautics Division
Minnesota Department of Transportation

Transportation Building, Room 417
John Ireland Blvd.
St. Paul, MN 55155

Minnesota Department of Transportation
Transportation Building, Room 809
St. Paul, MN 55155
(612) 296-1680

Minnesota Geological Survey
University of Minnesota
2642 University Avenue
St. Paul, MN 55114-1057
(612) 373-3372

## Mississippi

Division of Tourism
Mississippi Department of Economic
    Development
P. O. Box 849
Jackson, MS 39205
(601) 354-6715
(800) 647-2290

Mississippi State Highway Department
Transportation Planning Division
P. O. Box 1850
Jackson, MS 39205
(601) 354-7176

Regional Planning Branch
Mississippi Research & Development
    Center
P. O. Drawer 2470
Jackson, MS 39205
(601) 982-6606
NCIC State Affiliate

Mississippi Department of Natural
    Resources
Bureau of Geology
P. O. Box 5348
Jackson, MS 39216
(601) 354-6228

Mississippi Aeronautics Commission
400 Robert E. Lee Building
P. O. Box 5
Jackson, MS 39205
(601) 359-1270

## Missouri

Missouri Division of Tourism
301 W. High Street
Truman State Office Building
P. O. Box 1055
Jefferson City, MO 65101
(314) 751-4133

Division of Geology & Land Survey
Missouri Department of Natural
    Resources
P. O. Box 250
Rolla, MO 65401
(314) 364-1752
NCIC State Affiliate

Missouri Highway & Transportation
    Department
Aviation Division
P. O. Box 270
Jefferson City, MO 65102

## Montana

Travel Promotion Division
Montana Department of Commerce
1424 9th Ave.
Helena, MT 59620
(406) 444-2654

Montana Department of Highways
Program Development Division
Planning & Statistics Bureau
2701 Prospect Ave.
Helena, MT 59620
(406) 444-6115

Montana Bureau of Mines & Geology
Montana College of Mineral Science
    & Technology
Main Hall, Room 200
Butte, MT 59701
(406) 496-4167
NCIC State Affiliate

Montana Aeronautics Division
P. O. Box 5178
Helena, MT 59601
(406) 444-2506

## Nebraska

Travel & Tourism Division
Nebraska Department of Economic
    Development
P. O. Box 94666
Lincoln, NE 68509
(402) 471-3111
(800) 742-7595 (within Nebraska)
(800) 228-4307 (nationwide)

Nebraska Department of Roads
Planning Division
P. O. Box 94759
Lincoln, NE 68509-4759
(402) 473-4519

Conservation & Survey Division
113 Nebraska Hall
University of Nebraska
Lincoln, NE 68588
(402) 472-3471
NCIC State Affiliate

Information & Education Division
State Game & Parks Commission
P. O. Box 30370
Lincoln, NE 68503
(402) 464-0641

Nebraska Department of Aeronautics
P. O. Box 82088
Lincoln, NE 68501
(402) 471-2371

Nebraska Public Service Commission
301 Centennial Mall South
P. O. Box 94927
Lincoln, NE 68509
(402) 471-3101

## Nevada

Nevada Commission on Tourism
Capitol Complex
Carson City, NV 89710
(702) 885-4322

Nevada Department of Transportation
1263 S. Stewart St.
Carson City, NV 89712
(702) 885-3449

Geologic Information Specialist
Nevada Bureau of Mines & Geology
University of Nevada
Reno, NV 89557
(702) 784-6691
NCIC State Affiliate

## New Hampshire

Division of Forests & Lands
105 Loudon Rd., Prescott Park
P. O. Box 856
Concord, NH 03301
(603) 271-3456

New Hampshire Division of Parks &
    Recreation
Prescott Park, Building #2
105 Loudon Rd.
Box 856
Concord, NH 03301
(603) 271-3254

Office of State Geologist
117 James Hall
University of New Hampshire
Durham, NH 03824
(603) 862-1216

Office of Vacation Travel
New Hampshire Department of
    Resources & Economic Development
P. O. Box 856
Concord, NH 03301
(603) 271-2665

New Hampshire Department of Public
    Works & Highways
Planning & Economics Division
P. O. Box 483
Concord, NH 03301

New Hampshire Aeronautics Commission
Municipal Airport
Concord, NH 03301
(603) 271-2551

**New Jersey**

New Jersey Department of Transportation
1035 Parkway Ave. CN600
Trenton, NJ 08625
(609) 292-3105

New Jersey Division of Tourism
CN826
Trenton, NJ 08625
(609) 292-2470

Division of Economic Development
Department of Commerce & Economic
  Development
CN823
Trenton, NJ 08625-0823
(609) 292-7757

Department of Environmental Protection
New Jersey Geological Survey
1474 Prospect St. CN029
Trenton, NJ 08625
(609) 292-2576
NCIC State Affiliate

**New Mexico**

Tourism & Travel Division
New Mexico Economic Development &
  Tourism Department
Bataan Memorial Building
Santa Fe, NM 87503
(505) 827-6230
(800) 545-2040

New Mexico Bureau of Mines & Mineral
  Resources
Campus Station
Socorro, NM 87801
(505) 835-5420

New Mexico State Highway Department
P. O. Box 1149
Santa Fe, NM 87503
(505) 983-0668

New Mexico Transportation Department
Aviation Division
P. O. Box 579
Santa Fe, NM 87504-0579
(505) 827-4590

University of New Mexico
Technology Applications Center
2500 Central Avenue, S.E.
Albuquerque, NM 87131
(505) 277-3622
NCIC State Affiliate

**New York**

Department of Environmental
  Conservation
50 Wolf Road
Albany, NY 12205

Division of Tourism
New York State Dept. of Commerce

One Commerce Plaza
Albany, NY 12245
(518) 474-4116
(800) CALL NYS (all Northeastern
  States except Maine)

Map Information Unit
New York State Department of
  Transportation
State Campus, Building 4, Room 105
Albany, NY 12232
(518) 457-3555

New York State Office of Parks,
  Recreation & Historic Preservation
Agency Building #1
Empire State Plaza
Albany, NY 12238
(518) 474-0456

**North Carolina**

North Carolina Department of
  Transportation
P. O. Box 25201
Raleigh, NC 27611

North Carolina Division of Aviation
Department of Transportation
P. O. Box 25201
Raleigh, NC 27611
(919) 733-2491

North Carolina Department of
  Transportation
Office of Public Affairs
P. O. Box 25201
Raleigh, NC 27611
(919) 733-3463

Department of Natural Resources &
  Community Development
Geological Survey Section
Division of Land Resources
P. O. Box 27687
Raleigh, NC 27611
(919) 733-2423
NCIC State Affiliate

North Carolina Dept. of Transportation
Location & Survey
P. O. Box 25201
Raleigh, NC 27611
(919) 733-7241

**North Dakota**

North Dakota State Water Commission
State Office Building
209 E. Boulevard Ave.
Bismarck, ND 58501
(701) 224-2750
NCIC State Affiliate

North Dakota Geological Survey
University Station
Grand Forks, ND 58202-8156
(701) 777-2231

Planning Division
North Dakota State Highway Dept.
600 E. Boulevard Ave.
Bismarck, ND 58505-0178
(701) 224-3534 (map sales)

North Dakota Tourism Promotion
Capital Grounds
Bismarck, ND 58505
(701) 224-2525
(800) 472-2100 (within North Dakota)
(800) 437-2077 (nationwide)

**Ohio**

Ohio Department of Transportation
25 S. Front St., Room B100
Columbus, OH 43215
Map Sales, Room B100
  (614) 446-4430
Public Information Office, Room 308
  (614) 466-7170

Division of Geological Survey
Ohio Department of Natural Resources
Fountain Square, Building B
Columbus, OH 43224
(614) 265-6605

Office of Travel & Tourism
Department of Development
P. O. Box 1001
Columbus, OH 43216
(614) 466-8844

Ohio Department of Natural Resources
Publications Center
Fountain Square, Building B
Columbus, OH 43224
(614) 265-6608

Ohio Department of Natural Resources
Division of Parks & Recreation
Fountain Square
Columbus, OH 43224
(614) 265-7000

**Oklahoma**

Marketing Services Division
Oklahoma Tourism & Recreation Dept.
500 Will Rogers Building
Oklahoma City, OK 73105
(405) 521-2406

Oklahoma Department of Transportation
Reproduction Branch
200 N. E. 21st St.
Oklahoma City, OK 73105
(405) 521-2586

Oklahoma Geological Survey
University of Oklahoma
830 Van Vleet Oval, Room 163
Norman, OK 73019
(405) 325-3031

Oklahoma Aeronautics Commission
Department of Transportation Bldg.
200 N.E. 21st St.
Oklahoma City, OK 73105
(405) 521-2377

**Oregon**

Tourism Division
Economic Development Department
595 Cottage St., N.E.
Salem, OR 97310
(503) 373-1200
(800) 547-7842 (Outside Oregon)

Oregon Department of Geology &
  Mineral Industries
1005 State Office Building
Portland, OR 97201
(503) 229-5580

Oregon State Parks & Recreation Division
525 Trade St., S.E.
Salem, OR 97310
(503) 378-6305

Oregon State Library
Public Services
Salem, OR 97310
(503) 378-4277
NCIC State Affiliate

**Pennsylvania**

Pennsylvania Dept. of Commerce
Bureau of Travel Development
416 Forum Building
Harrisburg, PA 17120
(717) 787-5453

Pennsylvania Dept. of Transportation
Bureau of Strategic Planning
Room 912, Transportation & Safety Bldg.
Harrisburg, PA 17120
(717) 787-4247

Pennsylvania Dept. of Environmental
  Resources
Bureau of Topographic & Geological
  Survey
P. O. Box 2357
Harrisburg, PA 17120
(717) 787-2169
NCIC State Affiliate

Pennsylvania Bureau of Aviation
Department of Transportation
Capital City Airport
New Cumberland, PA 17070
(717) 783-2280

**Puerto Rico**

Puerto Rico Dept. of Transportation
  & Public Works
Photogrammetry & Geodesy Section
Minillas Government Center
G.P.O., Box 8218
San Juan, Puerto Rico 00910

(809) 726-5390

**Rhode Island**

Sea Grant Depository
Pell Marine Science Library
University of Rhode Island
Narragansett, RI 02882
(401) 792-6539
NCIC State Affiliate

Tourist Promotion Division
Department of Economic Development
7 Jackson Walkway
Providence, RI 02903
(401) 277-2601
(800) 556-2484 (Maine through
  West Virginia & Northern Ohio)

Rhode Island Dept. of Transportation
Planning Division
368 State Office Building
Smith Street
Providence, RI 02903
(401) 277-2694

**South Carolina**

Division of Tourism
South Carolina Dept. of Parks,
  Recreation & Tourism
Suite 110
1205 Pendleton St.
Columbia, SC 29201
(803) 758-2536

Map Sales, Traffic Engineering Division
South Carolina Dept. of Highways
  & Public Transportation
P. O. Box 191
Columbia, SC 29202
(803) 758-3001

Division of State Parks
Department of Parks, Recreation &
  Tourism
Suite 110, Edgar A. Brown Building
1205 Pendleton St.
Columbia, SC 29201
(803) 758-3622

South Carolina Aeronautics Commission
P. O. Drawer 1987
Columbia, SC 29202
(803) 758-2766

South Carolina Land Resources
Conservation Commission
2221 Devine St., Suite 222
Columbia, SC 29205
(803) 758-2823
NCIC State Affiliate

**South Dakota**

South Dakota Geological Survey
Science Center
University of South Dakota

Vermillion, SD 57069
(605) 624-4471

South Dakota Dept. of Transportation
State Highway Building
Pierre, SD 57501
(605) 773-3267

South Dakota Department of Game,
  Fish, & Parks
Anderson Building
Pierre, SD 57501
(605) 224-3485

**Tennessee**

Tennessee Department of Tourist
  Development
P. O. Box 23170
Nashville, TN 37202
(615) 741-2158

Tennessee Dept. of Conservation
Division of Geology
G-5 State Office Building
Nashville, TN 37219
(615) 741-2726

Tennessee Dept. of Transportation
Information Office
700 James K. Polk Building
505 Degderick St.
Nashville, TN 37219
(615) 741-2331

Division of State Parks
Department of Conservation
701 Broadway
Nashville, TN 37203
(615) 742-6667

Tennessee Division of Geology
701 Broadway
Nashville, TN 37203
(615) 742-6696

**Texas**

Texas Travel & Information Division
State Dept. of Highways & Public
  Transportation
11th & Brazos Streets
Austin, TX 78701
(512) 475-2877

Texas Bureau of Economic Geology
University of Texas at Austin
University Station, Box X
Austin, TX 78712
(512) 471-1534

Texas Natural Resources Information
  System
P. O. Box 13087
Austin, TX 78711
(512) 475-3321
NCIC State Affiliate

## Utah

Utah Travel Council
Council Hall, Capitol Hill
Salt Lake City, UT 84114
(801) 533-5681

Utah Geological & Mineral Survey
Department of Natural Resources
606 Black Hawk Way
Salt Lake City, UT 84108
(801) 581-6831
NCIC State Affiliate

Utah Department of Transportation
Office of Community Relations
4501 South, 2700 West
Salt Lake City, UT 84119
(801) 965-4104

Division of Parks & Recreation
1596 West North Temple
Salt Lake City, UT 84116
(801) 533-6012

Division of Aeronautical Operations
Department of Transportation
135 North 2400 West
Salt Lake City, UT 84116
(801) 533-5057

## Vermont

Agency of Transportation
Planning Division
133 State St.
Montpelier, VT 05602
(802) 828-2671

Office of State Geologist
Agency of Environmental Conservation
Heritage II, State Office Bldg. P. O.
79 River St.
Montpelier, VT 05602
(802) 828-3365

Agency of Environmental Conservation
Dept. of Forests, Parks & Recreation
Heritage II
79 River St.
Montpelier, VT 05602
(802) 828-3471

Operations Division
Vermont Agency of Transportation
State Administration Building
133 State St.
Montpelier, VT 05602
(802) 828-2828

Vermont Travel Division
Agency of Development & Community
  Affairs
134 State St.
Montpelier, VT 05602
(802) 828-3236

## Virgin Islands

Division of Tourism
Virgin Island Dept. of Commerce
Box 6400 – Charlotte Amalie
St. Thomas
U. S. Virgin Islands 00801
(809) 774-8784

## Virginia

Virginia State Travel Service
202 N. Ninth St., Suite 500
Richmond, VA 23219
(804) 786-2051

Dept. of Highways & Transportation
1221 E. Broad St.
Richmond, VA 23219
(804) 786-2838

Virginia Dept. of Conservation &
  Economic Development
Natural Resource Building
P. O. Box 3667
Charlottesville, VA 22903
(804) 293-5121
NCIC State Affiliate

Commonwealth of Virginia
Department of Aviation
4508 S. Laburnum Ave.
P. O. Box 7716
Richmond, VA 23231
(804) 786-3685

Division of State Parks
1201 Washington Building
Capitol Square
Richmond, VA 23219
(804) 786-6140

## Washington

Washington Dept. of Transportation
Transportation Building, KF-01
Olympia, WA 98504
(206) 753-2150

State of Washington Water Research
  Center
Washington State University
Pullman, WA 99164-3002
(509) 335-5531

Washington State Parks & Recreation
  Commission
7150 Clearwater Ln, KY-11
Olympia, WA 98504
(206) 753-5755

Washington State Library
Information Services Division
Documents Section
State Library Building, AJ-11
Olympia, WA 98504
(206) 753-4027 or 5590
NCIC State Affiliate (User Services)

Department of Natural Resources
Division of Management Services
Photos, Maps & Reports Section QW-21
Public Lands Building
Olympia, WA 98504
(206) 753-5338
NCIC State Affiliate
  (Data Acquisitions)

Department of Natural Resources
Bureau of Surveys & Maps
1102 S. Quince EV-11
Olympia, WA 98504
(206) 753-5337

## West Virginia

West Virginia Dept. of Highways
Systems Planning Division
Corridor & Project Planning Section
1900 Washington St., East
Charleston, WV 25305
(304) 348-2764

Division of Parks & Recreation
Department of Natural Resources
State Office Building 3, Room 311
1800 Washington St., East
Charleston, WV 25305
(304) 348-2764

Governor's Office of Economic &
  Community Development
Travel Division
State Capitol Building
Charleston, WV 25305

West Virginia Geological & Economic
  Survey
West Virginia Cartographic Center
Mont Chateau Research Center
P. O. Box 879
Morgantown, WV 26507-0879
(304) 594-2331
NCIC State Affiliate

## Wisconsin

Division of Tourism
P. O. Box 7606
Madison, WI 53707
(608) 266-2161
(800) ESCAPES (within WI, Chicago, &
  N. IL, MN, IA, MI)

Wisconsin Dept. of Transportation
Special Services Section
P. O. Box 7916
Madison, WI 53707
(608) 266-0309

Wisconsin Geological Survey
Map Sales
University of Wisconsin
1815 University Ave.
Madison, WI 53705
(608) 263-7389

Maps
Wisconsin Dept. of Transportation
Document Sales
3617 Pierstorff St.
P. O. Box 7713
Madison, WI 53707-7713
(608) 266-8921

Wisconsin State Cartographer
144 Science Hall
550 N. Park St.
University of Wisconsin
Madison, WI 53706
(608) 262-3065
NCIC State Affiliate

The American Geographical Society
Collection of the University of Wisconsin–
  Milwaukee Library
P. O. Box 399
Milwaukee, WI 53201
(414) 963-6282/963-7775

**Wyoming**

Wyoming Travel Commission
Cheyenne, Wy 82002
(307) 777-7777

Geological Survey of Wyoming
P. O. Box 3008
University Station
Laramie, WY 82071
(307) 742-2954

Wyoming Highway Department
Public Information Office
P. O. Box 1708
Cheyenne, WY 82002
(307) 777-7267

Aeronautics Commission
State of Wyoming
Cheyenne, WY 82002
(307) 777-7481

Wyoming State Engineer
Barrett Building
Cheyenne, WY 82002
(307) 777-7354
NCIC State Affiliate

# E. State Mapping Advisory Committees

*Several states have created state mapping advisory committees to determine the mapping needs of their respective states and to communicate these to the U. S. Geological Survey. Additionally, these committees may schedule workshops and publish newsletters which provide up-to-date information on the availability of cartographic information.*

**Alabama**

Dr. Ernest A. Mancini
State Geologist
Geological Survey of Alabama
University, Alabama 35486
(205) 349-2852

**Alaska**

Mr. Douglas Mutter
Alaska Department of Natural Resources
Division of Technical Services
3601 C Street
Anchorage, Alaska 99503
(907) 786-2377

**Arizona**

Mr. Robert Adams
Arizona Department of Highways
206 South Seventh Street
Phoenix, Arizona 85007
(602) 255-7239

**California**

Mr. Kenneth L. Woodward
Chief, Support Branch
Division of Planning
Department of Water Resources
Post Office Box 388
Sacramento, California 95802
(916) 445-9965

**Delaware**

Mr. Thomas E. Pickett
Chairman

State Mapping Advisory Committee
Delaware Geological Survey
University of Delaware
Newark, Delaware 19716
(302) 451-2833

**Hawaii**

Mr. Paul Nuha
Acting Chairman
Hawaii State Mapping Advisory
  Committee
State Land Surveyor
Dept. of Accounting and General Services
Survey Division
Post Office Box 119
Honolulu, Hawaii 96810
(808) 548-7422

**Idaho**

Mr. Ray Miller
Supervisor
Technical Services Section
Department of Lands
State House
Boise, Idaho 83720
(208) 334-3816

**Iowa**

Mr. Raymond R. Anderson
Remote Sensing Analysis
Iowa State Mapping Advisory Committee
Iowa Geological Survey
123 N. Capitol Street
Iowa City, Iowa 52242
(319) 338-1173

**Illinois**

Dr. Richard E. Dahlberg
Chairman
Illinois Mapping Advisory Committee
Department of Geography
Northern Illinois University
De Kalb, Illinois 60115
(815) 753-0631

**Kansas**

Dr. James R. McCauley
Chairman
Kansas Mapping Coordinating
  Committee
Kansas Geological Survey
1930 Constant Avenue
Campus West
University of Kansas
Lawrence, Kansas 66046-2598
(913) 864-4991, ext. 328

**Maine**

Dr. Walter A. Anderson
Chairman
Maine Mapping Advisory Committee
Department of Conservation
State House Station 22
Augusta, Maine 04333
(207) 289-2801

**Maryland**

Dr. Kenneth N. Weaver, Director
Maryland Geological Survey
The Johns Hopkins University
Baltimore, Maryland 21218

(301) 338-7084

**Michigan**

Mr. R. Thomas Segall
State Geologist/Chairman
Michigan Mapping Advisory Committee
Geological Survey Division
Michigan Department of Natural
  Resources
Post Office Box 30028
Lansing, Michigan 48909
(517) 373-0977

**Mississippi**

Dr. Donald Williams
Chairman
Mississippi Advisory Committee
Geography Department
University of Southern Mississippi
Post Office Box 5051, Southern Station
Hattiesburg, Mississippi 39406
(601) 266-4729

**Missouri**

Dr. Keith Wedge
Chairman
Missouri Mapping Advisory Committee
Department of Natural Resources
Post Office Box 250
Rolla, Missouri 65401
(314) 364-1752

**Nebraska**

Dr. Ronald C. Rundquist
Chairman
Nebraska Mapping Advisory Committee
Conservation and Survey Division
University of Nebraska–Lincoln
Lincoln, Nebraska 68558
(402) 472-3471

**Nevada**

Mr. John Schilling
Director/State Geologist
Nevada Bureau of Mines and Geology
University of Nevada–Reno
Reno, Nevada 89557-0088
(702) 784-6691

**New Jersey**

Mr. Lawrence Schmidt
Acting Director, Planning Group
State of New Jersey Department of
  Environmental Protection
Office of the Commissioner
CN 402
Trenton, New Jersey 08625
(609) 292-2885

**New Mexico**

Mr. Michael H. Inglis
Manager, Remote Sensing
Technology Applications Center
University of New Mexico
2500 Central Avenue, S.E.
Albuquerque, New Mexico 87131
(505) 277-3622

**North Carolina**

Mr. Steven Conrad
Division of Land Resources
Department of Natural Resources and
  Community Development
Post Office Box 27687
Raleigh, North Carolina 27611
(919) 733-3833

**Oregon**

Mr. John D. Beaulieu
Chairman
State Mapping Advisory Committee
Deputy State Geologist
Department of Geology and Industries
1069 State Office Building
Portland, Oregon 97201
(503) 229-5580

**South Carolina**

Mr. Villard Griffin
Professor of Geology
Clemson University
Clemson, South Carolina 29631
(803) 656-3438

**Texas**

Mr. Tommy Knowles
Chairman

Texas Mapping Advisory Committee
Post Office Box 13087, Capitol Station
Austin, Texas 78711
(512) 884-3011

**Utah**

Ms. Genevieve Atwood
Director
Utah Geological and Mineral Survey
606 Black Hawk Way
Salt Lake City, Utah 84108
(801) 581-6831

**Vermont**

David Butterfield
Chairman
Vermont Mapping Advisory Committee
Department of Water Resources and
  Environmental Engineering
Heritage II, River Street
Montpelier, Vermont 05602

**Washington**

Mr. Donald Karnes
Assistant Division Manager
Photo, Maps, and Reports Section
Department of Natural Resources
Public Land Building OW-21
Olympia, Washington 98504
(206) 753-5340

**Wisconsin**

Dr. M. E. Ostrom
Director/State Geologist
Wisconsin Geological and Natural
  History Survey
3817 Mineral Point Road
Madison, Wisconsin 53705
(608) 263-7384

**Wyoming**

Mr. George Christopulos
State Engineer
State of Wyoming
State Engineer's Office (037)
122 W. 25th, Herschler Building
Cheyenne, Wyoming 82002
(307) 777-7354

# F. Map Societies

*Map Societies are a recent phenomena in this country and represent the increasing interest in cartographic information. The two oldest are in New York and Washington, D.C. where both grew out of the local Special Libraries Association chapters. These groups have a varied membership and varied interests representing map collectors, railroad buffs, genealogists, dealers and librarians. Listed below are those known at the time of publication.*

## California Map Society

California Map Society
12021 Wilshire Blvd.
Box 2008
West Los Angeles, CA 90025
Publications: Directory of Cartographic
Resources in California, 1st ed., 1984.
Free CMS Bulletin (Occasional),
CMS Newsletter (Quarterly)
Dues:
  $10 Regular
    $5 Students & Seniors
  $10 Institutional
  $100 Sustaining
    $25 Contributing Sponsor
  $500 Life

## Chicago Map Society

Chicago Map Society
60 W. Walton St.
Chicago, IL 60610
Publications: World Directory of
Dealers in Antiquarian Maps, George
Ritzlin, ed., 2nd ed., 1980. $5.00.
Chicago Mapmakers: Essays on the
Rise of the City's Map Trade, Michael
P. Conzen, ed., Chicago Historical
Society for the Chicago Map Society,
1984. $12.00. Mapline subscription
included in membership.
Dues: $10
Meetings: Monthly Sept.–May, Fellow's
Lounge, Newberry Library, 3d
Tuesday each month

## International Map Collectors Society

International Map Collectors Society
1a Camden Walk
Islington Green
London, N1 8DY
Publications: International Map
Collectors Society Journal, Yasha
Beresiner, ed., P. O. Box 70, London
N3 3QQ, England. Quarterly. Free to
members.
Dues:
  $28 (1984)
  $500 Life Membership
Meetings: Main meeting held at the
Annual London Map Fair & Symposium;
bimonthly meetings conducted at
various locations.

## Map Society of the Delaware Valley

Map Society of the Delaware Valley
c/o Robert Hornick
Secretary/Treasurer
2401 Pennsylvania Ave. 18-B-30
Philadelphia, PA 19130
Dues:
  $15
Meetings: Five a year, Sept.–May

## Michigan Map Society

Michigan Map Society
Clements Library
University of Michigan
Ann Arbor, MI 48109

Publications: Mapline subscription
included in membership (Mapline,
The Newberry Library, 60 W. Walton,
Chicago, IL 60610, $5.00 annual
subscription, ISSN 0196-0881)
Dues:
  $10
Meetings: Monthly Sept.–May, 3rd
week of every month at Clements
Library

## New York Map Society

New York Map Society
c/o the Map Division
New York Public Library
42nd Street & Fifth Avenue
New York, NY 10018
Dues:
  $10
Meetings: Monthly, 1st Saturday of the
month, Sept.–June, at the American
Museum of Natural History Room 129,
Central Park West & 79th Street

## Washington Map Society

Washington Map Society
c/o Robert Hansen
Secretary/Treasurer
3051 Idaho Ave., N.W.
Washington, D.C. 20016
Dues:
  $10 (1983/84)
Meetings: 3rd Tuesday of every month,
Sept. –May

## Map Resources Questionnaire

PLEASE PRINT OR TYPE

1. Please write in the Map Library Name
   Address, Telephone Number and
   Responsible Person

   _____

   _____

   _____

   _____

2. What are the usual services hours for
   this collection?

   _____

3a. What is the total number of persons
   employed in this collection during the year?
   (in FTE numbers)

   |  | Full Time | Part Time |
   |---|---|---|
   | Prof. | _____ | _____ |
   | Non-Prof. | _____ | _____ |

   (includes students)

   b. If only part of the responsible person's time is devoted to maps,
   indicate approximate percentage:                              _____%

   c. What is the square footage of floor space given to
   the map collection?                                          _____

4. Please indicate the size of your map collection for each of the following items as of
   June 30, 1983.

   | Maps | _____ | Serial Titles | _____ |
   |---|---|---|---|
   | Air photos & imagery | _____ | Microforms | _____ |
   | Atlases | _____ | Computer Tapes | _____ |
   | Globes | _____ | Books (e.g. Gazetteers, Cartobibliographies, etc.) | _____ |

5a. Is your collection comprehensive geographically, or is it specialized by area?

   Comprehensive _____ (Skip To Question 6)

   Specialized _____

   b. What specific geographical areas do you emphasize?   1. _____

   2. _____   3. _____

6a. Is your collection primarily comprehensive thematically, or is it specialized by specific subject matter?

   Comprehensive _____ (Skip to Question 7)

   Specialized _____

   b. What specific subjects do you emphasize? (e.g. geology, vegetation, soils, etc.)

   1. _____   2. _____   3. _____

7. Please characterize the chronological coverage of your map collection by providing approximate
   percentages below:

   Pre–1900 _____   Post–1900 _____   = 100%

8a. Do you have any special cartographic collections?

   Yes _____   No _____ (Skip to Question 9)

   b. If so, please list (use additional paper if necessary) _____

   _____

9. Is the map collection cataloged?   Yes _____   What percentage _____%   No _____

10. What classification system do you use?   LC _____   AGS _____   Other _____

11. Which utility do you use for cataloging maps? OCLC _____ RLG _____

   Other (specify) _____ None _____

12. In what format is your catalog (check all that apply)? Cards _____ COM _____

   Online _____ Computer Printout _____ Other (specify) _____

13. Does this collection use any of the following preservation techniques (check all that apply)?

   Encapsulation _____ Lamination _____ Chartex or Fabric Mounting _____

   Edging _____ Deacidification _____ Other (specify) _____

14. Is the map collection a designated depository for (please check):

   USGS (topo) _____     GPO      _____
   USGS (geol) _____     NOS      _____
   DMA (topo) _____     NOAA     _____
   DMA (aero) _____     Canada (topo) _____
   DMA (hydro) _____     Canada (geol) _____

Others (specify) _____

15a. To whom is your collection available? (check all that apply)

   Public _____     Faculty _____
   Students _____     Other _____

   b. Do maps circulate from your collection? Yes _____ No _____ (Skip to 15e)

   c. To whom does your collection circulate? (check all that apply)

   Public _____     Faculty _____
   Students _____     Other _____

   d. What is the average annual circulation for: Maps _____ Books _____

   Aerial Photographs _____ Others (specify) _____

   e. What is the average number of persons using this collection each month? _____

16. Are materials available on interlibrary loan? Yes _____ No _____

17. Please check the copying facilities available for library materials?

   Xerox _____     Photographic reproduction _____
   Microform _____
   Dyeline _____     Other (specify) _____

18a. How many 5-drawer map cabinets do you have (If none, indicate 0) _____

   b. How many vertical map cabinets do you have? (If none, indicate 0) _____

   c. Other types of cabinets (specify) _____

   d. Please list any specialized map reading equipment available for the map collection?

   _____

19. Please list titles and frequency of publications issued by the map collection?

   _____

20. Please list other map collections or contact persons in your area, on campus, or within the library system that should be contacted for this survey:

   _____

Please return to:
   David A. Cobb
   418 University Library
   University of Illinois
   Urbana, IL 61801

_____
Name of Person Completing Survey

# Special Collections Index

*Listed below are those collections unique to specific libraries and not all of the special collections listed under each entry. For example, it is assumed that someone looking for aerial photographs of Nebraska will refer to the Nebraska section. This index, however, provides a key to named collections: i.e., Novacco (Newberry Library), Cavagna (University of Illinois), etc.*